This exhaustive enquiry into the covenant of works is divided into three parts. As a result of this the construction of the doctrine is made clearer. The author's plain style and thoroughness is evident throughout. For example in part one he takes the reader beyond the history of the Reformation to Augustine and Aquinas. But also the contemporary issue of the distinction between the question of contract versus covenant, and whether the term 'covenant of works' is warranted, is discussed. The exegetical part focusses on the significance of Sinai, and on particular verses used in both Testaments to support of the covenant of works. The final part contains an exposition of the doctrine of imputation. Such a straightforward style and its detail mean that the book is a truly interdisciplinary work. A reader studying this important topic will be aided by what is in effect three books in one. Even though a reader may take a view other the author's, he will find himself benefited by the learned detail that Professor Fesko has amassed.

PAUL HELM
Emeritus Professor of the
History and Philosophy of Religion,
King's College, London

For too long among evangelical scholars the doctrine of the covenant of works has been dismissed out of hand as an unwarranted dogmatic imposition upon the text of Scripture. It is high time to challenge that unthinking assertion, and so we rejoice at the publication of Dr J. V. Fesko's, *Adam and the Covenant of Works*. It is both a welcome defense, and a contemporary restatement of this much maligned, yet fundamental component of the Reformed system. With customary comprehensiveness, and in a way that most helpfully sets up the exegetical and systematic discussions to follow, Dr Fesko traces the major contours of the development of the covenant of works idea throughout church history. The exegetical work at the heart of the book, demonstrating the biblical *bona fides* for the doctrine of the prelapsarian covenant, is supremely useful. The measured denial of the place of grace in the covenant of works, though it will not persuade all, is a model of catholic-spirited debate, and the evaluation of Kline's views of 'the divine council' in Genesis 1:26, and the dogmatic significance of a more canonical Trinitarian alternative is most welcome. This is a valuable resource for students and preachers, and an important contribution to the recovery of confidence in a vital doctrine.

DAVID STRAIN
Senior Minister of First Presbyterian Church, Jackson, Mississippi
Chairman of the Board of Christian Witness to Israel

ADAM AND THE COVENANT OF WORKS

J. V. FESKO

MENTOR

Copyright © J. V. Fesko 2021

hardback ISBN 978-1-5271-0728-1
ebook ISBN 978-1-5271-0850-9

10 9 8 7 6 5 4 3 2 1

Published in 2021
in the
Mentor Imprint
by
Christian Focus Publications Ltd,
Geanies House, Fearn, Ross-shire,
IV20 1TW, Great Britain.

www.christianfocus.com

Cover design
by
Daniel Van Straaten

Printed
by
Bell & Bain, Glasgow

Dedicated
to
the faculty of
Reformed Theological Seminary,
Jackson, Mississippi

❖CONTENTS❖

Abbreviations viii

Acknowledgements xi

Preface xiii

Introduction xvii

PART I – History

I.1: Terms 1

I.2: Do This and Live 13

I.3: Adam's Faith 43

I.4: Covenant or Contract? 55

I.5: Grace in the Covenant of Works 77

I.6: The Covenant of Works and Sinai 107

PART II – Exegesis

II.1: Written on the Heart (Rom. 2:14-15) 161

II.2: In the Day that You Eat (Gen. 2:16-17) 183

II.3: Do This and Live (Lev. 18:5) 199

II.4: They Broke the Everlasting Covenant (Isa. 24:5) .. 217

II.5: Like Adam They Broke the Covenant (Hosea 6:7) .. 239

II.6: These Are Two Covenants (Gal. 4:24) 263

II.7: Adam, Israel, and Christ (Rom. 5:12-21) 281

II.8: Captive to the Law (Rom. 7:16) 301

PART III – Doctrine

III.1: Statement of the Doctrine 317

III.2: The Covenant of Works and Sinai 339

III.3: Justification and the Covenant of Works 357

III.4: Grace and Merit in the Covenant of Works 377

III.4a: Excursus on Genesis 1:26 419

Conclusion 435

Bibliography 441

Subject Index 477

Scripture Index 489

ABBREVIATIONS

AB	Anchor Bible
ACCS	Ancient Christian Commentary Series
ANF	Ante-Nicene Fathers
BCOTWS	Baker Commentary on the Old Testament Wisdom Series
BDB	Brown, Driver, Briggs, *Hebrew Lexicon*
BECNT	Baker Exegetical Commentary on the New Testament
BNTC	Black's New Testament Commentary
ca.	*circa* ('about')
CBQ	*Catholic Biblical Quarterly*
CCSS	Catholic Commentary on Sacred Scripture
Cf.	*confero* ('compare')
chp.	Chapter
CNTC	Calvin's New Testament Commentaries
comm.	exegetical comment on
CP	*Confessional Presbyterian*
CTJ	*Calvin Theological Journal*
CTR	*Criswell Theological Review*
CTS	Calvin Translation Society
EBC	Expositor's Bible Commentary
e.g.	*exempli gratis* ('for example')
esp.	Especially
ESV	English Standard Version
ExpT	*Expository Times*
ff.	Following
fol., fols.	folio, folios
HALOT	Hebrew and Aramaic Lexicon of the Old Testament
HapTR	*Hapshin Theological Review*
ICC	International Critical Commentary
i.e.	*id est* ('that is')
IJST	*International Journal of Systematic Theology*
JBL	*Journal of Biblical Literature*
JETS	*Journal of the Evangelical Theological Society*
JLS	*Journal of Legal Studies*

JMM	*Journal of Markets and Morality*
JPSTC	Jewish Publication Society Torah Commentary
JRT	*Journal of Reformed Theology*
JSNT	*Journal for the Study of the New Testament*
JSOT	*Journal for the Study of the Old Testament*
JTS	*Journal of Theological Studies*
KJV	King James Version
LCL	Loeb Classical Library
Lect.	*Lecture*
LW	Luther's Works
LXX	Septuagint
MAJT	*Mid-America Journal of Theology*
NAC	New American Commentary
NAK	*Nederlands Archief voor Kerkgeschiedenis*
NAS	New American Standard Version
NCBC	New Century Bible Commentary
NET	New English Translation
NIB	New Interpreter's Bible
NICNT	New International Commentary on the New Testament
NICOT	New International Commentary on the Old Testament
NIGTC	New International Greek Testament Commentary
NIV	New International Version
NKJ	New King James Version
NLT	New Living Translation
NLT-SE	New Living Translation – Second Edition
NPNF[1]	Nicene Post-Nicene Fathers, first series
NPNF[2]	Nicene Post-Nicene Fathers, second series
NRSV	New Revised Standard Version
NTS	*New Testament Studies*
OTL	Old Testament Library
p., pp.	Page, pages
PNTC	Pillar New Testament Commentary
PRR	*Presbyterian and Reformed Review*
PTR	*Princeton Theological Review*

q., qq.	Question, questions
re.	Regarding
RefR	*Reformed Review*
rep.	Reprint
RSV	Revised Standard Version
serm.	Sermon
SJT	*Scottish Journal of Theology*
s.v.	*sub verbum* ('under the word')
TBR	*The Bavinck Review*
TJR	*The Journal of Religion*
TNIV	Today's New International Version
TNTC	Tyndale New Testament Commentary
TOTC	Tyndale Old Testament Commentary
trans.	Translated by
TrinJ	*Trinity Journal*
TynB	*Tyndale Bulletin*
vol.	Volume
VT	*Vetus Testamentum*
VUL	Vulgate
WA	*D. Martin Luthers Werke* (Weimar)
WBC	Word Biblical Commentary
WCF	Westminster Confession of Faith
WLC	Westminster Larger Catechism
WSC	Westminster Shorter Catechism
WTJ	*Westminster Theological Journal*
WUNT	Wissenschaftliche Untersuchungen zum Neuen Testamentum
ZAW	*Zeitschrift für die Alttestamentliche Wissenschaft*

❧ ACKNOWLEDGEMENTS ☙

FRIEDRICH Nietzsche once wrote, 'A good writer possesses not only his own spirit but also the spirit of his friends.'[1] I am thankful for my friends who are willing to give of their time, impart their wisdom, and challenge my thinking. This is the means by which I can share in their spirit, and as Proverbs says, 'Iron sharpens iron, so one man sharpens another' (27:17). Friends have read portions or the entirety of this work in its various stages and provided me with valuable feedback and encouragement: Guy Waters, Miles Van Pelt, Richard Muller, Mike Allen, David VanDrunen, Matthew Barrett, Ligon Duncan, Harrison Perkins, Brian Hecker, Ryan McGraw, Jonathan Cruse, David Strain, Paul Helm, and Keith Mathison. Thanks to all of you who sacrificially gave of your time to help me make this book better. I have benefited from your feedback, collegiality, and brotherly love. I also want to thank my teaching assistant, Levi Berntson, for carefully proof reading the book.

I also give thanks to my wife and children, who are always a constant source of love, encouragement, and support. Thank you, Anneke, for your continual love for me. Unlike Eve, you always seek to encourage me to be a better husband, father, and Christian. To my children, thank you for blessing my life, bringing me joy, and for giving me a reason to write. I pray that you would learn the truths of the covenant of works and hold them near and dear to your hearts.

---

1. Friedrich Nietzsche, *Human, All Too Human: A Book for Free Spirits* (Cambridge: Cambridge University Press, 1996), 92.

Thank you to the MacKenzies and the whole team at Christian Focus for your encouragement and support over the years – for your willingness to publish my work.

I dedicate this book to the faculty at Reformed Theological Seminary, Jackson, Mississippi. I am so grateful for how you have received me into your fold – warmly, sincerely, and joyfully. You are a group of learned, godly, and humble professors, and I am honored to work alongside of you in service of Christ's church. Despite your incredible giftedness, acumen, and accomplishments, you are all courageous, yet gentle, kindhearted souls, and I consider it a privilege to serve with you. As we work together to prepare future pastors, leaders, and counselors, my prayer is that our faithful triune Lord will use us to His glory and for the edification of His church. We can all give thanks that our efforts are not in vain because the faithful last Adam has completed the work of the first.

> We thinke that *Paradise* and *Calvarie*,
>   *Christs* Crosse, and Adams tree, stood in one place;
> Looke, Lord, and finde both *Adams* met in me;
>   As the first *Adams* sweat surrounds my face,
>   May the last *Adams* blood my soule embrace.[2]

---

2. John Donne, 'Hymne to God My God, in My Sicknesse,' in *Donne: Poems and Prose* (New York: Alfred A. Knopf, 1995), 177.

~: PREFACE :~

THIS volume constitutes the second installment in a projected three volumes on the doctrines of the covenants of redemption, works, and grace, which mirrors my three-volume historical series covering the same topics.[1] My method is to study the history of each of the covenants in order to inform my own doctrinal construction. As with my study of the covenant of redemption, I feel as if I have received an entire theological education as I have researched the covenant of works. As John Webster has observed, 'What inhibits Christian theology is not only the generally inhospitable intellectual and institutional environment in which it has to flourish but its lack of roots in the traditions of Christian belief and practice which are the soil in which it can grow.'[2] Despite the fact that many without and within the Reformed tradition have made it fashionable to question, discredit, or disavow the covenant of works, my historical exploration has both steeled my convictions about the biblical truthfulness of the doctrine and revealed that many of the criticisms against it are unfounded. The various expositions of the doctrine also uncover a number of insights that have been buried in the ground and covered by weeds of disregard. My hope is that I have been able both to unearth buried kernels of truth as well as benefit from them in my own doctrinal formulation.

---

1. J. V. Fesko, *The Trinity and the Covenant of Redemption* (Fearn: Mentor, 2016); idem, *The Covenant of Redemption: Origins, Development, and Reception* (Göttingen: Vandenhoeck & Ruprecht, 2015); idem, *The Covenant of Works: Origins, Development, and Reception* (Oxford: Oxford University Press, 2020).

2. John Webster, *The Culture of Theology*, ed. Ivor J. Davidson and Alden C. Mc-Cray (Grand Rapids: Baker Academic, 2019), 44.

Whenever writing doctrinal works, I begin by listening quietly to the church throughout the ages as she teaches me about the oak of Scripture, then trace the truth through the roots and branches of redemptive history in Scripture, and ultimately stand back and draw a representation of that oak to show others the beauty and symmetry of God's Word. In seeing the beauty of God's Word, then people would rise up, thank, and worship our triune God. I constantly remind myself that tradition must not be the dead faith of the living, but the living faith of the dead. Christ gave teachers to the church in every age in the wake of His ascension, thus we ignore them to our impoverishment (Eph. 4:11). This tradition is by no means magisterial or infallible and always stands beneath the authority of Scripture. Scripture is vital to right doctrine because 'theology' beholden to autonomous reason or dead traditionalism is merely anthropology, rather than a communal, covenantal, and churchly reading of Scripture. The Bible is the boulder God throws in our path that crushes our idols and idolatries by which God arrests our hearts and minds to hold them captive to His Word.[3] Again, as Webster notes: 'Theology has its controlling center in exegesis of Holy Scripture; Holy Scripture is the Word of God; the Word of God summons us to faithful reading.'[4] But theology is more than reading and listening, as we must speak God's words back to Him as a child repeats his father's words all in the effort of learning how to talk. We can then take those words that trace the divine word and address them to the church and the world at large. But we must always be careful that our theology rightly interprets God's Word. As Thomas Aquinas once observed: 'Whatever is not according to Christ should be rejected.'[5]

My hope is that this book will contribute in a small way to the ongoing discussions about covenant theology, and the covenant of works in particular. The fact that there are so few monographs on

---

3. Webster, *The Culture of Theology*, 71, 74.

4. Webster, *The Culture of Theology*, 65.

5. Thomas Aquinas, *Commentary on the Letters of St. Paul to the Philippians, Colossians, Thessalonians, Timothy, Titus, and Philemon*, Latin / English Edition of the Works of St. Thomas Aquinas, trans. F. R. Larcher (Lander, WY: The Aquinas Institute for the Study of Sacred Doctrine, 2012), §§95-96 (pp. 108-09).

the covenant of works despite its wide attestation in the Reformed tradition exposes the need for greater reflection upon this vital doctrine. I use the English Standard Version unless otherwise noted, and at times I quote the biblical text that appears in cited works. All confessions and catechism quotations unless otherwise noted come from Jaroslav Pelikan and Valerie Hotchkiss, eds, *Creeds and Confessions of Faith in the Christian Tradition*, 3 vols. (New Haven, CT: Yale University Press, 2003). All translations are mine unless otherwise noted.

❦INTRODUCTION❧

EVEN though they no longer live and walk among us, dead theologians continue to speak through their written testimony. Shelves lined with books comprise a seemingly endless maze in which countless voices speak to one another in their effort to understand God's revelation. One shelf within this labyrinthine library is dedicated to understanding the conditions in which God originally created Adam and Eve. Did He create our first parents in a covenant, command them to obey, and if they were faithful, He would grant them eternal life? In seeking an answer to this question, we can pull a book off the shelf and eavesdrop on one conversation. In *Palæmon's Creed Reviewed and Examined*, eighteenth-century Presbyterian David Wilson argued that the distinction between the covenants of works and grace was merely the difference between the law of works and the gospel upon which the apostle Paul rests much of his reasoning in his epistles to the Romans and Galatians. 'For it must be evident to every one who attentively considers the scope of the apostle's reasoning in those places where he opposes the *promise*, or covenant of grace, to the *law*, that the distinction which he makes betwixt them tallies exactly, or rather is the very same with that distinction betwixt the covenant of works and the covenant of grace.' The differentiation between the two covenants did not owe 'its rise only to the fond conceit of some systematic divines' as some mistakenly claimed.[1] Wilson and his debate partner were on opposite sides of the aisle

---

1. David Wilson, *Palæmon's Creeds Reviewed and Examined*, 2 vols. (London: George Keith, 1762), I:59.

– Wilson believed the covenant of works was biblical whereas his debate partner did not. Telling is Wilson's remark that the doctrine's critic rejected 'what is contained in the confessions of all the Reformed churches, and has hitherto been taught by all sound Protestant divines, concerning the covenant of works.'[2] In other words, the covenant of works was a prized, well-received, biblical doctrine among Reformed churches but there was a rising tide of criticism that would reach its high water mark in the twentieth century within the very heart of the Reformed church.

As we return Wilson's book back to the shelf it reveals that some within the Reformed church believed that the doctrine of the covenant of works should be forgotten. It was a well-intended but failed effort to understand the opening act of the drama of redemption. On the other hand, what if Wilson is correct? What if the covenant of works is a term theologians apply to various ideas that the Scriptures raise in connection to Adam's initial creation and probation in the garden? What if the covenant of works is a vital part of biblical revelation? This book argues that Wilson is correct and along with him the historic Reformed tradition: the covenant of works is a fundamental piece of biblical revelation. While the doctrine has borne a number of different terms (e.g., covenant of life, covenant of works, *foedus naturae*, creation covenant, covenant of nature, first covenant, Adamic covenant), theologians have argued that God's relationship to Adam was more than an act of creation and bald probation. God made creatures in His image, gave them the creation, and entered into a loving covenantal bond with them. As common as this doctrine was among early modern Reformed theologians, critics arose and ultimately rejected it. Why did they discard the covenant of works? Briefly examining the chief criticisms against the covenant of works sets the stage for retrieving the doctrine, which is the chief aim of this book.

Critics

Karl Barth (1886-1968) is perhaps one of the most famous opponents of the covenant of works. He rejected the doctrine

---

2. Wilson, *Palæmon's Creed*, 60-61.

because he believed it contaminated theology with a principle of Pelagianism. Barth writes:

> The first place is taken by the strange spectacle of man in Paradise to whom eternal life is promised as a reward which he has earned, whose works can perfectly fulfill the command of God (even if his obedience is not yet secure), to whom God is just as much bound by this fulfillment as he [Adam] is to God, between whom and God the relationship is clearly that of a *do ut des* [I give, so you will give]. And this relationship is supposed to be the original form of the covenant.[3]

Barth does not explicitly use the term, but his complaint focuses upon the supposed contractual nature of the covenant. The *quid pro quo* relationship does not accord with Barth's Christocentric understanding of God's covenantal dealings with humanity. In his assessment, this contractual element distorts the rest of God's covenants and never departs. Instead, Barth believed that there was only one covenant, the covenant of grace which was mediated exclusively through Christ. According to Barth there was no covenantal relationship apart from Christ at any point, whether before or after the fall. Barth favored first-generation Reformed theologians because of their supposedly purer formulation of the covenant, but they soiled it with their erroneous doctrine of double predestination.[4] Barth therefore rejected all things natural (natural theology, natural law, the covenant of works) and maintained that all of God's interaction with creation was through the one covenant of grace in Christ, the only elected and rejected man.[5]

John Murray (1898-1975), erstwhile professor of systematic theology at Westminster Theological Seminary, Philadelphia, Pennsylvania, is one of the best-known conservative Reformed critics of the covenant of works. He stands in a long line of Scottish theologians who sought to unseat the doctrine. Murray argued that covenants were promissory in character based upon the fact that the first use of *berith* ('covenant') appears in God's dealings with

---

3. Karl Barth, *Church Dogmatics*, 14 vols., ed. G. W. Bromiley and T. F. Torrance (Edinburgh: T & T Clark, 1936-68), IV/1:62.

4. Barth, *Church Dogmatics*, IV/1:58.

5. Barth, *Church Dogmatics*, IV/1:59, 97, 140, 267.

Noah, not before. Hence, because God required Adam's obedience, His relationship with the first man was not covenantal, though of course it was marked by divine grace. Murray preferred the term *Adamic Administration* because of the supposedly non-covenantal character of the pre-fall context.[6]

James B. Torrance (1923-2003) followed in Murray's footsteps with the thesis that post-Reformation Calvinists foisted the idea of *contract* (a mutual agreement between equals) upon the biblical concept of covenant (a promise). Torrance was inspired by Murray but also by Barth. Torrance agreed with Barth's assessment that later Calvinists supposedly inverted John Calvin's (1509-1564) gospel-law understanding of redemption and contaminated it with the law-gospel structure through the infection of the covenant of works. In other words, a law-gospel understanding aligns the law with the covenant of works and the gospel with the covenant of grace. In Barth's view, there is no covenant of works and thus no pre-fall context where the law takes priority to grace. Rather, since all of God's dealings pre- or post-fall are part of the covenant of grace, fallen or not, all people first encounter the grace of God and then the law, thus gospel-law, not law-gospel. By adding the covenant of works, later Calvinists supposedly displaced God's grace in Christ and introduced legalism, among other errors, into Reformed theology.[7] Despite the fact that historians have thoroughly dismantled Torrance's claims, some still rely on his discredited thesis.[8]

New Testament professor Douglas Campbell is fond of Torrance's essays, as they 'were an interpretive epiphany for'

---

6. John Murray, 'Adamic Administration,' in *Collected Writings*, 4 vols. (Edinburgh: Banner of Truth, 1977), II:50-51; idem, 'Covenant Theology,' in *Collected Writings*, IV:216.

7. James B. Torrance, 'Covenant or Contract? A Study of the Theological Background of Worship in Seventeenth-Century Scotland,' *SJT* 23 (1970): 51-76; idem, 'The Concept of Federal Theology – Was Calvin a Federal Theologian?' in *Calvinus Sacrae Scripturae Professor: Calvin as Confessor of Holy Scripture*, ed. Wilhelm H. Neusner (Grand Rapids: Eerdmans, 1994), 15-40.

8. For critique of Torrance's claims, see Richard A. Muller, *After Calvin: Studies in the Development of a Theological Tradition* (Oxford: Oxford University Press, 2003), 63-104, esp. 175-90.

him.[9] He controversially claims that much of Lutheran and classic Reformed theology suffers from individualism, rationalism, and contractualism.[10] Campbell informs his criticism of classic Reformed theology from Torrance's work where he 'points out the fundamentally contractual structure of this system's soteriology and the consequent theological difficulties and cultural alliances that such a model can generate.'[11] Campbell takes his cue from Torrance and then describes classic Reformed theology in the following manner: 'This model has a pronounced binary structure: one is supposed to move from an unsaved, "unjustified" condition to a saved, "justified" condition by means of the exercise of "faith."'[12] Campbell calls the classic Reformed understanding of the covenants *Justification theory*, and believes that it is bad theology because of its supposedly contractual nature.[13] Disproving Campbell's broader claims is beyond the scope of this book, but what is of particular interest are his assertions about the supposed contractual nature of historic covenant theology, especially as it relates to the covenant of works.[14] In short, Campbell does not engage any primary source reading but rests his whole rejection of classic Reformed covenant theology upon Torrance's earlier work.

Another theologian who follows in Murray's footsteps is Andrew McGowan. Like Murray, McGowan believes that the 'in Adam / in Christ' teaching of Scripture does not require a covenantal underpinning and is better categorized as 'headship theology.'[15] Like

---

9. Douglas A. Campbell, *The Deliverance of God: An Apocalyptic Rereading of Justification in Paul* (Grand Rapids: Eerdmans, 2009), xxx.

10. Campbell, *Deliverance of God*, 7.

11. Campbell, *Deliverance of God*, 14-15.

12. Campbell, *Deliverance of God*, 15.

13. Campbell, *Deliverance of God*, 36.

14. For critique of Campbell on his doctrine of justification, see R. Michael Allen, *Justification and the Gospel: Understanding the Contexts and Controversies* (Grand Rapids: Baker Academic, 2013), 17, 35-36, 42-45, 102-04, 128-29, 167-69; Michael Horton, *Justification*, 2 vols. (Grand Rapids: Zondervan, 2018), II:60, 66-68, 164-68, 174-80, 220-22, 237-42, 297-99, 301, 317-20, 418-20, 434-35, 460-64

15. A. T. B. McGowan, *Adam, Christ and Covenant: Exploring Headship Theology* (London: Apollos, 2016), 2.

Campbell's uncritical use of Torrance's erroneous historiography, McGowan relies on questionable secondary sources to build his own dogmatic claims.[16] Additionally, McGowan expresses sympathies with Barth's criticisms of classic Reformed covenant theology. McGowan writes: 'Only when we have described God's free act of reconciliation in Christ can we turn to consider the covenantal relationship which God has set in place as part of the outworking of his sovereign and gracious electing action.'[17] McGowan believes that Barth rejects the 'notion of a "mutually binding contract,"' and as such, the 'use of this language of "contract" was later rejected by scholars in the Barth tradition.' McGowan then references Torrance's rejection of Reformed covenant theology which failed to see that 'the covenant was primarily gracious, based on love and not law.'[18] In his appraisal, McGowan contends that Barth was right to insist on the priority of grace over law, though he nowhere accounts for the philosophical Idealism that drove Barth to this conclusion.[19]

McGowan is but one of several other contemporary critics of the covenant of works. Recently Michael Williams, professor of systematic theology at Covenant Theological Seminary, has written against the idea that Adam could merit eternal life in the covenant of works. Like the earlier disapprovals, Williams believes that the language of merit and contract is self-centered. 'Merit invites us to think in mercenary, self-centered ways,' writes Williams, 'placing worth upon one's labor and the reward to which one is entitled upon completion of the labor or service, I believe that it is inappropriate for the depiction of the biblical covenant relationship between God and man.'[20] To be sure, Williams still maintains that Adam and God were in covenant, but any attempt to incorporate merit (the idea that Adam

---

16. McGowan, *Adam, Christ and Covenant*, 13. McGowan relies on the criticized theories of David Weir, *Origins of the Federal Theology in Sixteenth-Century Reformation Thought* (Oxford: Oxford University Press, 1990); cf. Richard A. Muller, 'Review of David Weir, *Origins of the Federal Theology*,' *TJR* 72/4 (1992): 597-98.

17. McGowan, *Adam, Christ and Covenant*, 23.

18. McGowan, *Adam, Christ and Covenant*, 25.

19. McGowan, *Adam, Christ and Covenant*, 35.

20. Michael Williams, 'Adam and Merit,' *Presbyterion* 35/2 (2009): 87-94, esp. 89.

earns the reward of eternal life) fails to see that God's interaction with Adam is not *quid pro quo*. He argues: 'Contractual relationships are oriented toward merit, as contracts focus upon reward rather than persons. God's covenant, however, is always focused upon the relationship between parties.'[21] This leads Williams to conclude: 'The doctrine of adamic merit and the notion of a Garden probation that the doctrine necessitates are fatally flawed, a reading of Genesis 1-2 that is contrary to the natural reading of the text, for it is one that arises from a dogmatic prejudice rather than cooperation with the text.'[22] Williams leaves the idea of an Adamic covenant intact but he empties it of much of its classic content. This is not to grant that classic Reformed theology employs the concept of merit as Williams implies, but he does pair it with the idea of probation, which lies at the heart of the historic Reformed covenant of works.

To this chorus of dissent, one may add the voice of New Testament scholar N. T. Wright. Wright has argued that there is much wrong with traditional Reformed theology because it has supposedly encouraged a Platonized understanding of salvation, an impulse that eschews earth in favor of an idealized heaven. Correlatively, Wright believes that much of the thinking and preaching about the cross in the present day has assumed the covenant of works. He targets the Westminster Confession of Faith as the chief embodiment of the doctrine. He acknowledges that there are different varieties of Reformed theology that agree with his own assessment, and thus have avoided using the term *covenant of works*. Wright does not identify who he might have in mind, though perhaps he has someone like Murray in view. Nevertheless, Wright's principal problem lies with what he calls the 'works contract.'[23] Wright provides a basically accurate but nonetheless threadbare description of historic Reformed covenant theology ('works contract'). God gave to Adam and Eve the command to keep a moral code in order to maintain their continuing life in

---

21. Williams, 'Adam and Merit,' 88-89.

22. Williams, 'Adam and Merit,' 90.

23. N. T. Wright, *The Day the Revolution Began: Reconsidering the Meaning of Jesus's Crucifixion* (San Francisco, CA: Harper One, 2016), 74.

the garden. Failure would mean their death. The works contract was then repeated with Israel through the Mosaic law, but like Adam and Eve, Israel failed. Finally, Jesus entered the scene and obeyed the moral law perfectly, paid the penalty of the broken law, and secured redemption. 'The overarching arrangement (the "works contract") between God and humans remained the same,' Wright avers, 'but Jesus had done what was required.'[24] Even though such explanations regularly appeal to the first three chapters of Romans, Wright counters that this all has nothing to do with Paul's letter. Righteousness is not about a moral status for one who has kept the 'works contract' perfectly, but rather the covenant faithfulness of God and about determining who belongs to the global family of Abraham.[25] Like Williams, Wright acknowledges that God and Adam were in covenant, but this is not a covenant of works but a *covenant of vocation*: 'The vocation in question is that of being a genuine human being, with genuinely human tasks to perform as part of the Creator's purpose for his world. The main task of this vocation is "image-bearing," reflecting the Creator's wise stewardship into the world and reflecting the praises of all creation back to its maker.'[26]

There are a number of factors that unite the aforementioned detractors of the doctrine. First, with the exception of Murray, there is generally a shallow engagement with primary sources. Few examine early modern Reformed works to see what they actually say about the covenant of works, whether exegetically or theologically. One of the common claims is that the doctrine supposedly rests on thin exegetical ice—maybe one verse—Hosea 6:7. But a survey of various works quickly dispels this accusation. As subsequent chapters will show, there is a large exegetical underpinning for the covenant of works. A second related imprecision is the doctrine's supposed contractual nature, which appears to be the principal

---

24. Wright, *Revolution*, 75.

25. Wright, *Revolution*, 75. Also see idem, *What St. Paul Really Said: Was Paul of Tarsus the Real Founder of Christianity?* (Grand Rapids: Eerdmans, 1997); idem, *Paul and the Faithfulness of God*, 2 vols. (Minneapolis, MN: Fortress Press, 2013), 796-856.

26. Wright, *Revolution*, 76.

complaint. Granted, early modern Reformed theologians use the word *contract* to describe and discuss the covenant of works, but this use of terminology is far from a smoking gun. Rather, one should ask whether *contract* means the same thing in the early modern and modern contexts. The problem with the contract versus covenant thesis is that detractors of the covenant of works fail on two fronts: they impose a modern definition of *contract* upon early modern uses of the term and they insufficiently factor what the Bible has to say about the nature of covenants. As this book proceeds with its argument, it will demonstrate the historical, exegetical, and theological deficiencies in the criticisms against the covenant of works.

Aims

The chief aim of this book is to recover the doctrine of the covenant of works. This is not to say that the doctrine has completely vanished from the contemporary scene. In recent years several works have been published defending the doctrine.[27] There are also several recent contributions that defend classic Reformed covenant theology.[28] At the same time, in the history of the doctrine there have been relatively few monographs devoted exclusively to the covenant of works. To my count there are only five entries that expound the doctrine from the sixteenth- through nineteenth-centuries.[29] There are, of

---

27. See, e.g., Richard C. Barcellos, *The Covenant of Works: Its Confessional and Scriptural Basis* (Palmdale, CA: Reformed Baptist Academic Press, 2016); idem, *Getting the Garden Right: Adam's Work and God's Rest in Light of Christ* (Cape Coral, FL: Founders Press, 2017); Rowland S. Ward, *God and Adam: Reformed Theology and the Creation Covenant* (2003; Lansvale, Australia: Tulip Publishing, 2019).

28. Guy P. Waters, J. Nicholas Reid, and John R. Muether, *Covenant Theology: Biblical, Theological, and Historical Perspectives* (Wheaton, IL: Crossway, 2020); Richard P. Belcher Jr., *The Fulfillment of the Promises of God: An Explanation of Covenant Theology* (Fearn: Mentor, 2020); Michael Brown and Zach Keele, *Sacred Bond: Covenant Theology Explored*, 2nd ed. (Grand Rapids: Reformed Fellowship, 2019); Michael Horton, *Introducing Covenant Theology* (Grand Rapids: Baker, 2009).

29. See Thomas Boston, *A View of the Covenant of Works from the Sacred Records*, 2nd ed (Edinburgh: John Gray, 1775); John Colquhoun, *A Treatise on the Covenant of Works* (Edinburgh: Thomsons, Brothers, 1821); William Lusk, *Discourses on the*

course, numerous treatments of the doctrine within broader works on covenant theology or sections in systems of theology. But given the lack of focused attention upon this doctrine and its pervasive rejection within the Reformed church, circumstances call for a full-orbed treatment and retrieval.

In this work I defend the thesis that the covenant of works is biblical and a necessary element for a right understanding of God, the world, Christ, and our redemption. Wilhelmus à Brakel (1635-1711) once noted the importance of the doctrine: 'For whoever errs here or denies the existence of the covenant of works will not understand the covenant of grace, and will readily err concerning the mediatorship of the Lord Jesus. Such a person will readily deny that Christ by his active obedience has merited a right to eternal life for the elect.'[30] Understanding the nature of the triune God's interaction with Adam ultimately sets the stage for the work of the last Adam, Jesus. Even though critics disparage the doctrine as cold and contractual, in reality it is all about the love of God. First Samuel 18:3 records these words about Jonathan's covenant with David, but they also say as much about God's covenant with Adam: 'Then Jonathan made a covenant with David, because he loved him as his own soul.' In other words, Adam was not God's equal, but God still showered him in the gifts of creation *ex nihilo*, made Adam and Eve in His very own image, and entered into holy communion with them by dwelling with them in the garden of Eden, the first earthly temple. God commanded Adam and Eve to be fruitful, fill all the earth, subdue it, and not to eat from the tree of knowledge.

The covenant of works was both the place where Adam and Eve were supposed to obey God's commands and to love Him. But obedience and love do not contradict one another but comprise two different sides of the same coin. Love and obedience lie at the heart of God's covenants with His people: 'You shall love the LORD your

---

Covenant of Works, the Fall of Man, and Original Sin (Troy, NY: N. Tuttle, 1832); James Duncan, *A Treatise on the Covenant of Works, Man's Fall and his Recovery through Jesus Christ* (Pittsburgh, PA: S. Engles & Co., 1813); John Love, *The Covenant of Works: Its Nature and End. A Discourse* (Aberdeen: G. & R. King, 1848).

30. Wilhelmus à Brakel, *The Christian's Reasonable Service*, 4 vols., trans. Bartel Elshout (Morgan, PA: Soli Deo Gloria, 1992): I:355.

God with all your heart and with all your soul and with all your might' (Deut. 6:5). Or in the words of Christ, 'If you love me, you will keep my commandments' (John 14:15). But in the light of Adam's apostasy, the covenant of works is not about an anthropocentric approach to God but ultimately about Jesus. Adam was a type of the one who was to come (Rom. 5:14), which means that the last Adam succeeded where the first failed. 'When Christ came into the world, he said ... "Behold, I have come to do your will, O God"' (Heb. 10:5-7; Ps. 40:6-8). As Jesus told His disciples: 'As the Father has loved me, so have I loved you. Abide in my love. If you keep my commandments, you will abide in my love, just as I have kept my Father's commandments and abide in his love' (John 15:9-10). Succinctly stated, the covenant of works sets the stage for the work of Christ. There is no redemption apart from creation, no last Adam without the first. There is no God-man without the first man. Every brush stroke, color, and hue in Adam's portrait points forward to God's saving love in Christ, excepting, of course, Adam's sin.

Plan

In order to prove this book's thesis, the book proceeds in three parts: history, exegesis, and doctrine. Part I presents a survey of key historical questions that establishes subsequent exegetical and doctrinal discussions.[31] Exploring the history of doctrine ensures that constructive theology is not merely a monologue but rather an ongoing dialogue with the church throughout the ages.

Part I

Part I explores six key issues: terminology, Leviticus 18:5, Adam's faith, covenant versus contract, grace in the covenant of works, and the connection between the Adamic and Mosaic covenants. Chapter I.1 explores the question of terminology. The *covenant of works* is one of the most common terms for the pre-fall God-Adam relationship, but it is not the only one. Theologians used a number of different terms to capture the various aspects of God's

---

31. For a historical survey of the history of the doctrine, see J. V. Fesko, *The Covenant of Works: Origins, Development, and Reception* (Oxford: Oxford University Press, 2020).

covenant with Adam; this chapter examines the reasons behind the different names theologians employed.

Critics claim that the covenant of works is a one-text doctrine, but one of the chief exegetical pillars, among many, is Leviticus 18:5, 'Do this and live.' Chapter I.2 presents a history of the use of this text from Thomas Aquinas (1225-1274), John Calvin, and a host of other early modern Reformed theologians to show how this Old Testament verse plays an important role in understanding Adam's pre-fall probation. Chapter I.3 investigates the question of Adam's faith. Early modern Reformed theologians believed that Adam had a general faith in God. But unlike faith in Christ, an extraspective faith that rests, receives, and accepts His work for salvation, Adam's faith was different. Adam's legal faith versus the faith of the covenant of grace is the difference between law and gospel: a general trust in God's Word that leads to obedience in the pre-fall context versus trusting in the all sufficient work of Christ for salvation in a post-fall world.

As much as modern critics inveigh against early modern theologians for supposedly confusing contract and covenant, chapter I.4 surveys these two concepts to prove that the critics have misunderstood both ideas. The Enlightenment significantly reconfigured the idea of contracts and some, such as James Torrance, have failed to realize that they read early modern texts through modern eyes. In early modernity, contracts and covenants were overlapping categories. Moreover, like covenants, contracts could take on different characteristics – they could be purely promissory or marked by requirements of mutual obligation. Just because a theologian uses the word *contract* does not mean he has imposed foreign commercial or cultural ideas upon the biblical text. In the early modern period contracts were the setting for displaying Christian virtues such as love and faithfulness, whereas in the modern period such motivations evaporated under the hot sun of rationalism. Contracts 'evolved' to become all about self-interest devoid of love and virtue.

The covenant of works supposedly turned Adam into God's equal, but such claims do not account for the way that many early modern Reformed theologians frequently appealed to divine grace even within the covenant of works. Such an appeal is not unique to Reformed theology but has precedent in the theology of Augustine (354-430), who believed that God created Adam and Eve in a state of grace. But as theologians integrated covenant with the pre-fall context, the conversation shifted from grace to the liberality of God's promise. Chapter I.5, therefore, surveys the question of grace in the covenant of works to uncover the different ways that early modern Reformed theologians explained how an infinite and transcendent God condescended to create and covenant with a finite creature. Chapter I.6 addresses one of the most complicated and debated issues related to the covenant of works, namely, its connection to the Mosaic covenant. This chapter uncovers a least a dozen different ways that theologians explain how the covenant of works relates to the Mosaic covenant. Despite the numerous opinions, there is a great degree of charity and flexibility that theologians exercised towards each other over this difficult question. Understanding the nexus between Adam and Moses reveals that, far from being a one text doctrine, Reformed theologians were reading the creation narrative within the broader context of the Pentateuch and canon of Scripture.

Part II
Part II examines eight passages that serve as an exegetical foundation for the covenant of works: Romans 2:14-15, Genesis 2:16-17, Leviticus 18:5, Isaiah 24:5, Hosea 6:7, Galatians 4:24, Romans 5:12-21, and Romans 7:1-6. Going back more than one hundred fifty years, critics have derided advocates of the covenant of works for supposedly inventing the doctrine from the debated translation of one verse, 'Like Adam they transgressed the covenant' (Hosea 6:7). An inspection of works that explain the doctrine, however, easily reveals that there is a whole host of biblical texts to which theologians appeal. Part II engages a number of these texts with fresh exegesis to establish the legitimacy of the doctrine. Chapter II.1 covers Romans 2:14-15, which speaks about the law written on the heart of all human beings. This naturally revealed law constitutes part of the legal basis for the covenant of works. Adam knew of the requirement to obey God because it was inscribed

upon his heart, which means that natural law is a vital part of bearing God's image and the knowledge that obedience would yield a reward. Chapter II.2 explains the significance of Genesis 2:16-17, God's command not to eat from the tree of knowledge. Reading this passage within the broader context of the Pentateuch, however, is crucial for recognizing its covenantal character. There are intra-canonical links between Genesis and Deuteronomy that reveal that God entered into a covenant with Adam.

Whereas Part I surveys the history of the exegesis of Leviticus 18:5, chapter II.3 revisits this passage exegetically. Through an examination of the subsequent intra-canonical interpretation of Leviticus 18:5 in Ezekiel 20:1-26, Nehemiah 9:29, Luke 10:25-28, Galatians 3:10-12, and Romans 10:5, the chapter shows that this verse teaches the covenant of works and is not a reference to the third (or normative) use of the law as John Murray claims. In other words, Leviticus 18:5 reveals that perfect obedience to the law of God yields the reward of eternal life, and as such, addresses the nature of Adam's pre-fall work. Chapter II.4 explores the prophet Isaiah's important statement, 'The earth lies defiled under its inhabitants; for they have transgressed the laws, violated the statutes, broken the everlasting covenant' (24:5). Interpreters have offered a number of different explanations for Isaiah's reference to the 'everlasting covenant,' but this chapter explains that Isaiah refers to God's covenant with Adam. Chapter II.5 ventures into the contested interpretation of Hosea 6:7. Critics of the covenant of works dismiss this verse as irrelevant for a host of reasons, but this chapter suggests that a careful reading provides explicit testimony of God's covenant with Adam. The chapter provides a brief history of interpretation and then exegetes the text to prove that Hosea refers to an Adamic covenant.

Another principal passage to which advocates of the covenant of works have historically appealed is Galatians 4:24, 'These women are two covenants. One is from Mount Sinai, bearing children for slavery; she is Hagar.' Chapter II.6 demonstrates that when Paul refers to Mount Sinai and the Mosaic covenant as Hagar, he taps into the stream of the covenant of works. In other words, even though the Mosaic covenant is part of the covenant of grace, it reminds Israel that the covenant of works still hangs over the heads of all people, whether Jew or Gentile. Among the cloud of passages that support the covenant of works, Romans 5:12-21 is one of the more commonly cited, and hence chapter II.7 exegetes this text. Theologians rightly quote this text in support of the covenant of works chiefly because of the Adam-Christ parallels that Paul describes. The doctrine of imputation lies at the heart of Romans 5, and imputation is a covenantal concept. How are all people subject to Adam's disobedience, and conversely how do believers benefit from Christ's obedience? The covenantal imputation of sin and righteousness provides the answer to these two questions. But fundamental to Paul's argument is both the doctrine of imputation and the specific terminology he employs. Paul uses Old Testament terminology for covenantal violation when he describes Adam's sin. Like Hosea 6:7, Paul's language is more direct evidence that God and Adam were in covenant. Romans 7:1-6 is the last examined passage in Part II. Chapter II.8 explains that when Christ redeems sinners from the bondage of the law, He frees them from the covenant of works. That Paul uses the covenantal imagery of marriage is no coincidence. Only death releases a person from the covenantal bonds of marriage, and therefore only Christ's death frees all people, Jew or Gentile, from the bond of the covenant of works.

Part III

Part III takes the exegetical foundation established in Part II and builds the doctrine of the covenant of works upon it in four chapters: a statement of the doctrine, the covenant of works and Sinai, the doctrine of justification, and grace and merit. Chapter III.1 takes all of the gathered exegetical data and organizes it to formulate the doctrine of the covenant of works by explaining its elements, promise, condition, penalty, sacraments, and present status. Chapter III.2 treads upon the highly controverted topic of the connections between the Adamic and Mosaic covenants. While the better part of wisdom might suggest avoiding the subject altogether, the fact that so many Reformed theologians engage the issue reveals its importance. A right understanding of the garden's connections to Sinai establishes a number of theological issues including the intra-canonical exegetical footing for the covenant of works, the universal human obligation to it, and the work of the last Adam as the only one who can redeem sinners from its curse. Chapter III.3 treats the topic of justification by faith alone, which might seem out of place given that the doctrine features prominently in the covenant of grace. Nevertheless, proponents of the covenant of works regularly invoke the doctrine of justification. This is not an error but rather illustrates two points. First, the doctrine of justification has its roots in Genesis 1-2, not Genesis 15. In other words, a biblical theology of justification must drill beyond Abraham's profession of faith to God's commands to Adam and Eve. Second, the origins of justification in Genesis 1-2 reveal that eschatology is born in the covenant of works, not the covenant of grace. Alternatively stated, eschatology precedes soteriology. Before sin ever entered the world, God gave Adam the promise of eschatological life in the covenant of works.

Chapter III.4 revisits the questions raised in chapter I.5 regarding grace in the covenant of works. Despite the common Reformed claims that Adam required God's grace, other Reformed theologians have proposed a superior idea. Rather than grace, the covenant, God's love, and the liberality of His promise provide a better alternative. In a post-Barthian world where Christology and grace swallow all other categories, God's love, benevolence, and the gifts of creation are a better way to account for God's initial covenantal dealings with Adam. Reserving God's grace for the post-fall world preserves the differences between nature and grace, creation and redemption, and most importantly protects the *man* in the God-*man*. But imperative in understanding God's relationship to Adam and how a mere creature could secure eternal life by his finite obedience is remembering that the covenant of works involves the triune God, specifically the Holy Spirit. The Spirit's work in Adam's covenant is an often-overlooked element in the pre-fall world. Thus, accounting for the doctrine of the Holy Spirit in the covenant of works is paramount for a robust account.

Conclusion

As popular as it is to reject the covenant of works, upon a closer examination the historic Reformed doctrine provides significant biblical insights for understanding humanity's initial creation. The covenant of works offers a thick account of Adam's initial creation and helps us to understand the nature of Christ's work of redemption. In the words of Herman Bavinck (1854-1921): 'Adam was not only obligated to keep the law but was confronted in the covenant of works with that law as the way to eternal life, a life he did not yet possess. But Christ, in virtue of His union with the divine nature, already had this eternal and blessed life. This life He voluntarily relinquished. He submitted Himself to the law of the covenant of works as the way to eternal life for Himself and His own.'[32] The covenants of works and grace are nothing more than terms that house a great storehouse of biblical information that relates to the first and last Adams. It behooves the church, therefore, to enter into the theological library labyrinth of the ages past to recover the doctrine of the covenant of works.

---

32. Herman Bavinck, *Reformed Dogmatics*, trans. John Vriend, ed. John Bolt, vol. 3 (Grand Rapids: Baker Academic, 2006), 379.

❦ PART I ❧
History

∽ I.1 ∽

Terms

Introduction

Reformed theology has long used and cherished covenantal
language for Adam's relationship with God. Criticism of
this language has arisen only relatively recently, for example, in
the twentieth century. John Murray (1898-1975) rejected the idea
of a covenant of works and instead preferred to refer to God's
pre-fall dealings with humanity as the *Adamic Administration*.
He advocated this change in terminology because the Bible does
not explicitly apply the term *covenant* to the Adamic state, and he
did not want to employ the term *works* to describe it. Although
Adam was under a divine probation, Murray nevertheless wanted
to register the idea that it was not a contract or compact.[1] If
Murray was pressed to employ the term *covenant* to describe
the pre-fall Adamic state, then he preferred *covenant of life*,
which was a term used by the Westminster Shorter and Larger
Catechisms.[2] Murray's rejection and preference of designations
raises an interesting question about the various terms early modern
Reformed theologians used to either label or describe the pre-fall

---

1. John Murray, 'Adamic Administration,' in *Collected Writings*, 4 vols. (Edinburgh: Banner of Truth, 1977), II:47-59, esp. 50.

2. *The Humble Advice of the Assembly of Divines, Now by Authority of Parliament Sitting at Westminster, Concerning a Larger Catechisme* (London: A. M., 1648), q. 20; *The Humble Advice of the Assembly of Divines, Now by Authority of Parliament Sitting at Westminster, Concerning a Shorter Catechism* (London: J. F., 1648), q. 12.

Adamic state. While *covenant of works* was certainly common, it was by no means the only term used. This chapter, therefore, presents a brief reconnaissance of the various terms used for the pre-fall covenant.

In short, theologians employed vocabulary based ultimately on personal preference, but they nevertheless chose different terms for the pre-fall covenant based upon how they identified the sequential place, nature, basis, condition, or goal of the covenant. But regardless of the rationale, theologians never made terminology a test of orthodoxy. Even then, this succinct survey provides an opportunity to better understand the rationale behind the Adamic covenant; it showcases the fact that it was a doctrinal construct rather than an explicit teaching of Scripture.[3] In other words, theologians arrived at the shores of this doctrine by way of good and necessary consequence. The chapter first surveys a collection of numerous terms that theologians employed to designate or describe the Adamic covenant. The survey is not exhaustive but illustrative to provide examples of the different terms that appear in early modern treatments of the Adamic covenant. Second, the chapter examines two high orthodox Reformed theologians, Francis Turretin (1623-1687) and Herman Witsius (1636-1708), in order to get a closer look at how they arrived at their respective decisions regarding the proper label for the Adamic covenant. The chapter then concludes with some observations about the various terms early modern theologians applied to the pre-fall covenant.

Survey of Terms

One of the earliest designations for the Adamic covenant comes from Roman Catholic theologian, Diego Lañyez (1512-1565), who spoke of the 'first and second covenants' (*primo et secondi pacti*). Sequence appears to be the motivating factor in this choice, as Adam's covenant is naturally first and the 'covenant of the grace

---

3. On this point, see e.g., Richard A. Muller and Roland A. Ward, *Scripture and Worship: Biblical Interpretation and the Directory for Worship* (Phillipsburg, NJ: P & R, 2007), 69-81; J. V. Fesko, *The Theology of the Westminster Standards: Historical Context and Theological Insights* (Wheaton, IL: Crossway, 2014), 86-90.

of God' (*pacti gratiae Dei*) comes second.[4] The choice, therefore, is practical. Another rationale for choosing terminology lies in soteriological categories and the relationship between law and gospel. Martin Luther (1483-1546) famously distinguished between the categories of law and gospel.[5] The law makes demands and the gospel gives promises. Other theologians such as Zacharias Ursinus (1534-1583), who studied with Lutheran theologian Philip Melanchthon (1497-1560), picked up this distinction and employed it in his own theology.[6] In his Larger Catechism, Ursinus poses the question, 'What is the difference between law and the gospel?' He replies: 'The law contains the natural covenant [*foedus naturale*] ... The gospel, however, contains the covenant of grace [*foedus gratiae*].'[7] Ursinus layers the natural covenant and covenant of grace over the categories of law and gospel, which was a trend that appears in several early modern Reformed treatments of the Adamic covenant. Ursinus' use of the terms *natural* juxtaposed with *grace*, however, owes its origins to the long-standing doctrinal pair of nature and grace, common to patristic and medieval theology.[8]

Nevertheless, Thomas Cartwright (1534-1603), for example, succinctly states: 'The lawe and the ghospell, otherwise called the

---

4. Diego Lañyez, 'Disputatio de justitia imputata,' in *Jacobi Lainez Disputationes Tridentiae*, vol. 2, ed. Harmannus Grisar (Regensberg: Feliciania Rauch, 1886), II.v (p. 159), II.xxxvii (p. 189).

5. Robet Kolb, 'Luther's Hermeneutics of Distinctions: Law and Gospel, Two Kinds of Righteousness, Two Realms, Freedom and Bondage,' in *The Oxford Handbook of Martin Luther's Theology*, eds. Robert Kolb, Irene Dingel, and L'Ubomír Batka (Oxford: Oxford University Press, 2014), 168-86.

6. Derk Visser, 'Ursinus, Zacharias,' in *The Oxford Encyclopedia of the Reformation*, 4 vols., ed. Hans. J. Hilderbrand (Oxford: Oxford University Press, 1996), IV:202-03.

7. Zacharias Ursinus, *Larger Catechism*, q. 36, in *An Introduction to the Heidelberg Catechism: Sources, History and Theology*, ed. Lyle D. Bierma, et al. (Grand Rapids: Baker, 2005); idem, *Summa Theologiae*, in *Der Heidelberger Katechismus und Vier Verwandte Katechismen* (Leipzig: Georg Böhme, 1907), 156.

8. See, e.g., Augustine, *A Treatise on Nature and Grace*, in NPNF[1] V:116-54; Paul Helm, 'Nature and Grace,' in *Aquinas Among the Protestants*, eds. David VanDrunen and Manfred Svensson (Oxford: Wiley Blackwell, 2018), 229-48.

Covenant of Woorkes and the Covenant of grace.'[9] George Walker (ca. 1581-1651), a Westminster divine, discusses the importance of distinguishing between 'the knowledge of the true difference of the Old and New Testament, the Covenant of Workes, and the Covenant of Grace, the Law and the Gospel.'[10] The identification between law and gospel and the two covenants (works and grace) appeared as early as Ursinus in early orthodoxy and persisted, therefore, into the beginning stages of high orthodoxy, evident in Walker's statement but also present in the works of others, such as James Ussher (1581-1656) and Henry Finch (ca. 1558-1625).[11] In concert with the connection between law and gospel and the two covenants, some theologians employed the term *foedus naturale*. Perhaps due in part to his time at Heidelberg and the influence of Ursinus, Franciscus Gomarus (1563-1641) labels the two periods as the natural and supernatural covenants (*naturale et supernaturale*).[12] Although, these terms could also find their inspiration from Gomarus' University of Leiden colleague Francis Junius (1545-1602) and his influential work on prolegomena where he divides theology into natural and supernatural categories.[13] According to Junius, natural theology dealt with things that

---

9. Thomas Cartwright, *A Short Catechism*, in *Cartwrightiana*, ed. Albert Peel and Leland H. Carlson (London: George Allen and Unwin Ltd., 1951), 159.

10. George Walker, *The Manifold Wisedome of God: In the Divers Dispensation of Grace by Jesus Christ* (London: John Bartlet, 1640), 2-3.

11. James Ussher, *A Body of Divinitie, or The Summe and Substance of Christian Religion* (London Tho. Downes and Geo. Badger, 1645), 123; [Henry Finch], *The Summe of Sacred Divinitie* (London: William Stansby, 1625?), I.xv (p. 223). Note, Finch's *Summe of Sacred Divinitie* has been erroneously attributed to John Downame (1571-1652). On Finch's authorship of the *Summe of Sacred Divinitie*, see Randall J. Pederson, *Unity in Diversity: English Puritans and the Puritan Reformation, 1603-1689* (Leiden: Brill, 2014), 89-90 n. 2, 123-27; Richard A. Muller, *Calvin and the Reformed Tradition: On the Work of Christ and the Order of Salvation* (Grand Rapids: Baker Academic), 223 n. 176.

12. Franciscus Gomarus, *Oratio De Foedere Dei*, in *Opera Theologica Omnia* (Amsterdam: Joannis Janssonsius, 1664), 2; cf. Michael A. Hakkenberg, 'Gomarus, Franciscus,' in *The Oxford Encyclopedia of the Reformation*, 4 vols., ed. Hans. J. Hilderbrand (Oxford: Oxford University Press, 1996), II:181-82.

13. Francis Junius, *A Treatise on True Theology*, trans. David Noe (Grand Rapids: Reformation Heritage Books, 2014), 145-68.

are common to all humans, and this was Adam's state when his nature was intact.[14] Conversely, after the fall and the corruption of nature, humans required inspired or supernatural theology to rescue them.[15] Gomarus, it appears, takes these two categories and unites them to the covenant concept to designate the natural and supernatural covenants.

Another source for the Adamic covenant comes from 1 Corinthians 15:45-46: 'The first man Adam was made a living soul; the last Adam was made a quickening spirit. Howbeit that was not first which is spiritual, but that which is natural; and afterward that which is spiritual' (KJV). The fact that Paul contrasts the two periods as natural versus spiritual led theologians like John Cameron (ca. 1579-1625) to call the Adamic covenant the *foedus naturae* ('covenant of nature'), which he contrasted with the *foedus gratiae* ('covenant of grace').[16] Theologians who employed Cameron's covenant theology, such as Edward Leigh (1602-1671) and Thomas Goodwin (1600-1680), therefore, also used the same term for the Adamic covenant. Leigh, for example, contrasts the *foedus naturale* with the *foedus evangelicum*, rather than the covenant of grace.[17] But Leigh also denominates the Adamic covenant as a *foedus legale* ('legal covenant'), a term also used by Alexander Morus (1616-1670), namely, *l'Alliance légale*.[18] There was a degree of flexibility in terminology among the adherents to the covenant of works evident in Leigh's use of *foedus naturale* and *foedus legale*,

---

14. Junius, *True Theology*, thesis 16 (p. 147), thesis 17 (p. 151).

15. Junius, *True Theology*, thesis 18 (p. 154), thesis 20 (p. 160).

16. John Cameron, *Certain Theses, or, Positions of the Learned John Cameron, Concerning the Threefold Covenant of God with Man*, in Samuel Bolton, *The True Bounds of Christian Freedome* (London: P. S., 1656), thesis VII (p. 356); idem, *De Triplici Dei Cum Homine Foedere Theses* (Heidelberg: 1608); idem, *Ioh. Cameronis S. Theologiae in Academia Salmuriensi Nuper Professoris, Praelectionum Tomus Tertius et Ultimus* (Saumur: Cl. Girard & Dan. Lerpiner, 1628), 611.

17. Edward Leigh, *A Treatise of the Divine Promises. In Five Books* (London: George Millar, 1633), II.i (pp. 63-64); Thomas Goodwin, *Of the Creatures, and the Condition of Their State by Creation*, in *The Works of Thomas Goodwin*, 12 vols. (1861-1866; Eureka, CA: Tanski Publications, 1996), I.iii (vol. VII, pp. 22-23).

18. Leigh, *Divine Promises*, II.i (p. 63); see J. P. Gaberel, *Histoire de L'Elglise de Geneve*, 3 vols. (Geneva: Joël Cherbuliez, 1858-62), III:121-23.

an elasticity that also marks Robert Rollock (1555-1599). Rollock calls the Adamic covenant a *foederis legalis* ('legal covenant'), but he also uses the interchangeable terms *foedus naturae sive operum* ('covenant of nature or works').[19] But at the same time, Rollock's preference was for the term *foedus operum* because works were the condition of this covenant and hence the best term to describe it, a choice shared by others such as Johannes Heidegger (1633-1698).[20]

If Rollock decided to use the term *covenant of works* because Adam's obedience was the condition, other theologians were motivated by the covenant's telos. Westminster divine George Walker employed the terms *covenants of works and grace* in tandem with law and gospel, but he also used several other terms for the Adamic covenant: 'the covenant of natural life and blessings.'[21] Henry Finch interchangeably employed the terms *law* and the *covenant of works*, but he also readily used *life* as a term to describe the Adamic state: 'With the Creatures, who are thus to doe his will, it hath pleased God to make a Covenant which is called the Covenant of Workes: A Covenant of life (or blessedness) to the doers: of death (or of a curse unto transgressors).'[22] Obadiah Sedgwick (ca. 1600-1658) called the covenant of grace, the *covenant of life*, but this was the term the Westminster Catechisms apply to the covenant of works.[23] It seems that Walker, Finch, and Sedgwick

---

19. Robert Rollock, *Some Questions and Answers about God's Covenant and the Sacrament That is a Seal of God's Covenant*, trans. and ed. Aaron Clay Denlinger (Eugene, OR: Pickwick Publications, 2016), q. 2 (p. 21); idem, *Quaestiones et Responsiones Aliquote de Foedere Dei* (Edinburgh: Henry Charter, 1596); idem, *Analysis Logica in Epistolam Pauli Apostoli ad Galatas* (London: Felix Kyngston, 1602), 55.

20. Rollock, *God's Covenant*, qq. 14-15 (p. 24); Johannes Heidegger, *Medullae Theologiae Christianae* (Zurich: David Gessner, 1697), IX (p. 69).

21. Walker, *Manifold Wisedome of God*, 2-3.

22. [Finch], *Summe*, I.xv (p. 222).

23. Obadiah Sedgwick, *The Bowels of Tender Mercy Sealed in the Everlasting Covenant* (London: Adoniram Byfield, 1661), I.ii (p. 7); Westminster Shorter Catechism, q. 12. A number of theologians called the covenant of grace the covenant of life (see., e.g., William Lawne, *An Abridgement of the Institution of Christian Religion Written by M. John Calvin* [Edinburgh: Thomas Vautrollier, 1585], III.xxi.1; Jeremais Bastingius, *An Exposition Upon the Catechisme of the Lowe*

all recognized that life was the goal of both the covenants of works and grace and thus employed the term for both states, but the Westminster divines eventually settled on the *covenant of works* in the Confession and *covenant of life* in the Catechisms.[24] The Westminster Confession acknowledged that theologians were not decided on the precise term for the covenant of grace, which they note was one of the commonly used designations.[25] The same terminological plasticity is true of the covenant of works.

Turretin and Witsius

Turretin exemplifies the terminological flexibility that was common among early modern Reformed theologians. Turretin defines a covenant as 'a mutual agreement between two or more persons concerning the mutual bestowal of certain goods and offices for the sake of common utility.'[26] He qualifies this definition and acknowledges that in the Adamic covenant there is 'no equality or proportion between God and man,' but that through His 'infinite condescension' God 'willed to enter into a covenant with his creatures.'[27] This definition and qualification reveal that Turretin does not baldly apply the term *covenant* to the pre-fall state without careful consideration of the parties. In other words, despite the common criticisms that the covenant of works implied that God and man were equals, Turretin recognizes they are not and that the only way humanity could participate in such an arrangement is if God voluntarily and willingly condescended to His creature.

Countryes [Cambridge: John Legatt, 1589], q. 74; George Walker, *Socinianisme in the Fundamentall Point of Justification Discovered, and Confuted* [London: John Bartlet, 1641], 53; Samuel Rutherford, *The Covenant of Life Opened: or, A Treatise of the Covenant of Grace* [Edinburgh: Robert Broun, 1655]).

24. *The Humble Advice of the Assembly of Divines, Now by Authority of Parliament sitting at Westminster, Concerning a Confession of Faith* (London: Company of Stationers, 1647), VII.i; Shorter Catechism, q. 12; Larger Catechism, q. 20.

25. Westminster Confession, VII.iii.

26. Francis Turretin, *Institutes of Elenctic Theology*, 3 vols., trans. George Musgrave Giger, ed. James T. Dennison Jr. (Phillipsburg, NJ: P & R, 1992-97), VIII.iii.1; idem, *Institutio Theologiae Elencticae* (Edinburgh: Robert Carter, 1847).

27. Turretin, *Institutes*, VIII.iii.1.

With this definition in mind, Turretin describes the double covenant (*foedus geminum*) proposed in the Scriptures as: *naturae et gratiae, operum et fidei, legale et evangelicum* ('nature and grace, works and faith, legal and evangelical').[28] Turretin readily acknowledges a number of different designations for what theologians commonly labeled the covenants of works and grace. He identified these pairs of terms for the twofold covenant because the distinction rested on the different relations (*schesi*) that God had to His creation, whether as Creator and Lord (*Creator et Dominus*) versus Redeemer and Father (*Redemptor et Pater*), as well as the diverse states of humanity, either as perfect (*creatura integra*) or as a fallen creature (*lapsa*). There were also different modes of obtaining eternal life and happiness (*vitam et felicitatem*), either through proper or imputed obedience. In the former God requires perfect obedience from Adam whereas the latter rests on the grace of God in Christ alone. The former is from the hand of a just Creator and the latter from a merciful Redeemer. God gave the former to innocent man without a mediator and the latter to fallen man through the work of a mediator.[29]

The following table illustrates the twofold covenant that Turretin observes in Scripture and why there are various common terms for the Adamic covenant:

Category	Covenant of Nature, Works, or Legal Covenant	Covenant of Grace, Faith, or Evangelical Covenant
God	Creator and Lord	Redeemer and Father
Humanity	Perfect	Fallen creature
Mode of life and happiness	Proper obedience	Imputed obedience
Requirement	Perfect obedience (works)	Obedience of another (faith) – grace of God alone

---

28. Turretin, *Institutes*, VIII.iii.4.
29. Turretin, *Institutes*, VIII.iii.4.

Category	Covenant of Nature, Works, or Legal Covenant	Covenant of Grace, Faith, or Evangelical Covenant
Divine role	Just creator	Merciful redeemer
Human condition	Innocent man without a mediator	Fallen man with mediator

The pre- and post-fall conditions, therefore, warrant the use of the different pairs of terms to denote the covenants of works and grace. That being said, Turretin does have a preferred term for the Adamic covenant. Based on the distinctions between the pre- and post-fall God and man relations, Turretin presents the following definition: 'The covenant of nature [foedus naturae] is that which the Creator made with innocent man as his creature, concerning the giving of eternal happiness and life under the condition of perfect and personal obedience.' He prefers the term foedus naturae, not because the covenant arises from the natural obligation (obligatione naturali) that was incumbent upon man at his initial creation, but because God founded the covenant on man's nature (in natura hominis) as he was first created by God and 'on his integrity or powers' (in illius integritate seu viribus).[30]

Witsius has a similar elasticity regarding the proper designation of the Adamic covenant. Like Turretin, Witsius provides a basic definition of a covenant: 'A covenant of God with man, is an agreement between God and man, about the way of obtaining consummate happiness; including a commination [threat] of eternal destruction, with which the contemner of the happiness, offered in that way, is to be punished.'[31] He then dissects a covenant into its three constituent elements: (1) a promise, (2) designation or prescription, and (3) penal sanction.[32] From within this general

---

30. Turretin, Institutes, VIII.iii.5.

31. Herman Witsius, Economy of the Covenants Between God and Man, 2 vols., trans. William Crookshank (1822; Escondido, CA: Den Dulk Foundation, 1992), I.i.9; idem, De Oeconomia Foederum Dei Cum Hominibus, 2nd ed. (Leeuwarden: J. Hagenaar, 1685).

32. Witsius, Economy of the Covenants, I.i.10.

framework, like Turretin, Witsius argues that Scripture reveals 'two covenants of God with man.'[33] He then identifies the first covenant: *Foedus Operum, quaod alias naturae, vel legale dicitus; & Foedus Gratiae* ('The Covenant of Works, otherwise called the Covenant of Nature, or the Legal; and the Covenant of Grace').[34] He also acknowledges that the covenant of works is called *legis & naturae* ('of the law and of nature') because God prescribed the covenant by the law and required works as its condition, which were founded on and coeval with nature.[35] Like Turretin, Witsius acknowledges the different terms by which theologians commonly denote the Adamic covenant, but he prefers the *foedus operum* instead of the *foedus naturae* as his term of choice.

Witsius opts for *foedus operum* because the apostle Paul mentions the *legem operum, & legem fidei* ('the law of works, and the law of faith') in Romans 3:27. By these principles the apostle identifies that a person can attain salvation by means of works or faith. Witsius compares and contrasts the two covenants to demonstrate where they agree and disagree. They agree in terms of their contracting parties (God and man), the promise of eternal life, the requirement of perfect obedience, and the same final cause, namely, the glory of God. They differ, however, in the following ways:[36]

Category	Covenant of Works	Covenant of Grace
Relation to God	Supreme law-giver	Merciful redeemer
Mediator	None	Jesus Christ
Condition	Perfect obedience	Perfect obedience of Christ
Man	Working (*ergazmeno*), and the reward given as debt (*ex debito*)	As believing (*credens*), and reward given by free grace (*donata kata charin*)

---

33. Witsius, *Economy of the Covenants*, I.i.14.

34. Witsius, *Economy of the Covenants*, I.i.15.

35. Witsius, *Economy of the Covenants*, I.ii.1.

36. Witsius, *Economy of the Covenants*, I.i.15.

Category	Covenant of Works	Covenant of Grace
Conditional or absolute	Conditional	Absolute
Telos	Manifestation of the holiness, goodness, and justice of God evident in His liberal promise and the recompense of reward	Praise of the glory of His grace (Eph. 1:6) and the revelation of His unsearchable wisdom found in Christ

Witsius and Turretin have a similar analysis of the differences between the covenants of works and grace, but Witsius nevertheless reveals his preference for the *foedus operum* as his desired designation for the Adamic covenant. Neither theologian gives the slightest hint of disapprobation for other common designations but nevertheless exhibits a partiality for different terms.

Conclusion

William Shakespeare once asked, 'What's in a name? that which we call a rose By any other name would smell as sweet?' Regardless of the name, early modern Reformed theologians agreed regarding the existence of the covenant of works. They did not agree on the precise terminology for this doctrine. They agreed that God and Adam were in covenant, but how they should label and describe this covenant was an issue of minor difference. Colleagues such as Turretin and Heidegger have very similar explanations of the doctrine but nevertheless landed on different terms, the *foedus naturae* for the former and the *foedus operum* for the latter. Some chose their term because of sequence – it was the first covenant in relation to the second, the covenant of grace (Lañyez). Others believed the covenants of works and grace were synonymous with law and gospel (Cartwright, Walker, Ussher, and Finch). Some opted for *foedus naturale* or *foedus naturae* because it contrasted with the *foedus gratia* or the *foedus evangelicum*; or, as a term *foedus naturae* highlighted the basis of covenant, namely, created nature (Leigh and Turretin). Another motivating factor in choice was the condition of the covenant, that is, Adam's obedience, hence they chose the term covenant of *works* (Rollock, Heidegger, and Witsius). And still yet others decided to label the covenant according to its telos, and hence the covenant of *life* (Westminster Assembly, Downame, Sedgwick, and Walker). A number of these theologians could also use multiple terms interchangeably (e.g., Rollock). Despite their different terminological choices, early modern Reformed theologians were united in their belief that God and Adam were in covenant.

~: I.2 :~

Do This and Live

Introduction

One of the most consistently cited texts in support of the covenant of works is Leviticus 18:5, 'Ye shall therefore keep my statutes, and my judgments: which if a man do, he shall live in them: I am the LORD' (KJV).[1] Theologians either cite this text directly or they appeal to it through their citations of two Pauline texts: 'The law is not of faith: but, The man that doeth them shall live in them' (Gal. 3:12 KJV) and, 'For Moses describeth the righteousness which is of the law, That the man which doeth those things shall live by them' (Rom. 10:5 KJV). The Westminster Confession of Faith (1647) cites these two latter texts as the first and second of three in support of the covenant of works.[2] In contrast to the claims of a number of nineteenth- and twentieth-century critics, the citation of Leviticus 18:5 is counter-evidence that the covenant of works was a one-verse doctrine. Hosea 6:7 was not the only verse to which early modern Reformed theologians appealed. But exactly how proponents of the doctrine get from a text embedded in the Mosaic covenant in a post-fall context to the pre-fall Adamic context is an important question. Is this not an example of poor exegesis

---

1. This chapter is an expanded version of an earlier essay, J. V. Fesko, 'Do This and Live: the Reformation of Biblical Exegesis,' *HapTR* 6 (2017): 9-28.

2. *The Humble Advice of the Assembly of Divines, Now by Authority of Parliament Sitting at Westminster, Concerning a Confession of Faith* (London: Company of Stationers, 1647), VII.ii.

or even worse, eisegesis? This chapter surveys the early modern interpretation of Leviticus 18:5 to demonstrate that proponents of the covenant of works cited the text in support of the doctrine because they read it against a larger canonical backdrop. They used the analogy of Scripture and the Bible's own intra-canonical interpretation of Leviticus 18:5 and thus believed that the verse was applicable to Adam's pre-fall state.

In order to prove this thesis, this chapter first begins with an exposition of Thomas Aquinas' (1225-1274) interpretation of Leviticus 18:5 to provide a useful comparative foil against Reformation and post-Reformation exegesis of Leviticus 18:5. Second, the chapter examines the exegesis of John Calvin (1509-1564) and Peter Martyr Vermigli (1499-1562). Calvin is by no means the normative theologian of the Reformed tradition, but his exegetical, theological, and homiletical corpus provides sufficient evidence for comparison with Aquinas and later post-Reformation views. Calvin's exegesis of this verse stands in continuity with later post-Reformation views that cited it in support of the covenant of works. The same continuities also appear in Vermigli's commentary on Romans 10:5. Thus Vermigli provides another point of comparison with Aquinas and later post-Reformation views. Third, the chapter examines the post-Reformation exegesis of Leviticus 18:5 through the commentary of Andrew Willet (1562-1621). Willet is a name few know today but he was a well-known theologian and exegete in his own day.[3] His peers recognized him as a talented textual critic, hence his commentary on Romans serves as an excellent window on the development and ongoing discussion regarding the exegesis of Leviticus 18:5.[4] Fourth, the chapter surveys a number of post-Reformation theologians to see how they enlisted this verse in the service of the covenant of works. Fifth, and last, the chapter concludes with some summary observations about the early modern Reformed interpretation of Leviticus 18:5.

---

3. On Willet's exegesis, see Darren M. Pollock, *Polemical Hermeneutics: Andrew Willet's 1611 Hexapla on Romans* (Göttingen: Vandenhoeck & Ruprecht, 2017).

4. 'Willet, Andrew,' in *Dictionary of National Biography*, ed. Sidney Lee, vol. 61 (London: Smith, Elder, & Co., 1900), 288-92.

Thomas Aquinas

Most theologians engage Leviticus 18:5 through the apostle Paul's quotation of it in Romans 10:5 and Galatians 3:12, and Aquinas is no exception. In his exegesis of Romans 10:5, Aquinas explains that when Paul writes, 'for Moses wrote,' that the apostle was proving a truth of which his fellow Jews were ignorant, 'that God's justice is more perfect than that of the law.' Aquinas argues that Paul contrasts the differences between legal justice (*iustitiae legalis*) and the justice of faith (*iustitiae fidei*).[5] Aquinas appeals to Paul's quotation of Leviticus 18:5 to explain legal justice. Aquinas also connects Leviticus 18:5 to another biblical use of the text in Ezekiel 20:13, 'They cast away my judgments, which if a man do, he shall live in them.'[6] This is an important citation because it reveals that Aquinas was aware of other quotations of the text and seeks to establish its meaning through intra-canonical exegesis. Nevertheless, the first point that Aquinas raises is that one must obey the law lest he become liable to the punishment of death. He appeals to Hebrews 10:28, that anyone who violates the law of Moses dies without mercy, and Leviticus 20:9, which states that the one who curses his parents is liable to death.[7] His second point is that God instituted the Mosaic law for the regulation of the present life because it promised temporal blessings, 'bodily regulations imposed until a time of reformation' (Heb. 9:10).[8] Aquinas' general point is, the law requires obedience and offers temporal blessings as rewards and levels death as the penalty for its transgression.

But Aquinas was aware that his exegetical conclusions appeared to contradict Christ's interaction with the rich young ruler. The ruler asked Jesus, 'What good deed must I do to have eternal life?' (Matt. 19:16). Jesus responded, 'If you would enter life, keep

---

5. Thomas Aquinas, *Commentary on the Letter of Saint Paul to the Romans*, trans. F. R. Larcher, ed. J. Mortensen and E. Alarcón (Lander, WY: The Aquinas Institute for the Study of Sacred Doctrine, 2012), lect. X.i, §820 (p. 280).

6. Aquinas, *Romans*, lect. X.i §821 (p. 280).

7. Aquinas, *Romans*, lect. X.i §821 (p. 280).

8. Aquinas, *Romans*, lect. X.i §822 (p. 280).

the commandments.' To avoid the apparent discrepancy, Aquinas employs a hermeneutical distinction: 'Christ's words must be understood according to the spiritual sense of the law [*spiritualem sensum legis*], a sense which refers to faith in him. But Paul's words refer to the inward sense of the law [*interiorem legis sensum*] according to which the law makes no mention of eternal life.'[9] Medieval exegetes commonly employed the distinction between the literal and spiritual sense of the text, an interpretive principle that dates back to Origen (185-254). The literal sense was the natural and plain reading of a biblical text whereas theologians subdivided the spiritual sense into three different categories: the allegorical, moral (or tropological), and anagogical. All together these four senses of Scripture go by the term, *quadriga*.

According to Aquinas, the literal sense of Scripture is its obvious meaning, the things to which the word directly points. When Scripture speaks of rocks, it refers to rocks – hard stony things. The allegorical sense reveals something beyond the literal. When Moses hit the rock and water flowed from it, the text refers to a literal rock but allegorically to Jesus, the one from whom flows living water. When the text refers to things we ought to do, we must read it in a moral sense. When Jesus instructs the crowd not to throw rocks at the adulterous woman because they too are guilty of sin, the tropological sense is that we ought not to judge others. The anagogical sense is when a text refers to our eternal glory.[10] According to Aquinas, God gave the law as a means by which to inform people inwardly what ought to be done, but by means of the Holy Spirit God 'inclines the affection to act aright.'[11] In other words, the different senses of the law address different ends – the spiritual sense points people to their need for faith in Christ

---

9. Aquinas, *Romans*, lect. X.i §822 (p. 280).

10. Thomas Aquinas, *Summa Theologica* (Allen, TX: Classic Reprints, 1948), Ia q. 1 art. 10; cf. Henri de Lubac, *Medieval Exegesis*, 3 vols. (1959; Grand Rapids: Eerdmans, 1998), II:1-40.

11. Aquinas, *Romans*, lect. VIII.i §602 (p. 204); cf. Gilles Emery, 'The Holy Spirit,' in *Reading Romans with St. Thomas Aquinas*, eds. Mathew Levering and Michael Dauphinais (Washington D. C.; The Catholic University of America Press, 2012), 154.

and thus eternal life, whereas the inward sense instructs people how they should act and thus holds out the temporal benefits of obedience. Thus, in Matthew 19:16-17, when Christ refers to the law and eternal life, one must read this statement according to its anagogical sense. That is, Christ points ultimately to eternal life and not to the law as a means by which one attains it.[12]

Aquinas presents similar exegesis of Paul's other quotation of Leviticus 18:5 in his epistle to the Galatians: 'But the law is not of faith: but he who does those things shall live in them' (Gal. 3:12). In the larger context of Galatians 3:12 Aquinas explains that Paul places man under a curse if he relies on the works of the law. 'It is one thing to be of the works of the law,' writes Aquinas, 'and another to observe the law.'[13] If a person is of the works of the law, then he places his trust and hope in them. But the law only begets knowledge of sin and offers no help by which one might escape it. Hence, anyone who is of the works of the law lies under a curse.[14] Even if Paul has ceremonial and moral works in view, works do not make one just before God. Only a supernaturally infused habit of faith makes one just before God.[15] The law merely commands what is right but does not give the virtue necessary to perform its obligations. Hence, those who rely on the works of the law lie under its curse.[16] The patriarchs were of the works of the law, which means that they lived during the period of redemptive history when God instituted the ceremonial law, but they did not rely on them. Rather, they were 'saved by faith in one to come, by trusting in His grace and by fulfilling the law at least spiritually.'[17]

Aquinas establishes his exegesis by presenting Paul's syllogism from Galatians 3:11-12:

---

12. Cf. De Lubac, *Medieval Exegesis*, II:179-222.

13. Thomas Aquinas, *Commentary on the Letters of Saint Paul to the Galatians and Ephesians*, trans. F. R. Larcher and M. L. Lamb, ed. J. Mortensen and E. Alarcón (Lander, WY: The Aquinas Institute for the Study of Sacred Doctrine, 2012), §135 (p. 66).

14. Aquinas, *Galatians*, lect. III.iv §135 (pp. 66-67).

15. Aquinas, *Galatians*, lect. III.iv §136 (p. 67).

16. Aquinas, *Galatians*, lect. III.iv §§137-38 (pp. 67-68).

17. Aquinas, *Galatians*, lect. III.iv §138 (p. 68).

Major premise: the just man lives by faith
Minor premise: the law is not of faith
Conclusion: No one is justified by the law.[18]

Some object to this conclusion because James clearly states: 'Was not Abraham our father justified by works?' (James 2:21). But Aquinas explains there are two different senses for the term *to justify*. It can refer to the execution and manifestation of justice, that is, a person's works prove he is justified, or it refers to the infused habit of justice. God does not justify a person by works but rather through the infused habit of justice and by the grace of faith. This latter sense of the term *to justify* (*iustificare*) is what Paul has in mind here in Galatians 3:11-12 and Romans 4:2.[19]

Paul supports his major premise, the just man lives by faith, from scriptural authority, namely, Habakkuk 2:4 (cf. Rom. 1:17; Heb. 10:38). He then addresses the minor premise, the law is not of faith, and introduces his quotation of Leviticus 18:5. The one who performs the moral and ceremonial precepts of the law will live in them, but as with his exegesis of Romans 10:5, Aquinas notes that the law does not promise eternal blessings but only temporal benefits, 'earthly and present things.' To substantiate this point Aquinas appeals to Isaiah 1:19 (KJV), 'If you be wiling [*sic*] and will hearken to me, you shall eat the good things of the land.' But a mere performance of the law finds its motivation in cupidity or fear, and hence is only a carnal keeping of the law. Those who do the works of the law shall live in them, 'Namely, in the present life, i.e., will be immune from temporal death and will be preserved in the present life.'[20]

In summary, Aquinas exegetes Leviticus 18:5 through an examination of the immediate context and its broader canonical context. He employs other corollary texts to support his conclusions. The law holds forth the prospects of temporal life and blessings should one obey its commands, but in the hands of Christ in its spiritual, or anagogical sense, it holds out the prospects of

---

18. Aquinas, *Galatians*, lect. III.iv §140 (p. 68).

19. Aquinas, *Galatians*, lect. III.iv §141 (pp. 68-69).

20. Aquinas, *Galatians*, lect. III.iv §144 (pp. 69-70).

eternal life. While one should not accuse Aquinas of imposing an arbitrary interpretation on Leviticus 18:5, his exegesis of the text ultimately rests on the medieval fourfold sense of Scripture to reach his exegetical and theological conclusions. Aquinas believed justification was a lifelong process and thus required the continued use of the law.[21] If one concluded that Christ taught obedience to the law as the means of gaining eternal life, then there would be no need for God's grace. Conversely, if Paul eliminated the use of the law in justification, then there was no means by which believers could seek their justification. Hence, apart from this fourfold interpretive distinction, Aquinas faces a contradiction between Christ and Paul. Christ teaches that observing the law secures eternal life whereas Paul teaches that observing the law only leads to temporal life. The quadriga leaves Aquinas' doctrine of justification intact.

John Calvin

As a second-generation Reformer, Calvin was convinced of the need to move away from the hermeneutics of the quadriga. He gave priority to the literal or natural sense of Scripture.[22] In his commentary on 2 Corinthians 3:6, 'For the letter kills, but the Spirit gives life,' Calvin voices his objection to allegorical exegesis:

> This passage has been distorted and wrongly interpreted first by Origen and then by others, and they have given rise to the most disastrous error that Scripture is not only useless but actually harmful unless it is allegorized. This error has been the source of many evils. Not only did it open the way for the corruption of the natural meaning of Scripture but also set up boldness in allegorizing as the chief exegetical virtue. Thus many of the ancients without any restraint played all sorts of games with the sacred Word of God, as if they were tossing a ball to and fro .... The terms *letter* and *Spirit*

---

21. See Alister McGrath, *Iustitia Dei: The Christian Doctrine of Justification*, 3rd ed. (Cambridge: Cambridge University Press, 2005), 63-67.

22. Susan Schreiner, *Are You Alone Wise? The Search for Certainty in the Early Modern Era* (Oxford: Oxford University Press, 2010), 81; also David Steinmetz, *Calvin in Context*, 2nd ed. (Oxford: Oxford University Press, 2010), 269; Richard A. Muller, *Post-Reformation Reformed Dogmatics*, 4 vols. (Grand Rapids: Baker, 2003), II:469-90.

have nothing to do with methods of expounding Scripture but with its force and fruit.[23]

Calvin was unwilling to assign multiple senses to Scripture.[24] In fact, at points Calvin so stressed the literal sense that he was unwilling to identify types of Christ in passages where other Reformers saw them.[25] Theologians, such as Lutheran Aegidius Hunnius (1550-1603), were highly critical of Calvin on this point.[26] Given his rejection of the quadriga, Calvin does not appeal to the internal and spiritual senses of the law as Aquinas does. So, then, how does Calvin explain Leviticus 18:5?

Like Aquinas, Calvin argues that Paul compares and contrasts the righteousness of faith and the righteousness of works. And like Aquinas, he detects a tension between how Paul elsewhere speaks of the law agreeing with faith, yet here in this passage he places them in stark opposition. Like Aquinas, Calvin also employs a twofold distinction, but not Aquinas' internal and spiritual sense. Rather, Calvin argues that the term *law* can either mean the doctrine of Moses in general, or other times it refers to precepts, rewards, and punishments.[27] In this particular case Paul set forth the precepts of the law in order to drive people to repentance. This requires that Paul establish the nature of the law – what a person can expect if he fulfills it and conversely what to expect if he violates it. Like Aquinas, Calvin fans out to other portions of Scripture to explain Paul's meaning. He appeals to John 1:17, 'The law was

---

23. John Calvin, *The Second Epistle of Paul the Apostle to the Corinthians and the Epistles of Timothy, Titus and Philemon*, CNTC, eds. David Torrance and T. F. Torrance (1960; Grand Rapids: Eerdmans, 1996), comm. 2 Cor. 3:6 (p. 43).

24. John Calvin, *Galatians, Ephesians, Philippians, & Colossians*, CNTC, eds. David W. Torrance and T. F. Torrance (1960; Grand Rapids: Eerdmans, 1996), comm. Gal. 4:22 (pp. 84-85); Muller, *Post-Reformation Reformed Dogmatics*, II:472.

25. See, e.g., Sujin Pak, *Judaizing Calvin: Sixteenth-Century Debates over the Messianic Psalms* (Oxford: Oxford University Press, 2009).

26. Aegidius Hunnius, *Calvinus Iudaizans* (Wittenberg: Welacus, 1593); idem, *Judaizing Calvin*, trans. Paul A. Rydecki (Bynum, TX: Repristination Press, 2012); also see Muller, *Post-Reformation Reformed Dogmatics*, II:471-72.

27. John Calvin, *Romans and Thessalonians*, CNTC, eds. David W. Torrance and T. F. Torrance (1960; Grand Rapids: Eerdmans, 1996), comm. Rom. 10:5 (pp. 222-23).

given by Moses; grace and truth came by Jesus Christ.' When the Scriptures use the term *law* in contrast to Christ, it does not refer to the doctrine of Moses in general but to its narrower meaning, namely precepts, rewards, and punishments.[28]

Despite some initial similarities between them, Calvin radically departs from Aquinas when he claims: 'The passage is taken from Lev. 18:5, where the Lord promises eternal life to those who will keep his law.' In fact, though he does not mention him by name, Calvin might have Aquinas in view when he writes: 'We see that Paul has also taken the passage in this sense, and not of temporal life only, as some hold.'[29] Calvin, however, could simply be rejecting what was by the sixteenth-century a common medieval interpretation of Leviticus 18:5. To prove his point, Calvin presents a syllogism:

Major premise: Since no man attains the righteousness prescribed by the law, unless he has exactly fulfilled every part of it,

Minor premise: All men always fall short of this perfection,

Conclusion: It is vain for anyone to strive for salvation in this way.[30]

The law is of no use for sinners for their justification, therefore, because of their inability to meet its condition. How then do sinners lay hold of eternal life? They do so through the righteousness of faith – they lay hold of the perfect law-fulfilling righteousness of Christ by faith alone.[31]

Calvin's exegesis of Galatians 3:10-12 echoes Aquinas' interpretation, but there are, of course, some significant differences. Like Aquinas, Calvin argues that Paul presses the antithesis between salvation by works versus faith in Christ. Calvin notes Paul's citation of Habakkuk 2:4. As with his quotation in Romans 1:17, Habakkuk 2:4 proves that Paul believed faith and works in justification are totally antithetical. Calvin explains how the 'law is not of faith,' and comments that, in one sense, faith and the law

---

28. Calvin, *Romans*, comm. Rom. 10:5 (p. 223).

29. Calvin, *Romans*, comm. Rom. 10:5 (p. 223).

30. Calvin, *Romans*, comm. Rom. 10:5 (pp. 223-24).

31. Calvin, *Romans*, comm. Rom. 10:6 (p. 224).

go hand in hand in the Christian life, but not in the doctrine of justification. In the arena of justification, faith and the law stand in stark antithesis: 'You can easily unite fire and water than reconcile the two statements that men are justified by faith and by the law. The law is not of faith, that is, it has a method of justifying a man which is completely foreign to faith.'[32] In the simplest of terms, you *do* the law and *believe* the gospel.

Calvin quickly stipulates, however, that faith is never idle and always 'works through love' (Gal. 5:6), but not in the doctrine of justification: 'It is not our doctrine that the faith which justifies is alone. We maintain that it is always joined with good works. But we contend that faith avails itself for justification.'[33] Calvin writes:

> For the present question is not whether believers ought to keep the law as far as they can (which is beyond all doubt), but whether they obtain righteousness by works; and this is impossible. Moreover, if anyone objects, 'Since God promises life to the doers of the law, why does Paul deny that they are righteous?' the answer is easy. None is righteous by the works of the law, because there is none who does them. We admit that the doers of the law, if there were any, would be righteous. But since that is a conditional agreement, all are excluded from life because no one offers the righteousness that he ought. We must bear in mind what I have already said, that to do the law is not to obey it in part, but to fulfill everything that belongs to righteousness.[34]

In his argument, Paul sets forth two mutually exclusive paths to justification: one by perfect obedience to the law and the other by faith in Christ. The fact that Paul opposes Leviticus 18:5 against Habakkuk 2:4 supports his claim. For Calvin, Leviticus 18:5 holds forth the prospect of eternal life. In this vein, Calvin explicitly argues that the Mosaic covenant *qua* law promises eternal life to the obedient. In other words, Calvin believed that the Mosaic administration of the law sets forth a covenant governed by a works principle, eternal life through obedience: 'Nor can it be denied, that

---

32. Calvin, *Galatians*, comm. Gal. 3:11 (p. 54).

33. Calvin, *Galatians*, comm. Gal. 5:6 (p. 96).

34. Calvin, *Galatians*, comm. Gal. 3:12 (pp. 54-55).

the reward of eternal salvation, as promised by the Lord, awaits the perfect obedience of the Law (Deut. 30:19).'[35]

In his sermon on the same passage Calvin emphasizes the same points that he makes in his commentary. Calvin confronted Roman Catholic claims about justification because he believed they created an erroneous mixture of God's grace and the believer's good works.[36] As in his commentary, he informed his congregation of the antithesis between faith and works in justification.[37] In his sermon, however, he appeals to an additional text heretofore absent from his exegesis of either Romans 10:5 or Galatians 3:10-12, that is, Romans 2:13, 'Not the hearers of the law, but the doers of it shall be justified.'[38] He uses this text to buttress his claim that one *does* the law and *believes* the gospel. Here, as in his Galatians commentary, Calvin highlights the harmony of law and gospel in the Christian life but in justification, he states that they 'can no more be joined together than fire and water.'[39]

Calvin's explanation of Matthew 19:16-17 also parallels his exegesis of Romans 10:5 and Galatians 3:10. The rich young ruler had too much confidence in his ability to fulfill the law. Christ therefore confronted him with the demands of the law. The law requires perfect obedience, and hence Calvin quotes two texts, Leviticus 18:5, 'He that does these things shall live by them,' and Deuteronomy 30:19, 'I call heaven and earth to witness that I have this day showed you life.'[40] Unlike Aquinas, Calvin believed that Paul and Jesus spoke with one voice. The law rewards perfect obedience with eternal life.

---

35. John Calvin, *Institutes of the Christian Religion*, 2 vols., trans. Henry Beveridge (Edinburgh: Calvin Translation Society, 1845), II.vii.3.

36. John Calvin, *Sermons on Galatians*, trans. Arthur Golding (1574; Audubon, NJ: Old Paths Publications, 1995), serm. XVIII (pp. 374-75).

37. Calvin, *Sermons on Galatians*, serm. XVIII (p. 376).

38. Calvin, *Sermons on Galatians*, serm. XVIII (p. 385); cf. idem, *Romans*, comm. Rom. 2:13 (p. 47).

39. Calvin, *Sermons on Galatians*, serm. XVIII (p. 387); cf. idem, *Galatians*, comm. Gal. 3:11 (p. 54).

40. John Calvin, *A Harmony of the Gospels: Matthew, Mark and Luke*, and James and Jude, eds. CNTC, vol. 2, David W. Torrance and T. F. Torrance (1960; Grand Rapids: Eerdmans, 1996), comm. Matt. 19:16-17 (pp. 253-54).

In his lectures on the Pentateuch, Calvin goes into greater theological detail in his treatment of Leviticus 18:5. He first rejects the medieval nominalist concept of merit in justification – that God does not accept a person's works based on their dignity or merit but on the basis of His covenant.[41] But then, once again, he argues that Moses presents two ways of justification – either through obedience to the law or by faith in Christ. As in his Romans commentary, he does not mention names but nevertheless rejects the idea that Leviticus 18:5 promises only temporal life. Calvin claims that proponents of this view, perhaps even Aquinas, feared that some would subvert this passage and claim that God grounded salvation in the merit of works. Rather, because of sin and corruption, fallen sinners are unable to meet the requirements of the law.[42] In other words, with a proper anthropology and doctrine of sin, theologians would not erroneously understand Leviticus 18:5 or the other places where this verse appears in Scripture (e.g., Rom. 10:5, Gal. 3:12). Given human sinfulness, they are unable to offer the requisite obedience and can in no way contribute to their justification. Calvin, therefore, rejects Roman Catholic soteriology: 'The rantings of the Popish theologians about partial righteousness are frivolous and silly, since God embraces at once all the commandments; and who is there that can boast of having thoroughly fulfilled them?'[43]

Although Calvin does not immediately engage Ezekiel 20 in his exegesis of Romans 10:5 or Galatians 3:12 as Aquinas does, he does deal with the text in his lectures. This lacuna of Ezekiel may be due to the fact that he did not lecture on this book until nearly the end of his life.[44] Nevertheless, he largely repeats conclusions he reached

---

41. John Calvin, *Commentaries on the Last Four Books of Moses Arranged in the Form of a Harmony*, trans. Charles William Bingham, CTS, vol. 3 (rep.; Grand Rapids: Baker, 1993), 203. Cf. McGrath, *Justitia Dei*, 198-201.

42. Calvin, *Harmony*, comm. Lev. 18:5 (p. 204).

43. Calvin, *Harmony*, comm. Lev. 18:5 (p. 205).

44. Wulfert de Greef, *The Writings of John Calvin, Expanded Edition: An Introductory Guide*, trans. Lyle D. Bierma (Louisville: Westminster John Knox, 2008), 92-93. Calvin does, however, connect Leviticus 18:5, Ezekiel 20:11, Romans 10:5, and Galatians 3:12 in his sermon on Deuteronomy 6:25, which dates 31 July 1555 (John Calvin, *Sermons de M. Jean Calvin sure le V. livre de Moyse nommé*

in his commentaries on Romans or Galatians. He rejected the notion that Leviticus 18:5 referred to temporal life. The prophet Ezekiel simply holds forth the twofold path of justification, law or faith, as Paul does in Romans 10:5-6. Calvin writes: 'We see, therefore, although God promised salvation to his ancient people, if they only kept the law, yet that promise was useless, since no one could satisfy the law and perform God's commands.'[45] Within this context Calvin connects Ezekiel 20:11 both to Romans 10:5 and Leviticus 18:5, but also to Deuteronomy 30:15.

His sermons on Deuteronomy illuminate Calvin's understanding regarding how long life in the land related to the promise of eternal life. Calvin was aware that Deuteronomy 30:15 gives the immediate impression that long life in the land is the reward for obedience. Yet, Calvin explained to his congregation:

> It is true that this present life is not the full measure or perfection of the blessings that God has promised us. It is only but a taste of them. Death is but a sign of God's wrath. The state of the life to come is the perfection both of good and bad. But Moses speaking unto the people that were under the figures and shadows of the law [*les figures et ombrages de la Loy*], named life, and thereunto added this word of blessing to signify that, by serving God the people should be blessed in all manner of felicity. And on the other hand, that they could expect misfortune, if they turned away from the service of God.[46]

So, while Aquinas appealed to the spiritual sense of the law, Calvin instead argued that the relationship between temporal and eternal life was that of figures and shadows, or type and antitype – long life in the land foreshadowed eternal life.

There are a number of similarities and dissimilarities between Calvin and Aquinas' respective exegesis of Leviticus 18:5. Both reject

---

Deuteronome [Geneva: 1567], 187; idem, *Sermons on Deuteronomy*, trans. Arthur Golding [London: Henry Middleton, 1583], serm. L [p. 301]).

45. John Calvin, *Commentaries on the Prophet Ezekiel*, 2 vols., CTS (rep.; Grand Rapids: Baker, 1993), lect. LXI (pp. 297-98).

46. Calvin, *Sermons sur Deuteronome*, 1007; idem, *Sermons on Deuteronomy*, serm. CLXXII (p. 1066). I have updated the Golding translation in comparison with the French original.

the idea of salvation by works, situate the text within its immediate and broader canonical context, and use corollary texts to explain its significance. Calvin's explanation of Leviticus 18:5 radically differs from Aquinas' because Calvin has a different conception of the nature and function of the law and a different doctrine of justification. Both Aquinas and Calvin identify a role for the law in the Christian life, but for Aquinas, who merges justification and sanctification, the law serves as the means by which believers seek their justification and sanctification. Aquinas rejects salvation by works, a strict *quid pro quo*, and instead argues that the only way one's works become acceptable is through the antecedent grace of God and an infused habit of grace. Calvin, on the other hand, distinguishes between justification and sanctification and thus retains a role for the believer's good works in sanctification but not justification. Aquinas therefore maintains a role for the law in the believer's justification whereas Calvin rejects it. But Aquinas runs into difficulty when he finds the seemingly contradictory statements of Jesus and Paul. Aquinas relieves the tension through the quadriga and the anagogical sense of the law. Calvin, on the other hand, generally rejects the medieval fourfold sense of Scripture; he instead posits an antithesis between obedience and faith in justification. Instead of employing the so-called spiritual sense of the text, Calvin instead argues in terms of typology.

In the broadest theological terms, Aquinas mixes law and gospel whereas Calvin distinguishes them. In the doctrine of justification Calvin places law and gospel in antithesis. In his *Institutes*, which represents the definitive doctrinal distillation of his exegesis, Calvin writes:

> But they observe not that in the antithesis between Legal and Gospel righteousness [*antithesi legalis & Evangelicae iustitiae*], which Paul elsewhere introduces, all kinds of works, with whatever name adorned, are excluded (Gal. 3:11-12). For he says that the righteousness of the Law consists in obtaining salvation by doing what the Law requires, but the righteousness of faith consists in believing that Christ died and rose again.[47]

_____

47. Calvin, *Institutes*, III.xi.14; idem, *Institutio Christianae Religionis* (Geneva: Robert Stephanus, 1559).

Calvin posited an antithesis between law and gospel: the gospel makes promises whereas the law makes promises under the condition of works.[48] Or more simply, the law makes demands. The law and gospel have two different types of righteousness, and whoever attempts to mix them 'crowns Christ with a wreath of thorns.'[49] Hence, the distinction between law and gospel, and their antithesis in justification, is vital to Calvin's soteriology.[50] The differences between Aquinas' and Calvin's respective soteriologies rests in their exegesis of Scripture and different understandings of the function of the law. The quadriga enabled Aquinas to hold two seemingly antithetical understandings of the law together, whereas apart from this hermeneutical principle, Calvin had to find another way to relate law and gospel. Calvin opposed law and gospel in justification but united them in sanctification. Even though he distinguished between justification and sanctification, he believed they were inseparably joined through the believer's union with Christ – the *duplex gratia*.[51]

Peter Martyr Vermigli

In his commentary on Romans, Vermigli interprets Paul's use of Leviticus 18:5 in Romans 10:5 in a similar fashion to Calvin. In the context of commenting on Romans 10:3-4, Vermigli explains that Paul identifies two paths of righteousness: the righteousness of God revealed through faith (Rom. 3:21-22) and justification by works (Rom. 4:2; cf. Phil. 3:9).[52] In the wake of the fall, no one

---

48. John Calvin, *Antidote to the Council of Trent*, in *Tracts*, vol. 3, trans. Henry Beveridge (Edinburgh: Calvin Translation Society, 1851), 156.

49. Calvin, *Institutes*, III.xi.12.

50. Calvin, *Institutes*, III.xi.17.

51. See, e.g., Cornelis Venema, *Accepted and Renewed in Christ: The Twofold Grace of God and the Interpretation of Calvin's Theology* (Gottingen: Vandenhoeck & Ruprecht, 2007); Richard A. Muller, *Calvin and the Reformed Tradition: On the Work of Christ and the Order of Salvation* (Grand Rapids: Baker, 2012), 202-43.

52. Peter Martyr Vermigli, *Most Learned Commentaries of D. Peter Martir Vermilius ... Upon the Epistle of S. Paul to the Romanes* (London: John Daye, 1558), fol. 316v; idem, *In Epistolam S. Paul Apostoli ad Rom. D. Petir Martyris Vermiliji*, 3rd ed. (Basil: Peter Pernius, 1568), 462.

can be justified by works, which is true even of believers because their good works are imperfect and they follow justification.[53] That being said, Vermigli observes the antithesis between justification by works versus faith – they are opposites.[54] Vermigli was aware of the patristic exegesis of John Chrysostom (ca. 349-407), who argued that the righteousness of the law and faith are one and the same.[55] To counter Chrysostom's exegesis, Vermigli points out that Paul appeals to the authority of Moses to demonstrate that he was not presenting something novel. That is, even Moses spoke of the two paths of justification. To this end Paul quotes Leviticus 18:5; Vermigli also notes the text's appearance in Ezekiel 20. He explains that Leviticus 18:5 informed Israel that the law required perfect obedience, and contra Augustine (354-430), Vermigli believed that this spotless obedience could secure eternal, not merely temporal, life.[56] Vermigli rejected Augustine's interpretation because of Christ's statements to the rich young ruler, namely, he asked what he must do to attain eternal life. Christ quoted Leviticus 18:5 in response (Matt. 19:16ff).[57] In Vermigli's assessment, the law requires exact obedience whereas the gospel requires the lively and effectual assent of faith.[58] Vermigli writes: 'The promises of the Lawe are given by supposition or condition of works going before. So that if these workes be not performed, the promises are made voyd.'[59] In short, the righteousness of the law consists in doing, whereas the righteousness of the gospel comes by believing.[60] Vermigli's exegesis mirrors Calvin's, and stands in contrast to Aquinas' interpretation.

---

53. Vermigli, *Romanes*, fol. 317v; idem, *Rom.*, 463.

54. Vermigli, *Romanes*, fol. 317r; idem, *Rom.*, 464.

55. Vermigli, *Romanes*, fol. 318r; idem, *Rom.*, 465; cf. John Chrysostom, *The Homilies of St. John Chrysostom on the Epistle of St. Paul to the Romans*, Homily XVII, in NPNF¹ XI:472-73.

56. Vermigli, *Romanes*, fol. 318r; idem, *Rom.*, 465-66.

57. Vermigli, *Romanes*, fol. 319v; idem, *Rom.*, 466.

58. Vermigli, *Romanes*, fol. 319v; idem, *Rom.*, 466.

59. Vermigli, *Romanes*, fol. 319v; idem, *Rom.*, 466.

60. Vermigli, *Romanes*, fol. 319v; idem, *Rom.*, 466.

Andrew Willet

Unlike Aquinas, Calvin, and Vermigli, Willet does not have a verse-by-verse exegesis of Romans, but instead presents a six-fold engagement: (1) text critical issues, (2) argument and method, (3) various questions, (4) doctrines, (5) controversies, and (6) moral uses.[61] In his treatment of Romans 10 Willet addresses the question, 'What life, temporall or spirituall is promised to the keepers of the law, v. 5?'[62] His answer to this question is divided into two major parts: a concise history of exegesis and his own exegesis of the text in question.

In his brief history of exegesis, Willet identifies two answers to the question of whether Leviticus 18:5 promised temporal or eternal life. Under the former, Willet identifies Origen, Theodoret (393-457), Ambrose (ca. 340-397), and Anselm (ca. 1033-1109), as proponents of the temporal life view.[63] The law merely promised escape from corporal death for transgression of the law for those guilty of idolatry, adultery, and murder. Since the law threatened death for violation of these commands, the person who obeyed the law would be free from its penalty. Thus, in this manner, the person who does them shall live (temporally) in them. Augustine contended that the spiritual life of faith was in view, namely, that he who received justification by faith performed the righteous deeds of the law, and thus in this manner lived in the commandments.[64] Willet rejects this interpretation because he believed Augustine confounded the law and the gospel. In his mind, Paul only addressed the righteousness that the law requires. To support his critique, Willet appeals to Chrysostom, who argued that people should have

---

61. Andrew Willet, *Hexapla: That Is, A Six-fold Commentarie upon the most Divine Epistle of the Holy Apostle S. Paul to the Romanes* (London: Leonard Greene, 1620).

62. Willet, *Romanes*, 438.

63. Origen, *Commentary on the Epistle to the Romans: Books 6-10*, trans. Thomas P. Scheck (Washington, D. C.; The Catholic University of America Press, 2002), VIII.ii.2; Theodoret of Cyrus, *Commentary on the Letters of St. Paul*, vol. 1, trans. Robert Charles Hill (Brookline, MA: Holy Cross Orthodox Press, 2001), 107.

64. Augustine, *On the Spirit and Letter*, in NPNF[1], chp. 51 (XXIX) (vol. V, pp. 105-06).

been justified by their law-keeping, but because of their sinfulness it was impossible to keep the law.[65]

After his concise history of exegesis, Willet pivots to the text in question. He first appeals to Matthew 19:16, 'If thou wilt enter into life keepe the commandments,' which according to Willet refers to eternal life. Willet concludes this because the rich young ruler asked the question, 'Good Master, what good thing shall I do, that I may have eternal life?' Willet knows of other possible interpretations, such as that offered by Jesuit theologian and exegete, Benedict Pererius (1535-1610). According to Pererius, Christ's words apply to the justified man and refer to faith working through love, but Willet responds: 'But Christ there speaketh not of the iustice of faith working by love, but of such keeping and observing of the commandements, as the law required, if any could have attained unto it: for as the question was, not of believing, but of doing, *What shall I doe*, so Christ maketh his answer, of such iustice, as was required by the law.'[66] Leviticus 18:5, therefore, holds forth the prospect of eternal life. But Willet was also aware of the text's appearance in Ezekiel 20:25, 'So I gave them statutes that were not good, and judgments whereby they should not live.' In other words, did the text's appearance in Ezekiel 20:25 undermine his interpretation because the prophet states that the law is 'not good'? Willet responds by acknowledging that the law promises life but due to humanity's weakness, they are unable to keep the law, and thus the law 'is not good' because it brings death to transgressors, 'See, I have set before thee this day life and good, and death and evil' (Deut. 30:15). For those who had the power to keep the law, it was life, but in reality, no one has this power. Hence, the law was death to transgressors. Willet cites Antoine de la Faye (1540-1615), professor of philosophy and theology at Geneva, to support his claim.[67] Given

---

65. Willet, *Romanes*, 438; cf. Chrysostom, *Homilies on the Epistle of St. Paul to the Romans*, in NPNF[1], Homily XVII (vol. 11, p. 473).

66. Willet, *Romanes*, 438; cf. Benedict Pererius, *Secundus Tomus Disputationum in Sacram Scripturam Continens Centum Octoginta Octo Disputationes Super Eipstola Beati Pauli ad Romanos* (Ingolstadt: Adam Sartorius, 1603), com. Rom. 10, disp. I.iii (pp. 1052-53).

67. Willet, *Romanes*, 438; cf. Antoine de la Faye, *In D. Pauli Apostoli Epistolam ad Romanos Commentarius* (Geneva: Peter and Jacob Chouet, 1608), 431-33.

human sinfulness, Leviticus 18:5 was 'not good.' The defect lies with fallen human nature, not the law of God. This text, therefore, supports Willet's exegesis of Leviticus 18:5.

In the following question Willet asks, 'Whether Paul did of purpose alleadge that place of Moses, Deuter. 30.12 or allude only unto it.'[68] The text in question states, 'It is not in heaven, that thou shouldst say, Who shall go up for us to heaven, and bring it unto us, that we may hear it and do it?' At first glance this question might appear irrelevant for the interpretation of Leviticus 18:5, but among the things that Willet addresses is the debate over whether Paul speaks of the literal or mystical sense of the law. In other words, he deals with questions that pertain to the medieval quadriga. Willet first identifies those who speak of the law in the literal sense, which includes Theodoret and Chrysostom. He next identifies those who contend that Paul speaks of the mystical sense of the law, such as Roman Catholic theologian Robert Bellarmine (1542-1621).[69] According to this view, Deuteronomy was a type of the gospel, which would include a second or new law. The Israelites need not seek heaven or the furthest parts of the earth for the knowledge of Christ because it was near to them in the law. But Willet responds: 'But Moses speaketh not of the precepts of the law in that place, is evident, because he sheweth the facilities of them: *it is in thy mouth and heart to doe it, etc.* but it was not so easie a thing to performe the Law.'[70]

Willet engages and dismisses a third view, which claims that Paul was arguing from the lesser (the law) to the greater (the gospel), and as such, if Moses commended the law to Israel, how much more would this be true of the gospel? Like Calvin, Willet argues that Paul posits an antithesis between the law and gospel: 'The Apostle sheweth the justice of faith to be a farre different thing from the iustice and righteousness of the law, and therefore not to differ onely as the lesse and greater, but as things of a divers

---

68. Willet, *Romanes*, 438.

69. Robert Bellarmine, *De Gratia et Libero Arbitrio*, in *De Controversiis Christianae Fidei*, vol. 3 (Lyon: Johannes Pillehotte, 1610), V.vi (cols. 601-04).

70. Willet, *Romanes*, 439.

nature.'[71] Willet concludes that, in this portion of Romans 10 Paul cites Deuteronomy 30:12 but intersperses his citation with his own authoritative apostolic exposition. Important to note, however, is that Willet dismisses any effort to employ a mystical interpretation of the text. Willet engages the history of interpretation, relies on the grammatical-historical meaning of the text, employs the immediate context, and compares it with other scriptural texts from both the Old and New Testaments to inform his own interpretation.

Post-Reformation Interpretation

Other post-Reformation voices joined the chorus and interpreted Leviticus 18:5 to similar conclusions as Calvin, Vermigli, and Willet. But in contrast to these three exegetes, theologians coordinated law and covenant, which gave the earlier exegesis a new covenantal hue. In concert with Reformation views, later exegetes and theologians such as Matthieu Virel (1561-1595), David Pareus (1548-1622), Franciscus Gomarus (1563-1641), Guillaume Bucanus (d. 1603), and Johannes Wollebius (1589-1629) connected Leviticus 18:5 with the promise of eternal, not temporal, life.[72] In agreement with Calvin, Vermigli, and Willet, exegetes and theologians such as Petrus de Witte (1622-1669) and John Davenant (1572-1641) cite Leviticus 18:5 when they explain the differences between the law and the gospel. De Witte writes: 'The Law promiseth eternal life to them, that are righteous in themselves, and keep the Commandments perfectly, by their own power. Lev. 18:5. Matt. 19:17. *Wilt thou enter into life, keep the Commandments*.'[73] Like his predecessors, de Witte informs his

---

71. Willet, *Romanes*, 439.

72. Matthieu Virel, *La Religion Chrestienne* (Geneva: Eustace Vignon, 1586), 15; David Pareus, *Davids Parei in Divinam ad Romanos S. Pauli Apostoli Epistolam Commentarius* (Geneva: Paulus Marcellus, 1617), 80; Franciscus Gomarus, *Analysis et Explicatio Epistolae ad Romanos* (Amsterdam Johannes Janssonius, 1644), 19; Guillaume Bucanus, *Institutiones Theologicae* (Geneva: Jacob Stoer, 1625), XIX.ix (p. 188); Johannes Wollebius, *Compendium Theologiae Christianae*, I.xiii, in *Reformed Dogmatics*, trans. John W. Beardslee (Oxford: Oxford University Press, 1965), 76.

73. Petrus de Witte, *Catechizing Upon the Heidelberge Catechisem, of the Reformed Christian Religion* (Amsterdame: Gillis Joosten Saeghman, 1664), 124. Also see John Davenant, *An Exposition of the Epistle of St. Paul to the Colossians*, trans. Josiah Allport (London: Hamilton, Adams, and Co., 1831), 262.

understanding of Leviticus 18:5 by comparing it with Christ's statements to the rich young ruler.

But where the connections between Calvin and the later tradition emerge most prominently is when one considers the parallels between their respective characterizations of the two types of righteousness. Recall that Calvin contrasted the antithesis between legal and evangelical righteousness (*antithesis legalis & Evangelicae iustitiae*) present in Paul's use of Leviticus 18:5 in Galatians 3:11-12.[74] This is the very antithesis that theologians invoke but draped in the doctrine of the covenant. Lucas Trelcatius (1573-1607), for example, explains that there are two subordinate parts of God's testament, the one *legal* (Lev. 18:5) and the other *evangelical.*[75] One of the delegates to the Synod of Dort (1618-19), Johannes Maccovius (1588-1644) explains the relationship between the two ways of righteousness in the following manner:

> The spiritual covenant is twofold: either legal or evangelical [*legale, vel Evangelicum*]. In the legal covenant God promises eternal life to those who fulfill the law, Lev. 18.5: '(You shall keep my statutes and my ordinances): by doing which a man shall live in them.' God established this covenant in paradise with innocent man. Our first parents have violated this covenant, and therefore, they have become guilty of eternal death …. In the evangelical covenant God promises to be our God in Jesus Christ, i.e., that He will bless us with every spiritual blessing and in return requires from us that we walk honestly before his eyes.[76]

Theologians and exegetes such as Giovanni Diodati (1576-1649) and James Ussher (1581-1656) looked at the Adamic state in comparison with the post-fall state and recognized that there was

---

74. Calvin, *Institutes*, III.xi.14.

75. Lucas Trelcatius, *A Briefe Institution of the Common Places of Sacred Divinitie* (London: Francis Burton, 1610), II (p. 283).

76. Johannes Maccovius, *Scholastic Discourse: Johannes Maccovius (1588-1644) on Theological and Philosophical Distinctions and Rules*, eds. Willem van Asselt, et al. (Apeldoorn: Instituut voor Reformatieonderzoek, 2009), XII.iv-v (pp. 224-27); idem, *Distinctiones et Regulae Theologicae ac Philosophicae* (Oxford: Robert Blagravius, 1656).

a different governing principle, law versus faith, and thus aligned Leviticus 18:5 with the covenant of works to contrast it with the covenant of grace.[77] In one sense, there is nothing new about such observations. To recognize the two paths of righteousness, works versus faith, goes as far back as at least Aquinas, who contrasted legal versus the righteousness of faith (*legalis & iustitiae fidei*) in his exegesis of Romans 10:5.[78] What was arguably new, was placing these categories under the rubric of covenant.

When Herman Witsius (1636-1708) or Francis Turretin (1623-1687) explained the covenant of works, they appealed to Leviticus 18:5 with its affixed promise of eternal life, which served as Adam's moral standard. Witsius explains that the covenant of works is 'otherwise called, *of the law* and *of nature*,' because God prescribed the covenant '*by the law*, requiring *works* as the condition,' and founded it upon and made it 'coeval with *nature*' (Lev. 18:5; Deut. 27:26).[79] Turretin explains the covenant of works in similar fashion when he writes:

> The law of works had the promise of heavenly and eternal life; therefore also the law prescribed to Adam. In each instance, it is the same law as to substance. The former is evident from 'who doeth these things, shall live by them' (Lev. 18:5); 'if thou wilt enter into life' (namely, the heavenly) 'keep the commandments' (Mt. 19:16-17); and 'the commandment was ordained to life' (Rom. 7:10) assuredly, not earthly, but heavenly. Since however, after the fall, the law can justify no one, this promise must necessarily have had place in upright Adam.[80]

Not only does Turretin explain the covenant of works in terms of the pre-fall function of the law, but he also cites texts across

---

77. Giovanni Diodati, *Pious and Learned Annotations Upon the Holy Bible* (London: Nicolas Fussell, 1651), comm. Lev. 18:5; James Ussher, *A Body of Divinity* (London: R. J. for Jonathan Robinson, 1702), 110.

78. Aquinas, *Romans*, lect. X.i §820 (p. 280).

79. Herman Witsius, *Economy of the Covenants Between God and Man*, trans. William Crookshank, 2 vols. (1822; Escondido, CA: Den Dulk Foundation, 1990), I.ii.1; cf. III.viii.46; I.iii.22.

80. Francis Turretin, *Institutes of Elenctic Theology*, trans. George Musgrave Giger, ed. James T. Dennison, Jr. (Phillipsburg, NJ: P & R, 1992-97), VIII.vi.4.

the canon – a string that has precedence at least as far back as Aquinas. The collation of these texts was not new but rather the manner of interpreting them was. Aquinas mixed faith and works whereas the Reformed distinguished them.

One of the clearest and most succinct presentations of the collation of law and covenant comes from David Dickson's (1583-1662) commentary on the Westminster Confession. In his treatment of the chapter on the law (XIX) he gives four reasons why Socinians err in their rejection of the covenant of works:

1. The Scriptures clearly describe the righteousness of the law (Lev. 18:5; Rom. 10:5; Gal. 3:12; Ezek. 20:11, 13). Whoever keeps the law will live in them.

2. When Christ answered the rich young ruler, He responded in terms of the covenant of works, by which He promised him eternal life should he fulfill the law (Matt. 19:17; Luke 10:28).

3. God created humanity in righteousness, holiness, and immortality, according to His image (Gen. 1:26; 9:6; Eccles. 7:29; Eph. 4:24; Col. 3:9-10). As a part of His image, God gave Adam the law of nature, which was engraved on his heart (Rom. 2:14-15). In addition to the image and law of nature, God also gave Adam a positive command that required his obedience and promised life, but conversely threatened death for its transgression. The consequences of success and failure would fall upon his offspring (Gen. 2:17; Rom. 6:23; 5:12-13).

4. There are a number of places in Scripture that deny that God justifies believers by the law but rather by faith through the righteousness of Christ (Rom. 3:20-21, 28; Gal. 2:16; 3:10-13; Phil. 3:9; Rom. 8:2-3).[81]

These four reasons reveal that the covenant of works was certainly not a one-text doctrine and that theologians did not misuse Leviticus 18:5. Rather, Leviticus 18:5 was part of a larger web of

---

81. David Dickson, *Truth's Victory Over Error* (Edinburgh: John Reid, 1684), 137-39.

texts that revealed the respective functions of law in the pre- and post-fall contexts.

Early modern Reformed theologians were in general consensus regarding the significance of Leviticus 18:5, but they did not agree on all points. John Cameron (ca. 1579-1625) believed that the covenant of works only held forth temporal life as its reward.[82] Later, Westminster divine Thomas Goodwin (1600-1680) argued in this Cameronian vein that Leviticus 18:5 spoke of merely extended temporal life as the reward of the covenant of works.[83] But important to note is that he still enlisted the text in support of the covenant of works. Not all of the divines, however, cited this text in this manner. Some, such as Edmund Calamy (1600-1660), believed that since God delivered Leviticus 18:5 within the context of the covenant of grace, it did not embody a works-principle but merely held out the importance of evangelical obedience (Mal. 7:21; Rev. 22:14; James 1:25).[84] Calamy still affirmed the covenant of works, but he did not appeal to Leviticus 18:5 to support the doctrine. He instead initially cites Job 25:4, Romans 3:23, 3:29, and 5:12.[85]

Another dissenter was John Ball (1585-1640), who believed that Leviticus 18:5 addressed evangelical obedience. Ball writes:

> These words, *Doe this and live*, must not be interpreted as if they did promise life upon a condition of perfect obedience, and for works

---

82. John Cameron, *Ioh. Cameronis S. Theologiae in Academia Salmuriensi Nuper Professoris, Praelectionum Tomus Tertius et Ultimus* (Saumur: Cl. Girard & Dan. Lerpiner, 1628); thesis XIX (pp. 614); idem, *Certain Theses, or, Positions of the Learned John Cameron, Concerning the Threefold Covenant of God with Man*, in Samuel Bolton, *The True Bounds of Christian Freedome* (London: P. S., 1656), 365.

83. Thomas Goodwin, *Of the Creatures, and the Condition of Their State by Creation*, in *The Works of Thomas Goodwin*, 12 vols. (1861-1866; Eureka, CA: Tanski Publications, 1996), II.vi (vol. VII, pp. 49-51). On the debate over eternal versus temporal life as the reward of the covenant of works, see Mark A. Herzer, 'Adam's Reward: heaven or Earth?' in *Drawn into Controversie: Reformed Theological Diversity and Debates within Seventeenth-Century British Puritanism*, eds. Michael A. G. Haykin and Mark Jones (Göttingen: Vandenhoeck & Ruprecht, 2011), 162-82; J. V. Fesko, *The Covenant of Works: Origins, Development, and Reception* (Oxford: Oxford University Press, 2020), 73-94.

84. Edmund Calamy, *Two Solemn Covenants* (London: Thomas Banks, 1645), 15.

85. Calamy, *Two Solemn Covenants*, 1-2.

done in such exactnesse as is required: but they must be expounded Evangelically, describing the subject capable of life eternall, not the cause why life and salvation is conferred: and by doing sincere, uniforme, unpartiall obedience, not exact fulfilling of the Law in every title is to be understood.[86]

Ball then lists a number of texts to support his claim that the verse addresses evangelical rather than legal obedience (Pss. 112:1; 106:3; 119:1-2; James 1:25; Rom. 2:7). He also enlists other texts, such as Romans 2:13, 'The doers of the Law are justified,' which also refers to evangelical obedience. That is, it refers to the justification of those who 'of sincere and upright walking, and shew who are justified, and to whom the promises of life pertaine, but not why they are justified.'[87] Like Calamy, Ball promoted the covenant of works but appealed to texts other than Leviticus 18:5 in support of the doctrine, including Genesis 2:16, Romans 5:17, 1 Corinthians 15:22, 47.[88] To be sure, Ball cites the maxim, 'Do this and live,' as that which characterizes the covenant of works, which was a 'perfect systeme of good.'[89] But to acknowledge that the 'do this and live' principle marks the covenant of works is not the same thing as saying that Leviticus 18:5 speaks of the covenant of works.

Ball held a minority view and thus he was not without his critics. Francis Roberts (1609-1675), author of the massive work on covenant theology, *Mysterium et Medulla Bibliorum*, objected to Ball's exegesis. He believed that Leviticus 18:5 said more than Ball's claim that it spoke of God's fatherly approbation of the believer's sincere works. He agreed that the passages to which Ball appealed (Pss. 112:1; 106:3; 119:1-2; James 1:25; and Rom. 2:7) could be interpreted in an evangelical manner, but Leviticus 18:5 did not fit this category. Roberts objected because the apostle Paul juxtaposed doing with believing in justification with this text in Romans 10:5 and Galatians 3:12. Roberts notes that in these two Pauline texts

---

86. John Ball, *A Treatise of the Covenant of Grace* (London: G. Miller, 1645), 136-37.

87. Ball, *Covenant of Grace*, 137.

88. Ball, *Covenant of Grace*, 6-14.

89. Ball, *Covenant of Grace*, 9-10.

'the Apostle purposely compares the *righteousness of works* and the *righteousness of faith* together (saith *Calvin Comm ad Rom. 10:5-6*) that he may better shew the repugnancy of them to one another. *Partly*, because the curse is denounced upon the least failing, *Deut. 27:26. Gal. 3:10.* But failings in Evangelical obedience are *Covered*, not *Cursed.*'[90] Roberts did not object to Ball's interpretation on dogmatic grounds but instead presented exegetical observations to counter his conclusions. Moreover, another important element in Robert's argument is his appeal to Calvin. Roberts rightly noted the agreement between both of their explanations of Romans 10:5. In other words, this is evidence of continuity between Calvin's and High Orthodox understandings of Leviticus 18:5. Calvin does not explicitly advocate the covenant of works but he has pieces that constitute the core of the doctrine.

Besides the dissenting views of Cameron and Goodwin (temporal life) and Calamy and Ball (evangelical obedience), there were other dissenting views. Westminster divine Samuel Bolton (1606-1654) provides a taxonomy of six different views on Leviticus 18:5. Bolton explains:[91]

1. 'Do this and live' refers both to the moral and ceremonial law, which was Israel's gospel.

2. Leviticus 18:5 does not abstractly address the law but reveals law and promise.

3. God did not command Israel, 'Do this and live,' but rather 'do and live in doing.' Israel may have lived in obedience, though they could not live by obedience.

4. Leviticus 18:5 was a repetition of the covenant of works by repeating the law of the covenant to Israel after He had

---

90. Francis Roberts, *Mysterium et Medulla Bibliorum. The Mysterie and Marrow of the Bible* (London: George Calvert, 1657), 773.

91. Samuel Bolton, *The True Bounds of Christian Freedome. Or a Treatise Wherein the Rights of the Law Are Vindicated, the Liberties of Grace Maintained; and Severall Late Opinions Against the Law Are Examined and Confuted* (London: P. S., 1656), 154-60; Brent C. Ferry, 'Works in the Mosaic Covenant: A Reformed Taxonomy' (ThM Thesis: Westminster Theological Seminary, 2009), 36.

given them the promise of life. God repeats the covenant of works to challenge Israel to be saved either by working or believing.

5. Leviticus 18:5 refers only to temporal and prosperous life in the land of Canaan.

6. God spoke 'do this and live' immediately to Israel but ultimately to Christ, who fulfills all righteousness for believers.

Bolton rejects all of these views and gives his own interpretation. He recognized that the law and gospel stand in opposition, but in the end the law served the purposes of the gospel. God gave the law to cause sinners to see their own shortcomings and drive them to Christ. Citing the exegesis of Vermigli and Heinrich Alting (1583-1644), Bolton admits that if you look upon the law separately, it stands opposed to the promises. But if you look at it in relation to the promises, it has a subservient role.[92] Bolton's explanation of Leviticus 18:5 mirrors his subservient view of the Mosaic covenant. That is, the Mosaic covenant is neither of the covenants of works nor grace but rather a third covenant; the Mosaic covenant is subservient to the covenant of grace.

Like other exegetes, Bolton confirms this conclusion through the analogy of Scripture and Christ's interaction with the young man (Matt. 19:16-17). It is impossible for sinners to fulfill the law perfectly (Rom. 8:3), but Christ did not present the law's demands so that the young man could fulfill them but to show him it was impossible. Citing Calvin in support of his conclusion, Bolton writes:

> When men will be *Saviours* of themselves, when they look for righteousnesse by the Law; Christ bids them goe and *keep* the Commandements, *servanda mandata*, and this to *humble* them, and to bring them to him. But if men be once *humbled*, and broken in the sight of sinne, then *[Omissa legis mentione gratia promissione solatur*, saith Calvin, 3 *lib. Instit. Capd. De Merced.*] without mention of the Law at all, hee *comforts* them with the free *promises* of Grace:

---

92. Bolton, *True Bounds*, 157-58.

Then he saith, Come to me all that are weary and heavy laden and I will ease you. And the Spirit of the Lord is upon me to preach liberty to the Captive, &c.[93]

So, despite their opposition, ultimately the law and gospel worked in concert within the broader context of God's redemptive plan.

Bolton's taxonomy is interesting at several levels. The taxonomy reveals that, despite the majority view that interpreted Leviticus 18:5 as a revelation of the law and thus a suitable text to support the covenant of works, there were other minority views. Unfortunately, Bolton fails to identify the names of those who hold the different views, whether any of the views overlap, or the extent to which these views were held. The second and third views (Leviticus 18:5 reveals law and promise and that Israel was supposed to live *in* obedience rather than *by* obedience) might apply to Calamy and Ball, and the fourth and fifth view (temporal life) likely applies to Aquinas, Cameron, and Goodwin. Nevertheless, Bolton's own view stands in continuity with the earlier exegesis of Calvin and Vermigli, confirmed by his appeal to them, and it stands in harmony with the overall majority opinion on the interpretation of Leviticus 18:5. In this majority view, the text presents the demand for perfect obedience in order to yield the blessing of eternal life. Such an interpretation addresses the nature of the law in the pre- or post-fall state and thus serves as exegetical support for the covenant of works.

Conclusion

The exegetical labors of Calvin, Vermigli, and Willet reveal that Reformed theologians exegeted Leviticus 18:5 within the broader canonical context rather than in isolation. They not only examined it within its immediate context, but they compared it with other Old Testament passages such as Ezekiel 20 and New Testament passages such as Christ's interpretation in Matthew, and Paul's use of the text in Galatians and Romans. From this larger context, they concluded that the Scriptures placed doing the law and believing the gospel in antithesis in the point of justification. Doing versus believing marks the two paths of righteousness – works versus

---

93. Bolton, *True Bounds*, 160; cf. Calvin, *Institutes*, III.xviii.9.

faith. This was not a new contribution to the history of exegesis, as Aquinas made the same observations about *legalis vel iustitia fidei*. What distinguished Aquinas from the Reformers is that they posited different solutions as to how the two categories related. Aquinas detected a possible conflict between the teaching of Paul and Jesus and resolved it by means of the quadriga. Leviticus 18:5 literally referred to temporal blessings but according to its spiritual sense it referred to eternal life. In contrast to the Reformers, Aquinas believed that apart from the grace of God a person could not perform the requisite works for one's justification. Calvin, Vermigli, Willet and a host of post-Reformation theologians believed that Paul's contrast was not between works and grace-powered works but between performing the law versus trusting in the all-sufficient work of Christ. Within the context of the two-Adams, doing falls on the Adam side of the register and believing on Christ's side. In other words, doing marks the covenant of works and believing characterizes the covenant of grace.

The surveyed history of Leviticus 18:5 in early modern Reformed theology also presents important background for the twentieth-century rejection of the covenant of works, particularly by John Murray (1898-1975). Murray assigned Leviticus 18:5 to the third, or normative, use of the law.[94] In line with the minority view of Calamy and Ball, Murray believed that Leviticus 18:5 spoke about evangelical obedience. But what makes Murray's claims unique is the belief that Paul quoted Leviticus 18:5 out of context. It was fine to apply the principle of 'do this and live' to Adam, but it had no place in a post-fall world.[95] He claimed that Leviticus 18:5 'is, of itself, an adequate and watertight definition of the principle of legalism.'[96] Such claims do not appear in any of the surveyed early modern appeals to the verse. Murray arguably isolates Leviticus 18:5 rather than employing the analogy of Scripture to interpret it. Rather than compare it with Ezekiel 20, Matthew

---

94. John Murray, 'Leviticus 18:5,' in *The Epistle to the Romans*, NICNT, vol. 2 (Grand Rapids: Eerdmans, 1965), 251-52.

95. Murray, 'Leviticus 18:5,' 250.

96. Murray, 'Leviticus 18:5,' 251.

19:16-17, according to Murray, Paul instead borrows the words of Leviticus 18:5 to describe the spirit of legalism. With such a different exegetical method, Murray was inevitably drawn to different theological conclusions. Murray removed key exegetical pillars of the doctrine, which caused its contraction in his body of doctrine.

~: I.3 :~

Adam's Faith

Introduction

One of the topics of discussion that arises under the broader rubric of the covenant of works is the question of Adam's faith. Given that late sixteenth- and early seventeenth-century Reformed theologians placed Adam in the covenant of works, does this mean there was no place for a doctrine of faith? Reformed theologians happily acknowledged that Adam had faith, but this does not mean that Adam's faith was the same as the doctrine of faith peculiar to the covenant of grace. In fact, Reformed theologians acknowledged that Adam's faith and the doctrine of faith of the covenant of grace were two entirely different things. In order to understand the differences between faith under the respective covenants of works and grace, this chapter surveys the views of two Westminster divines, Thomas Goodwin (1600-1680) and Samuel Rutherford (1600-1661), as both explain the nature of Adam's faith, but do so employing different terms and from different formulations of the covenant of works. The former argues that the telos of the covenant of works was extended temporal life in the garden whereas the latter argues it was eternal life. Despite their different views, Goodwin and Rutherford similarly argue that Adam's faith is different than the doctrine of faith of the covenant of grace. The chapter also briefly surveys the views of a number of other sixteenth- and seventeenth-century theologians and documents to show how many distinguished between legal and evangelical faith. In short, this chapter demonstrates that Adam's faith is a general trust in God and His Word whereas evangelical faith is to trust in the person and work of Christ in order to lay hold of His alien righteousness for the pardon of sins, justification, and eternal life.

Goodwin on Natural and Supernatural Faith

Adam's Natural Faith

In his extensive treatment of the covenant of works Goodwin devotes the better part of an entire chapter to the nature of Adam's faith. In Goodwin's mind, it was necessary to distinguish Adam's natural faith from the gift of supernatural faith that the Spirit works in the hearts of those who participate in the covenant of grace. The two faiths have some similarities, but they also have significant and noteworthy differences. Goodwin's explanation of Adam's faith comes on the heels of numerous arguments that he makes to substantiate the claim that Adam's state in the garden was entirely natural. Goodwin embraced the views of John Cameron (ca. 1579-1625) and the idea that Adam's reward was purely natural – extended temporal life in the garden was his reward, not eternal life as other theologians argued. Goodwin followed Cameron's view of 1 Corinthians 15:45ff, that Adam was of the earth and Jesus was the heavenly man. Adam was natural and Christ was supernatural. Therefore, Adam's reward could only be natural since only the supernatural blessing of eternal life could come through Christ. Given these parameters, Goodwin wanted to explain Adam's natural faith and distinguish it from the supernatural faith of the covenant of grace.

Goodwin begins his argument with two points. First, knowing God according to grace comes only through revelation and is thus completely beyond man's natural capacities. Faith is a supernatural gift of the Holy Spirit. Second, the light of faith is above the light of nature, or the infused common principles of reason.[1] Here

---

1. Thomas Goodwin, *Of The Creatures, and The Condition of Their State by Creation*, in *The Works of Thomas Goodwin*, 12 vols. (1861-66; Eureka, CA: Tanski Publications, 1996), II.vii (vol. VII, p. 54).

Goodwin refers to the idea of common notions (*koinai ennonai*), that all human beings have a shared knowledge of God's law by virtue of their creation in the divine image and its inscription on the heart.[2] Romans 2:14-15 is a commonly cited text to support the idea of common notions. In addition to the light of nature, Goodwin acknowledges that God gave Adam other revelation in the form of verbal commands regarding taking dominion over the earth, not eating from the tree of knowledge, the Sabbath, as well as God's creation of his wife, Eve. Because God revealed these things to Adam, which were ostensibly inaccessible to Adam through the light of nature, God therefore required faith of Adam in His Word.[3] This was not the same faith of the covenant of grace.

Goodwin explains Adam's natural faith in five points. First, everything that God revealed to Adam was within the scope of nature and natural knowledge. Even within a post-fall context, for example, when one person believes the claims of another, he exercises faith in that person, which is not a supernatural act. There are natural acts of faith. Second, God created Adam for communion within a natural world, not a supernatural one. Even Adam's conversations, or prayers, with God were a part of his natural duties in an unfallen world.[4] Third, when God revealed His Word to Adam, it was not above his nature to receive or comprehend it. According to the dictates of nature God existed, was true, faithful, just, and powerful in all His works. This knowledge was a part of the 'law written in his heart,' which was a constituent element of the divine image (cf. Eph. 4:24-25). Thus, Adam's ability to receive and accept God's Word was 'from the power of an inbred light.'[5] Fourth, when God spoke Adam knew it was God by the 'light of sanctified reason,' which in this context refers, not to the regenerative work of the Holy Spirit, but to Adam's unfallen condition. After the fall, of

---

2. For a historical overview of the use of common notions in Reformed theology, see J. V. Fesko, *Reforming Apologetics: Retrieving the Classic Reformed Approach to Defending the Faith* (Grand Rapids: Baker Academic, 2019), 27-48.

3. Goodwin, *Of the Creatures*, II.vii (vol. 7, p. 54).

4. Goodwin, *Of the Creatures*, II.vii (vol. 7, pp. 54-55).

5. Goodwin, *Of the Creatures*, II.vii (vol. 7, p. 55).

course, the light of his reason was dimmed by the noetic effects of sin.[6] Fifth, and finally, when God revealed knowledge to Adam it was all natural, not supernatural. This knowledge consisted of God's nature and attributes, the precepts of His will, and the privileges God granted to Adam. Goodwin thus concludes: 'So as, put all these five considerations together, the conclusion is that all the faith which Adam had may well be resolved into natural light, as the first principle and foundation of it, although further revealing and confirming what else the light of nature could not, or would not so easily have known.'[7]

Supernatural Faith

Goodwin, therefore, presented these five points to describe the nature of Adam's faith, though even then, he was not necessarily convinced this was the best term.[8] Nevertheless, he employed the term but also explained in four points how the supernatural faith of the covenant of grace differs from Adam's faith. First, Adam's context was entirely natural because this is the nature of the covenant of works. This covenant is, after all, a *foedus naturae*. God bases everything in the covenant of works upon Adam's nature—his justification, reward, and divine image—were purely natural. It would be odd, therefore, if there was a principle of supernatural faith in Adam.[9] Here Goodwin's argument stands in stark contrast to the Roman Catholic ideas of a *donum superadditum*, namely, that God gave Adam superadded gifts of faith, hope, and love, in a pre-fall context.[10]

Second, even if God gave Adam a supernatural faith, it would have been entirely superfluous. Goodwin comes to this conclusion

---

6. Goodwin, *Of the Creatures*, II.vii (vol. 7, p. 55).

7. Goodwin, *Of the Creatures*, II.vii (vol. 7, p. 56).

8. Goodwin, *Of the Creatures*, II.vii (vol. 7, p. 56).

9. Goodwin, *Of the Creatures*, II.vii (vol. 7, pp. 56-57).

10. Cf. Thomas Aquinas, *Summa Theologica* (rep.; Allen, TX: Christian Classics, 1948), Ia q. 95 art. 1; *Ex Omnibus Afflictionibus* (1 Oct 1567), and *Cum Occasione* (31 May 1653), in *Compendium of Creeds, Definitions, and Declarations on Matters of Faith and Morals*, ed. Heinrich Denzinger, 43rd ed. (San Francisco: Ignatius Press, 2012), §§1901-80, esp. 1921, and §§2001-07.

because, whether Protestant or Roman Catholic, theologians who argue that God gave Adam the 'superadded supernatural grace' of faith do so to facilitate Adam's ability to attain or merit heaven. Medieval theologians, such as Thomas Aquinas (1225-1274), therefore distinguish between pre-fall natural and supernatural gifts. But heaven as Adam's goal is a non-sequitur. That is, Adam's reward was purely natural and therefore a supernatural faith to attain or merit heaven was unnecessary. If indeed Adam's reward was heaven, then Goodwin acknowledges that he would have required a supernatural faith. But supernatural faith, argues Goodwin, prepares sinners who are absent from the Lord for heaven (2 Cor. 5:7). Faith gives people hope of things unseen (Heb. 11:1). God's presence for Adam contrasts with His absence for participants in the covenant of grace.[11]

Third, supernatural faith provides believers with a taste of knowing God, something that Adam already possessed. Moreover, since Adam's telos was purely natural, had Adam received the supernatural revelation of heaven as his telos but been unable to reach it by means of his natural gifts, he would have been filled with an unsatisfied longing. He would have been perfectly complete within his natural realm but nevertheless miserable because he would have been unable to fulfill the longing for heaven. Fourth, the faith of the covenant of grace is of a higher order (*altioris ordinis*) because it offers a taste of heaven. By supernatural faith believers can behold Christ and eternal life (2 Cor. 3:18). This is one of the biggest differences between natural and supernatural faith according to Goodwin. Adam only beheld the attributes, work, and effects of God through the infused natural knowledge and hence ultimately only obscurely beheld God. Through supernatural faith, on the other hand, believers obtain a taste of the age to come (Heb. 6:4-5), the Holy Spirit. At this point in his argument, Goodwin concludes with a quotation from Cameron's theses on covenant theology: '*Faith* which exact justice in the *covenant* of Nature presupposes, is from God (as the Schooles speakes) by way of Nature: whereas

---

11. Goodwin, *Of the Creatures*, II.vii (vol. 7, p. 57).

the *faith* which is required in the *Covenant* of grace, is from God too; but so as by way of *supernaturall* grace.'[12]

Given his quotation of Cameron, reviewing the inspiring source of Goodwin's own understanding of Adam's pre-fall faith provides a concise overview of the differences between natural and supernatural faith. According to Cameron, pre- and post-fall faith differ in four points:[13]

Difference	Covenant of Nature	Covenant of Grace
Foundation	Presupposes a perfect human nature, and thus has no place in post-fall humanity.	The promise made in Christ.
Nature vs. grace	Presupposes nature (*per modum naturae*)	Presupposes supernatural grace (*per modum gratia supernaturalis*)
Mutability vs. immutability	Adam's righteousness (*iustitia*) was mutable	Our holiness (*sanctitas*) is immutable and eternal because it flows from an immutable and eternal principle, the Spirit of Grace.
Pre- vs. post-fall nobility	Adam's nature was perfect but beneath the holiness begotten by faith in Christ	The holiest saint falls short of Adam's original righteousness, but this occurs due to the weakness of one's faith. But nevertheless, post-fall faith is far higher than pre-fall faith and grants access to a higher holiness than Adam's original state.

---

12. Goodwin, *Of the Creatures*, II.vii (vol. 7, pp. 58-59); cf. John Cameron, *De Triplici Dei Cum Homine Foedere Theses*, in *Ioh. Cameronis S. Theologiae in Academia Salmuriensi Nuper Professoris, Praelectionum Tomus Tertius et Ultimus* (Saumur: Cl. Girard & Dan. Lerpiner, 1628), thesis XIV (p. 613-14); idem, *Certain Theses, or, Positions of the Learned John Cameron, Concerning the Threefold Covenant of God with Man*, in Samuel Bolton, *The True Bounds of Christian Freedome* (London: P. S., 1656), 362-63.

13. Cameron, *Threefold Covenant*, thesis XIV (pp. 362-63); idem, *Triplici Foedere*, 613-14; also Richard A. Muller, 'Divine Covenants, Absolute and Conditional: John Cameron and the Early Orthodox Development of Reformed Covenant Theology,' *MAJT* 17 (2006): 41.

In a nutshell, there are two major reasons why Cameron and Goodwin differentiate between natural and supernatural faith. First, Adam's state was natural, thus his reward was natural. Second, the covenants of works and grace differ in terms of their object – Adam's obedience versus the promise of Christ's work through the gospel. The object of Adam's faith was God's Word – he had to trust God's Word but ultimately rest in his own obedience whereas participants in the covenant of grace must trust in the work of another, Jesus Christ.

Comparative Analysis

As clear as Goodwin and Cameron are, the question naturally arises, Is not this particular construction dependent upon their shared presupposition that Adam's telos was entirely natural? In other words, Goodwin and Cameron excise the need for supernatural faith because they presupposed a natural telos in the covenant of works. How normative can this formulation of Adam's faith truly be given that Goodwin and Cameron's doctrine of the covenant of works was a minority view within the early modern Reformed tradition? What might other theologians who posited a heavenly telos for Adam in the covenant of works say? Despite disagreements over the precise character of Adam's reward (natural vs. supernatural), Reformed theologians were in basic agreement regarding the question of Adam's faith. They did not use all the same arguments or terminology, but there was large-scale substantive agreement among them. One of the common distinctions that theologians employed was a *legal* versus an *evangelical* or *justifying* faith among the many other different uses of the term *faith* in Scripture. In other words, theologians exegetically and contextually defined the term and doctrine of faith and did not apply one definition or concept in their exegesis or doctrinal formulations.

John Downame (1571-1652) notes the different types of faith that occur in the Scriptures. Sometimes the term *faith* denotes:

- The doctrine (Acts 6:7; Gal. 3:2, 23; Rom. 12:6).
- Fidelity or faithfulness (Rom 3:3).

- A persuasion to believe in God (Heb. 11), which is more properly a justifying faith.

- Of miracles, a general or historical faith, a legal faith, a temporary faith, which are all different from a true lively and justifying faith, 'Whereby the Believe doth apprehend and apply unto himselfe particularly Christ and his righteousness and merits.'[14]

Others such as James Ussher (1581-1656) offer similar explanations of the different types of faith that appear in the Bible.[15] Theologians, therefore, who believed that Adam's reward was eternal life nevertheless differentiated between pre- and post-fall faith and did so through a different set of exegetically sourced distinctions.

Samuel Rutherford believed that Adam's reward was eternal life but distinguished between Adam's faith and the faith of believers in the covenant of grace. In his exposition of the book of James, Rutherford explains the difference between a lively and dead faith.[16] He engaged this subject because of Arminian and Socinian doctrines of faith. According to Rutherford, saving faith lays hold of an object, in this case, righteousness, apart from the works of the law (Rom. 3:21-22).[17] The Scriptures clearly state that we are justified by faith, not by love, alms, repentance, or deeds.[18] And faith, according to Rutherford, is to believe in Christ, lean on God, to come to Him 'by way of affiance,' and to receive Christ. None of these things can be said of love, repentance, or new obedience.[19]

---

14. John Downame, *The Christian Warfare Against the Devill World and Flesh Wherein is Described Their Nature, the Maner of their Fight and Meanes to Obtaine Victory* (London: William Stansby, 1634), III.xviii (p. 332).

15. James Ussher, *A Body of Divinitie, or the Summe and Substance of Christian Religion* (London: Thom. Downes and Geo. Badger, 1645), 196-200. I am grateful to Harrison Perkins for drawing my attention to this passage in Ussher's work.

16. Samuel Rutherford, *The Covenant of Life Opened: Or, A Treatise of the Covenant of Grace* (Edinburgh: Robert Broun, 1654), I.xix (p. 168).

17. Rutherford, *Covenant of Life*, I.xix (pp. 172-73).

18. Rutherford, *Covenant of Life*, I.xix (p. 174).

19. Rutherford, *Covenant of Life*, I.xix (pp. 174-75).

To illustrate his point further, Rutherford expands his description of faith to include consent to Christ's lordship and obedience to His government. If this is the nature of faith,

> Then well may *Adam*, in the Covenant of Works, be said to be justified and saved by faith; for if to believe in *God Redeemer*, and if this surrendering be the obedience of works by which we are justified and saved and perfectly righteous before God, upon the same reason to believe in God Law-giver and Creator in the Covenant of Works, and for *Adam* to surrender himself Covenant wayes, by a legall faith shall be the law of obedience of works by which *Adam* is justified and saved, and so he is saved by Law faith, as we are by Gospel-faith.[20]

Key to Rutherford's statement is the way he describes the nature of Adam's justification and his legal faith. Adam's faith was ultimately marked by obedience, not a trust in and resting upon Christ and His righteousness for salvation. Rutherford contrasts Adam's *legal faith* with *gospel faith*, which parallels Goodwin's categories of natural and supernatural faith. In Rutherford's judgment, the Arminian and Socinian error was that they mistakenly replaced the gospel faith of the covenant of grace with Adam's legal faith of the covenant of works.

Rutherford further elaborates this point when he explains what type of faith the gospel requires in contrast to legal faith. Legal faith is obedience to a command, whether those commands are revealed internally to the mind or externally.[21] Rutherford does not invoke the specific terminology here, but he likely has in view the natural law inscribed upon Adam's heart and the positive commands verbally given by God. Rutherford therefore explains: 'So *Adam* had a habit or habitual power to believe the Law and the Gospel upon supposition, should it be revealed.' In other words, Adam could have faith in God's law and even the gospel if God had revealed it to him. Rutherford then writes: 'Its folly to say *Adam* stood in need, before he fell, of a supernatural power to believe Evangelick truths, if he beleeved *God* to be true, he had such a

---

20. Rutherford, *Covenant of Life*, I.xix (p. 175).
21. Rutherford, *Covenant of Life*, I.xxiv (p. 205).

power as to believe all was true, that God should reveal.' Rutherford does not mention him by name, but he likely has Goodwin in the crosshairs with this statement, since Goodwin believed that heaven was beyond Adam's natural faith. Nonetheless, according to Rutherford: 'Adam had a faith of dependencie, to rely upon God in all possible evils feared.'[22]

By way of stark contrast, 'The promise of life is not made to Law-faith more then to Law-love, or Law-fear, or Law-desire, more then to any other, but the promise is made to Evangelick-faith that layes hold on CHRIST as our righteousnesse.'[23] To support this claim Rutherford appeals to several texts and authorities. He notes that Adam was given the ability to secure eternal life through his obedience, by obeying God's commands (Gal. 3:13; Ezek. 20:11). He then cites Ludwig Lavater (1527-1586), who writes: 'There is no absurditie if it be said men shall live, that is merit by free paction, life eternall.' He also appeals to John Calvin's (1509-1564) commentary on Ezekiel: 'If a man keep the Law, he needs not the Grace of Christ.'[24] In other words, Adam's faith is legal and thus very different from the gospel faith of the covenant of grace. Even though Rutherford and Goodwin disagreed on the particulars and the specific theological route, they both agreed on the final outcome. Adam's faith was a general trust in God and His Word and his beatitude within the covenant of works rested upon his own obedience and fidelity. Conversely, gospel faith is a specific trust in the person and work of Christ and beatitude in the covenant of grace ultimately rests upon laying hold of Christ's righteousness – the alien righteousness of another. Or in the words of the Westminster Confession, 'The principall Acts of saving faith, are, Accepting, Receiving, and Resting upon Christ alone for Justification, Sanctification, and Eternall life, by vertue of the Covenant of Grace.'[25]

---

22. Rutherford, *Covenant of Life*, I.xxiv (p. 205).

23. Rutherford, *Covenant of Life*, I.xxiv (p. 205).

24. Cf. John Calvin, *Commentaries on the Prophet Ezekiel*, 2 vols., CTS (rep.; Grand Rapids: Baker, 1993), lect. LXI (pp. 297-98).

25. *The Humble Advice of the Assembly of Divines, Now by Authority of Parliament Sitting At Westminster, Concerning a Confession of Faith* (London: Company of Stationers, 1647), XIV.ii.

Other theologians made this same type of distinction between legal and evangelical faith. Antonius Walaeus (1573-1639) maintains that legal faith is interchangeable with justification through the law whereas evangelical faith seeks justification through the gospel. The embodiment of legal faith is Leviticus 18:5, namely, the one who does the commandments will live by them. Conversely, evangelical faith comes through the gospel of Christ.[26] Johannes Cocceius (1603-1669) makes a similar observation when he explains that legal faith (*fides legalis*) simply believes in the promises of the law, that is, the one who does them shall live in them. This type of faith, argues Cocceius, cannot justify a person.[27] With some theologians, the desire to preserve the unique nature of the doctrine of faith was so great, that they proposed alternative terms for the covenant of grace. Francis Roberts (1609-1675), for example, contrasts the covenant of works with the covenant of faith.[28] He prefers the term *covenant of faith* to the usual *covenant of grace* because it is the condition of the covenant in contrast to the condition of works for the Adamic covenant. Moreover, in his judgment, it more closely aligns with Paul's terms, the law of works and the law of faith (Rom. 3:27).[29]

Conclusion

When a theologian invokes the category of Adam's faith it does not mean that this is the same concept as faith in Jesus. Reformed covenant theologians were quite clear and distinguished between Adam's general trust in God and His Word versus a specific trust in the person and work of Christ. Despite their disagreements over the particulars of the covenant of works, they clearly delineated between legal faith, which was ultimately obedience to the law, versus gospel faith, which is to believe and trust in Jesus for the

---

26. Antonius Walaeus, *Loci Communes S. Theologiae Autore D. Antonio Walaeo* (Leiden: Adrian Whyngarden, 1647), 416.

27. Johannes Cocceius, *Summa Theologiae Ex Scripturis Repetita* (Geneva: Samuel Chouët, 1665), VIII.xxii.46 (p. 278).

28. Francis Roberts, *Mysterium & Medulla Bibliorum. The Mysterie and Marrow of the Bible* (London: George Calvert, 1657), I.i (p. 2).

29. Roberts, *Mysterium & Medulla*, II.ii (p. 61).

forgiveness of sins, justification, and eternal life. The difference between legal and evangelical faith is the same difference between the early-Reformation categories of law and gospel. Theologians simply accounted for the difference of law and gospel in a pre- and post-fall world. The distinction between legal and evangelical faith was another front in the battle between Reformed and Roman Catholic theologians.

~: I.4 :~

Covenant or Contract?

Introduction

As contemporary readers investigate early modern concepts of covenant they inevitably run across language and terminology that ruffles their feathers. Numerous early modern theologians interchangeably employ the terms *covenant* and *contract* and contemporary readers object. Most notably James B. Torrance's (1923-2003) 1970 essay, claimed that seventeenth-century theologians confused contracts with covenants and introduced a theological aberration into the pristine theology of the Protestant Reformation.[1] Torrance's basic claim is that a covenant is an unconditional promise whereas a contract is a mutual agreement. According to Torrance, seventeenth-century Reformed theologians confused these two categories, which led them to construe God's dealings with humanity in terms of the covenants of works and grace. Torrance writes: 'This distinction between a Covenant of Works and a Covenant of Grace was unknown to Calvin and the Reformers – nor indeed would Calvin ever have taught it. The very distinction implies the confusion between a *covenant* and a *contract* – the one Latin word *foedus* meaning both and hence obscuring the distinction.'[2] Did early

---

1. James B. Torrance, 'Covenant or Contract? A Study of the Theological Background of Worship in Seventeenth-Century Scotland,' *SJT* 23 (1970), 51-76.

2. Torrance, 'Covenant or Contract?' 61-62. See also, idem, 'The Concept of Federal Theology – Was Calvin a Federal Theologian?' in *Calvinus Sacrae Scripturae*

modern Reformed theologians confuse covenants with contracts? The simple answer to this question is, no. This chapter provides the detailed answer to this question.

This chapter argues that contemporary historians such as Torrance have misunderstood early modern covenants and contracts; they have imposed anachronistic definitions of these terms upon early modern sources and thus misrepresented their claims. This chapter demonstrates that covenants and contracts were synonymous biblical and theological concepts, but that ultimately context determines the nature of these covenants and contracts, not superimposed definitions. As Quentin Skinner (1940-) has argued, only a contextual reading of a concept or term provides accurate assessment.[3] To prove this thesis, this chapter first surveys Torrance's claim. Second, it provides a broad critique of Torrance's argument. Third, the chapter engages primary sources to demonstrate the erroneous nature of Torrance's thesis. It identifies the various interchangeable terms that early modern theologians employed to denote and explain biblical covenants, including covenant, contract, bargain, compact, alliance, and the like. Fourth, the chapter explores the various theological uses of these terms to prove that early modern Reformed theologians did not distort the biblical notion of covenant. In this respect, there are two crucial elements that historians must factor: (1) contextual indicators that a theologian uses to define his terms. In other words, not all covenants are the same – they have different characteristics. (2) Many contemporary critics fail to account for the early modern – modern shift in the meaning and significance of the term *contract*. Early modern contracts are zebras whereas modern contracts are horses. They look similar but in truth are different animals altogether. The chapter then concludes and highlights the importance of reading early modern sources within their historical, cultural, and theological context to avoid misrepresenting their claims.

Professor: Calvin as Confessor of Holy Scripture, ed. Whilelm H. Neuser (Grand Rapids: Eerdmans, 1994), 15-40.

3. Quentin Skinner, 'Meaning and Understanding in the History of Ideas,' *History and Theory* 8/1 (1969): 3-53, esp. 40.

Torrance's Claims

Torrance's basic claim is that seventeenth-century Reformed theologians confused covenants with contracts. Torrance presents his argument in three steps: (a) his basic claim and definition of terms, (b) a survey of several biblical texts, and (c) a theological construction and critique of early modern covenant theology.

Definition of Terms

Torrance defines a covenant in the following manner: 'Theologically speaking a covenant is a promise binding two people or two parties to love one another *unconditionally*.'[4] He appeals to the English service book of 1549 to corroborate his claim, namely, that those who enter into the estate of marriage do so, 'for better for worse.' Unconditionally, in Torrance's view, drastically sets a covenant apart from a contract. 'A contract,' writes Torrance, 'is a *legal* relationship in which two people or two parties bind themselves together on mutual *conditions* to effect some future result. It betokens a mutual bargain, a compact, a business deal, grounded on certain terms or conditions with some future state of affairs in mind. It takes the form, "If ... if ... then ...," as in the business world.'[5] Torrance acknowledges that in Scottish law *covenant* and *contract* mean the same thing, but he nevertheless avers that, theologically speaking, one must not confuse the two.

Biblical Survey

Torrance admits that there are many different types of covenants in the Bible. First, there are *bilateral* covenants, such as the covenant between David and Jonathan – a bond between equals. Such a covenant is a *suntheke* according to Torrance. Second, there are *unilateral* covenants, such as when one of Israel's new kings made a covenant with the nation. Such a covenant is a *diatheke*. With these two biblical observations Torrance claims: 'God's dealings with men in Creation and in Redemption—in grace—are those of Covenant and not of contract.' In divine love

---

4. Torrance, 'Covenant or Contract?' 54.

5. Torrance, 'Covenant or Contract?' 54.

God initiates, announces, confirms, and establishes the covenant and the form of His declaration appears in the indicative: 'I will be your God and you shall be my people.' The term for God's covenants, therefore, is always *diatheke*. This was the discovery of the early Reformers, such as John Calvin (1509-1564) and John Knox (ca. 1513-1572).[6] In his view, 'The God of the Bible is a Covenant-God not a contract-god.'[7]

Critique of Early Modern Covenant Theology
In his critique of early modern Reformed covenant theology Torrance claims the introduction of the twofold covenants, works and grace, created the context for the distortion of the biblical doctrine of the covenants.[8] He presents several claims in defense of his argument. First, he argues that according to Calvin, all of God's interactions with people are on the basis of grace, 'There has been only one eternal covenant of grace promised in the Old Testament and fulfilled in Christ.'[9] As covenant theology developed, however, theologians supposedly introduced conditions throughout the covenantal landscape and hence Torrance concludes that a more accurate description of seventeenth-century Reformed covenant theology is *contract* theology. In each of the now three covenants God requires a condition: the covenant of redemption – the Son's obedience, the covenant of works – Adam's obedience, and the covenant of grace – faith and repentance from His people. According to Torrance, repentance is the condition, if someone wants their sins forgiven.[10] Torrance cites *The Sum of Saving Knowledge*, written by David Dickson (ca. 1583-1663) and James Durham (1622-1658), as evidence of the devolution of covenant theology because the document speaks of the 'covenant or contract' and speaks of conditions for all three covenants.[11]

---

6. Torrance, 'Covenant or Contract?' 54-55.

7. Torrance, 'Covenant or Contract?' 56.

8. Torrance, 'Covenant or Contract?' 61-62.

9. Torrance, 'Covenant or Contract?' 62.

10. Torrance, 'Covenant or Contract?' 62-63.

11. Torrance, 'Covenant or Contract?' 63.

According to Torrance, the synthesis between Christianity and culture was the driving force behind the corruption of covenant theology. He appeals to Samuel Rutherford's (1600-1661) *Lex Rex* and one of the ideas that he defended, namely, that law binds king and people together. The seventeenth-century witnessed the rise of the social contract, which were developed in great detail by John Locke (1632-1704) and Jean-Jacques Rousseau (1712-1778).[12] When theologians allowed these cultural notions of contract to seep into their concept of covenant, the very legalism in salvation they feared so much entered through their unwitting use of contract.[13] In addition to the *Sum of Saving Knowledge*, Torrance mentions the names of other theologians to buttress his claims including Cocceius, Preston, Ames, Ball, and Witsius. In Torrance's analysis, Zacharias Ursinus (1534-1583) supplies a smoking gun: 'A covenant in general signifieth a mutual contract or agreement of two parties joined in the covenant, whereby is made a bond or obligation on certain conditions for the performance of giving or taking something with the addition of outward signs and tokens.'[14] In his mind, such a definition pushes grace to the background and creates the so-called *federal scheme* where theologians radically dichotomized nature and grace: 'This separation between Nature and Grace amounts to a reversion to the pre-Reformation medieval view that *grace presupposes nature* and *grace perfects nature* – a departure from the great emphasis of the Reformation that nothing is prior to grace.'[15] This distortion introduces a host of negative side-effects, such as limited atonement, a loss of the doctrine of union with Christ, an overemphasis on the believer's subjective reception of grace rather than on Christ's objective work, the false distinction between the visible and invisible church, and an impoverishment of worship.[16]

---

12. Torrance, 'Covenant or Contract?' 64.

13. Torrance, 'Covenant or Contract?' 63.

14. Torrance, 'Covenant or Contract?' 66; cf. Zacharias Ursinus, *The Summe of Christian Religion*, trans. D. Henrie Parry (Oxford: 1601), 218. Note, though, that Torrance draws this quotation from John Murray, *The Covenant of Grace* (London: Tyndale Press, 1954), n. p.

15. Torrance, 'Covenant or Contract?' 67.

16. Torrance, 'Covenant or Contract?' 67-71.

Critique of Torrance's Claims

Torrance wrote his essay in 1970, and a number of historians have critiqued his claims based upon a close reading of the historical evidence.[17] Torrance's approach has a number of shortcomings. First, Torrance presents a superficial engagement of primary sources. He only offers a few basic quotes and statements. In his mind, the mere presence of the term *contract* or *condition* is *prima facie* evidence of theological devolution. Torrance never engages in a contextual reading of these terms to determine their precise meaning or use. By way of contrast, Richard Muller surveys the lexical and exegetical arguments of two theologians, Herman Witsius (1636-1708) and Wilhelmus à Brakel (1635-1711), to show that their own work looks nothing like Torrance's analysis.[18] While one may disagree with Witsius and à Brakel's exegesis, he should not accuse them of synthesizing Christianity and culture or confusing covenants with contracts apart from evidence.

Second, Torrance imposes a dogmatic definition of *covenant* and *contract* apart from significant historical or biblical exegesis. For his definition of *contract*, for example, he does not present sufficient historical research to corroborate his claim. Are all early modern contracts mutual agreements? Similarly, when he sets forth biblical evidence for his definition of covenant, he alludes to two biblical texts and then concludes that David's covenant with Jonathan is a *suntheke* whereas the Bible always presents the term *diatheke* for God's covenants with His people. The problem with his claim, however, is that the Septuagint employs the term *diatheke*, not

---

17. Richard A. Muller, 'The Covenant of Works and the Stability of Divine Law in Seventeenth-Century Reformed Orthodoxy: A Study in the Theology of Herman Witsius and Wilhelmus à'Brakel,' *CTJ* 29 (1994): 75-101. Also see J. Mark Beach, *Christ and the Covenant: Francis Turretin's Federal Theology as a Defense of the Doctrine of Grace* (Göttingen: Vandenhoeck & Ruprecht, 2007), 335-36; Andrew A. Woolsey, *Unity and Continuity in Covenantal Thought: A Study in the Reformed Tradition to the Westminster Assembly* (Grand Rapids: Reformation Heritage Publishing, 2012), 136-38; Brannon Ellis, 'The Eternal Decree in the Incarnate Son: Robert Rollock on the Relationship Between Christ and Election,' in *Reformed Orthodoxy in Scotland: Essays on Scottish Theology 1550-1700*, ed. Aaron C. Denlinger (London: Bloomsbury T & T Clark, 2014), 45-65.

18. Muller, 'Covenant of Works,' 80-87.

suntheke, when David and Jonathan make a covenant (1 Sam. 20:8; 23:18; cf. 18:3).

Third, Torrance pits Calvin against the so-called 'Calvinists,' which in itself is a specious claim given that the Reformed tradition never established Calvin as its normative theologian.[19] On this point Torrance makes several claims about Calvin's own theology, such as the fact that Calvin would have never taught the covenant of works because he believed that all God's dealings were on the basis of grace.[20] Calvin, of course, did not teach the formal doctrine of the covenant of works – it is anachronistic to his historical context. To claim that Calvin would have never taught the doctrine, however, rests on speculation and ignores the parallels between Calvin and the later Reformed doctrine of the covenant of works.[21]

Fourth, Torrance imposes his Barthian understanding of the one eternal covenant of grace over the early Reformed tradition and then criticizes seventeenth-century theologians for departing from this mythical norm.[22] But while Torrance did stand within Barthian covenant theology, Torrance stands in a long-line of Scottish theologians who were critical of early modern covenant theology, one that stretches from nineteenth-century theologians John Kelly, David Russell, and John Eagleton, the twentieth century with John Murray (1898-1975), and the twenty-first century with Andrew McGowan.[23]

---

19. Richard A. Muller, *Calvin and the Reformed Tradition: Studies in the Work of Christ and the Order of Salvation* (Grand Rapids: Baker, 2012), 51-69; idem, 'Demoting Calvin: The Issue of Calvin and the Reformed Tradition,' in *John Calvin, Myth and Reality: Images and Impact of Geneva's Reformer*, ed. Amy Nelson Burnett (Eugene, OR: Cascade, 2011), 3-17.

20. Torrance, 'Covenant or Contract?' 61-62.

21. See, e.g., Peter A. Lillback, *The Binding of God: Calvin's Role in the Development of Covenant Theology* (Grand Rapids: Baker, 2001). 276-304.

22. Cf. Torrance, 'Covenant or Contract?' 62; e.g., Woolsey, *Unity and Continuity*, 138.

23. David Russell, *A Familiar Survey of the Old and New Covenants* (Edinburgh: Waugh and Innes, 1824); John Kelly, *The Divine Covenants* (London: Jackson, Walford, & Hodder, 1851); John Eagleton, *Thoughts on the Covenant of Works: An Epistolary Address to Junior Ministers of the Gospel of All Denominations* (Edinburgh: R. Baynes, 1829); Andrew McGowan, *Adam, Christ and Covenant: Exploring Headship Theology* (Leicester: Apollos / InterVarsity Press, 2016).

These four defects alone constitute sufficient ground to dismiss Torrance's claims, but there is more to the story of the supposed difference between covenants versus contracts. Moreover, rather than repeat the previously critiqued aspects of Torrance's claims, the rest of the chapter provides further evidence to substantiate the claim that seventeenth-century theologians did not confuse covenants with contracts.

Terms

There is no dispute that early modern Reformed theologians liberally and interchangeably use the terms covenant, contract, compact, alliance, or bargain in their explanation of God's covenantal activity in the Bible. A few examples sufficiently illustrate this point. John Preston (1587-1628) comments on Genesis 17:7 and God's covenant with Abraham, which he describes as 'a Covenant, a compact and agreement.'[24] In one of the more popular covenantal works of the early seventeenth century, Edward Fisher (fl. 1627-1655) comments on Romans 7:4-6 in the following manner: 'The Apostle in the beginning of the seventh Chapter of the *Epistle* to the *Romans*, compares this compact bargain or covenant between a man in the state of nature, and the Law, as it is the Covenant of works, to the compact or covenant that is made between man and wife in marriage, and this death to their death.'[25] In this one statement Fisher uses compact and bargain as synonyms for *covenant*. Other early modern theologians unflinchingly use *covenant* and *contract* interchangeably.[26] The same is true of English as well as Latin texts, which often use *foedus, pactum, contractus, conventio*, and *consensus mutuus* as synonyms.[27] Early modern theological dictionaries and

---

24. John Preston, *The New Covenant Or the Saints Portion* (London: Nicolas Bourne, 1639), 313.

25. Edward Fisher, *The Marrow of Modern Divinity* (London: G. Calvert, 1645), 59.

26. Patrick Gillespie, *The Ark of the Covenant Opened* (London: Tho. Parkhurst, 1677), 6; Jeremias Bastingius, *An Exposition Upon the Catechisme of the Lowe Countryes* (Cambridge: John Legatt, 1589), 153. See also, Richard Baxter, *Christian Directory* (1846; Morgan, PA: Soli Deo Gloria, 1996), IV.xix (pp. 827-46, esp. 827, 829, 830).

27. See, e.g., Johannes Heidegger, *Corpus Theologiae Christianiae*, 2 vols. (Zurich: Heideggerian Office, 1732), IX.xv, xviii (pp. 306-07); Leonard Riissen, *Summa*

lexicons likewise identify these as synonymous terms. In his lexicon, Johannes Cocceius (1603-1669) defines the Hebrew term *berith* as *foedus* and *conventio*.[28] Celebrated Hebraist Johannes Buxtorf Sr. (1564-1629) defines *berith* as *foedus* or *pactum*.[29] In lexicographer Thomas Wilson's (1563-1622) *Christian Dictionarie* he defines *covenant* in the following manner: 'League or Agreement betweene two or more parties.'[30] Does the mere presence of the term *contract* or its equivalents invalidate the presented definitions? Have these early modern theologians confused covenants with contracts as Torrance alleges? The answer to these questions is, no.

The mere presence of terms like contract, agreement, pact, bargain does not automatically invalidate a theologian's claims. Noteworthy is the fact that with some, such as the lexicons or dictionaries, critics would easily spot eisegesis if the presented biblical texts did not accurately and contextually explain the terms. Under his entry for *covenant*, for example, Wilson lists a number of different references to show the varied use of the term in Scripture: the sign and pledge of God's covenant (Gen. 17:4), our promises made to God (Neh. 9:38), an agreement God makes with man for his salvation (Jer. 32:40), the Word of God (Ps. 25:10, 14; Exod. 19:5), the promise between a man and woman to enter into the estate of marriage (Mal. 2:14), circumcision (Gen. 17:13), and the tables of the covenant (Rom. 9:4).[31] Unlike Torrance, who only alludes to two different biblical texts, Wilson cites numerous examples in his entry for *covenant*.

Another factor is the exegetical nature of the various offered definitions. In his massive thousand-page-plus work on covenant

---

Theologiae Didactico-Elencticae (Berne: Daniel Tschiffel, 1703), IX.xii (p. 231); Petrus Van Mastricht, *Theoretica-Practica Theologia*, 9th ed., vol. 1 (Utrecht: W. van der Water, et al., 1724), III.xii.2 (p. 413).

28. Johannes Cocceius, *Lexicon et Commentarius Sermonis Hebraici et Chaldaici* (Frankfurt: Balthasar Christophor Wust, 1689), s. v. *berith* (pp. 115-16).

29. Johannes Buxtorf Sr., *Lexicon Hebraicum et Chaldaicum* (Basil: Johannes Konig, 1663), s.v. *berith* (p. 88).

30. Thomas Wilson, *A Christian Dictionarie* (London: W. Iaggard, 1612), s. v. *covenant* (p. 68).

31. Wilson, *Christian Dictionarie*, 68-69.

theology, Francis Roberts (1609-1675) presents detailed exegetical spadework common to early modern explanations of covenant. Roberts explains that the term *covenant* comes from the Hebrew term *berith*, which has several potential root origins including *barar*, to purify or make-clear, *berath*, which means firmness, or perhaps *barah*, which means to choose, or *bara*, to strike, cut, or divide. After considering these different options, he finally decides that its root term is *kerith*, which means 'to strike' or 'smite.' He supports this claim by recognizing that the Bible frequently joins the term *berith* with the term *carat*, which means to 'strike a covenant.' He bases this on a catena of texts including Exodus 24, Genesis 15:9, 10, 17, and Jeremiah 34:18-20.[32] Roberts then explores the Greek term *diatheke*, which he notes that the Septuagint employs throughout the Old Testament, except in Deuteronomy 9:15, where the LXX elides the term. But he observes that *diatheke* can also mean a *testament*, as in a last will and testament, but that context determines whether one should translate it as *covenant* or *testament*. He then lists all of the occurrences of *diatheke* in the New Testament.[33] Beyond this, Roberts explains the various English and Latin equivalents and their etymologies for the term, which include covenant, league, *foedus, pactum, testamentum*, and *conventio*.[34]

Far from imposing a one-size fits all definition, Roberts gives a nuanced lexical and exegetical discussion of the term to support his theological claims. He notes that a covenant is an agreement between God and man but that 'God condescends and stoops down to us, and we bare worms ascend up to God, and so meet one

---

32. Francis Roberts, *Mysterium et Medulla Bibliorum: The Mysterie and Marrow of the Bible, viz. God's Covenants with Man* (London: George Calvert, 1657), I.ii.1 (pp. 10-11). For an overview of Roberts' covenant theology, see Won Taek Lim, 'The Covenant Theology of Francis Roberts' (PhD Diss., Calvin Theological Seminary, 2000).

33. Roberts, *Mysterium et Medulla Bibliorum*, I.ii.1 (p. 11).

34. Roberts, *Mysterium et Medulla Bibliorum*, I.ii.1 (p. 13). Patrick Gillespie presents a similar carefully nuanced exposition of the eight different ways that covenant can be defined in Scripture (see Patrick Gillespie, *Ark of the Testament Opened, or The Secret of the Lord's Covenant Unsealed in a Treatise of the Covenant of Grace* [London: R. C., 1681], 61-74). My thanks to Ryan McGraw for drawing my attention to this passage in Gillespie's work.

another friendly and familiarly.'[35] God and man, therefore, are not equals in divine-human covenants. Building upon the idea of God's condescension in all divine-human covenants, he notes in agreement with Amos 3:3, 'can two walk together, except they be agreed?,' that 'concord is the foundation of all *contracts*.'[36] God alone initiates the covenant because He is its author, and hence it is a 'gratuitous agreement,' which once again reflects God's condescension. In this sense God's covenant is a promise.[37] While it is true that Roberts introduces the idea of conditions, or stipulations, the precise nature of these conditions is all-important. While all of God's covenants have conditions, not all conditions are the same. A condition of personal, perfect, and perpetual obedience in the covenant of works is not the same as the necessary condition of faith for the covenant of grace. In Roberts' formulation, God required Adam's perfect obedience in order to secure eternal life, but God's provision of the covenant of works was an act of grace: 'Gods entering into covenant with Adam before his fall, was an act of divine grace and favor, not of debt.'[38] By way of contrast, the covenant of grace (or *faith* in Roberts' construction), is 'a wonderful compound and contrivance of meer grace' because, among other things, Christ entirely secures the blessings as covenant surety.[39]

When he writes of the conditions of the covenant of grace, Roberts provides an extensive and highly nuanced discussion that defies an overly simplified explanation as we find with Torrance's criticisms. Roberts employs a scholastic distinction between *antecedent* and *concomitant conditions*. He further subdivides antecedent conditions into three categories: meritorious, impulsive, and preparatory. The Roman Catholic insistence upon the necessity of good works for salvation is a *meritorious antecedent condition* to

---

35. Roberts, *Mysterium et Medulla Bibliorum*, I.i.2 (p. 7).

36. Roberts, *Mysterium et Medulla Bibliorum*, I.ii.2 (p. 14).

37. Roberts, *Mysterium et Medulla Bibliorum*, I.ii.2 (p. 15).

38. Roberts, *Mysterium et Medulla Bibliorum*, I.ii.2 (p. 23). See also Harrison Perkins, *Catholicity and the Covenant of Works: James Ussher and the Reformed Tradition* (Oxford: Oxford University Press, 2020), 110-12.

39. Roberts, *Mysterium et Medulla Bibliorum*, II.ii.2 (pp. 105-06).

one's justification. In other words, the sinner must provide his good works before God finally justifies him before the divine bar. An *impulsive antecedent condition* is when God shows mercy to someone because of his divinely foreseen faith. The Arminians, according to Roberts, advocate these types of antecedent conditions. Roberts acknowledges the legitimacy of *preparatory antecedent conditions* of entering into covenant with God, such as regeneration, faith, and justification, but he stipulates that God Himself provides all of these conditions.[40] Conversely, *concomitant conditions* such as self-denial, repentance, continued belief in God's promises, and the like are all consequences of entering into God's covenant: 'Conditions consequent, or Following Gods taking man into Covenant with himself, are such Duties or Performances, as God requires from a people in Covenant with him, and *which flow from a true Covenant-state, as the proper Fruits, effects, and Consequents thereof*.'[41] Consequent conditions are very different from antecedent conditions. In other words, just because a theologian invokes the term *condition* does not automatically indicate that the covenant has devolved into a bald *quid pro quo*. In this case, St. Augustine's (354-430) famous maxim best explains the nature of consequent conditions, namely, 'Grant what you command, and command what you will.'[42]

Uses

At this stage in the survey, the evidence reveals that early modern formulations and definitions of covenants hinge on lexical study, careful exegesis of the biblical text, and fine-toothed scholastic distinctions. That being said, what of the penchant for identifying covenants as *contracts*? Is this the Achilles heel in early modern covenant theology? Once again, the simple answer is, no. A more detailed answer requires two things: (1) a brief exploration of how the meaning of the term *contract* evolved from the Middle Ages through the early modern and modern eras, and (2) a survey of

---

40. Roberts, *Mysterium et Medulla Bibliorum*, II.ii.2 (pp. 113-14).

41. Roberts, *Mysterium et Medulla Bibliorum*, I.ii.2 (p. 118), emphasis added.

42. Augustine, *Confessions*, trans. Owen Chadwick (Oxford: Oxford University Press, 1991), 202.

the terms *covenant* and *contract* to see how theologians employ the terms. In the simplest of terms, once again, context is crucial. Just because a theologian invokes the term *contract* does not automatically mean a covenant has devolved into a *quid pro quo* between two equal parties. *Contract* is an elastic term that has a range of meanings that depend upon context within a text as well as the text's historical context.

Evolution of Contracts

The history of English common contract law has its origins in the Middle Ages in which the only way a person entered a contract was by incurring debt. But there was a shift in the early sixteenth century where the idea of a *nudum pactum*, or a 'nude contract,' gained ascendancy. A *nudum pactum* was a verbal promise without any token of exchange.[43] One early modern legal work reveals the evolutionary development of English contract law. Christopher St. Germain (1460-1540) penned a dialogue between a professor and a law student. In this dialogue, the student asks an important question: 'Howbeit it is not much argued in the laws of England what diversity is between a contract, a concord, a promise, a gift, a loan, or a pledge, a bargain, a covenant, or such other? For the intent of the law is to have the effect of the matter argued, not the terms.'[44] This sixteenth-century legal text records the terminological elasticity for contracts. The chief concern was not for the specific term employed but only the substance of the matter. In other words, contracts take on many different forms. There is no one set definition or term. But legal historians have noted that, in the evolutionary development of contracts, the sixteenth-century observed a shift from debt to promissory oaths.[45] Historians

---

43. Victoria Kahn, *Wayward Contracts: The Crisis of Political Obligation in England, 1640-1674* (Princeton: Princeton University Press, 2004), 44; A. W. B. Simpson, *A History of the Common Law of Contract: The Rise of the Action of Assumpsit* (Oxford: Clarendon Press, 1987), 381-83.

44. Christopher St. Germain, *The Doctor and the Student*, ed. William Muchall (Cincinnati: Robert Clarke and Co., 1886), 174-75.

45. On this shift, see David Ibbetson, 'Sixteenth Century Contract Law: *Slade's Case* in Context,' *Oxford JLS* 4/3 (1984): 295-317.

ranging from Oliver Wendell Holmes (1841-1935) to A. W. B. Simpson (1931-2011) note this shift in the meaning of *contract*. In his history of contracts, Holmes observes: 'The common element of all contracts might be said to be a promise.'[46]

Like biblical covenants, however, early modern contracts take on a number of different forms depending on the context. Holmes provides an example of a contract as an act of kindness – a contract where, out of sheer kindness a truckman offers to carry and deliver a cask of brandy from Boston to Cambridge at no expense. Such an arrangement constitutes a contract because the truckman promises to carry the cask of brandy from one location to another and, even though at no expense, the owner of the cask has the right to hold the truckman accountable should he fail to fulfill his promise.[47] Theologian and legal theorist Hugo Grotius (1583-1645) notes this fact in his famous treatise on maritime law, *On the Law of War and Peace* (1631). In his treatment of promises, Grotius argues that 'bare promises,' or unilateral promises are not legally binding whereas promises that include an 'exchange of considerations' are binding.[48] Grotius then describes the different types of contracts: 'Some simple acts are merely kind, others are reciprocal. The kindnesses either are unmixed or involve a kind of mutual obligation. Unmixed kindnesses are either fulfilled in the present, or are directed to the future.'[49] Contracts, of course, were frequently pure *quid pro quo* arrangements, but different types appeared in every corner of life such as marriage, government, and theology. Early moderns looked upon marriage as both a covenant and contract because they often involved the giving of significant dowries as well as affections and promises of unconditional love, which stands in contrast to Torrance's analysis that claims that a marriage is only a covenant.[50] Henry Finch (ca. 1558-1625), for

---

46. Oliver Wendell Holmes Jr., *The Common Law* (London: Macmillan & Co., 1882), 289; also Simpson, *Common Law of Contract*, 199-247, 406-88.

47. Holmes, *The Common Law*, 290.

48. Hugo Grotius, *On the Law of War and Peace*, ed. Stephen C. Neff (Cambridge: Cambridge University Press, 2012), II.xi.1 (p. 186).

49. Grotius, *On the Law of War and Peace*, II.xii.2 (p. 202).

50. Torrance, 'Covenant or Contract?' 54.

example, defines the marriage contract as 'a promise of both the parties to marrie the one with the other.'[51] Marriage was a covenant of love between husband and wife but also a legal contract.[52] In fact some early modern texts, such as Margaret Cavendish's (ca. 1623-1673) *The Contract*, employed the language of contract to argue for equality between husband and wife in the marriage relationship as well as to account for love as the motivation for political obligation in political contracts.[53] Early modern writers used the marriage relationship as a metaphor to argue for the need of love in political contracts between people and their sovereign.[54] Early modern Christian jurists, such as John Selden (1584-1654), a participant in the Westminster Assembly, urged for fidelity in contracts because political leaders at the time treated them as disposable. Sovereigns only kept their contracts so long as it suited them.[55]

Selden's observations were part of an early modern trend that runs counter to Torrance's claims about the direction of influence between Christianity and culture. Torrance argues that the surrounding culture infected the biblical notion of covenant by introducing contract into the equation.[56] But, in fact, the opposite is the case. Victoria Kahn argues that covenant theology imposed the idea of a heavenly contract between God and His people as the prism through which Christians were supposed to conduct their lives.[57] In other words, the Bible influenced culture; theologians did

---

51. [Henry Finch], *The Summe of Sacred Divinity* (London: William Barrett, n. d.), 201.

52. On the legal, social, and political dimensions of early modern marriages among the social elite, see Heather Parker, "'At their perfect age": Elite Child Betrothal and Parental Control, 1430-1560,' in *Children and Youth in Premodern Scotland*, eds. Janay Nugent and Elizabeth Ewan (Woodbridge, Suffolk, UK: The Boydell Press, 2015), 173-86.

53. Kahn, *Wayward Contracts*, 173.

54. Kahn, *Wayward Contracts*, 174.

55. John Selden, *John Selden and His Table Talk*, ed. Robert Waters (New York: Eaton & Mains, 1899), s. v. contracts, 96-97. For similar comments regarding general fidelity in contracts in various circumstances, see Baxter, *A Christian Directory*, IV.xix (pp. 827-46).

56. Torrance, 'Covenant or Contract?' 61.

57. Kahn, *Wayward Contracts*, 33.

not impose culture on the Bible. In this vein, Scottish Presbyterians enacted the Solemn League and Covenant (1638) to preserve the doctrine, worship, discipline, and government of Scotland and seek the reform of the same in England and Ireland.[58] Note the title in which *league* and *covenant* appear as synonyms. One of the Westminster divines, Cornelius Burges (1589-1665), regularly preached before the House of Commons and urged them to renew the covenant with God in one of the famous 'fast sermons.' Burges viewed English history through the lens of Deuteronomy, and thus called the nation to covenant fidelity to God.[59] Another Westminster divine, Joseph Caryl (1602-1673) preached a sermon before the House of Commons to instruct them on the nature of biblical covenants to inform their political activities. As with other early modern works, Caryl rehearses the finer points of the lexical, exegetical, and theological nature of biblical covenants all in preparation for their own entering into covenant with God.[60]

The seventeenth century witnessed significant cultural, political, and theological changes and permanently altered the way people conceived of their relationship to government. In the Middle Ages, people did not consent to government but simply acknowledged its reality and existence. Neither Aristotle (384-322 B.C.) nor Thomas Aquinas (1225-1274) incorporated contract into their treatments of government. Subjects obeyed their sovereigns, not because they were supposed to keep their contracts, but because divine and natural law taught there was a political hierarchy.[61] But in the wake of the Protestant Reformation and the razing of social, political, and ecclesiastical hierarchies, people now related to government in terms of consent and contract. But at the same time philosophers sought to secularize the concept of contract. Thomas Hobbes (1588-1679) in his famous *Leviathan* (1651) complained that covenant theology,

---

58. *A Solemn League and Covenant, for Reformation, and Defence of Religion* (London: Edward Husbands, 1643).

59. Kahn, *Wayward Contracts*, 114-15.

60. Joseph Caryl, *The Nature, Solemnity, Grounds, Property, and Benefits of a Sacred Covenant* (London: John Rothwell, 1643); also Kahn, *Wayward Contracts*, 118-19.

61. Kahn, *Wayward Contracts*, 9.

natural law theory, and common law were the causes of the civil war between Charles I (1600-1649) and the Presbyterian Parliament. He laid the blame at the feet of their inflammatory preaching.[62] Others such as David Hume (1711-1776) ridiculed seventeenth-century contract law because it presupposed promises between the contracted parties.[63] Hume writes: 'Two men, who pull the oars of a boat do it by agreement or convention, tho' they have never given promises to each other.'[64] In short, Enlightenment philosophers like Hobbes, Hume, and Locke removed the promissory character of contracts.[65] According to some, Hobbes is the chief Enlightenment representative for recognizing that everything moderns perceived was wrong with early modern contract theory. No longer would contracts operate within church and community, marked by love, and promises, but the secular person turned away from theology to moral obligation grounded solely on rational self-interest.[66]

This evolutionary development of contract theory from the Middle Ages to the modern era is relevant for the proper comprehension of early modern covenantal texts that invoke terms like contract, bargain, compact, or league. Given the changes in the meaning of the term, one should not hastily assume, as does Torrance, that early modern contracts or the theological use of the term has the same uniform meaning from one historical context to another. Part of the problem with Torrance's analysis is he imposes a modern notion of contract upon early modern texts and then dismisses them as theological aberrations. But if this brief reconnaissance

---

62. Kahn, *Wayward Contracts*, 135; cf. Thomas Hobbes, *Leviathan*, ed. Richard Tuck (Cambridge: Cambridge University Press, 1996), XV (p. 111).

63. Kahn, *Wayward Contracts*, 279.

64. Cf. David Hume, *A Treatise of Human Nature* (1888; Mineloa, NY: Dover Publications, 2003), III.ii.2 (p. 348); idem, *Of Original Contract*, in *Political Essays*, ed. Knud Haakonssen (Cambridge: Cambridge University Press, 1994), 186-201.

65. On the philosophical shifts behind the change to contracts between the medieval, early modern, and modern periods, see James Gordley, *The Philosophical Origins of Modern Contract Doctrine* (Oxford: Oxford University Press, 1991).

66. Larry May, 'Hobbes,' in *Ethics in History of Western Philosophy*, ed. Robert J. Cavalier, James Gouinlock, and James P. Sterba (New York: St. Martin's Press, 1989), 125-54.

of the development of contract theory informs the exploration of early modern theological texts, then usage and context are all-determinative in the assessment of early modern covenant theology.

Covenants and Contracts in Early Modern Works

As the survey of Roberts' treatment of covenants revealed, covenants are varied things and the same goes for the use of the term *contract* in early modern theological works. William Ames (1576-1633) succinctly states that 'a reciprocall promise is a contract,' which captures the promissory character of early modern notions of contract.[67] Ames invokes the concept of reciprocity but this does not automatically disqualify the term from serving as an adequate synonym for *covenant*. Scottish theologian David Dickson presents God's covenant or contract in unconditional terms: 'Because bound in all bands *with us*, of nature, of grace and good will, of the Fathers gift and appointment, and his own Covenant and special Contract with us. So that albeit an uncouth man may possiblie leave a stranger in his journey alone, yet Christ cannot chuse to do so to us: but for the Bands betwixt him and us, he will never leave us, nor forsake us.'[68] God's contract with His people is unconditional and as such, early modern theologians speak of it in terms of love and hope. Downame writes: 'There is a mutual contract passed between us: for the Lord promiseth His grace, love, favour, protection, and all the benefits of this life, and the life to come; and the Church for her part promiseth her love to God, conjugal faith, and dutiful obedience.'[69]

---

67. William Ames, *The Marrow of Sacred Divinity* (London: Henry Oberton, 1642), 381; see similar statement by Giovanni Diodati, *Pious and Learned Annotations Upon the Holy Bible* (Nicolas Fussell, 1651), comm. Josh. 24:27; Roberts, *Mysterium Bibliorum*, III.ii (p. 739).

68. David Dickson, *An Exposition of All St. Pauls Epistles with an Explanation of Those Other Epistles of the Apostles, St. James, Peter, John & Jude* (London: Francs Eglesfield, 1659), 258.

69. John Downame, *Lectures Upon the Foure First Chapters of the Prophecie of Hosea* (London: William Welby, 1608), 42; idem, *The Christian Warfare Against the Devill World and Flesh* (London: William Stansby, 1634), 775; similarly, Joseph Hall, *Contemplations Upon the Principal Passages of the Holy Story*, in *The Works of Joseph Hall B. of Norwich* (London: M. Flesher, 1647), 858.

One can assume the basic semantic overlap between *covenant* and *contract* in early modern theology but must factor the context of the term's use to comprehend its meaning and significance. Keeping this in mind, one of the more important qualifiers theologians introduced was the distinction between *covenant* and *testament*. For some theologians, these terms were interchangeable but for others there was a significant difference.[70] In his commentary on Romans, Andrew Willet (1562-1621) makes the following observation: 'The Hebrew word *berith*, signifieth both *suntheke*, a compact or covenant made between parties, as *Aquila* translateth, as *Hierome* witnesseth, *in Malach.* 2. And *diatheke*, a testament, or disposition of one's last will, as the word is used by the Apostle. Heb. 9:17.'[71] Willet compares the Greek translation of the Old Testament by Aquila of Sinope (fl. 130) with Jerome's (327-420) translation to substantiate his definition of covenant. Contra Torrance, he did not derive this data from his surrounding culture but rather ancient translations of the Bible.

A number of early modern theologians employed the concept of *testament* both in Bible translation and their expositions of the covenant of grace to explain the covenant's unconditional nature. Seventeenth-century theologians were explicit that God and man were not equals, which the Westminster Confession captures in its opening statement in its treatment of the covenant: 'The distance between God and the Creature is so great, that although reasonable creatures do owe obedience unto him as their Creator, yet they could never have any fruition of him as their Blessednesse and Reward, but by some voluntary condescension on Gods part, which he hath been pleased to express by way of Covenant' (VII.i).[72]

---

70. Johannes Cocceius, for example, strongly distinguished between *covenant* and *testament*, which was unique (see Brian J. Lee, *Johannes Cocceius and the Exegetical Roots of Federal Theology: Reformation Developments in the Interpretation of Hebrews 7-10* [Göttingen: Vandenhoeck & Ruprecht, 2009]).

71. Andrew Willet, *Hexaplan: That is, A Six-fold Commentary Upon the Most Divine Epistle of the Holy Apostle S. Paul to the Romans* (Cambridge: Leonard Greene, 1620), 6.

72. *The Humble Advice of the Assembly of Divines, Now by Authority of Parliament Sitting at Westminster Concerning a Confession of Faith* (London: Company of Stationers, 1647). All subsequent quotations from the Confession come from this edition.

God condescended in both covenants, but the covenant of grace particularly manifests a testamentary character. Westminster divine William Gouge (1575-1653), for example, presents a careful exegesis of Hebrews 9:16-17, 'For where a testament is, there must also of necessity be the death of the testator. For a testament is of for after men are dead: otherwise it is of no strength at all while the testator liveth.' From his exegesis, he explains the differences between a covenant and testament: 'A covenant is an agreement between at least two parties, whereas a testament is the declaration of one party.' He also concludes: 'A covenant uses conditions on both sides, and a testament consists purely of the favor and grace of the testator.'[73] In other words, as a testament, the covenant of grace is unconditional – it is a pure gift.[74]

The Westminster Confession captures the testamentary character of the covenant of grace when it states: 'This Covenant of Grace is frequently set forth in Scripture by the name of a Testament, in reference to the death of Jesus Christ the Testator, and to the everlasting inheritance, with all things belonging to it, therein bequeathed' (VII.iv). This statement echoes English Bible translations of the period, such as the Geneva (1560) and King James (1611). As noted above, the King James translates Hebrew 9:16-17 as a reference to a *testament*, as does the Geneva. The Geneva, however, reveals the interchangeability of *testament* and *covenant* with the following marginal note: 'This proveth that Christ must dye, because the covenant or testament is of none effect without the death of the testator.'[75] In similar fashion, the *Annotations of Dort* explain Hebrews 9:16-17 as follows:

> *And therefore he is the Mediator of the New Testament*, the Hebrew word *berith*, which *Jeremy* useth, chap. 31. Signifies in general any kind of Covenant or contract, whether the same be made betwixt

---

73. William Gouge, *A Learned and Very Useful Commentary on the Whole Epistle to the Hebrewes* (London: T. W. and S. G. for Joshua Kirton, 1655), XCIV (pp. 194-95).

74. Kahn, *Wayward Contracts*, 50-51.

75. *The Bible and Holy Scriptures Conteyned in the Olde and Newe Testament* (Geneva: Rouland Hall, 1560), loc. cit.

two parties, or by one party, only, as Testaments use to be, whereof examples by be read, *Gen.* 6.18. *Job* 31.1. Now that this Covenant is a Testament, the Apostle sets down as certain, because it comes from Gods side alone.[76]

The *Annotations* identify *covenant* and *contract* as synonyms but then qualify the definition based upon the particular text in question, which in this case denominates the covenant as an unconditional testament.

Conclusion

The mere appearance of the term *contract* cannot determine the nature of an early modern Reformed understanding of covenant. The surveyed historical record reveals that context and usage are all-determinative. Far from the picture that early modern theologians erroneously imposed their cultural experiences upon the biblical text and distorted the doctrine of covenants, the evidence reveals something entirely different. Torrance's thesis of covenant-contract confusion fails due to several factors: erroneous biblical exegesis, imposing Barthian notions of covenant upon early modern theological formulations, an insufficiently exegetical definition of covenant, an anachronistic modern definition of contract, and an insufficient reading of primary sources. This chapter reveals, therefore, that, with early modern theological texts, the choice between covenant or contract is a false dichotomy. In the historical investigation of covenant theology, historians must account for the early modern – modern terminological tectonic shift in the meaning of *contract* to avoid misunderstanding the term and pitting it against *covenant*. For systematic theologians, the challenge is slightly different. Given the shift in meaning, it seems inadvisable to employ the term *contract* or *bargain* in constructive theology because moderns do not hear promissory oath, but something less. Nevertheless, this chapter highlights the need to reconstruct the historical thought-world in which theologians lived in order adequately to understand their claims. Just because a historian

---

76. Theodore Haak, ed., *The Dutch Annotations on the Whole Bible* (London: Henry Hills, 1657), comm. Heb. 9:16-17.

reads a text in his native tongue does not mean he possesses the requisite skills for accurate comprehension and interpretation. Sometimes early modern English is a foreign language.

~: 1.5 :~

Grace in the Covenant of Works

Introduction

*T*he common historical narrative among many contemporary Reformed theologians is that the sixteenth-century Reformers completely broke with the Roman Catholic under-standing of Adam's pre-fall estate. Reformers such as John Calvin (1509-1564), we are told, rejected the so-called nature-grace dualism of medieval theology and simply affirmed the goodness of Adam's pre-fall nature. The facts of history, however, present a very different picture. Reformed theologians did not entirely break with their catholic heritage but only initially addressed areas where there were perceived errors, such as in the doctrines of justification, predestination, and the church. Other doctrinal areas largely remained untouched, such as the lion's share of theology (proper), christology, or in this case, pre-fall anthropology. In other words, first and second-generation Reformed theologians largely accounted for Adam's pre-fall constitution in terms of a common catholic Augustinian-Thomistic view. They divided God's gifts into the categories of natural and supernatural, argued that God's grace was necessary for Adam to merit anything, and that Adam's natural created state was insufficient to reach the supernatural end of eternal life. It was only through the introduction of the doctrine of the covenant of works that Reformed theologians began to discuss Adam's pre-fall estate in terms of the doctrine of the covenant rather than ontology and grace.

77

This chapter seeks to prove that there are a variety of views on how theologians explain Adam's pre-fall relationship with God within the early modern Reformed tradition, but that with the introduction of the doctrine of the covenant, Reformed views shifted from ontological to covenantal categories to explain Adam's nature, and in what sense he could merit eternal life. First and second-generation Reformed theologians largely retain a traditional Augustinian-Thomist nature-grace construct. Early orthodox theologians begin to employ the doctrine of the covenant, and some excise the nature-grace construct altogether, and others still retain it. There is a mixture of views in High Orthodoxy in which some virtually repristinate an Augustinian-Thomist nature-grace construct within the context of the covenant of works and others entirely reject it and only employ the covenant to account for how pre-fall Adam can merit eternal life. Rather than discuss Adam's merit in terms of the disproportionality between creature and creator and the necessity to elevate human nature by divine grace to enable Adam to attain eternal life, theologians instead employ the doctrine of the covenant. Adam can merit eternal life because God, in His goodness and beneficence, has promised Adam eternal life on the condition of his obedience.

To prove the thesis that there is a diversity of views that shifts from ontological to covenantal categories, this chapter first surveys the pre-fall anthropology of Thomas Aquinas (1225-1274). One must establish a baseline for the common Augustinian-Thomist understanding so that he can recognize it when it later appears among Reformed theologians. It may come as a surprise, but some High Orthodox theologians invoke Aquinas' express terminology to explain Adam's pre-fall estate. Second, the chapter surveys the views of Calvin, Peter Martyr Vermigli (1499-1562), key Reformation era confessions, and the view of Martin Luther (1483-1546). Luther provides an interesting foil to compare against Reformed views. Third, the chapter surveys the views of Early Orthodox theologians including Robert Rollock (ca. 1555-1599) and Johannes Wollebius (1589-1629). Fourth, the chapter explores the views of High Orthodox views in the Westminster Confession of Faith (1647), Anthony Burgess (d. 1664), Samuel

Rutherford (ca. 1600-1661), John Ball (1585-1640), John Owen (1616-1683), Francis Turretin (1623-1687), and Willhelmus à Brakel (1635-1711), and the Late Orthodox views of Salomon Van Til (1643-1713), Johannes Braun (1628-1708), and Benedict Pictet (1655-1724). The chapter concludes with analysis as to what accounts for the shift within later early modern Reformed theology – why the tradition moves away from ontology to covenant in its explanation of Adam's pre-fall estate.

Aquinas on Grace Before the Fall

Most theologians are familiar with the Roman Catholic concept of merit in terms of its twofold distinction: *condign* merit is full merit—a person actually earns his reward—there is proportionality between the work and the earned reward.[1] *Congruent* merit, on the other hand, is half merit—a person does not actually earn his reward—there is disproportionality between the work offered and the reward. In simpler terms, with condign merit a student earns the grade of 'A' by answering all of the exam questions correctly. With congruent merit, the professor grades on a curve – though the student only answered half of the questions correctly, the professor nevertheless gives him an 'A.' The distinction between condign and congruent merit ultimately has foundations in anthropology. Merit is not simply a question of determining the value of a particular work of obedience but also establishing the source of the obedience. Who brings the act of obedience forward for evaluation? What is he capable of doing? Is he capable of condign or only congruent merit? These questions are especially important when we consider Adam's place in his pre-fall estate.

To be sure, we tread upon hotly contested ground in Roman Catholic theology. There is significant debate concerning what Aquinas taught regarding the natural desire to see God. In other words, does pre-fall humanity have a natural desire to pursue the beatific vision, or is this desire only the result of infused sanctifying

---

1. For a broad overview of Aquinas' views on merit, see Joseph P. Wawrykow, *God's Grace and Human Action: 'Merit' in the Theology of Thomas Aquinas* (Notre Dame: University of Notre Dame Press, 1995).

grace? The literature is legion, and opinions are sharply divided over the precise answer to this question.[2] I leave such debates to the side and instead offer a general account of Aquinas' answer to this question. Simply stated, Aquinas believed that humanity's end must be proportionate to his nature. A pre-fall natural state must have a natural end; in order to attain the supernatural end of the beatific vision God must grant pre-fall humanity a gift of infused supernatural grace. Only with supernatural grace can natural man reach a supernatural end – such a supernatural means is proportionate to its supernatural end. Aquinas, of course, offers a significant amount of theological argumentation to prove this point.

In his *Summa Theologica*, Aquinas addresses the foundational question regarding whether Adam was created in a state of grace. He acknowledges that some theologians deny that Adam was created in such a state, but that God bestowed grace upon Adam after his creation before he sinned. Nevertheless, in his mind, Ecclesiastes 7:29, 'God made man upright,' proves that God endowed humanity with righteousness and thus grace: 'It is clear that also the primitive subjection by virtue of which reason was subject to God, was not a merely natural gift, but a supernatural endowment of grace; for it is not possible that the effect should be of greater efficiency than the cause.'[3] Aquinas bases his argument on the earlier opinions of Augustine (354-430). In his *City of God*, Augustine claims that as soon as Adam and Eve sinned, they forfeited their gift of divine grace.[4]

Aquinas builds off Augustine's opinion and answers the question whether anyone can merit eternal life apart from grace. Aquinas

---

2. Cf. e.g., Henri De Lubac, *The Mystery of the Supernatural* (1967; New York: Herder & Herder, 1998); Steven A. Long, *Natura Pura: On the Recovery of Nature in the Doctrine of Grace* (New York: Fordham University Press, 2010); Lawrence Feingold, *The Natural Desire to See God According to St. Thomas Aquinas and His Interpreters* (Ave Maria, FL: Sapientia Press, 2010); John Milbank, *The Suspended Middle: Henri de Lubac and the Renewed Split in Modern Catholic Theology*, 2nd ed. (Grand Rapids: Eerdmans, 2005); see the symposium interacting with Feingold's *Natural Desire*, in *Nova et Vetera*, English Edition 5/1 (2007).

3. Thomas Aquinas, *Summa Theologica* (rep.; Allen, TX: Christian Classics, 1948), Ia q. 95 art. 1.

4. Aquinas, *Summa Theologica*, Ia q. 95 art. 1; cf. Augustine, *City of God*, XIII.13, in NPNF[1] II:251.

distinguishes between man's 'state of perfect nature' and a 'state of corrupt nature.' He focuses his attention on the first state – Adam's pre-fall condition. According to Thomas, there is only one reason why man cannot merit eternal life without grace by his natural endowments, namely, because his merit depends upon divine pre-ordination. Aquinas explains: 'Now no act of anything whatsoever is divinely ordained to anything exceeding the proportion of the powers which are the principles of its act; for it is a law of Divine providence that nothing shall act beyond its powers.' By Adam's natural powers he can attain a connatural end, but only by infused grace can he achieve a supernatural end.[5] Aquinas supports his argument with exegetical appeal to 1 Corinthians 2:9: 'What no eye has seen, nor ear heard, nor the heart of man imagined, what God has prepared for those who love him.'[6]

Aquinas employs this Pauline text to make the point that eternal life is a good that exceeds the proportion of humanity's created nature – he bases this upon the idea that eternal life and the beatific vision exceeds natural human knowledge. 'And hence,' writes Aquinas, 'it is that no created nature is a sufficient principle of an act meritorious of eternal life, unless there is added a supernatural gift, which we call grace.'[7] In several other places Aquinas offers exegetical argumentation to make his case, such as in his explanation of 2 Corinthians 5:5: 'He who has prepared us for this very thing is God, who has given us the Spirit as a guarantee.' In his comments on this text, Aquinas argues that our desire to preserve our earthly tabernacle (our physical bodies) is a natural desire, but the motivation to put on a heavenly tabernacle (our resurrected bodies) is not a natural desire but comes from God. Aquinas writes:

> The reason for this is that upon every nature follows a desire suited to the end of that nature, as something heavy naturally tends downward and seeks to rest there. But if a thing's desire is above its nature, that thing is not moved to that end naturally, but by something else, which

---

5. Aquinas, *Summa Theologica*, IaIIae, q. 62 art. 3.

6. Aquinas, *Summa Theologica*, IaIIae q. 114 art. 2.

7. Aquinas, *Summa Theologica*, IaIIae, q. 114 art. 2.

is above its nature. Now it is evident that to enjoy eternal glory and to see God by his essence, although it is appropriate to see God by his essence, although it is appropriate to a rational creature, is above its nature. Therefore, the rational creature is not moved to desire this by nature, but by God himself, who makes us for this very thing.[8]

The combined point of these two texts (1 Cor. 2:9 and 2 Cor. 5:5) is that the beatific vision is beyond man's natural desires and hence must be God-given.

Aquinas, however, does not merely marshal exegetical arguments but also rests his claims upon a philosophical principle. At several points throughout his theological corpus, Aquinas invokes Aristotle's (384-322 B.C.) claims about proportionality. Aquinas employs two distinctions that he develops through an Aristotelian grid: passive and obediential potency. A passive potency can only be realized through its own active power.[9] An obediential potency can be realized by virtue of external assistance. Aquinas explains: 'Now it must be born in mind that in the human soul, as in every creature, there is a double passive power: one in comparison with a natural agent; – the other in comparison with the first agent, which can reduce any creature to a higher act than a natural agent can reduce it, and this is usually called the obediential power of a creature.'[10] A stone only has the passive potency to lie still or to fall if dropped from a height, but it has an obediential potency of becoming a human being if God so wills it.[11]

In several places Aquinas draws upon Aristotle to confirm this distinction. Aquinas writes:

According to natural perfection, however, man could fittingly know God only from creation. This is clear from the following. In any genus a passive power extends only to those things to which an active

---

8. Thomas Aquinas, *Commentary on the Letters of Saint Paul to the Corinthians* (Lander, WY: Aquinas Institute for the Study of Sacred Doctrine, 2012), comm. 2 Cor. 5:5, chp. 5, lect. II (§160).

9. Thomas Aquinas, *Summa Contra Gentiles*, 5 vols. (1956; Notre Dame: University of Notre Dame Press, 1975), III:45.6.

10. Aquinas, *Summa Theologica*, IIIa q. 11 art. 1.

11. Feingold, *Natural Desire*, 107.

power extends. Therefore, the Commentators [Averroes commenting on Aristotle's *Metaphysics*, bk. IX] says that there is no passive power in nature for which there is not a corresponding active power. In human nature, however, there is a double power for understanding: one passive, which is the possible intellect, and the other active, which is the agent intellect. Consequently, the possible intellect according to the natural process is in potency only to those form which become actually intelligible through the agent intellect .... Thus it is that by our natural power we can know God and other immaterial substances only through sensible things. But, in the state of innocence, man, by reason of the perfection of grace, receives a knowledge of God by means of an internal inspiration due to the irradiation of divine wisdom.[12]

By his natural powers, man can know God from nature, but in order to see the immaterial God Adam required the grace of God to implant an impression upon the mind – seeing the immaterial God was beyond Adam's natural potency but becomes an obediential potency by God's grace. Aquinas did not promote a new idea with this distinction, as it likely originated well before his time in the theology of Augustine.[13]

What Aquinas only mentions in passing in the above-cited quote (Aristotle's *Metaphysics*), takes a more prominent place at other points in his work. For example, in his *Summa Theologica* Thomas writes: 'What we can do with the Divine assistance is not altogether impossible to us; according to the Philosopher [Aristotle], "What we can do through our friends, we can do, in some sense, by ourselves [*Nicomachean Ethics*, III.iii]"'[14] But Aquinas avers, it is better to achieve a greater good, even if reliant upon the grace of God, than to accomplish a lesser good merely by natural powers. Again, Aquinas writes: 'The nature that can attain perfect good, although it needs help from without in order to attain it, is of more noble condition than a nature which cannot attain perfect good, but attains some imperfect good, although it

---

12. Thomas Aquinas, *Truth*, 3 vols. (1952; Eugene: Wipf & Stock, 2008), q. 18, art. 2.

13. Feingold, *Natural Desire*, 108-10.

14. Aquinas, *Summa Theologica*, IaIIae q. 109 art. 4 ad. 2.

need no help from without in order to attain it, as the Philosopher [Aristotle] says (*De Caelo*, II.xii).'[15] Through repeated reference to Aristotle, Aquinas finds corroborative evidence that pre-fall man has no passive potency for the beatific vision.

Based, therefore, upon two chief texts (1 Cor. 2:9 and 2 Cor. 5:5) and the Aristotelian principle of proportionality, Aquinas maintains that pre-fall humanity is incapable of attaining the beatific vision. 'Man cannot,' writes Aquinas, 'with his purely natural endowments, fulfill the precept of the love of God.'[16] Pre-fall man needs grace to render obedience unto God. Noteworthy is that there is a sense in which Aquinas' discussion about pre-fall man is abstract given that, since God ordained man for a supernatural end, he did not have any other option. God's grace is therefore a necessary correlate of creation. In fact, some have described Thomas' anthropology as possessing an 'unstable ontological constitution,' which necessitates the stabilizing principle of God's grace in the pre-fall estate. Generally speaking, pre-fall man in some sense wants to see God but cannot do so by his natural powers – he leans, therefore, towards God without a natural means to fulfill the desire apart from God's grace.[17]

Comparison with Historic Reformed Views

Reformation

The Reformation brought significant changes to many elements within the broader Christian body of doctrine, but early on there were elements that went unmodified. One such element was the pre-fall anthropology. John Calvin, for example, was never shy of departing with the Roman Catholic Church in areas where he perceived problems. Nevertheless, he still embraced an Augustinian-Thomist understanding of pre-fall Adam's need for divine grace. In his reflection upon the sacramental nature of the tree of life, Calvin writes:

---

15. Aquinas, *Summa Theologica*, IaIIae q. 5 art. 5 ad. 2.

16. Aquinas, *Summa Theologica*, IaIIae, q. 109 art. 4 ad. 3; Feingold, *Natural Desire*, 130.

17. De Lubac, *Mystery of the Supernatural*, 113; Feingold, *Natural Desire*, 399-400.

But if Adam's hitherto innocent, and of an upright nature, had need of monitory signs to lead him to the knowledge of divine grace [*divinę gratiae*], how much more necessary are signs now, in this great imbecility of our nature, since we have fallen from the true light? Yet I am not dissatisfied with what has been handed down by some of the fathers, as Augustine and Eucherius, that the tree of life was a figure of Christ, inasmuch as He is the Eternal Word of God: it could not indeed be otherwise a symbol of life, than by representing him in figure. For we must maintain what is declared in the first chapter of John (John 1:1-3) that the life of all things was included in the Word, but especially the life of men, which is conjoined with reason and intelligence. Wherefore, by this sign, Adam was admonished, that he could claim nothing for himself as if it were his own, in order that he might depend wholly upon the Son of God, and might not seek life anywhere but in him.[18]

Calvin clearly posits the necessity of God's grace in Christ for pre-fall Adam, and Adam's failure to recognize his need for Christ, represented in the tree of life, was the impelling cause of his fall.[19] Calvin's argument sounds very similar to Aquinas'. He posits upright Adam nevertheless had need of divine grace before the fall in order to obey God's command not to eat from the tree of knowledge. Moreover, Calvin specifically states that Adam 'could claim nothing for himself as if it were his own,' which parallels Aquinas' concept of natural potency – according to Adam's natural powers he could not attain the beatific vision. The only way Adam could obey was not to seek 'life anywhere but in him,' in Christ – even in a pre-fall context. This parallels Aquinas' concept of obediential potency – by God's grace Adam could render obedience proportionate to the supernatural end of the beatific vision.

---

18. John Calvin, *Commentary on Genesis*, CTS (rep.; Grand Rapids: Baker, 1993), comm. Gen. 2:9 (p. 117); idem, *Commentarii Ioannis Calvini in Quinque Libros Mosis. Genesis Seorsum: Reliqui Quatvor in Formam Harmonias Digesti* (Geneva: Gaspar de Hus, 1573), 16.

19. Calvin has a twofold understanding of Christ's role in the pre- and post-fall contexts. In the former, Christ serves as the cosmic mediator, whereas in the latter He serves as the redemptive mediator. For examination and explanation of this distinction, see Oliver D. Crisp, *Revisioning Christology: Theology in the Reformed Tradition* (Aldershot: Ashgate, 2011), 23-42.

Calvin is more specific when he addresses the question of Adam's pre-fall state in his *Institutes*. Calvin writes:

> I feel pleased with the well-known saying which has been borrowed from the writings of Augustine, that man's natural gifts were corrupted by sin, and his supernatural gifts withdrawn; meaning by supernatural gifts the light of faith and righteousness, which would have been sufficient for the attainment of heavenly life and everlasting felicity. Man, when he withdrew his allegiance to God, was deprived of the spiritual gifts [*spiritualibus donis*] by which he had been raised to the hope of eternal salvation. Hence it follows, that he is now an exile from the kingdom of God, so that all things which pertain to the blessed life of the soul are extinguished in him until he recover them by the grace of regeneration. Among these are faith, love to God, charity towards our neighbor, the study of righteousness and holiness. All these, when restored to us by Christ, are to be regarded as adventitious and above nature [*praeter naturam*]. If so, we infer that they were previously abolished.[20]

Calvin's explanation of Adam's pre-fall estate is consonant with an Augustinian-Thomist understanding. Both Calvin and Aquinas claim that Adam had natural and supernatural gifts. With Aquinas, Calvin affirms that only by the supernatural gifts would Adam have been able to attain heavenly life. Only the grace of regeneration restores these supernatural gifts, which are, both before and after the fall, 'above nature' (*praeter naturam*). Calvin clearly affirms a nature-grace construct in his pre-fall anthropology. Adam's righteousness was a supernatural, not natural, gift, which means it was not part of the image of God but was superadded.

In spite of these similarities between Calvin and Aquinas, there are nevertheless two noteworthy observations. First, unlike Aquinas, Calvin locates God's pre-fall grace in the cosmic, not redemptive, mediatory office of Christ. Second, whatever similarities exist between Aquinas and Calvin likely point, not to Calvin's direct dependence upon Aquinas, but to their common catholic

---

20. John Calvin, *Institutes of the Christian Religion*, 2 vols., trans. Henry Beveridge (Grand Rapids: Eerdmans, 1957); idem, *Institutio Christianae Religionis* (Geneva: Robert Stephanus, 1559), II.ii.12.

Augustinian heritage. Recall that the natural-obediential potency distinction originates with Augustine, and in his comments on Genesis 2:9 Calvin approvingly cites Augustine's explanation of the significance of the tree of life – a sacramental sign pointing to Christ in the pre-fall estate as well as his citation in the *Institutes* to delineate between Adam's natural and supernatural gifts.

Peter Martyr Vermigli was a second-generation Reformer who also embraced an Augustinian-Thomistic understanding of Adam's pre-fall estate.[21] In his commentary on Aristotle's *Nicomachean Ethics*, Vermigli takes issue with Aristotle's inability to recognize human depravity because he did not possess faith in Christ or have the light of the Scriptures. Vermigli believed, consequently, that Aristotle incorrectly argued that people could develop virtues on their own. Rather, Vermigli countered that when God created man He equipped and adorned him with virtues – they are God-given. The fall damaged man's virtues and the only way to reacquire them is by God's grace, not through our own efforts: 'It is not always true that we must have actions before we acquire virtues. We say this because of the first man and also because of those whom God immediately infuses with virtues from the moment of their conversion.'[22] Vermigli clearly states that God infuses virtues and this is true both of pre- and post-fall humanity.

If there is any doubt, Vermigli, like Calvin, distinguishes between Adam's natural and supernatural pre-fall gifts. Vermigli writes: 'Adam was so created of God, that he was capable of that supernaturall felicitie [*capax supernaturalis foelicitatis*]; who nevertheless setting light by the commandments of God, was despoiled of all those supernatural gifts [*dotibus supernaturalis*], and was left to the first state of his owne nature.'[23] Vermigli

---

21. For an overview of Vermigli's anthropology, see John Patrick Donnelly, *Calvinism and Scholasticism in Vermigli's Doctrine of Man and Grace* (Leiden: Brill, 1976).

22. Peter Martyr Vermigli, *Commentary on Aristotle's Nicomachean Ethics* (Kirksville, MO: Truman State University Press, 2006), 296-97.

23. Peter Martyr Vermigli, *The Common Places of the Most Famous and Renowned Divine Doctor Peter Martyr*, trans. Anthonie Marten (London: 1583), II.i.5 (p. 217); idem, *Loci Communes D. Petri Martyris Vermilii* (London: Thomas Vautroller, 1583), 125.

distinguishes between Adam's natural and supernatural gifts, and in the fall Adam lost his supernatural gifts and was left to the state of his own nature. This falls along the Augustinian-Thomist pre-fall nature-grace line.

Shadows of this Augustinian-Thomistic understanding of Adam's pre-fall estate also appear in several key Reformed confessions, such as the Gallican (1559) and Belgic (1561) confessions. Calvin, Theodore Beza (1519-1605), and Pierre Viret (1511-1571) composed the Gallican Confession for the Reformed churches of France. Concerning the creation of man the Gallican Confession states: 'We believe that man was created pure and perfect in the image of God, and that by his own guilt he fell from the grace which he received [*déchu de la grâce qu'il avait reçue*]' (IX).[24] The confession does not explain Adam's state in terms of natural and supernatural gifts but does invoke the term *grace* in the pre-fall context, which is the broader rubric for the Augustinian-Thomist pre-fall anthropology. In fact, in parallel with Aquinas, the Gallican Confession cites Ecclesiastes 7:29 to support the claim that Adam was created in grace.[25]

A more specific phrase appears in the Belgic Confession, written by Guy de Bres (ca. 1522-1567). It affirms that God made Adam in His image, and as such he was good, just and holy, 'able by his own will to conform in all things to the will of God.' But the confession then stipulates, 'But when [Adam] was in honor he did not understand it and did not recognize his excellence [*mais quand il a été en honneur, il n'en a rien su; et n'a pas reconnu son excellence*].' The Belgic couples this pre-fall ignorance with the subsequent loss of gifts as a result of the fall: 'He lost all his excellent gifts [*a perdu tous ses excellents dons*] which he had received from God, and he retained none of them except for small traces which are enough to make him inexcusable' (XIV).[26] These statements do not automatically commit the Belgic Confession to an Augustinian-Thomist nature-grace construct, but

---

24. The French original from the Gallican Confession is cited from Philip Schaff, *Creeds of Christendom*, 3 vols., 6th ed. (1931; Grand Rapids: Baker, 1990), III:365.

25. Cf. Aquinas, *Summa Theologica*, Ia q. 95 art. 1.

26. The French original of the Belgic Confession taken from Schaff, *Creeds of Christendom*, III:398.

they are harmonious with it. That Adam 'did not understand' his state and that he 'lost all his excellent gifts' as a result of the fall points in the direction of the Augustinian-Thomist nature-grace construct, which recognizes that Adam had natural and supernatural gifts.

Before we examine later Reformed views, we should note that not all Protestant Reformers embraced the common Augustinian-Thomist construction of Adam's pre-fall estate. One such dissenting voice was Martin Luther. In his commentary on Genesis, which he began writing in 1535, Luther takes issue with 'the scholastics,' and their view of pre-fall Adam. Luther writes: 'The scholastics [scholastici] argue that original righteousness [iusticia originalis] was not part of man's nature [connaturalis] but, like some adornment, was added to man as a gift [donum], as when someone places a wreath on a pretty girl.'[27] Luther objected to this construction on the grounds that he believed that righteousness was natural to Adam's creation: 'Let us rather maintain that righteousness [iusticiam] was not a gift [donum] which came from without [ab extra], separate from man's nature, but that it was truly part of his nature, so that it was Adam's nature to love God, to believe God, to know God, etc. These things were just as natural for Adam as it is natural for the eyes to receive light.'[28] The fact that Luther invokes 'the scholastics,' and the illustration of the eye's ability to receive light, likely points to the fact that he had Aquinas specifically in view. Another possibility is that Luther was interacting with theological opinions common to Aquinas and other medieval theologians.

Nevertheless, in his *Summa Contra Gentiles* Aquinas explains the difference between active and passive potencies and invokes the illustration of eyesight. Aquinas draws a parallel between the active and passive potencies of the eyes and the possible and agent intellect. Briefly, the *possible intellect* is a person's ability to know information, and the *agent intellect* is the ability to abstract information through

---

27. Martin Luther, *Lectures on Genesis: Chapters 1-5*, in LW, vol. 1, ed. Jaroslav Pelikan (St. Louis: Concordia Publishing House, 1958), comm. Gen. 3:7 (pp. 164-65); idem, *D. Martin Luthers Werke*, vol. 42 (Weimar: Herman Böhlaus, 1911), 123. The Weimar edition is hereafter abbreviated as WA.

28. Luther, *Lectures on Genesis*, comm. Gen. 3:7, in LW 1:165, WA 42:124.

sensory perception. Hence, the eyes have the passive potency to perceive light but can only actualize that passive potency if the eyes are illumined by light. Similarly, the possible intellect can receive information through the agent intellect.[29] Aquinas employs these arguments to prove that a passive potency can be realized only through its active power. He applies these categories to pre-fall Adam to make the point that Adam does not have the active potency to obey God apart from infused sanctifying grace. Yet, Luther takes this same field of discourse, namely eyesight, and argues the diametrically opposite point. Righteousness is not a superadded gift but was 'as natural for Adam as it is natural for the eyes to see light.' Luther writes: 'For just as it is the nature of the eye to see, so it was the nature of reason and will in Adam to know God, to trust God, and to fear God.' Luther grants that as a result of the fall, man's eyesight has been damaged and requires the grace of God to restore proper function, but God's grace is a post-fall, not pre-fall, necessity.[30] Regardless of the precise target, whether it was Aquinas or other medieval theologians, Luther rejected the Augustinian-Thomist nature-grace construct. Righteousness and the desire to see God were a part of Adam's natural pre-fall constitution.

In another interesting contrast, Luther takes the opposite position of Calvin. Calvin, recall, maintained that the tree of life was a sacramental sign that pointed to Christ, and that Adam's chief fault was that he failed to rely upon Him.[31] In contrast to this view, Luther writes: 'Before Adam's fall it was not necessary for him to have Christ, because he was righteous and without sin, just as the angels have no need of Christ. If Adam had not fallen, it would not have been necessary for Christ to become our Redeemer.'[32] Luther goes on to write: 'If Adam had not fallen, he

---

29. Aquinas, *Summa Contra Gentiles*, III:45.6; cf. Bernard Wuellner, S. J., *Dictionary of Scholastic Philosophy* (Fitzwilliam, NH: Loreto Publications, 2012), s. v. *intellect* (p. 62).

30. Luther, *Lectures on Genesis*, comm. 3:7, in LW 1:165.

31. Calvin, *Genesis*, comm. Gen. 2:9 (p. 117).

32. Martin Luther, *Disputation on Justification*, in LW, vol. 34, ed. Lewis Spitz (Philadelphia: Muhlenberg Press, 1960), 185.

would have entered the kingdom of heaven without Christ.'[33] Adam had no need of Christ because he had not sinned and God created him in a state of righteousness, a state by which he could have secured eternal life through his obedience. Unlike Calvin, Luther only conceives of Christ as a redemptive, not cosmic, mediator.

Early Orthodoxy

One of the earliest proponents of the covenant of works was Scottish theologian Robert Rollock (ca. 1555-1599). Unlike earlier Reformation theologians, such as Calvin, who spoke of Adam's pre-fall state merely under terms of natural law, Rollock coordinated law and covenant such as in the theology of Wolfgang Musculus (1497-1563).[34] The coordination of covenant and creation gave theologians a different category to work with. Under the dominant Augustinian-Thomist paradigm, theologians largely dealt with Adam's relationship to God in terms of ontology. Rollock factors the covenant in Adam's creation, which offered a different way of accounting for his relationship to God. In his catechism on the covenants, Rollock explains that the basis of the covenant of works is 'a good, holy, and upright nature, of the kind which was in man at creation.' Rollock, in contrast to the Augustinian-Thomist paradigm, attributes Adam's wisdom, holiness, and justice to 'nature' (q. 6).[35] Rollock specifies that the condition of the covenant of works is 'good works, which ought to proceed from that good, holy, and upright nature' (q. 8). Rollock clearly places naturally produced works in opposition to grace when he answers the question why faith in Christ and works

---

33. Luther, *Disputation on Justification*, in LW 34:187.

34. Jordan J. Ballor, *Covenant, Causality, and Law: A Study in the Theology of Wolfgang Musculus* (Göttingen: Vandenhoeck & Ruprecht, 2012).

35. Aaron C. Denlinger, trans., 'Robert Rollock's Catechism on God's Covenants,' *MAJT* 20 (2009): 105-29; Robert Rollock, 'Excursus: De Foedere Dei,' in *Analysis Dialectica ... in Pauli Apostolis Epistolam ad Romanos* (Edinburgh: Robert Waldegrave, 1594), 161-63. All subsequent quotations from Rollock's Catechism are taken from Denlinger's translation. For similar arguments and conclusions regarding Rollock's views, see Harrison Perkins, *Catholicity and the Covenant of Works: James Ussher and the Reformed Tradition* (Oxford: Oxford University Press, 2020), 99-103.

proceeding from grace and regeneration are precluded from the covenant of works: 'Because the virtues of man's nature, and the worlds proceeding from those virtues, cannot coexist with the grace of Christ and the works of grace' (q. 10).

So, if Rollock precludes grace from the pre-fall context, how does he explain the specific status of Adam's good works, the means by which he would have procured eternal life? Rollock denies the fact that Adam's works would be meritorious; in the covenant of works Adam's obedience was first and foremost his duty and an expression of gratitude (q. 12; Rom. 11:35; Luke 17:10). Moreover, even though Adam's works would have proceeded from an upright nature, they would not have been meritorious strictly speaking. Only when a work is unrequired can it be considered meritorious, but since Adam's work was required both by nature and by virtue of the covenant, it is not meritorious (q. 13). Rollock's understanding of merit finds parallel expressions in Zacharias Ursinus (1534-1583) and William Perkins (1558-1602). All three affirm the impossibility of man to merit truly and strictly anything from God.[36] So even though Rollock eliminates grace from Adam's pre-fall estate, he nevertheless characterizes Adam's works in a manner similar to congruent merit, though his view bears similarities to how other Reformed theologians argue for *meritum ex pacto*, merit by way of covenant. Namely, Adam's works are not truly meritorious but only considered meritorious by God or according to the terms of the covenant.[37] At the same time, Rollock's use of covenant and the shift towards *ex pacto* merit echoes the earlier medieval Scotist and nominalist view of sacramental efficacy.[38] Nonetheless, there is a sense in which Rollock's position represents a shifting paradigm – he no longer rests his view of Adam's pre-fall state exclusively

---

36. Zacharias Ursinus, *The Commentary of Dr. Zacharias Ursinus on the Heidelberg Catechism* (1852; Phillipsburg: P & R, n. d.), q. 91 (pp. 485-88); William Perkins, *A Reformed Catholike* (Cambridge: John Legat, 1598), 104-05.

37. See Harrison Perkins, '*Meritum ex pacto* in the Reformed Tradition: Covenantal Merit in Theological Polemics,' *MAJT* 31 (2020): forthcoming.

38. Richard A. Muller, *Dictionary of Latin and Greek Theological Terms: Drawn Principally from Protestant Scholastic Theology*, 2nd ed. (1985; Grand Rapids: Baker Academic, 2017), s. v. *ex pacto* (p. 114).

upon ontology given his use of the doctrine of the covenant, but neither does he fully employ the doctrine of the covenant to explain the nature and function of Adam's obedience.[39]

Other Early Orthodox theologians incorporated the doctrine of the covenant in their explanation of Adam's pre-fall estate, but they still retained the Augustinian-Thomistic paradigm. Johannes Wollebius (1589-1629), for example, maintains the bi-covenantal architecture of the covenants of works and grace.[40] But in contrast to Rollock, Wollebius distinguishes between natural and supernatural gifts: 'The gifts of the image of God were partly natural and partly supernatural.'[41] The natural gifts were the invisible substance of the soul and its faculties, the intellect and will.[42] The supernatural gifts, on the other hand, were: 'Clarity of intellect, freedom of will and rectitude [*voluntatis libertas et rectitudo*], conformity [to reason] on the part of the whole person, and dominion over the lower creatures.'[43] Wollebius identifies Adam's 'rectitude' as a supernatural gift, and ultimately identifies Adam's pre-fall state as one of grace. The fall was not due to 'the withholding of some special grace by which man might have remained innocent, for there was no obligation to give even the grace that God did give man; he received, in fact, the ability to act as he willed, although not that of willing as he could.'[44] God gave Adam grace in the pre-fall garden, which was chiefly manifest in the supernatural gift of an upright intellect.

Jacob Arminius (1560-1609) debated the nature of Adam's pre-fall state with Francis Junius (1545-1602). In an Augustinian-

---

39. See comments by Denlinger, 'Robert Rollock's Catechism,' 108.

40. Johannes Wollebius, *Compendium Theologiae Christianae*, in *Reformed Dogmatics*, ed. John W. Beardslee (Oxford: Oxford University Press, 1965), I.viii.1 (p. 64); idem, *Compendium Theologiae Christianae* (Basil: Joh. Jacob Genathus, 1633), 61. Note, reference to the Latin edition will follow with the page number to the 1633 edition.

41. Wollebius, *Compendium*, I.viii.8 (p. 65).

42. Wollebius, *Compendium*, I.viii.9 (p. 65).

43. Wollebius, *Compendium*, I.viii.10 (p. 65), translation emended; cf. idem, *Compendium*, 63.

44. Wollebius, *Compendium*, I.ix.1.1 (p. 67).

Thomist fashion Arminius divided Adam's pre-fall gifts into natural and supernatural categories The supernatural aspects of Adam's nature were *superinfused grace (gratiam superinfusam)*.[45] There was no state in which God creates humanity in a state of pure nature (*puris naturalibus*).[46] Junius largely agreed with Arminius on these points, as he believed that man could only achieve a natural end according to his natural powers and thus required supernatural powers to attain a supernatural end.[47] Junius writes: 'Towards the former end Adam could make way by nature: towards the latter he could be elevated by grace.'[48]

High and Late Orthodoxy

In the period of High Orthodoxy, the same trends continue with theologians employing the common Augustinian-Thomist pre-fall anthropology. One such theologian was Westminster divine Anthony Burgess. Burgess is an important figure not only because of his significant contribution to the creation of the Westminster Standards but also because of his own impressive theological works. One of the most notable of his contributions was his *Vindicae Legis* (1646), a series of lectures on the law of God. Burgess delivered these lectures because of the encroaching threat of antinomianism, though Burgess does delve into matters related to Adam's pre-fall estate. Burgess writes:

> Yet, though it were a Covenant of works, it cannot be said to be of merit. Adam though in innocency, could not merit that happinesse which God would bestow upon him: first, because the enjoying of God, in which Adams happinesse did consist, was such a good, as did farre exceed the power and ability of man. It's an infinite good, and all that is done by us is finite. And then in the next place, Because even then Adam was not able to obey any command of God, without

---

45. Jacob Arminius, *Conference with Junius*, X, in *The Works of James Arminius*, 3 vols. (1875; Grand Rapids: Baker, 1996), III:109; idem, *Iacobi Arminiii … amica cum D. Francisco Iunio de praedestinatione per litteras habita collatio*, in *Opera Theologica* (Leiden: Godefridus Basson, 1629), 521.

46. Arminius, *Conference with Junius*, XI, *Works*, III:136.

47. Arminius, *Conference with Junius*, XII, *Works*, III:138.

48. Arminius, *Conference with Junius*, XII, *Works*, III:138.

the help of God. Though some will not call it grace, because they suppose that onely cometh by Christ; yet all they that are orthodox do acknowledge a necessity of God's enabling Adam to that which was good, else he would have failed. Now then, if by the help of God Adam was strengthened to do the good he did, he was so farre from meriting thereby, that indeed he was the more obliged to God.[49]

Burgess incorporates an element absent from Aquinas, namely, the doctrine of the covenant of works. But in spite of this difference, Burgess makes his point regarding Adam's inability to merit along Augustinian-Thomist lines.

Adam's goal was supposed to be enjoying God as his chief happiness – the beatific vision. And like Aquinas, Burgess believed that, according to his natural powers, the reward of the covenant of works exceeded Adam's natural powers and abilities. The only way that Adam could achieve the goal was by the grace of God, though Burgess stipulates that some Reformed theologians did not want to call this assistance *grace*. To call this assistance grace like Aquinas before him does not appear to bother Burgess. Although, Burgess does not describe this pre-fall grace as infused sanctifying grace as Aquinas does. Nevertheless, Burgess and Aquinas both maintain the disproportionality between Adam's natural created state and the reward of Adam's obedience – the beatific vision. They both resolve the disproportionate relationship through the dispensation of pre-fall divine grace.

Other Westminster divines, such as Samuel Rutherford, affirm similar beliefs but approach it in a slightly different manner. In his *Covenant of Life Opened*, Rutherford explains:

Life is either considered as the end, or secondly as a free reward. In the former respect. To live an intellectuall life in obeying God, was to Adam so created a connaturall end, as to burn, is to fire, and to give light, to the Sunne. And God may put the respect of a reward upon any obediential end. But that Adam should have such an eminent life, for the reward of his obedience as a communion with God, which is farre above his obedience, is the free donation of God: nor is there

---

49. Anthony Burgess, *Vindicae Legis: or, A Vindication of the Morall Law and the Covenants* (London: Thomas Underhill, 1647), lect. XIII (p. 129).

any necessary connexion between Adams perfect obedience, and so high and eminent a life, nor can this Covenant, as touching such a promise, be written in his heart. God then never loved to make any Covenant, yea even that of Works, without some acts and out goings of grace, and the hyre was grace.[50]

Once again, like Burgess, Rutherford follows Augustinian-Thomist lines in his explanation of Adam's pre-fall estate and nature. Unlike Burgess, Rutherford does not locate any ontological inability or deficiency in Adam's pre-fall nature. He, like Aquinas, identifies Adam's natural end as a life lived in obedience to God; the natural end of man is not the beatific vision. Rutherford signals this by invoking the Thomist term *connatural*. This was the very distinction that Luther rejected.[51] The only way man can achieve the blessed reward of the covenant of works is due to God's 'free donation,' which Rutherford identifies as 'out goings of grace.' Rutherford places a disproportionate relationship between Adam's obedience and the reward; hence, Adam requires God's grace to reach a supernatural end. God does not elevate Adam's nature but rather his works.

Other theologians of the period offer similar constructions. John Ball, for example, wrote one of the more oft-cited works on covenant theology. He addresses the subject of Adam's obedience and its relationship to the reward. In his explanation of Leviticus 18:5, 'Do this and live,' Ball, in a manner similar to Rollock, explains that Adam's obedience would have been rewarded in strict justice but it would not have been according to merit. Citing Luke 17:10, namely that we are all unprofitable servants and that Adam would have merely performed his duty rather than perform a work worthy of great reward, God simply rewarded Adam's obedience as if it were sufficient. Ball maintains that Adam's obedience was his 'Homage-penny, a thing before the command indifferent unto which he had a natural inclination, from which he was now to abstaine, because God ... here interposed himself and reserved this as an Homage unto

---

50. Samuel Rutherford, *The Covenant of Life Opened: or, A Treatise of the Covenant of Grace* (Edinburgh: Robert Broun, 1654), I.vii (p. 22).

51. Cf. Aquinas, *Summa Theologica*, IaIIae, q. 62 art. 3; Luther, *Lectures on Genesis*, comm. Gen. 3:7, in LW 1:164-65; idem, WA: 42:123.

himself.'[52] Ball does not invoke the specific term, but his argument echoes the categories of condign and congruent merit. Ball does not connect the value of Adam's obedience to the covenant. Adam, strictly speaking, would not have offered condign merit, otherwise he would have actually merited the reward. Rather, his merit would have been congruent – God looked upon it as if it were worthy.

Like Thomas before him, Ball employs a similar pre-fall anthropology when he posits natural and supernatural state for Adam's pre-fall estate:

> The subject of this Covenant [of works] is man intire and perfect, made after the Image of God in Righteousnesse and true holinesse, furnished not only with a reasonable soule and faculties beseeming, but with divine qualities breathed from the whole Trinity, infused into the whole man, lifting up every faculty and power above his first frame, and inabling and fitting him to obey the will of God intirely, willingly, exactly, for matter and measure.[53]

Ball clearly states that Adam was first created, what he calls Adam's 'first frame,' and that he was then subsequently elevated by divine qualities 'infused into the whole man.' Ball is aware of the potentially controversial nature of his claim: 'Whether this was natural or supernaturall unto the first man, is a question needlesse to be disputed in this place, and peradventure if the termes be rightly understood, will be no great controversie.'[54]

---

52. John Ball, *A Treatise of the Covenant of Grace* (London: Edward Brewster, 1645), 10. A Continental contemporary, Johannes Maccovius (1588-1644), made similar claims about merit, though his discussion pertains specifically to the rewarding of post-fall post-conversion works (Johannes Maccovius, *Scholastic Discourse: Johannes Maccovius on Theological and Philosophical Distinctions and Rules*, trans. Willem J. van Asselt, et al [Apeldoorn: Instituut voor Reformatieonderzoek, 2009], XV.vii [p. 251]). Moreover, when Maccovius discusses the covenant, he seems to invoke *ex pacto* concepts when he states that humans are not truly in a covenant with God but only analogically so: 'The covenant between God and the creatures is not a covenant in a proper sense but only in an analogical sense. It is a pact by which God promises man something and in turn stipulates something that must be done by him' (Maccovius, *Scholastic Discourse*, XII.i [p. 225]). He does not invoke categories of grace but rather divine promise as the basis for the reward of the covenant.

53. Ball, *Covenant of Grace*, 11.

54. Ball, *Covenant of Grace*, 11.

John Owen accounted for Adam's pre-fall estate in a similar manner. Owen believed that the covenant of works required obedience, but this obedience had to be undergirded by grace given the disproportional relationship between the merit of obedience and the reward.[55] Owen elsewhere explains that both the covenants of works and grace contained grace, but in different degrees. The covenant of grace was 'ordered in all things,' which means that it contains all necessary benefits to ensure the salvation of the elect.[56] This was not so regarding the covenant of works: 'The first covenant with Adam was ordered in grace, but not in all grace; it was ordered in righteousness, holiness, and innocency, but not ordered in the grace of perseverance: and failing in that grace, the whole covenant failed.'[57] Owen affirmed the doctrine of the covenant of works, but in Augustinian-Thomist fashion still rested his understanding of merit upon Adam's ontology.

In contrast to these covenantal Augustinian-Thomist views, there were other High and Late Orthodox Reformed theologians who made a greater use of the covenant to answer the question regarding how Adam could possibly secure the reward of the covenant of works through his obedience. Signs of divergence on the relationship between Adam, God, covenant, and reward appear in the Westminster Confession of Faith (1647). Unlike Aquinas, Burgess, Rutherford, Ball, and Owen, the Confession does not explicitly invoke the term *grace* to describe Adam's pre-fall estate. Rather, the Confession merely speaks of God's voluntary condescension by way of covenant (VII.i). Moreover, in stark contrast to Aquinas, the Confession takes a very different tack regarding Adam's pre-fall abilities: 'Man, in his state of Innocency, had freedom, and power, to will, and to do that which was good, and

---

55. John Owen, *An Exposition of the Epistle to the Hebrews*, vol. 6, in *The Works of John Owen*, vol. 22, ed. William H. Goold (1855; Edinburgh: Banner of Truth, 2010), 69.

56. John Owen, 'The Everlasting Covenant, Sermon I,' in *The Works of John Owen*, vol. 9, ed. William H. Goold (1850-53; Edinburgh: Banner of Truth, 1998), 418.

57. Owen, 'Everlasting Covenant,' 9:419; cf. Ryan M. McGraw, *A Heavenly Directory: Trinitarian Piety, Public Worship and a Reassessment of John Owen's Theology* (Göttingen: Vandenhoeck & Ruprecht, 2014), 149nn 58-60.

well pleasing to God; but yet, mutably, so that he might fall from it' (IX.ii). Likewise, in its explanation of creation, the Confession states: 'After God had made all other creatures, he created man, male and femal, with reasonable and immortall souls, indued with knowledge, righteousnesse and true holiness, after his own Image, having the Law of God written in their hearts, an power to fulfill it' (IV.ii). The Confession does not invoke the concept of a natural and supernatural pre-fall state, nor does it say that Adam lacked the ability or desire for the goal of the covenant of works.

The closest the Confession gets to addressing questions of merit appears in its treatment of post-fall works from within the context of applied soteriology. The Confession's chapter on good works follows the chapters on Effectual Calling (X), Justification (XI), Adoption (XII), Sanctification (XIII), Saving Faith (XIV), and Repentance Unto Life (XV). Moreover, the Confession states that good works are the 'fruits and evidences of a true and lively faith' (XVI.ii). The context is clearly post-fall and redemptive and does not directly address Adam's pre-fall state. But there are certainly traces of the on-going discussion about merit in this chapter:

> We cannot, by our best Works, merit pardon of sin, or eternall life at the hand of God, by reason of the great disproportion that is between them and the glory to come; and, the infinite distance between us and God, whom, by them, we can neither profit, nor satisfie for the debt of our former sins, but, when we have done all we can, we have done but our duty, and are unprofitable servants (XVI.v).[58]

These are all themes that appear in the discussions and debates about Adam's pre-fall state: the inability to merit eternal life, the disproportionality between the merit and the reward, the infinite distance between God and man, as well as invoking Luke 17:10. But this entire statement falls after the Confession's rejection of works of supererogation (XVI.iv) and factors the fall and sin into the equation. Notably, none of these subjects appear in the Confession's discussion of Adam's pre-fall state.

---

58. Cf. Obadiah Sedgwick, *The Bowels of Tender Mercy Sealed in the Everlasting Covenant* (London: Adoniram Byfield, 1661), II.v.1 (pp. 460-61).

The Confession, therefore, does not preclude concepts of pre-fall grace but neither does it require them. The lack of terminological precision and purposefully ambiguous statements reveals two things regarding Adam's pre-fall estate: (1) theologians were not agreed on the language and theological concepts to explain the precise nature of the relationship between obedience and reward, and (2) Reformed theologians were moving away from a common Augustinian-Thomistic understanding through greater use of the doctrine of the covenant. One potential contributing factor to the development of Reformed understanding of Adam's pre-fall estate was the debates that were occurring within Roman Catholic circles over these very issues. During the Early Orthodox period Roman Catholic theologians Michael Baius (1513-1589) and later Cornelius Jansen (1585-1638) rejected the distinction between pre-fall natural and supernatural love. They believed this was a corruption that arose from Aristotelian philosophy.[59] Baius in his work *Prima Hominis Justitia* (1566) argued that participation in the divine nature was due to Adam's natural un-fallen integrity, not due to its elevation by grace.[60] Baius was condemned for his view by Pope Pius V (1504-1572) in the papal bull *Ex Omnibus Afflictionibus* (1567).[61] Jansen developed Baius' views at much greater length in his treatise *De Status Purae Naturae*. He believed that Adam's natural end was eternal life.[62] Like Baius, Jansen was condemned by Pope Innocent X (1574-1655) in his papal bull *Cum Occasione* (1653).[63]

Although these debates occurred within the Roman Catholic Church, Reformed theologians were aware of Baius and Jansen. The possibility exists that these debates were a contributing factor towards moving away from an Augustinian-Thomist understanding

---

59. Feingold, *Natural Desire*, 284.

60. Michael Baius, *Prima Hominis Justitia*, in *Michaelis Baii Opera* (Colon: Balthasar Egmont, 1696), I.iv-xi (pp. 55-63); Feingold, *Natural Desire*, 278.

61. *Ex Omnibus Afflictionibus* (1 Oct 1567), in *Compendium of Creeds, Definitions, and Declarations on Matters of Faith and Morals*, ed. Heinrich Denzinger, 43rd ed. (San Francisco: Ignatius Press, 2012), §§1901-80, esp. 1921.

62. Cornelius Jansen, *De Statu Purae Naturae*, I.xv, in *Cornelii Iansenii Episcopi Iprensis Augustinus*, vol. 2 (Louvain: Jacob Zeger, 1640), cols. 745-52; Feingold, *Natural Desire*, 278.

63. *Cum Occasione* (31 May 1653), in *Denzinger, Compendium*, §§2001-07.

of Adam's pre-fall state.[64] Jansen's massive work *Augustinus*, for example, was published in 1640, just a few short years before the Westminster Assembly began its confession-writing labors. Turretin specifically cites Jansen's *Augustinus* on the question of whether Adam was created in a state of pure nature.[65] To what degree these debates influenced Reformed views is a matter beyond the scope of this modest chapter, but it nevertheless reveals that Adam's pre-fall state was a subject of lively debate in Roman Catholic circles and these debates may have caused Reformed theologians to think carefully through the issues.

Nevertheless, further evidence of the doctrinal shift on Adam's pre-fall estate appears in later seventeenth-century theologians such as Francis Turretin. Turretin very clearly states that Adam 'had the power to perform the prescribed duty' of the covenant of works.[66] Turretin believed that Adam was naturally bound to obey God given his status of one of God's creatures, but that the covenant of works imposed a stronger federal bond upon him,

> By the powers received in creation – he could perform it, although in order that he might actually perform it, he still needed the help of God [*auxilio Dei*] both to actuate these faculties and powers and to preserve them from change. This help did not tend to the infusion of any new power, but only to exercising the efficacy of that power which he had received.[67]

Turretin unmistakably steers clear of the notion of infused grace like that advocated by Aquinas and Ball. He also does not invoke

---

64. See, e.g., Theophilus Gale, *The True Idea of Jansenisem, Both Historick And Dogmatick* (London: E. Calvert, 1669); Samuel Annesley, *The Morning Exercises at Cripplegate*, vol. 6 (1675; London: Thomas Tegg, 1844), serm. XXV (p. 560); Melchior Leydekker, *Melchioris Leydeckeri de Historia Jansenismi* (Utrecht: Francis Halmam, 1695).

65. Francis Turretin, *Institutes of Elenctic Theology* (Phillipsburg: P & R, 1992-97), V.ix.4-5, XIV.xiv.2.

66. Turretin, *Institutes*, VIII.iii.11; cf. J. Mark Beach, *Christ and the Covenant: Francis Turretin's Federal Theology as a Defense of the Doctrine of Grace* (Göttingen: Vandenhoeck & Ruprecht, 2007), 106-19.

67. Turretin, *Institutes*, VIII.iii.14; idem, *Institutio Theologicae Elencticae*, 3 vols (Edinburgh: John D. Lowe, 1847).

the category of grace but merely states that Adam had to rely upon 'the help of God.'

When it comes to the question of proportionality, or more specifically the supposed disproportionality between the obedience and reward, Turretin takes a fully covenantal route. Turretin explains that within a covenant there are mutual obligations, in this case, obligations for Adam and God. Adam owed his obedience to God both by virtue as his status as one of God's creatures as well as the covenant. On God's side, the covenant was gratuitous 'as depending upon a pact or gratuitous promise by which God was bound not to man, but to himself and to his own goodness, fidelity, and truth.' Strictly speaking, therefore, God would not have been in Adam's debt if he had fulfilled the requirements of the covenant of works. Rather, God was ultimately indebted to His own fidelity and the promise that He made. Turretin explains: 'If the apostle seems to acknowledge this right or debt (Rom. 4:4), it must be understood in no other than a respective sense; not as to the proportion and condignity of the duty rendered to God by man (Rom. 8:18; Luke 17:10), but to the pact of God and justice (i.e., the fidelity of him making it).'[68] In other words, had Adam been faithful, he would have received the reward, not due to the proportionality between the obedience and reward but 'from the pact and liberal promise of God.'[69] Rather than rotate around the axis of ontology and Aristotelian principles of proportionality, Turretin's doctrine revolves around covenant and God's goodness and fidelity to fulfill His covenant promises. Turretin acknowledges the ontological disproportionality between God and man and between the obedience and promised reward, but does not build upon these principles.

Johannes Cocceius (1603-1669), Herman Witsius (1636-1708), Salomon Van Til, Johannes Braun, à Brakel, and Pictet conceive of merit *ex pacto* in similar fashion to Turretin.[70] Pictet, for example, grants the basic premise of the disproportionality between God

68. Turretin, *Institutes*, VIII.iii.16.

69. Turretin, *Institutes*, VIII.iii.17.

70. Herman Witsius, *Economy of the Covenants Between God and Man*, 2 vols., trans. William Crookshank (1822; Escondido: Den Dulk Foundation, 1990), I.i.14-15, ii.1-3; I.ix.16; Johannes Cocceius, *Summa Theologiae*, in *Opera Omnia*, vol. 7 (Amsterdam: 1701), XXII.xxiii-xxiv, xxvii-xxviii (p. 206).

and man. Hence, strictly speaking, there cannot be a true covenant between God and man if one defines a covenant as a mutual agreement between two parties. By virtue of man's status as creature, he owes obedience to God and conversely, God owes nothing to man. 'But God, under the influence of pure kindness [*Deus sua sola benignitate*],' writes Pictet, 'was pleased by means of a covenant, to invite into communion with himself, and by this bond of love and mutual agreement, more effectually to win over his creature, who was already subject, and owed every thing to him.'[71] Pictet addresses the disproportionality between God and man by means of the covenant.

Other Reformed theologians reject the distinction between condign and congruent merit because all human beings are unprofitable servants even in a pre-fall state according to Luke 17:10, which precludes condign merit. Van Til precludes congruent merit because God is no respecter of persons – God does not show partiality to anyone (Job 34:19; Gal. 2:6-7). Hence, the only available remaining category is *meritum ex pacto* – merit by virtue of God's covenantal promise.[72] Braun offers similar reasons for opting for *meritum ex pacto*. In contrast to Van Til, Braun rejects condign merit because God is no respecter of persons and because no person could offer works truly worthy of God given the disproportionality between creator and creature. He rejects congruent merit because he denies that Adam received sanctifying grace (*gratia gratum faciens*). Instead, Adam's merit was *ex pacto* insofar as it was the stipulation of the covenant, which was given solely by the good pleasure of God (*ex mero beneplacito Dei*).[73] À Brakel specifically addresses the question of

---

71. Benedict Pictet, *Christian Theology* (London: R. B. Seeley and W. Burnside, 1834), VII (p. 153); idem, *Theologia Christiana* (London: R. Baynes, 1820), VII. iv (p. 130).

72. Salomon Van Til, *Theologiae Revelatae Compendium*, in *Theologiae Utrisque Compendium* (Leiden: Jordan Luchtmans, 1704), II.ii (pp. 87-88).

73. Johannes Braun, *Doctrina Foederum sive Systema Theologiae* (Amsterdam: Abraham van Somer, 1691), vol. I, part III, VIII.ii.13 (pp. 259-60); cf. Aaron C. Denlinger, *Omnes in Adam Ex Pacto Dei: Ambrogio Catarino's Doctrine of Covenantal Solidarity and Its Influence on Post-Reformation Reformed Theologians* (Göttingen: Vandenhoeck & Ruprecht, 2010), 239-44.

Adam's pre-fall powers and takes the diametrically opposed path as Aquinas: Adam 'was adorned with the image of God, consisting of a flawless knowledge of God, righteousness, and holiness. He therefore certainly knew both condition and promise, and was capable of fulfilling the condition.'[74] À Brakel mentions nothing of supernatural grace added to Adam's original created condition but only writes of his perfection and both the ability and knowledge of eternal life as a constitutive part of the image of God.[75]

Conclusion

The surveyed evidence reveals that there are several different ways that Reformed theologians explain Adam's pre-fall estate. There are at least five different views, though some of these categories arguably overlap in various ways. Theologians:

1. Carry over an Augustinian-Thomist nature-grace construct (Calvin, Vermigli, the Gallican and Belgic confessions).

2. Reject the nature-grace construct and argue that righteousness was completely natural to Adam given his status as a creature made in God's image (Luther).

3. Employ the doctrine of the covenant, maintain the opposition between grace and works in the pre-fall context, but nevertheless contend that Adam was unable to merit truly anything before God, which is similar to the doctrine of congruent merit (Rollock), though all of the elements of *ex pacto* merit are present as with later Reformed theologians (Turretin, Witsius, Pictet, Van Til, Braun, and à Brakel).

4. Employ the doctrine of the covenant to explain Adam's pre-fall estate but still retain the Augustinian-Thomist nature-grace construct either in terms of natural and supernatural

---

74. Wilhelmus à Brakel, *The Christian's Reasonable Service*, 4 vols. (Morgan, PA: Soli Deo Gloria, 1992), I:364.

75. Cf. Herman Bavinck, *Reformed Dogmatics*, 4 vols. (Grand Rapids: Baker, 2003-07), II:539-48, 569-70; IV:729; Steven J. Duby, 'Working with the Grain of Nature: Epistemic Underpinnings for Christian Witness in the Theology of Herman Bavinck,' *TBR* 3 (2012): 60-84, esp. 69-71.

gifts (Wollebius, Arminius, Junius, Burgess, and Ball) or the divine elevation of the efficacy of Adam's obedience (Rutherford).

5. Explain Adam's ability to merit in terms of divinely given grace, but nevertheless distinguish between pre- and post-fall grace. The former is imperfect and lacks the grace of perseverance, while the latter is perfected and contains said grace (Owen).

This overall taxonomy reveals an important aspect of the reception and use of the doctrine of the covenant of works.

The common assumption is that Reformed theologians rejected the so-called nature-grace dualism of Roman Catholicism. This popular narrative has virtually become a fact that requires no evidence. History reveals a much different picture. Initially, theologians saw little need to alter their understanding of their common catholic Augustinian-Thomist pre-fall anthropology. The only category they employed was ontology. Theologians had to account for Adam's (in)ability somehow to secure eternal life through his obedience and the only recourse they had to explain the difference between the creator and creature was elevating Adam's pre-fall nature by grace so he could lay hold of a supernatural end. Even Luther's rejection of the nature-grace construct only left him with the goodness of Adam's created nature to explain how he might attain eternal life. Luther only had recourse to ontology.

Once theologians coordinated the doctrine of the covenant with Adam's pre-fall estate, there was another category to account for the disproportionate relationship between the infinite creator and the finite creature. Rollock made steps forward by setting aside the nature-grace construct by making use of the doctrine of the covenant. Evidence of the shifting tides on these issues appears in the Westminster Confession, which in contrast to the Gallican Confession, does not invoke the category of grace to explain Adam's pre-fall estate but only God's voluntary condescension in covenant. Moreover, the only time the Westminster Confession discusses the disproportionality between human merit and the reward of eternal life is in the post-fall context. This evidence reflects the divines' agreement on ruling out merit to fallen humanity but the vague language of a voluntary condescension by way of covenant was sufficiently ambiguous to allow for a diversified orthodoxy on this subject. Recall Burgess' comments that there were some theologians who declined to describe Adam's pre-fall estate in terms of grace. The move away from the Augustinian-Thomist understanding of Adam's pre-fall estate fully flowered in the latter seventeenth century when theologians simply spoke in terms of *ex pacto* merit. All of this evidence points to the fact that, as a matter of history, the early modern Reformed tradition exhibits a degree of diversity on the nature of Adam's pre-fall relationship with God. Ontology and covenant represent two opposite poles with mediating positions in between, all of which arguably falling within the bounds of early modern confessional orthodoxy.

~: I.6 :~

The Covenant of Works and Sinai

Introduction

One of the most disputed questions surrounding the covenant of works is the precise nature of the relationship between the Adamic and Mosaic covenants. Westminster divine Anthony Burgess (d. 1664) commented: 'I do not find in any point of divinity, learned men so confused and perplexed (being like Abraham's ram, hung in a bush of briars and brambles by the head) as here.'[1] While there is a general agreement on the main features of the covenant of works among advocates of the doctrine from the early modern to the modern period, the same cannot be said of how the Adamic covenant relates to the Mosaic covenant. This chapter therefore presents an overview of a number of views that theologians held from the sixteenth until the nineteenth centuries to show the variety of opinion on the matter. This survey is by no means exhaustive but merely illustrative.[2] This chapter aims to demonstrate that

---

1. Anthony Burgess, *Vindiciae Legis: or, A Vindication of the Morall Law and the Covenants* (London: Thomas Underhill, 1647), 229.

2. For a survey on the various early modern Reformed views on the relationship between the Adamic and Mosaic covenants, cf., e.g., Brenton C. Ferry, 'Works in the Mosaic Covenant: A Reformed Taxonomy,' in *The Law is Not of Faith: Essays on Works and Grace in the Mosaic Covenant*, eds. Bryan D. Estelle, J. V. Fesko, and David VanDrunen (Phillipsburg, NJ: P & R, 2009), 76-105; idem, 'Works in the Mosaic Covenant: A Reformed Taxonomy,' (ThM Thesis, Westminster Theological Seminary, 2009); Mark Jones, 'The "Old" Covenant,' in *Drawn into Controversie: Reformed Theological Diversity and Debates Within Seventeenth-Century British*

Reformed theologians believed that the covenant of works appeared both in the pre-fall and Sinai contexts. To borrow language from *The Marrow of Modern Divinity*, 'the Morall Law may in some sence be said to be the Law of workes ... the Law of workes, and the Covenant of works, are all one.'[3] In other words, the moral law, the covenant of works, and the Mosaic covenant are in some sense related. 'In some sense,' is another way of saying, 'This is a difficult issue to untangle.' The ensuing survey of various views demonstrates this claim.

The chapter begins with an examination of how Heinrich Bullinger (1504-1575), John Calvin (1509-1564), Wolfgang Musculus (1497-1563), and Peter Martyr Vermigli (1499-1562) characterized the Mosaic covenant. These theologians contribute to later formulations of the relationship between the Adamic and Mosaic covenantal administrations. The chapter then surveys the views of William Perkins (1558-1602) and Amandus Polanus (1561-1610). These two theologians both formally advocated the covenant of works, but unlike later formulations, Perkins did not apply it to the pre-fall context whereas Polanus did. But both Perkins and Polanus called the Mosaic covenant the covenant of works. These formulations contrast with the views of John Cameron (ca. 1579-1625) and Edward Leigh (1602-1671). Cameron argued that the Mosaic covenant was distinct from the covenants and works and grace. In other words, rather than a common twofold covenant scheme, works and grace where the Mosaic covenant is part of the covenant of grace, Cameron maintained a threefold scheme: the covenant of works, Mosaic covenant, and covenant of grace, where the Mosaic covenant is not part of the covenant of grace. Leigh adopted many aspects of Cameron's views, but not his construction of the Mosaic covenant. Both, however, drew connections between Sinai and Adam. The third section of this chapter treats Cameron's and Leigh's views. Fourth, the chapter surveys the views of a

---

Puritanism, eds. Michael A. G. Haykin and Mark Jones (Göttingen: Vandenhoeck & Ruprecht, 2011), 183-203; Sebastian Rehnmann, 'Is the Narrative of Redemptive History Trichotomous or Dichotomous?' *NAK* 80/3 (2000): 296-308.

3. Edward Fisher, *The Marrow of Modern Divinity* (London: 1645), 7.

number of Westminster divines. There were at least five different views represented at the assembly. Fifth, the chapter explores the formulations of Francis Turretin (1623-1687) and Herman Witsius (1636-1708). Both were continental Reformed theologians but constructed the relationship between the Adamic and Mosaic covenants in different ways. Both used scholastic distinctions to demonstrate how the covenant of works appeared at Sinai. Sixth, the chapter investigates the views of a number of eighteenth and nineteenth-century theologians, including Thomas Boston (1676-1732), James Buchanan (1791-1857), John Colquhoun (1748-1827), Robert Shaw (1795-1863), and Charles Hodge (1797-1878). The chapter concludes with some observations about the variegated character of this aspect of the doctrine of the covenant of works.

Bullinger, Calvin, Musculus, and Vermigli

Heinrich Bullinger

One of the Reformation's important pillars was the successor to Ulrich Zwingli (1484-1531), Heinrich Bullinger. Before Calvin's *Institutes* reached their definitive 1559 edition, Bullinger's own *Decades* presented the first complete summary of Reformed doctrine. Ever since Zwingli's initial efforts to demonstrate the unity of the testaments in his defense of infant baptism against the Anabaptists, Reformed theologians sought to prove the unity of the testaments. Bullinger does this in his treatment of the use, fulfillment, and abrogation of the law where, among other things, he sought to show the similarities and differences between the Old and New Testaments.[4] Among the similarities, Bullinger explained that Old Testament saints shared the same sacraments, invocation of God, the same hope, expectation, inheritance, Spirit, faith, and doctrine as New Testament saints. All of God's saints are one people and are 'under one only testament.' Such is the agreement, but Bullinger explains the disagreement by what was at that time a common theological distinction: 'In the very substance

---

4. Heinrich Bullinger, *The Decades of Henry Bullinger*, 2 vols., trans. Thomas Harding (1849-52; Grand Rapids: Reformation Heritage Books, 2004), III.viii (vol. II, p. 236). Note, volume and page number references refer to the nineteenth-century Parker edition division, not the two volumes of the reprint edition cited here.

[*substantia*], truly, thou canst find no diversity: the difference which is betwixt them doth consist in the manner of administration [*modo administrandi*], in a few accidents [*accidentibus*], and certain circumstances [*circunstantiis*].'[5] Bullinger recognizes that there are elements in the Old Testament that pass away and that are accidental or circumstantial connected primarily with the mode of administration. Bullinger characterizes these accidental qualities in the following manner: 'For to the promise or doctrine of faith, and to the chief and principal laws, there were annexed certain external things [*accesererunt externa*], which were added until the time of amendment [*tempus correctionis*].'[6] Bullinger employs a substance-accidents distinction common to theology that goes back at least to Augustine (354-430) to explain the differences and similarities between the testaments.[7] This is a distinction that Reformed theologians employ for centuries to come to explain the relationship between the Adamic and Mosaic covenants.

John Calvin

In his definitive 1559 edition of the *Institutes of the Christian Religion* Calvin deals with the subject of unity of salvation in both the Old and New Testaments; namely, salvation is by grace alone through faith alone in Christ alone. However, Calvin notes that there is a difference between the testaments: 'The covenant [*foedus*] made with all the fathers is so far from differing from ours in reality and substance [*substantia et re*], that it is altogether one and the same: still the administration [*administratio*] differs.'[8] This statement presents a programmatic understanding of the relationship between the testaments. Like Bullinger, Calvin affirms that salvation is the

---

5. Bullinger, *Decades*, III.viii (vol. II, p. 293); idem, *Sermonum Decades Quinque de Potissimis Christianae Religionis Captibus, in Tres Tomos* (Zurich: Christoph Froschoverus, 1557), 148.

6. Bullinger, *Decades*, III.viii (vol. 2, p. 294); idem, *Sermonum Decades*, 148.

7. See, e.g., Augustine, *On the Trinity*, V.v, in NPNF[1] III: 89.

8. John Calvin, *Institutes of the Christian Religion*, trans. Henry Beveridge (Grand Rapids: Eerdmans, 1957), II.x.2; idem, *Institutio Religionis Christianae* (Geneva: Robert Stephanus, 1559). Cf. Andrew A. Woolsey, *Unity and Continuity in Covenantal Thought: A Study in the Reformed Tradition to the Westminster Assembly* (Grand Rapids: Reformation Heritage Books, 2012), 253-343, esp. 253-76.

same in substance but differs in administration. Calvin calls the one trans-testamental covenant the *spiritual covenant* (*spirituale foedus*).[9] All of God's elect participate in this the *spirituale foedus*.[10] The spiritual covenant unites all believers in the mode of salvation, but Calvin gave full force to the idea that the *administratio* differed between the testaments. He argues that with the dispensation of the Mosaic covenant God introduced two separate covenants, the *foedus legale* and the *foedus evangelicum*, which he connects to the respective ministries of Moses and Christ.[11] It seems that the *foedus evangelicum* is one and the same with the *spirituale foedus*, as both rest on the work of Christ. The *foedus legale*, however, or the Old Testament (*Vetus testamentum*) refers to the solemn method of confirming the covenant comprehended under ceremonies and sacrifices. Since there is nothing substantial in it, until we look beyond it, the apostle contends that it behooved to be annulled and become antiquated, to make room for Christ, the surety of a better covenant, by whom the eternal sanctification of the elect was once purchased, and the transgression which remained under the Law wiped away.[12]

The *foedus legale*, therefore, containing these ceremonies and sacrifices, was temporary, and thus gave way to Christ; it was part of the *administratio*, not the *substantia et re* of the *foedus evangelicum* or *spirituale foedus*.[13]

Calvin argued that the law reveals human sin and renders sinners inexcusable, but at the same time it shows that a perfect righteousness is the only means by which 'a man may be deemed and pronounced righteous at the divine tribunal.' Calvin, therefore, further states: 'Nor can it be denied, that the reward of eternal salvation, as promised by the Lord, awaits the perfect obedience

---

9. Calvin, *Institutes*, II.x.7.

10. Calvin, *Institutes*, II.xi.2.

11. Calvin, *Institutes*, II.xi.4.

12. Calvin, *Institutes*, II.xi.4.

13. John Calvin, *Galatians, Ephesians, Philippians, and Colossians*, trans. T. H. L. Parker, ed. David W. Torrance and T. F. Torrance, CNTC (1965; Grand Rapids: Eerdmans, 1996), comm. Gal. 4:1 (p. 71); idem, *Commentarii in Epistolam Pauli ad Galatas* (Geneva: Jean Girard, 1548), 59.

of the Law (Deut. 30:19).'[14] Calvin clearly stipulates that sinful human beings cannot fulfill this requirement, but it does not mitigate the fact that the law holds forth the promise of eternal life for perfect obedience. Once again, this is part of the *foedus legale* and is accidental to the substance of the *foedus evangelicum*. Like Bullinger, Calvin identifies the legal character of the Mosaic covenant and distinguishes it from the spiritual covenant that unites all believers by means of an Aristotelian distinction between substance and accidents. Calvin's comments regarding the legal and evangelical covenants coalesce in his exegesis of Galatians 4:24, where Paul identifies Sarah and Hagar as two covenants. 'Doctrine is the mother by whom God begets us,' writes Calvin, and this doctrine is twofold: 'legal and evangelical.'[15] He again invokes the language of the legal and evangelical covenants and identifies them with Hagar and Sarah respectively.[16]

Calvin explains that the legal covenant (or Hagar) birthed the holy prophets and other believers, but not to a permanent slavery; God only placed them under this covenant as a schoolmaster for a time. God concealed their freedom under the veil of ceremonies and sacrifices. Outward appearances only revealed slavery, yet inwardly these saints were free in the sight of God. This inward and outward distinction corresponds to the substance-accidents relationship between the legal and evangelical covenants. So, their slavish birth under the law did not prevent Old Testament saints from having Jerusalem, the evangelical covenant (Sarah), as their mother in spirit. Calvin then makes an important qualification when he writes: 'But those who cleave to the bare law and do not know it as a schoolmaster to bring them to Christ, but rather make it a barrier against coming to Him, are the Ishmaelites born to slavery.'[17] Calvin follows Paul's argument and thus explicitly identifies Hagar (the legal covenant) with Sinai. Calvin's exegesis is important because this argumentation

---

14. Calvin, *Institutes*, II.vii.3.

15. Calvin, *Galatians*, comm. 4:24 (pp. 85-86).

16. Calvin, *Galatians*, comm. 4:24 (p. 86).

17. Calvin, *Galatians*, comm. 4:24 (p. 86).

regarding the two different covenants (legal versus evangelical) eventually evolves into an explanation of the relationship between the Adamic and Mosaic covenants in the later reception of the covenant of works.

Wolfgang Musculus

Musculus plays an important part in the evolution of Reformed covenant theology because he was one of the main sixteenth-century theologians who integrated law and covenant.[18] Works such as Edward Fisher's (fl. 1627-55) *Marrow of Modern Divinity* picked up this combination of concepts and integrated it in its doctrine of the covenants.[19] In his treatment of the covenant of works Fisher links Musculus' comments regarding the close connection between law and covenant to the relationship between Leviticus 18:5 and Adam's pre-fall state. Fisher believed the 'do this and live' of Leviticus 18:5 applied to Adam; note that Leviticus 18:5 is a text from the Mosaic covenant, which means that Fisher saw a close connection between these two covenants. Nevertheless, Fisher appeals to Musculus in the following manner: 'Adam, Lo, to the intent that thou mayest live, I have given thee liberty to eat, and I have given thee abundantly to eat, let all the fruits of paradse [sic] be in thy power, one tree except, which see thou touch not, for that I keep to my own Authority, the same is the Tree of the Knowledge of Good and Evil, if thou touch it the meate thereof shall not bring life, but death.'[20] Fisher's statement is not a quotation from Musculus but rather a summary of what Musculus explains in his treatment of the law of nature.

Musculus identifies the law of nature as that which God engrafts into the human reason, and that which the apostle Paul writes about in Romans 2:14-15.[21] The law of nature is how people who do not have the written law can nevertheless make sound moral

---

18. Wolfgang Musculus, *Common Places of Christian Religion* (London: 1563), fol. 118r.

19. Fisher, *Marrow of Modern Divinity*, 6.

20. Fisher, *Marrow of Modern Divinity*, 6-7; cf. Musculus, *Common Places*, fol. 31.

21. Musculus, *Common Places*, fol. 31v.

judgments.[22] Musculus derives the concept both from Scripture and finds corroborating support from Thomas Aquinas (1225-1274), whom he positively mentions.[23] Musculus distinguishes the law of nature from the law given by words, the written law, and the law of the Spirit.[24] Adam received both the law of nature, written on his heart but also the law given by words, evident in the commands to be fruitful, multiply, fill the earth, as well as the prohibition against eating from the tree of knowledge.[25] Musculus concludes that the various ordinances that God gave to Adam and Eve (e.g., to be fruitful) have the force of a law. This was not his opinion alone, but also that of Basil the Great (330-379).[26] Musculus recognizes that law governed Adam's state in the garden. These manifestations of the law are of a piece with the Decalogue, which God delivered through Moses at Sinai, because they are all manifestations of and participation in God's eternal law, a Thomistic concept.[27] Musculus is important because he presses the point that the moral law runs through all of God's dealings with humanity. This is a contributing factor to the eventual placement of the covenant of works at Sinai and also undergirds the later confessional codification in the Westminster Confession's explanation of the law.

Peter Martyr Vermigli

A similar pattern unfolds in Vermigli's understanding of law. Vermigli defines the law of God as His commandment, wherein He expresses both His will and disposition, or nature.[28] Like Musculus,

---

22. Musculus, *Common Places*, fol. 31r; cf. Jordan J. Ballor, *Covenant, Causality, and Law: A Study in the Theology of Wolfgang Musculus* (Göttingen: Vandenhoeck & Ruprecht, 2012), 196-98.

23. Musculus, *Common Places*, fol. 30r; cf. e.g., Michael Baur, 'Law and Natural Law,' in *The Oxford Handbook of Aquinas*, eds. Brian Davies and Eleonore Stump (Oxford: Oxford University Press, 2012), 238-54.

24. Musculus, *Common Places*, fol. 30v.

25. Musculus, *Common Places*, fols. 32-33.

26. Musculus, *Common Places*, fol. 32r.

27. Musculus, *Common Places*, fols. 34r, 30r; cf. Thomas Aquinas, *Summa Theologica* (rep.; Allen, TX: Christian Classics, 1948), Ia IIae q. 91.

28. Peter Martyr Vermigli, *Common Places of the Most Famous and Renowned Divine Doctor Peter Martyr* (London: 1574), II.iii.1 (p. 280).

Vermigli acknowledges that God has written His law on the hearts of all people, a truth Paul explains in Romans 2:14-15. In his exegesis of this text, Vermigli explains that the Gentiles did the things the law required even though they did not possess the law of Moses.[29] In the broader context of Paul's Romans 2 argument, Vermigli notes that there was a connection between the law of nature and the Decalogue. In fact, Vermigli argues that the law endures through both the Old and New Testaments. Paul here does not contradict his teaching elsewhere that only faith in Christ brings salvation, but rather merely points out that the Gentiles have a form of the law written on their hearts that is a piece of the law delivered at Sinai.[30]

Summary

Bullinger, Calvin, Musculus, and Vermigli present important pieces of the root system that later flowers into the covenant of works, but in particular, they also address matters that demonstrate the connections between the Adamic and Mosaic contexts. Bullinger employed the substance versus accidents distinction to explain the similarities and differences between the testaments. Calvin recognized the legal character of the Mosaic covenant and distinguished it from the one trans-testamental spiritual or evangelical covenant. Musculus and Vermigli recognized the relations between the various manifestations of the law and thus saw the organic connections between the natural or Adamic law and the Mosaic law. These four Reformers present ideas that later theologians combine to draw the connections between Adam and Moses.

Perkins and Polanus

William Perkins

Perkins was one of the first theologians explicitly to use the term *covenant of works* (*foedus operum*), but his view is not perfectly consonant with later early modern iterations of the doctrine. In

---

29. Peter Martyr Vermigli, *Most Learned and Fruitful Commentaries of D. Peter Martir Vermilius ... Upon the Epistle of S. Paul to the Romanes* (London: John Daye, 1558), comm. Rom. 2:14-15 (fol. 44).

30. Vermigli, *Most Learned Commentaries*, comm. Rom. 2:14-15 (fol. 44r); cf. Stephen Grabill, *Rediscovering the Natural Law in Reformed Theological Ethics* (Grand Rapids: Eerdmans, 2006), 98-121.

fact, evidence suggests that Perkins was actually closer to Calvin than to later early modern Reformed theologians on the question of the covenant of works. Perkins undoubtedly employs the terms *covenants of works and grace*, but he does not use them the same way that later theologians do. In his *Golden Chaine* he covers the entire Decalogue and when he transitions to the doctrine of salvation he writes: 'Hitherto the covenant of workes, and of the Law, who followeth the covenant of Grace' (*Hactenus de foedere operum et de lege; sequitur foedus gratiae*).[31] In other words, the covenant of works is a post-fall phenomenon.[32] There are two chief pieces of evidence that corroborate this conclusion.

First, in his chapter on humanity's creation in the pre-fall state, he neither invokes the category of covenant nor the term *covenant of works* (*foedus operum*). He outlines the dignity of man in four parts: (a) that God made him in His own image, (b) God gave him dominion over all of the creatures, (c) the decency of his body, and (d) the labor of the body without pain or grief.[33] He clearly affirms that God issues commands regarding the trees of life and knowledge, and that this revelation constituted an 'examination and trial of man's obedience.'[34]

Second, Perkins follows his treatment of humanity's creation and pre-fall state with chapters on sin and the fall (X), man's fall

---

31. William Perkins, *A Golden Chaine, or The Description of Theologie, Containing the Order of the Causes of Salvation and Damnation, According to Gods Woord* (London: Edward Alde, 1595), XXXI (fol. O3r); idem, *Armilla Aurea, id est, Theologiae Descriptio Mirandam Seriem Causarum et Salutis et Damnationis Iuxta Verbum Des Proponens* (Cambridge: John Legatt, 1591), fol. O4r.

32. Aaron Clay Denlinger, 'Introduction,' in Robert Rollock, *Some Questions and Answers About God's Covenant the Sacrament That Is a Seal of God's Covenant: With Related Texts*, ed. and trans. Aaron Denlinger (Eugene, OR: Pickwick Publications, 2016), 6-7 n. 19; Jan Van Vliet, *The Rise of Reformed System: The Intellectual Heritage of William Ames* (Milton Keynes: Paternoster, 2013), 33-34; cf. Woolsey, *Unity and Continuity*, 466-72; Harrison Perkins, *Catholicity and the Covenant of Works: James Ussher and the Reformed Tradition* (Oxford: Oxford University Press, 2020), 94-99; idem, 'Reconsidering the Development of the Covenant of Works: A Study in Doctrinal Trajectory,' *CTJ* 53/2 (2018): 289-317, esp. 302-09.

33. Perkins, *Golden Chaine*, IX (fol. B7).

34. Perkins, *Golden Chaine*, IX (fol. B7r).

and disobedience (XI), original sin (XII), actual sin (XIII), the punishment of sin (XIV), election and Christ as its foundation (XV), Christ's two natures (XVI), the distinction of His natures (XVII), and Christ's birth (XVIII), before he introduces the Decalogue (XIX).

Only under his treatment of the Decalogue does he introduce the doctrine of the covenant: 'Gods covenant, is his contract with man, concerning life eternall, upon certain conditions.' He then distinguishes the two different covenants: 'Againe, there are two kindes of this covenant. The covenant of works, and the covenant of grace' (Jer. 31:31-33). According to Perkins, the covenant of works is 'Gods covenant, made with condition of perfect obedience, and is expressed in the morrall [sic] Law. The Morrall Law, is that parte of Gods word, which commandeth perfect obedience unto man, as well in his nature, as in his actions, and forbideth the contrarie. Rom. 10:5.' The law has two parts, the edict, which commands obedience, and the condition binding people to obedience. 'The condition,' writes Perkins, 'is eternall life to such as fulfill the Lawe: but to transgressors, everlasting death.' Perkins makes the explicit connection between the Decalogue and covenant of works when he states that the former 'is an abridgement of the whole Lawe, and the covenant of workes. Exod. 34:27.'[35]

Perkins' characterization of the Mosaic covenant parallels Calvin's earlier explanation; the only difference between Calvin and Perkins are the terms they use. Calvin calls the Mosaic covenant the *foedus legale* and Perkins labels it the *foedus operum*. Further confirmation that the two theologians held parallel views regarding the Mosaic covenant appears in Perkins' exegesis of Galatians 4:24, Sarah and Hagar and the two covenants. Perkins explains that Hagar and Sarah are the covenants of works and grace respectively.[36] Perkins writes:

The two Testaments are the Covenant of workes, and the Covenant of grace, one promising life eternall to him that doth all things

---

35. Perkins, *Golden Chaine*, XIX (fol. E6).

36. William Perkins, *A Commentarie or Exposition, Upon the Five First Chapters of the Epistle to the Galatians* (Cambridge: John Legat, 1604), 344-45.

contained in the law: the other to him that turns and believes in Christ. And it must be observed, that Paul saith, *they are two*, that is, two in substance, or kind. And they are two, sundrie waies. The law, or covenant of workes, propounds the bare iustice of God, without mercie: the covenant of grace, or the Gospel, reveales both the iustice and mercie of God, or the iustice of God giving place to his mercie.[37]

Perkins spells out additional ways to delineate the diverse function of obedience versus faith, which appears in the following table:[38]

Covenant of Works (Law)	Covenant of Grace (Gospel)
The law requires inward and perfect righteousness in nature and action.	Propounds imputed justice, which gives place to God's mercy.
Promises life on the condition of works	Promises remission of sins and everlasting life upon the condition that sinners rest on Christ by faith.
The law was written on tables of stone	The Gospel is written on the tables of our hearts (Jer. 31:31-33; 2 Cor. 3:3).
The law was in nature by creation	The Gospel is above nature and revealed after the fall.
The law has Moses as a mediator (Deut. 5:27).	Christ is the mediator of the New Testament (Heb. 8:6).
Dedicated by the blood of beasts (Exod. 24:5).	Dedicated by the blood of Christ (Heb. 9:12).

Again, there are several noticeable things in Perkins' exegetical treatment of Galatians 4:24.

First, his exegesis parallels Calvin's exegesis – the only difference appears to be the nomenclature he uses. Calvin does not call the Mosaic covenant the *foedus operum* but rather the *foedus legale*. This terminological difference is nominal and not substantive. Second,

---

37. Perkins, *Galatians*, 347.

38. Perkins, *Galatians*, 347.

Perkins does not appeal to the Adamic context or argue that the covenant of works originates in the pre-fall state; the covenant of works is a post-fall reality. Third, like Calvin, Perkins contrasts the differences between the law and gospel. Calvin not only uses these terms but also labels them the two doctrines, the legal and evangelical.[39] Fourth, in similar fashion to Calvin, Musculus and Vermigli, Perkins appeals to the doctrine of creation for the origins of the law. Fifth, recall in his discussion of the moral law that Perkins appealed to Romans 10:5 to substantiate the claim that the law requires perfect obedience, exegesis consistent with both Calvin and later advocates of the covenant of works.[40]

These five points reveal important information about Perkins' place in the development of the covenant of works. Strictly speaking, Perkins does not advocate the covenant of works as the doctrine later develops or appears, for example, in the works of Robert Rollock (1555-1599).[41] Rollock clearly taught that the covenant of works was a pre-fall phenomenon. These five points also show that Perkins' views closely parallel those of Calvin on law and gospel and the nature of the Mosaic covenant. But for the purposes of this chapter, Perkins' formulation of the Mosaic covenant and the label he applies to it, *foedus operum*, provide one of the links in the chain of the development of the covenant of works. Perkins labels the Mosaic covenant the covenant of works because he detects a works principle in it, that is, the idea that perfect obedience to the law secures eternal life. But

---

39. Calvin, *Galatians*, comm. 4:24 (pp. 85-86).

40. Cf. e.g., Calvin, *Institutes*, II.vii.3; idem, *Sermons on Galatians*, trans. Arthur Golding (1574; Audubon, NJ: Old Paths Publications, 1995), serm. XVIII (pp. 374-76, 385, 387); idem, *Commentaries on the Last Four Books of Moses Arranged in the Form of a Harmony*, trans. Charles William Bingham, CTS, vol. 3 (rep.; Grand Rapids: Baker, 1993), comm. Lev. 18:5 (pp. 204-05); Johannes Maccovius, *Scholastic Discourse: Johannes Maccovius (1588-1644) on Theological and Philosophical Distinctions and Rules*, eds. Willem van Asselt, et al. (Apeldoorn: Instituut voor Reformatienderzoek, 2009), XII.iv-v (pp. 224-27); Francis Roberts, *Mysterium et Medulla Bibliorum. The Mysterie and Marrow of the Bible* (London: George Calvert, 1657), 773.

41. E.g., Robert Rollock, *A Treatise on Effectual Calling*, in *Select Works of Robert Rollock*, 2 vols., ed. William M. Gunn (1844-49; Grand Rapids: Reformation Heritage Books, 2008), XXV (vol I, p. 175).

as subsequent sections below demonstrate, theologians extend the covenant of works into the pre-fall context and then carefully explain how the continuities and discontinuities relate between the Adamic and Mosaic covenants. Even though few theologians echoed Perkins' formula, this is not to say that his view was a complete outlier. Others such as Nicholas Byfield (1579-1622) identifies the covenant of works with the law, which he connects to the Old covenant.[42]

Amandus Polanus

Polanus appears to have a similar understanding of the covenant of works as Perkins, though he extends the doctrine to the pre-fall state. In his small work *The Substance of Christian Religion*, Polanus does not raise the doctrine of the covenant in his treatment of humanity's creation. He writes about the image of God and pre- and post-fall man.[43] There are then a number of intervening chapters that treat providence, good, evil, divine permission, and election, before he discusses the law of nature. Like Calvin, Musculus, and Vermigli, Polanus argues that God engraved His law on Adam's heart in his initial creation, but he does not appeal to the doctrine of the covenant.[44] In concert with the earlier tradition, Polanus discusses the differences between law and gospel. Within this context he begins to tread upon what eventually becomes the well-worn path of the covenant of works. The law, according to Polanus, is the command of God and that which instructs humans regarding what they must do and not do; it requires perfect obedience and promises eternal life to those who obey the law (Matt. 19:16-19; 7:12; Lev. 18:5; Ezek. 20:11; Rom. 10:5; Gal. 3:10; Deut. 27:26; James 2:10).[45] Even though Polanus appeals to a catena of texts commonly associated with the covenant of works, he still does not raise the subject.

---

42. Nicholas Byfield, *The Pattern of Wholesome Words* (London: Samuel Mun, 1618), 206.

43. Amandus Polanus, *The Substance of Christian Religion, Soundly Set Forth in Two Bookes* (London: John Oxbridge, 1595), 23-24; idem, *Partitiones Theologicae* (Geneva: Peter Albertus, 1623).

44. Polanus, *Substance of Christian Religion*, 45-46.

45. Polanus, *Substance of Christian Religion*, 51.

Only when Polanus treats soteriology does he address the doctrine of the covenant. Polanus defines covenant as 'a bargaine [*pactum*] which God hath made with men, in which God promiseth to men some good, & requireth of them again, that they performe those things which he commandeth.'[46] The twofold covenant is either of works or grace. Polanus defines the covenant of works (*foedus operum*) as 'a bargaine of God made with men concerning eternall life, to which is both a condition of perfect obedience adjoined, to be performed by man, & also a threatning of eternall death if he shal not performe perfect obedience' (Gen. 2:17).[47] Up to now, his explanation mirrors Perkins' view, but unlike the Elizabethan theologian, Polanus cites Genesis 2:17. What was true of the law, namely that it held out the promise of eternal life to the one who perfectly obeyed, was true both of the Mosaic and, now, Adamic covenants. Hence, Polanus extended the covenant of works into the pre-fall context, but like Perkins, he also believed that the Mosaic covenant presented the covenant of works. Polanus writes: 'The repetition of the covenant of works is made by God (Exod. 19:5. Deut. 5:2. 1 King 8:21. Heb. 8.9).' God repeated the covenant of works at Sinai for four reasons: (1) to stir up people to obedience, (2) that every mouth might be stopped for failing to obey perfectly (Rom. 3:19), (3) to reveal human sin (Rom. 3:19-20, 7:7-11), and (4) to drive sinners to Christ for restoration through the covenant of grace (Gal. 3:22, 5:23).[48] Polanus argues the same points in his massive *Syntagma Theologiae*. But especially as it relates to the topic of this chapter, Polanus again states: 'God repeated this same covenant with the people of Israel through Moses.'[49]

Summary

To this point all of the Reformation-era pieces of the puzzle appear in Perkins and Polanus. Law and gospel present different

---

46. Polanus, *Substance of Christian Religion*, 87-88; idem, *Partitiones*, 108.

47. Polanus, *Substance of Christian Religion*, 88; idem, *Partitiones*, 108.

48. Polanus, *Substance of Christian Religion*, 88.

49. Amandus Polanus, *Syntagma Theologicae Christianae* (Hanau: Johannes Aubrius, 1615), VI.xxxiii (p. 450B): 'Idem fedus repetivit Deus cum populo Israëlitico per Mosen.'

ways of receiving eternal life, and the Mosaic covenant contains both ways but with a greater emphasis on the law. Calvin called it the *foedus legale* and Perkins labeled it the *foedus operum*, or covenant of works. Polanus used the term, *foedus operum*, but located the origins of the covenant in the pre-fall state. He maintained, however, that the covenant of works was present at Sinai because God repeated the covenant of works through Moses. There is a sense in which scholastic distinctions have fallen to the wayside regarding the relationship between law and gospel or the covenants of works and grace. Bullinger and Calvin, for example, employed the distinction between substance and accidents to explain how the *foedus legale* and *foedus evangelicum* occupied the same patch of redemptive history. Apart from qualification or distinction Polanus states that God repeated the covenant of works through Moses. As willing as Polanus was to draw upon medieval theology, he did not apply terminological distinctions. Despite these differences, Calvin, Perkins, and Polanus all recognize that the Mosaic covenant presents the idea that perfect obedience to the law yields eternal life.

Cameron and Leigh

John Cameron

Cameron introduced the idea of a threefold covenant. In addition to the covenants of works and grace, Cameron argued the Mosaic covenant was subservient to the covenant of grace. Hence, the Mosaic covenant was neither of the covenants of works nor grace but was a *tertium quid*.[50] Cameron also introduced the idea that Adam's reward and goal was extended temporal life in the garden rather than eternal life.[51] These two points stand in contrast to the earlier tradition. Calvin, for example, believed that the

---

50. John Cameron, *De Triplici Dei Cum Homine Foedere Theses*, in *Ioh. Cameronis S. Theologiae in Academia Salmuriensi Nuper Professoris, Praelectionum Tomus Tertius et Ultimus* (Saumur: Cl. Girard & Dan. Lerpiner, 1628), thesis VII (p. 611); idem, *Certain Theses, or, Positions of the Learned John Cameron, Concerning the Threefold Covenant of God with Man*, in Samuel Bolton, *The True Bounds of Christian Freedome* (London: P. S., 1656), 356.

51. Cameron, *Threefold Covenant*, thesis IX (pp. 357-58).

foedus legale was related to the *foedus spirituale* or *evangelicum* in terms of substance and accidents. That being said, how much of a difference exists between saying that the Mosaic covenant is temporary and accidental and thus not of the substance of the *foedus evangelicum* versus that it is a *tertium quid?* In both formulations the Mosaic covenant becomes obsolete with the advent of Christ. In both formulations believing Israelites participated in both covenants: the *foedus legale* and *foedus spirituale* for Calvin, and the covenant of grace and subservient covenant for Cameron. For all of its appearances of novelty, Cameron's threefold covenant does not appear all too different from Calvin's scholastic distinction; Cameron's subservient covenant appears to be a distinction under a different name.

Given Cameron's formulation, one might expect that he therefore does not claim that the covenant of works reappears at Sinai if the Mosaic covenant is a *tertium quid.* Cameron nevertheless argues that the covenant of works reappears in the Mosaic (or subservient) covenant. Cameron believed that God presented the goal of extended temporal life to both Adam and Israel, Adam in the garden and Israel in the promised land.[52] Cameron believed that Adam's and Israel's states foreshadowed the benefits and offices of Christ through words and types.[53] But even then, the Adamic covenant only accidentally by reason of the fall, points sinners to Christ; it did not point to Christ in its pre-fall function because Adam had no need of a mediator.[54] This is the extent of the connections that Cameron believed existed between the Adamic and Mosaic (subservient) covenants. He believed there were significant differences between them.[55] So, it is fair to say that Cameron saw connections between the two covenants, but he did not go as far as to say that the Mosaic covenant was the covenant of works or that God repeated it at Sinai.

---

52. Cameron, *Threefold Covenant,* theses LXXX-LXXXI (pp. 400-01).

53. Cameron, *Threefold Covenant,* theses XXVI-XXVII (pp. 368-69).

54. Cameron, *Threefold Covenant,* thesis LVIII (p. 389).

55. Cameron, *Threefold Covenant,* thesis XLVI (pp. 383-84).

Edward Leigh

Leigh incorporated a number of the elements of Cameron's threefold covenant theology, but he demurred in identifying the Mosaic covenant as subservient to the covenant of grace. He instead drew upon the formulations of Johannes Scharpius (1572-1648) to argue that the Mosaic covenant was part of the one trans-testamental covenant: 'The Covenant [of Grace] is but one for substance, yet in divers respects and circumstances it is either Old or New.'[56] This is the same scholastic distinction that Bullinger and Calvin employed, but Leigh attributes it to Scharpius.[57] Leigh argues that the primary term for the Old Testament is the law because its chief element is the law of Moses, and conversely the New Testament is the gospel because its main component is the message of salvation. Echoing the earlier law-gospel distinction of Calvin and even the terms he applies to the Mosaic covenant, Leigh writes: 'The forme of the Covenenant is in the one Legall, in the other Evangelicall.'[58] Leigh's point, like Calvin, is to demonstrate that the Old and New covenants do not 'differ essentially as the Covenant of works and grace, but *modo administrandi*, in manner of administration.'[59] Leigh, therefore, resorts to the form-matter or substance-accidents distinction to explain how law and gospel relate in the Mosaic covenant.

The Westminster Assembly

The Westminster Standards (Confession and Catechisms) is a clearing house for the covenant of works, as not only did multiple views feed into the assembly's deliberations when they wrote their chapter on the covenant, but the Standards distill the various opinions to their essential components.[60] As noted

---

56. Edward Leigh, *A Treatise of the Divine Promises. In Five Bookes* (London: George Millar, 1633), II.i (p. 70).

57. Cf. Johannes Scharpius, *Cursus Theologicus in Quo Controversiae Omnes de Fidei Dogmatibus* (Geneva: Francis Nicolaus, 1622), 354-55.

58. Leigh, *Divine Promises*, II.i (p. 71).

59. Leigh, *Divine Promises*, II.i (p. 74).

60. This section on the Westminster Assembly is taken from J. V. Fesko, *The Theology of the Westminster Standards: Historical Context and Theological Insights* (Wheaton, IL: Crossway, 2014), 144-58.

above, theologians saw connections between the law of nature, Adam, and the Decalogue. Edward Fisher, for example, succinctly states: '*Adam* heard as much in the garden, as *Israel* did at *Sinai*, but onely in fewer words, and without thunder.'[61] Ursinus offers a similar analysis:

> The *moral law* is a doctrine harmonizing with the eternal and unchangeable wisdom and justice of God, distinguishing right from wrong, known by nature, engraven upon the hearts of creatures endowed with reason in their creation, and afterwards often repeated and declared by the voice of God through his servants, the prophets; teaching what God is and what he requires, binding all intelligent creatures to perfect obedience and conformity to the law, internal and external, promising the favor of God and eternal life to all those who render perfect obedience, and at the same time denouncing the wrath of God and everlasting punishment upon all those who do not render this obedience, unless remission of sins and reconciliation with God be secured for the sake of Christ the mediator.[62]

Ursinus and Fisher echo the same principle advocated by Calvin, Vermigli, and Musculus. Namely, the moral law runs through all of God's covenantal dealings with humanity. The Westminster divines recognized the truth of the idea and thus state: 'God gave to Adam a Law, as a Covenant of Works, by which he bound him, and all his posterity to personall, entire, exact, and perpetual obedience; promised life upon the fulfilling, and threatened death upon the breach of it.'[63] Important to note are the series of texts the divines offer in support of this statement: Genesis 1:26-27; 2:17; Romans 2:14-15; 10:5; 5:12, 19; Galatians 3:10, 12; Ecclesiastes 7:29; and Job 28:28. One should note the interweaving of texts that deal with both natural

---

61. Fisher, *Marrow of Modern Divinity*, 9.

62. Zacharias Ursinus, *Commentary of Dr. Zacharias Ursinus on the Heidelberg Catechism*, trans. G. W. Williard (1852; Phillipsburg: P & R, n. d.), 490-91.

63. *The Humble Advice of the Assembly of Divines, Now by Authority of Parliament Sitting at Westminster, Concerning a Confession of Faith* (London: Company of Stationers, 1647), XIX.i.

law and the covenant of works, as the proof texts reveal that they are at a minimum closely identified if not outright synonymous. Romans 2:14-15 was a text commonly understood as a reference to natural law; Calvin for example explains: 'Paul contrasts nature with the written law, meaning that the Gentiles had the natural light of righteousness, which supplied the place of the law by which the Jews are taught, so that they were *a law unto themselves.*'[64]

The Confession then proceeds to situate the moral law in subsequent redemptive history: 'This Law,' referring to the law given to Adam 'as a Covenant of Works,' 'after his fall, continued to be a perfect rule of righteousnesse, and, as such, was delivered by God upon Mount Sinai, in ten Commandments, and written in two Tables.'[65] The divines also acknowledge that 'this Law,' that which was delivered to Adam and subsequently to Israel, is 'commonly called Moral.'[66] As noted in the introduction to this chapter, in his *Marrow of Modern Divinity*, Fisher has his legalist dialogue partner state the following: 'But, Sir, you said that the Morall Law may in some sence be said to be the Law of workes, and you have also said, that the Law of workes, and the Covenant of works, are all one, by which it should seem, that the Morall Law may in some sence be said to be this covenant of workes, made with all mankinde before *Adams* fall.'[67] Fisher accedes to this statement and cites George Downame (ca. 1563-1634) in support of the identification of the moral law with the covenant of works.

---

64. John Calvin, *Romans and Thessalonians*, CNTC (1960; Grand Rapids: Eerdmans, 1996), loc. cit., Rom. 2:14-15 (p. 48). Similar comments appear in other commentators such as Philip Melanchthon, *Commentary on Romans*, trans. Fred Kramer (St. Louis: Concordia, 1992), comm. Rom. 2:14-15 (pp. 89-90); Giovanni Diodati, *Pious and learned annotations upon the Holy Bible: plainly expounding the most difficult places thereof* (London: Nicolas Fussell, 1651), comm. Rom. 2:14; Andrew Willet, *Hexapla: That is, a six-fold commentarie upon the most divine epistle of the holy apostle S. Paul to the Romanes* (Cambridge: Leonard Greene, 1620), comm. Rom. 2:14-15 (pp. 115-25), Rom. 13:8 (p. 620).

65. Westminster Confession, XIX.ii.

66. Westminster Confession, XIX.iii.

67. See, e.g., Fisher, *Marrow of Modern Divinity*, 7.

Downame contends that the law can be understood in a number of different senses: it can mean the *Torah*, which can mean the whole teaching of the Old Testament, but it can also refer simply to the covenant of works: 'More strictly and properly the Law signifieth the covenant of workes, which is also called the Law of workes, Rom. 3.27. which upon condition of perfect and perpetuall obedience promiseth justification and salvation to the observers thereof (Rom 10.5. Gal. 3.12. Lev. 18.5. Ezek. 20.11. Acts 13.38. Rom. 3.20, 28).[68] Downame further elaborates upon these points as he contrasts the differences between the law and the gospel. In opposition to Roman Catholic theologian Robert Bellarmine (1542-1621), Downame writes:

> For the first: he cavilleth with *Calvin* and *Chemnitius* and others, as though they understood simply by the Law of workes, that which requireth workes, and by the Law of faith, which requireth faith: as if the Law of faith did not also require workes, and the Law of workes did not also require faith: whereas our writers disginguish the two covenants of God, that is, the Law and the Gospell, whereof one is the covenant of workes, the other, the covenant of grace: doe teach, that the Law of workes is that, which to justification requireth workes, as the condition thereof: the Law of faith that, which to justification requireth faith, as the condition thereof. The former saith, doe this, and thou shalt live, *Rom.* 10.5, *Gal.* 3.12. *Mat.* 19.17. the latter believe in Christ, and thou shalt be saved, *Iohn* 3.16. *Act* 16.31.[69]

One should note the overlap between the Confession's proof texts and those offered by Downame, as well as Fisher's explanation. The Confession codifies the common opinion on the connection and association of the moral law, the covenant of works, and the Decalogue given in the Mosaic covenant.

A matter of significant debate, however, was the precise relationship between the Adamic and Mosaic covenants. One of the divines, Samuel Bolton (1606-1654), acknowledges that there were a number of different positions on this matter:

---

68. George Downame, *A Treatise of Justification* (London: Nicolas Bourne, 1633), VII.iv.4 (p. 465).

69. Downame, *A Treatise of Justification*, VII.ii.6 (p. 443).

Threefold: Mixed	Threefold: Covenant of Works Repeated	Threefold: Subservient	Twofold
1. Covenant of nature	1. Covenant of nature	1. Covenant of nature	1. Covenant of works
2. Covenant of grace	2. Covenant of promise (or grace)	2. Covenant of grace	2. Covenant of grace.[70]
3. Sinai is mixed: nature and grace	3. Sinai is a covenant of works	3. Sinai is a subservient, neither of the covenant of works or grace	

Bolton explains that the mixed view held that there were three different covenants in Scripture: a covenant of nature with Adam, the covenant of grace, and that the Mosaic covenant was a mixed covenant of nature and grace. A second view held that there were covenants of nature and grace, but that the Mosaic covenant was a repetition of the covenant of works. A third view held to the covenants of nature and grace, but that the Mosaic covenant was neither part of the covenant of nature or grace, but was a *tertium quid* (a third alternative). Bolton notes that the most common scheme was a twofold view: covenants of works and grace.

Westminster divine Edmund Calamy (1600-1666) offers another layer of views that differs slightly from Bolton's arrangement:

Fourfold (Simpson)	Threefold (Burroughs)	Twofold (Pope)	Threefold (Burgess)	Twofold (Calamy)
1. Covenant of works (Adam)	1. Covenant of works with Adam	1. Covenant of works with Israel with no prior covenant, i.e., no covenant with Adam	1. Covenant of works	1. Covenant of works

---

70. Bolton, *True Bounds of Christian Freedome*, 128-29.

128

Fourfold (Simpson)	Threefold (Burroughs)	Twofold (Pope)	Threefold (Burgess)	Twofold (Calamy)
2. Covenant of grace (Abraham)	2. Covenant of works with Israel	2. Covenant of grace	2. Covenant of grace with Israel	2. Covenant of grace.[71]
3. Covenant of works (Israel)	3. Covenant of grace through Jesus		3. A second covenant of grace	
4. Covenant of grace (new covenant)				

Calamy identifies the fourfold scheme with 'M. Sympson,' a likely reference to Sydrach Simpson (ca. 1600-1655), one of the divines. Simpson's view entailed four covenants: a covenant of works with Adam, a covenant of grace with Abraham, another covenant of works with Israel, and a covenant of grace, which was the new covenant. Calamy connects a second position with Jeremiah Burroughs (ca. 1600-1646), another Westminster divine. According to Calamy, Burroughs held a threefold scheme with a covenant of works with Adam, another covenant of works with Israel, and a covenant of grace through Christ.

Calamy identifies a third position with James Pope (fl. 1675) as its chief advocate.[72] Pope believed that there were only two covenants: a covenant of works with Israel with no previous covenant existing (there was no previous covenant with Adam) and a covenant of grace; his view echoes the earlier view of Perkins. Calamy associates the fourth position with Westminster divine, Anthony Burgess, who supposedly held a threefold view. In this

---

71. Edmund Calamy, *Two Solomne Covenants Made Between God and Man: viz. The Covenant of Workes, And the Covenant of Grace* (London: Thomas Banks, 1646), 1-2; Jones, 'The "Old" Covenant,' 187.

72. See James Pope, *The unveiling of Antichrist. Or, Antichrist stript naked out of all his Scripture-attyre, by Which He Hath Deceived the Christian World* (London: Henry Overton, 1646).

view there was a covenant of works with Adam, a covenant of grace with Israel, and a second covenant of grace beyond that made with Israel. The fifth, and last position, Calamy claims as his own, which was the common twofold view: covenants of works and grace.

Several things need to be said about these taxonomies, especially Calamy's. Upon closer examination there is some imprecision in the reported views. Calamy states that he heard the first two views in person, one reported before a committee of the assembly and the other given in a sermon. Calamy gathers the other views from written works. So Calamy possibly misunderstood a person's views. This is a likelihood given what he reports about his fellow divines, Jeremiah Burroughs and Anthony Burgess. Recent analysis of Burroughs' view has recognized it as similar to the position of Cameron, one that Bolton identifies as the threefold (subservient) scheme.[73] Burroughs writes:

> The administration of the Law to them it was under another notion, it was to bring them to Christ, and that they might come to see their inability of keeping of that Covenant, and come to understand Christ so much the more, and to be driven unto Christ by having the Law presented to them, God did never intend by giving of the Law to the people of the Jews that it should be a Covenant of eternal life to them; indeed there was this in the administration of it somewhat different from us, some special Covenant about their living in *Canaan*, and about mercies in that promised Land, beyond that that we have in the Law, as we find in the new Testament, the (I say) had this annexed to it.[74]

Burroughs contends that the administration of the Law, the Mosaic covenant, had different elements 'annexed' to the covenant that New Testament believers no longer live under.

Burroughs makes this point clearer as he propounds the nature of the Mosaic covenant:

> The Law that was first given unto *Adam* and written in his heart, afterwards even obliterated, then it was transcribed by the same hand

---

73. Jones, 'The "Old" Covenant,' 187.

74. Jeremiah Burroughs, *Gospel Conversation* (London: Peter Cole: 1653), 47; Jones, 'The "Old" Covenant,' 187.

in tables of stone and given unto them chiefly to shew them their misery, and their need of Christ; to be a preparation for Christs coming into the world; and with this one addition beyond what we have in the new Testament, that there was a temporal covenant annexed unto it, that concern'd their living prosperously in the Land of *Canaan*, (& so far we are delivered even from the Law as it was given by *Moses*, that is, from the connexion of the Covenant that was added unto the delivering of the Law) concerning their happy and comfortable condition in the Land of *Canaan* upon the keeping of their Law.[75]

This is the element that echoes Cameron's own formulation: the Mosaic covenant was neither of the covenants of works or grace, but a third covenant, subservient to the covenant of grace; this view, incidentally, was also Bolton's.[76] Confirmation that Bolton held to the subservient view comes from the fact that he published Cameron's *Theses on the Threefold Covenant of God with Man* in an English translation as an appendix to his *True Bounds of Christian Freedom*.[77] Other theologians who have been identified with the threefold (subservient) view include Westminster divines Thomas Goodwin (1600-1680) and Obadiah Sedgwick (ca. 1600-1658), as well as John Owen (1616-1683), Samuel Petto (1624-1711), Edward Fisher, and Richard Baxter (1615-1691).[78]

---

75. Burroughs, *Gospel Conversation*, 47.

76. Bolton, *True Bounds*, 130-31.

77. Note the subtitle of Bolton's work, *Whereunto is annexed a discourse of the learned John Camerons, touching the three-fold covenant of God with man, faithfully translated*; cf. John Cameron, *De Triplici Dei cum homine foedere theses* (Heidelberg: 1608). The appendix appears in Bolton, *True Bounds*, 351-401; cf. idem, *The True Bounds of Christian Freedom* (Edinburgh: Banner of Truth, 2001).

78. Obadiah Sedgwick, *The bowels of tender mercy sealed in the everlasting covenant* (London: Edward Mottershed, 1661), I.i-ii (pp. 1-7); Richard A. Muller, 'Divine Covenants Absolute and Condition: John Cameron and the Early Orthodox Development of Reformed Covenant Theology,' *MAJT* 17 (2006): 52; Jones, 'The "Old" Covenant,' 186, 194-202; Michael Brown, *Christ and the Condition: The Covenant Theology of Samuel Petto (1624-1711)* (Grand Rapids: Reformation Heritage Books, 2012), 87-104; Fisher, *Marrow of Modern Divinity*, 28-29. Baxter seems to lend his qualified approval of this view as well (Richard Baxter, *Aphorismes of Justification, With their Explication annexed. Wherein also is opened the nature of the Covenants, Satisfaction, Rightousnesse, Faith, Works, &tc* [London: Francis Tyton, 1649], thesis XXIX [pp. 144-46]).

Another weakness in Calamy's taxonomy is reflected in how he reports the views of fellow divine Anthony Burgess. Burgess does not posit two covenants of grace as Calamy claims. Burgess rattles through the various views: 'Some (as you have heard) make it [the Mosaic Covenant] a Covenant of workes, others a mixt Covenant, some a subservient Covenant; but I am perswaded to goe with those who hold it to be a Covenant of grace.'[79] But Burgess' view is somewhat nuanced and does not fall strictly into a twofold scheme, namely that there are only two covenants, one of works and the other of grace. Burgess writes:

> The Law (as to this purpose) may be considered more largely, as that whole doctrine delivered on Mount Sinai, with the preface and promises adjoined, and all things that may be reduced to it; or more strictly, as it is an abstracted rule of righteousnesse, holding forth life upon no termes, but perfect obedience. Now take it in the former sense, it was a Covenant of grace; take it in the later sense, as abstracted from *Moses* his administration of it, and so it was not of grace, but workes.[80]

So, Burgess places the Mosaic covenant in the covenant of grace in the broader spectrum of everything propounded at Sinai; but in the narrower view, taken out of the context of its administration, it is a covenant of works.

As reflected in Bolton's taxonomy, there were other views for which Calamy does not account. Bolton identifies a threefold scheme that presents the Mosaic covenant as a mixed covenant, one that has both the covenants of works and grace. George Walker (1581-1651), one of the Westminster divines, held this view: 'For the first part of the Covenant which God made with Israel at Horeb, was nothing else but a renewing of the old Covenant of works which God made with *Adam* in Paradise.'[81] But on the other hand, Walker also believed that there was a second part of the

---

79. Burgess, *Vindiciae Legis*, lect. XXIV (p. 232).

80. Burgess, *Vindiciae Legis*, lect. XXIV (p. 233).

81. George Walker, *The Manifold Wisedom of God in the Divers Dispensation of Grace by Jesus Christ, in the Old New Testament. In the Covenant of Faith. Workes. Their Agreement and Difference* (London: John Bartlet, 1640), XV (p. 128).

Mosaic covenant, which was more obscurely given in the Levitical laws, the tabernacle, and the ark, which were types of Christ. This dimension of the Mosaic covenant was more clearly set forth in the Deuteronomic version of the covenant, and 'was nothing else but a renewing of the Covenant of grace which he had before made with their Fathers, *Adam, Abraham, Isaac*, and *Iacob*.'[82]

Other theologians of the period, such as Peter Bulkeley (1583-1659), made distinctions similar to Walker's. Bulkeley believed that the 'Covenant of workes was then revealed and made knowne to the children of Israel, as being before almost obliterated and blotted out of mans heart, and therefore God renewed the knowledge of the Covenant of workes to them.'[83] Key to Bulkeley's statement is that the covenant of works was *revealed*, not that it was re-administered. Bulkeley also employs the wide-narrow distinction vis-à-vis the covenants of works and grace as they both relate to the Mosaic covenant: 'The Law is to be considered two wayes: First, absolutely, and by it selfe, as containing a covenant of works; Secondly, dependently, and with respect to the covenant of grace.'[84]

Even though at least four of the divines, Burroughs, Bolton, Sedgwick, and Goodwin, held to the threefold (subservient) view, and others such as Walker held the mixed view, the common position was a twofold scheme (works and grace), which was also the generally held view in the broader Reformed tradition.[85] John Ball (1585-1640), for example, writes: 'Most Divines hold the old and new Covenant to be one in substance and kind, to differ only in degrees.'[86] Westminster divines, such as Samuel Rutherford, also polemicized against views such as Cameron's threefold (subservient) scheme.[87] One of the reasons Rutherford argued against this view was because he believed that the Mosaic covenant was not

---

82. Walker, *Manifold Wisedom*, XV (pp. 128-29).

83. Bulkeley, *The Gospel-Covenant*, I.vii (p. 62).

84. Bulkeley, *The Gospel-Covenant*, I.vii (p. 63).

85. See Turretin, *Institutes*, XII.viii.6.

86. Ball, *Covenant of Grace*, VII (p. 95).

87. Samuel Rutherford, *Covenant of Life Opened, or A Treatise of the Covenant of Grace* (Edinburgh: Robert Broun, 1654), I.xi (pp. 57-58).

a covenant of works; he based his argument upon a number of different texts from Scripture. One such text was Deuteronomy 30:6 and the promise of a circumcised heart.[88] But even then, Rutherford admitted that the moral law was a covenant of works for the unregenerate.[89]

However, important to note are the different nuances that a theologian might employ in untangling this challenging issue. In a work commended by Westminster divine Edmund Calamy, Thomas Blake (ca. 1597-1657) stated his agreement with John Ball and Anthony Burgess that the Mosaic covenant was part of the covenant of grace.[90] But on the other hand, like Bulkeley and Walker, he also acknowledges the broad-narrow distinction when dealing with the Mosaic covenant: 'There are those phrases in Moses, which are ordinarily quoted, as holding out a covenant of Works, and in a rigid interpretation are no other; yet in a qualified sense, in a Gospel-sense, and according to Scripture-use of the phrase, they hold out a covenant of Grace, and the termes and conditions of it.'[91] If it is not already evident, all of the aforementioned views defy a neat and tidy taxonomy.

So, then, given the complexity of this issue and the varied opinions, what did the Westminster Assembly conclude? What does the Confession say on this matter? As previously noted, the Confession affirms the connection between the moral law, natural law, and the Decalogue as the summary of the moral law. The Shorter Catechism confirms this conclusion with two questions regarding the moral law:

Q. What did God at first reveal to man for the rule of his Obedience?

A. The rule God at first revealed to man for his Obedience, as, the Moral Law (Rom. 2:14-15, 10:5).

Q. Where is the Moral Law summarily comprehended?

---

88. Rutherford, *Covenant of Life*, I.xi (p. 61).

89. Rutherford, *Covenant of Life*, I.xi (p. 63).

90. Thomas Blake, *Vindiciae Foederis; or, A Treatise of the Covenant of God Entered with Man-Kinde*, 2nd ed. (London: Abel Roper, 1658), XXXIII (pp. 210-11).

91. Blake, *Vindiciae Foederis*, XXXIII (pp. 215-16).

A. The Moral Law is summarily comprehended in the Ten Commandments (Deut. 10:4).[92]

Beyond this the Confession addresses matters related to the relationship between the covenant of works and Mosaic covenant, though only briefly. The divines recognize that in the Old Testament the covenant of grace was 'differently administered' in comparison to the 'time of the Gospel' (VII.v). The divines employ a common Aristotelian distinction of *substance* and *accidents* to explain how Christ and the gospel is administered under both periods of redemptive history. They identify Christ as the 'substance' of the covenant of grace, revealed in various promises, prophecies, sacrifices, circumcision, and the like, all fore-signifying Christ to come.[93] Although they do not employ the term *accidents* to describe the different elements that attended the covenant of grace in the Old Testament, it is implied. During the New Testament, the earlier sacrifices, circumcision, types, and ordinances gave way to a simpler and clearer revelation of Christ, manifest in the 'Preaching of the Word, and the Administration of the Sacraments of Baptisme, and the Lords Supper.'[94]

That the accidentals of the Old Testament administration of the covenant of grace were stripped away is evident in what the Confession states about the other elements of the Law. Using the common threefold distinction of the moral, ceremonial, and civil law, the Confession states:

> Beside this Law, commonly called Moral, God was pleased to give to the people of Israel, as a Church under age, Ceremoniall Laws containing several typicall Ordinances, partly of worship, prefiguring Christ, his graces, actions, sufferings, and benefits, and partly holding forth divers instructions of moral duties. All which Ceremonial Laws are now abrogated, under the new Testament (XIX.iii).

> To them also, as a Body Politique, he gave sundry Judicial Laws, which expired together with the State of that people; not obliging

---

92. *The Humble Advice of the Assembly of Divines, Now by Authority of Parliament Sitting at Westminster Concerning a Shorter Catechism* (London: J. F., 1648), qq. 40-41.

93. Westminster Confession, VII.v-vi.

94. Westminster Confession, VII.vi.

any other now, further than the general equity thereof may require (XIX.iv).[95]

These accidental elements of the administration of the covenant of grace were removed once Christ, the 'substance,' had arrived. They were no longer necessary.

Beyond these statements, the divines explicitly exclude only one position regarding the relationship between the covenants of works and grace: 'There are not therefore Two Covenants of Grace, differing in substance, but one and the same, under various dispensations' (XIX.vi). The divines register an oblique rejection of the view of reputed antinomian Tobias Crisp (1600-1643). Crisp readily accepted the basic twofold covenantal scheme, a covenant of works and a covenant of grace, but he offered a unique formulation regarding the Mosaic covenant. Crisp believed that Christ is completely absent from the covenant of works because at its core is 'Do this and live,' which implies life upon the offering of perfect obedience and curse upon disobedience. On the other hand, Christ stands at the center of the covenant of grace, a covenant that in no way admits the works of the believer in any sense by which the sinner can somehow satisfy the demands of the law. Christ fulfills all of the necessary conditions of the covenant of grace.[96] Crisp believed, however, that the Mosaic covenant was unique. He did not believe that the Mosaic covenant was in any sense the covenant of works. The covenant of works, for example, demands perfect obedience and has no provision for the forgiveness of sins. On the other hand, the Mosaic covenant offers the forgiveness of sins (Num. 15:28).[97] Moreover, the Mosaic covenant had priests, which mediated sacrifice, atonement, and the forgiveness of sins; but the Aaronic priesthood paled in comparison to the greater priestly ministry of Christ, a priest according to the order of Melchizedek.

---

95. The threefold division of the law (moral, civil, and ceremonial) goes back at least to Aquinas, see *Summa Theologica* Ia IIae q. 99 art. 4.

96. Tobias Crisp, *Christ alone Exalted: Being the Compleat Works of Tobias Crisp, D. D. Containing XLII Sermons*, 2 vols. (London: William Marshall, 1690), vol. II, serm. II (pp. 246-47).

97. Crisp, *Christ alone Exalted*, vol. II, serm. II (p. 247).

Crisp offers these comments in his sermon on Hebrews 8:6, which speaks of the superiority of Christ's ministry over the old priestly order.[98] Crisp explains the relationship between the two priestly orders in terms of two different covenants of grace:

> The whole Administration of that Covenant which the Priests had to manage, was wholly and only matter of Grace: And though it were a Covenant of Grace, yet it is opposed to that Covenant which Christ in his own Person did mediate. Therefore the opposition which stands here, is not between the Covenant of Works, and the Covenant of Grace, but it is between the Covenant of Grace *weak, imperfect, unprofitable, disannulled*; and another Covenant of Grace that is *perfect, established,* and makes the comers thereunto perfect.[99]

Elsewhere, based upon his exegesis of Jeremiah 31:31, Crisp succinctly states: 'Here are two Covenants, a *New Covenant*, and the *Covenant he made with their Fathers.*'[100]

The question naturally arises, Why did the divines specifically exclude Crisp's view? From one vantage point there does not appear to be much indication that Crisp's view differs from the cornucopia of variations that existed at that time on the relationship between the Mosaic covenant and the covenants of works and grace. Crisp's view seems as reasonable as some of the other views. What difference is there, for example, between saying that there is one covenant of grace with legal accidents that fall away with the advent of Christ, who is the substance, and saying there are two covenants of grace? Crisp, after all, indicates that Christ is typified and foreshadowed in the weaker covenant of grace.[101] The most likely answer is that Crisp's view on the relationship between the covenants of works, grace, and the moral law struck and severed a nerve that the divines believed was vital to an orthodox soteriology.

Reformed theologians maintained, whether holding a three-fold or twofold covenantal scheme in their different variants, the

---

98. Crisp, *Christ alone Exalted*, vol. II, serm. II (pp. 246-47).

99. Crisp, *Christ alone Exalted*, vol. II, serm. II (p. 247).

100. Crisp, *Christ alone Exalted*, vol. II, serm. II (p. 250).

101. Crisp, *Christ alone Exalted*, vol. II, serm. II (p. 248).

perpetual necessity and binding nature of the moral law. Crisp, on the other hand, rejected the idea that the moral law was still binding upon believers. Crisp also denied the connection between the moral law and the Mosaic covenant:

> You see the Apostle from *Jeremiah* brings a direct distinction of two Covenants, *I will make a new Covenant, not according to the Covenant I made with their Fathers*. Here are two Covenants, a *New Covenant*, and the *Covenant made with their Fathers*. Some may think it was the Covenant of Works at the Promulgation of the Moral Law: But mark well that Expression of *Jeremiah*, and you shall see it was the Covenant of Grace.... For (saith he), *not according to the Covenant I made with their Fathers, although I was an Husband unto them*. How can God be considered as *Husband* to a People under the Covenant of Works, which was broken by Man in Innocency, and so became disannulled or impossible by the break of it? The Covenant of Works runs thus: *Cursed is every one that continueth not in all things that are written in the Book of the Law*; and, *in the day that thou sinnest thou shalt die the death*. Man had sinned before God took him by the hand to lead him out of the Land of *Egypt*, and Sin had separated Man from God; how then can God be called an *Husband* in the Covenant of Works? The Covenant therefore was not a Covenant of Works, but such a Covenant as the Lord became a *Husband* in, and that must be a Covenant of Grace: And yet saith the Lord, *I will make a new Covenant, not according to the Covenant I made with their Fathers, &tc.*[102]

For Crisp, the Mosaic covenant was a covenant of grace, but not the promulgation of the moral law. Moreover, when the Mosaic covenant was swept away with the advent of the second covenant of grace, the implication was that the moral law was no longer binding upon the believer. According to Crisp, the stronger covenant of grace had no conditions whatsoever; God supplied everything and man was entirely passive. Conditions were part of the covenant of works, not part of the stronger covenant of grace.[103]

---

102. Crisp, *Christ alone Exalted*, vol. II, serm. II (p. 250).

103. Cf. Francis Roberts, *Mysterium & medulla bibliorum. The mysterie and marrow of the Bible: viz. God's covenants with man, in the first Adam, before the fall: and in the last Adam Jesus Christ, after the fall* (London: George Calvert, 1657), II.ii.5 corollary IV (pp. 111-32).

In his *Vindiciae Legis*, Westminster divine Anthony Burgess specifically engages Crisp on this point. Citing Crisp in the margin, Burgess writes: 'Therefore it is a very wilde comparison of one* [in the margin, *Crisp], that a man under grace hath no more to doe with the Law, then an English-man hath with the lawes of Spain or Turkie.'[104] The divines understood that the moral law 'doth for ever binde all, as well as justified persons as others, to the obedience thereof.' They believed, 'Neither doth Christ, in the Gospel, any way dissolve, but much strengthen this obligation.'[105] But they are also quick to point out, 'Although true Beleevers be not under the Law as a Covenant of Works, to be thereby justified or condemned, yet, is it of great use to them, as well as to others; in that, as a Rule of life informing them of the will of God, and their duty, it directs, and binds them to walk accordingly.'[106] Note, for the unregenerate, the moral law was not a rule of life but a covenant of works, but the opposite was true for those who were in union with Christ. The divines perceived the threat to the perpetual binding nature of the moral law spread across the various covenants and therefore excluded Crisp's view. The Confession therefore only precludes one view, but this is not to say that the divines endorsed other views; rather, the Confession does not rule them out. The explicit statements of a confession are just as important as its omissions and silence. When a confession says nothing about a view, it often means the opinion is extra-confessional and thus a matter of doctrinal liberty, or individual opinion rather than the confessional position.

Turretin and Witsius

Francis Turretin
The same type of doctrinal liberty for various views did not mark the later reception of the covenant of works. Turretin and Johannes

---

104. Burgess, *Vindiciae Legis*, lect. I (p. 15); for the engagement of Crisp's views by another Westminster divine, see Rutherford, *Covenant of Life Opened*, II.x (pp. 344-48).

105. Westminster Confession, XIX.v.

106. Westminster Confession, XIX.vi.

Heidegger (1633-1698) created the Formula Consensus Helvetica (1675) as a bulwark against the perceived dangers of Salmurian theology. They specifically proscribed Cameron's threefold covenant view:

> We disapprove therefore of the doctrine of those who fabricate for us three Covenants, the Natural, the Legal, and the Gospel Covenant, different in their whole nature and pith; and in explaining these and assigning their differences, so intricately entangle themselves that they obscure not a little, or even impair, the nucleus of solid truth and piety; nor do they hesitate at all, with regard to the necessity, under the Old Testament dispensation, of knowledge of Christ and faith in Him and His satisfaction and in the whole sacred Trinity, to theologize much too loosely and not without danger.[107]

But one must carefully distinguish between rejecting the idea of the subservient covenant and that the covenant of works in some sense reappears in the Mosaic covenant. Turretin was averse to the former but amenable to the latter.

In his exposition of the covenant of the covenant of grace, Turretin argues that God dispensed the covenant after Adam's fall through to the consummation, but that He did so in different ways.[108] In particular, God administered the covenant of grace at Sinai 'under a rigid legal economy' (*rigida oeconomia legali*).[109] There was a twofold relation (*schesis*) – one that was legal, 'through which by a new promulgation of the law and of the covenant of works [*nova Legis et foederis operum promulgatione*], with an intolerable yoke of ceremonies, he wished to set forth what men owed and what was to be expected by them on account of duty unperformed.' The other relation was evangelical where the law was a schoolmaster to Christ (Gal. 3:24) and contained the 'shadow of things to come' (Heb. 10:1).[110] This twofold relation either appears according to its

---

107. Formula Consensus Helvetica, canon XXV, in A. A. Hodge, *Outlines of Theology* (1860; Edinburgh: Banner of Truth, 1991), 663.

108. Francis Turretin, *Institutes of Elenctic Theology*, trans. George Musgrave Giger, ed. James T. Dennison, Jr. (Phillipsburg, NJ: P & R, 1992-97), XII.vii.1.

109. Turretin, *Institutes*, XII.vii.31; idem, *Institutio Theologiae Elencticae*, 3 vols. (Edinburgh: John D. Lowe, 1847).

110. Turretin, *Institutes*, XII.vii.31.

'external economy of legal teaching or as to the internal truth of the gospel promise lying under it' (*externam oeconomiam paedagogiae legalis, vel quoad internam veritatem promisssionis Evangelicae*). 'The form' of this external economy, writes Turretin,

> was the pact added to that external dispensation, which on the part of God was the promise of the land of Canaan and of rest and happiness in it; and, under the image of each, of heaven and the rest (*sabbatismou*) in him (Heb. 4:3, 9); or of eternal life according to the clause, 'Do this and live.' On the part of the people, it was a stipulation of obedience to the whole law or righteousness both perfect (Deut. 27:26; Gal. 3:10) and personal justification by it (Rom. 2:13).[111]

Turretin's formulation arguably hearkens back to Bullinger's and Calvin's use of the substance-accidents distinction and echoes a number of points that Calvin makes, such as the law holding out the prospects of eternal life to the person who presents his perfect obedience. But Turretin differs from Calvin in that he explicitly appeals to the covenant of works and its renewed promulgation as the Mosaic covenant's external form and rigid legal economy.

Herman Witsius

Witsius added yet another wrinkle to what is already a complex collection of views. Witsius employed the long-standing distinction between substance and accidents to explain the differences between the administration of the one trans-testamental covenant: 'It is a matter of the greatest moment, that we learn distinctly to consider the covenant of grace, either as it is in its substance or essence [*substantia & essentia*], as they call it, or as it is in divers ways proposed by God, with respect to circumstantials [*circumstantialia*], under different economies. If we view the substance of the covenant, it is but only one, nor is it possible that it should be otherwise.'[112] Under the circumstantials, therefore, of the old economy of the

---

111. Turretin, *Institutes*, XII.vii.32.

112. Herman Witsius, *The Economy of the Covenants Between God and Man* (1822; Escondido, CA: Den Dulk Foundation, 1990), III.ii.1; idem, *De Oeconomia Foederum Dei cum Hominibus* (Basel: Johannes Rudolph, 1739).

covenant of grace, Witsius believed that the Mosaic covenant repeated the covenant of works: 'When the law was given from Mt. Sinai or Horeb, there was a repetition of the covenant of works.'[113] The purpose of the repeated covenant of works was to promote the covenant of grace, to drive sinners to Christ when they recognized they were incapable of meeting its demands.[114] At this point, though Witsius appeals to the covenant of works, he nevertheless believed that Calvin taught this function of the law at Sinai; he cites Calvin in support of the claim that only 'crass Israelites' misunderstood the purpose of the Mosaic covenant.[115] Witsius therefore argued that the Mosaic covenant served the covenant of grace through a pedagogical function by driving sinners to Christ, but it had a different aspect in respect to the unfolding of redemptive history.

When God made the Mosaic covenant with Israel, the nation promised to render their sincere obedience to all of its commands, and God in return would bless them with a temporal and eternal reward. The eternal reward was eschatological life if they would perfectly obey the law, which ultimately no one could fulfill. But the temporal reward was extended life in the land in consequence of their sincere obedience. This aspect of the Mosaic covenant addresses Israel as a nation, not the salvation of rank-and-file Israelites.[116] Witsius believed in its function as a national covenant, the Mosaic economy served as a type that both reached back and echoed Adam's state in the garden, but it also pointed forward to the blessings of heaven:

> But these very things certainly cease not, according to the sentiments of learned men, to be all of them types of the greatest things to the Christian church. The city of Jerusalem itself, the very temple with its whole pomp of ceremonies, though no longer in being, any more than Adam and the deluge, yet ought also to be considered by us

---

113. Witsius, *Economy of the Covenants*, IV.iv.48.

114. Witsius, *Economy of the Covenants*, IV.iv.49.

115. Witsius, *Economy of the Covenants*, IV.iv.52; cf. John Calvin, *Romans and Thessalonians*, trans. Ross Mackenzie, eds. David Torrance and T. F. Torrance, CNTC (1960; Grand Rapids: Eerdmans, 1996), comm. Rom. 10:4 (pp. 221-22).

116. Witsius, *Economy of the Covenants*, IV.iv.54.

Christians as types of the heavenly city and temple not made with hands. In a word, the whole of the Mosaic law, though abrogated as to any obligation of observance, ceases not to exhibit to us, for our instruction, a type of spiritual things.[117]

Given its typological function and its connection to the nation, Witsius argues the Mosaic covenant is neither of the covenant of works or grace but is a *tertium quid*, what he calls a 'covenant of sincere piety' (*foedus sincerae pietatis*). The Mosaic covenant presupposed the covenant of grace, because no one can promise sincere obedience to God apart from its assistance. But it also assumed the covenant of works because its attending terror through its signs, which would have motivated the Israelites to embrace God's covenant. 'This agreement therefore,' writes Witsius, 'is a consequent of the covenant of grace and of works; but was formally neither the one or the other' (cf. Josh. 24:22; 2 Chron. 15:12; 2 Kings 23:3; Neh. 10:29; Ps. 119:06).[118]

Summary

There is a sense in which Witsius bears many different elements that have appeared in the ongoing development of the discussion thus far. He employs the substance-accidents distinction like Calvin, argues that the Mosaic covenant serves the covenant of grace like Cameron's subservient covenant. But unlike Cameron, he believed that the Mosaic covenant offered the prospects of eternal life, not merely temporal life in the promised land. Like Turretin, Witsius argued that God repeated the covenant of works at Sinai, but said that because of the presence of the covenant of grace, it was a national covenant of sincere piety. In the big picture, Witsius' formulation does not differ from earlier versions; he, like others before him, recognizes that the covenant of works in some sense is present in the Mosaic covenant. He uses many of the same long-standing distinctions to explain how the covenants of works and grace relate at Sinai but also introduces new categories, such as the concept of a national covenant of sincere piety. Highlighting

---

117. Witsius, *Economy of the Covenants*, III.iii.4-5.

118. Witsius, *Economy of the Covenants*, IV.iv.54.

the Mosaic covenant's place vis-à-vis Israel as a nation versus individual Israelites is an emphasis that appears in the subsequent development of this aspect of the doctrine of the covenant of works.

Boston, Colquhoun, Shaw, Buchanan, and Hodge

Thomas Boston

In the eighteenth-century reception of the covenant of works theologians continued the discussion regarding the proper relationship between the Adamic and Mosaic covenants. In the case of Thomas Boston, the primary place where he deals with the issue is in his annotated republished edition of Fisher's *Marrow of Modern Divinity*.[119] Recall from the introduction of this chapter that Fisher argued that 'the Morall Law may in some sence be said to be the Law of workes ... the Law of workes, and the Covenant of works, are all one.'[120] Boston observes that the preface to the ten commandments, 'I am the Lord thy God, which have brought thee out of the land of Egypt, out of the house of bondage,' indicates that God gave the Israelites the covenant of grace at Sinai (cf. Gen. 17:7; 15:14; 17:1).[121] Boston also opines, however, 'But that the covenant of works was also, for special ends, repeated and delivered to the Israelites on mount Sinai, I cannot refuse.'[122]

Boston gives four reasons for the reappearance of the covenant of works. First, Galatians 4:24 indicates that there were two covenants. Second, the New Testament explains the Decalogue (Exod. 20) in terms of a works principle, 'If thou wilt enter into life, keep the commandments' (Matt. 18:17-19; cf. Luke 10:25-28; Deut. 27:26; Gal. 3:10). Third, the New Testament highlights the antithesis between law and grace, such as Galatians 3:12, 'the law is not of faith, but the man who doth them shall live in them.' Fourth, the law from Sinai was a covenant (Gal. 4:24; 3:17-18). Hence, Boston concludes that both covenants (works and grace)

---

119. Thomas Boston, *The Marrow of Modern Divinity in Two Parts by Edward Fisher with Notes by Mr. Thomas Boston*, 8th ed. (Falkirk: Patrick Mair, 1789).

120. Fisher, *Marrow of Modern Divinity*, 7.

121. Boston, *Marrow*, 72.

122. Boston, *Marrow*, 72.

were delivered at Sinai, the covenant of grace made with Abraham and the covenant of works made with Adam.[123] God administered both covenants, which reflects the two paths of justification. But Boston stipulated that one should not confound the two covenants, grace and works. 'The later,' writes Boston, 'was added to the former, as subservient unto it; to turn their eyes towards the promise, or covenant of Grace, God gave it to Abraham by promise.'[124] Boston uses Cameron's language of *subservience*, but in a different way. That is, he does not bracket the Mosaic covenant as a *tertium quid*, neither of the covenants of works nor grace. Rather, both covenants appear in the Mosaic economy, but the reappearance of the covenant of works is primarily to serve the ends of the covenant of grace. But like earlier theologians who believed the external form of the covenant was dominated by legal qualities, Boston came to the same conclusion: 'Hence it appears, that the covenant of grace was, both in itself, and in God's intention, the principal part of the Sinai transaction; nevertheless the covenant of works was the most conspicuous part of it, and law most open to the view of the people.'[125]

John Colquhoun

A similar construction appears in the work of John Colquhoun. In his *Treatise on the Law and the Gospel*, Colquhoun explains the nature of the law in the Mosaic covenant. Colquhoun begins with an undisputed fact, namely, the Decalogue was published in the form of a covenant. But he then claims that it was a mixed dispensation: 'In it, the covenant of grace was *repeated* and *published*; the covenant of works was awfully *displayed*, in subservience thereto; and a national covenant between God and the Israelites, who also made, as an *appendage* to the covenant of grace.'[126] Immediately evident are the parallels between Colquhoun and Boston, notably with the use of the term *subservience*, but there are also arguably traces of Witsius

---

123. Boston, *Marrow*, 73-74.

124. Boston, *Marrow*, 74.

125. Boston, *Marrow*, 74.

126. John Colquhoun, *A Treatise on the Law and the Gospel* (New York: Wiley & Long, 1835), 53.

when he designates the Mosaic covenant as a national covenant. But Colquhoun distinguishes between the *publication* of the covenant of grace and the *display* of the covenant of works. This slight difference allows him to preserve the unity of salvation throughout both testaments. Colquhoun begins his exposition of the law, for example, with the covenant of grace and the law's function as a rule and duty for believers. He notes the inversion of law and gospel within the context of the covenant of grace for believers: 'Instead of saying to them, Keep my commandments, that I may become your God; he, on the contrary, said to each of them, "I am the Lord thy God," therefore keep my commandments.' This is not the law as the covenant of works but the law of Christ; Colquhoun applies the term 'rule of life,' which comes from the Westminster Confession.[127]

Colquhoun then gives seven reasons as to why the Israelites received the covenant of grace:

1. The ten commandments are founded on the preface, 'I am the Lord thy God.'

2. Scripture describes the Israelites as the people of God, a peculiar treasure to Him, His first born, and the seed of Abraham.

3. God instructed Israel to inscribe the law on tablets of stone and store them in the ark, which represented the divine law as the covenant of works, but it would be fulfilled by Christ.

4. God could not make the covenant of works with Israel because, as fallen human beings, they had already violated it in Adam.

5. When Moses read the covenant to the people, he ratified it with the sprinkling of blood.

6. God instituted the ceremonial law, which has no other reference but the covenant of grace; they were types of the sacrifice of Christ.

7. Circumcision and Passover were two sacraments of the covenant of grace.[128]

---

127. Colquhoun, *Law and Gospel*, 54-55; cf. Westminster Confession XIX.vi.

128. Colquhoun, *Law and Gospel*, 55-62.

These seven points clearly reveal that God dealt with Israel on the basis of the covenant of grace, hence the *publication* of this covenant at Sinai.

> By way of contrast, God *displayed* the covenant of works at Sinai. The covenant was not renewed with them, yet it was, on that solemn occasion, repeated and *displayed* to them. It was not proposed to them, in order that they might consent, by their own works, to fulfil the condition of it; but it was displayed before them, in subservience to the covenant of grace, that they might see how impossible it was for them as condemned sinners, to perform that perfect obedience, which is the immutable condition of life in it.[129]

The reappearance of the covenant of works, therefore, served a pedagogical function to drive sinners to Christ and the covenant of grace. Hence, like Boston, the covenant of works was subservient, or served the greater purpose, of the covenant of grace.

Colquhoun gives seven reasons for why the covenant of works was displayed at Sinai:

1. The terror that accompanied the Mosaic covenant, thunder, lightning, the blasts of the trumpet, and the voice of God that bellowed out of the fire of Sinai revealed God's wrath against the human race for the breach of the covenant of works.

2. The law was written on tablets of stone, indicating that it was 'the ministration of death,' but deposited in the ark, it prefigured the law's fulfillment by the Messiah, who was the 'surety of a better covenant.'

3. The Scripture designates the law as a *covenant* according to Galatians 4:24 and therefore presented a different mode of attaining salvation, a mode inconsistent with the promise (Gal. 3:17). Hence the law at Sinai was the covenant of works.

4. According to Christ's instruction, the law given by Moses is the covenant of works (Matt. 19:17-19), and Paul confirms this in his epistles (Rom. 10:5; Deut. 27:26; Gal. 3:10; Lev. 18:5).

---

129. Colquhoun, *Law and Gospel*, 63.

5. The New Testament's opposition between law and grace confirms that the law in the form of a covenant of works was displayed at Sinai: 'The law was given by Moses, but grace and truth came by Jesus Christ' (John 1:17). And, 'The law is not of faith; but, The man that doeth them shall live in them' (Gal. 3:12). But this conclusion only applies to the law in its covenant form.

6. The law was written on tablets of stone to convince sinners of their sin and misery, before it could be written on their hearts as a rule of life.

7. Paul confirms the presence of the covenant of works in Galatians 4:24. Only the covenant of works engenders bondage.[130]

For these seven reasons Colquhoun concludes that God displayed the covenant of works at Sinai in the administration of the Mosaic covenant.

These seven points echo Boston's earlier formulation. Colquhoun also highlights the confessional nature of his view by raising the distinction between the law as a *covenant* versus a *rule* to explain how the two covenants function harmoniously. Colquhoun contends that we must view the law from a twofold point of view: 'Namely, as the law of Christ, or the law as a rule of life to believers, and, as the law as it is the matter of a covenant of works, to unregenerate sinners.'[131] The relevant passage from the Confession where this distinction appears states: 'Although true Beleevers be not under the Law as a Covenant of Works, to be thereby justified, or condemned; yet, is it of great use to them, as well as to others; in that, as a Rule of life informing them of the will of God, and their duty, it directs, and binds them to walk accordingly.'[132] If one is in Christ, he is in the covenant of grace and thus the law is a rule of life, but if he is unregenerate, then he is not in the covenant of grace and the law is therefore a covenant

---

130. Colquhoun, *Law and Gospel*, 64-69.
131. Colquhoun, *Law and Gospel*, 70-71.
132. Westminster Confession, XIX.iv.

of works. The law's dual capacity as a rule or covenant applies both to individuals and the Israelite nation. The Mosaic covenant was a national covenant, as it was peculiar to God and Israel alone. Jehovah the Son of God was the king and sovereign of Israel as a political body, which is another way of saying that He was their God and redeemer, and hence the law was a rule unto Israel. But Colquhoun also believed that this was consistent with the idea to view it at the same time as a covenant of works.[133]

Robert Shaw

Other Scottish theologians explained the Confession in this manner. In his commentary on the Confession's chapter on the law, Shaw notes that the 'law of the ten commandments was promulgated to Israel from Sinai in the form of a covenant of works.'[134] God did not intend to renew a covenant of works with Israel so they could seek eternal life through their obedience. Rather, the promulgation of the law as the covenant of works was supposed to show them the requirement for perfect obedience, demonstrate that they could not meet this standard, and thus drive them to the covenant of grace. Consequently, Shaw explains that the Mosaic covenant was a mixed dispensation. God revealed both covenants at Sinai; the covenant of grace appears in the preface to the Decalogue, 'I am the Lord thy God,' but the moral law was also displayed as a covenant of works to convince Israel of their sin. Shaw summarizes his argument in the following manner: 'The law, therefore, was published at Sinai as a covenant of works, in subservience to the covenant of grace. And the law is still published in subservience to the gospel, as "a schoolmaster to bring sinners to Christ, that they may be justified by faith" (Gal. 3:24).'[135] Only believers, therefore, obtain freedom from the law as a covenant of works; the unregenerate still remain under the law as a covenant of works bound to the standard of perfect obedience.[136]

---

133. Colquhoun, *Law and Gospel*, 72-73.

134. Robert Shaw *An Exposition of the Confession of Faith of the Westminster Assembly of Divines*, 8th ed. (Glasgow: Blackie and Son, 1857), 195.

135. Shaw, *Exposition*, 195.

136. Shaw, *Exposition*, 199.

James Buchanan

Another Scottish Presbyterian theologian, James Buchanan, promotes the idea that the covenant of works reappears at Sinai, but unlike Boston and Colquhoun, he initially strikes out on his own. Buchanan writes: 'The Law – considered as a national covenant, by which their continued possession of the land of Canaan, and of all their privileges under the Theocracy, was left to depend on their external obedience to it; – might be called a national Covenant of Works, since their temporal welfare was suspended on the condition of their continued adherence to it.'[137] Buchanan does not appeal to common distinctions, substance versus accidents, the law as a covenant versus a rule, or the internal versus external character of the Mosaic covenant. He instead takes the idea of a national covenant, which appeared in Witsius, Boston, and Colquhoun, and he combines it with the covenant of works – hence, the Mosaic covenant was a *national* covenant of works. This distinction acknowledges that the covenant of works is in some sense in the Mosaic covenant, but it removes it from the realm of soteriology. It is not *the* covenant of works per se but a *national* covenant of works. Buchanan makes this clear when he writes: 'It had no relation to the spiritual salvation of individuals, otherwise than as this might be affected by their retaining, or forfeiting, their outward privileges and means of grace.'[138]

But Buchanan's national covenant of works does not preclude him from addressing how the covenant of works in the Mosaic covenant relates to individuals. Buchanan writes: 'It may be considered, however, in another light, as a re-exhibition of the original Covenant of Works, for the instruction of individual Jews in the principles of divine truth; for in some such light it is evidently presented in the writings of Paul.'[139] Unlike his Scottish colleagues, Buchanan cites authorities at this point to support

---

137. James Buchanan, *The Doctrine of Justification: An Outline of Its History in the Church and of Its Exposition from Scripture* (1867; Edinburgh: Banner of Truth, 1991), 38.

138. Buchanan, *Justification*, 38-39.

139. Buchanan, *Justification*, 39.

his claim. He appeals to Herman Venema (1697-1787), John Erskine (1721-1803), William Warburton (1698-1779), Thomas Bell (1733-1802), and Adam Gib (1714-1788), who make similar arguments.[140] While Buchanan may have discovered these sources on his own, another likely scenario is that Erskine led Buchanan to at least two of them, as Erskine mentions Warburton and Venema in the preface to his work.[141]

Buchanan was well-read on the subject and through these works was exposed to a number of different voices and opinions on the matter. In his extensive exegesis of Galatians 4:24, for example, Bell cites Turretin, Boston, William Ames (1576-1633), Johannes Maccovius (1588-1644), Jonathan Edwards (1703-1758), Isaac Watts (1674-1748), and Melchior Leydekker (1642-1721), in support of the idea that the covenant of works reappeared at Sinai.[142] Bell also alludes to Cameron's view and rejects it.[143] Buchanan, therefore, believed he was on solid exegetical ground and that there were numerous authorities who supported the idea. He argued that the re-exhibition of the covenant of works produced 'a spirit of bondage unto fear,' and as such the desired effect was to

140. Herman Venema, *Dissertationum Sacrarum, Libri Tres* (Leiden: Samuel and Johannes Luchtmans, 1771), II.i (pp. 250-58); John Erskine, *Theological Dissertations* (London: Edward and Charles Dilly, 1765), 1-66; William Warburton, *The Divine Legation of Moses Demonstrated in Nine Books*, 10th ed., 3 vols. (London: A. Millar and J. and R. Tonson, 1765), V.iv-v (vol. II, pp. 489-514, vol. III, pp. 1-17), VI.vi (vol. III, pp. 199-266); Thomas Bell, *A View of the Covenants of Works and Grace* (Glasgow: Edward Khull & Co., 1814), 253-82; Adam Gib, *Kaina Kai Palaia. Sacred Contemplations* (Edinburgh: Neill and Company, 1788), 17-170.

141. Erskine, *Theological Dissertations*, ix.

142. Bell, Thomas. *A View of the Covenants of Works and Grace* (Glasgow: Edward Khull & Co., 1814), 258, 260-61, 262, 270. Cf. Turretin, *Institutes*, XI.xxiv.12; Boston, *Marrow*, 55-56; William Ames, *The Marrow of Theology*, trans. John Dykstra Eusden (Grand Rapids: Baker, 1968), I.xxxix.4; Johannes Maccovius, *Loci Communes Theologici* (Amsterdam: Ludovicus & Daniel Elzevirius, 1658), LVIII (pp. 500-03); Jonathan Edwards, *History of the Work of Redemption* (Edinburgh and Boston: Draper & Folsom, 1782), 67-68; Isaac Watts, *Faith and Practice Represented in Fifty-Four Sermons on the Principle Heads of the Christian Religion*, vol. 1 (London: John Oswald, 1739), 240-60; Melchior Leydekker, *Synopsis Theologiae Christianae, Libris VII* (Utrecht: Rudolph à Zyll, 1689), III.vii.15 (pp. 218-19).

143. Bell, *Covenants of Works and Grace*, 275.

drive people to the grace of Christ. But regardless of the presence of the covenant of works, Buchanan wanted to ensure his readers that 'The economy of Moses, whatever prominence it gave to the Law, was unquestionably a dispensation of the Covenant of Grace.'[144]

Charles Hodge

The above-surveyed theologians were all eighteenth- and nineteenth-century Scotsmen, but American theologians such as Charles Hodge also promoted the idea of the repetition of the covenant of works. Hodge engages this issue in the context of his commentary on 2 Corinthians 3:6, 'for the letter killeth, but the spirit giveth life.' How can a text that purportedly describes the covenant of grace be a death dealer? In terms of the text in question, why would Paul contradistinguish between the letter and the spirit and tout the superiority of the ministry of the new covenant? Like his predecessors, Hodge readily acknowledged that the covenant of grace underlays both the patriarchal and Mosaic dispensations, the Abrahamic and Mosaic covenants.[145] Hodge argues that when Paul contrasts the letter and the spirit he speaks of the antithesis between law and gospel (Rom. 7:6; Gal. 3:3; Rom. 2:27).[146] But Hodge asks how can Paul ascribe a legal character to the Mosaic covenant when it so plainly teaches the gospel.[147]

Hodge answers this question by pointing to the places where the Scriptures teach that the law requires perfect obedience (Rom. 10:5; Gal. 3:10, 12). It is in this vein that Hodge believes that Paul speaks of the law as the covenant of works and in this sense is a 'ministration of death.'[148] But how does the Mosaic covenant, which is part of the covenant of grace, also in some sense contain the covenant of works? Hodge argues that God presented the Mosaic economy

---

144. Buchanan, *Justification*, 39.

145. Charles Hodge, *1 & 2 Corinthians* (1857-59; Edinburgh: Banner of Truth, 1994), 430. Hodge also addresses the idea in his later-published systematic theology (cf. Charles Hodge, *Systematic Theology*, 3 vols. [New York: Scribner, Armstrong, and Co., 1876], II:374-76).

146. Hodge, *1 & 2 Corinthians*, 431.

147. Hodge, *1 & 2 Corinthians*, 432.

148. Hodge, *1 & 2 Corinthians*, 433.

with variegated purposes in mind and thus one must view it under different aspects. What may be true under one aspect might not be true of another.[149] Hodge then presents three different arguments to explain the different aspects of the Mosaic covenant. First, 'the law of Moses was, in the first place, a re-enactment of the covenant of works.' Hodge reminds his readers that a covenant is simply a promise suspended on a condition. In this case, the covenant of works is the promise of life suspended on the condition of perfect obedience. This is the very teaching of Christ, according to Hodge. When the young lawyer asked Christ how to obtain eternal life, Christ asked him, 'What is written in the law?' The lawyer rattled off a number of commandments. Christ then responded, 'Thou hast answered right, this do and thou shalt live' (Luke 10:26-28 KJV). Hodge succinctly states, 'This is the covenant of works.'[150] This is the principle that appears so prominently in the Mosaic covenant, a principle that gives it a legal character. Under this aspect, the Mosaic covenant is a ministration of death.[151]

Second, in line with earlier theologians (e.g., Witsius, Colquhoun, Buchanan, Shaw), Hodge describes the Mosaic economy as a national covenant: 'It presented national promises on the condition of national obedience.' Under this aspect the Mosaic economy is purely legal.[152] Third, but even though the Mosaic covenant contained a renewed revelation of the law, it also presented a renewed revelation of the gospel. The Mosaic covenant presented the priesthood and sacrifices as types and shadows of Christ's office and work, which presupposes faith, not works, as the condition of salvation. Identifying the particular aspect (legal or evangelical) is all-important in rightly understanding the Mosaic covenant. Hodge writes, 'As the old covenant revealed both the law and the gospel, it either killed or gave life, according to the light in which it was viewed.'[153]

---

149. Hodge, *1 & 2 Corinthians*, 433.

150. Hodge, *1 & 2 Corinthians*, 433.

151. Hodge, *1 & 2 Corinthians*, 434.

152. Hodge, *1 & 2 Corinthians*, 434.

153. Hodge, *1 & 2 Corinthians*, 434.

Summary

The formulations of the above-surveyed theologians reveal that some of the earlier seventeenth-century emphases made their way into expositions of the relationship between the Adamic and Mosaic covenants. Boston, for example, was tapped into the discussion through his annotations to Fisher's *Marrow of Modern Divinity*, and Colquhoun engaged Bell's work, which interacted with a number of seventeenth-century sources. This led the surveyed theologians to continue the idea that the covenant of works reappeared at Sinai. But in addition to individual sources, the Westminster Confession's use of the *covenant* versus *rule* distinction was one of the most common ways theologians accounted for the presence of the covenant of works at Sinai. There was an additional layer that some added, such highlighting the Mosaic covenant as a national covenant of works. Arguably, however, these explanations were simpler in comparison with the variegated views present at the Westminster assembly.

Analysis

What accounts for the common trend that theologians believed that the covenant of works in some sense reappeared at Sinai? The answer to this question provides one of the reasons, I believe, that accounts for the development of the covenant of works. The simplest answer is that theologians saw both legal and evangelical elements in the Mosaic covenant. In the earliest formulations theologians accounted for these two principles under the labels of law and gospel, but with the coordination of covenant with these categories, they morphed into the covenants of works and grace. At the same time, the discussion about the relationship between the Adamic and Mosaic covenants is not merely a theological tail wagging the exegetical dog. One of the things that drives this whole discussion is the exegesis of Galatians 4:24, Hagar and Sarah, and the two covenants, as well as the interpretation of Leviticus 18:5 (Gal. 3:10; Rom. 10:5).

In this vein Thomas Bell's comments are worth noting. Bell points out that the Westminster divines found all of their 'proofs of the covenant of works either from the garden or the mount, from Eden or from Sinai.' He thus explains:

But if that covenant was not given at Sinai, one class of these proofs must go for nothing, being quite foreign to the purpose for with they are adduced. In our Larger Cat. Quest. 93. having defined the moral law as a covenant of works, they expressly assert, Quest. 98. that this moral law was delivered by the voice of God upon mount Sinai, and written by him on two tables of stone. Whence I think we may infer that according to them, the Sinai law was a covenant of works. The moral law is the covenant of works. But that law was delivered on mount Sinai. Therefore the covenant of works was delivered there. True it is, these same Divines teach in our Confession of Faith, Chap. 19. sect. 2. that the law was delivered on mount Sinai as a perfect rule of righteousness. But these are no how contrary. The same law might be delivered both as a rule, and as a covenant.[154]

These comments are noteworthy because he touches on the fact that theologians argued from both Genesis and later portions of the Pentateuch (e.g., Lev. 18:5) for the validity of the covenant of works. If Leviticus 18:5 defined the nature of the pre-fall covenant of works, then by virtue of its appearance in the administration of the Mosaic covenant it must in some sense define God's covenantal dealings with Israel. Exegesis, therefore, drove the agenda as theologians sought to understand texts such as Leviticus 18:5 and Galatians 4:24 and how they worked with God's dealings with humanity both before and after the fall.

But this survey reveals the complexity of this issue, and leads to two noteworthy observations. First, it may be only a slight exaggeration to say that this chapter has touched briefly upon the numerous formulations that exist on the question of the relationship between the Adamic and Mosaic covenants. This chapter identifies at least thirteen different variations on this one issue with five different views at the Westminster assembly alone, though some of these variants might overlap in certain ways. Calvin, for example, is similar to Turretin, but the former does not specifically invoke the covenant of works given that the term is anachronistic for his time in the sixteenth century.

---

154. Bell, *Covenants of Works and Grace*, 261.

No.	View	Adherent(s)
1.	Substance – accidents, or administration	Bullinger, Calvin, Leigh, Scharpius
2.	Mosaic covenant is a covenant of works	Perkins, Pope
3.	Mosaic covenant repeats the Adamic covenant of works	Polanus
4.	The Mosaic covenant is neither of the covenant of works nor grace, but a third, subservient covenant	Cameron, Burroughs, Bolton, Goodwin, Sedgwick, Owen, Petto, Fisher, Baxter
5.	Mixed – the Mosaic covenant is a mixed covenant of both works and grace	Walker
6.	Fourfold – covenants with Adam, Abraham, works with Israel, and the new covenant	Simpson
7.	Twofold – covenants of works and grace	Calamy, Rutherford, Blake, Burgess
8.	Covenant of works is *revealed*, not re-administered at Sinai	Bulkeley
9.	Two covenants of grace	Crisp
10.	Substance and accidental promulgation of the covenant of works at Sinai	Turretin, Heidegger
11.	The Mosaic covenant is a covenant of sincere piety	Witsius
12.	The covenant of works was repeated or displayed and delivered at Sinai	Boston, Colquhoun, Shaw
13.	A national covenant of works	Buchanan, Hodge

In fact, one of the few attempts to provide a taxonomy of Reformed views identifies the following seven variations, some of which have not been covered in this chapter:

1. Material republication: that the moral law appears in both the pre- and post-fall covenantal administrations, where some distinguish between the form and matter of the law.

2. Formal republication: the form of the covenant of works appears in the Mosaic covenant.

   a. Relative: where the Mosaic covenant is relatively the covenant of works depending on one's relation to Christ. If he is an unbeliever, the Mosaic covenant is the covenant of works, if he is a believer, the law is a rule of life.

   b. Pedagogical: the covenant of works was given at Sinai to remind Israel about the covenant of works, reveal their sin, and show them their need for Christ.

   c. Hypothetical: the covenant of works was republished in coordination with 2.b. above, which showed the possibility that a person could merit eternal life. But this is purely hypothetical given the fallen human condition.

   d. Typological: the typological-heavy accents in the Mosaic covenant foreshadow Christ and His fulfillment of the broken covenant of works.

   e. Complex: the covenant of works and grace were republished together at Sinai.[155]

This taxonomy highlights the many varying dimensions of this theological discussion and the overlapping categories that might appear in any one view.

It is instructive, therefore, to observe the flexibility and charity that theologians exercised towards one another in attempting to untangle this knot. In addition to Burgess' comments about theologians being like the horns of Abraham's ram caught in a bramble on this issue, a number of other well-respected theologians

---

155. Ferry, 'Works in the Mosaic Covenant,' 69-77.

registered similar thoughts. Westminster divine Obadiah Sedgwick (1600-1658), for example, said this was 'somewhat a knotty question, and therefore I speak warily unto it.' Owen likewise averred: 'This is a subject wrapped up in much obscurity, and attended with many difficulties.' And Thomas Blake also commented: 'Some have so muddied the way, that it is not easie to proceed in any faire and clear order.'[156] The charity on this issue appears in the fact that the Westminster Confession only proscribes the view of Tobias Crisp, who oddly enough did not believe the Mosaic covenant was in any sense the covenant of works but a weakened covenant of grace. Only Turretin's and Heidegger's Formula Consensus barred the threefold covenant theology of Cameron, but the positive reception of this confessional document was extremely limited. But while Turretin and Heidegger objected to bracketing the Mosaic covenant as a *tertium quid*, they did not object to the idea that the covenant of works reappeared at Sinai.

Conclusion

Reformed theologians were in general agreement that the covenant of works in some sense appeared in the Mosaic covenant. They were divided, however, on the particular sense in which it appeared. Commitment to the idea that the moral law was shot through all of God's covenants, the antithesis between law and gospel, the exegesis of key texts such as Leviticus 18:5, Galatians 4:24, and 2 Corinthians 3:6, and coordinating covenant with law were contributing factors both to the development of the covenant of works and the ensuing discussion about the precise relationship between the Adamic and Mosaic covenants.

---

156. Ferry, 'Works in the Mosaic Covenant,' 24; cf. Obadiah Sedgwick, *The Bowels of Tender Mercy Sealed in the Everlasting Covenant* (London: 1661). 172; John Owen, *An Exposition of the Epistle to the Hebrews*, vol. 6, ed. William H. Goold (1855; Banner of Truth, 1991), 60; Thomas Blake, *A Treatise of the Covenant of God Entered with Man-kinde* (London: 1658), 296.

~: PART II :~

Exegesis

~: II.1 :~

Written on the Heart
(Rom. 2:14-15)

Introduction

In the twentieth century, the theological concept of natural law no longer waxed but instead waned in Reformed theological works.[1] The shadow of German Idealism loomed large over the landscape. Theologians were less inclined to appeal to multiple *foci* in their theological works as starting points, such as Scripture, God, creation, and the categories of natural and supernatural revelation. They instead followed the tenets of idealism and employed singular starting points, such as the doctrine of Christ. The monistic tendency of the single starting point appears most famously in Karl Barth's (1886-1968) *Church Dogmatics*, where Christ is not merely the center of his soteriology but of his entire theological system – the singular starting point for all theological knowledge.[2] Barth therefore legendarily shut the door to natural theology in his famous *Nein!* to Emil Brunner (1889-1966).[3] This

---

1. On the place of natural law in historic Reformed theology, see Stephen J. Grabhill, *Rediscovering the Natural Law in Reformed Theological Ethics* (Grand Rapids: Eerdmans, 2006); and David VanDrunen, *Natural Law and the Two Kingdoms: A Study in the Development of Reformed Social Thought* (Grand Rapids: Eerdmans, 2009).

2. Richard A. Muller, 'A Note on "Christocentrism" and the Imprudent Use of Such Terminology,' *WTJ* 68 (2006): 253-60.

3. Emil Brunner and Karl Barth, *Natural Theology: Comprising 'Nature and Grace' by Professor Dr. Emil Brunner and the reply 'No!' by Dr. Karl Barth* (rep.; Eugene, OR: Wipf & Stock, 2002).

shift in the use and appreciation of natural categories made inroads into various doctrines, but especially in the covenant of works. One of the more commonly cited biblical texts in support of the early modern Reformed doctrine of the covenant of works was Romans 2:14-15: 'For when Gentiles, who do not have the law, by nature do what the law requires, they are a law to themselves, even though they do not have the law. They show that the work of the law is written on their hearts, while their conscience also bears witness, and their conflicting thoughts accuse or even excuse them.' Yet, by the twentieth century exegetical footing had changed.

Due in part to the idealist-influenced methodology and shifting biblical interpretive principles, theologians no longer connected Romans 2:14-15 with the covenant of works. Both advocates and critics of the doctrine deemed Romans 2:14-15 exegetically irrelevant. In his treatment of the doctrine, Louis Berkhof (1873-1957) interacts with numerous biblical texts to substantiate the existence of the covenant of works (Gen. 3:15; Hosea 6:7; Rom. 7:10; 10:5; Gal. 3:13; Rom. 5:12-21; Job 31:33; Lev. 18:5; Ezek. 20:11, 13, 20; Luke 10:28; and Gen. 3:22), but Romans 2:14-15 is not among them.[4] The only places that Berkhof engages the text is when he connects it to dispensationalism's period of 'conscience' and common grace, particularly *iustitia civilis* (civil righteousness).[5] In a similar vein, in his rejection of the covenant of works, John Murray (1898-1975) whittled the doctrine's exegetical support largely to one text, namely Hosea 6:7. In lieu of the covenant of works Murray presents his own 'Adamic Administration' but nowhere appeals to Romans 2:14-15.[6]

In contrast to the contemporary preterition, this chapter defends the thesis that Romans 2:14-15 is a vital exegetical pillar that bears the doctrinal weight of the covenant of works. In short, Romans 2:14-15 teaches that God writes the basic content of the

---

4. Louis Berkhof, *Systematic Theology: New Combined Edition* (1932, 1938; Grand Rapids: Eerdmans, 1996), 211-18.

5. Berkhof, *Systematic Theology*, 290, 441, 443.

6. John Murray, 'Adamic Administration,' in *Collected Writings of John Murray*, vol. 2 (Edinburgh: Banner of Truth, 1977), 47-59.

moral law on the hearts of all people. In concert with the positive and negative commands (fill the earth, and subdue it and not to eat from the tree of knowledge), the heart-inscribed law of God constitutes the legal demands of the covenant of works. God wrote His law on Adam's heart and thus naturally and supernaturally revealed the requirements of the covenant of works: obey the law and submit to the authority of your covenant Lord and you will secure eternal life. In the post-fall context, the natural law still exists and functions, but due to sin people no longer have the ability to secure eternal life according to the terms of the covenant of works. This does not mean, however, that the covenant of works disappears from the stage of redemptive history. The permanency of the heart-inscribed law still serves as a testimony of the covenant of works and continues to provide a basis of judgment at the great assize. But how, precisely, the covenant of works functions in the post-fall world awaits arguments presented later in this chapter.

In order to demonstrate the thesis that Romans 2:14-15 is an exegetical basis for the covenant of works, this chapter first begins with a broad overview of the immediate context of Paul's statements regarding the heart-inscribed knowledge of the law. Second, the chapter examines Romans 2:14-15 to explain what Paul means when he writes that Gentiles do *by nature* what the law requires, that the law is written on human hearts, and how this knowledge interacts with the human conscience. Third, the chapter offers theological analysis of how Paul's attestation to natural law functions within the covenant of works both before and after the fall, in the Adamic and Mosaic covenants. The chapter then concludes with summary observations about the importance of Romans 2:14-15 and natural law for the covenant of works.

Broader Context

Romans 2:14-15 appears in the context of the opening of Paul's letter to the church at Rome. The apostle announced the chief purpose of his letter in his thesis statement: 'For I am not ashamed of the gospel, for it is the power of God for salvation to everyone who believes, to the Jew first and also to the Greek. For in it the righteousness of God is revealed from faith to faith, as it is written, "The righteous shall live by faith'" (Rom. 1:16-17, trans. mine). God reveals His saving righteousness in the gospel, but at the same time there is a flip side to His saving activity – His judgment against wickedness: 'For the wrath of God is revealed from heaven against all ungodliness and unrighteousness of men, who by their unrighteousness suppress the truth' (Rom. 1:18). In order to legitimize God's judgment on human wickedness, Paul points to the ways in which sinful human beings reject the knowledge of God. Rather than worship the one, true, living God, people instead worship idols and in a narcissistic stupor gaze into the mirror of their fellow human beings and become enamored with their own image (Rom. 1:19-32).

In chapter two Paul transitions from human wickedness to God's judgment that justly falls on sinners (Rom. 2:2). Paul then introduces the nature of God's judgment:

> He will render to each one according to his works: to those who by patience in well-doing seek for glory and honor and immortality, he will give eternal life; but for those who are self-seeking and do not obey the truth, but obey unrighteousness, there will be wrath and fury. There will be tribulation and distress for every human being who does evil, the Jew first and also the Greek, but glory and honor and peace for everyone who does good, the Jew first and also the Greek. For God shows no partiality (Rom. 2:6-11).

Paul's teaching echoes Old Testament expectations, namely, that God will judge human beings for their actions and repay them according to their deeds (Ps. 62:12; Prov. 24:12; Hosea 12:2; Job 34:11; Eccles. 12:14; Jer. 17:10).[7] In rendering this judgment, Paul stresses three things: (1) that God is impartial and fair (Rom. 2:2, 5, 11), (2) that His judgment will fall on both Jew and Gentile alike (Rom. 2:9, 10), and (3) that this judgment will be according to works (Rom. 2:6). Commentators are in broad agreement on these three points but opinions splinter when it comes to defining *Jew* and *Gentile* in this context and the precise nature of judgment according to works.

---

7. Douglas J. Moo, *The Epistle to the Romans*, NICNT (Grand Rapids: Eerdmans, 1996), 136; Scott W. Hahn, *Romans*, CCSS (Grand Rapids: Baker, 2017), 24.

Space prohibits an exhaustive dissection of the different views on these two disputed issues; hence, I will not explore them in great detail, as others have ably done this.[8] Nevertheless, regarding the first issue, suffice it to say that the overall context of Paul's opening argument lends itself to the fact that Paul speaks about non-Christian Jews and Gentiles and the universal standard that all people must meet regardless of who they are. Paul's later statements in Romans 3 confirm this when he writes that 'every mouth may be stopped, and the whole world may be held accountable to God' (Rom. 3:19). Mere possession of the law is insufficient for one's salvation and thus Jews do not automatically have a built-in advantage over the Gentiles.[9] Rather, Paul sets forth the principle that God will judge every person by his works. Note, however, that he has not yet introduced his exposition of justification by faith but only explains how God's standard of judgment functions.[10] Paul does not cite Leviticus 18:5, but he appeals to its principle, namely, perfect obedience secures eternal life (cf. Luke 19:16-17; Rom. 10:5; Gal. 3:10-14).[11] John Calvin (1509-64) explains:

> They [the Jews] gloried in their unique knowledge of the law, because they perceived that it was the rule of righteousness (Deut. 4:1). To refute this mistaken impression he asserts that the hearing or the knowledge of the law is not of such consequence as to afford righteousness, but that works must be brought forth in accordance with the saying, 'He that doeth them shall live in them' (Lev. 18:5; cf. Rom. 10:5; Gal. 3:12). The sense of this verse, therefore, is that if righteousness is sought by the law, the law must be fulfilled, for

---

8. So Moo, *Romans*, 140-42; Thomas R. Schreiner, *Romans*, BECNT (Grand Rapids: Baker, 1998), 119-23.

9. Schreiner, *Romans*, 118.

10. Moo, *Romans*, 141-42.

11. Joseph Fitzmyer, *Romans*, AB (New York: Doubleday, 1992), 308; Charles Hodge, *Romans* (1835; Edinburgh: Banner of Truth, 1989), 54; Robert Haldane, *Romans* (1874; Edinburgh: Banner of Truth, 1996), 89; Schreiner, *Romans*, 119; C. K. Barrett, *The Epistle to the Romans*, 2nd ed., BNTC (Peabody, MA: Hendrickson, 1991), 47; David VanDrunen, *Divine Covenants and Moral Order: A Biblical Theology of Natural Law* (Grand Rapids: Eerdmans, 2014), 239, 246-47.

the righteousness of the law consists in the perfection of works. Those who misinterpret this passage for the purpose of building up justification by works deserve universal contempt.[12]

This is how the law functions, or more specifically, these are the terms of the covenant of works.[13] But judgment according to works raises a relevant and expected question. How can God universally hold all people accountable for keeping the law if only Jews received it at Sinai? How can God legitimately hold Gentiles accountable for a legal standard they do not know? These questions set the stage for Paul's statements in Romans 2:14-15.

Paul presents a distinction that corresponds to the categories of Jew and Gentile: 'For all who have sinned without the law will also perish without the law, and all who have sinned under the law will be judged by the law' (Rom. 2:12). 'Without the law' corresponds to the Gentiles and 'under the law' to the Jews. The Gentiles are without the Torah and the Jews are under it. In other terms, the Gentiles are outside of the Mosaic covenant and the Jews are under this covenant. Paul's statements elsewhere confirm this characterization: 'Remember that you [Gentiles] were at that time separated from Christ, alienated from the commonwealth of Israel and strangers to the covenants of promise' (Eph. 2:12).[14] Whether one is, therefore, outside or under the Mosaic covenant and in possession of the Torah, he must nevertheless perform the law in order to secure a verdict of *justified*: 'For it is not the hearers of the law who are righteous before God, but the doers of the law who will be justified' (Rom. 2:13). This statement conceptually echoes Leviticus 18:5's 'do this and live,' and Paul's other pithy aphorism, 'The law is not of faith' (Gal. 3:12). Just as in Galatians 3, however, in the broader context Paul quotes Psalm 143:2 to remind his readers that due to sin no person can travel the path of justification by works: 'For by works of the law no human being will be justified in his sight, since through the law comes the knowledge of sin'

---

12. John Calvin, *Romans and Thessalonians*, CNTC (1960; Grand Rapids: Eerdmans, 1996), 47.

13. Charles Hodge, *Romans*, 50.

14. Moo, *Romans*, 145; Fitzmyer, *Romans*, 305.

(Rom. 3:20; cf. Gal. 3:11).[15] This begs the question, How can God hold Jews and Gentiles both accountable before the divine bar if only the Jews have received the Torah? Paul presents his answer in Romans 2:14-15.

Romans 2:14-15

Paul writes: 'For when Gentiles, who do not have the law, by nature do what the law requires, they are a law to themselves, even though they do not have the law. They show that the work of the law is written on their hearts, while their conscience also bears witness, and their conflicting thoughts accuse or even excuse them' (Rom. 2:14-15). In the history of the exegesis of these two verses, commentators have presented three interpretive alternatives. Paul refers to: (1) Gentiles who fulfill the law and are saved apart from faith in Christ (Pelagius); (2) Gentile Christians who fulfill the law because they are in union with Christ (Augustine); or (3) Gentiles who perform some aspects of the law but who are not saved.[16] Within the larger context of his argument, the third alternative is the best solution for a number of reasons. To say, for example, that Gentiles could perform the law and thus secure their salvation apart from Christ would overturn Paul's entire argument (e.g., Rom. 1:18-32; 3:1-20). Therefore, Pelagius' view is incorrect. Similarly, while Christians do in some sense fulfill the law (e.g., Rom. 13:8-10), they only do so through the indwelling power of the Spirit (Rom 7:6; 8:4; Gal. 3:5; 5:18). Paul clearly states here that these Gentiles 'by nature do what the law requires' (Rom. 2:14).[17] There are three things that explain Paul's point in Romans 2:14-15: (1) Gentiles do what the law requires *by nature*, (2) this law is 'written on their hearts,' and (3) it is a function of their conscience.

First, Paul appeals to the natural law that all people have, though in this case his point is especially relevant for Gentiles (cf. Rom.

---

15. Moo, *Romans*, 147.

16. Moo, *Romans*, 148-49; cf. Pelagius, *Pelagius's Commentary on St. Paul's Epistle to the Romans* (Oxford: Clarendon, 1998), 72-73.

17. Moo, *Romans*, 149; Fitzmyer, *Romans*, 306; VanDrunen, *Divine Covenants*, 232.

1:32).[18] Natural law was a common concept among Roman, Greek, and Jewish writers in Paul's historical context.[19] Cicero (106-43 B.C.), for example, writes: 'Law is the highest reason implanted in Nature, which commands what ought to be done and forgives the contrary. This reason, when firmly fixed and perfected in the human mind, is Law.'[20] According to Greek philosophers, the natural law or 'unwritten law' is the basis for legal and social order, which means that there are universal moral standards.[21] In fact, at this particular point Paul's language in Romans 2:14-15 likely comes from stock phrases that were common to Aristotle (384-322 B.C.). In technical exegetical terms,

---

18. Hahn, *Romans*, 27; Schreiner, *Romans*, 122-23; Barrett, *Romans*, 49-50. Murray does not invoke the category of natural law but substantively appeals to the concept when he claims that Gentiles, 'by reason of what is implanted in their nature, confront themselves with the law of God' (John Murray, *The Epistle to the Romans*, NICNT [Grand Rapids: Eerdmans, 1968], 73). But where Murray possibly demurs from natural law is when he only claims that the Gentiles have their 'moral nature,' which takes 'the place of the revealed law possessed by the Jews' (Murray, *Romans*, 73-74). In other words, Murray does not appeal to natural law but rather humanity's upright nature. The two concepts are arguably similar but absent in Murray's argument is any appeal to historical examples of natural law with which Paul was likely familiar. Murray, it seems, does not want to admit the category of natural law into Paul's argument. Furthermore, he specifically notes that Paul does not say that God wrote His law on Gentile hearts but the *work* of the law, 'things required and stipulated by the law .... Prescriptions of the law are inscribed and ingenerated with that which is deepest and most determinative in their moral and spiritual being' (Murray, *Romans*, 74-75). Murray gets as close as he can to natural law concepts without appealing to them. This may be his effort to distance himself from the perceived connections between natural law and Roman Catholic theology. In truth, however, natural law categories are common to both Roman Catholic and Reformed theology (see VanDrunen, *Natural Law and Two Kingdoms*; Grabill, *Rediscovering Natural Law in Reformed Theological Ethics*). Käsemann takes a similar approach to Murray, though he explicitly rejects any connection between Paul and first-century natural law views. Instead, in contrast to the written law of the Jews, the Gentiles 'have an analogue to the *graphe* and are accountable to this as the Jews are to the Torah received by them' (Ernst Käsemann, *Commentary on Romans* [Grand Rapids: Eerdmans, 1980], 64).

19. For natural law views among post-Apostolic Jewish writers, see David Novak, *Natural Law in Judaism* (Cambridge: Cambridge University Press, 1998).

20. Cicero, *De Legibus*, I.vi.18, in *On the Republic, On the Laws*, LCL, vol. 16, trans. C. W. Keyes (Cambridge: Harvard University Press, 1943), 317; Fitzmyer, *Romans*, 310.

21. Moo, *Romans*, 150.

Paul echoes Aristotle.[22] There are three key phrases in Paul's text that first appear in Aristotle:[23]

Romans 2:14-15	Aristotle
They are a law to themselves [*eautois eisin nomos*]	The refined and free man will have this manner, being, as it were, *a law to himself* [*oion nomos on eauto*] (*Nichomachean Ethics* IV.viii.10).
The work of the law [*to ergon tou nomou*]	First, that justice is real and beneficial, but not that which (only) appears (to be just); nor the written law either, for it does not do *the work of the law* [*ergon to tou nomou*] ... And that it belongs to the better man to use and abide by the unwritten rather than the written (laws) (*Art of Rhetoric*, I.xv.7, [1375b]).
accuse or even excuse [*kategorountoun he kai apologoumenon*]	First, then, let us speak of the laws, how one must use (them) when persuading and dissuading, and *accusing and excusing* [*kategorountai kai apologoumenon*] ... (*Rhetoric* I.xv [1375a]).

These three phrases occur in both Aristotle and Paul, and notably, there are no analogues in the Septuagint. The absence of these phrases from the Septuagint is significant, because it means that Paul was not drawing on the Old Testament when he employed them in Romans. It does not conclusively prove he was dependent on Aristotle, but at a minimum it does point to the fact that he was using extra-biblical data. But there are important considerations that support the claim that Paul echoed Aristotle.

Along these lines Hellenistic Jews, such as Philo of Alexandria (25 B.C.- A.D. 50), wrote of the same concept: 'And right reason is an infallible law engraved not by this mortal or that and, therefore, perishable as he, nor on parchment or slabs, and, therefore soulless

---

22. C. John Collins, 'Echoes of Aristotle in Romans 2:14-15: Or, Maybe Abimelech Was Not So Bad After All,' *JMM* 13/1 (2010): 124.

23. Collins, 'Echoes of Aristotle,' 129-30.

as they, but by immortal nature on the immortal mind, never to perish.'[24] In texts that date from the early second century A.D., Palestinian Jews appealed to the concept of natural law to explain how the patriarchs were able to obey the law even though they had not formally received it as Israel did at Sinai: 'For at that time the unwritten law was in force among them, and the works of the commandments were accomplished at that time, and the belief in the coming judgment was brought about, and the hope of the world which will be renewed was built at that time, and the promise of the life that will come later was planted.'[25] This is not to say that Paul's use of natural law is exactly the same as his first-century counterparts but rather that he appeals to the concept and even uses some of the same terminology.

Calvin offers a useful explanation of Paul's appeal to natural law by connecting it to the Stoic concept of *prolepsis*:

> Since, therefore, all nations are disposed to make laws for themselves of their own accord, and without being instructed to do so, it is beyond all doubt that they have certain ideas of justice and rectitude, which the Greeks refer to as *prolepsis* [preconception], and which are implanted by nature in the hearts of men. Therefore they have a law without the law; for although they do not have the written law of Moses, they are by no means completely lacking in the knowledge of right and justice. They could not otherwise distinguish between vice and virtue, the former of which they restrain by punishing it, while commending the latter, and showing their approval of it, and honoring it with rewards. Paul contrasts nature with the written law, meaning that the Gentiles had the natural light of righteousness, which supplied the place of the law by which the Jews are taught, so that they were *a law unto themselves.*[26]

---

24. Philo, *Every Good Man Is Free*, 46, in *Philo*, LCL, vol. IX, trans. F. H. Colson (1941; Cambridge: Harvard University Press, 1985), 37; Moo, *Romans*, 150 n. 34.

25. 2 (Syriac Apocalypse of) Baruch, 57:2-3, in *The Old Testament Pseudepigrapha*, 2 vols., ed. James H. Charlesworth (New York: Doubleday, 1983), I:641; Moo, *Romans*, 150 n. 34.

26. Calvin, *Romans*, 48. For nearly identical explanation, see Philip Melanchthon, *Commentary on Romans*, trans. Fred Kramer (St. Louis: Concordia, 1992), 88-90. For a contemporary advocate that Paul employs Stoic categories, see J. W. Martens, 'Romans 2.14-16: A Stoic Reading,' *NTS* 40 (1994): 55-67. Also

Given the nature of the concept to which Paul appeals and the overlapping terminology between Paul and Aristotle, Calvin makes a valid observation that is generally true. Whether he appeals specifically to Aristotelian or Stoic notions of natural law is immaterial. Rather, Paul appeals to common first-century ideas about natural law to prove that Gentiles know God's law by virtue of their creation in God's image.

Second, Paul notes that the Gentiles do by nature what the law requires and that the work of the law is 'written on their hearts.' Paul explains that God has written the 'work of the law,' that is, the conduct required by the law, on Gentile hearts. Some commentators such as Augustine have argued that this is evidence that Paul writes of Gentile Christians because he mentions the work of the law written on the hearts, which invokes Jeremiah's new covenant and the law written on the hearts of the redeemed (31:33).[27] Yet, the immediate context of Paul's statement precludes this interpretive possibility. Paul says that the Gentiles 'do by nature what the law requires' and that Gentile consciences accuse or excuse their conduct.[28] Jeremiah's prophecy is about a new redemptive work, a work wrought by the Spirit, not something that is natural to all people let alone the sole work of conscience. The Spirit convicts Christians, yet Paul mentions nothing of the Spirit's work here.[29] By stating, therefore, that by nature the work of the law is written on the heart, Paul appeals to creational or Adamic categories. When God created human beings, He inscribed His law on their hearts.[30]

---

see Troels Engberg-Pedersen, *Paul and the Stoics* (Louisville, KY: Westminster John Knox Press, 2000). My thanks to Guy Waters for alerting me to Engberg-Pedersen's work.

27. Moo, *Romans*, 152. For more recent advocates of this view, see N. T. Wright, 'The Law in Romans 2,' in *Paul and the Mosaic Law*, ed. James D. G. Dunn (Grand Rapids: Eerdmans, 1996), 131-50; Robert Jewett, *Romans* (Minneapolis: Fortress, 2007), 213; C. E. B. Cranfield, *Romans*, ICC, 2 vols. (Edinburgh: T & T Clark, 2001), I:152, 158-59; Simon Gathercole, 'A Law Unto Themselves: The Gentiles in Romans 2.14-15 Revisited,' *JSNT* 85 (2002): 27-49.

28. Fitzmyer, *Romans*, 310.

29. VanDrunen, *Divine Covenants*, 233, 248-51.

30. Haldane, *Romans*, 90-91.

By virtue of their creation in God's image, all human beings possess the knowledge of this law. The Old Testament provides testimony to this fact.[31] When Abraham lied to Abimelech and told him that Sarah was his sister, God warned Abimelech in a supernaturally revealed dream not to violate her because she was in fact Abraham's wife.[32] When Abimelech confronted Abraham, he said: 'You have done to me things that ought not to be done' (Gen. 20:9). God's supernatural revelation to Abimelech confirmed what the king knew, namely, that a man should not have sexual relations with another man's wife. The dream also revealed to Abimelech something he did not know, namely, that Abraham and Sarah were married.

God, therefore, used the work of the law inscribed on Abimelech's heart and the king even appealed to this when he confronted Abraham's sin. Abimelech did not cite the Torah but merely what was commonly known and practiced as upright conduct. In fact, God Himself testified to Abimelech's morality in the incident: 'Yes, I know that you have done this in the integrity of your heart, and it was I who kept you from sinning against me. Therefore I did not let you touch her' (Gen. 20:6-7). God restrained him but, in some sense, Abimelech's conduct was upright; he acted in the integrity of his heart (בתם־לבבך), which is terminology used to describe morally outstanding Old Testament saints (Gen. 6:9; 17:1; Job 1:1, 8; 2:3).[33] In fact, in this case, the pagan king acted with greater moral integrity than the redeemed patriarch.[34] Abraham dreaded Abimelech because he believed there was 'no fear of God' among the king's people (Gen. 20:11). 'Fear of God' does not designate

---

31. On the significance of the Genesis 20 narrative for natural law, see VanDrunen, *Divine Covenants*, 148-61, 279-80; idem, *A Biblical Case for Natural Law* (Grand Rapids: Acton Institute, [2006]), 42-49; Novak, *Natural Law in Judaism*, 47-50.

32. Bruce K. Waltke, *Genesis: A Commentary* (Grand Rapids: Zondervan, 2001), 285.

33. Gordon J. Wenham, *Genesis 16-50*, WBC, vol. 2 (Dallas, TX: Word Books, 1994), 71.

34. Cf. Meredith G. Kline, *Genesis: A New Commentary*, ed. Jonathan G. Kline (Peabody, MA: Hendrickson, 2016), 76; Martin Luther, *Lectures on Genesis 12-20*, LW, vol. 3 (St. Louis, MO: Concordia, 1961), 323-24; Gerhard von Rad, *Genesis*, rev. ed. (Philadelphia: The Westminster Press, 1961), 228; Waltke, *Genesis*, 285.

a person is a member of the covenant or one who professed faith in the one, true, living God. The phrase is the common way to describe one who has 'reverence and regard for the most elementary moral norms, whose severe guardian was everywhere considered to be the divinity.'[35] For example, Ugarit and Egyptian marriage contracts considered adultery a 'great sin.'[36] This is just one example of a pagan employing the naturally inscribed law upon his heart.[37] What the Old Testament presents in an extended narrative, Paul gives with didactic precision: 'Gentiles ... by nature do what the law requires.'

Third, Paul demonstrates how this natural law functions within each person: 'Their conscience also bears witness, and their conflicting thoughts accuse or even excuse them' (Rom. 2:15). Here when Paul writes of 'conscience' (συνείδησις), he employs a term that comes from the Greek world, not the Old Testament. The term came from Stoic philosophy, although Paul only uses it in terms of its popular rather than its technical meaning.[38] The conscience interacts with the heart-inscribed knowledge of the law and either excuses one's conduct as being moral or accuses a person for his immoral actions.[39] As with Abimelech, his conscience did not allow him knowingly to violate Sarah. All people possess this capacity by virtue of their creation because God has written this knowledge on their hearts. Romans 2:14-15, therefore, fits into Paul's overall argument by explaining the way that God holds Gentiles accountable. Thus, 'For all who have sinned without the law will also perish without the law, and all who have sinned under the law will be judged by the law' (Rom. 2:12). This means, that since the Gentiles 'do by nature what

---

35. Von Rad, *Genesis*, 229; see also Waltke, *Genesis*, 285-86; Nahum Sarna, *Genesis*, Jewish Publication Society Torah Commentary (Philadelphia: Jewish Publication Society, 1989), 142-43.

36. Waltke, *Genesis*, 286; Sarna, *Genesis*, 143.

37. For other expositions of natural law in the Old Testament, see VanDrunen, *Divine Covenants*, 39-208, 263-414; Matthew Levering, *Biblical Natural Law: A Theocentric and Teleological Approach* (Oxford: Oxford University Press, 2012), 22-68, esp. 58-62.

38. Moo, *Romans*, 152; Barrett, *Romans*, 50; cf. Käsemann, *Romans*, 65-66.

39. Murray, *Romans*, 75; cf. VanDrunen, *Divine Covenants*, 253-57.

the law requires' (Rom. 2:14), what is written on their hearts has similar moral content of the Torah.[40]

Theological Analysis

The Adamic and Mosaic covenants are a dual delivery mechanism and explain how God holds all people accountable to the same moral standard at the final judgment, whether Jew or Gentile (Rom. 2:16).[41] This is what Reformed theologians argued and enshrined in several of their confessional documents.[42] Reformed theologians contend that God does not administrate His law apart from a covenant, though they may distinguish but not separate law and covenant. Conversely, the administration of God's law is covenantally binding. The next chapter explores Genesis 1:28 and 2:16-17 as the formal administration of the Adamic covenant. Read in context, the divine command prohibiting eating from the tree of knowledge bears all of the characteristics of an administration of covenantally binding law. Nevertheless, how does Romans 2:14-15 and the natural law inscribed on the heart function in connection with the covenant of works?

As noted in the introduction, Reformed theologians commonly appealed to Romans 2:14-15 as exegetical warrant for the existence of the covenant of works. One of the clearest examples of this trend appears in the Westminster Confession's treatment of the moral law, which intersects with the covenant of works. The Confession states: 'God gave to Adam a Law, as a Covenant of Works, by which he bound him, and all his posterity to personal, entire, exact, and perpetuall obedience, promised life upon the fulfilling, and threatened death upon the breach of it, and endued him with power and ability to keep it.'[43] The divines cite a web of texts to support this claim: Genesis 1:26-27; 2:17; Romans 2:14-15; 10:5; 5:12, 19;

---

40. Fitzmyer, *Romans*, 309; Schreiner, *Romans*, 122; VanDrunen, *Divine Covenants*, 251-53, 282-366.

41. Hahn, *Romans*, 26.

42. Irish Articles, §21; Savoy Declaration, VII.ii; Second London Confession, XIX.i.

43. *The Humble Advice of the Assembly of Divines, Now By Authority of Parliament Sitting at Westminster Concerning a Confession of Faith* (London: Company of Stationers, 1647), XIX.i.

Galatians 3:10, 12; Ecclesiastes 7:29; and Job 28:28. This series of texts presents the chief elements that appear in Paul's appeal to natural law as the means by which God judges Gentiles, those who are without the Torah. The divines appeal to Genesis 1:26-27 and 2:17 to note the supernaturally revealed commands of God to Adam.

Appended to the proscription against eating from the tree of knowledge is the sanction of death. The divines connect these Genesis texts with Paul's authoritative interpretation of Adam's fall, particularly Romans 5:12 and 19: 'sin came into the world through one man' and 'by the one man's disobedience many were constituted sinners' (trans. mine). The sin-death connection easily explains why Adam was subject to the sanction, as he was the one who violated God's command. It is not immediately evident, however, as to why all people suffer the consequence of death unless there is something that binds Adam and his progeny. In this case, Paul states that God κατεστάθησαν ('constituted') many as 'sinners.' God created a connection between Adam and his offspring and thus holds all people accountable for his infraction of the divine prohibition. The divines also appeal to Leviticus 18:5, 'do this and live,' which appears embedded in Galatians 3:12 and Romans 10:5 to demonstrate how the law functions. Specifically, obedience procures blessing and disobedience secures sanction. The divines believed that Adam had the moral capacity to obey, which appears in their citation of Ecclesiastes 7:29 and Job 28:28, 'God made man upright' and 'Behold, the fear of the Lord, that is wisdom, and to turn away from evil is understanding.' But the divines also acknowledged that God's positive command of dominion (be fruitful, multiply, fill the earth and subdue it) and His prohibition (do not eat from the tree of knowledge) were not the only means by which He established the covenant of works. Nestled in the string of biblical texts is Romans 2:14-15. God both gave Adam supernaturally revealed commands but also inscribed the requirements of the covenant of works on his heart.

Now, when I say that God inscribed the requirements of the covenant of works on Adam's heart, this statement necessitates an important qualification. In Paul's explanation of the moral law, he equates the heart-inscribed 'work of the law' with the demands of the Torah, particularly the Decalogue. The Decalogue does not contain the creation commands (the dominion mandate and the prohibition). These are the specific terms of the covenant of works. Instead, when I say that God inscribed the requirements of the covenant of works on Adam's heart, I mean that He recorded its general requirements. That is, God inscribed the necessity to live ethically and an essential morality, follow God's commands, and honor Him as the covenant Lord. This reading makes sense given what Paul states in Romans 1:18-32. That is, the work of the law is pre-Decalogue in nature. In broad terms, God writes the moral law on Adam's heart, which serves as the channel through which the specific commands function. The moral law is the superhighway on which the traffic of the dominion mandate and prohibition were supposed to travel. However, while one may distinguish the natural and supernatural law, we must remember that they inseparably work in concert both before and after the fall.

The divines follow Paul's argumentation in Romans 2:14-15 when they write about the connections between the pre- and post-fall delivery of the moral law: 'This law, after his fall, continued to be a perfect rule of righteousnesse, and, as such, was delivered by God on Mount Sinai, in Ten Commandments' (XIX.ii). They recognized the organic connection between the naturally revealed law, which functioned as a part of the covenant of works, and the supernaturally revealed law, which served as a part of the covenant of grace's Mosaic covenant. But the organic connection between the Adamic and Sinaitic forms of the moral law does not mean that God administered the covenant of works *simpliciter* in both contexts. In the Adamic context God administered the covenant of works in order to give Adam the opportunity to secure eternal life (WCF VII.ii). In the post-fall framework, the divines state that the moral law continued to serve as 'a perfect rule of righteousnesse.' That is, God intended the law to function as a *rule*, not as a *covenant*.[44] There is a distinct difference between these two

44. On this point see, e.g., John Colquhoun, *A Treatise on the Covenant of Works* (Edinburgh: Thomsons, Brothers, 1821), 15-17; idem, *A Treatise on the Law and the Gospel* (New York: Wiley & Long, 1835), 20, 36-37; James Buchanan, *The Doctrine of Justification: And Outline of Its History in the Church, and of Its Exposition*

categories. As a *covenant*, the law demands personal, perpetual, and perfect obedience in order for one to secure justification and eternal life. As a *rule*, however, the moral law serves as a guide for the Christian life that shows what conduct is pleasing to God as well as the misconduct that is displeasing to Him.

The divines capture this rule versus covenant distinction in the following statement:

> Although true Beleevers be not under the Law as a Covenant of Works, so to be thereby justified, or condemned, yet, it is of great use to them, as well as to others; in that, as a Rule of life informing them of the will of God, and their duty, it directs, and binds them to walk accordingly; discovering also the sinful pollutions of their nature, hearts, and lives; so as examining themselves thereby, they may come to a further conviction of, humiliation for, and hatred against sin; together with a clearer sight of the need they have of Christ, and the perfection of his obedience (XIX.vi).

This means that the covenant of works does not disappear or fade away with Adam's fall. The formula of 'perfect obedience yields eternal life' perpetually endures – the covenant of works reappears in the dark clouds of Sinai and reminds sinners of their need to obey God's law. The fact that sinners carry the law inscribed on their hearts is another permanent reminder – the conscience continues to excuse or accuse the sinner's conduct. The only thing that defangs the law as a covenant of works is one's relationship to Christ. If a person is in union with Christ and thus a participant in the covenant of grace, then the law is no longer a covenant of works by which to be justified or condemned. Only in Christ does the law become a rule of life. Hence the divines state that only 'true Beleevers' possess the law as a rule rather than a covenant.

Throughout the Bible various passages acknowledge the existence of the two paths to eternal life – either doing the law or believing in

---

from Scripture (Edinburgh: T & T Clark, 1867), 158, 287, 356; Robert Shaw, *An Exposition of the Confession of Faith of the Westminster Assembly of Divines*, 8th ed. (Glasgow: Blackie and Son, 1857), 198-99; William Cunningham, *Historical Theology: A Review of the Principal Doctrinal Discussions in the Christian Church Since the Apostolic Age*, vol. 2, 3rd (Edinburgh: T & T Clark, 1870), 88, 359-60.

Christ. As the subsequent chapter on Leviticus 18:5 explains, both Christ and Paul appeal to these two paths. A lawyer stood up and asked Jesus: 'Teacher, what shall I do to inherit eternal life?' Jesus prodded him with a question about what the law teaches, which the lawyer answered: 'You shall love the Lord your God with all your heart and with all your soul and with all your strength and with all your mind, and your neighbor as yourself.' Jesus then responded with Leviticus 18:5, 'You have answered correctly; do this, and you will live.' The apostle Paul quotes Leviticus 18:5 to the same effect when he writes: 'But the law is not of faith, rather "The one who does them shall live by them"' (Gal. 3:12).

Another place where Paul addresses the two principles, however, is in Romans 3:27: 'What then becomes of our boasting? It is excluded. By what kind of law? By a law of works? No, but by the law of faith.' Within the context of Romans 3, Paul emphasizes the point that only faith in Christ saves sinners: 'For we hold that one is justified by faith apart from works of the law' (Rom. 3:28). If faith alone saves sinners, then the sinner's works do not play a role in his justification. Correlatively, if God excludes the sinner's works, then he has no ground for boasting. Hence Paul's statements at the beginning of Romans 4: 'For if Abraham was justified by works, he has something to boast about, but not before God. For what does the Scripture say? "Abraham believed God, and it was counted to him as righteousness"' (Rom. 4:2-3; cf. Gen. 15:6). This is why Paul states that our boasting is excluded (Rom. 3:27). But important to note is why God excludes our boasting: 'By a law of works? No, but by the law of faith' (διὰ ποίου νόμου; τῶν ἔργων; οὐχί, ἀλλὰ διὰ νόμου πίστεως) (cf. Rom. 8:2). Here Paul uses his ever-elastic term νόμος, which in most contexts denotes *law*, but in this context refers to *principle, system, order,* or even *method of salvation*.[45] That is, the

---

45. For overviews of various interpretations, see Moo, *Romans*, 247-50; Cranfield, *Romans*, 219-20; and Jewett, *Romans*, 297. Many commentators agree that Paul uses the term νόμος in this non-literal sense (so Hodge, *Romans*, 100; Calvin, *Romans*, 78-79; Moo, *Romans*, 248-50; Fitzmyer, *Romans*, 363; Murray, *Romans*, 122-23; Melanchthon, *Romans*, 103; Käsemann, *Romans*, 103; Hahn, *Romans*, 49; Jewett, *Romans*, 297-98). Others believe it is a reference to the Torah (Schreiner, *Romans*, 201-02; Cranfield, *Romans*, 220).

principle of works admits boasting because the sinner secures his own redemption. Again, if Abraham was justified by works, he would have something to boast about. But the principle of faith, resting in the work of Christ, presents no opportunity for personal boasting. There is a works νόμος and a faith νόμος in a post-fall world, but in the pre-fall world there was only a works νόμος, and God both revealed this principle through His supernaturally administered commands to Adam and by the naturally revealed law inscribed on his heart.

In the Westminster Standards the divines observe a second idea regarding the relationship between the naturally and supernaturally revealed law. Namely, while the natural and supernatural law have similar content, the heart-inscribed law and the Torah are not exactly the same. The Westminster Shorter Catechism presents the following series of questions and answers that once again demonstrates the organic links between the Adamic and Sinaitic covenants, but there is an important qualification regarding their relationship:

Q. What did God at first reveal to man as the rule for his Obedience?

A. The rule that God first revealed to man for his Obedience, was, the Moral Law (Rom. 2:14-15; 10:5).

Q. Where is the Moral Law summarily comprehended?

A. The Moral Law is summarily comprehended in the Ten Commandments (Deut. 10:4).

Q. What is the sum of the Ten Commandments?

A. The sum of the Ten Commandments is, to Love the Lord our God, with all our heart, with all our soul, with all our strength, and with all our minde: and our neighbor as our selves (Matt. 22:37-40).[46]

---

46. *The Humble Advice of the Assembly of Divines Now by Authority of Parliament Sitting at Westminster, Concerning a Shorter Catechism* (London: J. F., 1648), qq. 41-42. Note, I cite the original edition of the catechism, though it does not have question numbers. I employ the traditional numbering system for ease of reference to subsequent numbered editions.

These three questions capture the same nexus between the natural and supernatural law. The divines once again appeal to Romans 2:14-15 to substantiate the existence of the moral law in its natural form and coordinate it with Romans 10:5 (Lev. 18:5) to explain that its principle (νόμος) is works, or obedience.

But when they draw the moral law's connections to Sinai, they add a necessary qualification to distinguish the content of the natural versus supernatural forms: the moral law is *summarily comprehended* in the Decalogue. In other words, the divines do not claim that the moral law is precisely the same in the Adamic and Sinaitic covenants. The moral law can be quite expansive and thus the Decalogue is a summary of its contents. Conversely, the Torah has other legal dimensions that go beyond the scope of the natural law, such as the judicial and ceremonial laws. This qualification, I believe, echoes the distinction that Paul employs in Romans 2:14-15 when he states that the Gentiles do not have the Torah but nevertheless do what it requires; they show that the work of the Torah (τὸ ἔργον τοῦ νόμου) is written on the heart. The *Torah* versus the *work of the Torah* captures the distinction between the naturally and supernaturally revealed law, which the divines echo when they explain that the Decalogue is a summary of the moral law. The divines appeal to Christ's summary of the law, which is the same summary Luke presents (10:26-28) in Christ's response to the lawyer's question about eternal life. The moral law, therefore, appears in both natural (Adamic) and supernatural forms (Mosaic). As Geerhardus Vos (1862-1949) notes, 'At Sinai it was not the "bare" law that was given, but a reflection of the covenant of works revived, as it were, in the interests of the covenant of grace continued at Sinai.' There is an organic link between the natural and supernatural law because, in Vos' analysis, 'The natural relation in which man stands to God and this just claim made by the Creator, remain valid, also at each later stage and are presupposed in each act, including the covenant of grace.'[47]

---

47. Geerhardus Vos, 'The Doctrine of the Covenant in Reformed Theology,' in *Redemptive History and Biblical Interpretation: The Shorter Writings of Geerhardus Vos*, ed. Richard B. Gaffin, Jr. (Phillipsburg, NJ: P & R, 1980), 255.

Conclusion

Romans 2:14-15 is a vital exegetical pillar for the covenant of works. Paul's affirmation that God has written the law on the hearts of all people confirms the universally binding nature of God's creation order. When God gave Adam the commands to be fruitful, fill and subdue the earth and the prohibition not to eat from the tree of knowledge, they worked in concert with the naturally revealed law. Adam by nature knew the basic requirements of God's law; by virtue of his creation in God's image Adam knew that he had to submit to his covenant Lord. By nature he knew that obedience would yield a reward. His conscience would excuse or accuse him in his conduct. In the words of James Ussher (1581-1656), the law of God was 'chiefly written in his heart at his creation, and partly also uttered in his eare in Paradise.'[48] The natural law and supernaturally revealed commands constituted the legal terms of the covenant of works.

---

48. James Ussher, *A Body of Divinitie, or The Summe and Substance of Christian Religion* (London: Thomas Downes and George Badger, 1645), 124.

~: II.2 :~

In the Day that You Eat
(Gen. 2:16-17)

Introduction

*W*hen God created Adam and Eve He placed them in the garden and spoke of the possibility of great blessing but also of the risk of curse: 'And the LORD God commanded the man, saying, "You may surely eat of every tree of the garden, but of the tree of the knowledge of good and evil you shall not eat, for in the day that you eat of it you shall surely die"' (Gen. 2:16-17).[1] Adam and Eve had a head-on collision with God's command and plunged the world into sin and death. The prohibition against eating from the tree of knowledge was the occasion for Adam and Eve's sin. For this reason, early modern Reformed theologians appealed to this verse as a *locus classicus* for the covenant of works. But in the twentieth century Reformed theologians were not persuaded by the claims of their forefathers. John Murray (1898-1975) famously rejected the doctrine of the covenant of works and one of the chief reasons was that the word *covenant* did not appear in Genesis 1–3; the term made its first appearance in Genesis 6:18 where God made a covenant of Noah.[2] In Murray's assessment, since the

---

1. Portions of this chapter are drawn from J. V. Fesko, *Death in Adam, Life in Christ: The Doctrine of Imputation* (Fearn: Mentor, 2016), 233-70.

2. John Murray, 'Adamic Administration,' in *Collected Writings of John Murray*, vol. 2 (Edinburgh: Banner of Truth, 1977), 47-59, esp. 48.

term was absent from Genesis 1–3, the doctrine was nonexistent. While Murray's observation is correct—the term *covenant* does not appear in Genesis 1–3—he nevertheless operated with a different hermeneutical methodology than his early modern counterparts. The difference appears in the way that some early modern Reformed theologians appealed to Genesis 2:16-17 as an exegetical support for the covenant of works.

Francis Turretin (1623-1687), for example, cites Genesis 2:16-17 but he correlates it with other texts from the rest of the canon to explain how the divine command functions (cf. Deut. 27:26; Ezek. 20:11; Matt. 19:17; Gal. 3:12).[3] Turretin's strategy was different from Murray's method. Turretin and other early modern Reformed theologians read Genesis 2:16-17 in the broader context of the canon, especially the Pentateuch, not merely the narrow context of Genesis 1–3.[4] Genesis 1–3 is not an island; this patch of Scripture is part of a greater canonical whole. We do not come to the creation narrative apart from this broader context. Israelites wandering in the wilderness on the heels of exodus and the Sinai covenant would have heard the Genesis 2:16-17 prohibition in a very different way than Murray's interpretative method suggests.

The thesis of this chapter is that Genesis 2:16-17 constitutes a part of the formal establishment of the covenant of works. God's creative acts constitute the material establishment of the covenant of works. Adam knew by nature what God's law required and the blessings that would result from his obedience. But the communication of the divine prohibition in concert with the commands to be fruitful, fill the earth, and subdue it (Gen. 1:28) comprised the

---

3. Francis Turretin, *Institutes of Elenctic Theology*, trans. George Musgrave Giger, ed. James T. Dennison Jr. (Phillipsburg, NJ: P & R, 1992-97), VIII.iii.7.

4. See, e.g., John Downame, *The Summe of Sacred Divinitie* (London: William Stansby, 1625?), I.xv (pp. 225-26); Edward Leigh, *A Treatise of the Divine Promises. In Five Bookes* (London: George Millar, 1633), II.i (p. 64); James Ussher, *A Body of Divinitie, or The Summe and Substance of Christian Religion* (London: Tho. Downes and Geo. Badger, 1645), 125; Samuel Rutherford, *The Covenant of Life Opened: Or, A Treatise of the Covenant of Grace* (Edinburgh: Robert Broun, 1654), I.ix (p. 50); Anthony Burgess, *Vindiciae Legis: or, A Vindication of the Morall Law and the Covenants* (London: Thomas Underhill, 1647), 233.

formal establishment of the covenant of works. One can distinguish the material and formal causes of the institution of the Adamic covenant, but they cannot be separated because one cannot function without the other. Doctors can distinguish heart and lungs and the different functions they serve but human beings cannot exist apart from either. In the words of James Ussher (1581-1656), the law of God was chiefly written in Adam's heart at his creation, and partly also uttered in his ear in paradise.[5] Or in the words of the Irish Articles (1615), 'Man being at the beginning created according to the image of God (which consisted especially in the wisdom of his mind and the true holiness of his free will), had the covenant of the law ingrafted in his heart, whereby God did promise unto him everlasting life upon condition that he performed entire and perfect obedience unto His Commandments, according to that measure of strength wherewith he was endued in his creation, and threatened death unto him if he did not perform the same' (art. XXI). The naturally and supernaturally revealed law worked in concert as the legal terms of the covenant of works in the pre-fall context.

To demonstrate this thesis, this chapter proceeds along the following lines. First, it explains the positive and negative commands, Genesis 1:28 and 2:16-17, as comprising the blessings and curses of God's interaction with Adam. Second, the chapter examines these blessings and curses in the broader canonical context, especially within the framework of the Pentateuch. In short, Genesis 1–3 should not be read in isolation from the rest of the Pentateuch but rather these three chapters form the first part of an inclusio that finds its counterpart in Deuteronomy 28–34. Adam's ejection from paradise anticipates Israel's expulsion from the promised land – the two sections mutually inform one another. Third, the chapter concludes with some observations regarding the significance of Genesis 2:16-17 as a proof text for the covenant of works.

Be Fruitful and Do Not Eat

As the previous chapter explained, there is a close relationship between the covenant of works and the *imago Dei*. God prototypically

---

5. Ussher, *Body of Divinitie*, 124.

inscribed His law on Adam's heart, a reflection of His own moral character. By virtue of his creation in God's image, Adam knew right from wrong and the necessity of obedience. In concert with this natural revelation, God also supernaturally revealed a positive command: 'And God blessed them. And God said to them, "Be fruitful and multiply and fill the earth and subdue it, and have dominion over the fish of the sea and over the birds of the heavens and over every living thing that moves on the earth"' (Gen. 1:28). We should not separate humanity's image-bearing from the command to exercise dominion over the earth. God's command functions as an organic explanation of the chief elements of what it means to be an image bearer.[6] The chief element of bearing God's image is ruling over the creation, but humanity's rule was not for an indefinite period of time – it had a terminus, a goal. They were supposed to subdue the earth and fill it, tasks that imply a necessary terminus. In theological terms, there was an eschatological goal to their labors, which means there is telos that is inherent to humanity's image bearing. This eschatological aspect finds its origins in God's Sabbath-rest at the conclusion of His own creation work (Gen. 2:1-4). As God works and rests, so creatures made in His image work and rest. A subsequent chapter in Part III will address this point in greater detail.

Important are the parallels between God's creative activity and Adam's exercise of dominion over the creation. Adam initially exercised dominion over the creation when he named all of the animals (Gen. 2:18-19). In the ancient Near East, to name something was to have authority over it. Adam's kingly activity points back to God's own authoritative naming activity.[7] God spoke the cosmos into existence. He said, 'Let there be light,' and there was light. He called the light *day* and the darkness *night* (Gen. 1:3-4). God exercised dominion over the creation by virtue of His kingly fiats, but these were not bare utterances of raw creative power but were ultimately *covenantal* declarations. God speaks

---

6. David VanDrunen, *Divine Covenants and Moral Order: A Biblical Theology of Natural Law* (Grand Rapids: Eerdmans, 2014), 48-50; also J. Richard Middleton, *The Liberating Image: The Imago Dei in Genesis 1* (Grand Rapids: Brazos, 2005), 50-55.

7. Graeme Auld, '*Imago Dei* in Genesis: Speaking in the Image of God,' *ExpT* 116 (2005): 259-62; VanDrunen, *Divine Covenants*, 51.

through the prophet Jeremiah and states: 'Thus says the LORD: If you can break my covenant with the day and my covenant with the night, so that day and night will not come at their appointed time, then I will reject the offspring of Jacob and David my servant and will not choose one of his offspring to rule over the offspring of Abraham, Isaac, and Jacob' (Jer. 33:25-26). God announces through the prophet that His covenant fidelity to Israel and David, especially in the covenant promise to give David an heir to sit upon his throne and rule over Israel (2 Sam. 7:14ff), is as strong as His covenant with the day and the night – covenantal events that first unfolded in the opening verses of the Bible.

Other instances of the convergence of creation and covenant occur in Psalm 148:5-6: 'For he commanded [צוה] and they were created. And he established them forever and ever; he gave a decree [חק], and it shall not pass away.' The parallel between *command* and *decree* points to the fact that God's verbal creative acts parallel the covenantal administration of His laws. Similar parallels occur in Psalm 147:18-19 with a seamless transition from creation to covenant: 'He sends out his word [דברו], and melts them; he makes his wind blow and the waters flow. He declares his word to Jacob, his statues and rules [חקיו ומשפטיו] to Israel.'[8] When God issues commands, He does so as a king, as Lord of His covenantally binding Word. In every command there is a tacit covenantal obligation, whether in the case of God's fiat to create light and darkness or in His commands to Adam and Eve to be fruitful and subdue the earth.[9]

But the positive command was not the only Word that God delivered to Adam. He also supernaturally revealed a prohibition: 'And the LORD God commanded the man, saying, "You may surely eat of every tree of the garden, but of the tree of the knowledge of good and evil you shall not eat, for in the day that you eat of it you shall surely die"' (Gen. 2:16-17). If God blessed Adam and Eve through the administration of the dominion mandate, then its counterbalancing

---

8. Middleton, *Liberating Image*, 67.

9. Kevin Vanhoozer, *First Theology: God, Scripture, and Hermeneutics* (Downers Grove: InterVarsity Press, 2002), 200-01.

side was the specter of curse, in this case the prospect of death for violating God's command.[10] God bound His command to the tree of knowledge. This tree did not have magical properties that imparted death to the one who devoured its fruit but was a visible sign and seal of God's command. What God's Word was to his ears, the tree was to Adam's eyes. In fact, the parallels between the description of God's law and the tree of knowledge suggest this connection. The law of God makes the simple wise and enlightens the eyes (Ps. 19:7-8). These are the very characteristics that drew Eve to eat from the forbidden fruit: 'So when the woman saw that the tree was good for food, and that it was a *delight to the eyes*, and that the tree was to be desired *to make one wise*, she took of its fruit and ate' (Gen. 3:6; emphasis).[11] The trees of the garden, therefore, functioned in the same fashion as signs of the covenant, such as the rainbow, circumcision, or the Sabbath (Gen. 9:13-16; 17:9-14; Exod. 31:13).

The form of the prohibition presents another important element that ties it to divine covenantal activity, particularly with the lexeme: 'You shall not eat' (לא תאכל). The negative particle 'You shall not' (לא) followed by the imperfect form of the verb 'eat' (תאכל) is the common pattern for the prohibitions of the Decalogue. For example: 'You shall not murder' (Exod. 20:13). In addition to these syntactical features, a motive clause immediately follows the proscription: 'For [כי] in the day that you eat of it you shall surely die.' A prohibition + motive clause appears in the second, third, and fourth commandments (Exod. 20:5, 7, 11).[12] The command against eating from the tree of knowledge has the same form as God's later covenantal laws.

Another aspect of the prohibition that points towards the presence of a covenant is the penalty, namely, death: 'For in the

---

10. Meredith G. Kline, *Genesis: A Commentary* (Peabody, MA: Hendrickson, 2016), 20.

11. D. J. A. Clines, 'The Tree of Knowledge and the Law of Yahweh,' *VT* 24 (1974): 8-14.

12. Gordon J. Wenham, *Genesis 1-15*, WBC, vol. 1 (Dallas, TX: Word Books, 1987), 67; B. Gemser, 'The Importance of the Motive Clause in Old Testament Law,' *VT Supplement* 1 (1953): 50-66; cf. Umberto Cassuto, *A Commentary on the Book of Genesis: Part One* (Jerusalem: Magnes Press, 1998), 124.

day that you eat of it you shall surely die.' Two factors place this consequence within the conceptual orbit of the covenant: (1) that it constitutes the counterbalance to blessing, and (2) that elsewhere in the Old Testament death is covenantal curse. Genesis 1:28 characterizes the dominion mandate as a blessing: 'And God blessed them' (ויברך אתם אלהים). And death most certainly comprises covenant curse in other parts of the Old Testament: 'I call heaven and earth to witness against you today, that I have set before you life and death, blessing and curse' (Deut. 30:19). This verse places life and death in parallel with blessing and curse. The pair of blessing and curse appears as the dual outcomes of God's covenantal activity (cf. Gen 12:3; 27:29; Num. 24:9). This blessing-curse pattern prominently appears in the re-administration of the Mosaic covenant before Israel entered the promised land:

> See, I am setting before you today a blessing and a curse: the blessing, if you obey the commandments of the LORD your God, which I command you today, and the curse, if you do not obey the commandments of the LORD your God, but turn aside from the way that I am commanding you today, to go after other gods that you have not known. And when the LORD your God brings you into the land that you are entering to take possession of it, you shall set the blessing on Mount Gerizim and the curse on Mount Ebal (Deut. 11:26-29).

God sets forth blessing and curse, contingent on obedience versus disobedience; this is the same formal dynamic that appears in the creation command and prohibition. If obedient, Adam would have known the blessings of the dominion mandate, or if disobedient he would experience the curse of death (cf. Exod. 20:7; 31:14; Lev. 24:16).[13]

One last factor points towards covenantal activity in Genesis 1–3, namely, the revelation of God's name, *Yahweh Elohim* in conjunction with covenant curse (Gen. 2:16; cf. Gen. 2:4; Exod. 3:14ff). Note the connection between covenant, curse, and the divine name in Deuteronomy 29:12 (MT 11, trans. mine), which states:

---

13. Bruce K. Waltke, *Genesis: A Commentary* (Grand Rapids: Zondervan, 2001), 87.

לעברך בברית יהוה אלהיך ובאלתו אשר יהוה אלהיך כרת עמך היום

So that you may enter the covenant of the LORD your God and into his oath-curse which the LORD your God has made with you this day (cf. 1 Sam. 14:24; 1 Kings 8:31; 2 Chron. 6:22).

In this one statement we find the covenant name of God, the terms for covenant (ברית), making a covenant (כרת), and oath-curse (אלה).[14] An Israelite would not hesitate to think that Adam was in anything but a covenantal relationship with God given the presence of God's covenantal name along with a threatened curse of death for violating His command. This would especially be the case in light of the parallels between God's command not to eat of the tree of knowledge and the similarly worded commands of the Decalogue, which when combined with the covenant name, point in the direction of a covenantal relationship (Exod. 20:1-17, esp. cf. Exod. 20:2; Gen. 2:16).

Therefore, within the immediate context of Genesis 1–3, there are six factors that signal the presence of a covenant:

1. God gave Adam and Eve a blessing with the administration of the dominion mandate (Gen. 1:28).

2. Adam's naming activity paralleled God's own covenantal creative activity as he exercised dominion over the creation.

3. The prohibition against eating from the tree of knowledge is the counterbalance to the blessing and exhibits the covenantal consequences of blessing and curse, life and death that appear in later parts of the Pentateuch.

4. The prohibition has the same syntactical form as the prohibitions of the Decalogue, the heart of the Mosaic covenant.

5. The presence of the tree of knowledge (and tree of life) function in similar fashion to other signs of God's covenants.

6. The narrative invokes the covenant name of God, *Yahweh Elohim*, as the preface to the divine prohibition and threat of curse, which anticipates later covenant-curse formulations.

---

14. Anne Marie Kitz, *Cursed Are You! The Phenomenology of Cursing in Cuneiform and Hebrew Texts* (Winona Lake: Eisenbrauns, 2014), 13, 26-27; cf. HALOT, I:51.

These six elements in and of themselves represent sufficient grounds to conclude that there was a covenant between God and Adam. But there is greater corroborating evidence when one examines Genesis 1:28 and 2:16-17 in the broader context of the Pentateuch.

The Broader Context

As noted in the introduction, Genesis 1–3 and Deuteronomy 28–34 form an inclusio.[15] The creation narrative should never be severed from the rest of the canon, especially the closing chapters of the Pentateuch. If the Mosaic covenant provides a benchmark for covenantal activity, then all signs point to the presence of covenant in Genesis 1–3. To recognize that Adam and Eve were in a covenant has precedent in ancient Jewish tradition: 'The Lord created human beings out of earth .... He bestowed knowledge upon them, and allotted to them the law of life. He established with them an eternal covenant, and revealed to them his decrees' (Sirach 17:1, 11-12). In fact, patristic theologians such as Augustine (354-430) gleaned the concept of an Adamic covenant from Sirach's interpretation of Genesis 2:16-17: 'All living beings become old like a garment, for the covenant from of old is, "You must die!"' (Sirach 14:17).[16] Sirach claimed that Genesis 2:17's threatened sanction of death was evidence of the existence of a covenant.[17] Another example of Jewish claims of a covenant in Eden appears in *Genesis Rabbah*, a rabbinic commentary. The commentary argues that Adam's failure to keep God's commandment and his subsequent exile foreshadow Israel's similar failures. *Genesis Rabbah* 19:9 explains:

> It is written, 'But they are like a man [Adam], they have transgressed the covenant' (Hosea 6:7) 'They are like a man,' specifically, 'like the first man.' [We shall now compare the story of the first man in Eden with the story of Israel in its land.] 'In the case of the first man, I brought him into the garden of Eden, I commanded him, he

---

15. Seth D. Postell, *Adam as Israel: Genesis 1–3 as the Introduction to the Torah and Tanakh* (Cambridge: James Clarke and Co., 2012), 3-4; also Terence E. Fretheim, *The Pentateuch* (Nashville, TN: Abingdon, 1996), 53-63, esp. 56-58.

16. Augustine, *City of God*, XVI.xxvii, in NPNF², II:326.

17. John G. Snaith, *Ecclesiasticus: or The Wisdom of Jesus Son of Sirach* (Cambridge: Cambridge University Press, 1974), 74-75.

violated my commandment, I judged him to be sent away and driven out .... So too in the case of his descendants, I brought them into the Land of Israel, I commanded them, they violated my commandment, I judged them to be sent out and driven away.'[18]

Such inter-testamental and post-biblical comparisons between Israel and Adam originate from the prophetic intra-canonical exegesis of the creation narrative: 'But like Adam they [Israel] transgressed the covenant' (Hosea 6:7a).[19] A subsequent chapter addresses Hosea 6:7 in greater detail to substantiate this claim.

Nevertheless, hermeneutically, one must therefore avoid reading Genesis 1–3 in isolation from the rest of the Old Testament, but especially Deuteronomy. Israelite readers knowledgeable of the Pentateuch, evident by the Jewish sources cited above, read the creation narrative within the context of Israel's covenantal charter, Deuteronomy, and observed many parallels between Eden, Sinai, and Gerazim and Ebal.[20] In addition to foreshadowing the last Adam, God's faithful son (Rom. 5:14), Genesis 1–3 anticipates Israel's failure to keep the Mosaic covenant and their future exile from the promised land. Both Adam and Israel point to Jesus, the

---

18. *Genesis Rabbah: The Judaic Commentary to the Book of Genesis*, trans. Jacob Neusner, 3 vols. (Atlanta: Scholars Press, 1985), 19.9 (vol. I, 208-09); also Postell, *Adam as Israel*, 6-7; Carlos Bovell, 'Genesis 3:21: The History of Israel in a Nutshell,' *ExpT* 115 (2004): 361-66.

19. Byron G. Curtis, 'Hosea 6:7 and Covenant-Breaking like/at Adam,' in *The Law Is Not of Faith: Essays on Works and Grace in the Mosaic Covenant*, eds. Bryan D. Estelle, J. V. Fesko, and David VanDrunen (Phillipsburg: P & R, 2009), 170-209.

20. On the inter-textual symbiotic relationship between Genesis 1–3 and Deuteronomy see, e.g., Mary Douglas, *Purity and Danger: An Analysis of the Concepts of Pollution and Taboo* (London: Routledge & Kegan Paul, 1966), 41-57, esp. 55ff; T. Stordalen, *Echoes of Eden: Genesis 2–3 and Symbolism of the Eden Garden in Biblical Hebrew Literature* (Leuven: Peeters, 2000), 33; Trygve N. D. Mettinger, *The Eden Narrative: A Literary and Religio-Historical Study of Genesis 2–3* (Winona Lake: Eisenbrauns, 2007), xii, 49-50, 57; John Van Steters, *Prologue to History: The Yahwehist as Historian in Genesis* (Louisville: Westminster John Knox, 1992), 127-29; Norbert Lohfink, *The Christian Meaning of the Old Testament* (Milwaukee: Bruce Publishing Co., 1968), 58-62. Note, one need not adopt the higher text-critical stance of commentators who posit a late-date for the Genesis material in order to accept the interpretive relationship between Genesis 1–3 and the rest of the Pentateuch, especially Deuteronomy.

last Adam – the only one in a post-fall world who completed Adam's failed work. Adam's failure to subdue the seditious serpent, his temptation, covenant apostasy, and subsequent exile is Israel's story in miniature.[21] Adam's apostasy and exile in Genesis 1–3 forms an inclusio with Israel's foretold apostasy and exile in Deuteronomy 32:1-43. This sets up God's work in the 'last days' where He will rectify Adam's and Israel's failures (Deut. 30:6).

The following six details support the claim that Genesis 1–3 must be read within the context of the Pentateuch:[22]

1. Genesis 1–3 was literarily composed in such a manner as to anticipate the Mosaic covenant.

   a. The pattern of creation, fall, and restoration in Genesis 1–3 anticipates the preparations for the construction of the tabernacle (Exod. 25–31) and the fall and restoration of Israel after the golden calf incident (Exod. 32–34).[23]

   b. The structure of the curses and their effects on the serpent, woman, and man (Gen. 3:14-19) anticipate the Purity Code of Leviticus 11–15.

   c. The language used to describe Adam and Eve's retreat was composed in the light of God's theophany on Mt Sinai and Israel's withdrawal (cf. Gen. 3:8; Exod. 20:18-21). Just as God covered Adam and Eve's nakedness (Gen. 3:21), God concludes the administration of the law with a command to cover their nakedness in worship (Exod. 20:26).

---

21. Postell, *Adam as Israel*, 3-4, 130.

22. Postell, *Adam as Israel*, 108-19.

23. See also Gordon J. Wenham, 'Sanctuary Symbolism in the Garden of Eden Story,' in *I Studied Inscriptions from Before the Flood: Ancient Near Eastern, Literary and Linguistic Approaches to Genesis 1-11*, eds. Richard S. Hess and David Toshio Tsumura (Winona Lake, IN: Eisenbrauns, 1994), 399-404; Peter J. Kearney, 'Creation and Liturgy: The P Redaction of Ex 25-40,' *ZAW* 89 (1977): 375-87, esp. 375-78; Moshe Weinfeld, 'Sabbath, Temple and Enthronement of the Lord,' in *Mélanges Bibliques et Orientaux en l'honneur de M. Henri Cazelles*, ed. A. Caquot and M. Delcor (Neukirchen-Vluyn: Neukirchener Verlag, 1981), 501-12; *Midrash Rabbah, Numbers*, vol. 1 (London: The Soncino Press, 1983), Num. 12:13 (pp. 483-84); G. K. Beale, *The Temple and the Church's Mission: A Biblical Theology of the Dwelling Place of God* (Downers Grove: IVP Academic, 2004), 31-38.

    d. The woman's sin foreshadows the tenth commandment (cf. Gen. 3:6; Deut. 5:21; Exod. 20:17).

2. The vocabulary that describes Adam's paradisiacal responsibilities (to tend and keep the garden) also appear in the description of the priestly duties (cf. Gen. 2:15; Num. 3:7-8; 4:23-24, 26).[24]

3. As noted above, the prohibition against eating the fruit of the tree of knowledge bears the same characteristics as the Decalogue (cf. Gen. 2:16-17; Exod. 20:1-17).

4. The theme of food features prominently in both portions of the Pentateuch. The dietary restriction of Genesis 2:16-17 foreshadows the laws of Leviticus 11. For example, the fact that Eve told the serpent that they were instructed not to touch the fruit from the tree of knowledge is the same language that appears in Leviticus 11:8 and Deuteronomy 14:8. These are the only three places in the Pentateuch where the terms 'do not eat' and 'do not touch' appear together.

5. Both Adam and Israel contingently dwell in their respective locations. God told Adam to obey, receive blessing, and thus live (Gen. 1:28; 3:24). Conversely, he was told if he disobeyed he would suffer exile and death (Gen. 2:16-17). Israel was told they would enjoy long life in the land if they obeyed, and contrariwise they would suffer exile and death if they disobeyed. Leviticus 18:5 summarizes 'the obedience yields life' formula for both Adam and Israel.

6. Adam's disobedience resulted in curse (Gen. 3:14-19), exile (Gen. 3:22-24), and death, versus similar consequences for the violation of the Mosaic covenant: curse (Deut. 28:15-68), exile (Deut. 28:36, 41, 64, 68), and death (Deut. 28:45, 48, 53-57, 63).

These thematic and terminological connections stand out prominently and confirm that Genesis 1–3 must be read in the context of the Pentateuch in order to produce a thick reading of the text.

---

24. See also, Wenham, 'Sanctuary Symbolism,' 401.

A quarantined reading of Genesis 1–3 misses the rich texture and depth the rest of the Pentateuch provides. And in particular, divorcing Genesis 1–3 from the Pentateuch wounds the ligaments that connect these opening chapters to the doctrine of the covenant. Each of these six points grow from the covenantal soil of Exodus, Leviticus, Numbers, and Deuteronomy.

One of the strongest pieces of evidence that confirms covenantal activity in Genesis 1–3 is the thematic and terminological links with the ending of Deuteronomy. These connections form the two bookends of an inclusio. The inclusio involves Genesis 1–3 and Deuteronomy 28–34 and presents the following five points of contact:[25]

1. There are clusters of terms that are peculiar to Genesis 1–3 and Deuteronomy 32–33 that do not appear anywhere else in the Old Testament. For example, the following terms only appear in Genesis 1:1–2:4 and Deuteronomy 32 and 33:

   a. Heaven and earth (ארץ and שמים) (Gen 1:1, 15, 17, 20, 26, 28, 30; 2:1, 4; Deut. 32:1)

   b. Void / waste (תהו) (Gen. 1:2; Deut. 32:10)

   c. Hover (רחף) (Gen. 1:2; Deut. 32:11)

   d. Vegetation and plants // grass and herbs (עשב and דשא) (Gen. 1:11, 12; Deut. 32:2)

   e. Sea creature // serpent (תנין) (Gen. 1:21; Deut. 32:33).

2. Genesis 1–11 and Deuteronomy 29–34 present a theologically pessimistic outlook on human beings in general and Israel more specifically. Like Israel, God places Adam in a favorable environment, which is contingent on obedience to law with death and exile as the threatened and fulfilled punishment.[26] Genesis 6:5, for example, notes that God saw 'that every intention [כל־יצר] of the thoughts of [man's] heart

---

25. Postell, *Adam as Israel*, 136-48.

26. Joseph Blenkinsopp, 'P and J in Genesis 1:1–11:26: An Alternative Hypothesis,' in *Fortunate Are the Eyes that See*, ed. Astrid B. Beck, et al. (Grand Rapids: Eerdmans, 1995), 1-15, esp. 4, 7.

was only evil continually.' This is the same type of evaluation that God makes of Israel: 'For I know what they are inclined [יצרו] to do even today, before I have brought them into the land that I swore to give' (Deut. 31:21; cf. Deut. 31:20, 27-29). There are only three evaluations of the intentions of the human heart in the Pentateuch (Gen. 6:5; 8:21; and Deut. 31:21).

3. Genesis 1 opens and Deuteronomy 34 closes the Pentateuch with an emphasis on unconquered land. The unsubdued creation stood before Adam (Gen. 1:28) and the undefeated promised land lay before Israel (Deut. 34:1-5).

4. Both Genesis 3 and Deuteronomy 34 end with the problem of exile. God cast Adam and Eve out of the garden (Gen. 3:23-24), and Deuteronomy ends with the prospects of Israel's impending exile and Moses' banishment from the promised land (Deut. 34:5).

5. At the macro level, a number of commentators have noted that the Pentateuch is arranged in such a manner to place Leviticus at the center, flanked by the inner ring of Exodus and Numbers, and the outer ring of Genesis and Deuteronomy. Both Genesis and Deuteronomy close with a blessing of the twelve tribes (Gen. 49 // Deut. 33) followed by the deaths of Jacob and Moses respectively and their burials (Gen. 50 // Deut. 34). Moses and Jacob recognize that the days were drawing near for them to die (Gen. 47:29; Deut. 31:14) and they will both 'lie with their fathers' (Gen. 47:30; Deut. 31:16). Both men call a new leader (Joseph and Joshua respectively) after their deaths (Gen. 47:29; Deut. 31:14). Both death scenes mention the land of Canaan (Gen. 49:30; Deut. 32:49). Jacob dies in exile and Moses dies in exile.[27]

---

27. Christophe Nihan, *From Priestly Torah to Pentateuch: A Study in the Composition of the Book of Leviticus* (Tübingen: Mohr Siebeck, 2007), 69-76; John H. Sailhamer, *The Pentateuch as Narrative* (Grand Rapids: Zondervan, 1995), 35-37; Hans Ulrich Steymans, 'The Blessings in Genesis 49 and Deuteronomy 33: Awareness of Intertextuality,' in *South African Perspectives on the Pentateuch*

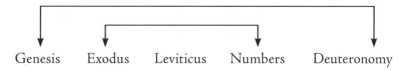

Genesis   Exodus   Leviticus   Numbers   Deuteronomy

These foregoing five points do not prove the existence of an Adamic covenant. Rather, they demonstrate that Genesis is an organic part of the Pentateuch and that no one book was supposed to be isolated from the other four books.

In other words, critics such as Murray read Genesis 1–3 as if the rest of the Pentateuch did not exist, which is ironically similar to higher text-critical readings. They bypass the literary context of the first three chapters and read it in chronological succession as if the reader was not supposed to peer over the wall of the third chapter to see what follows. Hence, if the term *covenant* does not appear in the first three chapters, then the idea must not exist. Yet, if the above surveyed connections mean anything, it is that the Pentateuch is a literary unit. Rather than five individual books, the Pentateuch is one book with five interconnected chapters. Any one part should be read in the light of the whole. Israelites that were tuned in to the frequencies of the Pentateuch would have noted the links between the various parts, in this case, the inclusio of Genesis 1–3 and Deuteronomy 29–34. They would have noted the similarities between Adam's and Israel's circumstances, and they would have placed the various pieces of Adamic furniture within a covenantal house, the natural domicile of God's interaction with Israel and one of the dominant themes of the Pentateuch.

Conclusion

When God issued His command and prohibition, they were not a manifestation of the bare law but rather came clothed in the garments of covenant. Early modern Reformed theologians were right to read Genesis 2:16-17 within the larger matrix of the Pentateuch. They recognized the connections between the implicit references to covenant and their explicit appearances in

---

Between Synchrony and Diachrony, eds. Jurie le Roux and Eckart Otto (London: T & T Clark, 2007), 71-89, esp. 72, 73-78; Fretheim, *Pentateuch*, 57.

later portions of the Bible. The pairing of blessing and curse, the similarities between the prohibition of eating from the tree of knowledge and the Decalogue's proscriptions, and the signs of the trees of life and knowledge all pointed towards the existence of an Adamic covenant. In addition to these flags, this chapter has presented other indicators that confirm the early modern contention that Adam and God were in covenant. But the conclusion that there was an Adamic covenant was not the opinion of sixteenth and seventeenth century Reformed theologians alone, but a common view among the Jews of the inter-testamental as well as post-apostolic periods, evident from the statements from Sirach and *Genesis Rabbah*. In sum, like the chief rule of real estate (location, location, location), context, context, context is the principal maxim of hermeneutics. In this case, the context of the Pentateuch is all-determinative for a proper covenantal reading of Genesis 2:16-17. The context confirms that God and Adam were in a covenantal relationship.

~: II.3 :~

Do This and Live
(Lev. 18:5)

Introduction

*L*eviticus 18:5 is perhaps the text most commonly appealed to in support of the covenant of works, but in the contemporary period it is probably one of the least understood.[1] The text states, 'You shall therefore keep my statutes and my rules; if a person does them, he shall live by them: I am the LORD' (Lev. 18:5). But how can a text embedded in the Mosaic covenant speak to the pre-fall Adamic covenant? If God clearly administered the Mosaic covenant in the wake of His gracious redemption of Israel from Egypt, how can Leviticus 18:5 have anything to do with a pre-fall covenant of works? In short, the Scriptures set forth two paths to being declared righteous before the divine bar, doing versus believing, or obeying the law perfectly versus believing in the gospel and trusting in the all-sufficient work of Christ. The Scriptures set forth these two paths in a number of different places, but one of the chief texts where the obedience–eternal life connection appears is Leviticus 18:5. This one text surprisingly appears a number of times in both the Old and New Testaments and shows that *if* one can perfectly obey the law, then he can secure eternal life.

---

1. Portions of this chapter come from J. V. Fesko, 'The Republication of the Covenant of Works,' *CP* 8 (2012): 197-212.

In order to demonstrate this interpretation of Leviticus 18:5, this chapter first sets the stage with the objections of twentieth-century Reformed theologian, John Murray (1898-1975). Murray believed that Leviticus 18:5 addressed matters related to the third, or normative, use of the law; it is not about a works-principle (i.e., obedience secures a reward). After examining Murray's view, the chapter presents counter-exegesis to explain why Murray's view is incorrect. The chapter then confirms this counter-exegesis by surveying five key texts: Ezekiel 20:1-26, Nehemiah 9:29, Luke 10:25-28, Galatians 3:10-12, and Romans 10:5, which are all texts that cite and interpret Leviticus 18:5. The chapter explains the theological significance of Leviticus 18:5 and how it relates to the covenant of works. The chapter concludes with some summary observations about Leviticus 18:5 and how it supports the doctrine of the covenant of works.

John Murray's Rejection

A small minority of early modern Reformed theologians objected to Leviticus 18:5 as exegetical proof for the covenant of works; they argued it addressed evangelical rather than legal obedience. That is, it applied to the covenant of grace, not to the covenant of works.[2] In more recent years, John Murray has argued that Leviticus 18:5 does not at all speak to the covenant of works for a number of reasons. Murray contends, first, that the original context is one of grace; Leviticus 18 echoes other passages such as Exodus 20:1-17 and Deuteronomy 5:6-21. These passages begin with the announcement of God's redemption of Israel. Murray believes therefore that Leviticus 18:5 'refers not to the life accruing from doing in a legalistic framework but to the blessing attendant upon obedience in a redemptive and covenant relationship to God.'[3]

Second, Murray argues that the only way Leviticus 18:5 and 'do this and live' could be used in antithesis to faith is if Paul misquoted

---

2. E.g., Edmund Calamy, *Two Solemn Covenants* (London: Thomas Banks, 1646), 15, 19; John Ball, *A Treatise of the Covenant of Grace* (London: G. Miller, 1645), 136-37.

3. John Murray, 'Appendix B: Leviticus 18:5,' in *Romans*, NICNT (1959, 65; Grand Rapids: Eerdmans, 1968), 249.

the verse; according to Murray in its original context Leviticus 18:5 refers to the third (or normative) use of the law. Briefly, there are three uses of the law traditionally recognized by Reformed theology: (1) the pedagogical use of the law, which drives the sinner to Christ by showing him how far he falls short of the requirements of the law; (2) the civil use of the law – its employment in the regulation of government and society; and (3) the normative use of the law, which shows Christian believers what conduct is acceptable and pleasing to God – it is a guide for the Christian life. Murray writes: 'It has been maintained that here is not strictly *quotation* in support of his argument but "a free employment of the words of Moses, which the apostle uses as an apt substratum for his own course of thought."'[4] For Murray, 'do this and live' could apply to Adam under the 'Adamic Administration,' but in a post-fall world it has no place.[5] In fact, Murray contends that Leviticus 18:5 'is, of itself,' an adequate and watertight definition of the principle of legalism.'[6] In summary, Murray believes that Paul has taken Leviticus 18:5 out of context to echo the erroneous teaching of the Judaizers and their misinterpretation of the law so he can disprove it.[7] We can note two things about Murray's exegesis: (1) it is perhaps one of the best examples of a rejection of Leviticus 18:5 as a proof text for the covenant of works; and (2) Murray's exegesis runs counter to the historic Reformed appeal to this verse.[8]

Leviticus 18:5

The key question regarding the original context of Leviticus 18:5 is whether, as Murray contends, it falls under the third use of the law. Does the text explain how a member of the covenant of grace benefits

---

4. Murray, 'Leviticus 18:5,' 251-52.

5. Murray, 'Leviticus 18:5,' 250.

6. Murray, 'Leviticus 18:5,' 251.

7. So also Moisés Silva, *Interpreting Galatians: Explorations in Exegetical Method*, 2nd ed. (Grand Rapids: Baker, 2001), 193-94; Nils Alstrup Dahl, *Studies in Paul: Theology for the Early Christian Mission* (1977; Eugene, OR: Wipf & Stock, 2002), 159-77.

8. See J. V. Fesko, *Covenant of Works: Origins, Development, and Reception* (Oxford: Oxford University Press, 2020).

from the blessings of the covenant of life by being obedient, or is something else in view? Murray argues that the Lord's declaration at the beginning of the chapter sets us in the context of grace and hence the third use of the law is in view. But is this conclusion necessarily so? Within its original context, the text begins with God's announcement, 'I am the LORD your God' (Lev. 18:2), but such a statement is not an indicator that what follows falls under the pedagogical or normative use of the law. Rather, these words simply indicate the divine source of the law; Israel must follow these laws because they are the statutes of the covenant Lord.[9] The divine pronouncement, 'I am the LORD your God,' also harkens back to the administration of the Decalogue, which reminds the Israelites that God is the source of both: the Levitical legislation is of the same weight and importance as the law given at Sinai.[10]

Second, Murray does not consider Leviticus 18:5 in the broader context of the chapter, which clearly sets forth a works-principle regarding Israel's tenure in the land:

> Do not make yourselves unclean by any of these things, for by all these the nations I am driving out before you have become unclean, and the land became unclean, so that I punished its iniquity, and the land vomited out its inhabitants. But you shall keep my statutes and my rules and do none of these abominations, either the native or the stranger who sojourns among you (for the people of the land, who were before you, did all of these abominations, so that the land became unclean), lest the land vomit you out when you make it unclean, as it vomited out the nation that was before you (Lev. 18:24-28).

God establishes a relationship between keeping His rules and Israel's tenure in the land. Ask the simple question, Why was Israel cast out of the land? And there is a simple response: They disobeyed God's laws. This echoes Adam's state in the garden and subsequent expulsion. The same relationship existed for the

---

9. Jacob Milgrom, *Leviticus*, AB, 3 vols. (New Haven: Yale UP, 1991-2000), 1517.

10. Milgrom, *Leviticus*, 1518; John E. Hartley, *Leviticus*, WBC (Dallas: Word, 1992), 291-93; cf. Rashi, *Leviticus*, The Pentateuch and Rashi's Commentary, trans. Abraham ben Isaiah and Benjamin Sharfman (Brooklyn: S. S. & R. Publishing, 1949), 173.

previous tenants of the land. The rest of the chapter's legislation explains why the land vomited out the Canaanites: they committed sexual immorality (Lev. 18:6-23; cf. Dan. 9).[11]

Third, a grammatical element within the chapter itself suggests that this legislation was binding both upon the Israelites as the covenant people of God and Gentiles sojourning within the land. Leviticus 18:5a states: 'You shall therefore keep [ושמרתם] my statutes and rules.' The text employs a second person masculine singular perfect sufformative suffix. But the latter half of the verse then shifts to a masculine third person singular verb: 'If a person does [יעשה] them, he shall live by them' (Lev 18:5b). The shift in pronouns and persons indicates that both Jew and Gentile were bound by these laws, which verse 26 confirms: 'But you shall keep my statutes and my rules and do none of these abominations, either the native or the stranger [והגר] who sojourns among you.' Another consideration is that the text specifically states that the 'man' (האדם) who does them will live by them, which generalizes this command.[12] At this point there are a number of exegetical features that do not fit Murray's exegesis. How, for example, can Leviticus 18:5 be the third use of the law if God applies it to the sojourner in the land, one who is not a member of the covenant of grace? The point is, *pace* Murray, that both Jew and Gentile (covenant and non-covenant member) must live in subjection to the law otherwise the land will vomit them out (cf. Amos 1–2).

Beyond these three issues, there is the pressing question regarding what it means to *live*. The text states: 'If a person does

---

11. That God was driving out the Canaanites draws the reader back to the Noahide incident when Ham's sons lost their right to the land of Canaan because of their sexual immorality (contra Milgrom, *Leviticus*, 1520; cf. Gen. 9:22; 10:6; Lev. 18:7-17; Bruce K. Waltke, *Genesis: A Commentary* [Grand Rapids: Zondervan, 2001], 149; Umberto Cassuto, *A Commentary on the Book of Genesis*, Part Two [Jerusalem: Magnes Press, 1997], 151-52; Nahum Sarna, *Genesis*, JPSTC [Philadelphia: JPS, 1989], 66; Claus Westermann, *Genesis 1-11*, trans. John J. Scullion, S. J. [Minneapolis: Fortress, 1994], 488; Gordon J. Wenham, *Genesis 1-15*, WBC [Waco: Word Books, 1987], 199-200).

12. Milgrom, *Leviticus*, 1522; Preston M. Sprinkle, *Law and Life: The Interpretation of Leviticus 18:5 in Early Judaism and in Paul*, WUNT (Tübingen: Mohr Siebeck, 2008), 28-29.

them, he shall live by them.' To what form of life does the verse refer? Does it refer to temporal life in the land or something else, such as eternal life? Note that within the context of chapter 18 the one who violates the laws suffers the curse of the covenant (Lev. 18:29). If disobedience earns a person covenant curse, then the converse must also be true that obedience earns Israel covenant blessing. This is a conclusion agreed upon by commentators both old and new.[13] In context this promise is specifically given to the nation of Israel who was a party to the Mosaic covenant, which was tied to their tenure in the land. In the light of the New Testament, Israel's tenure in the land typifies the obedience of Christ, the one who will obey the law and be justified by His works. But before we turn to the New Testament, there are two other places in the Old Testament that cite Leviticus 18:5, the books of Ezekiel and Nehemiah.

Ezekiel 20:1-26

Leviticus 18:5 resurfaces in Ezekiel 20 where the prophet covers Israel's time in Egypt (vv. 5-9), the desert (vv. 10-17), and the subsequent generations (vv. 18-26).[14] In verses 10-13 God explains through the prophet that He gave Israel a clear revelation of this law with a synonymous parallelism: 'I gave them my statutes // and // made known to them my rules' (v. 11a). Then, in the latter half of the verse Ezekiel quotes Leviticus 18:5: 'If a person does them, he shall live' (v. 11b). The prophet's application of Leviticus 18:5 refers to the whole law, not merely to laws pertaining to sexual immorality, as in the original context. What happened to the first generation in the desert? The prophet explains: 'But the house of Israel rebelled against me in the wilderness. They did not walk in my statutes but rejected my rules, by which, if a person does them, he shall live; and my Sabbaths they greatly profaned. "Then I said I would pour out my wrath upon them in the wilderness, to make

---

13. Wenham, *Genesis*, 253; contra Milgrom, *Leviticus*, 1522-23. Cf. Baruch A. Levine, *Leviticus*, JPSTC (Philadelphia: JPS, 1989), 119; Rashi, *Leviticus*, 174; Sprinkle, *Law and Life*, 31-34.

14. See Daniel Block, *The Book of Ezekiel Chapters 1-24*, NICOT (Grand Rapids: 1997), 630-33.

a full end of them'" (v. 13). This formula does not fit the third use of the law as Murray contends, as Israel's disobedience is not met with grace but justice and covenant curse (cf. Ezek. 18:9, 17, 19, 21; 33:15; Deut. 6:24f; 30:15-19).[15]

According to the prophet the later generations were just like their fathers: 'But the children rebelled against me. They did not walk in my statutes and were not careful to obey my rules, by which, if a person does them, he shall live; they profaned my Sabbaths. "Then I said I would pour out my wrath upon them and spend my anger against them in the wilderness'" (v. 21). Once again Ezekiel quotes Leviticus 18:5 and the formula continues: wrath meets disobedience, not the grace of the forgiveness of sins and sanctification as with the third use of the law. The verses that follow make it abundantly clear that the third use of the law is not at all in view. The prophet writes:

> Moreover, I swore to them in the wilderness that I would scatter them among the nations and disperse them through the countries, because they had not obeyed my rules, but had rejected my statutes and profaned my Sabbaths, and their eyes were set on their fathers' idols. Moreover, I gave them statutes that were not good [לא טובים] and rules by which they could not have life [לא יחיו בהם], and I defiled them through their very gifts in their offering up all their firstborn, that I might devastate them. I did it that they might know that I am the Lord (Ezek. 20:23-26).

Were this not a quote from Scripture, people might otherwise be surprised at the fact that the prophet would say that God's statutes were 'not good' and they were rules by which 'they could not have life.'[16] Verses 23-26 are an intentional contrast with what we find in verses 11-13; these latter verses contrast Israel's failure vis-à-vis the life offered in the earlier portion of the chapter that quotes Leviticus 18:5.[17] Would we consider the third use of the law as 'not

---

15. Moshe Greenberg, *Ezekiel 1-20*, AB (New York: Doubleday, 1983), 366; cf. Walther Eichrodt, *Ezekiel* (Philadelphia: Westminster, 1965-66), 267-68.

16. Block, *Ezekiel 1-24*, 639-40; Ellen F. Davis, *Swallowing the Scroll: Textuality and the Dynamics of Discourse in Ezekiel's Prophecy* (Sheffield: Sheffield Academic Press, 1989), 113-14.

17. Cf. Greenberg, *Ezekiel*, 368-70; G. A. Cooke, *The Book of Ezekiel*, ICC (1936; Edinburgh: T & T Clark, 1970), 218-19.

good'? At this point the defect lies not with the sinner, however true it is that sinful man is unable to fulfill the requirements of the law; rather the prophet places the 'defect' upon the divinely given law – it is 'not good.' While I will address these matters below, how can one hold these seemingly contradictory estimations of God's law together? How can the law at the same time be good (e.g., Rom. 7:12) and 'not good' (Ezek. 20:25)?

Nehemiah 9:29

The broader historical context of the book of Nehemiah is the post-exilic return to the promised land. The land vomited Israel out due to their idolatry and sin. In terms of the oath that Israel swore at the bases of Mts. Gerazim and Ebal, God visited the curses of the covenant upon the people (Deut. 28:1-68, esp. vv. 15, 32-34, 36-37, 64). In the ninth chapter Nehemiah rehearses Israel's history and recounts: the creation (v. 6), God's covenant with Abraham (vv. 7-8), the exodus (vv. 9-15), Israel's post-exodus idolatry (vv. 16-19a), the wilderness wanderings (vv. 19b-21), and the conquest of the nations that culminated in securing the promised land (vv. 22-26). Nevertheless, in spite of God's redemptive mercy and long-suffering with her hard-heartedness, Israel persisted in her disobedience (v. 26), so God gave them into the hands of their enemies (v. 27); Israel repented for a short time before she returned to her rebellious ways (v. 28). And so, Nehemiah avers:

> And you warned them in order to turn them back to your law. Yet they acted presumptuously and did not obey your commandments, but sinned against your rules, which if a person does them, he shall live by them, and they turned a stubborn shoulder and stiffened their neck and would not obey. Many years you bore with them and warned them by your Spirit through your prophets. Yet they would not give ear. Therefore you gave them into the hand of the peoples of the lands (Neh. 9:29-30).

Nehemiah explicitly captures the connection between Israel's (dis) obedience and long life in the land versus exile; he directly links Leviticus 18:5 to the prospects of long life in the land through his quotation of the text.

But beyond the quotation of Leviticus 18:5, Nehemiah uses the text as a fulcrum to contrast God's righteousness in all He does with what the Israelites do and do not do. Nehemiah highlights the contrast in the following chiastic structure:

A Praise (5b)

   B Confession in the form of historical retrospect (vv. 6-31)

   X Petition (32)

   B¹ Confession of present sin (vv. 33-35)

A¹ Lament (vv. 36-37).[18]

Within this chiasm, Nehemiah presents the contradictory actions of God versus Israel:[19]

B	B¹
'You [LORD] are righteous … you have kept your promise'	v. 33
'You made [עשה] the heaven' (v. 6) 'You made [עשה] a name for yourself' (v. 10) 'the wonders that you performed [עשה] among them' (v. 17) 'In your great mercies you did not make [עשה] and end of them' (v. 31).	v. 33
'They had made [עשה] for themselves a golden calf … and had committed [עשה] great blasphemies' (v. 18). 'That they might do [עשה] with them [inhabitants of the land] as they would' (v. 24). 'They committed [עשה] great blasphemies' (v. 26). 'But after they had rest they did [עשה] great evil' (v. 28).	v. 34 (2x)
Your law [תורה], vv. 26, 29 (2x).	v. 34

---

18. Mark A. Throntveit, *Ezra-Nehemiah* (Louisville, KY: John Knox Press, 1992), 102.

19. Throntveit, *Ezra-Nehemiah*, 106.

B	B¹
'They acted presumptuously and did not obey your commandments, but sinned against your rules, which if a person does [עשׂה] them, he shall live by them' (v. 29; cf. v. 16).	v. 34
Warning, vv. 26, 29, 30.	v. 34
Turn, repent, vv. 17, 26, 28 (2x), 29	v. 35
Kingdoms, v. 22.	v. 35

Nehemiah pounds a steady and rhythmic drumbeat of what God does (עשׂה) and what the people do (עשׂה), and in particular what they do not do as it pertains to Leviticus 18:5, 'The person who does [עשׂה] them, he shall live by them.' Had they 'done' the law, God would have given them life.[20] There is a definite connection between 'do this and live' and long life in the land, but this does not exhaust the significance of this text as the subsequent New Testament interpretation attests.

Luke 10:25-28

Leviticus 18:5 appears in the gospels, specifically when a lawyer asked Christ, 'What must I do to inherit eternal life?' (Luke 10:25). Jesus asked the lawyer, 'What is written in the Law?' to which the lawyer responded: 'You shall love the Lord your God with all your heart and with all your soul and with all your strength and with all your mind, and your neighbor as yourself' (Luke 10:27). How did Jesus respond? He quotes Leviticus 18:5: 'You have answered correctly; do this, and you will live' (Luke 10:28; cf. Lev. 18:5 LXX). That the totality of the law is in view is evident by the lawyer's quotation of Deuteronomy 6:5 and Leviticus 19:18; but Christ's response also holds out eternal life as the goal of obedience to the law. Key in this exchange is what follows, in that the lawyer,

---

20. A. Andrew Das, *Paul, the Law, and the Covenant* (Grand Rapids: Baker, 2000), 254-55.

'desiring to justify himself' (v. 29), asked Jesus who his neighbor was.[21] In other words, this exchange demonstrates that a person can either be justified by works or by faith in Christ, though the former is now impossible in a post-fall world. Christ's use of Leviticus 18:5 also illustrates that, taken by itself, the verse sets forth the principle of the covenant of works – obedience yields eternal life.

A similar pattern unfolds in Matthew 19:16-17 (// Mark 10:17-22 // Luke 18:18-23) where a man approached Christ and asked Him, 'Teacher, what good deed must I do to have eternal life?' (Matt. 19:16; cf. 25:46). Christ responded, 'If you would enter life, keep the commandments' (Matt. 19:17). When the man asked what commandments he had to keep (Matt 19:18), Christ pointed to the so-called second table of the law and its prohibitions against murder, adultery, theft, false witness, the command to honor one's parents, and to love one's neighbor (Matt. 19:18b-19; cf. Exod. 20:12-16; Lev. 19:18).[22] Christ does not specifically cite Leviticus 18:5's lexeme, 'do this and live,' but the principle is nevertheless present when Christ points to the connection between keeping the commandments and entering eternal life.[23] This approach stands in comparison to the humble faith of which Christ speaks in the immediately preceding verses (Matt. 19:10-15).[24] Either one enters the kingdom of heaven through a God-given child-like faith, or he must perfectly fulfill the law's commands.

---

21. E. Earle Ellis, *The Gospel of Luke*, NCBC (1966; Grand Rapids: Eerdmans, 1996), 161; I. Howard Marshall, *The Gospel of Luke*, NIGTC (Grand Rapids: Eerdmans, 1978), 444; Alfred Plummer, *The Gospel According to S. Luke*, ICC (1901; Edinburgh: T & T Clark, 1977), 285; cf. Darrell L. Bock, *Luke*, 2 vols., BECNT (Grand Rapids: Baker, 1996), 1026-27; G. K. Beale and D. A. Carson, eds., *New Testament Commentary on the Use of the Old Testament* (Grand Rapids: Baker, 2007), 321-22; Joseph A. Fitzmyer, *The Gospel According to Luke (X-XXIV)*, AB (New York: Doubleday, 1985), 881.

22. W. D. Davies and D. C. Allison, *Matthew*, ICC, 3 vols. (London: T & T Clark, 2006), III:43.

23. Donald A. Hagner, *Matthew 14-28*, WBC, vol. 33b (Dallas, TX: Word Books, 1995), 557.

24. D. A. Carson, *Matthew: Chapters 13-28*, EBC (Grand Rapids: Zondervan, 1995), 422-23.

For fallen sinners, of course, the only open path is that of faith (Matt. 19:26).[25]

Galatians 3:10-12

When Paul cites Leviticus 18:5 in Galatians 3:12, he does so in concert with Christ's use and interpretation of the verse. Paul writes in the verses immediately before verse 12: 'For all who rely on works of the law are under a curse; for it is written, "Cursed be everyone who does not abide by all of the things written in the Book of the Law, and do them." Now it is evident that no one is justified before God by the law for, "The righteous shall live by faith." But the law is not of faith, rather "The one who does them shall live by them"' (Gal. 3:10-12). Paul sets two principles in opposition to one another, doing versus believing.[26]

Paul quotes Habakkuk 2:4, 'The righteous shall live by faith.' Paul's quotation does not align with the Septuagint, which translates

---

25. Carson, *Matthew*, 424.

26. Beale and Carson, *Commentary*, 803. Contra Ridderbos, who argues, 'There is no conflict between Hab. 2 and Lev. 18 either, so long as the root of life is sought in the grace of God and thus in faith' (Herman N. Ridderbos, *The Epistles of Paul to the Churches of Galatia*, NICNT [Grand Rapids: Eerdmans, 1953], 125). Ridderbos' interpretation rests on the assumption that Paul employs the Judaizers' misunderstanding of the law, which if adopted makes Paul's argument unintelligible, especially in the light of the broader intra-canonical interpretation of Leviticus 18:5. Moreover, in line with his argument from Galatians 3:10ff, Paul quotes the Old Testament, not the Judaizers (cf. e.g. Douglas J. Moo, *Galatians*, BECNT [Grand Rapids: Baker, 2013], 208-09; A. Andrew Das, *Galatians* [St. Louis: Concordia, 2014], 324; Richard Longenecker, *Galatians*, WBC [Dallas: Word, 1990], 120). Others have sought to minimize the supposed tensions between the antithesis between doing and believing by claiming that Paul dismisses reliance on 'works of the law' as reference to circumcision, food laws, and Sabbath observance, Jewish identity markers, not works-righteousness. When Paul says that one must 'abide by *all* things written in the Book of the Law' (Gal. 3:10), he does not have perfect obedience to the law in view but rather simply meant living within the provisions of the law, including employing the provisions for sin, namely, sacrifice and atonement (so James D. G. Dunn, *The Epistle to the Galatians*, BNTC [Peabody, MA: Hendrickson, 1993], 171-74). Such an argument hinges on the thoroughly disproven claim that 'works of the law' only refers to the so-called Jewish identity markers and not general adherence to the law (see, e.g., Moisés Silva, 'Faith versus Works of the Law in Galatia,' in *Justification and Variegated Nomism*, vol. 2, ed. D. A. Carson, et al. [Grand Rapids: Baker, 2004], 217-48).

the text in such a manner to refer to God's faithfulness, 'the righteous shall live by my faithfulness' (δὲ δίκαιος ἐκ πίστεώς μου ζήσεται). Rather, Paul quotes the Hebrew text, namely, 'The righteous shall live by his faith.'[27] Paul places a link between faith and righteousness. But Paul then identifies a second path to righteousness, namely, through doing the law: 'But the law is not of faith, rather "The one who does them shall live by them"' (Gal. 3:12). To be clear, Paul may mark this path to righteousness, but sin is an obstacle, 'Now it is evident that no one is justified before God by the law' (Gal. 3:11a). The path to performing the law to secure one's justification may be obstructed by sin which renders it impossible for fallen human beings, but this does not negate the fact that the path still exists. In the sin-fallen world, the only way to be right with God is by believing the gospel, not performing the law.[28]

Another point to note is the harmony that exists between the interpretations of Christ and Paul. Christ told the lawyer that if he obeyed the law, he could obtain eternal life. This was in fact the very question posed to Him, 'What must I do to inherit eternal life? [ζωὴν αἰώνιον]' (Luke 10:25). In line with Christ's teaching, Paul quotes Leviticus 18:5, which states that the person who obeys the law 'shall live' (ζήσεται) (Gal. 3:12; cf. Luke 10:28). This is not merely reference to temporal life in the land, as some early modern and modern commentators have suggested.[29] Rather, nothing short of eschatological life is in view given the overall context of Paul's argument and how he juxtaposes Habakkuk 2:4 with Leviticus 18:5. Three points bear this conclusion, which appear in the following table:[30]

---

27. Thomas Schreiner, *Galatians*, ZECNT (Grand Rapids: Zondervan, 2010), 207-08.

28. Schreiner, *Galatians*, 211.

29. So, e.g., John Cameron, *Certain Theses, or, Positions of the Learned John Cameron Concerning the Threefold Covenant of God*, in Samuel Bolton, *The True Bounds of Christian Freedome* (London: P. S., 1656), theses LXXX-LXXXI (pp. 400-01); James D. G. Dunn, *The Theology of Paul the Apostle* (Grand Rapids: Eerdmans, 1998), 152-54, 374-75; idem, *Galatians*, 175-76; cf. Moo, *Galatians*, 208-09; Das, *Galatians*, 323.

30. Beale and Carson, *Commentary*, 801.

Category	Habakkuk 2:4	Leviticus 18:5
Articular subject	ὁ δίκαιος (the righteous)	ὁ ποιήσας (the one who does)
Prepositional phrase	ἐκ πίστεως (by faith)	ἐν αὐτοῖς (in them)
Both have the same main verb	ζήσεται (will live)	ζήσεται (will live)

Given the parallel between the two verses, the life in view of Habakkuk 2:4 is the same life in view for Leviticus 18:5. Yes, when a person places his faith in Christ, he is in possession of right and title to eternal life in the present (Rom. 5:20-21).[31] Nevertheless, the present extends into an eschatological future (cf. Luke 23:43). *Now* in its immediate context, Leviticus 18:5 presented the prospects of long life in the land, but the ultimate referent was to eternal life; long life in the land was typical of the antitypical reality of eschatological life.[32]

Romans 10:5

In the broader context of Romans 10:5 Paul demonstrates that Israel failed to establish right standing with God, as he reveals that his heart's prayer is that Israel would be saved (Rom. 10:1). But what is the specific nature of Israel's failure? Paul explains: 'For, being ignorant of the righteousness of God, and seeking to establish their own, they did not submit to God's righteousness' (Rom 10:3). Paul intentionally contrasts Israel's attempts to achieve righteousness (Rom 9.30-31) with God's righteousness (τοῦ θεοῦ δικαιοσύνην). What is the remedy for Israel's failure? Paul writes: 'For Christ is the end of the law for righteousness to everyone who believes' (Rom. 10:4), by which he establishes an antithesis between works and faith, or doing and believing.

---

31. Schreiner, *Galatians*, 209, 211.

32. Schreiner, *Galatians*, 212-14; see also Simon Gathercole, 'Torah, Life, and Salvation: Leviticus 18:5 in Early Judaism and the New Testament,' in *From Prophecy to Testament: The Function of the Old Testament in the New*, ed. C. A. Evans (Peabody, MA: Hendrickson, 2004), 126-45.

Paul then appeals to Leviticus 18:5: 'For Moses writes about the righteousness that is based on the law, that the person who does the commandments shall live by them' (Rom. 10:5). Paul's appeal to Leviticus 18:5 cannot be an instance of the so-called 'misinterpretation theory,' where Paul assumes the erroneous legalistic opinion of his opponents to disprove it, nor is Paul merely borrowing these words out of context, as Murray argues. Paul states: 'Moses writes about the righteousness *that is based on the law* (Μωϋσῆς γὰρ γράφει τὴν δικαιοσύνην τὴν ἐκ [τοῦ] νόμου)' (emphasis).[33] Nowhere does Paul introduce a passage with such a Scripture quotation formula only to misquote the text.[34] Paul writes of the principle found in the law, such as Deuteronomy 6:25, 'And it will be righteousness for us, if we are careful to do all this commandment before the LORD our God, as he has commanded us.'[35] Paul echoes this principle earlier in Romans: 'For it is not the hearers of the law who are righteous before God, but the doers of the law who will be justified' (Rom. 2:13). Paul also states Μωϋσῆς γὰρ γράφει ('For Moses writes'), which is in the present active indicative, conveying the idea that Leviticus 18:5 is still binding even now.[36]

In the broader context of Romans 10, Paul moves from the righteousness that is based upon the law (the one who does them shall live by them) to the righteousness that comes by faith, verses

33. For a survey of the various views on Romans 10:5 and bibliography, see Sprinkle, *Law and Life*, 168-70.

34. Schreiner, *Galatians*, 213; Beale and Carson, *Commentary*, 655.

35. J. A. Thompson, *Deuteronomy*, TOTC (Downers Grove: IVP, 1974), 127; J. G. McConville, *Deuteronomy*, AOTC (Downers Grove: IVP, 2002), 144-45; Moshe Greenberg, 'Some Postulates of Biblical Criminal Law,' in *A Song of Power and the Power of Songs: Essays on the Book of Deuteronomy*, ed. Duane L. Christensen (Winona Lake: Eisenbrauns, 1993), 288; Jeffrey H. Tigay, *Deuteronomy*, JPSTC (Philadelphia: JPS, 2003), 81; Moshe Weinfeld, *Deuteronomy 1-11*, AB (New York: Doubleday, 1991), 349; *pace* Meredith G. Kline, *Treaty of the Great King: The Covenant Structure of Deuteronomy* (Grand Rapids: Eerdmans, 1963), 67.

36. Beale and Carson, *Commentary*, 655; cf. Steven E. Runge, *Discourse Grammar of the Greek New Testament: A Practical Introduction for Teaching and Exegesis* (Peabody, MA: Hendrickson, 2010), 130, 132-33. My thanks to my colleague, Miles Van Pelt, to alerting me to Runge.

6-10: 'For with the heart one believes and is justified, and with the mouth one confesses and is saved' (v. 10; cf. Gal. 3:12; Hab. 2:4; Lev. 18:5). Paul succinctly restates what we have found in Ezekiel: Israel's failure to 'do this and live' (Ezek. 20:11, 13, 21) will be fulfilled by God (Ezek. 36-37).[37] So Paul states that Israel's failed attempts to achieve righteousness on its own (Rom. 9:30-31) has been fulfilled by God in Christ (Rom. 10:6-10; Deut. 20:12-14) and is available to anyone who believes in Him.

Theological Significance

After this survey of Leviticus 18:5 and the five different places it later appears in the Old and New Testaments, we are better informed to answer the question as to how a text embedded in the Mosaic covenant can address Adam's pre-fall state. Just because Leviticus 18:5 appears in the Mosaic covenant, which is part of the covenant of grace, does not automatically preclude the possibility that it speaks to Adam's pre-fall state. Leviticus 18:5 reveals one of two paths available for one's justification, either works or faith. In the pre-fall context, Leviticus 18:5 therefore applies to Adam's state because the only way to attain eternal life was through his obedience to God's commands: to be fruitful, multiply, fill the earth, subdue it, and not to eat from the tree of knowledge (Gen. 1:28; 2:16-17). Leviticus 18:5 therefore sets forth the Adamic path to eternal life, confirmed especially by Christ's quotation of this text when the lawyer asked Him, 'What must I do to inherit eternal life?' (Luke 10:25).

But if Leviticus 18:5 applies to Adam's pre-fall state, what role does it play in a post-fall world, specifically within the covenant of grace and the Mosaic covenant? When Paul appeals to Leviticus 18:5 in Romans 10:5, he specifically states, 'For Moses writes.' This lexeme is in the present tense which indicates that the Adamic path to justification still stands. In a post-fall world, the covenant of works hangs over the heads of all human beings both in terms of its penalty and to press sinners with the demands of the law – the need for perfect righteousness, impeccable obedience to the law.

---

37. Sprinkle, *Law and Life*, 38.

Within the administration of the Mosaic covenant, Leviticus 18:5 stands as a reminder to Israel and ultimately to the whole world that perfect obedience to the law was necessary but unreachable because of sin; in this manner, then, God revealed their inability to meet the law's demands and Israel's need for Christ. This was the way that both Jesus and Paul used Leviticus 18:5; it was not a revelation of the gospel of salvation by grace through faith alone in Christ alone. Rather, it was a revelation of the protological function of the law, namely, that obedience secures blessing and disobedience warrants curse.[38] More specifically, Adam's obedience would have secured eternal life.

In the Mosaic covenant, Israel's obedience would have secured long life in the land, which finds its antitypical reality in eternal life. This is not to say that Israel could have merited eternal life through their good works – far from it. Rather, it showed that the Adamic path was still open should one be able to render perfect obedience to the law. Corporately, Israel typified the person and work of Christ, the one who was 'born under the law' (Gal. 4:4) and who came to 'fulfill the law' (Matt. 5:17). In the post-fall context Leviticus 18:5 functions in its role as pedagogue, hence the prophet Ezekiel calls God's law 'not good' (Ezek. 20:23-26). Whatever moral speed one might build up in the effort to run up the hill of God's law, he can never reach the top. Hence, due to human sin God's law is 'not good,' or in the words of Paul, the Mosaic covenant was 'a ministry of death, carved in letters of stone' (2 Cor. 3:7). Only Christ removes the specter of death because He suffers the curse of the law on behalf of those who believe in Him. But the path of Christ is one of faith, not works, believing, not doing. The righteous will live by his faith, whereas the law is not of faith.

Conclusion

Leviticus 18:5 taps into a vein that runs from pre-redemptive through redemptive history to the consummation. In pre-fall

---

38. David VanDrunen, *Divine Covenants and Moral Order: A Biblical Theology of Natural Law* (Grand Rapids: Eerdmans, 2014), 308.

context the principle of Leviticus 18:5 appears, namely, obedience secures eternal life. In the post-fall world stained by sin, the principle still exists and God therefore reminds Israel and the rest of the world, 'The person who does them, will live by them,' to remind them of the law's demands and their need for a savior. Whether in Leviticus 18:5, Ezekiel 20, Nehemiah 9:29, Luke 10:25-28, Galatians 3:10-11, or Romans 10:5, the message is consistently the same: perfect obedience secures eternal life. God created Adam and gave him commands to perform, which reflected the 'do this and live' principle. Thus, Leviticus 18:5 aptly captures the pre-fall Adamic state and serves as an important exegetical pillar for the covenant of works.

~: II.4 :~

They Broke the
Everlasting Covenant
(Isa. 24:5)

Introduction

*A*s the foregoing chapters have noted, there are a number of
passages of Scripture that serve as exegetical proof texts
for the covenant of works. In more recent years one passage that
theologians have added to this collection of texts is Isaiah 24:5, 'The
earth lies defiled under its inhabitants; for they have transgressed the
laws, violated the statutes, broken the everlasting covenant.' Some
modern exegetes contend that Isaiah references the Adamic covenant
in his prophetic indictment. But this conclusion is not uncontested
since theologians have argued that Isaiah instead refers to other
covenants, such as the Abrahamic, Noahic, or Mosaic covenants.
Others refuse to identify any one covenant because Isaiah has no
single covenant in view but instead generally condemns humanity
for its sinfulness in covenantal terms. Simply stated, pick any one
covenant and the human race has broken it. As the exposition below
attests, there are reasonable arguments for each of the different
interpretations of this passage given that there are arguably allusions
to multiple covenants in Isaiah's statement. Nevertheless, this
chapter defends the thesis that the best explanation for Isaiah's
indictment rests in the Adamic covenant. Within the overall context

217

of Isaiah's prophecy, he charges the Gentile nations, which he summarizes in Isaiah 24:5-6, namely, given humanity's violation of the Adamic covenant, God has brought its covenant sanction upon them, namely, death. Only God's redemption and mercy will deliver them from this curse when He swallows death in victory.

To prove this thesis the chapter first surveys the different views on Isaiah 24:5. Second, it argues that the two best explanations for Isaiah 24:5 are either the Adamic or Noahic covenant. But the former edges out the latter for two reasons: death is the chief topic of Isaiah 24–27 and the apostle Paul's use of Isaiah's apocalypse (Isa. 24–27). The chapter then concludes with some observations regarding Isaiah 24:5 and the covenant of works.

Survey of Different Views

There are five different views regarding the interpretation of Isaiah 24:5, namely, that the prophet refers to the: Adamic covenant, the Noahic covenant, the Abrahamic covenant, the Mosaic covenant, and that there is no specific covenant in view.

Adamic Covenant

E. J. Young (1907-1968), former Old Testament professor at Westminster Theological Seminary (Philadelphia), is among those who believe that Isaiah 24:5 refers to the Adamic covenant. He notes that the verse's opening phrase, 'As for the earth – it has become profane under its inhabitants,' employs language typically associated with the pollution of the promised land (Num. 35:33; Deut. 21:19; Jer. 3:9; Ps. 106:38). But now the prophet applies this language beyond Palestine to the entire earth. In Young's mind, the geographic extent of sin only has one origin: Adam's fall in the garden. Eden is where Adam transgressed the covenant, and the earth thus fell under a curse (Gen. 3:17). Young states that the prophet defines humanity's transgression as a violation of laws, statutes, and the everlasting covenant.[1] But how, precisely, do the nations transgress God's laws? Young provides two answers.

---

1. E. J. Young, *The Book of Isaiah*, 3 vols. (Grand Rapids: Eerdmans, 1969), II:156; so also William J. Dumbrell, *Covenant and Creation: A Theology of the Old Testament Covenants* (1984; Carlisle: Paternoster Press, 2000), 74.

First, all people have God's laws written on their hearts, and thus Isaiah says 'they have transgressed laws.' Young does not directly appeal to the concept of natural law but notes that this was a common explanation among early modern Reformed commentators such as Campegius Vitringa (1669-1722), who wrote a significant commentary on the prophet Isaiah with few peers in terms of depth of his exegetical analysis.[2] Vitringa observes that when the Old Testament refers to the Mosaic law it often employs the phrase the 'laws of the Lord,' but here Isaiah only speaks of 'laws, statutes, and eternal covenant.' This means, therefore, that the prophet only refers to the law of nature and of the nations (*ius naturae et gentium*), which Israel shares in common with the Gentile nations. The people of the earth are guilty of breaking the natural law, conscience, and common law.[3] Young also notes that Rabbinic interpreters such as Ibn Ezra (1089-1167) presented similar arguments. Ibn Ezra explains Isaiah's reference to 'the laws' (תורת) as those 'which are dictated by common sense, in which all agree.' Similarly, Isaiah's use of 'ordinance' (חק) refers to 'the laws of God, contained in the natural order of things; and this is likewise the meaning of ברית עולם "the covenant of the universe."'[4] But according to nineteenth-century scholars, such as Wilhelm Gesenius (1786-1842), conceptions of natural law were supposedly alien to the Hebrew mind because they only knew of specially revealed laws.[5]

Rejections of natural law notwithstanding, Young admitted a variant of the category because of Paul's statements in Romans 2:14-15. He distinguishes between natural law and the 'work of the law' written on their hearts, which means that

> Gentiles do by natural instinct those things which are prescribed by the Law. In so doing, they show that, by reason of what is actually

2. See Charles Telfer, *Wrestling with Isaiah: The Exegetical Methodology of Campegius Vitringa (1659-1722)* (Göttingen: Vandenhoeck & Ruprecht, 2016).

3. Campegius Vitringa, *Commentarius in Librum Jesiae*, vol. 2 (Leeuwarden: Franciscus Halma, 1720), 11.

4. Ibn Ezra, *The Commentary of Ibn Ezra on Isaiah*, vol .1, ed. M. Friedländer (London: Society of Hebrew Literature, 1873), 109.

5. Young, *Isaiah*, II:156 n. 23; cf. Wilhelm Gesenius, *Commentar über den Jesaia* (Leipzig: Friedrich Christian Willhelm Vogel, 1821), 764.

implanted in their nature, they reveal the Law of God unto themselves; and this fact shows that the work of the Law is written on their own hearts. In transgressing those things prescribed in the Law, however, it may be said that the Gentiles were actually transgressing the Law itself. Here, the plural is used to show that the Gentiles had transgressed divine commands and ordinances, and also that their sins were many and varied.[6]

The work of the law written on the heart at humanity's creation is one way all people 'have transgressed laws' and renders them liable to divine judgment. In their rebellious ways, sinners change God's statutes – they re-write God's laws in their own image; they have treated God's laws as if they did not exist.[7]

Second, because of humanity's sinful ways they are all guilty of 'making void the covenant of eternity.'[8] The lexeme ברית עולם was first used to describe the Noahic covenant after the flood; it was universal, as God made it with Noah, his children, and all creatures (Gen. 9:9-10). The covenant was also eternal (Gen. 9:11). But the covenant was also unconditional, in that God presented no stipulations to activate the promises. How, therefore, could someone violate the Noahic covenant?[9] Young also takes issue with Calvin's interpretation (see below), who believed that Isaiah referred to the Mosaic covenant. Young did not agree with Calvin because Isaiah has more than Israel in view. 'The earth lies defiled under its inhabitants,' refers to all people, not merely the Jews. The frustration of this eternal covenant is something global, not peculiar to Israel alone. For these two reasons (the works of the law written on the heart and the reference to the global guilt for violating the eternal covenant), Young believes that Isaiah speaks of the Adamic covenant. The prophet uses language common to the Mosaic covenant to characterize humanity's transgression and guilt

---

6. Young, *Isaiah*, II:157. For the distinction between natural law and works of the law written on the heart, Young appeals to the exegesis of his Westminster colleague, John Murray (see John Murray, *Romans*, vol. 1, NICNT [Grand Rapids: Eerdmans, 1959], 74).

7. Young, *Isaiah*, II:157.

8. Young, *Isaiah*, II:156.

9. Young, *Isaiah*, II:157.

they possess by virtue of Adam's covenantal transgression and their own personal sins, which warrants curse and judgment (Isa. 24:6).[10]

Noahic Covenant

A number of recent commentators believe that Isaiah refers to the Noahic covenant.[11] So, David VanDrunen recognizes that there are good reasons for seeing the Mosaic covenant as the possible referent but that the Noahic covenant has fewer obstacles to overcome.[12] He presents at least five reasons why the Noahic covenant best explains Isaiah 24:5. First, the universal context ('the earth') of Isaiah 24 and the prophet's interest in the Gentile nations (Isa. 13–23) favors a Noahic rather than Mosaic context. All of the nations are in covenant with God through the Noahic covenant; they are not participants in the Mosaic covenant. Second, Isaiah's message of cosmic unraveling presents the antithetical parallel to the covenantally promised global stability (Gen. 8:22). Third, the consequential curse of Isaiah 24:6 finds its origins in the withdrawal of the curse in the Noahic covenant (Gen. 8:21). Fourth, when Isaiah speaks of the opening of the 'windows of heaven' (Isa. 24:17), this corresponds to their shutting at the conclusion of Noah's flood (Gen. 8:2; 7, 11). And, fifth, the prophet's call to the people to enter their chambers and shut the door behind them until God's wrath has passed by (Isa. 26:20) alludes to Noah closing his family inside the ark until the flood concluded.[13] VanDrunen, notes, however, that there are at least two objections that require answers.

---

10. Young, *Isaiah*, II:158.

11. E.g., Christopher R. Seitz, *Isaiah 1-39* (Louisville, KY: John Knox Press, 1993), 179-82; John D. Watts, *Isaiah 1-33*, WBC, vol. 24 (Nashville, TN: Thomas Nelson, 1985), 318; Walter Brueggemann, *Isaiah 1-39* (Louisville, KY: Westminster John Knox Press, 1998), 192; Steven D. Mason, 'Another Flood? Genesis 9 and Isaiah's Broken Eternal Covenant,' *JSOT* 33/2 (2007): 177-98; Daniel R. Streett, 'As It Was in the Days of Noah: The Prophets' Typological Interpretation of Noah's Flood,' *CTR* 5 (2007): 42-46; Robert B. Chisholm, 'The "Everlasting Covenant" and the "City of Chaos": Intentional Ambiguity and Irony in Isaiah 24,' *CTR* 6/2 (1993): 237-53.

12. David VanDrunen, *Divine Covenants and Moral Order: A Biblical Theology of Natural Law* (Grand Rapids: Eerdmans, 2014), 193.

13. VanDrunen, *Divine Covenants*, 194.

First, when Isaiah speaks of 'laws' and 'statutes,' such language echoes common elements of the Mosaic covenant. At the same time, these terms are not exclusively Mosaic and are common to Abraham's conduct in his covenant with God (Gen. 26:5). God also uses the term *statute* to describe the fixed natural order of the sun, moon, and stars (Jer. 31:35-36), which nevertheless bears strong covenantal connotations read in the broader context of Jeremiah's prophecy (33:20-21). In other words, there is a larger cosmic covenantal order beyond the Mosaic covenant.

Second, Isaiah speaks of the frangibility of the 'eternal covenant,' which is uncharacteristic of the Noahic covenant. But VanDrunen counters that breaking any everlasting covenant creates a cognitive dissonance. This may be a rhetorical point in Isaiah's prophecy, namely, that humanity has broken a seemingly unbreakable covenant, which only underscores their wickedness. In the end, however, VanDrunen admits that the Noahic covenant is infrangible, but that there is nothing extraordinary about God pointing out the natural law elements borne by the Noahic covenant and holding humanity accountable for its violation 'while the earth remains' (Gen. 8:22). If Isaiah 24–27 describes the consummation of the age, then God has kept His Noahic promises and preserved the earth until its conclusion and never destroying it by waters of judgment.[14] VanDrunen, therefore, believes that the Noahic covenant best explains Isaiah's statement, but at the same time he acknowledges that his reference to the 'everlasting covenant' is intentionally ambiguous. He notes that both the Noahic and Mosaic covenants are unintelligible apart from the original covenant that Adam broke. If the violation of the Adamic covenant warranted the judgment of the world that was suspended but not abandoned, 'then this original covenant must not lurk far out of the picture in 24:5.'[15]

Abrahamic Covenant

The advocates who argue that Isaiah refers to the Abrahamic covenant date back to the sixteenth- and seventeenth centuries.

---

14. VanDrunen, *Divine Covenants*, 194-95.

15. VanDrunen, *Divine Covenants*, 195.

Wolfgang Musculus (1497-1563), for example, notes that the prophet arraigns the Israelites for their transgressions of God's laws, which the Scriptures place under the rubric of covenant (ברית). But the Abrahamic covenant lies at the root of God's covenantal dealings with Israel: 'And God said to Abraham, "As for you, you shall keep my covenant, you and your offspring after you throughout their generations .... So shall my covenant be in your flesh an everlasting covenant"' (Gen. 17:9, 13).[16] This is the same view that the Synod of Dort (1618-19) puts forth in its annotations on the Bible. The annotations of Dort argue that Isaiah speaks of the covenant God made with Abraham in Genesis 17 and renewed with Israel in Exodus 24.[17] The Westminster Assembly's (1643-1655) annotations note that this is a common view among some expositors but nevertheless opts for a reference to the Mosaic covenant. Noteworthy are the different views that were common: the Abrahamic covenant (Gen. 17:7, 13, 14), Mosaic covenant (Exod. 24:7-8; Jer. 11:2, 4), or natural law (Ps. 119:89; Matt. 5:18); at this period the covenant of works was apparently not an extant option, though natural law was a constituent element of the covenant of works in early modern Reformed theology.[18] This means that the interpretive option of the covenant of works was substantively present in the early modern period under the category of natural law.

Mosaic Covenant
John Calvin (1509-1564) is among those who argue that Isaiah refers to the Mosaic covenant. Calvin notes that Isaiah characterizes the earth as defiled or polluted on account of its inhabitants. 'There is a kind of mutual bargain between the land and the husbandmen [*mutuum quodammodo commercium inter terram et agricolas / traffique commune entre la terre & les laboureurs*],' writes Calvin, 'that it gives

---

16. Wolfgang Musculus, *In Esaiam Prophetam Commentarii* (Basil: ex Officina Heruagianus, 1557), 379.

17. Theodore Haak, ed. *The Dutch Annotations Upon the Whole Bible* (London: Henry Hills, 1657), comm. Isa. 24:5.

18. *Annotations Upon All the Books of the Old and New Testaments* (London: Evan Tyler, 1657), comm. Isa. 24:5.

back with usury what it has received.' If people sow righteousness, then the earth returns a bountiful harvest, but if they disseminate wickedness then it becomes barren; sin disrupts the 'regular order of nature.'[19] Isaiah specifies the reason why the earth lies in a polluted state, 'Because they have transgressed the laws.' Isaiah employs the term תורת, which refers to the Law and God's divine instruction, which contains His commandments and promises.[20] Calvin thus translates Isaiah's use of חק as 'ordinance,' which denotes ceremonies or morals but opts to render it as 'commandments,' because it covers 'everything that belongs to the rule of a holy life.'[21] Thus far Calvin translates Isaiah 24:5 as, 'The earth is polluted on account of its inhabitants, because they have transgressed the laws, they have changed the commandments.'

When Calvin arrives at the last portion of the verse, 'they have broken the everlasting covenant,' he explains that the term ברית refers to a 'covenant and contract' (*foedus et pactum / l'alliance*), which is limited to those 'contracts' where the Lord promised to be the God of His people. Calvin lists three texts from the Mosaic covenant: Exodus 19:6, 29:45, and Leviticus 26:12.[22] Calvin believes that the Mosaic covenant fills Isaiah's prophetic horizon and that Israel alone is in the crosshairs of his indictment. Israel has been disobedient and broken the holy covenant. This means that Calvin understands Isaiah 24:5 to say, 'The earth is polluted on account of its inhabitants, because Israel has transgressed the laws, they have changed the commandments, they have broken the everlasting Mosaic covenant.' The prophet calls the covenant

---

19. John Calvin, *Commentary on the Book of the Prophet Isaiah*, vol. 1, CTS (rep.; Grand Rapids: Baker, 1993), 169; idem, *Commentaires sur le Prophete Isaïe* (Genève: Adam Rivery & Jean Rivery, 1552), 311; idem, *Commentariorum in Isaiam Prophetam, 1-39*, in *Joannis Calvini Opera Quae Supersunt Omnia*, vol. 42, ed. Edouard Cunitz, et al. (Braunschweig: C. A. Schwetschke, 1863), 401. More recent advocates of this view are Dan Johnson, *From Chaos to Restoration: An Integrative Reading of Isaiah 24-27*, JSOT Sup 61 (Sheffield: Journal for the Study of the Old Testament, 1988), 25-29; and Donald C. Polaski, 'Reflections on a Mosaic Covenant: The Eternal Covenant (Isaiah 24:5) and Intertextuality,' *JSOT* 77 (1998): 55-73.

20. Calvin, *Isaiah*, 169.

21. Calvin, *Isaiah*, 170.

22. Calvin, Isaiah, 170; idem, Isaïe, 311; idem, Isaiam, 401.

'everlasting' because it was 'perpetual and inviolable' and was 'to be in force in every age.' Israelite fathers were supposed to transmit in uninterrupted succession to their children the knowledge of the Mosaic covenant and its requirements, but since Israel failed in this task God was going to overthrow and bring a curse upon them.[23] 'Therefore hath the curse devoured the earth' (Isa. 24:6 KJV). But Calvin avers, God did not have generic curses in view but the specific sanctions of the Mosaic covenant (Lev. 26:16; Deut. 28:15). But even though Calvin thinks the Mosaic covenant stands front and center, he nevertheless casts a line back to the creation and the fall of Adam: 'We know that the earth was cursed on account of the transgression of our first parent, so that it brought forth thorns and thistles instead of fruits' (Gen. 3:17-18). Calvin implies that God mitigated the effects of the curse and partially smothered it with the Mosaic covenant, but in view of Israel's failures, He was going to unleash the full force of the curse upon the inhabitants of the earth.[24]

Generic Covenantal Reference

As one can see from the three previously surveyed views, there are elements and allusions from different covenants in the Old Testament, thus some scholars conclude that no one covenant is in view. Alec Motyer, for example, explains that the beginning of verse 5 reveals the earth's defiled state, a condition that began on the heels of Adam's fall and the consequential 'thorns and thistles' (Gen. 3:18) infecting the earth. Sin defiles the earth; rather than yielding fruit as God originally intended (Gen. 2:15), it became a wilderness under the pollution of humanity's sin – the ultimate form of toxic waste.[25] Motyer makes two connections to the Adamic context as subtexts to Isaiah's denunciation and argues that the prophet provides three reasons behind humanity's guilt. First, they have transgressed revealed truth. They have עבר ('crossed over') or 'transgressed' (παραβαίνω LXX and NT) laws; the Old and

---

23. Calvin, *Isaiah*, 170-71.

24. Calvin, *Isaiah*, 171.

25. J. Alec Motyer, *The Prophecy of Isaiah: An Introduction and Commentary* (Downers Grove: InterVarsity Press, 1993), 198.

New Testaments use these terms specifically for the violation of expressly revealed laws. Therefore, the first ground of humanity's guilt is that they have refused to live by God's divine revelation.[26] Second, as Calvin noted, people violated (lit. 'altered') God's laws; they introduced their own humanly-sourced morality in lieu of God's laws.

And third, they broke God's everlasting covenant; the prophet specifically uses the term פרר, which is terminology for covenant violation (Deut. 31:20; cf. Num. 30:8-9). Related to this is that Isaiah uses the term 'everlasting covenant,' which is a term applied to the Noahic covenant (Gen. 9:16), God's covenant dispensation extending back to Abraham (Ps. 105:10), the Sabbath in the Mosaic covenant (Lev. 24:8), the Davidic covenant (2 Sam. 23:5), and the new covenant (Isa. 55:3).[27] These different elements lead Motyer to the following conclusion:

> While this whole passage is resonant with flood motifs, it would be mistaken to tie this covenant reference in any way exclusively to Noah, even though its ambience starts with him. Every covenant dispensation had its regulatory aspect, however undeveloped it may have been in comparison with the normative Mosaic system. This may be why Isaiah used the plural *laws*, so as to cover every period and aspect of covenant law-giving. Even Abraham who lived under the broadest of divine precepts (Gen. 17:2), is said to have kept the Lord's 'laws' (Gen. 26:5). In essence, the annulling of the covenant was the refusal to live in the fellowship which God opened.[28]

For humanity's covenant infidelity, God imposes covenant curse upon them (Lev. 26:25-45; Deut. 11:26-28; 28:15ff; Dan. 9:11; Zech. 5:3).[29] But in parallel with the Noahic covenant, not everyone will fall under God's judgment; some will escape (Isa. 24:13-16; cf. Gen. 6:5-8). Motyer consequently sees Isaiah 24:5 as a kaleidoscope of multiple covenantal images dancing before the eyes. No one covenant dominates but this montage conveys the

---

26. Motyer, *Isaiah*, 199.

27. Motyer, *Isaiah*, 199.

28. Motyer, *Isaiah*, 199.

29. Motyer, *Isaiah*, 199.

fact that all humanity is guilty of sin regardless of the covenantal administration, hence God will judge them for their infidelity.

Analysis

While there are elements that commend each of the foregoing views, the best view that explains Isaiah 24:5 is that the prophet refers to the Adamic covenant. The ideal way to demonstrate this claim is to examine the series of concentric circles around Isaiah 24:5: the verse itself, the broader context of Isaiah 24–27, the larger environment of Isaiah's prophecy, and the scope of the canon of Scripture, particularly the apostle Paul's pronouncements on similar themes.

Isaiah 24:5
Isaiah states: 'The earth lies defiled under its inhabitants; for they have transgressed the laws, violated the statutes, broken the everlasting covenant' (24:5). These statements point in a global or universal direction rather than the limited scope of the Mosaic covenant as Calvin argues. 'The earth [אֶרֶץ] lies defiled under its inhabitants.' The term אֶרֶץ can have a limited reference to the promised land, but in this case two factors point to the earth.[30] First, the immediate context of Isaiah 13–23 sets the stage for the prophet's condemnation of the Gentile nations, not merely Israel. Isaiah (23:17), for example, mentions the Gentile city of Tyre, which is in modern day Lebanon, before he transitions to chapter 24 and his repeated mention of the earth: 'Behold, the LORD will empty the earth and make it desolate .... The earth shall be utterly empty and utterly plundered; for the LORD has spoken His Word. The earth mourns and withers; the world languishes and withers; the highest people of the earth languish' (Isa. 24:1-4). Second, Isaiah democratizes the impending judgment: 'And it shall be, as with the people, so with the priest; as with the slave, so with his master; as with the maid, so with her mistress; as with the buyer, so with the seller; as with the lender, so with the borrower; as with the creditor, so with the debtor' (Isa. 24:2). All walks of life and economic stations fall under God's curse for their sins.

---

30. Cf. Polaski, 'Reflections on a Mosaic Covenant,' 61.

Another element of Isaiah 24:5 is the prophet's use of the lexeme, 'everlasting covenant [ברית עולם].' VanDrunen rightly notes that God applies this term to the postdiluvian Noahic covenant (Gen. 9:16), and so the prophet's use of Noahic imagery might point in this direction. But this term alone is not decisive for locating the Noahic covenant in Isaiah 24:5 as the Old Testament uses it for multiple covenants as the following table shows:

Abrahamic covenant	'And I will establish my covenant between me and you and your offspring after you throughout their generations for an *everlasting covenant*, to be God to you and to your offspring after you .... both he who is born in your house and he who is bought with your money, shall surely be circumcised. So shall my covenant be in your flesh an *everlasting covenant* .... God said, "No, but Sarah your wife shall bear you a son, and you shall call his name Isaac. I will establish my covenant with him as an *everlasting covenant* for his offspring after him"' (Gen. 17:7, 13, 19; cf. 1 Chron. 16:17; Ps. 105:10).
Davidic covenant	'For does not my house stand so with God? For he has made with me an *everlasting covenant*, ordered in all things and secure. For will he not cause to prosper all my help and my desire' (2 Sam. 23:5)?
New covenant	'Incline your ear, and come to me; hear, that your soul may live; and I will make with you an *everlasting covenant*, my steadfast, sure love for David' (Isa. 55:3; cf. 61:8). 'I will make with them an *everlasting covenant*, that I will not turn away from doing good to them. And I will put the fear of me in their hearts, that they may not turn from me' (Jer. 32:40; cf. 50:5). 'I will remember my covenant with you in the days of your youth, and I will establish for you an *everlasting covenant*' (Ezek. 16:60; cf. 37:26).

The book of Leviticus also attaches the term to the Sabbath in the Mosaic covenant: 'Every Sabbath day Aaron shall arrange it before the Lord regularly; it is from the people of Israel as an everlasting covenant' (Lev. 24:8, trans. mine).

The fact that Isaiah uses this term is not automatically determinative for identifying the specific covenant in view. Rather, 'everlasting covenant' means that it is enduring and does not pass away until it runs its divinely appointed course. God instituted circumcision, for example, as an everlasting covenant, which saw its fulfillment with the advent of Christ (Gen. 17:13; cf. Acts 7:8). The lexeme ברית עולם, therefore, simply means that the violated covenant persists – it was not temporary. One possible option is that the term עולם does not mean 'everlasting,' but 'ancient' (cf. e.g., Gen. 6:4) as Meredith Kline suggests.[31] But taken together עולם ברית most likely means that the Adamic covenant persists until the consummation both in terms of its requirements, rewards, and consequences for violation. Other portions of Scripture confirm this as the Adamic works-principle surfaces in the midst of the Mosaic covenant (Lev. 18:5) and in Christ's and Paul's teaching: perfect obedience secures eschatological life (cf. Luke 10:28; Gal. 3:12; Rom. 10:5). Moreover, Paul succinctly states that Christ was born 'under the law' (Gal. 4:4), which corroborates the conclusion that the terms of the Adamic covenant still persist.

The last element that deserves attention is that the inhabitants of the earth have 'transgressed the laws' and 'violated the statutes.' The Old Testament never uses the term תורת ('laws') for the Mosaic covenant, though the two are associated (e.g., Judg. 2:1; Ps. 111:5, 9; Exod. 31:16).[32] But as VanDrunen correctly points out, the book of Genesis uses the term to characterize Abraham's obedience to God's commandments (Gen. 26:5); this occurs long before the administration of the Mosaic covenant. The same pattern applies to the term חק ('statute'). The vast majority of the occurrences refer to the laws of the Mosaic covenant, but the term can refer

---

31. Meredith Kline, 'Death, Leviathan, and the Martyrs: Isaiah 24:1–27:1,' in *Essential Writings of Meredith G. Kline*, ed. Jonathan G. Kline (Peabody, MA: Hendrickson, 2017), 225; cf. HALOT, I:799.

32. Polaski, 'Reflections on a Mosaic Covenant,' 57.

to general laws (Gen. 47:22, 26). These two terms might therefore point to the Mosaic covenant, but the broader global context points in a different direction. The best explanation for the meaning of these two terms ('laws' and 'statutes') does not come from the immediate context but from the larger canonical context, especially Paul's use of Isaiah.

Isaiah 24–27

At this stage the two best contenders are the Adamic or Noahic covenants, not Calvin's Mosaic covenant or Motyer's indefinite covenant view. Isaiah refers to a covenant that the inhabitants of the earth have violated, and the Bible only knows of two such universal covenants, the Adamic or Noahic. The inhabitants of the earth were not in covenant with God at Sinai; this was a relationship restricted to Israel alone. While Isaiah employs language that evokes other covenants, such as 'everlasting covenant,' 'laws,' and 'statutes,' the global indictment points away from an indefinite referent and to either the Adamic or Noahic covenants. The larger context of Isaiah 24–27, however, leads away from the Noahic covenant and to the Adamic covenant because of its chief topic, namely, death. Kline points out that Isaiah 24–27 has been called 'Isaiah's apocalypse,' and that the chief subject is Yahweh's victory over death.[33] The centerpiece of the prophet's apocalypse is Isaiah 25:6-8:

> On this mountain the LORD of hosts will make for all peoples a feast of rich food, a feast of well-aged wine, of rich food full of marrow, of aged wine well refined. And he will swallow up on this mountain the covering that is cast over all peoples, the veil that is spread over all nations. He will swallow up death forever; and the Lord GOD will wipe away tears from all faces, and the reproach of his people he will take away from all the earth, for the LORD has spoken.[34]

The conquest of death finds its counterpart in Isaiah 24:1-3, but especially in the violation of the everlasting covenant, which merits covenantal sanction: 'Therefore a curse devours the earth, and its

---

33. Kline, 'Death, Leviathan, and the Martyrs,' 217; also Chisholm, 'The "Everlasting Covenant,"' 237.

34. Kline, 'Death, Leviathan, and the Martyrs,' 219-20.

inhabitants suffer for their guilt; therefore the inhabitants of the earth are scorched, and few men are left' (Isa. 24:6). The Old Testament attaches the entrance of death to the violation of the Adamic, not the Noahic, covenant. Adam introduced both death and curse to the creation (Gen. 2:16-17; 3:17) and Isaiah prophesies about the apocalyptic reversal of this covenantal judgment.

Canonical Connections to Paul
Some theologians such as Geerhardus Vos (1862-1949) have noted the integral relationship between the prophet Isaiah and the apostle Paul. Vos has suggested that Isaiah's princely mind finds its counterpart in the apostle's writings: 'Paul seems to have felt the congeniality of Isaiah's mind to his own. He quotes from him often and with that fine spiritual insight which penetrates beyond the surface meaning of a passage into the innermost mind of the author and divines the subtle shade of his momentary thought and feeling.'[35] In short, Isaiah is Paul's Old Testament mirror image given the similarity of the doctrinal themes they both address, and this is especially true with regard to Isaiah's apocalypse.[36] Isaiah 24:4, for example, states: 'The earth mourns and withers; the world languishes and withers,' which finds its Pauline counterpart in Romans 8:22: 'For we know that the whole creation has been groaning together in the pains of childbirth until now.'[37] Kline explains that in Isaiah 26:16-18 God's people battle against their enemy until God grants them deliverance through resurrection (Isa. 26:19), a theme that pulsates in Romans 8 with the creation's eager expectation of the revelation of the sons of God by resurrection (Rom. 8:23).[38]

In the Corinthian context, Paul specifically cites Isaiah 25:8 in his victory taunt against death: 'When the perishable puts on the imperishable, and the mortal puts on immortality, then shall come

---

35. Geerhardus Vos, 'Some Doctrinal Features of the Early Prophecies of Isaiah,' *PRR* 8 (1897): 462.

36. On Paul's use of Isaiah, see J. Ross Wagner, *Heralds of the Good News: Isaiah and Paul in Concert in the Letter to the Romans* (Leiden: Brill, 2003).

37. Kline, 'Death, Leviathan, and the Martyrs,' 222-23; also Douglas J. Moo, *The Epistle to the Romans*, NICNT (Grand Rapids: Eerdmans, 1996), 514.

38. Kline, 'Death, Leviathan, and the Martyrs,' 223.

to pass the saying that is written: "Death is swallowed up in victory"' (1 Cor. 15:54).[39] In the Corinthian and Romans contexts, Paul's doctrinal rhapsodies on Christ's victory over death originate from reflection on the Adamic ancestry of death. Paul, for example, writes:

> Thus it is written, 'The first man Adam became a living being'; the last Adam became a life-giving Spirit. But it is not the spiritual that is first but the natural, and then the spiritual. The first man was from the earth, a man of dust; the second man is from heaven. As was the man of dust, so also are those who are of the dust, and as is the man of heaven, so also are those who are of heaven. Just as we have borne the image of the man of dust, we shall also bear the image of the man of heaven (1 Cor. 15:45-49, trans. mine).

Adam, the man of dust, introduced death and the last Adam is the one who, in Isaianic terms, swallows death in victory through His resurrection. Within this immediate context Paul quotes Genesis 2:7, 'The first man Adam became a living being,' in conjunction with his use of Isaiah 25:8, 'Death is swallowed up in victory.'[40] The Adamic, not Noahic, narrative is the primary subtext of Isaiah's apocalypse. In fact, Isaiah's apocalypse was no minor interest for Paul but was a chief element in his explanation of Israel's eschatological redemption in Romans 9–11 (Rom. 11:26-27; cf. Isa. 27:8-9).[41] Paul's use of Isaiah does not merely consist of a few scattered phrases but undoubtedly rests in the whole complex of Isaiah 24–27.

The Isaianic reflections on death and the culpability of humanity for its presence in the world find another Pauline counterpart in Romans 5:12-21. Paul clearly states that death entered the world through Adam's sin: 'Therefore, just as sin came into the world through one man, and death through sin, and so death spread to all men because all sinned' (Rom. 5:12). Crucial is that God takes Adam's covenantal transgression and imputes it to all humanity.

---

39. Kline, 'Death, Leviathan, and the Martyrs,' 219, 224.

40. G. K. Beale and D. A. Carson, eds., *The New Testament Commentary on the Use of the Old Testament* (Grand Rapids: Baker, 2007), 747-48.

41. Beale and Carson, *Commentary*, 676; Moo, *Romans*, 727-29; Wagner, *Heralds of the Good News*, 294-98.

All human beings are guilty of violating the covenant of works on two grounds: (1) Adam's imputed sin and guilt, and (2) their own personal violations of God's law, the knowledge of which they possess by virtue of the inscription of the law upon their hearts. In Kline's analysis:

> What the prophet says in the context of 24:4 must be recognized as a significant source for the covenantal theology of death in Romans 5:12 and the verses that follow. Isaiah deals there with death as a curse. Like Paul, Isaiah teaches that death entered the world through the entrance of sin—indeed, through the sin of breaking 'the ancient covenant' in Eden—and that death so passed unto all men, devouring the earth's population, generation after generation.[42]

As Isaiah states, 'The earth lies defiled under its inhabitants; for they have transgressed the laws, violated the statutes, broken the everlasting covenant. Therefore a curse devours the earth .... The earth staggers like a drunken man; it sways like a hut; its transgression lies heavy upon it, and it falls, and will not rise again' (Isa. 24:5-6a, 20).

The fact that Paul employs the same term that appears in the Septuagint's translation of Isaiah to characterize Adam's sin further confirms the connections between Isaiah 24 and Romans 5:12-21. As the subsequent chapter on Romans 5:12-21 demonstrates, Paul distinguishes between sin (ἁμαρτία) and transgression (παράβασις), or covenantal violation. God imputes Adam's παράβασις to all humanity, and in this manner 'all sinned' (Rom. 5:12). But at the same time all humans violate natural law: 'For when Gentiles, who do not have the law, by nature do what the law requires, they are a law to themselves, even though they do not have the law' (Rom. 2:14).[43] Contra Gesenius and others, such as Johnson, who claim that natural law is 'against the spirit of Hebraism which knows no law superior to the revealed law'

---

42. Kline, 'Death, Leviathan, and the Martyrs,' 225; see also idem, *Kingdom Prologue: Genesis Foundations for a Covenantal Worldview* (Overland Park, KS: Two Age Press, 2000), 14.

43. John N. Oswalt, *The Book of Isaiah: Chapters 1-39*, NICOT (Grand Rapids: Eerdmans, 1986), 446.

and that it 'runs completely contrary to the Hebrew mind,' Paul's own use of natural law is contrafactual evidence.[44] Gesenius takes Vitringa to task for relying on the earlier exegesis of Ibn Ezra who, like Moses Maimonides (1135-1204), supposedly added his 'philosophical education to the base of the biblical documents.'[45] In other words, Ibn Ezra superimposed natural law categories on Isaiah's text.

Yet, as earlier chapters demonstrate, natural law categories are not foreign to the Old Testament. Paul's discussion of the 'work of the law' written on the heart does not arise *de novo* with his letter to Rome. As a number of scholars have pointed out, natural law categories appear repeatedly in the Old Testament. David Novak argues Cain intuitively knew that his murder of Abel was wrong. The Genesis narrative never states that he received a positive command, 'Thou shalt not murder,' yet God held him accountable for his sinful act. God countered Cain's claim that he was not his brother's keeper with his punishment and exile, which in effect declared, 'You are your brother's keeper and you rejected your duty by murdering him.'[46] The same natural law pattern unfolds in Abraham's interaction with the pagan king Abimelech and the Egyptian midwives who feared God more than Pharaoh.[47] Moreover, closer to Isaiah 24:5, VanDrunen surveys the broader context of Isaiah's oracles against the nations (Isa. 13-23) and asks the pertinent question of what moral standard does the prophet use as the basis for his indictments? Certainly not the Mosaic law, as Isaiah never invokes it against them.[48] To borrow Gesenius' objection against natural law, What *positive Gesetz* ('positive law') does the prophet cite against the

---

44. Gesenius, *Jesaia*, 764: 'vollkommen gegen den Geist des Hebraismus, weicher kein adhere Gesetz kennt, als das geoffenbarte;' Johnson, *Chaos*, 43.

45. Gesenius, *Jesaia*, 764: 'öfter seine philosophicshe Bildung zur Unseit in die biblischen Urkunden tragen will.'

46. David Novak, *Natural Law in Judaism* (Cambridge: Cambridge University Press, 1998), 33-34.

47. Novak, *Natural Law*, 47-50. See also VanDrunen, *Divine Covenants*, 263-81. Note, there is debate among scholars whether the midwives were Hebrew or Egyptian. Novak persuasively argues that the midwives were Egyptian.

48. VanDrunen, *Divine Covenants*, 178-90, esp. 186-89.

nations in Isaiah 13–23?[49] The answer is, none, which means that God holds them accountable for their violations of the natural law, or in Pauline terms, the work of the law written on their hearts.

Imputed Adamic sin and violations of natural law, then, are the means by which the inhabitants of the earth have 'transgressed the laws [παρέβησαν τὸν νόμον], violated the statutes, [and] broken the everlasting covenant' (Isa. 24:5); note the Septuagint translation of Isaiah uses the verbal form of παράβασις, which anticipates Paul's use of the noun in Romans 5:14 when he describes Adam's sin. Imputed sin, guilt, and personal sins account for the legal ground for the continued imposition of the covenantal sanction of death. These covenantal transgressions trigger the curse; note Isaiah 24:6's עַל־כֵּן / διὰ τοῦτο. This pattern does not fit the Noahic covenant. Under the Noahic covenant sin does not warrant curse as it does in the Adamic or Mosaic dispensations.[50] True, those who shed the blood of man receive their just punishment, but this is a planned part of God's covenantal administration, not a violation that warrants covenant-breaking curse as described in Isaiah 24:5-6. Adam's covenantal breach triggered the curse of his exile from the garden as did Israel's sins, which prompted their exile from the land. In the words of Jeremiah, Israel broke the Mosaic covenant (Jer. 31:20); or in Hosea's characterization, 'like Adam [Israel] broke the covenant' (Hosea 6:7). When people commit murder, they suffer penalty but this does not break the Noahic

---

49. Gesenius, *Jesaia*, 764.

50. Some, such as Mason, argue this very point. Namely, the Noahic covenant is not purely promissory but 'bilateral,' and thus like other biblical covenants has responsibilities and sanctions, and thus curses (Mason, 'Another Flood?' 180, 183, 184-86, 194-95; idem, *'Eternal Covenant' in the Pentateuch: The Contours of an Elusive Phrase* [New York: T & T Clark, 2008], vii, 47-87, esp. 87). Others, such as Blenkinsopp, claim that Isaiah reshapes the purely promissory Noahic covenant into a bilateral covenant (Joseph Bleninsopp, *Isaiah 1-39*, AB [New York: Doubleday, 2000], 351-52). For those who argue the Noahic covenant is unilateral, see, e.g., James Barr, 'Reflections on the Covenant with Noah,' in *Covenant as Context: Essays in Honour of E. W. Nicholson*, ed. A. D. H. Mayes and R. B. Salters (Oxford: Oxford University Press, 2003), 11-22, esp. 12-13; Gerhard Von Rad, *Genesis: A Commentary*, rev. ed. (Philadelphia: The Westminster Press, 1972), 133-34; Bruce K. Waltke, *Genesis: A Commentary* (Grand Rapids: Zondervan, 2001), 144-45.

covenant – the rainbow remains in the sky. *Pace* VanDrunen, 'the curse on the earth consequent upon violation of the covenant (Isa. 24:5-6)' does not correspond 'to the withdrawal of the curse in the Noahic covenant' (Gen. 8:21).[51] Death unabatedly continues to devour generation after generation of Adam's descendants all under Noah's rainbow. The Noahic covenant does not remove the Adamic curse of death but rather is a stay of execution, the final judgment postponed.

If the Adamic covenant offers, then, the best explanation for Isaiah's universal death-swallowing curse, what of the different allusions to the Noahic covenant? As noted above, there are definite intertextual referents to God's covenantal dealings with Noah: calling the Adamic covenant an 'everlasting covenant' (Isa. 24:5; cf. Gen. 9:16), invoking Noahic language that 'the windows of heaven are opened' (Isa 24:18; cf. Gen. 8:2; 7:11), and the call for God's people to enter their chambers until the flood of His wrath has passed (Isa. 26:20; cf. Gen. 7:16) all fit Noahic patterns.[52] Nevertheless, it is not merely that the Adamic covenant lurks nearby while Noah takes center stage, *pace* VanDrunen.[53] Rather, Isaiah conveys the apocalyptic denouement of Adam's death-producing covenantal transgression in Noahic hues.[54] Adam stands center stage and Noah is supporting cast. This pattern unfolds in the New Testament where Jesus and Peter depict the consummation in terms of Noah's world-ending flood (Luke 17:26-37; 2 Pet. 3:1-7).[55]

Conclusion

Splintered interpretations reveal that Isaiah 24:5 is a challenging passage of Scripture to interpret. Exegetes have located virtually every biblical covenant in this verse with the exception of the new

---

51. VanDrunen, *Divine Covenants*, 194.

52. VanDrunen, *Divine Covenants*, 193-94; Kline, 'Death, Leviathan, and the Martyrs,' 235.

53. VanDrunen, *Divine Covenants*, 195.

54. Similarly, Oswalt, *Isaiah*, 446.

55. Bruce K. Waltke, *An Old Testament Theology: An Exegetical, Canonical, and Thematic Approach* (Grand Rapids: Zondervan, 2007), 300-01; also Streett, 'As It Was in the Days of Noah,' 33-34.

and Davidic covenants. The fact that all of God's covenants bear some similarities accounts for some of this interpretive chaos. Earlier chapters have noted, for example, the similarities between the Adamic and Mosaic covenants. And this chapter has observed that the Noahic covenant has left an indelible impression on the Old and New Testaments, so much so that Isaiah, Jesus, and Peter all characterize the consummation in Noahic terms. Nevertheless, the fact that Isaiah deals with the Gentile nations (Isa. 13–23) and the whole earth (Isa. 24:1-6) and not Israel alone, precludes the Abrahamic and Mosaic covenants as viable interpretive options. That Isaiah also reveals God's victory over death (Isa. 25:8) and that Paul picks up this very theme and juxtaposes it with the Adamic context (1 Cor. 15:42-58; Rom. 5:12-21), both confirm that the Adamic covenant is the best interpretive option for Isaiah 24:5.

There are at least two important implications of this exegetical conclusion. First, once again, contrary to critics of the doctrine, it does not rest on one isolated text such as Hosea 6:7. The doctrine has an exegetical foundation that is spread throughout the canon of Scripture. Even among those interpreters who chose other options, such as Calvin (Mosaic covenant), VanDrunen (Noahic covenant), or Motyer (no specific covenant), all three recognize that the God-Adam relationship lies close at hand and invoke it to explain their exegesis. When Paul explains the presence of death in the world and the work of Christ as its remedy, he looks back at the garden of Eden through the prism of Isaiah's prophecy; he borrows the prophet's language about God swallowing death in victory. Second, as Kline notes, Paul's covenantal federalism does not arise *de novo* in his own work but has roots that reach deep into the Old Testament. This means that the covenant of works is not a foreign imposition on the biblical text but a doctrine that grows organically from it. In this particular case, Isaiah identified humanity's violation of the Adamic covenant as the reason why they universally suffered the curse of death.

~: II.5 :~

Like Adam They Broke
the Covenant
(Hosea 6:7)

Introduction

*I*n the history of the doctrine of the covenant of works Hosea
6:7 has played a prominent but nevertheless debated role.
Does the text say, 'But like Adam they transgressed the covenant'
(ESV, ASV, NAS, NIV, NLT; VUL; German *Bibel*, Wycliffe,
Coverdale, Bishop's Bible), or 'But they like men have transgressed
the covenant' (KJV; NKJ; LXX; Geneva), or 'At Adam they broke
the covenant' (NET, NRSV, RSV, TNIV)?[1] Does the prophet
speak of Adam, people in general, or a physical location? The answer
to this question is not insignificant. If the text refers to Adam,
the first human being, then it is an explicit biblical reference to
the covenant of works.

While the outcome of this debated question is important, at
the same time it does not single-handedly determine whether
the covenant of works exists despite the claims of a number of

---

1. For some of these references, see Byron G. Curtis, 'Hosea 6:7 and Covenant-
Breaking like/at Adam,' in *The Law is Not of Faith: Essays on Works and Grace
in the Mosaic Covenant*, ed. Bryan D. Estelle, J. V. Fesko, and David VanDrunen
(Phillipsburg, NJ: P & R, 2009), 170-209, esp. 178-80.

nineteenth- and twentieth-century critics. The covenant of works does not hinge on one specific text, let alone Hosea 6:7. Rather, the doctrine rests on multiple exegetical pillars. Remove any one pillar and the doctrinal edifice still has other multiple points of support. Most advocates of the covenant of works have historically acknowledged that the doctrine was a theological construct; in historic hermeneutical terms, the doctrine is a good and necessary consequence (WCF I.vi).

Does the fact that the doctrine rests on multiple exegetical pillars mean that Hosea 6:7 is therefore superfluous? If the text has been the location of a pitched exegetical battle with no one position emerging as the clear and uncontested victor, why not altogether bypass the verse in question? While some theologians over the years have done precisely that, this chapter presents the thesis that Hosea 6:7 does indeed refer to Adam, the first human being, and thus is an explicit reference to a pre-fall Adamic covenant. The reference to Adam, however, is part of a double-entendre where the prophet refers both to the first man and to a murderous event at the city of Adam. This chapter proves this thesis by first presenting a brief history of the exegesis of Hosea 6:7. Second, the chapter gives an overview of the larger context of Hosea where the verse in question appears. Third, the chapter offers exegesis of Hosea 6:7. Fourth, the chapter briefly discusses the theological implications of Hosea's invocation of Adam as a negative comparative foil for Israel and its significance for the covenant of works. Last, the chapter concludes with some observations about the importance of Hosea 6:7 for the covenant of works.

History of Exegesis

The interpretive debate seesaw for Hosea 6:7 begins in the post-apostolic period with comments that come from *Genesis Rabbah*:

> It is written, 'But they are like a man [Adam], they have transgressed the covenant' (Hosea 6:7). 'They are like a man,' specifically, like the first man. [We shall now compare the story of the first man in Eden with the story of Israel in its land.] 'In the case of the first man, I brought him into the garden of Eden, I commanded him, he violated my commandment, I judged him to be sent away and driven

240

out' .... 'So too in the case of his descendants, I brought them into the Land of Israel, I commanded them, they violated my commandment, I judged them to be sent out and driven away'....[2]

Genesis Rabbah was written between A.D. 300-500 and is a midrash (an ancient Jewish commentary) on Genesis. And at this point in the commentary, the author appeals to Hosea 6:7 as the basis for a comparison between Adam and Israel. The commentary notes the potential ambiguity in Hosea's original statement with the inclusion of the indefinite article, *a* man, but then specifies that the intended man is Adam. Around the same timeframe, within the Christian community, Jerome (347-420) translated the Vulgate and rendered it as a reference to Adam: *ipsi autem sicut Adam transgressi sunt pactum* ('They like Adam transgressed the covenant'). Jerome's translation was one of the chief exegetical means by which the concept of an Adamic covenant entered the theological stream of the church. Early modern Roman Catholic theologian Cornelius à Lapide (1567-1637) glosses Hosea 6:7 as 'the first parents in paradise violated the covenant with God.'

Lapide cites a number of patristic and medieval exegetes who argue the same conclusion including Jerome, Cyril (ca. 376-444), Rupert of Deutz (ca. 1075-1129), Hugh of St. Victor (ca. 1096-1141), and Nicholas of Lyra (ca. 1270-1349). Lapide did not blindly follow tradition but also noted that the Septuagint rendered the verse as a common reference to humanity, 'Like men they transgressed the covenant.'[3] Cyril, for example, writes:

> We should at all points be very zealous in investigating the truth; in this case we need to say that in the place of *like someone* the Hebrew text says 'like Adam' *breaking a covenant*, so that we may

---

2. *Genesis Rabbah: The Judaic Commentary to the Book of Genesis*, trans. Jacob Neusner, 3 vols. (Atlanta: Scholars Press, 1985), 19.9 (vol. I, 208-09); also Seth D. Postell, *Adam as Israel: Genesis 1-3 as the Introduction to the Torah and Tanakh* (Cambridge: James Clarke and Co., 2012), 6-7; Carlos Bovell, 'Genesis 3:21: The History of Israel in a Nutshell,' *ExpT* 115 (2004): 361-66.

3. Cornelius à Lapide, *R. P. Cornelii A Lapide e Societate Jesu, Sacrae Scripturae Olim Lovanni, Postea Romae Professoris, Commentaria in Duodecim Prophetas Minores* (ex Typographia Balleoniana, 1761), *loc. cit.* Hosea 6:7 (p. 111); Richard A. Muller, *Post-Reformation Reformed Dogmatics*, 4 vols. (Grand Rapids: Baker, 2003), II:437.

understand that the *breaking* by the people of Israel was like that committed by Adam. While it was granted to him, remember, to have a relationship with God, to live without [fear of] corruption, (143) and to be regaled with the delights of paradise, he paid no need to the divine commandment; he then took a turn for the worse, and was unexpectedly deprived of his former condition. So, too, with *them* that is the people of Israel .... But since like the first man—Adam, that is—they fell headlong into apostasy, *they* too, will be completely estranged from the one who was in the habit of making them prosper, *having broken a covenant.*[4]

In addition to Lapide, there were other sixteenth-century Roman Catholics who appealed to Hosea 6:7 to substantiate the existence of an Adamic covenant. Ambrogio Catharinus (1483-1553), a delegate to the Council of Trent and one of the first advocates of a fully federal imputation of Adam's sin partially rested his claims on Hosea 6:7.[5]

In Protestant circles there were voices for and against the Adamic referent in Hosea 6:7. John Calvin (1509-1564) famously rebuffed the Adamic interpretation:

> Others explain the words thus, 'They have transgressed as Adam the covenant.' But the word, Adam, we know is taken indefinitely for men. This exposition is frigid and diluted, 'They have transgressed as Adam the covenant;' that is, they have followed or imitated the example of their father Adam, who had immediately at the beginning transgressed God's commandment. I do not stop to refute this comment; for we see that it is in itself vapid.[6]

In Calvin's view, this particular text did not make reference to Adam, but other theologians were not of the same opinion. Even

---

4. Cyril of Alexandria, *Commentary on the Twelve Prophets*, vol. 1, trans. Robert C. Hill, The Fathers of the Church (Washington, D. C: Catholic University of America Press, 2007), 143.

5. Paolo Sarpi, *Historia del Concilio Tridentino* (London: Giovani Billio, 1619), 170; idem, *The Historie of the Councel of Trent*, trans. Nathanael Brent (London: Robert Barker and John Bill, 1620), 175. See also Aaron Denlinger, *Omnes in Adam Ex Pacto Dei: Ambrogio Catarino's Doctrine of Covenantal Solidarity and Its Influence on Post-Reformation Reformed Theologians* (Göttingen: Vandenhoeck & Ruprecht, 2010).

6. John Calvin, *Commentary on Hosea*, CTS (rep.; Grand Rapids: Baker, 1993), 235.

though the doctrine of the covenant did not prominently feature in Martin Luther's (1483-1546) theology, he nevertheless agreed with Jerome's interpretation of Hosea 6:7; the verse referred to Adam: 'They do as their father did. He transgressed the covenant he had received. Thus they have transgressed my covenant.'[7] Despite this acknowledgement of an Adamic referent, this seed never flourished in Luther's theology. This covenantal infertility did not characterize the exegesis and theology of Reformed theologians.

At the turn of the seventeenth century a number of Reformed theologians began to appeal to Hosea 6:7 as evidence of a pre-fall Adamic covenant. William Whitaker (1548-1595) acknowledged that Hosea 6:7 referred to a pre-fall covenant between God and Adam.[8] Alexander Nowell (ca. 1507-1602) also interpreted the text in a similar manner. Nowell cites Hosea 6:7 and Romans 5:19 when he explained the nature of Adam's fall: 'He the issue of the earth, not contented that he was made according to the image of God, with intolerable ambition, and pride sought to make himself equal with the majesty of God. Finally, he withdrew himself from allegiance to his Creator (Gen. 3:11; Hosea 6:7; Rom. 5:19), yea, and malapertly shook off his yoke.'[9] There were others, however, such as Lambert Daneau (ca. 1530-1595) that opted for the generic human referent.[10]

There were voices for and against the Adamic referent in the Reformed tradition. Evidence that the text had a mixed reception in support of the covenant of works appears in the fact that the Westminster divines did not cite Hosea 6:7 in either the Confession or Catechisms. The Confession cites Galatians 3:12, Romans 10:5 and 5:12, 19-20 to support its statement in

---

7. Martin Luther, *Lectures on the Minor Prophets*, Luther's Works, vol. 18, ed. Hilton C. Oswald (St. Louis, MO: Concordia, 1975), comm. Hosea 6:7 (p. 33).

8. Cf. William Whitaker, *Tractatus … De Peccato Originali* (Johannes Legat, 1600), 42-43, 76; Denlinger, *Ex Omnes Adam*, 233-35.

9. Alexander Nowell, *A Catechism Written in Latin by Alexander Nowell, Dean of St. Paul's*, trans. Thomas Norton (1570; Cambridge: Cambridge University Press, 1853), 149.

10. Lambert Daneau, *A Fruitfull Commentarie on the Twelve Small Prophets* (Cambridge: University of Cambridge, 1594), comm. Hosea 6:7 (p. 431).

VII.ii, and they cite Genesis 1:26, 2:17, Romans 2:14-15, 10:5, 5:12, 19-20, Galatians 3:10, 12, Ecclesiastes 7:29, Job 28:18 at XIX.i.[11] The Shorter Catechism cites Genesis 2:16-17, Romans 5:12, 1 Corinthians 15:21-22.[12] The original Larger Catechism does not cite proof texts.[13] The fact that the Confession and Shorter Catechism cite slightly different texts is likely due to the fact that different theologians were involved in the process of writing each respective document. The individuals involved did not necessarily share the same exegetical opinions even though they agreed on the doctrine. Nevertheless, noteworthy is the fact that Hosea 6:7 is missing. Hosea 6:7's absence is something that would change as the seventeenth century marched on. In the latter part of the century, numerous theologians appealed to the text as exegetical proof of the covenant of works including Francis Turretin (1623-1687), Petrus Van Mastricht (1630-1706), Johannes Heidegger (1633-1698), Leonard Riissen (ca. 1636-1700), Johannes Cocceius (1603-1669), Wilhelmus à Brakel (1635-1711), and Herman Witsius (1636-1708).[14]

---

11. *The Humble Advice of the Assembly of Divines Now by Authority of Parliament Sitting at Westminster Concerning a Confession of Faith* (London: Company of Stationers, 1647).

12. *The Humble Advice of the Assembly of Divines Now by Authority of Parliament Sitting at Westminster Concerning a Shorter Catechism* (London: J. F., 1648).

13. *The Humble Advice of the Assembly of Divines Now by Authority of Parliament Sitting at Westminster Concerning a Larger Catechism* (London: Evan Tyler, 1648).

14. Francis Turretin, *Institutes of Elenctic Theology*, 3 vols., trans. George Musgrave Giger, ed. James T. Dennison Jr. (Phillipsburg, NJ: P & R, 1992-97), VIII.iii.8; Petrus Van Mastricht, *Theoretica-Practica Theologia*, 9th ed., vol. 1 (Utrecht: W. van der Water, et al., 1724), XII.i (p. 413); Johannes Heidegger, *Corpus Theologiae Christianae* (Zurich: Officina Heidegerriana, 1732), IX.vi (p. 303); idem, *Medullae Theologiae Christianae* (Zurich: David Gessner, 1697), IX.iii (p. 69); Leonard Riissen, *Summa Theologiae Didactico-Elencticae* (Berne: Daniel Tschiffel, 1703), IX.xii (p. 231); Johannes Cocceius, *The Doctrine of the Covenant and Testament of God*, trans. Casey Carmichael (Grand Rapids: Reformation Heritage Books, 2016), I.iii (pp. 20-21); Wilhelmus à Brakel, *The Christian's Reasonable Service*, 4 vols., trans. Bartel Elshout (Morgan, PA: Soli Deo Gloria, 1992), I:365-66; Herman Witsius, *Economy of the Covenants Between God and Man: Comprehending a Body of Divinity*, 2 vols., trans. William Crookshank (1822; Escondido, CA: Den Dulk Foundation, 1991), I.viii.1; Cf. Richard A. Muller, *Post-Reformation Reformed Dogmatics*, 4 vols. (Grand Rapids: Baker, 2003),

While not all theologians who appealed to the text present exegesis, there was undoubtedly a suitable awareness of the nuts and bolts of how one hermeneutically arrived at the conclusion that Hosea 6:7 spoke of Adam. Wilhelmus à Brakel presents five points in favor of his exegesis of the disputed text. Even though אדם can be translated as either *Adam* or *man*, à Brakel opts for the former because, first, he believes that rendering the term *man* would rob the statement of its intended emphasis. Of what force would the comparison be if Israel violated the covenant like other men who were also members of the covenant? In order for them to violate the covenant they would need to belong to it.

Second, in Genesis, Deuteronomy (32:8) and 1 Chronicles 1:1 the term אדם is the proper name *Adam*. This is especially the case in Job 31:33, 'If I covered my transgressions as Adam [כאדם].' À Brakel notes that there is no controversy over the translation of Job 31:33, which is an express statement about Adam's effort to cover his sins. This is the same grammatical construction that appears in Hosea 6:7, 'They like Adam [כאדם] have transgressed the covenant.' À Brakel employs the Reformation principle of using clearer passages to interpret less clear passages.

Third, Hosea 6:7 does not employ an emphatic ה and that such grammatical markers are typically not employed with proper names. If the term אדם should be translated as *man*, then one might expect to find the term marked by a ה. Fourth, based on other texts of Scripture, one can conclude that Adam was in covenant with God and that Hosea 6:7 corroborates these other references.

Fifth, and finally, the referent to Adam fits well within Hosea's overall argument. The prophet's intention was to demonstrate the magnitude of Ephraim's and Judah's sin by identifying the origin and an example of it. Their own breach of their covenant originated with Adam and was therefore all the more reprehensible. Adam threw caution to the wind and recklessly and faithlessly broke the covenant. Israel followed in the similitude of Adam's transgression

II:436-41; Willem Van Asselt, *The Federal Theology of Johannes Cocceius (1603-69)* (Leiden: Brill, 2001), 250.

by treacherously violating God's covenant with them.[15] À Brakel, therefore, did not baldly appeal to the text but offered exegetical and theological rationale to arrive at his conclusion.

Such exegetical patterns continued in the eighteenth and nineteenth centuries as theologians such as Thomas Boston (1676-1732), Adam Gib (1714-1788), John Brown of Haddington (1722-1787), and James Hogg (ca. 1658-1734) appealed to Hosea 6:7 in support of the covenant of works.[16] In most cases these theologians either appealed to the text or echoed earlier exegesis. But in Boston's case, he checked with a number of authorities. Like theologians before him, he notes the parallel lexeme, כאדם ('like Adam') in Job 31:33, 'If I covered my transgressions as Adam.' But he also cites Psalm 82:7, 'But ye shall die like Adam.'[17] Boston surveyed numerous other exegetes and translations to arrive at his conclusion, including 'the Vulgate, Tirgurine, Castalio, Arias Montanus, Rabbi Solomon, Grotius, and the Dutch translation.'[18] He examined various translations, such as the Vulgate and the Dutch *Statenvertaling*, as well as consulting rabbinic authorities to arrive at his conclusion that Hosea 6:7 spoke of Adam.

By the nineteenth century, however, support for the covenant of works began to wane. Reformed theologians such as John Colquhoun (1748-1827) appealed to Hosea 6:7, but critics began to line up and dismissed both the doctrine and exegesis that saw Adam referenced in the disputed verse.[19] John Eagleton (1785-1832), for example, rejected any claims that the Scriptures teach the covenant of works,

---

15. À Brakel, *Christian's Reasonable Service*, I:365-66.

16. Thomas Boston, *A View of the Covenant of Works from the Sacred Records* (Edinburgh: John Gray, 1775), 5-7; Adam Gib, *Kaina kai Palaia: Sacred Contemplations in Three Parts* (Philadelphia: W. Young and J. McCulloch, 1788), 81; John Brown of Haddington, *A Compendious View of Natural and Revealed Religion in Seven Books* (Glasgow: John Bryce, 1782), 217; James Hog, *A Letter to a Gentleman Detecting the Errors Vented at this Time* (Edinburgh: William Brown and William Dicky, 1716), 11.

17. Boston, *Covenant of Works*, 6.

18. Boston, *Covenant of Works*, 54-55.

19. John Colquhoun, *A Treatise on the Covenant of Works* (Edinburgh: Thomsons, Brothers, 1821), 6.

though he admitted that theologians appeal to Hosea 6:7. Eagleton granted that the text might say, 'They, like Adam, have transgressed the covenant,' but that such a translation does not say 'Adam fell by transgressing the covenant of works which promised eternal life to his obedience, and threatened his disobedience with eternal death.' Instead, Eagleton employed the strictest positivist reading. The text, he argues, does not say *covenant of works* but ברית. This means that the text refers to a purification (Eagleton's definition of ברית), not a mutual agreement with conditional rewards and sanctions.[20] Even then, Eagleton rejects the idea that אדם is a proper name and instead refers to *men*. Israel, like common men, walked in the ways of the nations and conducted themselves sinfully.[21]

By the twentieth century Reformed theologians were somewhat evenly split. Those who advocated the covenant of works commonly appealed to Hosea 6:7 and critics of the doctrine dismissed the idea that the disputed text spoke of Adam. Critics include Herman Hoeksema (1886-1965), and John Murray (1898-1975); proponents include Geerhardus Vos (1862-1949), Louis Berkhof (1873-1957), and B. B. Warfield (1851-1921).[22] In fact, Warfield wrote a brief but comprehensive essay that traced the history of interpretation of the text and presented exegesis in favor of the Adamic referent. In his typically adroit manner, Warfield surveys every period of church history, rabbinic sources, and contemporary scholarship as well as the various exegetical options. In the end, he remarks: 'We

---

20. John Eagleton, *Thoughts on the Covenant of Works: Epistolary Address, to the Junior Ministers of the Gospel of All Denominations* (London: R. Baynes, 1829), 95. See similar conclusions in John Kelly, *The Divine Covenants: Their Nature and Design; or, The Covenants Considered as Successive Stages in the Development of the Divine Purposes of Mercy* (London: Jackson, Walford, & Hodder, 1861), 13-20.

21. Eagleton, *Covenant of Works*, 95-96.

22. Herman Hoeksema, *Reformed Dogmatics* (1966; Grand Rapids: Reformed Free Publishing Association, 1985), 220-21; John Murray, 'Adamic Administration,' in *Collected Writings*, vol. 2 (Edinburgh: Banner of Truth, 1977), 49; Geerhardus Vos, *Reformed Dogmatics*, 5 vols., ed. Richard B. Gaffin, Jr., et al. (Bellingham, WA: Lexham Press, 2012-14), II:36; Louis Berkhof, *Systematic Theology: New Combined Edition* (1932, 1938; Grand Rapids: Eerdmans, 1996), 214-16; B. B. Warfield, 'Hosea VI.7: Adam or Man?' in *The Selected Shorter Writings*, 2 vols., ed. John E. Meeter (rep.; Phillipsburg, NJ: P & R, 2001), I:116-29.

do not think we should err therefore, if we adopted the translation, "Like Adam." But if we should err, we should err in a great and goodly company.'[23]

This overview of the history of the interpretation of Hosea 6:7 reveals several important factors. First, interpreting Hosea 6:7 as a reference to Adam and a pre-fall covenant was not the proprietary exegesis of Reformed theologians. It originated in post-apostolic rabbinic interpretation and patristic exegesis, such as with Jerome's Vulgate. An important qualification to make, however, is that just because exegetes acknowledged the existence of an Adamic covenant does not mean they were advocates of the early modern Reformed doctrine of the covenant of works. It does mean, however, that Reformed theologians were not alone in recognizing that Hosea 6:7 spoke of a pre-fall Adamic covenant.

Second, beyond patristic exegetes, medieval and sixteenth-century Roman Catholic theologians also interpreted Hosea 6:7 as a reference to an Adamic covenant. Third, when Reformed theologians appealed to Hosea 6:7 as evidence of the covenant of works, it was not the solitary exegetical proof text. Hosea 6:7 was part of a larger web of passages that theologians employed to argue for the doctrine's existence.

Fourth, just because a theologian argued for an Adamic referent does not mean that he was an advocate of the covenant of works; conversely, just because a theologian promoted the covenant of works did not automatically mean he appealed to Hosea 6:7 or believed it had an Adamic referent. The lines of opinion on this question crisscross in many different directions. One cannot say that just because he holds to the covenant of works automatically means he will interpret Hosea 6:7 in a particular manner. That being said, there are respectable reasons to defend the idea that Hosea 6:7 reveals the existence of a pre-fall Adamic covenant.

Context

In order to exegete Hosea 6:7, we must first set the stage for the broader context of the verse in question. Hosea was called by God

---

23. Warfield, 'Hosea VI.7,' 129.

to prophesy the destruction and exile of Israel when the nation was at the height of its wealth during the reign of Jeroboam II (793-753 B.C.). Hosea famously inaugurated his ministry through a living parable when he married an adulterous woman, Gomer.[24] One of the most defining characteristics of the book is the subtext of Deuteronomy 4:20-31, which encapsulates Israel's history on which the prophet bases his message. This means that the Mosaic covenant, with its attendant curses and blessings, is a significant theme within the book of Hosea.[25] The prophet's essential message is that God's wrath will fall on Israel for her sin and violation of the Mosaic covenant, but eschatological blessing and reconciliation will follow His judgment.[26] Covenant, therefore, looms large on Hosea's horizon; it is the fulcrum on which the prophet moves the curses against Israel and holds out the hope of God's faithfulness to His people in spite of their sin.

The prophet presents his oracles first through his parabolic marriage and children (1:2–3:5), and then his prophetic oracles in chapters 4–14. Hosea levels charges against Israel (chp. 4), against the priests and people (chp. 5), and issues a call to repentance (6:1-3). In the heart of his prophecies Hosea indicts the people with breaking God's covenant in chapters 6:4–11:11. The concluding section of his book brings further accusations against Israel, a deceptive people (11:12–12:14), he heralds the end of God's compassion in the present (chp. 13), and holds out the hope of restoration and renewal (chp. 14). The text in question, therefore, comes in the midst of Hosea's charge that Israel has broken the terms of the Mosaic covenant; thus God will visit the covenant sanctions on the people for their infidelity.

Within the immediate context of Hosea 6:7, the prophet calls the nation to repentance (Hosea 6:1-3), but on the heels of this cry God asks a rhetorical question with a pair of synonymous parallelisms that acknowledge the fleeting covenant loyalty of Israel and Judah:

24. Douglas Stuart, *Hosea-Jonah*, WBC, vol. 31 (Waco, TX: Word Books, 1987), 9.

25. Walter Brueggemann, *Tradition for Crisis: A Study in Hosea* (Richmond, VA: John Knox Press, 1968), 13-25.

26. Stuart, *Hosea-Jonah*, 6-8, xxxii-xlii.

What shall I do with you, O Ephraim?
What shall I do with you, O Judah?
Your love is like a morning cloud,
like the dew that goes early away (HOSEA 6:4).

Israel and Judah are fundamentally unfaithful – they lack the desired covenant love (חסד) (Hosea 6:6). Because of their sin and faithlessness God hemmed them in through the ministry of His prophets. But in particular, Hosea invokes the language of Deuteronomy and the terms of the Mosaic covenant: 'I have slain them by the words of my mouth, and my judgment goes forth as the light' (Hosea 6:5). In particular, the lexeme 'words of my mouth' (אמרי־פי) reflects the curses of the Mosaic covenant: 'Give ear, O heavens, and I will speak, and let the earth hear the words of my mouth [אמרי־פי]' (Deut. 32:1). Heeding God's voice was the means by which Israel would receive blessing or conversely curse for their disobedience (cf. Deut. 28:1-6, 15-35).[27] God reveals His desire is not for rebellion but for covenant love: 'For I desire steadfast love and not sacrifice, the knowledge of God rather than burnt offerings' (Hosea 6:6). God was disinterested in the veneer of formalism and lip service to His covenant, a common theme in the messages of other prophets and even Christ Himself (Amos 5:21-24; Isa. 1:12-17; Micah 6:6-8; Matt. 9:13; 12:7).[28]

Like Adam, Like Men, or At Adam?

This brings us to the shores of the verse in question. Does Hosea say: 'But like Adam,' 'But like men,' or 'At Adam they transgressed the covenant'? In the history of the interpretation of the verse, the first two options have been the dominant choices, but in recent years the third has become a contender, largely in part because of the latter half of the verse: 'But [like Adam or men, or at Adam] they transgressed the covenant; *there they dealt faithlessly with me*' (Hosea 6:7, emphasis). That Hosea 6:7a might refer to a place rather than people or a person is due to the locative adverb in Hosea 6:7b, namely, שׁם ('there'). There is evidence for all three variants, thus it proves helpful to review the

---

27. Stuart, *Hosea-Jonah*, 109-10.

28. Stuart, *Hosea-Jonah*, 110.

other two options before defending the thesis that 'like Adam,' is a part of Hosea's intended meaning.

At Adam

Two of the more recent defenders of the 'at Adam' option are Francis Andersen and David Noel Freedman in their Anchor Bible commentary on Hosea. They appeal to the immediate context and the statement in verse 9: 'As robbers lie in wait for a man, so the priests band together; they murder on the way to Shechem; they commit villainy.' They believe this verse is determinative for the context and dictates that the passage is about a murderous band of priests who committed their crime near Adam (cf. Josh. 3:16). Andersen and Freedman surmise that Adam is a town at the Jordan crossing on the road connecting Shechem to the Israelite cities of Succoth and Mahanaim. Thus, while this gang of priests was on the road from the Transjordan to Shechem, they perpetrated murder at Adam, or conversely priests from Adam could have killed travelers on their way to Shechem. 'There,' at Adam, 'they transgressed the covenant.'[29] Other interpreters arrive at the same conclusion by suggesting that the text כ 'like' be emended to the preposition ב 'in,' or 'at,' to suggest 'at Adam.' Julius Wellhausen (1844-1918) was the first to suggest this possibility.[30] This emendation is a reasonable suggestion given that the two letters are similar in shape. Despite being a late-comer to the interpretive history of this verse, it seems to be the favored view among many contemporary commentators.[31]

Like Men

One of the oldest advocates of the 'like men' view dates back to the Septuagint, which renders the verse: αὐτοὶ δέ εἰσιν ὡς ἄνθρωπος

---

29. Francis I. Andersen and David Noel Freedman, *Hosea*, AB, vol. 24 (New York: Doubleday, 1980), 435-39.

30. Curtis, 'Hosea 6:7,' 181-82.

31. So James Luther Mays, *Hosea: A Commentary* (Philadelphia: The Westminster Press, 1969), 99-101; David Allan Hubbard, *Hosea: An Introduction and Commentary*, Tyndale Old Testament Commentary (Downers Grove: InterVarsity Press, 1989), 128-29; A. A. Macintosh, *Hosea: A Critical and Exegetical Commentary* (Edinburgh: T & T Clark, 1997), 236-39; cf. Hans Walter Wolff, *Hosea* (Minneapolis: Fortress, 1974), 121-22; Derek Kidner, *Love to the Loveless: The Message of Hosea* (Downers Grove: InterVarsity Press, 1981), 67-69.

παραβαίνων διαθήκην ('But they are as a man transgressing the covenant'). This is also the view of Calvin, the 1560 Geneva Bible, and the 1611 King James Bible.[32] In more recent years John Murray advocated the view but he does not present any substantive exegesis; he merely claims that the verse can be interpreted as a reference to people rather than to Adam.[33] Despite its commonality in the inter-testamental era as well as in the early modern period, the view has fallen out of favor. One, therefore, must reach back to the early modern exegetes to uncover the interpretive rationale in opting for 'like men' as the most likely choice.

Among early modern exegetes, Westminster divine Jeremiah Burroughs (1600-1646) provides a detailed explanation of this interpretation. Burroughs notes that there is good reason to read the lexeme as 'like Adam' given Paul's statements in Romans 5:14, namely, that there were those who 'had not sinned after the similitude of Adam's transgression.' So, as Adam was ejected from the garden, so too the Israelites should be cast out of the promised land. But Burroughs observes that noted Hebraist François Vatable (d. 1547) and Jewish convert to Christianity and leading Hebraist Immanuel Tremellius (1510-1580) argue that Hosea 6:7 can mean, 'They have broken my covenant as a man, they thought that I had been as their fellow creature.'[34] But rather than a reference to a generic 'man,' Burroughs observes: 'But the words are more usually read, as in our books, 'But they like men have transgressed the covenant;' that is, not as I, who, like a God, have kept covenant; but they, like such men as themselves, i.e., weak, inconstant, frail, unfaithful creatures, have transgressed' (Job 31:33).[35] Burroughs does not elaborate as to why he cites Job 31:33, a text commonly cited in favor of the Adam reading. Nevertheless, he argues that אדם should be translated as 'man' in their corrupt state, as weak and frail rather than as godly saints.

---

32. Curtis, 'Hosea 6:7,' 178-80.

33. Murray, 'Adamic Administration,' 49.

34. Jeremiah Burroughs, *An Exposition of the Prophecy of Hosea*, ed. Thomas Hall, Edward Reynolds, and James Sherman (1643, 1843; Beaver Falls, PA: Soli Deo Gloria, n.d.), 334.

35. Burroughs, *Hosea*, 334.

They have acted like ordinary men and have thus transgressed God's covenant. Burroughs takes Hosea 6:7b's שָׁם ('there') as a reference to the promised land, to Canaan. Hence, 'They like men have transgressed my covenant; there in Canaan they have dwelt treacherously.' He believed, therefore, that Hosea's immediate reference was to the Mosaic covenant. Burroughs cites the Septuagint's rendering of Hosea 6:7b, κατεφρόνησέν μου ('they despised me') to explain the nature of Israel's covenantal transgression. Burroughs, therefore, was in dialogue with noted linguistic experts, different versions of the Old Testament, such as the Septuagint and likely the Vulgate, and thus arrived at the conclusion that 'like men' was the best interpretive option. One should note that Burroughs was an advocate of the covenant of works, hence his doctrinal convictions did not predetermine his exegesis.[36]

Like Adam
There are certainly good reasons to adopt either the 'at Adam' or 'like men' interpretations of Hosea 6:7a, but at the same time I believe there are three strong reasons that commend the idea that the statement refers to Adam: (1) other occurrences of the כְּאָדָם lexeme, (2) Hosea's numerous echoes and allusions to Genesis, especially the creation narrative, and (3) the apostle Paul's comparison of Adam and Israel. Within the context of the Old Testament, the first reason is the appearance of the same lexeme in Job 31:33, 'If I have covered my transgressions as Adam [כְּאָדָם], By hiding my iniquity in my bosom' (NKJV). Job contrasts his own transparency regarding his sin with Adam's efforts to hide his sin with fig-leaves (Gen. 3:7-8).[37] Similarly, Boston cites Psalm 82:7 in addition to Job 31:33, 'But ye shall die like Adam [כְּאָדָם].'[38]

---

36. Burroughs, *Hosea*, 334.

37. David J. A. Clines, *Job 31-37*, Word Biblical Commentary, vol. 18a (Nashville, TN: Thomas Nelson, 2006), 1030; cf. Tremper Longman III, *Job*, Baker Commentary on the Old Testament Wisdom and Psalms (Grand Rapids: Baker, 2012), 356 n. 11; Manfred Oeming, 'To Be Adam or Not to Be Adam: The Hidden Fundamental Anthropological Discourse Revealed in an Intertextual Reading of *Adam* in Job and Genesis,' in *Reading Job Intertextually*, ed. Katharine Dell and Will Kynes (New York: Bloomsbury, 2013), 19-29, esp. 26-27.

38. Boston, *Covenant of Works*, 6.

On Psalm 82:7 patristic, early modern, and modern translations opt for a generic reading of כאדם, that is, 'like men you shall die' (ESV; KJV; NAS; NET; NIV; NLT; NRSV; TNIV; NKJV; VUL 81:7). Modern commentators arrive at the same conclusion.[39] Although some commentators note the possibility that it is a reference to Adam. Derek Kidner, for example, states: 'This could be translated "like Adam", but the parallel expression, "like any prince", is too general to make this likely. "Like man"… is nearer the mark.'[40] Yet, Kidner's admission lends credence to Boston's appeal to the text as supporting evidence of the Adamic reading of Hosea 6:7a.

While the interpretation of Hosea 6:7a does not hinge on Psalm 82:7, it provides further corroborating evidence that other portions of the Old Testament use Adam as a comparative foil. Briefly, the overall context of the Psalm is suggestive of an Adamic reference. God sits in the congregation of the mighty and judges among the gods (Ps. 82:1). He brings judgment against the rulers of Israel, whom He designates as *gods* (אלהים) (cf. John 10:34).[41] While the comparison between mere men and princes is a possible reading, the more powerful contrast is between Adam and princes: 'Nevertheless, like Adam you shall die, and fall like any prince.' When we take into account, moreover, that the Old Testament employs נפל ('fall') for human leaders in sudden, disastrous deaths in battle or execution, then the verse aptly describes Adam's kingly fall (cf. Exod. 19:21; 33:28; Josh. 8:25; Judg. 8:10; 12:6; 20:44, 46; 1 Sam. 4:10; 31:8; 2 Sam. 1:19, 25, 27; 3:38; 11:7; 21:9; 1 Kings 22:20; Isa. 14:12;

---

39. Hans-Joachim Kraus, *Psalms 60-150* (Minneapolis: Fortress, 1993), 154; Marvin E. Tate, *Psalms 51-100*, WBC, vol. 20 (Dallas, TX: 1990), 338-39; Arthur Weiser, *The Psalms: A Commentary* (Philadelphia: The Westminster Press, 1998), 560; Charles Augustus Briggs, *A Critical and Exegetical Commentary on the Book of Psalms*, ICC, 2 vols. (Edinburgh: T & T Clark, 1976), II:216-17; Mitchell Dahood, *Psalms II: 51-100*, AB (New York: Doubleday, 1968), 268-71; also note John Calvin, *The Book of Psalms*, vol. 2, CTS (rep.; Grand Rapids: Baker, 1981), 335.

40. Derek Kidner, *Psalms 73-150*, TOTC (Downers Grove: InterVarsity Press), 299.

41. D. A. Carson and G. K. Beale, eds., *The New Testament Commentary on the Old Testament* (Grand Rapids: Baker, 2007), 465-66.

Jer. 20:4).[42] Israel's leaders will 'fall' like other tyrants, chiefs, princes, and the like. They will fall as Adam did from his kingly throne.[43] The significance of this interpretation is that, at three key points in the Old Testament, writers make comparisons with Adam: Job did not hide his sin like Adam, Israel's judges would fall like Adam for their sin, and Israel broke the covenant like Adam. But there are still several other factors that commend the 'like Adam' interpretation.

The second reason supporting the 'like Adam' reading involves the immediate context of Hosea and intertextual allusions to the creation narrative. In recent years Francis Landy has proposed the text's connections to the creation narrative, but he only offers a few suggestions such as God's desire for Israel to possess His knowledge, a possible allusion to Adam's efforts to acquire knowledge against God's will (cf. Hosea 6:6; Gen. 3:6).[44] But more recently others have presented more compelling evidence of the links between Hosea and Genesis, and the fall narrative in particular. Byron Curtis identifies the following links:[45]

- Hosea 1:9 and 2:23 (25 MT) invokes the covenant formula, 'You are not my people, and I am not your God,' which first appears in Genesis 17:7-8.[46]

- Hosea 1:10 says that the number of the Israelites will be as the sand of the sea, which echoes Genesis 22:17.

- Hosea 2:18 (20 MT) states: 'And I will make for them a covenant on that day with the beasts of the field, the birds of the heavens, and the creeping things of the ground,' which resonances the Noahic covenant and the creation account (Gen. 1, 9:10).

---

42. On Adam's kingly office, see e.g., David VanDrunen, *Divine Covenants and Moral Order: A Biblical Theology of Natural Law* (Grand Rapids: Eerdmans, 2014), 380-85.

43. Tate, *Psalms 51-100*, 338.

44. Francis Landy, *Hosea* (Sheffield: Sheffield Academic Press, 1995), 84-85.

45. Curtis, 'Hosea 6:7,' 189-90.

46. Rolf Rendtorff, *The Covenant Formula: An Exegetical and Theological Investigation* (Edinburgh: T & T Clark, 1998), 14-15.

- Hosea 4:3 references 'the beasts of the field and the birds of the heavens, and even the fish of the sea,' which duplicates the language of Genesis 1:28, 30.

- Hosea 9:6 and especially 10:8 employs the same exact terminology associated with the consequences of the fall: 'The high places of Aven, the sin of Israel, shall be destroyed. Thorn and thistle shall grow up on their altars' (cf. Gen. 3:18).

These are just seven of sixteen total references to Genesis that Curtis amasses from Hosea, excluding Hosea 6:7. In short, Hosea knew the book of Genesis and employs its language and narratives as arrows against the recalcitrant Israelites.[47] In addition to these Genesis references, Curtis counts seventeen references to the Exodus-Deuteronomy complex, which means that Hosea was familiar with the other books of the Pentateuch.[48]

These intertextual echoes and allusions reveal that Hosea was well-acquainted with the Pentateuch, and especially the history of Adam and his fall.[49] In fact, Hosea 2:18, 21 has been identified as Hosea's version of the new covenant: 'And I will make for them a covenant on that day with the beasts of the field, the birds of the heavens, and the creeping things of the ground .... And in that day I will answer, declares the LORD, I will answer the heavens, and they shall answer the earth.'[50] Key here is that Hosea characterizes Israel's state in terms of Adam's fall, 'thorn and thistle shall grow up on their altars' (Hosea 10:8), and their redemption in terms of (new) creation. That Hosea would therefore depict Israel's sin in Adamic terms creates a hospitable context to read Hosea 6:7a as, 'Like Adam they transgressed the covenant.'

The third reason lies within the broader canon of Scripture and Paul's comparison between Adam and Israel in Romans 5. Many turn to Romans 5:12-21 and examine the Adam-Christ parallel that Paul expounds: 'Adam ... was a type of the one who was to come'

---

47. Curtis, 'Hosea 6:7,' 191-92.

48. Curtis, 'Hosea 6:7,' 192-93.

49. Curtis, 'Hosea 6:7,' 194; also Andersen and Freedman, *Hosea*, 439.

50. Curtis, 'Hosea 6:7,' 195; also Michael DeRoche, 'The Reversal of Creation in Hosea,' *VT* 31/4 (1981): 400-09.

(Rom. 5:14). This is certainly the chief focus of Paul's argument: 'For as by the one man's disobedience the many were constituted sinners, so by the one man's obedience the many will be constituted righteous' (Rom. 5:19, trans. mine). But in the opening words of Paul's argument the apostle nestles Israel in between Adam and Christ. While the next chapter explores the Adam-Israel-Christ connection in greater detail, suffice it to say that Paul identifies Adam and Israel as living under similar conditions: 'Death reigned from Adam to Moses, even over those whose sin was not like the transgression of Adam' (Rom. 5:14). Paul divides redemptive history into three periods: Adam to Moses, which has people who did not sin like Adam, life under Moses, where people did sin like Adam, and then Christ. For the purposes of Hosea 6:7, the first two periods are of interest.

The reason Paul compares Adam's state with the Israelites who lived under Moses is that both periods were characterized by law: God issued His positive commands and sanctions to Adam and to Israel through the Mosaic covenant. Those who lived before the inception of the Mosaic covenant did not live under these divinely revealed commands and sanctions. In fact, there is a possibility that Paul had Hosea 6:7 in mind when he compared Adam and Israel. The Septuagint of Hosea 6:7a states: ὡς ἄνθρωπος παραβαίνων διαθήκην ('like a man they transgressed the covenant'). This is the same language that Paul uses to characterize Adam's transgression (παράβασις) (Rom. 5:14). In fact, the New Testament uses the term παράβασις for a violation of covenant law (cf. Rom. 2:23; 4:15; Gal. 3:19; Heb. 2:2; 9:15; also 1 Tim. 2:14). The next chapter addresses this issue in greater detail. Nevertheless, as earlier chapters have argued, the parallels between Adam's commands and sanctions reflect the Mosaic covenant. In other words, Hosea is not the only biblical author to compare Adam's and Israel's covenantal state. Granted, Paul does not invoke the term *covenant* in his comparison, but the idea is substantively present. Paul would not characterize Israel's reception of the law any other way.

The biblical occurrences, the כאדם lexeme, Hosea's numerous echoes and allusions to Genesis, especially the creation narrative, and the apostle Paul's comparison of Adam and Israel confirm that 'like Adam' is a warranted exegetical conclusion: it fits both within the immediate, the Old Testament, and the New Testament contexts. Were Hosea 6:7a the only part of the prophet's statement, with this corroborating evidence one might be able to close the case on the proper interpretation of the disputed verse. But one of the obstacles to the 'like Adam' reading is Hosea 6:7b and the statement, 'There they dealt faithlessly with me.' How does the reference to Adam in Hosea 6:7a fit with the reference to a place in 6:7b? Byron Curtis has persuasively argued that Hosea has presented a double-entendre. One does not have to choose between 'like Adam' or 'at Adam,' but rather both are in view. At first, this may seem like an ill-fated attempt to have one's cake and eat it too, but there are two factors that support this claim.

First, Hosea is a punster – there are numerous points in his oracles where he employs polysemous wordplays. The best-known wordplays are those associated with the circumstances of his marriage and his children: 'Go, take to yourself a wife of whoredom and have children of whoredom, for the land commits great whoredom by forsaking the LORD' (Hosea 1:2). Although it is debated, here זנונים ('whoredom') possibly takes on different senses: literal prostitution and idolatry. One must therefore listen carefully and pay attention to each use of the word to follow the prophet's message. The same holds true for the names of Hosea's children: Jezreel means 'God sows,' which in Hosea's polysemous message now means God will scatter Israel (Hosea 1:4-5). Lo-Ruhammah and Lo-Ammi mean 'she who is not loved' and 'not my people,' respectively. In the case of the former, the name hints at the possibility that she is an illegitimate child, and so God applies the name to Israel – she will be rejected (Hosea 1:6-8). Lo-Ammi means both 'not my people' and 'he's no son of mine.'[51] Hosea's use of double-entendres with proper names is especially relevant both in his prophecy and especially regarding Hosea 6:7. Curtis provides a list of at least twenty-two different places where names have double meanings.[52]

---

51. Curtis, 'Hosea 6:7,' 201-02.

52. Curtis, 'Hosea 6:7, 204-05.

Second, Curtis argues that Hosea 6:7 constitutes a 'Janus' parallelism, which is a sufficiently ambiguous pun that can be read in two different ways. There might be three lines of poetry, for example, where the middle line is brilliantly uncertain, which acts as a fulcrum and causes the reader to pause, and consider the possible alternatives. Curtis cites Song of Songs 2:12 as an example of a symmetrical Janus parallelism:

> The flowers appear on the earth,
> the time of singing [הזמיר] has come,
> and the voice of the turtledove is heard in our land.

Here the term זמיר can mean either 'song' (2 Sam. 23:1) or 'pruning' (cf. Lev. 25:3).[53] Hence, the verse causes the reader to pause and consider a slightly different reading:

> The flowers appear on the earth,
> the time of singing/pruning has come,
> and the voice of the turtledove is heard in our land.

Hosea 6:7, on the other hand, is an example of an asymmetrical Janus parallelism:

> But like [their ancestor] Adam they transgressed the covenant;
> Like [the residents of the town of] Adam, there they dealt faithlessly with me.[54]

The Janus parallelism provides an answer that accounts for the whole verse and does not require an emendation of the text. It accounts for both 'like Adam' and the presence of the locative adverb שם ('there').[55] This reading also fits within Hosea's overall habit of using proper names as puns.

Theological Implications

If the presented exegesis is correct, then there are at least three important theological implications. First, there is explicit biblical

---

53. Curtis, 'Hosea 6:7,' 206.

54. Curtis, 'Hosea 6:7,' 207.

55. Curtis, 'Hosea 6:7,' 208; see also Duane Garrett, *Hosea, Joel*, NAC, vol. 19a (Nashville, TN: Broadman and Holman, 1997), 162-63.

evidence that points to the existence of a pre-fall Adamic covenant. But one must cautiously categorize the nature of this evidence. John Eagleton's criticism is valid to a certain extent, namely, that Hosea 6:7a does not state that Adam violated the covenant of works.[56] Numerous translations of the Scriptures, Christian and Jewish commentators, Lutheran, Roman Catholic, and Reformed theologians have all concluded that Hosea 6:7 speaks of the first man, Adam, and the covenant he broke. Just because an interpreter concludes that Adam is the proper interpretation does not mean he advocates the Reformed doctrine of the covenant of works. But then again, Eagleton's criticism assumes that the sole exegetical foundation for the covenant of works is Hosea 6:7; if this is the case, then his observation is significant. Yet, as the surveyed history of the text's interpretation demonstrates, this one verse was not immediately an exegetical mainstay for the doctrine. Rather, Reformed theologians later appealed to this verse because it was explicit evidence that God and Adam were in covenant prior to the fall. In order to establish what kind of covenant this was, they drew on numerous other passages. Recall the Westminster Confession cites Genesis 1:26; 2:17; Romans 2:14-15; 10:5; 5:12, 19-20; Galatians 3:10, 12; Ecclesiastes 7:29, and Job 28:18 in support of the covenant of works (VII.ii; XIX.i). In other words, the doctrine does not rest on this lone text despite the claims of some.[57] Hence, the Adamic reading of Hosea 6:7 attests to the existence of the covenant of works, but other passages of Scripture explain its specific nature.

Second, Hosea 6:7 anticipates the use of Paul's major epochs of biblical history. Despite the claims of some, Adam is not a minor player in the drama of redemptive history.[58] His shadow looms large over the Old Testament. The intra-canonical links between the creation and fall narratives and other portions of the Bible are

---

56. Eagleton, *Covenant of Works*, 95.

57. E.g., Philip Schaff, ed., *Creeds of Christendom*, 6th ed., 3 vols. (1931; Grand Rapids: Baker, 1990), I:484 n. 2.

58. See, e.g., Peter Enns, *The Evolution of Adam: What the Bible Does and Doesn't Say About Human Origins* (Grand Rapids: Brazos), 79-92.

significant. As noted in earlier chapters, the creation narrative and Deuteronomy 28–34 form an inclusio – they have an interpretively symbiotic relationship. Adam foreshadows Israel's existence and exile from the land.[59] Hosea was aware of the Adam-Israel bond and employed it several places in his prophecy. In narrative terms, even though Adam fell long ago, Israel continued to re-live his wretched story. In theological terms, the covenant of works does not fade into the mist of history but is an ever-present reality that affects all human beings. Israel's history is a microcosm of Adam's failure, a chronicle that showcases the universal sinful state of all human beings. Thus, Paul picks up the Adam-Israel history and adds the final concluding chapter, the story of the last Adam, Christ.

Third, if Hosea freely drew on the creation and fall narratives to characterize Israel's apostasy, then the road is a two-way street. That is, the theological traffic does not travel in one direction. If Adam's fall characterizes Israel's faithlessness, then conversely Israel's infidelity also illuminates Adam's sin. If Israel failed to show their covenant love (חסד) to God (Hosea 6:6), then the same is true of Adam. His sin, among other things, was a failure of covenant love.

Conclusion

Despite the historically divided opinions regarding the correct interpretation of Hosea 6:7, there is good reason to conclude that the prophet intended to invoke the name of Adam. He used Adam's name as a double-entendre to draw his audience back to the garden to recall the first man's apostasy and to see their own history in that light – the murderous events at Adam that demonstrated Israel's own covenant infidelity. But this text also explicitly reveals that God's covenantal activity did not first begin with Noah (Gen. 6:18); instead, God first entered into a covenant with Adam.

---

59. Postell, *Adam as Israel*, 149-68.

~: II.6 :~

These Are Two Covenants
(Gal. 4:24)

Introduction

Among early modern Reformed theologians, Galatians 4:24 is a commonly cited passage in support of the covenant of works, 'These women are two covenants. One is from Mount Sinai, bearing children for slavery; she is Hagar.' One of the most extensive treatments of this verse comes from Scottish theologian, Thomas Bell (1733-1802). Bell spends nearly two hundred pages explaining this one text.[1] Bell's case is extensive but his claim that Galatians 4:24 speaks to the covenant of works rests on several conclusions drawn from the text.

First, the patriarchal history is a typical representation of the Abrahamic and Mosaic covenants.[2] Second, the Mosaic covenant has appended curses, unlike the covenant of promise confirmed by Christ (Deut. 29:21).[3] Third, Paul identifies Sinai as a covenant that produces slaves, not free children.[4] Fourth, in the covenant of works God promised eternal life as the reward for perfect obedience

---

1. Thomas Bell, *A View of the Covenants of Works and Grace; and a Treatise on the Nature and Effects of Saving Grace* (Glasgow: Edward Khull, 1814), 3-185.

2. Bell, *Covenants of Works and Grace*, 55.

3. Bell, *Covenants of Works and Grace*, 87.

4. Bell, *Covenants of Works and Grace*, 88.

(Rom. 10:5; Gal. 3:10), whereas in the covenant of grace God freely promises eternal life through the vicarious suffering and obedience of Christ.[5]

These four points lead Bell to conclude that Paul has in view the covenants of works and grace when he explains that Sarah and Hagar are two different covenants. Bell goes on to list seven reasons why he believes his conclusion is correct.[6] Exploring Bell's reasons lies more within the realm of historical theology, but his common claim that Galatians 4:24 is exegetical proof for the covenant of works has merit and is basically sound. This chapter defends the thesis that Paul speaks of the covenant of works in Galatians 4:24. Stating the thesis is simple, but proving it is another matter.

Most contemporary exegetes do not draw any connections to the Adamic context let alone the covenant of works, hence at first appearance proving this chapter's thesis seems like a steep uphill climb. Nevertheless, the present-day absence of Adamic and Mosaic covenantal connections stands in stark contrast to their common linkage in the early modern period. The contemporary absence of Mosaic connections to the Adamic covenant is an instance where the church needs the fresh breeze of ages gone by to blow through our minds to remind us of forgotten truths. Hence, in order to prove this chapter's thesis, it first presents the broader context of Paul's arguments in Galatians; the broader context sets the stage for the capstone of Paul's polemic against works-righteousness. Second, the chapter examines Galatians 4:24 to explain the nature of the Hagar-Sarah typology and why Paul associates the Mosaic covenant with Hagar and slavery. One of the keys to connecting the Mosaic and Adamic covenants is that Paul characterizes being under the law as living under the 'elementary principles of the world' (στοιχεῖα τοῦ κόσμου). In short, Paul places the Mosaic covenant on the protological side of redemptive history; it is incompatible with the new creation and the eschatological age inaugurated by Christ. Alternatively stated, the Mosaic covenant is part of the present evil age and

---

5. Bell, *Covenants of Works and Grace*, 89.

6. Bell, *Covenants of Works and Grace*, 89-113.

is incompatible with the age to come. Third, the chapter sets forth several important theological distinctions to explain how Paul maintains the unity of salvation throughout the whole Old Testament but at the same time speaks negatively of the Mosaic covenant. Crucial here is an early modern theological distinction regarding Paul's understanding of the law, the law *qua* covenant is different from its role and function *qua* a rule for the Christian life. The chapter then concludes with some observations regarding the importance of Galatians 4:24 as a proof text for the covenant of works.

Broader Context

The broader context of Paul's anti-Judaizer polemic is vital to understanding Paul's argument in Galatians 4:24. The third and fourth chapters constitute the heart of his explanation of the doctrine of justification, where he contrasts works-righteousness with the righteousness that comes by faith. Paul juxtaposes Leviticus 18:5's 'do this and live' with Habakkuk 2:4's 'the righteous shall live by his faith.' Through these Old Testament quotations Paul explains that there are two mutually exclusive paths to justification, one by perfect obedience and the other by faith in Christ alone. The Judaizers did not realize they were conflating these two paths when they tried to combine the need for circumcision with faith in Christ in order to secure their salvation. On the one hand, such a move was understandable given Israel's long possession of circumcision as the sign of the covenant between God and His people. On the other hand, the Judaizers and the misled Galatians failed to recognize that, with the advent of Christ, God irreversibly moved the eschatological clock forward. The hands on the clock signaled that the age to come had dawned and that the sun was setting on the present evil age. A second failure for the Judaizers and deceived Galatians was in understanding the nature of the law's demands. A partial fulfillment, no matter how well intended, was insufficient. The law demands perfect obedience, and even for redeemed sinners, this is a peak too tall to ascend (Gal. 3:10). Hence Paul's quotation of David's psalm: 'By works of the law no one will be justified' (Gal. 2:16; cf. Ps. 143:2).

Galatians 4:24

In his effort to press the idea of the incompatibility of the two paths of justification Paul explains how the law functions in concert with the promises of the gospel. He begins this portion of his argument in Galatians 3:19 with his undoubtedly pressing question, 'Why then the law?' He presents his answer in the verses that follow, which has its capstone in his appeal to Hagar and Sarah: 'Now this may be interpreted allegorically: these women are two covenants. One is from Mount Sinai, bearing children for slavery; she is Hagar' (Gal. 4:24).

There is one preliminary issue that requires resolution before we proceed to examine Galatians 4:24b, namely, the nature of Paul's allegory. Scholars are divided on whether Paul uses the term ἀλληγορέω ('allegorically') to denote allegory or typology. Allegory is when one assigns an arbitrary interpretation to a biblical text that has nothing to do with the original historical context.[7] Conversely, typology is when historical persons, events, or places prefigure later events, places, or persons. Scholarship is divided on the question, but a suitable answer is that Paul employs typology in his divinely inspired commentary on the Old Testament text.[8] Ishmael and Isaac, for example, serve as types of children of slavery versus offspring of the promise (Gal. 4:21-23, 26-29; cf. 3:29), and these two participate in the broader matrix of the two principles of justification, either by law or by promise. Hence Paul connects Ishmael's mother, Hagar, with Mt. Sinai and Isaac's mother, Sarah, with Jerusalem above – these two women represent different covenants (Gal. 4:24, 26). F. F. Bruce explains that Paul

has in mind that form of allegory which is commonly called typology: a narrative from OT history is interpreted in terms of the new covenant, or (to put it the other way round) an aspect of the new covenant is presented in terms of an OT narrative. Typology

---

7. Thomas Schreiner, *Galatians*, ZECNT (Grand Rapids: Zondervan, 2010), 300.

8. Leonhard Goppelt, *Typos: The Typological Interpretation of the Old Testament in the New* (Grand Rapids: Eerdmans, 1982), 1-23, 139-40; F. F. Bruce, *The Epistle to the Galatians: A Commentary on the Greek Text* (Grand Rapids: Eerdmans, 1982), 217; cf. A. Andrew Das, *Galatians* (St. Louis: Concordia, 2014), 494-95.

presupposes that salvation history displays a recurring pattern of divine action: thus the exilic prophets portrayed their people's return from Babylon in terms of a second Exodus, and the NT writers portray the Christian redemption in terms both of the Exodus and the return from Babylon.[9]

As the arguments below substantiate, the Mosaic covenant is part of the Adamic side of Paul's two-age (Adam-Christ) understanding of history. This is why Hagar represents (allegorically, or typologically) works righteousness and therefore has roots that reach back to Adam with branches that extend to Moses. But the key question is, How can Paul negatively connect Hagar with the Sinai (or Mosaic) covenant when it is part of God's positive redemptive dealings with Israel? This is a challenging issue that requires careful attention to the text and several important and necessary interpretive distinctions.

Paul writes: 'These women are two covenants. One is from Mount Sinai, bearing children for slavery; she is Hagar. Now Hagar is Mount Sinai in Arabia; she corresponds to the present Jerusalem, for she is in slavery with her children. But the Jerusalem above is free, and she is our mother' (Gal. 4:24b-26). If Hagar is the Mosaic covenant, then what covenant does Sarah represent? Given the overall context, especially Paul's arguments in Galatians 3:15-18 and the fact that Sarah was Abraham's wife and mother of Isaac, the most likely reference is to the Abrahamic covenant (Gen. 15).[10] Some scholars contend that the contrast is not between the Mosaic (Hagar) and Abrahamic (Sarah) covenants, but the old and new covenants (cf. Jer. 31:31).[11] The choice here is not either/or but both/and. The Mosaic covenant is the old covenant (2 Cor. 3:14), and the new covenant is the fruition of the Abrahamic covenant (2 Cor. 3:6).[12] So, then, Hagar is the Mosaic (old) covenant and Sarah is the Abrahamic (new) covenant. How do these two

---

9. Bruce, *Galatians*, 217.

10. Schreiner, *Galatians*, 301.

11. Hans Dieter Betz, *Galatians: A Commentary on Paul's Letter to the Churches in Galatia* (Philadelphia: Fortress, 1979), 243; Longenecker, *Galatians*, 211.

12. Schreiner, *Galatians*, 301.

covenants relate to one another? In a post-fall context, when God deals with humans on the basis of grace, how can Paul characterize the Mosaic covenant as one that produces children of slavery? In theological terms, how can the Mosaic covenant, which is a part of the covenant of grace, produce children of slavery? The answer to these questions lies in Paul's earlier explanation of the role and function of the law.

Paul explains the law's function vis-à-vis God's promise to Abraham in Galatians 3:15-29, where he writes: 'The law, which came 430 years afterward, does not annul a covenant previously ratified by God, so as to make the promise void. For if the inheritance comes by the law, it no longer comes by promise; but God gave it to Abraham by a promise' (Gal. 3:17-18). The Sinai law came centuries after the Abrahamic covenant, but it does not overturn God's promises to the patriarch. As with his juxtaposition of doing versus believing, works versus faith, 'do this and live' versus 'the righteous shall live by faith,' Paul contrasts law versus promise (Gal. 3:10-11; cf. Rom. 10:5). Salvation does not come through law but through promise: 'For if the inheritance comes by the law, it no longer comes by promise' (Gal. 3:18). This means that in redemptive history, there are two diametrically opposed principles at work, law and promise principles, but these doctrines are not bare, but step onto the stage of redemptive history through God's covenantal dealings with Israel.[13] In this case, God's dealings with Abraham are covenantal, and thus Sarah represents the Jerusalem that is above which produces children of freedom. Contrariwise, Hagar represents the Sinai covenant, which is the covenantally administered law principle.

Given this information, one can gloss Paul's statement in Galatians 3:17-18 in the following manner: 'The [Mosaic covenant], which came 430 years afterward, does not annul a covenant previously ratified by God, so as to make the promise void. For if the inheritance comes by the [Mosaic covenant], it no longer comes by promise; but God gave it to Abraham by a promise.' In the latter half of Galatians 3, every time Paul uses the term *law*,

---

13. Betz, *Galatians*, 243.

one can gloss it as *Mosaic covenant*, which illuminates the nature of Paul's argument:

> Why then the [Mosaic covenant]? It was added because of transgressions, until the offspring should come to whom the promise had been made, and it was put in place through angels by an intermediary. Now an intermediary implies more than one, but God is one. Is the [Mosaic covenant] then contrary to the promises of God? Certainly not! For if a [covenant] had been given that could give life, then righteousness would indeed be by the [Mosaic covenant]. But the Scripture imprisoned everything under sin, so that the promise by faith in Jesus Christ might be given to those who believe. Now before faith came, we were held captive under the [Mosaic covenant], imprisoned until the coming faith would be revealed. So then, the [Mosaic covenant] was our guardian until Christ came, in order that we might be justified by faith. But now that faith has come, we are no longer under a guardian [i.e., the Mosaic covenant], for in Christ Jesus you are all sons of God, through faith (Gal. 3:19-26).[14]

Paul's overall point in Galatians 3–4 is not that the law *qua* law is a bad thing or in and of itself produces children of slavery. Paul clearly elsewhere testifies to the goodness and utility of the law in the Christian life (Rom. 7:12; 13:8, 10; Gal. 5:14). Rather, he labors to prove that the law *qua* covenant, specifically the Mosaic covenant, with its attending curses for failing to keep its rules, produces children of slavery. The chief error, therefore, of the Judaizers was that they believed Sinai was terminal, the telos of God's redemptive plan; they failed to see that it was a temporary stop before the final destination of Christ and the new covenant (Rom. 10:4).

But this still leaves the conclusion that the Mosaic covenant is different from the Abrahamic covenant. In Paul's earlier argument from Galatians 3:10-11, the law is the chief characteristic of the Mosaic covenant, hence his statement, 'the law is not of faith,' but instead, 'the one who does them, shall live by them' (Gal. 3:12; cf. Lev. 18:5). Other passages in the New Testament echo this depiction,

---

14. T. David Gordon, *Promise, Law, Faith: Covenant-Historical Reasoning in Galatians* (Peabody, MA: Hendrickson, 2019), 140-60.

such as when John writes: 'For the law was given through Moses; grace and truth came through Jesus Christ' (John 1:17). The function of the Mosaic covenant has two important corollaries: (1) that it is temporary and ultimately inferior to the Abrahamic and new covenants; and (2) that the Mosaic covenant has protological roots and thus has Adamic connections.

First, Paul clearly attests to the temporary and inferior nature of the Mosaic covenant. The Mosaic covenant was a late-comer, making its appearance 430 years after the Abrahamic covenant, which came directly from God: 'God gave it to Abraham by a promise' (Gal. 3:18). By way of contrast, the Mosaic covenant did not come directly from God but was administered by intermediaries: 'It was put in place through angels by an intermediary. Now an intermediary implies more than one, but God is one' (Gal. 3:19b-20). Angels and Moses stand as the intermediaries of the Mosaic covenant (Deut. 33:2 LXX; Ps. 68:17; Acts 7:53; Heb. 2:2).[15] In the divine economy, the Mosaic covenant had a planned obsolescence embedded in it: 'It was added because of transgressions, until the offspring should come to whom the promise had been made' (Gal. 3:19a). The temporary function of the Mosaic covenant was to drive people to Christ and the gospel: 'So then, the law was our guardian until Christ came, in order that we might be justified by faith' (Gal. 3:24).

Second, Paul associates the Mosaic covenant with 'the weak and worthless elementary principles of the world [στοιχεῖα τοῦ κόσμου]' (Gal. 4:9). Prior to the advent of Christ, Israel was 'enslaved to the elementary principles of the world [στοιχεῖα τοῦ κόσμου]' (Gal. 4:3). What does the term στοιχεῖα mean and why does Paul depict the Mosaic covenant in this manner? To be sure, this is one of the more controverted issues in Pauline studies. In classical Greek literature the 'elementary principles of the world' (στοιχεῖα τοῦ κόσμου) are earth, air, fire, or water (cf. 4 Macc. 12:13).[16] The term 'elements' (στοιχεῖα) alone can refer

---

15. Schreiner, *Galatians*, 241.

16. E.g., Philo, *On the Creation*, XVI.52, in *Philo*, LCL, vol. 1, trans. F .H. Colson and G. H. Whitaker (1929; Cambridge: Harvard University Press, 1991), 38-39; also Martinus C. de Boer, 'The Meaning of the Phrase *ta stoicheia tou kosmou* in Galatians,' NTS 53 (2007): 204-24, esp. 205, 207. For a survey of

to fundamental principles or rules for life.[17] In some instances, στοιχεῖα refers to angelic and demonic powers (cf. NRSV, NEB).[18] Given its usage in several other New Testament texts, however, one can determine a basic meaning of the term. In Colossians 2:8, Paul writes: 'See to it that no one takes you captive by philosophy and empty deceit, according to human tradition, according to the elemental spirits of the world [κατὰ τὰ στοιχεῖα τοῦ κόσμου], and not according to Christ.' In 2 Peter 3:10, the apostle writes: 'But the day of the Lord will come like a thief, and then the heavens will pass away with a roar, and the heavenly bodies [στοιχεῖα] will be burned up and dissolved, and the earth and the works that are done on it will be exposed.' Luke employs the term to refer to the regulations of the law: 'Take these men and purify yourself along with them and pay their expenses, so that they may shave their heads. Thus all will know that there is nothing in what they have been told about you, but that you yourself also live in observance of the law [στοιχεῖς καὶ αὐτὸς φυλάσσων τὸν νόμον]' (Acts 21:24; cf. Gal. 6:16; 5:25b).[19]

These references are consistent with the idea that τὰ στοιχεῖα τοῦ κόσμου refers to the original protological creation, and in this particular case to the creation law that appears both in the Adamic and Mosaic covenants.[20] The following points substantiate this connection. Peter connects the original creation with the στοιχεῖα,

---

ancient literature on this topic, see Eduard Schweizer, 'Slaves of the Elements and Worshipers of Angels: Gal 4:3, 9 and Col 2:8, 18, 20,' in *JBL* 107/3 (1988): 455-68, esp. 456-64.

17. E.g., Xenophon, *Memorabilia*, II.i.1, in *Xenophon: Memorabilia and Economics*, trans. E. C. Marchant, LCL (1923; Cambridge: Harvard University Press, 1959), 80-81; so Schweizer, 'Slaves of the Elements,' 466-68; J. Louis Martyn, *Galatians*, AB (New York: Doubleday, 1997), 395.

18. Schreiner, *Galatians*, 267-68; cf. Bo Reicke, 'The Law and This World According to Paul,' *JBL* 70/4 (1951): 259-76; Herman Ridderbos, *Galatians*, NICNT (Grand Rapids: Eerdmans, 1953), 153; Das, *Galatians*, 441-42.

19. Linda Belleville, '"Under law": Structural Analysis and the Pauline Concept of Law in Galatians 3:21-4:11,' *JSNT* 16 (1986): 53-78, esp. 67-68; Das, *Galatians*, 440.

20. Schreiner, *Galatians*, 268; cf. the similar holistic definition of James D. G. Dunn, *The Epistle to the Galatians*, BNTC (Peabody, MA: Hendrickson, 1993), 212-13.

the heavenly bodies that will burn up at the consummation – the original creation will be a thing of the past.[21] And Paul aligns the στοιχεῖα with traditions and regulations: 'Do not handle, Do not taste, Do not touch (referring to things that all perish as they are used) – according to human precepts and teachings' (Col. 2:21-22).[22] In some cases, the στοιχεῖα can refer to human traditions, such as in Colossians. But here in Galatians 4, Paul associates the στοιχεῖα with the Mosaic covenant.[23] In other words, the Mosaic covenant is in some sense a part of the στοιχεῖα, the original protological creation, and is thus incompatible with the new eschatological creation. The legal connections between the Adamic and Mosaic covenants appear, for example, in Paul's comparison between the two economies: 'Yet death reigned from Adam to Moses, even over those whose sinning was not like the transgression of Adam, who was a type of the one who was to come' (Rom. 5:14). The subsequent chapter on Romans addresses this point in greater detail, but important to note is that Paul groups Adam and Moses together and brackets the period in between as a time when people's 'sinning was not like the transgression of Adam.' That is, between Adam and Moses people did not exist under a state of expressly revealed commands with appended blessings and sanctions (cf., e.g., Gen. 2:16-17; Deut. 28:15).

So, then, how can Paul group the Adamic and Mosaic states together? How can the Judaizers' desire to embrace the law be a return under the στοιχεῖα τοῦ κόσμου? The answer comes from recognizing that the στοιχεῖα τοῦ κόσμου refers to the creation law that both Gentile and Jew share. Both Jew and Gentile have the creation law written on their hearts, whereas in contrast to the Gentile, the Jew also has the explicit testimony of the law through its reception in the Mosaic covenant. God in some sense repeats the Adamic creation law to Israel at Sinai.[24] This connection is in

21. Richard J. Bauckham, *Jude, 2 Peter*, WBC (Dallas: Word, 1983), 316.

22. N. T. Wright, *Colossians & Philemon*, TNTC (Grand Rapids: Eerdmans, 2002), 125-26.

23. Cf. Douglas J. Moo, *Galatians*, BECNT (Grand Rapids: Baker, 2013), 262-63.

24. David VanDrunen, *Divine Covenants and Moral Order: A Biblical Theology of Natural Law* (Grand Rapids: Eerdmans, 2014), 346-66, esp. 358-65; similar in a broad sense, Moo, *Galatians*, 262-63.

one fashion evident with the combination of terms in Paul's lexeme, στοιχεῖα τοῦ κόσμου. There is no debate over the term κόσμος – this term means 'world.' But if στοιχεῖα denotes 'rules' or 'regulations,' then on the surface it refers to regulations or laws somehow connected to the world. But what, precisely, is the connection?

Recall from the earlier chapter on Romans 2:14-15 that God inscribes the work of the law on the hearts of all people, which is part of the broader fabric of the created order (Rom. 1:19-21, 32). The revelation of the law in human hearts and the law-bound created order has ample attestation in biblical and extra-biblical texts. Psalm 104, for example, speaks of the orderly rhythms of the creation (cf. Sirach 16:26-28). Note the connection between law and creation in the Testament of Naphtali, a second-century B.C. extra-biblical text:[25]

> Sun, moon, and stars do not alter their order; thus you should not alter the Law of God by the disorder of your actions. The gentiles, because they wandered astray and forsook the Lord, have changed the order, and have devoted themselves to stones and sticks, patterning themselves after wandering spirits. But you, my children, shall not be like that: In the firmament, in the earth, and in the sea, in all the products of his workmanship discern the Lord who made all things, so that you do not become like Sodom, which departed from the order of nature.[26]

This text links creation and law and even suggests an explanation for Paul's statement regarding the Galatian Gentiles and the στοιχεῖα τοῦ κόσμου: 'Formerly, when you did not know God, you were enslaved to those that by nature are not gods. But now that you have come to know God, or rather to be known by God, how can you turn back again to the weak and worthless elementary principles of the world, whose slaves you want to be once more' (Gal. 4:8-9)? The Gentiles turned the creation-bound law into an idol rather than looked to the one by faith who ingrained the law in the world.

---

25. Reicke, 'The Law and This World,' 273-74.

26. Testament of Naphtali, 3.2-5, in *The Old Testament Pseudepigrapha*, 2 vols., ed. James H. Charlesworth (New York: Doubleday, 1983), I:812.

God manifested His laws, therefore, not only in the creation and on the human heart, but also to Israel through the Mosaic covenant. Paul suggests this when he describes the Gentiles, 'who do not have the law, by nature do what the law requires,' because they have the 'work of the law written on their hearts' (Rom. 2:14-15). The natural law and the law of the Mosaic covenant are substantively the same, and thus: 'For all who have sinned without the law will also perish without the law, and all who have sinned under the law will be judged by the law' (Rom. 2:12). All people, therefore, Jew or Gentile, lie under the Adamic or Mosaic forms of the law and are thus subject to its curse. Given that the Adamic and Mosaic forms of the law were connected and tied to the protological creation, it is unsuited for the curse-free eschatological age.[27]

Confirmation of the incompatibility of the Mosaic covenant with the new creation appears in the parallels that appear in Paul's characterizations of life under the στοιχεῖα and the law. Paul chides the Galatians for the desire to return to the elementary principles of the world: 'In the same way we also, when we were children, were enslaved to the elementary principles of the world [ὑπὸ τὰ στοιχεῖα τοῦ κόσμου]' (Gal. 4:3). Note the use of the same preposition when Paul addresses the Judaizers regarding the law: 'Tell me, you who desire to be under the law [οἱ ὑπὸ νόμον θέλοντες εἶναι]' (Gal. 4:21a). To be under (ὑπὸ) the law is the same thing as being under (ὑπὸ) the στοιχεῖα.[28] The blessing of the gospel is, 'God sent forth his Son, born of woman, born under the law [γενόμενον ὑπὸ νόμον], to redeem those who were under the law [ἵνα τοὺς ὑπὸ νόμον ἐξαγοράσῃ], so that we might receive adoption as sons' (Gal. 4:4b-5). Elsewhere Paul employs this same dynamic when he explains that the law no longer holds power over anyone who is in Christ: 'For sin will have no dominion over you, since you are not under law but under grace [οὐ γάρ ἐστε ὑπὸ νόμον ἀλλὰ ὑπὸ χάριν]' (Rom. 6:14). Christ redeems sinners from under the law, whether in Adamic or Mosaic forms. They are no longer subject to the curse and thus free from its Adamic (Gentile) or Mosaic (Jew)

---

27. VanDrunen, *Divine Covenants*, 347.

28. De Boer, 'The Meaning of the Phrase,' 209-14.

covenantal obligations. In short, the Mosaic covenant is part of the Adamic age and consequently has no place in the new creation.[29] Or in Paul's words, 'The world has been crucified to me, and I to the world' (Gal. 6:14). That is, the protological creation, or world, or 'present evil age,' with its Adamic and Mosaic στοιχεῖα are fading out of existence until they are no more and only the new creation remains (Gal. 1:4).[30]

The following table compares and contrasts Hagar and Sarah, the two different covenants and what they each represent:[31]

Hagar	Sarah
• Son of the slave woman: Ishmael	• Son of the free woman: Isaac
• 'according to the flesh'	• 'through the promise'
• Mosaic and Old covenant	• Abrahamic and New covenant
• Sinai and present Jerusalem	• Heavenly Jerusalem
• Slavery	• Freedom
• 'according to the flesh'	• 'according to the Spirit'
• Judaizers	• Christianity
• Adamic aeon	• Aeon of the last Adam
• Elements of the world, the protological creation	• New or eschatological creation
• Legal, law	• Evangelical, gospel
• Curse	• No curse
• Present evil age	• Age to come

One of the chief problems with the Judaizers is that they wanted to turn the clock of redemptive history back, as if Christ had never come, and live under the Adamic-Mosaic aegis. By believing that their justification hinged in part on their circumcision, they were trying to live under the legal demands of the law, which was impossible for two reasons: (1) sinners can never present perfect obedience to the law because of original and actual sin, and (2) Christ bore the curse of the law and fulfilled its legal demands on behalf of those who believe in Him. Hence Paul confronted the

---

29. VanDrunen, *Divine Covenants*, 346-65.

30. Das, *Galatians*, 443.

31. Betz, *Galatians*, 245; Das, *Galatians*, 498.

Judaizers with the slave-producing nature of the Mosaic covenant to show them their theological error.

Theological Analysis

In and of itself, the exegesis of Galatians 4:24 is a challenging issue, but clearly articulating the doctrinal implications of this text has vexed Reformed theologians for centuries. Paul definitely distinguishes the Mosaic covenant from the Abrahamic covenant, but how does one account for the salvation of Old Testament saints under each respective covenant if Sarah and Hagar represent two different principles, one legal and the other evangelical? Paul lucidly explains that Abraham was justified by grace alone through faith alone in Christ alone (Rom. 4:1-8). Moreover, given that he cites Habakkuk 2:4 in support of the doctrine of justification in Galatians 3:10-14 and contrasts it with Leviticus 18:5, one can safely assume that salvation remains the same throughout the Old Testament. That is, if Abraham's justification stands at the beginning and Habakkuk 2:4 lies near the end of the Old Testament, then all who believe in the gospel prior to Christ's first advent are saved in the same manner. Historically, Reformed theologians have accounted for the unity of salvation by claiming that God's salvific interaction with His elect immediately after Adam's fall is a part of the one trans-testamental covenant of grace.[32] This means that in some sense, the Mosaic covenant is part of the covenant of grace. So, then, how does one account for Paul's statements regarding the two covenants, Hagar and Sarah, and Sinai's connections to the Adamic state? The question is simple, but the answers are legion and at times complex.[33]

Sixteenth-century Reformers such as John Calvin (1509-1564) offer what would become a fairly common answer within the early modern and modern Reformed tradition. Calvin followed Paul in his argument by designating Hagar the legal covenant and Sarah the evangelical covenant, which aligns with Paul's explanation.

---

32. WCF, VII.v-vi, XI.vi; so also Ridderbos, *Galatians*, 176.

33. See J. V. Fesko, *The Covenant of Works: Origins, Development, and Reception* (Oxford: Oxford University Press, 2020).

The legal covenant produces slaves and the evangelical covenant produces free people. He further explains that the legal covenant birthed the holy prophets and other believers into a state of temporary slavery, as their true freedom was concealed under the veil of ceremonies and sacrifices. To all external observation, the Mosaic covenant revealed nothing but slavery. Inwardly, however, these Old Testament saints were free before God.[34] In his *Institutes* Calvin distinguishes between the *substance* of the spiritual covenant versus the *administration* of the external legal covenant: 'The covenant made with all the fathers is so far from differing from ours in reality and substance, that it is altogether one and the same: still the administration differs.'[35] In this sense Calvin could say that Adam's and Israel's covenantal states were similar – they were both under a legal economy.

Later theologians such as Francis Turretin (1623-1687) recognized the value in the substance-accidents distinction but explicitly factored the Adamic-Mosaic connection. In particular, God administered the covenant of grace as Sinai 'under a rigid legal economy.'[36] There was a twofold relation (*schesis*) – one that was legal, 'through which by a new promulgation of the law and of the covenant of works, with an intolerable yoke of ceremonies, he wished to set forth what men owed and what was to be expected by them on account of duty unperformed.' The other relation was evangelical where the law was a schoolmaster to bring us to Christ (Gal. 3:24) and contained the 'shadow of things to come' (Heb. 10:1).[37] This twofold relation either appears according to its 'external economy of legal teaching or as to the internal truth of the gospel promise lying under it.' 'The form' of this external economy, writes Turretin,

---

34. John Calvin, *Galatians, Ephesians, Philippians, and Colossians*, CNTC, trans. T. H. L. Parker, eds. David Torrance and T. F. Torrance (1968; Grand Rapids: Eerdmans, 1996), 86.

35. John Calvin, *Institutes of the Christian Religion*, trans. Henry Beveridge (Grand Rapids: Eerdmans, 1957), II.x.2.

36. Francis Turretin, *Institutes of Elenctic Theology*, trans. George Musgrave Giger, ed. James T. Dennison, Jr. (Phillipsburg, NJ: P & R, 1992-97), XII.vii.31.

37. Turretin, *Institutes*, XII.vii.31.

was the pact added to that external dispensation, which on the part of God was the promise of the land of Canaan and of rest and happiness in it; and, under the image of each, of heaven and the rest (*sabbatismou*) in him (Heb. 4:3, 9); or of eternal life according to the clause, 'Do this and live.' On the part of the people, it was a stipulation of obedience to the whole law or righteousness both perfect (Deut. 27:26; Gal. 3:10) and personal justification and by it (Rom. 2:13).[38]

Turretin, like Calvin, recognized the two co-existent principles at work, the legal and evangelical, law and promise, and explained their interrelation through a substance-accidents distinction. Such a distinction allowed theologians to preserve a number of things: (1) the unity of salvation across the testaments, (2) the points that Paul makes regarding Sarah and Hagar as two distinct covenants, and (3) drawing the connections between the Adamic and Mosaic covenants.

Another important theological distinction allowed early modern Reformed theologians to explain how the law was and was not binding on Christians. Paul speaks negatively about the law and aligns it with the στοιχεῖα; it is an instrument of bondage – Hagar is the matriarch of slaves. Conversely, Paul also positively writes of fulfilling the law (Rom. 13:8, 10; cf. James 2:8). How do these ideas cohere? As noted above, the answer comes in recognizing the law *qua* covenant versus the law *qua* a law. Or, in terms of a common early modern Reformed distinction, theologians recognize the difference between the law *qua* covenant versus *qua* rule. The Westminster Confession, for example, states: 'Although true believers be not under the law, as a covenant of works, to be thereby justified, or condemned; yet is it of great use to them, as well as to others; in that, as a rule of life informing them of the will of God, and their duty, it directs and binds them to walk accordingly.'[39] Believers are not subject to the law *as a covenant*, which requires perfect, personal, and perpetual obedience to secure eternal life. But when Christ delivers them from the law as a covenant, it still has relevance as a rule, a guide, for the Christian

---

38. Turretin, *Institutes*, XII.vii.32.

39. Westminster Confession, XIX.vi.

life. This is the type of distinction that Paul has in mind when he speaks negatively of the law as Hagar, the Sinai covenant, versus fulfilling the obligations of the law as a Christian. The former only brings death and slavery, whereas the latter is the fruit of one's redemption and union with Christ. Paul does not speak positively of the covenantally imbedded law; he does not speak well of Hagar unless she serves as the pedagogue to drive sinners to Christ.

Conclusion

In the simplest of terms, Hagar is a form of the covenant of works *redivivus*, a reminder that the requirements of the covenant of works, positive (perfect obedience) and negative (curse), still hang over the heads of all people, whether Jew or Gentile. Early modern Reformed theologians recognized this and thus rightly enlisted Galatians 4:24 as a text that confirmed the existence of the covenant of works. One of the principal errors of the Judaizers was that they thought there was no difference between the Abrahamic and Mosaic covenants.[40] In theological terms, they mistakenly conflated the covenants of works and grace; they erroneously tried to combine faith in Jesus with works. They did not approach the law in Christ who completely fulfilled the covenant on their behalf but as a covenant that they could fulfill. Paul challenged their flawed theology by showing the incompatibility of Leviticus 18:5's 'do this and live,' with Habakkuk 2:4's 'the righteous shall live by his faith.' He capped his argument by pushing aside the misguided notion that the Mosaic covenant was a friend. The Mosaic covenant was Hagar, a mother who only gave birth to slaves. The only way that Hagar would be a blessing is if by God's grace sinners recognized the echoes of the covenant of works in Sinai's foreboding clouds and menacing curses for disobedience. In remembering Adam's failure and God's judgment that thundered from Sinai's heights, they would flee to Sarah, she who held out Christ and who would welcome them with open arms, freedom, and the loving embrace of eternal life.

---

40. Ben Witherington, III, *Grace in Galatia: A Commentary on Paul's Letter to the Galatians* (Grand Rapids: Eerdmans, 1998), 243.

❦ II.7 ❧

Adam, Israel, and Christ
(Rom. 5:12-21)

Introduction

*A*mong the passages of Scripture to which Reformed theologians commonly appeal to support the covenant of works is Romans 5:12-21. This passage is significant because Paul places Adam and Christ in parallel to demonstrate the way in which the first Adam brought sin and death into the world through his disobedience and how Christ has undone the deleterious effects through His life, death, and resurrection. Within the Adam-Christ parallel Paul sets forth the two federal heads of history – either one is in union with Adam or with Christ. But buried in between the two massive peaks of Christ and Adam is a smaller but nevertheless important mountain, namely, Sinai. Paul divides history into three periods, from Adam to Moses, from Moses to Christ, and from Christ until the consummation.[1] The fact that Paul mentions Moses means that he appeals to God's covenantal transactions with Israel at Sinai in his effort to explain the nature of Adam's sin and the sins of subsequent human beings. The Adam-Israel connection provides important information that helps us understand the Adam-Christ relationship. The thesis of this chapter is that the Adam-Israel-Christ nexus provides two vital elements that demonstrate that God and

---

1. Joseph Fitzmyer, *Romans*, AB (New York: Doubleday, 1992), 109.

Adam were in covenant: (1) the Adam-Israel comparison proves that Adam was in covenant because Paul states they both existed under *nomos*-governed states, or more specifically, *covenants*; and (2) the Adam-Christ relationship demonstrates that God imputed the respective actions of each federal head to those whom they respectively represent, which is covenantal activity.

In order to prove this thesis, this chapter first examines the question of how the doctrine of the covenant appears in Romans 5:12-21 through the comparison between Adam's and Israel's *nomos*-governed states and the technical terminology Paul employs. The fact that Paul uses specific terms to distinguish sin under covenant legal provisions versus outside of covenant is key evidence for an Adamic covenant. Second, the chapter explores the nature of the two imputations that Paul presents. Third, the chapter ends with some summary observations about covenant and imputation in Romans 5.

Covenant

Romans 5 has historically been a chief focal point in the church's historic wrestling with the biblical text, whether in the Augustine-Pelagius dispute, the re-discovery of the gospel in the Reformation, discussions over imputation in the post-Reformation period, or with the deliberations over the New Perspective on Paul in the present.[2] Paul teaches weighty and significant matters in this densely packed chapter, specifically, how God relates the whole human race to one of two towering figures in redemptive history, Adam or Christ. How does the disobedience of one impact the human race, and contrariwise how does the one righteous act of Christ affect those who are in Him? But before we examine the nature of the double imputation that Paul explains in Romans 5:12-21 we must first explore what Paul has to say about the connections between Adam and Israel. Paul writes: 'Therefore, just as sin came into the world through one man, and death through sin, and so death spread to all men because all sinned – for sin indeed was in the world before the law was given, but sin is not counted where there is no law. Yet

---

2. For coverage of these debates, see J. V. Fesko, *Death in Adam, Life in Christ: The Doctrine of Imputation* (Fearn: Mentor, 2016), 31-170.

death reigned from Adam to Moses, even over those whose sinning was not like the transgression of Adam, who was a type of the one who was to come' (Rom. 5:12-14). The chief point of interest for this section specifically comes in Paul's statement, 'death reigned from Adam to Moses, even over those whose sinning was not like the transgression of Adam.' This one statement reveals that both Adam and Israel were under *nomos*-governed states; or in simpler terms, Adam and Israel were both in covenantal contexts. That Adam and Israel were in covenant with God is apparent on two grounds.

First, Paul compares and contrasts two periods of redemptive history when he states that death reigned from Adam to Moses. Readers familiar with key biblical narratives would easily explain why Adam died – he sinned (Gen. 2:16-17). Similarly, they would also be able to explain why Israelites might die – they too were subject to the sanctions of the law and in some cases, even death (e.g., Exod. 20:1-17; 21:12-17). Yet what about people that lived after Adam but before Moses? Why were they subject to death? The short answer is, because God imputes Adam's sin and guilt to all humanity. The next section addresses Paul's teaching on imputation. But for this section, the more pertinent question is, Why does Paul bracket out the people who lived after Adam but before Moses? Why does Paul say that their sin was unlike the transgression of Adam? Is not all sin the same? No, Paul specifically explains that all sin is not alike. In this particular case, the reason that Paul places a parenthesis around the interval between Adam and Moses is because their situation was different. Adam received explicit special revelation from God both in the form of the dominion mandate and the prohibition against eating from the tree of knowledge (Gen. 1:28; 2:16-17). Similarly, Israel stood at the foot of Sinai and received special revelation of God through giving of the law. As the chapter on Genesis 2:16-17 explained, it is significant that the embargo against eating from the tree of knowledge has the same syntactical form as the commandments in the Decalogue. Both Adam and Israel lived in states that were governed by God's specially revealed commands.

People who lived after Adam but before Moses, however, did not live in a covenantal context. There is no biblical record of specially revealed commands to this group of people; moreover Paul's statement here in Romans 5:13-14 explicitly states that they received no such revelation. This means that Adam's and Israel's states were comparable. At a minimum, as the thesis of this chapter states, they were both under *nomos*-governed conditions. The following diagram illustrates Paul's point:

Adam	Between Adam and Moses	Moses
'And God blessed them. And God said to them, "Be fruitful and multiply and fill the earth and subdue it, and have dominion over the fish of the sea and over the birds of the heavens and over every living thing that moves on the earth"' (Gen. 1:28). 'And the LORD God commanded the man, saying, "You may surely eat of every tree of the garden, but of the tree of the knowledge of good and evil you shall not eat, for in the day that you eat of it you shall surely die"' (Gen. 2:16-17).	No specially revealed commands	The Decalogue (Exod. 20:1-17) and the Book of the Covenant (20:19–23:33).

The legal parallels between Adam's and Israel's special *nomos*-governed contexts is sufficient proof to demonstrate that both were in covenant with God. Some might object, however, and argue that Israel's covenant context is clear given the means by which they received the law, namely, the Mosaic covenant. Adam's context, however, is not necessarily covenantal. He only received commands; Genesis 1–3 mentions nothing of a covenant.[3] While it is theoretically possible that God could administer His law apart from a covenant, two factors weigh against such a scenario: (a)

---

3. E.g., John Murray, 'Adamic Administration,' in *Collected Writings*, vol. 2 (Edinburgh: Banner of Truth, 1977), 47-59, esp. 48-49.

aside from the creation narratives, there is no biblical narrative where God administers His law apart from an explicitly stated covenant; and (b) Paul's language precludes such a conclusion.

This twofold observation raises the second point of this section, namely, the technical terms Paul employs in his explanation of Adam's and Israel's *nomos*-governed contexts. English translations try to capture the fact that Paul employs different words for sin: 'For sin [ἁμαρτία] indeed was in the world before the law was given, but sin [ἁμαρτία] is not counted where there is no law. Yet death reigned from Adam to Moses, even over those whose sinning [ἁμαρτήσαντας] was not like the transgression [παραβάσεως] of Adam' (Rom. 5:13-14a). The ESV uses two different English terms *sin* and *transgression* to capture Paul's shift in terminology. But to most readers, the two terms are largely synonymous and therefore of little theological significance. The same cannot be said of Paul's Greek terms. This is not merely literary variety but reflects important theological distinctions. Notable is that Paul applies the term ἁμαρτία to those who live during the Adam-Moses interval but employs the term παράβασις to characterize Adam's infidelity.

Why does Paul use two different terms? The simple answer is ἁμαρτία denotes moral failing in general, whereas παράβασις specifically denotes a covenantal violation. Some commentators make a more general observation regarding Paul's specific use of terms. Douglas Moo, for example, writes: 'Paul's use of "transgression," a term that he always associates with disobedience of an express commandment, shows that he refers to people who were not subject to the "law" that he speaks about in these verses. They were people who, unlike Adam, sinned without violating an express command of God to them.'[4] This is a solid observation, and handles the text more carefully than other commentators who

---

4. Douglas Moo, *The Epistle to the Romans*, NICNT (Grand Rapids: Eerdmans, 1996), 330; cf. also James D. G. Dunn, *Romans 1-8*, Word Biblical Commentary, vol. 38a (Dallas, TX: Word Books, 1988), 276; C. E. B Cranfield, *Romans: 1-8*, ICC (Edinburgh: T & T Clark, 2001), 283; C. K. Barrett, *The Epistle to the Romans: Revised Edition* (Peabody, MA: Hendrickson, 1991), 105; N. T. Wright, *Romans*, NIB, vol. 10 (Nashville, TN: Abingdon, 2002), 527; Thomas Schreiner, *Romans*, BECNT (Grand Rapids: Baker, 1998), 279; Fitzmyer, *Romans*, 418.

say nothing about Paul's terminology.[5] Nevertheless, the biblical text warrants a heartier statement regarding the significance of the term παράβασις.

A survey of New Testament texts where writers use παράβασις reveals that these moral infractions are covenantal in nature. The term παράβασις occurs in five other places in the New Testament:

- 'You who boast in the law dishonor God by breaking the law [παραβάσεως τοῦ νόμου]' (Rom. 2:23).

- For the law brings wrath, but where there is no law there is no transgression [οὐδὲ παράβασις]' (Rom. 4:15).

- 'Why then the law? It was added because of transgressions [τῶν παραβάσεων], until the offspring should come to whom the promise had been made, and it was put in place through angels by an intermediary' (Gal. 3:19).

- 'For since the message declared by angels proved to be reliable, and every transgression or disobedience [πᾶσα παράβασις καὶ παρακοὴ] received a just retribution' (Heb. 2:2).

- 'Therefore he is the mediator of a new covenant, so that those who are called may receive the promised eternal inheritance, since a death has occurred that redeems them from the transgressions [παραβάσεων] committed under the first covenant' (Heb. 9:15).

Four of the texts (Rom. 2:23, 4:15, Heb. 2:2, and 9:15), have the Mosaic covenant in view. In Romans 2:13 Paul charges the Jews for their violation of the Mosaic law; and in Romans 4:15 Paul explains how the blessings of salvation extend beyond the Jews.[6]

---

5. So, e.g., Robert Haldane, *Romans* (1874; Edinburgh: Banner of Truth, 1996), 209-10; Charles Hodge, *Romans* (1835; Edinburgh: Banner of Truth, 1989), 155-58; Philip Melanchthon, *Commentary on Romans* (St. Louis, MO: Concordia Publishing House, 1992), 134-35; Scott Hahn, *Romans*, CCSS (Grand Rapids: Baker, 2017), 82-86; John Murray, *The Epistle to the Romans*, NICNT (1962, 1965; Grand Rapids: Eerdmans, 1968), 187-91; Richard Longenecker, *The Epistle to the Romans*, NIGTC (Grand Rapids: Eerdmans, 2016), 592-93; John Calvin, *Romans and Thessalonians*, CNTC (1960; Grand Rapids: Eerdmans, 1996), 112-13.

6. Moo, *Romans*, 165-66, 276.

Hence, Paul's reference to the law is not generic but specific – the Mosaic covenantal law. The two Hebrews passages likewise have the same framework and Hebrews 9:15 explicitly invokes the πρώτη διαθήκη ('first covenant'), or Mosaic covenant.[7] In the fifth, Galatians 3:19, τῶν παραβάσεων ('the transgressions'), Paul argues that God added the Mosaic covenant in order to create the context for covenant violations. This might seem counterintuitive but is the same point that Paul makes in Romans: 'Now the law came in to increase the trespass' (Rom. 5:20a). In other words, the introduction of the Mosaic covenant exacerbates the problem of sin, which shows the need for Christ.[8] Nevertheless, in this context the term refers to violations of the Mosaic covenant.

In the sixth occurrence of the term, Paul again employs it to characterize the Adamic state: 'Adam was not deceived, but the woman was deceived and became a transgressor [παραβάσει γέγονεν]' (1 Tim. 2:14).[9] That Paul applies the term both to Adam and Eve only strengthens the claim that they were both in covenant with God. The verbal form of the term, παραβαίνω, occurs in three places: Matthew 15:2-3 and Acts 1:25. These occurrences still fit within the overall covenantal context. In Matthew, the Pharisees elevated their tradition to the level of God's commandment, and Christ challenged them on this point, evident in Matthew's use of an antithetical parallelism:

tradition (παράδοσιν) vs. command (ἐντολὴν) //
elders (πρεσβυτέρων) vs. God (τοῦ θεοῦ).[10]

---

7. Paul Ellingworth, *The Epistle to the Hebrews*, NIGTC (Grand Rapids: Eerdmans, 1993), 137-39, 459-61; William Lane, *Hebrews 1-8*, WBC, vol. 47a (Dallas, TX: 1991), 37-38; idem, *Hebrews 9-13*, WBC, vol. 47b (Dallas, TX: Word Books, 1991), 241-42.

8. Douglas J. Moo, *Galatians*, BECNT (Grand Rapids: Baker, 2013), 232-34.

9. I. Howard Marshall, *The Pastoral Epistles*, ICC (Edinburgh: T & T Clark, 1999), 464; George W. Knight III, *The Pastoral Epistles*, NIGTC (Grand Rapids: Eerdmans, 1992), 144.

10. W. D. Davies and D. C. Allison, *Matthew 8-18*, ICC (London: T & T Clark, 2006), 522.

And in Acts, Luke applies the term to Judas, who was guilty of apostasy, that is, violating the covenant (cf. Luke 22:29).[11]

When one casts a net over the Old Testament, the case only becomes stronger. In the Septuagint, the term appears in Psalm 101 [100 LXX]:3: 'I will not set before my eyes anything that is worthless. I hate the work of those who fall away [παραβάσεις]; it shall not cling to me.' In this context the Psalmist applies the term to apostates, but the context is still the Mosaic covenant: 'I will look with favor on the faithful in the land' (Ps. 101:6). In the Pentateuch, land and covenant go hand in hand (e.g., Gen. 15:18; Exod. 6:4; Lev. 26:42; Deut. 31:20). The verbal form of the term occurs thirty-four times and falls into one of three categories: covenant violation, breach of God's laws, or marital betrayal. The following table lists the occurrences and categories into which they fall:

Covenant Violation	Breaking God's Laws	Marital Betrayal
Josh. 7:11, 15; 23:16; 2 Kings 18:12; Hosea 6:7; 8:1; Isa. 24:5; Ezek. 16:59; 17:15-16, 18; 44:7.	Exod. 32:8; Lev. 26:40; Num. 14:41; 22:18; 24:13; 27:14; Deut. 1:43; 9:12; 9:16; 11:16; 17:20; 28:14; Josh. 11:15; 1 Sam. 12:21; 15:24; Ps. 119:119; Job 14:17; Jer. 5:28; Dan. 9:5; Isa. 66:24.	Num. 5:12, 19-20, 29.

Out of the thirty-four Old Testament occurrences only one instance lacks a covenantal context: 'You would call, and I would answer you; you would long for the work of your hands. For then you would number my steps; you would not keep watch over my sin; my transgression would be sealed up in a bag, and you would cover over my iniquity [παρέβην]' (Job 14:15-17). But even within this context, Job places his 'iniquity' within the context of God's 'call,' which would categorize this as a violation of God's Word, or law (cf. Deut. 28:14). The same holds true for uses of the verb for marital betrayals. In the Old Testament marriage is a covenantal relationship (Mal. 2:14).[12]

---

11. Cf. C. K. Barrett, *Acts*, vol. 1, ICC (Edinburgh: T & T Clark, 1998), 103-04.

12. Gordon P. Hugenburger, *Marriage as a Covenant: Biblical Law and Ethics as Developed from Malachi* (Grand Rapids: Baker, 1998).

Most revealing, however, are the dozen instances where the Old Testament employs the term in connection with violation of God's covenant:

- 'Israel has sinned; they have transgressed my covenant [παρέβη τὴν διαθήκην] that I commanded them' (Josh 7:11).

- 'And he who is taken with the devoted things shall be burned with fire, he and all that he has, because he has transgressed the covenant of the LORD [παρέβη τὴν διαθήκην κυρίου]' (Josh 7:15).

- 'If you transgress the covenant of the LORD your God [ἐν τῷ παραβῆναι ὑμᾶς τὴν διαθήκην κυρίου τοῦ θεοῦ ὑμῶν], which he commanded you' (Josh. 23:16).

- 'Because they did not obey the voice of the LORD their God but transgressed his covenant [παρέβησαν τὴν διαθήκην], even all that Moses the servant of the LORD commanded. They neither listened nor obeyed' (2 Kings 18:12).

- 'But like Adam they transgressed the covenant [παραβαίνων διαθήκην]' (Hosea 6:7).

- 'Because they have transgressed my covenant [παρέβησαν τὴν διαθήκην μου] and rebelled against my law' (Hosea 8:1).

- 'The earth lies defiled under its inhabitants; for they have transgressed the laws [παρέβησαν τὸν νόμον], violated the statutes, broken the everlasting covenant' (Isa. 24:5).

- 'For thus says the Lord GOD: I will deal with you as you have done, you who have despised the oath in breaking the covenant [παραβῆναι τὴν διαθήκην μου]' (Ezek. 16:59).

- 'Can he break the covenant [παραβαίνων διαθήκην] and yet escape?' (Ezek. 17:15).

- 'As I live, declares the Lord GOD, surely in the place where the king dwells who made him king, whose oath he despised, and whose covenant with him he broke [παρέβη τὴν διαθήκην μου], in Babylon he shall die' (Ezek. 17:16).

- 'He despised the oath in breaking the covenant [παραβῆναι διαθήκην]' (Ezek. 17:18).

- 'You have broken my covenant [παρεβαίνετε τὴν διαθήκην μου], in addition to all your abominations' (Ezek. 44:7).

These dozen references are significant not only because they employ verbal forms of Paul's term παράβασις but because they also coordinate covenant violation with other related concepts: breaking God's commands (Josh. 7:11; 23:16), not obeying the voice of the Lord, transgressing the laws that Moses gave Israel (2 Kings 18:12), and despising the covenantal oath (Ezek. 16:59, 17:18). Particularly noteworthy is that this is the very language that Hosea uses in his comparison between Adam's and Israel's sins against God.

This lexical data confirms the conclusion that Paul states that God and Adam were in covenant. Even though critics and proponents of the covenant of works have claimed that Hosea 6:7 is perhaps the only biblical text where an Adamic covenant has explicit warrant, Paul's use of παράβασις confirms that there is a third place in Scripture that explicitly places God and Adam in covenant: Hosea 6:7, Isaiah 24:5, and here in Romans 5:12-14.[13] In fact, Thomas Aquinas (1225-1274) makes this precise connection: '*Death ... reigned*, i.e., exercised its power over men, by bringing them to damnation *from Adam* through whom sin entered the world, *unto Moses*, under whom the law was given: *the law was given through Moses* (John 1:17), not only over those who sinned actually, but *even over them also who have not sinned, after the similitude of the transgression of Adam,* who sinned actually: *but like Adam they transgressed the covenant; there they dealt faithlessly with me* (Hosea 6:7).'[14] This means that one can legitimately gloss Romans 5:13-14a as follows: 'For sin indeed was in the world before the [Mosaic covenant] was given, but sin is not counted where there is no [covenant]. Yet death reigned from Adam to Moses, even over those whose sinning was not like [Adam's breach of the covenant].'

13. E.g., Murray, 'Adamic Administration,' 49.

14. Thomas Aquinas, *Commentary on the Letter of Saint Paul to the Romans*, trans. F. R. Larcher, vol. 37, Latin/English Edition of the Works of St. Thomas Aquinas (Lander, WY: Aquinas Institute for the Study of Sacred Doctrine, 2012), §424 (p. 144).

Paul does not say that there is no sin apart from covenant but rather that there are two types of sin: those that constitute a breach of a covenant, such as in the case of Adam and Israel, and those that violate the law of God inscribed on the hearts of all people: 'For all who have sinned without the law will also perish without the [Torah], and all who have sinned under the [Torah] will be judged by the law' (Rom. 2:12). Hence, those who lived in the interval between Adam and Moses are guilty of sin, as Paul clearly states, but they are guilty of ἁμαρτία, not παράβασις.

Imputation

But this raises a second question, namely, How can God hold accountable the people who lived after Adam but before Moses?[15] If they did not violate a covenant as Adam and Israel, why do they nevertheless die? The quick answer is, God imputes Adam's sin and guilt to all people, and hence all people are subject to the penalty of the Adamic covenant. In Romans 4 Paul focuses upon imputation at a personal soteriological level, or as it relates to the *ordo salutis*. But here in Romans 5 Paul rises above the terrain and offers a bird's eye view of the *historia salutis*. Paul's interest lies in addressing the corporate significance of the work of the first and last Adams, which he accomplishes by oscillating back and forth between Adam and Christ with his 'just as … so also' comparisons. Adam's actions have detrimental universal consequences and Paul explains how God in Christ has counteracted those effects. And though Paul's explanations follow his treatment of imputation in Romans 4, what he says here constitutes the theological foundation for all that has gone before since the opening of the epistle.[16] Paul discusses sin and righteousness, imputation, within the context of the one and the many – a theme shot through the whole passage.[17]

---

15. The following section was drawn from Fesko, *Death in Adam, Life in Christ*, 208-16.

16. Moo, *Romans*, 314-15.

17. S. Lewis Johnson, Jr., 'Romans 5:12 – An Exercise in Exegesis and Theology,' in *New Dimensions in New Testament Study*, eds. Richard N. Longenecker and Merrill C. Tenney (Grand Rapids: Zondervan, 1974), 301.

Paul opens his fifth chapter reflecting upon the significance of Christ's death and our justification, namely, that Christ has died for the ungodly (Rom. 5:1-11). He then transitions to explain the reason behind this salvation (Διὰ τοῦτο) through the antithetical parallelism between Adam and Christ (Rom. 5:12).[18] Paul writes: 'Therefore, just as sin came into the world through one man, and death through sin, and so death spread to all men because all sinned' (Rom. 5:12). Paul explains that sin is a foreign invader – it was not native to the original creation, which Genesis characterized as being 'very good' (Gen. 1:31). He lays the onus for this invasion upon Adam's shoulders, and does so with the phrase, δι' ἑνὸς ἀνθρώπου ('through one man').[19] The biblical narrative explicitly identifies Eve as the first one to sin, yet Paul lays the responsibility squarely upon Adam (Gen. 3:6; cf. 1 Tim. 2:13-14; 2 Cor. 11:3). Adam, not Eve, was the representative for humanity.[20] But in what way does Paul link the one man with οἱ πολλοί ('the many')?

The latter half of verse 12 involves the much-disputed meaning of ἐφ' ᾧ. Augustine (354-430) famously translated this phrase as, 'in whom.' That is, 'Just as sin came into the world through one man, and death through sin, and so death spread to all men; in whom [Adam] all sinned [in quo omnes peccaverunt].' Better grammatical analysis points us in a different direction. The disputed phrase most likely means because: 'Sin came into the world through one man, and death through sin, and so death spread to all men because all sinned' (emphasis; cf. 2 Cor. 5:4; Phil. 3:12). Moreover, the overall chiastic structure of this verse indicates that ἐφ' ᾧ has a causal meaning:[21]

A   sin (12a) produces
   B   death (12b)
   B¹ all die (12c)
A¹ because all sin (12d)

---

18. Johnson, Jr., 'Romans 5:12,' 301.

19. Johnson, Jr., 'Romans 5:12,' 302.

20. Moo, *Romans*, 319.

21. Moo, *Romans*, 321-22; Johnson, Jr., 'Romans 5:12,' 305.

In other words, in some sense God views all of humanity as guilty of sin because of Adam's one transgression. And while arguing that all humanity participated in Adam's sin is an accurate conclusion, we must drill down into text to determine the precise nature of this participation.[22] In what way has all humanity sinned (ἥμαρτον)?

Answering this question brings us to the shores of some heavily trafficked territory in the history of exegesis. There are largely four different views on the manner of humanity's participation in Adam's sin:[23]

(1) Imitation

Pelagius (fl. ca. 390-418) famously argued that there is no legal or ontological connection between Adam and humanity. Rather, the connection is imitative.[24] Adam's progeny imitate his sin – Adam is a bad moral example. A predecessor to Pelagius appears in 2 Baruch 54:19, 'Adam therefore is not the cause, save only of his own soul, but each of us has been the Adam of his own soul.' Advocates of this view include Albert Barnes (1798-1870), C. K. Barrett (1917-2011), Emil Brunner (1889-1966), and Rudolf Bultmann (1884-1976), as well as those who deny the historicity of Adam, such as Roman Catholics Daryl Domning and Monika Hellwig.[25] The problem with such exegesis is that it fails to engage the text responsibly. Paul makes the point six times that Adam's one sin caused the death of all people and that because of his sin ἁμαρτωλοὶ κατεστάθησαν οἱ πολλοί ('the many were constituted

---

22. Johnson, Jr., 'Romans 5:12,' 304.

23. Johnson, Jr., 'Romans 5:12,' 306-13.

24. Pelagius, *Pelagius's Commentary on St Paul's Epistle to the Romans*, trans. Theodore de Bruyn (Oxford: Clarendon Press, 1998), 92.

25. Albert Barnes, *Notes, Explanatory and Practical, On the Epistle of Romans* (New York: Leavitt, Lord, and Co., 1834), 127-29; C. K. Barrett, *Romans*, BNTC (Peabody: Hendrickson, 1991), 111; Emil Brunner, *The Christian Doctrine of Creation*, trans. Olive Wyon (London: 1952), 99; Rudolph Bultmann, 'New Testament and Mythology: The Mythological Element in the Message of the New Testament and the Problem of Its Re-interpretation,' in *Kerygma and Myth*, ed. Hans Werner Bartsch (New York: Harper & Row, 1961), 7; Daryl P. Domning and Monika K. Hellwig, *Original Selfishness: Original Sin and Evil in the Light of Evolution* (Aldershot: Ashgate, 2006).

sinners' trans. mine) (Rom. 5:12, 15, 16, 17, 18, 19). Moreover, Paul contrasts Adam's one sin with the on-going sin of others: 'Yet death reigned from Adam to Moses, whose sinning was not like the transgression of Adam' (Rom. 5:14).

(2) Realism

This view was first made famous by Augustine who, based upon his mistranslation of Romans 5:12, believed that all humanity was seminally present in Adam. In some sense, then, humanity was really truly physically present. In addition to Augustine, similar views appear in John Calvin (1509-1564), W. G. T. Shedd (1820-1894) and James H. Thornwell (1812-1862).[26] The pertinent question here is, Does Adam pass sin onto his progeny by virtue of numerical or representative unity? The overall thrust of Romans 5:12-21 does not appear to be numerical unity, especially when Paul states that the many were 'constituted,' or 'appointed sinners' (κατεστάθησαν) by virtue of Adam's one sin (Rom. 5:19). There is also the fact that Paul repeatedly emphasizes the effects of Adam's one sin, but if humanity was seminally present in Adam why do they not bear the guilt of Adam's subsequent sins since they ostensibly would have been seminally present for those acts as well? Last, a realistic theory of participation muddies the waters of the Adam-Christ parallel. Paul places Adam and Christ and the effects of their respective acts in antithetical parallel: 'For as by the one man's disobedience the many were constituted sinners, so by the one man's obedience the many will be constituted righteous' (Rom. 5:19, trans. mine). The means by which humanity participates in Adam's sin is the same manner in which believers participate in Christ's act of righteousness.

---

26. John Calvin, *The Epistles of Paul the Apostle to the Romans and to the Thessalonians*, CNTC (1961; Grand Rapids: Eerdmans, 1996), 112; idem, *Institutes of the Christian Religion*, trans. John Allen (Grand Rapids: Eerdmans, 1948), II.i.5-8; idem, John Calvin, *John 1-10*, CNTC (1960; Grand Rapids: Eerdmans, 1996), 66; W. G. T. Shedd, 'Original Sin,' in *Discourses and Essays* (Andover: W. F. Draper, 1856), 218-71; idem, *Dogmatic Theology*, 3 vols. (1888; Grand Rapids: Zondervan, 1969), II:168-260; James H. Thornwell, 'Nature of Our Interest in the Sin of Adam, Being a Review of Baird's Elohim Revealed,' in *Collected Writings*, vol. 1, ed. John B. Adger (Richmond: Presbyterian Committee of Publication, 1871), 515-68.

(3) Mediate Imputation

This view has been historically associated with Josua Placaeus (1596-1655).[27] Placaeus believed that humanity was guilty because they sinned; they did not sin because they were guilty. Is humanity's guilt antecedent or consequent? Do people sin because they are guilty, or are they guilty because they sin?[28] The main thrust of his argument is that humanity does not inherit Adam's guilt but a corrupt nature, and this corrupt nature leads them to sin. The so-called imputation occurs, therefore, through the means of an inherited corrupt nature. A noted advocate of this view is Henry Boynton Smith (1815-1877).[29] Once again, this view does not pay close attention to the details of the text. Paul states that death spread to all men because all sinned (ἥμαρτον). The Greek term ἁμαρτάνω does not mean *to be* or *become corrupt* (cf. e.g., Matt. 18:15; 1 Cor. 15:34; Titus 3:11; John 5:14). The theory also rides roughshod over the Adam-Christ parallel (Rom. 5:19). Moreover, if the main concern was that guilt follows sin rather than precedes it, the proposed solution of receiving a corrupt nature rather than the guilt of sin does not alleviate the perceived problem. To receive a corrupt nature presupposes some sort of guilt. In the end, though Placaeus called his view *mediate imputation*, in truth, he does away with the doctrine of imputation.[30]

(4) Immediate Imputation

This view appears in, among others, Francis Turretin (1623-1687), the Westminster Confession of Faith (1647), the Savoy Declaration (1658), Second London Confession (1689), and Charles Hodge (1797-1878).[31] Advocates of this view maintain that God immediately

---

27. Josua Placaeus, *De Imputatione Primi Peccatis Adami Josue Placaei in Academia Salmuriensi S. s. Theologiae Professoris Disputatio* (Saumur: Ioannem Lesnerium, 1661).

28. Hodge, *Romans*, 161, 164.

29. Henry Boynton Smith, *System of Christian Theology*, 2nd ed. (New York: A. C. Armstrong & Son, 1884), 306-17.

30. Turretin, *Institutes of Elenctic Theology* (Phillipsburg: P & R, 1992-97), IX.ix.5-6; cf. also Francis Turretin and Johannes Heidegger, *Formula Consensus Helvetica*, X-XII, in A. A. Hodge, *Outlines of Theology* (1860; Edinburgh: Banner of Truth, 1991), Appendix II (pp. 658-59).

31. Turretin, *Institutes*, IX.ix.11, 16; WCF VI.i; Savoy Declaration VI.i; Second London Confession, VI.iii; Charles Hodge, *Systematic Theology*, 3 vols. (rep.; Grand Rapids: Eerdmans, 1993), II:196-203.

(apart from any physical or real means) imputes both Adam's guilt and Christ's righteousness to those whom they represent. This view, in my judgment, best accounts for the exegetical data of Romans 5:12 and its immediate context.

Immediate imputation best explains a number of features in the text – there are five chief reasons.[32] First, Paul presents Adam and Christ as the respective representatives for humanity. Adam's dominion mandate (Gen 1:28) was not his alone but belonged to the human race. Hence, just as Christ's one act of obedience is representative and comprises the judicial ground for the justification of the elect, so Adam's one act of disobedience constitutes the judicial ground for the condemnation for those who are united to him.[33] Second, Paul implicitly relies upon the doctrine of immediate imputation when he describes humanity's legal state, a condition in which all people are born spiritually dead and under a curse – they are 'by nature children of wrath' (Eph. 2:3). Third, the concept of the one representing the many is not new or foreign to the Scriptures – Achan's sin (Josh. 7), David's sinful census (2 Sam. 24; cf. 1 Chron. 21), Daniel's vision of the Son of Man (Dan. 7), Leviticus 16 and the Day of Atonement (Lev. 16:21-22), and Isaiah's suffering servant (Isa. 53:11-12), and Joshua the high priest's investiture (Zech. 3:1-5; cf. Isa. 61:10) all feature the concept of immediate imputation.[34] One acts and the many bear the positive or negative consequences. Fourth, immediate imputation better accounts for the Adam-Christ parallels. Paul repeatedly states that the respective actions of *one* impact the many, either for life or death. Most pointedly, *all* die because *one* sinned. Fifth, immediate imputation best explains why Adam's progeny only bear the guilt and consequences of his first and not his subsequent sins.

Immediate imputation, therefore, best explains Romans 5:12-21, though there are several other elements in this passage that merit examination, namely, the historicity of Adam, the Old Testament background, and the covenantal context. One of the more important

---

32. For what follows, see Johnson, Jr., 'Romans 5:12,' 312-13.

33. Hodge, *Romans*, 170.

34. See Fesko, *Death in Adam, Life in Christ*, 175-96.

points in Romans 5:12-21 is that Paul compares two historical people, Adam and Christ, and two historical actions. Despite the efforts of some exegetes and theologians to categorize Adam as a mythic icon that explains the human fallen condition, such efforts must ignore the plain meaning of the text.[35] When Paul identifies Adam as a 'type [τύπος] of the one to come' (Rom. 5:14), he has in mind a comparison between historical, not mythical, realities. Such is the nature of biblical typology – it places Old Testament historical events, places, and people in an analogous relationship to New Testament historical events, places, and people.[36] To argue that Adam is a mythic figure or did not truly exist means Paul's argument ultimately crumbles.[37] How can God impute the non-existent mythical act of one non-historical mythical figure to the rest of humanity? If Adam did not exist, then there is no act of disobedience to impute, which means either there is no corporate solidarity with him and hence no corporate guilt, or that God created human beings defective with a predisposition towards sin. Such a conclusion not only strikes at the goodness of the creation but at the very heart of the doctrine of God. How can a holy and upright God create humanity with a proclivity towards sin and then hold them accountable if they were unable to act otherwise?

Another important feature is the Old Testament background to Paul's argument. As already noted, the concept of immediate imputation is not foreign to the Scriptures – it appears throughout the Old Testament. Beyond the broader connections to the Old Testament, there are a number of elements within Romans 5:12-21 that connect this passage to Isaiah 53. Through one (ἑνὸς) man, Adam, sin entered the world and 'death spread to all men because all sinned' (Rom. 5:12). Paul labels those affected by Adam's sin as τοὺς πολλοὺς

---

35. E.g., Peter Enns, *The Evolution of Adam: What the Bible Does and Doesn't Say about Human Origins* (Grand Rapids: Brazos, 2012), 79-87.

36. Leonhard Goppelt, *Typos: The Typological Interpretation of the Old Testament* (Grand Rapids: Eerdmans, 1982), 17-20; Richard M. Davidson, *Typology in Scripture: A Study of Hermeneutical τύπος Structures* (Berrien Springs, MI: Andrews University Press, 1981), 313-16.

37. D. A. Carson, 'Adam in the Epistles of Paul,' in *In the Beginning*, ed. Nigel M. de Cameron (Glasgow: Biblical Creation Society, 1980), 28-44.

('the many'). Conversely, echoing Isaianic themes, Paul explains: 'For the judgment following one trespass brought condemnation, but the free gift following many trespasses brought justification' (Rom. 5:16). In contrast to Adam's disobedience, Christ, the last Adam, offers His representative righteousness, or obedience, which brings justification. Paul oscillates back and forth between the actions of one and the effect upon the many, whether unto condemnation or justification. The fact that Paul mentions that the οἱ πολλοί 'will be constituted righteous' (δίκαιοι κατασταθήσονται οἱ πολλοί, Rom. 5:19, trans. mine) likely arises directly from Isaiah 53:11b (LXX).[38]

The last key observation is the covenantal context for Paul's argument. Paul operates within a covenantal framework, evident by his use of the term παράβασις, the one and the many, and his allusion to Isaiah 53, all of which grow out of the rich covenantal soil of the Old Testament. The covenant binds the one and the many together, and in other places in his epistles Paul references the concept (Rom. 9:4; 11:27; 1 Cor. 11:25; 2 Cor. 3:6, 14; Gal. 3:17; 4:24; Eph. 2:12). Moreover, Paul understood that Christ's intercessory work was connected to the fulfillment of Jeremiah's prophesied new covenant given that Christ identified His shed blood as that which ratified the new covenant (cf. Jer. 31:31-34; Matt. 26:28; Mark 14:24; Luke 22:20; 1 Cor. 11:25; cf. Heb. 9:15). All of these different elements, therefore, confirm that Paul's doctrine of imputation was informed by the Old Testament. Imputation was no novelty but rather went back into the earliest days of Israel's existence. Given the Adam-Christ parallel, it also stands to reason that Adam and humanity exist in covenantal relationship.[39]

---

38. Hofius, 'Fourth Servant Song,' 182; cf. Brian Vickers, *Jesus' Blood and Righteousness: Paul's Theology of Imputation* (Wheaton: Crossway, 2006), 122; Moo, *Romans*, 345-46; Albrecht Oepke, καθίστημι, in *Theological Dictionary of the New Testament*, vol. 3, ed. Gerhard Kittel (Grand Rapids: Eerdmans, 1965), 445; Charles Hodge, *Romans* (1835; Edinburgh: Banner of Truth, 1989), 173-74; Ben C. Dunson, *Individual and Community in Paul's Letter to the Romans* (Tübingen: Mohr Siebeck, 2012), 148-54; Sang-Won (Aaron) Son, *Corporate Elements in Pauline Anthropology: A Study of Selected Terms, Idioms, and Concepts in the Light of Paul's Usage and Background* (Rome: Pontifico Instituto Biblico, 2001), 61, 77.

39. Hodge, *Romans*, 156; Robert Haldane, *Romans* (1874; Edinburgh: Banner of Truth, 1996), 213, 232-33.

Theological Implications

The doctrinal implications of Romans 5:12-21 are significant for the covenant of works on two fronts. First, the doctrine of the covenant informs Paul's arguments in Romans 5:12-21, evident especially by his use of the term παράβασις. His Jewish audience familiar with the Septuagint would undoubtedly know the significance of this term and conclude that Adam's sin was a covenantal violation. While Paul does not use the term διαθήκη ('covenant') in this passage, παράβασις nevertheless has covenantal significance. There is a metonymical relationship between the two terms – to summon one is to invoke the other. For as Paul says, apart from covenantal law, there is no παράβασις (Rom. 4:15).

Second, some texts such as Hosea 6:7 provide legitimate exegetical footing to support the claim that God and Adam were in covenant, but here Paul adds crucial theological data to flesh out the nature of this covenant. Adam transgressed God's covenant and the aberrant fruit of his apostasy was imputed sin and guilt to all humanity. Paul's explanation of the Adam-Christ parallel is essentially a redemptive-historical exegesis of the creation-fall narrative that explains in great detail both the nature of God's covenant but its negative and positive effects. With Adam's transgression, God imputed his sin and guilt to all humanity; but with Christ's obedience, He imputes His righteousness to those who believe in Him (cf. Rom. 3:21-5:11). That Paul places Adam and Christ in parallel also suggests that Christ entered the sin-fallen world ὑπὸ νόμον ('under the law'), that is, under the provisions of the covenant of works. He is not only the Messiah but is also the ὁ ἔσχατος Ἀδὰμ ('last Adam') (1 Cor. 15:45). Eschatological life was the goal for Adam, but he failed to secure it for himself and his offspring because of his transgression; but Christ entered the Adamic covenant and was perfectly obedient and thus secured the reward of the covenant of works. So, while one should maintain the distinct loci of systematic theology so that no one loci swallows the other, nevertheless the covenant of works thus establishes anthropology, which is a significant element of christology. Whatever the Bible says of Adam applies to and, in some sense, informs the doctrine of Christ.

Third, the Adam-Israel connection is important for understanding the Adam-Christ parallel. The Mosaic covenant is clearly not the terminal destination for redemptive history but it is certainly a crucial stop along the way. The fact that Paul, like Hosea before him, compared Adam's and Israel's states means that they mutually inform one another because of their similar covenantal contexts. Paul does not say that Israel participated in the Adamic covenant *simpliciter*, that is, that like Adam they could have secured eternal life through their obedience. In a sin-fallen world Paul clearly indicates that no flesh shall be justified in the presence of God by works of the law (Rom. 3:20, 27-28). The inability to seek justification by works of the law is a significant discontinuity between the Adamic and Mosaic covenants. Nevertheless, as earlier chapters on Genesis 2:16-17 and Hosea 6:7 argue, there are sufficient continuities between the Adamic and Mosaic covenants to warrant their comparison.

Conclusion

Romans 5:12-21 is an important load-bearing text for the covenant of works because Paul concisely deals with the old and new creations, the first and last Adams. The passage speaks of the consequences of union with the two Adams – either one is in union with Adam or Christ. But given Paul's terminology and the double-imputation that he explains, this is a passage that has covenant written all over it. God administers His law by means of covenants, whether in the pre-fall or post-fall contexts. Another way of stating this conclusion is, when God dispenses His law, it is covenantally binding. When God issued the dominion mandate (Gen. 1:28) and told Adam, 'You may surely eat of every tree of the garden, but of the tree of the knowledge of good and evil you shall not eat, for in the day that you eat of it you shall surely die' (Gen. 2:16b-17), He bound Adam to His command – He was in covenant with His creature.

~: II.8 :~

Captive to the Law
(Rom. 7:1-6)

Introduction

Early modern Reformed theologians appeal to Romans 7:1-6 to support the doctrine of the covenant of works. When Westminster divine William Strong (d. 1654) explains that God binds every unregenerate person under the law as a covenant of works, he appeals to Paul's statements about being married to the law as a husband. Once God frees sinners from the law and unites them to Christ, they are then dead to the law.[1] Strong's contemporary, Edward Fisher (fl. 1627-55), explains Romans 7:4-6 in the following manner: 'The Apostle in the beginning of the seventh Chapter of the *Epistle* to the *Romans*, compares this compact bargain or covenant between a man in the state of nature, and the Law, as it is the Covenant of works, to the compact or covenant that is made between man and wife in marriage, and this death to their death.'[2] Both theologians believed Paul was dealing with law and covenant in this passage, and in particular, how God frees sinners from the bondage to the law. In other words, Paul deals with how God frees sinners from the effects and consequences of the broken covenant of works. Theologians such as Johannes

---

1. William Strong, *A Discourse of the Two Covenants: Wherein the Nature, Differences, and Effects of the Covenant of Works and of Grace Are Distinctly, Rationally, Spiritually and practically Discussed* (London: Francis Tyton, 1678), I.ii (p. 38).

2. Edward Fisher, *The Marrow of Modern Divinity* (London: G. Calvert, 1645), 59.

Cocceius (1603-1669), Matthew Henry (1662-1714), Charles Hodge (1797-1878), and Robert Haldane (1764-1842) understood Romans 7:1-6 in this manner.[3] If appeal to historical sources alone warranted doctrinal conclusions, then there is sufficient reason to recognize that Romans 7:1-6 discusses the covenant of works. Nevertheless, while history can inform, instruct, and illuminate, doctrine must ultimately rest on the exegesis of the Scriptures.

Hence, this chapter defends the thesis that Paul discusses the covenant of works in Romans 7:1-6 and the means by which Christ frees sinners from its bond. The chapter begins with an examination of the passage and then segues to analysis. In particular, it may not immediately strike the reader, but Romans 7:1-6 is a passage steeped in the doctrine of the covenant. Paul and his original audience undoubtedly breathed covenantal air and thus did not think twice about the idea; but contemporary readers who stand at a great historical distance must re-familiarize themselves with this fundamental category. In other words, sometimes one must state the obvious because too many have become unconscious of it.

Romans 7:1-6

The passage in question comes in the context of Paul's extended argument regarding the nature of redemption through Christ, in particular, the implications of the doctrine of justification. Paul's arguments in Romans 7:1-6 build off statements he makes in the previous chapter, specifically, 'For sin will have no dominion over you, since you are not under law but under grace' (Rom. 6:14).[4]

---

3. Johannes Cocceius, *Doctrine of the Covenant and Testament of God*, trans. Casey Carmichael (Grand Rapids: Reformation Heritage Books, 2016), III.lviii (pp. 58-59); Matthew Henry, *A Commentary on the Whole Bible: Romans to Revelation* (London: The Religious Tract Society, 1835), comm. Rom. 7:1-6 (pp. 38-40); Charles Hodge, *Romans* (1835; Edinburgh: Banner of Truth, 1989), 214-19; Robert Haldane, *Romans* (1874; Edinburgh: Banner of Truth, 1996), 277-84.

4. N. T. Wright, *Romans*, NIB (Nashville: Abingdon, 2002), 558; John Murray, *The Epistle to the Romans*, NICNT (1959, 1965; Grand Rapids: Eerdmans, 1968), 239; Robert Jewett, *Romans*, Hermenia (Minneapolis, MN: Fortress, 2007), 428; C. E. B. Cranfield, *Romans*, 2 vols., ICC (Edinburgh: T & T Clark, 2001), I:330; Joyce A. Little, 'Paul's Use of Analogy: A Structural Analysis of Romans 7:1-6,' *CBQ* 46 (1984): 82-83.

Paul explains that 'our old man was crucified with him [Christ] in order that the body of sin might be brought to nothing ... for one who has died has been justified from sin' (Rom. 6:6-7, trans. mine). This brings us to Romans 7:1 where Paul writes: 'Or do you not know, brothers—for I am speaking to those who know the law—that the law is binding on a person as long as he lives?' Paul establishes the fact that sinners lie under the dominion of the law, but once they are crucified with Christ, and are thus in union with Him, they are no longer under law but under grace. This explains Paul's statement, 'the law is binding on a person as long as he lives.'

But questions immediately arise regarding the law. What *law* does Paul have in mind? Interpretations vary and include: the law in general, or a legal system, Roman law because Paul was presumably writing to Roman citizens, the Mosaic law as the immediate context seems to demand, natural law, or all laws given to humanity including the command of Genesis 2:17.[5] The most likely answer is that Paul refers to the Mosaic law given that his use of νόμος up to this point has referred to this economy. This is a conclusion that interpreters as diverse as Thomas Aquinas (1225-1274), John Calvin (1509-1564), and other contemporary commentators adopt.[6] Even though Paul's audience was probably largely Gentile does not mean they would be utterly ignorant of the Mosaic law and thus sidelined.[7] Instead, within the context of his argument Gentiles could follow his argument stemming from earlier portions of his letter. In this case, he merely restates what

---

5. For references to the different views, see Joseph A. Fitzmyer, *Romans*, AB (New York: Anchor Bible, 1992), 455-56.

6. Thomas Aquinas, *Commentary on the Letter of Saint Paul to the Romans*, trans. F. R. Larcher (Lander, WY: The Aquinas Institute for the Study of Sacred Doctrine, 2012), chp. 7, lect. 1, §520 (p. 178); John Calvin, *Romans and Thessalonians*, CNTC, ed. T. F. Torrance and David W. Torrance (1960; Grand Rapids: Eerdmans, 1996), 137-38; e.g., Fitzmyer, *Romans*, 456; Wright, *Romans*, 558; Douglas J. Moo, *The Epistle to the Romans*, NICNT (Grand Rapids: Eerdmans, 1996), 411; Thomas R. Schreiner, *Romans*, BECNT (Grand Rapids: Baker, 1998), 346; Murray, *Romans*; C. K. Barrett, *The Epistle to the Romans*, rev. ed. (1957; Peabody, MA: Hendrickson, 2001), 126; James D. G. Dunn, *Romans 1-8*, WBC, vol. 38a (Dallas, TX: Word, 1988), 359.

7. Wright, *Romans*, 558.

he has explained before, namely, that sin and the law enslave them and Christ sets them free (Rom. 6:20-23). But one should not forget an important contextual element regarding the Mosaic law: God administers the law as a covenant, as Paul elsewhere clearly states (Gal. 4:21-27; cf., e.g., Deut. 29:21; Ps. 78:10; Isa. 24:5; Jer. 31:31-33). Paul is not interested in the law merely as a moral standard but in its redemptive historical role as the Mosaic covenant.

Paul illustrates this point in the verses that follow: 'Thus a married woman is bound by the law to her husband while he lives, but if her husband dies she is released from the law of marriage. Accordingly, she will be called an adulteress if she lives with another man while her husband is alive. But if her husband dies, she is free from that law, and if she marries another man she is not an adulteress' (Rom. 7:2-3). At this point, questions arise regarding the exact nature of Paul's appeal to marriage. Is this an allegory as Augustine (354-430), Philip Melanchthon (1497-1560), and Theodore Beza (1519-1605) suggest, where the husband represents corrupt human nature, and the wife is the soul? When the corrupt nature dies, the soul is free to marry another. Or, is the wife the church, and the husband the law, as Origen (184-253) and Chrysostom (d. 407) propose?[8] Nothing in the immediate context indicates that Paul introduces an allegory but only uses marriage as an illustration, or an example, of his point in verse 1.[9] So if Romans 7:2-3 is an illustration, what point does it convey?

The law indissolubly binds the husband and wife together save one exception, death. Hence Paul states that the law binds the woman to her husband 'while he lives,' and only his death

---

8. See Hodge, *Romans*, 216; cf. Augustine, *Augustine on Romans: Propositions from the Epistle to the Romans Unfinished Commentary on the Epistle to the Romans*, trans. Paul Frederiksen Landes (Chico, CA: Scholars Press, 1982), 13-14; Philip Melanchthon, *Commentary on Romans*, trans. Fred Kramer (St. Louis, MO: Concordia, 1992), 152-55; Theodore Beza, *Iesu Christi D. N. Novum Testamentum* (Geneva: Jacob Stadot, 1616), Rom. 7:1-6; Origen, *Commentary on the Epistle to the Romans: Books 6-10*, trans. Thomas P. Scheck (Washington, D. C: The Catholic University of America Press, 2002), VI.vii.2-19 (pp. 20-29); Chrysostom, *Homilies on Romans*, Homily XII, in NPNF[1] XI:416-27, esp. 418-20.

9. So Hodge, *Romans*, 216; Moo, *Romans*, 412; Wright, *Romans*, 558; Murray, *Romans*, 240.

releases her to marry another.[10] There are two noteworthy elements regarding Paul's illustration. First, he likely alludes to prescriptions of the Mosaic law when he writes of the ὕπανδρος ('married woman'), which is a term that appears in Numbers 5:20, 29 (LXX) (cf. Deut. 24:1-4; Prov. 6:24, 29).[11] The use of this word confirms that Paul does not have natural law, Roman law, or a general legal system in view but rather the legal stipulations of the Mosaic covenant. First-century Jews were familiar with this marriage principle from the Mosaic law.[12] But Paul connects this illustration to what he says about the law in Romans 6:9, 14, namely, that sin κυριεύσει ('rules over') sinners; it exercises a lordship over humanity through the law that ends only with death. In Old Testament Judaism wives had no right to divorce their husbands; only the husband's death freed them from the bond of marriage.[13]

Second, one should not forget that marriage was understood in covenantal terms. Both Old and New Testaments recognize this fact. The Old Testament characterizes God's relationship to Israel in terms of a marriage covenant: 'For your Maker is your husband, the LORD of hosts is his name' (Isa. 54:5; cf. 62:5; Jer. 3:1). The prophet Hosea embodied this idea in a living parable when he married his adulterous wife, Gomer, who represented idolatrous Israel (Hosea 3:1-5).[14] The most explicit reference that confirms the marriage-covenant connection appears in the prophet Malachi: 'But you say, "Why does he not?" Because the LORD was witness between you and the wife of your youth, to whom you have been faithless, though she is your companion and your wife by covenant' (Mal. 2:14).[15] The New Testament continues this theme in a higher key when it presents Jesus as the bridegroom who weds the

---

10. Moo, *Romans*, 413.

11. Fitzmyer, *Romans*, 457; Jewett, *Romans*, 431; Dunn, *Romans*, 360.

12. Schreiner, *Romans*, 347.

13. Schreiner, *Romans*, 347.

14. Scott W. Hahn, *Romans*, CCSS (Grand Rapids: Baker, 2017), 111.

15. Gordon P. Hugenburger, *Marriage as a Covenant: Biblical Law and Ethics as Developed from Malachi* (Grand Rapids: Baker, 1994), 27-47.

church (Matt. 25:1-13; John 3:28-29; Eph. 5:23-33; Rev. 19:7).[16] This marriage imagery overlaps with the New Testament's ideas about Christ as the mediator of the new covenant (cf. Jer. 31:31; Luke 22:20; 1 Cor. 11:25; 2 Cor. 3:6; Heb. 8:8, 13; 9:15; 12:24). Paul does not invoke the term *covenant* but it nevertheless stands quietly center stage both in terms of the apostle's appeal to the Mosaic covenant and the marriage covenant.[17]

Paul takes this covenant-marriage illustration and applies it to his Roman readers when he writes: 'Likewise, my brothers, you also have died to the law through the body of Christ, so that you may belong to another, to him who has been raised from the dead, in order that we may bear fruit for God' (Rom. 7:4). If death frees a wife from the marriage covenant to her husband, then death likewise frees a sinner from her covenantal bond to the law. Or, in Haldane's explanation: 'As, then, the covenant relation of a wife to her husband is dissolved by death, so believers are released from their covenant relation to the law by the death of Christ, with whom they died; for He died to sin, chp. vi. 10, and to the law having fulfilled it by His obedience and death, so that it hath no further demand upon Him.'[18] Noteworthy is that believers receive the legal benefit of Christ's law-neutralizing work through their justification, which is in order to their sanctification, or bearing fruit for God.[19] As Paul indicates this point with a result clause: 'But now we are released from the law, having died to that which held us captive, so that [ὥστε] we serve in the new way of the Spirit and not in the old way of the written code' (Rom. 7:6). Or, justification is the necessary prerequisite of sanctification. Either a person is under the law and thus not justified, or he is justified and hence not under the law (Rom. 6:7, 14).[20] But justification is

---

16. Hahn, *Romans*, 111.

17. See similar comments in Anders Nygren, *Commentary on Romans* (Philadelphia: Muhlenberg Press, 1944), 270-71.

18. Haldane, *Romans*, 280.

19. Jewett, *Romans*, 435.

20. David VanDrunen, *Divine Covenants and Moral Order: A Biblical Theology of Natural Law* (Grand Rapids: Eerdmans, 2014), 437-40.

not merely a soteric fact, one related solely to the individual sinner; it is also a redemptive-historical reality.

Paul further colors in the lines of his marriage-covenant illustration with the contrasting opaque and vivid hues of redemptive history: he compares the dark shades of the present evil age and the bright tones of the age to come, the new heavens and earth. Paul writes: 'For while we were living in the flesh, our sinful passions, aroused by the law, were at work in our members to bear fruit for death. But now we are released from the law, having died to that which held us captive, so that we serve not under the old written code but in the new life of the Spirit' (Rom. 7:5-6). Paul contradistinguishes between flesh, passions, law, death, and the old written code versus new life of the Spirit. Within the framework of his argument, Paul envisions the law, or Mosaic covenant, as part of the 'present evil age' (cf. Rom. 6:14; Gal. 1:4). Paul highlights this point when he characterizes the law as the 'old written code' and contrasts it with life in the Spirit.[21] This contrast raises at least two important points.

First, Paul's arguments here are a further extension of the two-Adam configuration he establishes in Romans 5:12-21. Sin enters the world through Adam, and because of his covenantal transgression (παράβασις), God counts all human beings as having sinned (Rom. 5:12-14). But Adam's apostasy was not the final word, as God sent the Word, the last Adam, to redeem sons and daughters of Adam: 'For as by the one man's disobedience the many constituted sinners, so by the one man's obedience the many will be constituted righteous' (Rom. 5:19, trans. mine). Christ redeems sinners from under the law by uniting with them through the indwelling of His Holy Spirit. Paul leads up to his arguments of Romans 7:1-6 by beating the continual drumbeat of the believer's death no less than seven times:

1. How can we who died to sin still live in it (Rom. 6:2)?

2. All of us who have been baptized into Christ Jesus were baptized into His death (Rom. 6:3).

---

21. Moo, *Romans*, 415; Dunn, *Romans*, 366-67.

3. We were buried therefore with Him [Christ] by baptism into death, in order that, just as Christ was raised from the dead by the glory of the Father, we too might walk in the newness of life (Rom. 6:4; cf. Col. 2:11-14).

4. For if we have been united with Him in a death like His, we shall certainly be united with Him in a resurrection like His (Rom. 6:5).

5. We know that our old man was crucified with Him in order that the body of sin might be brought to nothing (Rom. 6:6).

6. We have died with Christ, we believe that we will also live with Him (Rom. 6:8).

7. You also must consider yourselves dead to sin and alive to God in Christ Jesus (Rom. 6:11).

So, when Paul describes the believer's death to the law in terms of a dissolved marriage-covenant, he refers to the death of his Adamic existence, his 'old man,' and his subsequent marriage to Christ as a new creation in Him.[22]

Second, the Mosaic covenant is part of the Adamic side of the Adam-Christ ledger of redemptive history. The Mosaic covenant is undoubtedly part of the covenant of grace, since God intended and used it to drive sinners to Christ, indeed, to increase sin (Rom. 5:20-21). But it functions as a ministry of death; it is the old covenant, which becomes obsolete in the light of the new covenant (2 Cor. 3:7-18).[23] Some might object because they believe that the covenant of grace has all of its ties to the eschaton, to the new creation. The covenant of grace most certainly terminates in the new creation, but God initiates it on the heels of Adam's fall in the sin-darkened present evil age. The covenant of grace has many temporary elements that pass away with the advent of Christ and ultimately with the consummation of the age. When Paul writes to the Colossians and tells them not to let anyone

---

22. Wright, *Romans*, 559.

23. Wright, *Romans*, 561; Jewett, *Romans*, 436; cf. Charles Hodge, *1 & 2 Corinthians* (1857, 1859; Edinburgh: Banner of Truth, 1994), 432-35.

pass judgment on them regarding questions about food and drink, festivals, or the Sabbath, he explains: 'These are a shadow of the things to come, but the substance belongs to Christ' (Col. 2:17; cf. Rom. 10:4; Heb. 10:1).[24] This means that the Mosaic covenant is part of the covenant of grace but serves to highlight the substance of the covenant of grace, namely, Christ. Hence, the Mosaic covenant becomes obsolete with Christ's advent. Recall that Paul elsewhere likens the Mosaic covenant to the στοιχεῖα τοῦ κόσμου ('elementary principles of the world') from which the children of God have been freed by Christ (Gal. 4:3). Or in language closer to Paul's argument in Romans 7, 'You are not under law but under grace' (Rom. 6:14b).

Analysis

Covenant of Works

In short, in Romans 7:1-6 Paul explains the binding nature of the law and, as Strong and Fisher rightly explain, the apostle shows how the law functions as the covenant of works. Only the death of Christ releases the law's grip of the sinner and frees him to marry another. The Westminster Confession explains the believer's relationship to the law in a similar manner when it writes: 'Although true believers be not under the law, as a covenant of works, to be thereby justified, or condemned; yet it is of great use to them, as well as to others; in that, as a rule of life informing them of the will of God, and their duty, it directs and binds them to walk accordingly' (XIX.vi).[25] When God first gave Adam the moral law, He gave it to him as a covenant of works, 'by which he bound him and all his posterity to personal, entire, exact, and perpetual obedience' (WCF XIX.i). When Adam violated the covenant of works, it did

---

24. See, e.g., Douglas J. Moo, *The Letters to the Colossians and to Philemon*, PNTC (Grand Rapids: Eerdmans, 2008), 222-24; Peter T. O'Brien, *Colossians, Philemon*, WBC, vol. 44 (Waco, TX: Word Books, 1982), 139-41.

25. *The Confession of Faith and Catechisms of The Orthodox Presbyterian Church* (Willow Grove, PA: The Committee on Christian Education of the Orthodox Presbyterian Church, 2005). This edition of the confession cites Romans 6:14 and 7:4 as proof texts for this statement.

not disappear but continued to abide. When God gave the moral law to Israel in the form of the Mosaic covenant, it was supposed to serve as a 'perfect rule of righteousness' (WCF XIX.ii), that is, for regenerate Israelites the moral law served as a rule. But for unregenerate Israelites, the moral law served as 'a covenant of works, to be thereby justified, or condemned' (WCF XIX.vi). The confession employs the nomenclature of covenant theology to explain the dynamic of Romans 7:1-6. This means that the law *qua* the covenant of works never expires until the consummation of the age. Adam's infidelity does not eliminate its requirements or reward. Only Christ delivers sinners from the consequences of its violation through union with Him and full participation in the covenant of grace.

Some might object to this conclusion because Paul does not have the Adamic covenant primarily in view but the Mosaic covenant. How can Paul's comments apply to the Adamic covenant? Or, how can Paul's comments directed to those who know the law, i.e., Jews (Rom. 7:1), equally apply to Gentiles? How can Paul's reference to the Mosaic covenant expand to and include the Adamic covenant? The Old Testament highlights the fact that God has not given the Mosaic law to the Gentile nations: 'He declares his word to Jacob, his statutes and rules to Israel. He has not dealt thus with any other nation; they do not know his rules' (Ps. 147:19-20). Paul also recognizes this fact when he contrasts those who sin without the law with those who have the law (Rom. 2:12).[26] This does not mean, however, that Gentiles need not heed Paul's instruction in Romans 7:1-6. Rather, given Paul's explanation of the law in Romans 1-2, all people are under God's law, whether the Mosaic law for the Jew or natural law for the Gentile because through their God-informed conscience.[27] Whether Jewish or Gentile, apart from Christ they lie under the condemnation of the law. This is not to say, however, that there is no difference between the natural and Mosaic laws. Rather, Israel's state under the Mosaic law serves

---

26. Stephen Westerholm, *Israel's Law and the Church's Faith: Paul and His Recent Interpreters* (Grand Rapids: Eerdmans, 1988), 192.

27. Westerholm, *Israel's Law*, 193.

as a paradigmatic microcosm for all people.[28] What is true of Israel's existence under the Mosaic covenant is generally true of all humanity under the Adamic covenant. That is, no one, Jew or Gentile, can seek justification by means of the law. The only hope of redemption comes through the one who has fulfilled the law. Only in Christ does the law become a rule, a friend, and guide.

The Covenant of Works and Justification

Another important observation relates to the origins of the doctrine of justification. Some have sought to write a biblical theology of justification and have rightly begun in the garden of Eden and Adam's probation. But they do not explicitly draw out the idea inherent in probation, namely, success warrants justification and failure merits condemnation. Expositional emphasis falls on failure and condemnation; there is nothing wrong with this, as Adam did indeed fail.[29] But in Romans 7:1-6 Paul presents the idea that Christ fulfills the requirements of the covenant of works as well as pays the penalty for its violation: 'But now [νυνὶ δὲ] we are released from the law, having died to that which held us captive, so that we serve in the new way of the Spirit and not in the old way of the written code' (Rom. 7:6). Paul's νυνὶ δὲ ('but now') signals the in-breaking of the new creation work of the last Adam, he who was born under the law to fulfill all its obligations (Gal. 4:4; Matt. 5:17); these responsibilities originate in the Adamic context.[30] When God justifies Christ, therefore, He declares Him righteous vis-à-vis the legal requirements to which all human beings are bound, but especially to the precepts of the moral law revealed in the Mosaic covenant.

When God first created, He interspersed His activity with divine judgments of His work: 'And God said, "Let there be light," and there was light. And God saw that the light was good' (Gen. 1:3). His work culminated with the creation of humanity, male and

---

28. Westerholm, *Israel's Law*, 194; Moo, *Romans*, 417; VanDrunen, *Divine Covenants*, 354-58.

29. Brian Vickers, *Justification by Grace through Faith: Finding Freedom from Legalism, Lawlessness, Pride, and Despair* (Phillipsburg, NJ; P & R, 2013), 11-30.

30. Jewett, *Romans*, 437.

female, which He declared by a divine verdict that they were 'very good' (Gen. 1:31).[31] When God issued the commands to fill all the earth and subdue it and not eat from the tree of knowledge under pain of death (Gen. 1:28; 2:16-17), Adam's loving obedience should have elicited the divine verdict of 'justified,' and the Father's, 'This is my beloved Son in whom I am well pleased.' Adam's obedience would have unleashed the Spirit and the eschaton. Instead, Adam failed, and paved the way for 'one like the son of man' to come, to obey, and to unleash the Spirit and the new creation (cf. Ps. 8; Dan. 7:13; Matt 26:64; Mark 14:62; Luke 22:69; 1 Cor. 15:20-28, 42-49). Christ releases the new creation work of the Spirit through His own justification: 'Great indeed, we confess, is the mystery of godliness: He was manifested in the flesh, justified by the Spirit, seen by angels, proclaimed among the nations, believed on in the world, taken up in glory' (1 Tim. 3:16-17, trans. mine). The divine verdict that should have cascaded over Adam on the heels of his successful probation in the garden instead fell on Christ, the only begotten of the Father, the last Adam (Rom. 1:3-4). In the words of Hodge, 'It is the legal system, which says, "Do this and live," that Christ has abolished, and introduced another, which says, "He that believes shall be saved."'[32]

Conclusion

The word *covenant* does not appear in Romans 7:1-6 but Paul definitely engages the concept as he explains how the law is no longer binding on redeemed sinners. In this passage Paul demonstrates that people live under one of two masters, either law or grace, which is an extension of the respective reigns of Adam and Christ. Paul illustrates the virtually unbreakable connection between the sinner and the law, whether in its Adamic or Mosaic forms, whether for Gentiles or Jews. In his marriage illustration, Paul powerfully captures the fact that only death breaks the ties between the sinner

---

31. Mary Sylvia C. Nwachukwu, *Creation-Covenant Scheme and Justification by Faith: A Canonical Study of the God-Human Drama in the Pentateuch and the Letter to the Romans* (Rome: Editrice Pontifica Università Gregoriana, 2002), 58; Meredith G. Kline, *Images of the Spirit* (1980; Eugene, OR: Wipf and Stock, 1999), 112.

32. Hodge, *Romans*, 217.

and the law and this happens only through the work of Christ. In his illustration, the law does not die; rather, the sinner dies.[33] In other words, the covenant of works hangs over the collective heads of humanity – they can neither break free from its demands nor flee the consequences of its Adamic fracture. Humanity's slavery under the covenant of works finds a microcosmic illustration in Israel's similar bondage under the Mosaic covenant (Gal. 4:1ff). In the fallen state only Christ's perfect obedience and suffering can break the power of sin, which is the law (1 Cor. 15:56). So even though the term does not appear, Paul nevertheless addresses the nature of the covenant of works and the only way sinners can break free from its grip.

---

33. Murray, *Romans*, 242.

❖ PART III ❖
Doctrine

~: III.1 :~

Statement of the Doctrine

Introduction

Exegesis gathers the materials for constructive doctrinal formulation. Part II exegeted eight key texts: Romans 2:14-15, Genesis 2:16-17, Leviticus 18:5, Isaiah 24:5; Hosea 6:7, Galatians 4:24, Romans 5:12-21, and Romans 7:16. All of these texts reveal the existence of a covenant between God and Adam but there are other passages that should be factored. This chapter sets forth the formal statement of the doctrine but does not leave exegesis behind. In B. B. Warfield's (1886-1921) terms, the chapter takes the individual soldiers scattered throughout the biblical text and begins to organize them into armies.[1] Or as Geerhardus Vos (1862-1949) has illustrated it, the chapter takes the exegetical information from the unfolding *line* of redemptive history and draws a *circle* to demonstrate how all of the data theologically coheres and fits together.[2] This chapter therefore synthesizes the biblical data from Part II to formulate the covenant between God and Adam.[3] Before

---

1. B. B. Warfield, 'The Idea of Systematic Theology,' in *Studies in Theology* (Oxford: Oxford University Press, 1932), 49-87.

2. Geerhardus Vos, 'The Idea of Biblical Theology as a Science and as a Theological Discipline,' in *Redemptive History and Biblical Interpretation: The Shorter Writings of Geerhardus Vos*, ed. Richard B. Gaffin Jr. (Phillipsburg, NJ: P & R, 1980), 3-24.

3. This chapter traces the outline and content of Louis Berkhof, *Systematic Theology: New Combined Edition* (1932, 1938; Grand Rapids: Eerdmans, 1996), 211-18.

the chapter constructs the doctrine it must address matters of definition and terminology.

A historic definition of the covenant of works appears in the Westminster Confession of Faith (1646): 'The first covenant made with man was a covenant of works, wherein life was promised to Adam; and in him to his posterity, upon condition of perfect and personal obedience' (VII.ii). God made an agreement with Adam that He would reward his obedience with eternal life and that his faithful actions would also fall positively upon his offspring or negatively should he disobey. In technical terms, the covenant of works designated Adam as the federal head of humanity – God would impute his obedience or conversely his disobedience to those whom he represented. In this covenant God issued two commands: the dominion mandate (Gen. 1:28) and the prohibition of eating from the tree of knowledge (Gen. 2:16-17).

In the history of the doctrine a number of terms have been employed and some have objected to the designation *covenant of works*. The Westminster Shorter Catechism, for example, designates the Adamic covenant as a *covenant of life* (q. 12). As noted in Part I, theologians have called it the first covenant, natural covenant, covenant of nature, legal covenant, creation covenant, and Adamic covenant. Any one of these terms is suitable and captures important aspects of God's initial agreement with Adam. Nevertheless, the covenant of works is a preferable choice for two chief reasons.

First, the covenant rested in Adam's obedience, which Scripture labels as *works*. Works stand in opposition to *faith* and *belief*. Note, for example, Paul's juxtaposition of works verses faith: 'Now to the one who works, his wages are not counted as a gift but as his due. And to the one who does not work but believes in him who justifies the ungodly, his faith is counted as righteousness' (Rom. 4:4-5).

Second, *works* characterize the nature of the pre-fall covenant. God gave Adam work to do – he was supposed to be fruitful, multiply, fill all the earth, and subdue it (Gen. 1:28). He was supposed to labor for six days and then rest on the Sabbath (Gen. 2:3). As God worked and then entered His rest, so Adam was supposed to labor and then enjoy a weekly foretaste of his eternal rest to come each and every Sabbath. As Vos notes: 'The so-called "Covenant of Works" was nothing but an embodiment of the Sabbatical principle. Had its probation been successful, then the sacramental Sabbath would have passed over into the reality it typified, and the entire subsequent course of the history of the race would have been radically different.[4]

Going forward, the chapter proceeds by exploring: (1) the scriptural data that goes beyond the previously exegeted texts in Part II, (2) elements of the covenant of works, which includes its natural and covenantal components, its condition, penalty, and sacraments, and (3) the present status of the covenant of works. The chapter concludes with summary observations.

Scriptural Data

One of the hallmark features of the covenant of works is that theologians have long-noted that it is a doctrinal construct. In contrast to nineteenth and twentieth-century modernity, which was influenced by positivism and its insistence that the term *covenant* explicitly appear in Genesis 1–3, past generations of Reformed exegetes know no such strictures.[5] Herman Bavinck (1854-1921), for example, notes: 'Reformed scholars were never so narrow as to insist on the word "covenant" since the matter itself was certain: one may doubt the word provided the matter is safe (*de vocabulo dubitetur, re salva*). But hidden behind the opposition to the word was opposition to the matter itself. And this must never be surrendered inasmuch as covenant is the essence of true religion.'[6] In terms of historic Reformed hermeneutics,

---

4. Geerhardus Vos, *Biblical Theology: Old and New Testaments* (1948; Edinburgh: Banner of Truth, 2014), 140.

5. So, e.g., John Murray, 'Adamic Administration,' in *Collected Writings*, vol. 2 (Edinburgh: Banner of Truth, 1977), 49; Jeffrey J. Niehaus, 'An Argument against Theologically Constructed Covenants,' *JETS* 50/2 (2007): 259-73.

6. Herman Bavinck, *Reformed Dogmatics*, ed. John Bolt, trans. John Vriend, 4 vols. (Grand Rapids: Baker Academic, 2003-08), II:569. On the covenant of works as a doctrinal construct, see, e.g., Richard A. Muller, 'The Covenant of Works and the Stability of Divine Law in Seventeenth-Century Reformed Orthodoxy: A Study in the Theology of Herman Witsius and Wilhelmus à Brakel,' *CTJ* 29 (1994): 75-101; Thomas Boston, *A View of the Covenant of Works from the Sacred Records* (Edinburgh: John Gray, 1775), 3; E. J. Young, 'Confession and Covenant,' in *Scripture and Confession:*

theologians determined that God and Adam were in covenant by collating various biblical texts and determining that, on the whole, the Scriptures teach that this covenant exists. In the simplest of terms, they used Scripture to interpret Scripture; in theological terms, they arrived at the doctrinal conclusion by good and necessary consequence (WCF I.vi). The term *trinity*, for example, does not appear in the Bible, yet the entire Christian tradition recognizes the validity of the doctrine through good and necessary consequence. The term may be absent but is the concept materially and substantively present? Therefore, what biblical data points to the existence of a covenant?

Immediate Context
No one disputes that God and Israel were in covenant, thus the Mosaic covenant serves as a suitable benchmark to determine whether a covenant appears in Genesis 1–3.[7] There are a series of parallels between Genesis 1–3 and the Mosaic covenant that corroborate the existence of a covenant between God and Adam. God issued Adam and Eve commands to fill the earth and subdue it and not to eat from the tree of the knowledge of good and evil that parallels the administration of the law at Sinai (cf. Gen. 1:28, 2:17; Exod. 20:13-15). The trees of the garden (life and knowledge) signal the presence of a covenant, as they serve as signs of God's promise of eternal life and the administration of His command (law) not to eat from the tree of knowledge. The trees function in the same manner as other covenantal signs: the rainbow, circumcision, and the Sabbath (cf. Gen. 2:9; 9:13-16; 17:9-14; Exod. 31:13). As with the Mosaic covenant, Genesis 2:4 invokes the covenant name of God, Yahweh (Gen. 2:4; Exod. 3:14ff). In Genesis 1–3 and in the Mosaic covenant we find the blessing-curse formula – obedience and life versus disobedience and

---

A Book About Confessions Old and New, ed. John H. Skilton (Phillipsburg, NJ: P & R, 1973), 31-66, esp. 58; John Colquhoun, *A Treatise on the Covenant of Works* (Edinburgh: Thomsons, Brothers, 1821), 273; Geerhardus Vos, *Reformed Dogmatics*, 5 vols., ed. Richard B. Gaffin, Jr., et al. (Bellingham, WA: Lexham Press, 2012-14), II:35.

7. For a similar interpretive strategy, see Boston, *Covenant of Works*, 5; Colquhoun, *Covenant of Works*, 6; Adam Gib, *Kaina kai Palia: Sacred Contemplations in Three Parts* (Philadelphia, PA: W. Young and J. McCulloch, 1788), 84-85.

death (cf. Gen. 2:9, 16-17; Deut. 27:1–28:68). Within the immediate context of Genesis 1–3 the commands, the sacramental trees, the covenant name of God, and the blessing-curse formula all point to the existence of a covenant between God and Adam. Any Old Testament Israelite listening to the Genesis 1–3 text would hear features that he would immediately associate with the elements of the Mosaic covenant.

Broader Context

The Genesis 1–3 context is one piece that fits within the broader context of a much larger canonical puzzle. As common as it is for some detractors of the doctrine to isolate Genesis 1–3 from the rest of the Pentateuch, this broader canonical context is vital to reading the opening chapters of the Bible. There is in fact an inter-textual symbiotic relationship between Genesis 1–3 and the book of Deuteronomy.[8] Israelite readers knowledgeable of the Pentateuch read the creation narrative within the context of Israel's covenantal charter, Deuteronomy, and observed the many parallels between Eden, Sinai, and Gerazim and Ebal. In addition to foreshadowing the last Adam, God's faithful son (Rom. 5:14), Genesis 1–3 anticipates Israel's failure to keep the Mosaic covenant and their future exile from the promised land. Both Adam and Israel point to Jesus, the last Adam – the only one in a post-fall world who completed Adam's failed work.[9] Adam's failure to subdue the slithering serpent, his smooth-sounding words of seduction, Adam's sedition, and Adam and Eve's subsequent banishment are

---

8. So Mary Douglas, *Purity and Danger: An Analysis of the Concepts of Pollution and Taboo* (London: Routledge & Kegan Paul, 1966), 41-57, esp. 55ff; T. Stordalen, *Echoes of Eden: Genesis 2-3 and Symbolism of the Eden Garden in Biblical Hebrew Literature* (Leuven: Petters, 2000), 33; Trygve N. D. Mettinger, *The Eden Narrative: A Literary and Religious-Historical Study of Genesis 2-3* (Winona Lake: Eisenbrauns, 2007), xii, 49-50, 57; John Van Steters, *Prologue to History: The Yahwehist as Historian in Genesis* (Louisville, KY: Westminster John Knox Press, 1992), 127-29; Norbert Lohfink, *The Christian Meaning of the Old Testament* (Milwaukee, WI: Bruce Publishing, 1968), 58-62.

9. For a defense of this claim, see J. V. Fesko, *Last Things First: Unlocking Genesis 1–3 with the Christ of Eschatology* (Fearn: Mentor, 2007), 145-82. Also see Benjamin L. Gladd, *From Adam and Israel to the Church: A Biblical Theology of the People of God* (Downers Grove, IL: InterVarsity Press, 2019), 47-48, 78-91.

Israel's story in miniature.[10] Adam's apostasy and exile form an inclusio with Israel's prophesied apostasy and exile in Deuteronomy 32:1-43. Adam's and Israel's apostasies set the stage for the last days where the last Adam will rectify Adam's and Israel's failures (Deut. 30:6).

Elements of the Covenant of Works

The two participants in the covenant of works are the triune God and Adam as the federal covenant head (Rom. 5:12-21; 1 Cor. 15:22, 45; cf. 1 Tim. 2:13). In the covenant there is a twofold aspect to God's relationship to Adam, the natural and covenantal. Important to note, however, is that while these two aspects may be distinguished, they are inseparable.

The Natural Aspect

The biblical account describes Adam's creation and God's commands to be fruitful, multiply, fill the earth, subdue it, and not to eat of the tree of knowledge as a sequence of events. God first created Adam (Gen 2:7), gave him the command not to eat of the tree of knowledge (Gen. 2:16-17), created Eve (Gen. 2:22-23), and then gave them the dominion mandate (Gen. 1:28). In this vein the Westminster Shorter Catechism is correct when it asks and answers the question: 'What special act of providence did God exercise toward man in the estate wherein he was created?' The catechism answers: 'When God had created man, he entered into a covenant of life with him, upon condition of perfect obedience; forbidding him to eat of the tree of the knowledge of good and evil, upon pain of death' (q. 12). When God created Adam there was a natural aspect to their relationship: God is creator, Adam is creature. God is Lord, Adam is servant. As creator, God endowed Adam with His divine image. The image of God is both office and gifts. That is, as an image-bearer Adam's responsibility and office was to exercise dominion over the creation. Genesis 1:28 provides a definition of the office of that image: to rule over the fish of the

---

10. Seth Postell, *Adam as Israel: Genesis 1–3 as the Introduction to the Torah and Tanakh* (London: James Clarke & Co., 2011), 3-4, 108-19, 130, 134-48.

sea, birds of the heavens, and the whole earth.[11] But the image of God is not merely office or function but also entails the gifts that enabled Adam to carry out his office. To borrow language from the Westminster Larger Catechism, God created Adam and Eve 'after his own image, in knowledge, righteousness, and holiness, having the law of God written in their hearts, and power to fulfill it, and dominion over the creatures, yet subject to fall' (q. 17; see also WCF IV.ii).

A vital element of the covenant of works is that Adam possessed the law of God by virtue of being an image bearer. As Paul writes in Romans 2:14-15, 'For when the Gentiles who do not have the law, by nature do what the law requires, they are a law to themselves, even though they do not have the law. They show that the work of the law is written on their hearts, while their conscience also bears witness, and their conflicting thoughts accuse or even excuse them.' All people by virtue of their creation possess the law of God written on their hearts, whereas the Jews possessed the moral law in two modes: upon their hearts and through the administration of the law in the Mosaic covenant (Exod. 20; Deut. 5). The moral law inscribed upon Adam's heart was part of the natural bond between him and his creator. Adam recognized both from the testimony inscribed upon his heart and in his conscience his obligations to his maker, a testimony also writ large across the entire creation.[12] In his pre-fall state Adam and Eve knew who God was, knew what He required of them as His creatures, and could learn more about God by reading the book of creation, or as the Belgic Confession describes it, the book of nature.[13] Likewise, the Westminster Confession states, 'The light of nature showeth that there is a

---

11. David VanDrunen, *Divine Covenants and Moral Order: A Biblical Theology of Natural Law* (Grand Rapids: Eerdmans, 2014), 48-50; J. Richard Middleton, *The Liberating Image: The Imago Dei in Genesis 1* (Grand Rapids: Brazos, 2005), 50-55.

12. Bavinck, *Reformed Dogmatics*, IV:34.

13. Belgic Confession, art. II. See also Abraham Kuyper, 'The Natural Knowledge of God,' *TBR* 6 (2015): 73-112, esp. 73-74, 82-83; J. V. Fesko, *Reformed Apologetics: Retrieving the Classic Reformed Approach to Defending the Faith* (Grand Rapids: Baker Academic, 2019), 11-48.

God, who hath lordship and sovereignty over all, is good, and doth good unto all, and is therefore to be feared, loved, praised, called upon, trusted in, and served, with all the heart, and with all the soul, and with all the might' (XXI.i; cf. I.i).[14]

Hypothetically, in a purely natural state (*in naturalibus puris*), had Adam transgressed the moral law he would have been liable to punishment; and conversely, he would have received blessing and reward given his possession of the natural law and righteousness.[15] Adam would have known to obey God. As an image-bearer, he would have been inclined to love and serve Him. As James Ussher (1581-1656) explains in the Irish Articles (1615): 'Man being at the beginning created according to the image of God (which consisted especially in the Wisdom of his mind and the true Holiness of his free will) had the covenant of the law ingrafted in his heart: whereby God did promise unto him everlasting life, upon condition that he performed entire and perfect obedience unto his Commandments, according to that measure of strength wherewith he was endued in his creation, and threatened death unto him if he did not perform the same' (XXI).[16] In other words, Adam knew by virtue of his status as an image-bearer what God required of him. Abstractly considered, he did not know of the specific commands to fill the earth, subdue it, and not to eat from the tree. The specifics of Adam's work required the formal administration of the covenant. The natural aspect of Adam's relationship with God also has a horizontal dimension, in that Adam was the father of the human race (Acts 17:26).[17] There is a natural-biological bond between Adam and all human beings.[18]

---

14. Bavinck, *Reformed Dogmatics*, II:565, 567, 571.

15. David VanDrunen, 'Natural Law and the Works Principle Under Adam and Moses,' in *The Law Is Not of Faith: Essays on Works and Grace in the Mosaic Covenant*, ed. Bryan D. Estelle, J. V. Fesko, and David VanDrunen (Phillipsburg, NJ: P & R, 2009), 283-314, esp. 292-97; cf. Bavinck, *Reformed Dogmatics*, II:571.

16. See Harrison Perkins, *Catholicity and the Covenant of Works: James Ussher and the Reformed Tradition* (Oxford: Oxford University Press, 2020), 50-73.

17. Berkhof, *Systematic Theology*, 215.

18. This statement raises the question of recent scientific research that is beyond the scope of this chapter but has been addressed elsewhere, e.g., J. P. Moreland,

This natural bond is the means by which God conveys sinful corruption to all human beings (WCF VI.iii).[19]

The Covenantal Aspect

From the very outset God revealed that He was both creator and a covenant-making God. The Westminster Standards are correct to say that God condescended to Adam and Eve to make a covenant with them as a special act of providence, but given God's decree to create there is no possible world in which God creates apart from making this covenant with them. Given God's decree to create and enter into a covenant of works with humanity, its existence was an absolute necessity. There is no possible world where God creates Adam and Adam declines the covenant and remains *in naturalibus puris*. Pace Bavinck, the covenant and its promise of eternal life does not serve as a Reformed version of the *donum superadditum*.[20] That is, God does not first create Adam in a natural state and then give him the possibility of a supernatural end as an addendum to his natural existence. Pure nature versus Adam's state in covenant is merely a theological distinction so that one might understand how nature and covenant relate to one another. Nature and covenant are ultimately concreated realities and thus inseparable, though distinguishable. Like the faculty psychology, intellect and will are distinct faculties of the soul but are nevertheless inseparable.

To understand better the relationship between nature and covenant, we can designate Adam's image-bearing nature as the material cause of the covenant of works and the administration of the divine commands as its formal cause. That is, there is no covenant of works apart from Adam's natural endowments as an image bearer, but likewise there is no covenant with Adam apart from God's special act of providence. To force a choice between Adam created *in* versus *for* covenant imposes a false dilemma upon the biblical text – choosing between the two attempts to

---

et al., eds., *Theistic Evolution: A Scientific, Philosophical, and Theological Critique* (Wheaton, IL: Crossway, 2017), 363-402, 839-926.

19. WCF VI.iii.

20. See Bavinck, *Reformed Dogmatics*, II:571-72.

rend the seamless garment of creation and covenant.[21] When God formally administered the covenant, however, He commanded Adam and Eve to be fruitful, multiply, fill the earth, subdue it, and not to eat from the tree of knowledge (Gen. 1:28; 2:16-17). The connection between the material and formal causes of the covenant of works follows the pattern that unfolds in the creation narrative. God first creates and then verbally confirms what He has accomplished. God first created light and then declared that it was good; He then defined the light and the darkness by calling them day and night (Gen. 1:3-6). God created humans in His image and then verbally defined what it meant to be an image-bearer (Gen. 1:26-28). Likewise, God created humans in a covenantal state given the fact that they bore His image and then confirmed and formalized this state through His verbal commands (Gen. 1:28; 2:16-17). Vos explains that God's revelation follows this word-act-word pattern. First God speaks, then He acts, and then follows His actions with an interpretive word.[22] God declares that He will make humans (word, Gen. 1:26), then He makes Adam and Eve (act, Gen. 1:27), and then He verbally confirms and defines what He has done through His verbal commands (word, Gen. 1:18; 2:16-17).

In this covenant God constituted Adam as the representative and federal head of the human race. In the natural relationship there is an organic and biological connection between Adam and his offspring, but by virtue of the covenantal bond Adam is the federal head; the covenant unites all of humanity together. By means of the covenantal bond God imputes Adam's sin to all human beings and holds them guilty for Adam's transgression. Or, as the Westminster Confession states: Adam and Eve 'being the root of all mankind, the guilt of this sin was

---

21. For a brief overview of the history of the created *in* versus *for* covenant, see Joel R. Beeke and Mark Jones, *A Puritan Theology: Doctrine for Life* (Grand Rapids: Reformation Heritage Books, 2012), 221-24.

22. Geerhardus Vos, *Biblical Theology: Old and New Testaments* (1948; Edinburgh: Banner of Truth, 1996), 7; see also Matthew Barrett, *Canon, Covenant and Christology: Rethinking Jesus and the Scriptures of Israel* (Downers Grove, IL: IVP Academic, 2020), 45-47.

imputed.'[23] When God formally administered the covenant, He placed Adam and Eve under a temporary probation. Once Adam and Eve fulfilled the mandate, were fruitful, multiplied, filled all the earth, and subdued it, they would have secured God's promise of eternal life. It is, however, also possible that their probation could have had a shorter duration and, once passed, God would have allowed them to eat of the tree prior to the completion of the dominion mandate.

The Promise of the Covenant

God promises eternal life through the formal administration of the covenant. Some have argued that Genesis 1–3 contains no promise of eternal life.[24] No one contends that the promise of eternal life appears explicitly in the opening chapters of the Bible. When God, however, commanded Adam not to eat from the tree of knowledge (Gen. 2:16-17), the threatened curse of death implies that life was the reward for obedience. When God says, 'For in the day that you eat of it you shall surely die,' Adam would have lived had he obeyed the command. At some point he would have been permitted to eat from the tree of life. To eat from the tree of knowledge was to choose death. To obey God's command was to choose life. Adam's options anticipate Israel's later similar covenantal choice when God told Israel: 'I call heaven and earth to witness against you today, that I have set before you life and death, blessing and curse. Therefore choose life, that you and your offspring may live' (Deut. 30:19). While Adam lived in the garden, he enjoyed life and possessed righteousness by virtue of being an image bearer of God, but the life he had was mutable and his righteousness was unproven. If Adam was obedient to the command and passed the covenantal probation, he would have entered a confirmed state of eternal life and his righteousness would have been proven.

---

23. Westminster Confession, VI.iii. For a historical, exegetical, and theological treatment of the doctrine of imputation, see J. V. Fesko, *Death in Adam, Life in Christ: The Doctrine of Imputation* (Fearn: Mentor, 2016). Also see John Murray, *Imputation of Adam's Sin* (Phillipsburg, NJ: P & R, 1977).

24. For advocates of this view, see J. V. Fesko, *The Covenant of Works: Origins, Development, and Reception* (Oxford: Oxford University Press, 2020), chps. 5–7.

When Paul writes, 'The very commandment that promised life' (Rom. 7:10), his reference is to eternal, not temporal, life. Obedience to the law has eschatological life as its reward, as 'the Spirit is life because of righteousness' (Rom. 8:10). The law-obedience-eternal life connection stands behind Leviticus 18:5's principle of, do this and you shall live. Jesus later appeals to Leviticus 18:5 in His conversation with the lawyer who asked Him, 'Teacher, what shall I do to inherit eternal life?' Jesus asked the lawyer, 'What is written in the Law?' The lawyer responded: 'You shall love the Lord your God with all your heart and with all your soul and with all your strength and with all your mind, and your neighbor as yourself.' Jesus replied, 'You have answered correctly; do this, and you will live' (Luke 10:25-28; cf. Deut. 6:4; Lev. 18:5). The apostle Paul appeals to this same law-obedience-eternal life nexus in his explanation of the doctrine of justification: 'No it is evident that no one is justified before God by the law, for "the righteous shall live by faith." But the law is not of faith, rather "The one who does them shall live by them"' (Gal. 3:11-12; cf. Rom. 10:5). Human beings either attain eternal life by faith in Christ or through obedience to the law. In a fallen state sinners are incapable of perfect obedience to law but in the pre-fall state, this was a genuine possibility for Adam. God created Adam in His image and thus he was righteous (Eccles. 7:29).[25] Adam's rectitude means he was perfectly righteous and thus capable of obeying both naturally and supernaturally revealed law. Adam could love God and follow the natural law as it was inscribed on his heart and written in the creation, and he could obey the supernatural revelation that he received in the dominion mandate and command not to eat from the tree of knowledge. Or, in the words of the Westminster Confession, 'Man, in his state of innocency, had freedom, and power to will and to do that which was good and well pleasing to God; but yet, mutably, so that he might fall from it' (IX.ii).

The Condition of the Covenant

When God promised Adam eternal life, it was not an unconditional promise. The promise was conditioned upon Adam's prerequisite

---

25. Tremper Longman III, *The Book of Ecclesiastes*, NICOT (Grand Rapids: Eerdmans, 1998), 207.

obedience. Adam and Eve had to obey every manifestation of God's law, whether the naturally or supernaturally revealed commands: the moral law inscribed on their hearts and written in the creation, the dominion mandate, and the command not to eat from the tree of knowledge. The law is like a mirror, and thus to break one part is to break the whole mirror: 'For whoever keeps the whole law but fails in one point has become guilty of all of it' (James. 2:10; cf. Gal. 5:3; Matt. 5:18-19).[26] In the words of the Westminster Larger Catechism, God entered into a covenant of life with Adam 'upon condition of personal, perfect, and perpetual obedience, of which the tree of life was a pledge; and forbidding to eat of the tree of the knowledge of good and evil, upon the pain of death' (q. 20). Critics of the covenant of works, however, contend that the legal element of the covenant of works turns the relationship between God and Adam into a cold piece of business, a legal transaction and nothing more.[27] While some treatments of the covenant of works may be spartan, seeking an economy of words in the interest of pedagogical precision and clarity, the Bible does not pit legal and affective categories against one another.

Law and love go hand in hand and appear quite prominently in Israel's *Shema*: 'Hear, O Israel: The LORD our God, the LORD is one. You shall love the LORD your God with all your heart and with all your soul and with all your might. And these words that I command you today shall be on your heart' (Deut. 6:4-6). The legal aspects of the covenant of works do not cast a shadow of darkness over the fact that Adam's obedience was ultimately a manifestation of his love for God. As Herman Witsius (1636-1708) observes: 'The law of nature could be nothing but a precept of conformity to God, and of perfect love.'[28] Similarly, Wilhelmus à Brakel (1635-1711) avers: 'Adam doubtlessly had the most perfect law. The most

---

26. Douglas J. Moo, *The Letter of James*, PNTC (Grand Rapids: Eerdmans, 2000), 114.

27. So N. T. Wright, *The Day the Revolution Began: Reconsidering the Meaning of Jesus's Crucifixion* (San Francisco: Harper One, 2016), 74-76.

28. Herman Witsius, *Economy of the Covenants Between God and Man*, 2 vols. (rep.; Escondido, CA: The Den Dulk Foundation, 1990), I.iii.7.

perfect law is the law of love.'[29] The covenantal bond between Adam and God was also supposed to have a horizontal dimension with respect to Eve. As Paul writes: 'For the whole Law is fulfilled in one word: "You shall love your neighbor as yourself"' (Gal. 5:14; cf. Lev. 19:18). Paul similarly and succinctly states, 'Love is the fulfilling of the law' (Rom. 13:10b). As John Calvin (1509-1564) once characterized the law, it is a perpetual rule of love (*perpetuam charitatis regulam*), because God's 'eternal and immutable will is, that we are all to worship him and mutually love one another.'[30] This is true both of the post- as well as the pre-fall covenantal administrations of law. That God focused Adam's obedience on the solitary command not to eat from the tree of knowledge did not mean that Adam and Eve were not obligated to the natural law or dominion mandate. Rather, Adam's probation had its fulcrum in the tree of knowledge, the sacramental sign of God's law and commands. The tree pointed both to the dominion mandate and the command not to eat the fruit of the tree of knowledge. The great question that stood before Adam and Eve was, would they love God with all their heart, soul, mind, and strength? Would he rest in perfect union and communion with God, in the power of the Spirit, and obey His commands, or would Adam venture out on his own? Adam's failure, therefore, was not merely one of disobedience but ultimately one of love. He loved himself more than his covenant Lord.

The Penalty of the Covenant

God specifies that the penalty of the covenant of works was death. Adam undoubtedly suffered death, but some believe that God did not follow-through on His threat because Adam did not die on the day that he ate of the fruit (cf. Gen. 2:17; 5:5).[31] As common as this

---

29. Wilhelmus à Brakel, *The Christian's Reasonable Service*, 4 vols., trans. Bartel Elshout (Morgan, PA: Soli Deo Gloria, 1992), I:359.

30. John Calvin, *Institutes of the Christian Religion*, trans. Henry Beveridge (Grand Rapids, MI: Eerdmans, 1947), IV.xx.15; idem, *Institutio Christianae Religionis* (Geneva: Robert Stephanus, 1559).

31. So, e.g., Herman Gunkel, *Genesis* (Macon, GA: Mercer University Press, 1997), 10.

misunderstanding is, terms like *die* and *death* should be read within and defined by their canonical context. Adam physically died 930 years after his covenant apostasy in Eden. As God threatened, he returned to the dust of the earth (Gen. 3:19). But contrary to popular opinion, Adam and Eve died on the day that they ate of the fruit. Adam and Eve spiritually died, as they were both immediately aware of their nakedness and shame on the heels of their sin (Gen. 3:7). In Pauline terms, they both became children of wrath and were dead in their sin (Eph. 2:1-3). But they died in another way on the day that they ate of the fruit. Recall that Genesis 1–3 forms an inclusio with Deuteronomy 32:1-43 – both of God's sons (Adam and Israel) were placed in the presence of God, both committed covenantal apostasy, and both were exiled from His presence – Adam from the garden and Israel from the promised land. The garden of Eden was the temple of God and thus living within this sacred space was tantamount to life itself.[32] This is the way that Deuteronomy characterizes living in God's presence in the land: 'The LORD your God ... is your life and length of days' (Deut. 30:20). In fact, the Psalmist longs to dwell especially in the house of the Lord: 'One thing I have asked of the LORD, that I may dwell in the house of the LORD all the days of my life, to gaze upon the beauty of the LORD and to inquire in his temple' (Ps. 27:4; cf. Ps. 23:6). If the Old Testament idealized life as dwelling in God's presence in the temple, then conversely how does it characterize death? Ezekiel portrays Israel's exile as laying in a graveyard in a state of death – Israel lies in a barren valley as a pile of dry bones (Ezek. 37).[33]

Stated simply, presence is life and exile is death.[34] These connections appear a number of times in Deuteronomy. Exile is a

---

32. On the garden's status as the first earthly temple, see, e.g., G. K. Beale, *The Temple and the Church's Mission: A Biblical Theology of the Dwelling Place of God* (Downers Grove, IL: InterVarsity Press, 2004), 66-80; J. V. Fesko, *Last Things First: Unlocking Genesis 1–3 with the Christ of Eschatology* (Fearn: Mentor, 2007), 57-67; L. Michael Morales, *The Tabernacle Pre-Figured: Cosmic Mountain Ideology in Genesis and Exodus* (Leuven: Peeters, 2012), 51-120.

33. Stephen G. Dempster, *Dominion and Dynasty: A Theology of the Hebrew Bible* (Downers Grove, IL: InterVarsity Press, 2003), 126, 153.

34. R. W. L. Moberly, 'Did the Serpent Get it Right?' *JTS* 39/1 (1988): 1-27, esp. 18.

consequence of covenantal infidelity (Deut. 4:25-28; 28:58-68). Exile is the final consequence of Israel's utter abandonment of the covenant (Deut. 29:24) and a rejection of God's commands (Deut. 28:15, 58). In fact, exile is ultimately the result of idolatry (Deut. 4:25; cf. Prov. 5:5, 20-23; 7:21-27) and the violation of the first two commandments of the Decalogue (Deut. 28:20).[35] These violations cause Israel's destruction: 'I call heaven and earth to witness against you today, that you will soon utterly perish from the land that you are going over the Jordan to possess. You will not live long in it, but will be utterly destroyed' (Deut. 4:26; cf. 28:63). Israel suffers the consequences of the *lex talionis*, an eye for an eye (Deut. 19:21). If the individual suffers death for idolatry, then corporate death is the fitting punishment for national idolatry (Deut. 4:3; 13:2-6, 7-11, 13-16; 17:2-7).[36]

This canonical exegetical data informs us that a faithful Israelite would not have seen Adam's 930-year life as a stay of execution or that God somehow relented. Rather, he would have seen Adam's fate in a far worse light. From within their own context Israelites would have realized that, first and foremost, the threatened curse was exile from the garden – Adam would be cast out of paradise and forced to live East of Eden in a state of exilic death (cf. Num. 5:1-4; 12:1-15; 2 Kings 7:3-8).[37] He would be ejected from his dwelling in God's temple-presence. To be sure, Adam's death also entailed his spiritual and physical death. The noetic effects of sin disrupted all of his faculties and he eventually returned to the dust.

There are important corollaries in the recognition that the chief penalty for violating the covenant was exile from God's presence in the temple-garden. The Spirit is a crucial part of the covenant of works. The creation narrative announces the Spirit's presence in the opening words of the Bible: 'And the Spirit of God was hovering over the face of the waters' (Gen. 1:2). But we should not

---

35. Moberly, 'Did the Serpent Get it Right?' 16-17.

36. Kenneth J. Turner, *The Death of Deaths in the Death of Israel: Deuteronomy's Theology of Exile* (Eugene: Wipf & Stock, 2010), 225-26.

37. Cf. Moberly, 'Did the Serpent Get It Right?' 13-17; Mettinger, *Eden Narrative*, 58-59; Anne Marie Kitz, *Cursed Are You! The Phenomenology of Cursing in Cuneiform and Hebrew Texts* (Winona: Eisenbrauns, 2014), 138, 238-39; J. Pedersen, *Israel, Its Life and Culture*, vol. 1/1-2 (Oxford: Oxford University Press, 1926), 451-52.

think that the Spirit participated in the opening moments of the creation only to be rushed off-stage during the climactic scene of the first act. If the rest of the Bible gives us any clue, recognizing the garden as the first temple means that Eden was also the realm of the Spirit. God's Spirit typically dwells in the various temples scattered throughout Scripture.

The Spirit was present over the desert tabernacle in the form of a cloud by day and pillar of fire by night (e.g., Exod. 13:21; Num. 9:15-16; 11:25). In the context of constructing the post-exilic temple, the prophet Haggai connects God's temple with the presence of the Spirit: 'I am with you, declares the LORD of hosts, according to the covenant that I made with you when you came out of Egypt. My Spirit remains in your midst' (Hag. 2:4-5; cf. Neh. 9:19-20; Isa. 63:11-14).[38] In Ezekiel's prophecy, God promises to place His Spirit within His people and return them to the promised land (Ezek. 36:37). These types give way to the antitypical reality when tongues of fire rested upon the heads of the disciples at Pentecost (Acts 2:3-4), a fact confirmed by Paul's repeated statements about the people of God comprising His final dwelling place – the eschatological Spirit-filled temple (1 Cor. 3:16; 6:19; Eph. 2:22).[39]

If the temple is the location of the Spirit's presence, then this means that the Spirit imparts life to anyone within the confines of Eden's sacred space. Several places in Scripture confirm this Spirit-life connection. In the book of Job, for example, Elihu states: 'The Spirit of God has made me, and the breath of the Almighty gives me life' (Job 33:4). This text echoes themes present in the creation narrative, both in terms of the Spirit's participation in the creation of the cosmos (Gen. 1:2) as well as God breathing life into Adam's nostrils (Gen. 2:7). Conversely, the absence of God's Spirit means death: 'If he should set his heart to it and gather to himself his Spirit and his breath, all flesh

---

38. Meredith G. Kline, *Images of the Spirit* (1980; Eugene: Wipf & Stock, 1998), 15; J. Luzaraga, *Las Tradiciones de La Nube en la Biblia y en el Judaismo Primitivo* (Rome: Biblical Institute Press, 1973), 234-45.

39. G. K. Beale, 'The Descent of the Eschatological Temple in the Form of the Spirit at Pentecost: Part I,' *TynB* 56/1 (2005): 73-102; idem, 'The Descent of the Eschatological Temple in the Form of the Spirit at Pentecost: Part II,' *TynB* 56/2 (2005): 63-90.

would perish together, and man would return to dust' (Job. 34:14-15, trans. mine).[40] Elihu's comments present a reversal of the Spirit's participation in the creation and breathing life into Adam's nostrils. All of this means that if he disobeyed the covenantal command not to eat from the tree of knowledge, Adam would be sent into exile away from the presence of God and His life-giving Holy Spirit. This is why exilic death inexorably leads to physical death.

The Sacraments of the Covenant

In God's covenants, He typically provides an attending sign. In His covenant with Noah God made the rainbow the sign of His covenant (Gen. 9:16). In the Abrahamic covenant circumcision was the covenantal sign (Gen. 17:11). God appointed the Sabbath as the sign of the Mosaic covenant (Exod. 31:16-17). The kingly line of descendants is arguably the sign of the Davidic covenant, David's house and kingdom would be made sure forever (2 Sam. 7:16). If the Davidic line expired, then so too would God's covenantal promise. Baptism and the Lord's Supper are the signs of the new covenant (Matt. 26:28; Mark 14:24; Luke 22:20; cf. Exod. 24:8; Matt. 28:18-20; Col. 2:11-12). In all of these covenants the signs physically embody God's verbal promises. God promised not to destroy the earth by a flood again: 'When I bring clouds over the earth and the bow is seen in the clouds, I will remember my covenant that is between me and you and every living creature of all flesh' (Gen. 9:16). Likewise, when God promised to be a God to Abraham and his seed after him, circumcision was a sign of His promise (Gen. 17:12).

In His covenant with Adam, therefore, God gave to Adam the sign of the tree of knowledge, a visible manifestation of His law. Genesis 3:6 describes the fruit of the tree as 'good for food, a delight to the eyes, and desired to make one wise.' The Psalmist echoes this description when he writes about the law of God: the law of the God makes the simple wise, rejoices the heart, and enlightens the eyes (Ps. 19:8-9).[41] The tree of knowledge was a

---

40. Tremper Longman, III, *Job*, BCOTWP (Grand Rapids: Baker, 2012), 393-94; David J. A. Clines, *Job 21–37*, WBC, vol. 18a (Nashville: Thomas Nelson, 2006), 774.

41. D. J. A. Clines, 'The Tree of Knowledge and the Law of Yahweh,' *VT* 24 (1974): 8-14.

sacramental representation of God's law. The tree of life likewise served as a sacramental sign of the implicit promise of eternal life for Adam and Eve upon their successful probation.[42] Some have suggested that the two trees, the garden, and the Sabbath all served as the four sacraments of the covenant.[43] Some believe that the tree of life and the garden were the two sacraments, and still yet others maintain that the tree of life was the sole sacrament.[44] While these different choices have their merits, at the same time the best option recognizes that only the trees of life and knowledge were sacramental signs of the covenant of works. There is no inherent verbal promise associated with the garden. One might easily say that the garden is a type of heaven, but not a sacrament. Similarly, one may say that the Sabbath functions as a type of eternal life but not as a sacrament per se, as it functioned for Israel in the Mosaic covenant (Exod. 31:13; Ezek. 20:12, 20). And while the tree of life is surely a sign of the covenant, this one tree only captures half of the nature of the covenant, namely, the goal of eternal life. Taken together, however, both trees visibly augment the covenant blessings and sanctions: the tree of life visibly represented the eschatological glory that awaited the completion of Adam's successful probation, and the tree of knowledge signified the curse of the covenant that would fall upon Adam and all his offspring should he disobey. The trees were 'both perpetual admonitions and remembrancers of the probation our first parents were passing through, and of the Life and Death that waited on the issue. One of them was a means of strength, by the participation of it: similar to the use of the Sacrament of the Passover or the Lord's Supper. The other by the prohibition of it, the sight of it, and the refusal of it, a means of strength also.'[45]

---

42. Bavinck, *Reformed Dogmatics*, II:574-75.

43. So Witsius, *Economy of the Covenants*, I.vi.2

44. On the tree of life as the sole sacrament, see A. A. Hodge, *Outlines of Theology* (1860; Edinburgh: Banner of Truth, 1991), 314.

45. Robert J. Breckinridge, *The Knowledge of God Objectively Considered Being the First Part of Theology Considered as a Science of Positive Truth, Both Inductive and Deductive* (New York: Robert Carter & Brothers, 1585), 470.

The Present Status of the Covenant of Works

There are some who claim that the covenant of works has been 'wholly abrogated as a means to inherit eternal life.'[46] Such language is misleading and gives the impression that the covenant of works has been left behind amidst the rubble of the fallen kingdom of Adam. Yet, the Westminster Confession points in a different direction when it states: 'Man, by his fall, *having made himself incapable of life by that covenant*, the Lord was please to make a second, commonly called the covenant of grace' (VII.iii; emphasis). The Confession does not say that the covenant of works has been wholly abrogated but that *fallen* human beings have made themselves incapable of obtaining life by means of this covenant. That the promise of eternal life through the covenant of works still stands is evident by both Jesus' and Paul's appeal to Leviticus 18:5 (Luke 10:25-28; Rom. 10:5; Gal. 3:12). This means then that, positively, the promise of eternal life still stands for any sinless human being who can render perfect, personal, and perpetual obedience to the law. Jesus, the last Adam, is the one who was sent to take up the failed work of the first Adam.[47] Jesus was born under the law so that He might redeem sinners from its curse and complete Adam's work. Negatively, the violated covenant of works still hangs over the collective head of humanity – they still lie under its curse because of Adam's transgression, their federal head. All of Adam's race lies under the covenant of works and cannot be released from its obligation except through union and communion with the last Adam.[48]

Conclusion

Clockmakers have a twofold labor – they must ensure that a clock tells the proper time, which means that they must also understand how clocks are made. The same division of labor holds true for theologians. They should herald the message of Scripture, but in

---

46. E.g., Cornelis P. Venema, 'The Mosaic Covenant: A "Republication" of the Covenant of Works?' *MAJT* 21 (2010): 35-101, esp. 35, 68.

47. Berkhof, *Systematic Theology*, 218.

48. John Colquhoun, *A Treatise on the Covenant of Works* (Edinburgh: Thomsons, Brothers, 1821), 187.

order to do this they must understand how the different parts work together. This chapter has set forth the constituent parts of the Bible's teaching on the covenant between God and Adam. It has set forth the gears, wheels, and springs of the clock of Scripture. But lest one get lost in these details and lose sight of the larger picture, I conclude the chapter with a summary reflection on the covenant of works.

The triune God voluntarily condescended by creating and entering into a covenant with human beings through their representative, Adam. The gifts of creation and covenant were the place where love and law met. God wrote His rule of love on Adam's heart and throughout the creation. In love He also gave Adam his covenantal charter to seal the gift of the divine image he bore:

> Fill and subdue the earth – but perform this work in the anointing of the Spirit and in accordance with my will. You are my son and bear my image, thus go and fill the earth with my image to declare that I am sovereign over heaven and earth. The tree of knowledge will continually remind you to love me with all of your heart, soul, mind, and strength. As a sign of your love, do not eat from this tree. Manifest your love in *hesed*, covenant love and faithfulness, and I will confirm your fidelity – you will dwell eternally in immutable and indefectible union and communion. I will declare, 'This is my son in whom I am well pleased!' 'Well done, good and faithful servant.' Your covenant love will usher in a new heavens and earth for you and your offspring. Seek your own path, however, and you will die – you will live in exile from my life-giving presence until you return to the dust from whence you came.

Such is the nature of the covenant of works. Far from a cold legal transaction, the covenant of works is an arena of love – God's fatherly love for Adam, and Adam's filial love for God. But Adam chose his own way and failed to love his Father and covenant Lord. Still, all was not lost. One like Adam, the Son of Man, would come – He would take up Adam's abandoned work and fulfill it in love. Although Samuel spoke the following words to Saul, they can just as easily be said of the fall of Adam and the hope of the last Adam: 'You have done foolishly. You have not kept the command of the LORD your God, with which he commanded you. For then the LORD would have established your kingdom ... forever. But now your kingdom shall not continue. The LORD has sought out a man after his own heart, and the LORD has commanded him to be prince over his people, because you have not kept what the LORD commanded you' (1 Sam. 13:13-14). But this story awaits another time and covenant.

~: III.2 :~

The Covenant of Works and Sinai

Introduction

*T*he apostle Peter once wrote that there are some things in Paul's letters that are hard to understand (2 Pet. 3:16). This statement applies to many challenging doctrines, but especially to the question regarding the relationship between the covenant of works and the Mosaic covenant. Part I surveyed the sixteenth through nineteenth centuries and identified at least a dozen different views. Perhaps the cacophony of voices of some of the Reformed tradition's greatest theologians warrants an appeal to Proverbs 26:17, 'Whoever meddles in a quarrel not his own is like one who takes a passing dog by the ears.' If the greatest theological minds have been unable to reach a consensus, then perhaps the better part of wisdom is to walk away from the place where angels fear to tread? On the other hand, even if no clear consensus has emerged, the fact that so many Reformed theologians have engaged the question testifies to the importance of the issue. To argue that the Mosaic covenant provides contextual exegetical data to help readers determine that God and Adam were in covenant only addresses half of the theological equation. That is, how are the Adamic and Mosaic covenants similar? To walk away and not explain how they are dissimilar undoubtedly leaves many unanswered questions. Thus, this chapter aims to explain the relationship between the Adamic and Mosaic covenants.

This chapter argues that the covenant of works reappears in the Mosaic covenant. But such a thesis requires several important caveats. First, the Mosaic covenant is part of the covenant of grace. Ever since the fall and God's promise of the redeemer (Gen. 3:15), all of God's dealings with His people have been on the basis of grace. Second, as noted in the previous chapter, by the fall humans have made themselves incapable of obtaining eternal life by means of the covenant of works (WCF VII.iii). Third, to say that the covenant of works *reappears* does not mean that God re-administered the covenant of works and thus gave fallen human beings one more shot at eternal life. Rather, the reappearance of the covenant of works at Sinai serves three purposes: (a) it reminds fallen sinners of their liability for the broken covenant of works, (b) it shows Israel that they are incapable of perfect obedience to the law, and (c) it prophetically points to the horizon to reveal that one like Adam will come to fulfill the abandoned covenant of works. In order to prove the thesis that the covenant of works reappears at Sinai, the chapter proceeds in the following manner. It begins with a broad sweep of redemptive history to explore the typological connections between Adam, Israel, and Christ. It then examines 2 Corinthians 3:3-11, which is a relevant text for this question. The chapter then explores the theological implications of the harvested typology and exegesis. Finally, the chapter concludes with some summary observations about the relationship between the Adamic and Mosaic covenants.

Broader Typological Connections

In the big picture of redemptive history God had two sons, Adam (Luke 3:38) and Israel (Exod. 4:22; Hosea 11:1).[1] Adam was placed in the paradisiacal garden (Gen. 2:8-15), and the Pentateuch describes the promised land in terms evocative of Eden (Num. 24:5-9). In fact, according to recent scholarship, Numbers 24:5-9 'in the poetic hyperbole of prophetic oracles, Israel is Eden recultivated ... Eden has in fact materialized among Israel's

---

1. What follows is revised, updated, but originates from J. V. Fesko, 'The Republication of the Covenant of Works,' *CP* 8 (2012): 197-212, esp. 204, 210-12.

tents.'[2] Just as He walked in the garden (Gen. 3:8) so Yahweh walked among Israel (Lev. 26:12). God gave Adam a command not to eat of the tree of knowledge lest he die (Gen. 2:17) and He also gave Israel a series of commands with similar curses annexed to them (Deut. 7:12-13; 8:19). The earliest Jewish interpreters of the Old Testament identified these parallels between Adam and Israel and determined that Israel's tenure in the land was a recapitulation of Adam's probation in the garden. Jacob Neusner (1932-2016) identifies key themes within the *halakhah* (the normative law of the Oral Torah) such as the parallels between Eden and the promised land and Adam and Israel.[3] In the Jewish Oral Torah (specifically Sifra, the Halakic midrash to the book of Leviticus) there are reflections upon the prohibition against eating the fruit from any new tree for three years (Lev. 19:23). Neusner comments: 'Then the planting of every tree imposes upon Israel the occasion to meet once more the temptation that the first Adam could not overcome. Israel now recapitulates the temptation of Adam then, but Israel, the New Adam, possesses, and is possessed by the Torah .... So when Israel enters the Land, in exactly the right detail Israel recapitulates the drama of Adam in Eden.'[4]

To be clear, ancient Judaism's estimation of Israel's powers was far more optimistic than Scripture allows, but we should not miss the point that the earliest interpreters of the Bible observed the Adam // Israel parallels in the broader narrative of the Old Testament.[5] At the most fundamental level, New Testament authors

---

2. William P. Brown, *The Ethos of the Cosmos: The Genesis of Moral Imagination in the Bible* (Grand Rapids: Eerdmans, 1999), 214; cf. G. K. Beale, *The Temple and the Church's Mission: A Biblical Theology of the Dwelling Place of God* (Downers Grove: InterVarsity Press, 2004), 123-26.

3. Jacob Neusner, *The Halakhah: Historical and Religious Perspectives* (Leiden: Brill, 2002), 2.

4. Neusner, *Halakhah*, 8.

5. G. K. Beale, *We Become What We Worship: A Biblical Theology of Idolatry* (Downers Grove: IVP, 2008), 141-60, 213; Scott J. Hafemann, *Paul, Moses, and the History of Israel* (Milton Keynes: Paternoster, 2005), 228-29; Benjamin L. Gladd, *From Adam and Israel to the Church: A Biblical Theology of the People of God* (Downers Grove, IL: InterVarsity Press, 2019), 5-57.

recognize this point as there is a web of interconnected texts that link Adam, Israel, and Jesus: Adam is a type of the one who was to come (Rom. 5:14). Israel typified Christ, which Matthew confirms when he applies Hosea 11:1 to Christ's exodus from Egypt: 'Out of Egypt I called my son' (Matt. 2:15).[6] Both Adam and Israel typify Christ – this is undeniable. The type-antitype relationship between Adam, Israel, and Christ highlights the faithlessness of God's sons (Adam and Israel) and the faithfulness of God's only begotten Son, Jesus. To argue that the covenant of works does not reappear in the Mosaic covenant disrupts the typological trajectory that culminates in Christ. Stated alternatively, there are typological connections between Adam, Israel, and Jesus (the last Adam).

2 Corinthians 3:1-11

Part II presented exegesis of Leviticus 18:5 and the subsequent places in Scripture where this verse reappears: Ezekiel 20, Nehemiah 9:29, Luke 10:25-28, Galatians 3:10-12, and Romans 10:5. Even though some such as John Murray (1898-1975) have tried to argue that Leviticus 18:5 falls under the third (normative) use of the law, the intra-canonical use of this text points in the opposite direction. Leviticus 18:5 reveals that obedience yields reward (even eternal life) and punishment is the consequence of disobedience. For this reason, Reformed theologians enlisted this verse to support the doctrine of the covenant of works; and others such as John Calvin (1509-1564) argued that it spelled out one of the two ways to obtain eternal life, namely, by perfect obedience to the law. The Leviticus 18:5 thread is one of the chief pieces of evidence for the reappearance of the covenant of works with the Mosaic covenant. In other words, the revelation of the Mosaic covenant contains exegetical pieces of the covenant of works puzzle. Reformed theologians have naturally, therefore, wrestled to explain how the legal and evangelical elements at Sinai relate. How can the covenant of works not disrupt the integrity of the covenant of grace? How can two contradictory

---

6. See G. K. Beale, 'The Use of Hosea 11:1 in Matthew 2:15: One More Time,' *JETS* 55/4 (2012): 697-715.

paths to justification, works versus faith, share the same stage in redemptive history?

Charles Hodge (1797-1878) offers exegesis of 2 Corinthians 3 that is one example of how a Reformed theologian has handled these issues. Within the broader context of 2 Corinthians 3 Paul contrasts the old and new covenants by showing the superiority of the latter over the former. He compares the two by employing a rabbinic exegetical argument, a *qal wahomer* ('the light and the heavy'), which takes the form of, 'if X is … then how much more is Y?'[7] Paul compares the two covenants in the following manner:

Verses	Old Covenant	New Covenant
vv. 7-8	Now if the ministry of death, carved in letters on stone	will not the ministry of the Spirit have even more glory.
v. 9	For if there was glory in the ministry of condemnation,	the ministry of righteousness must far exceed it in glory.
v. 11	For if what was being brought to an end came with glory,	much more will what is permanent have glory.

Paul's statement about the 'ministry of death' cannot be reduced to the pedagogical use of the law; Paul clearly contrasts the old covenant, which was written on tablets of stone, with the new covenant, which is 'written not with ink but the Spirit of the living God' (vv. 3, 14).[8] There is more in view than the law's pedagogical function to drive sinners to Christ; instead, Paul highlights elements that deal with condemnation – something beyond the three uses of the law. Paul's characterization of the Mosaic covenant as a ministry of death stands in stark antithesis to the Jewish estimations of it as a 'gift of life.'[9] Paul's 'ministry of death' language parallels

---

7. Murray J. Harris, *The Second Epistle to the Corinthians*, NIGTC (Grand Rapids: Eerdmans, 2005), 279.

8. Harris, *Second Corinthians*, 279-80.

9. C. K. Barrett, *The Second Epistle to the Corinthians*, BNTC (1973; Peabody: Hendrickson, 1997), 115; Victor Paul Furnish, *II Corinthians*, AB (New York: Doubleday, 1984), 226-29; Margaret E. Thrall, *The Second Epistle to the Corinthians*, vol. 1, ICC (Edinburgh: T & T Clark, 1994), 240-41, 249.

other negative characterizations of the Mosaic covenant, such as when he connects it to Hagar who produces children of slavery versus the Abrahamic, which is Sarah (Gal. 4:24-25). It echoes Paul's characterization of the Mosaic covenant as living under the 'elementary principles of the world' (στοιχεῖα τοῦ κόσμου) (Gal. 4:3, 9). Likewise, Paul brackets out the sinners between Adam and Moses, 'whose sinning was not like the transgression of Adam' (Rom. 5:14). That is, Adam and Israel were both under covenantal administrations of law. Or in Hosea's terms, like Adam, Israel transgressed the covenant (Hosea 6:7). Returning to 2 Corinthians 3, if both the Mosaic and New covenants belong to the one covenant of grace, how do we relate them one to another?

Hodge draws attention to this antinomy by noting: 'Every reader of the New Testament must be struck with the fact that the apostle often speaks of the Mosaic law as a covenant of works; that is, presenting the promise of life on the condition of perfect obedience.'[10] Here Hodge has the present passage in mind as well as Galatians 3:10-12 and Romans 10:5, both of which quote Leviticus 18:5. Hodge, however, also notes that Paul maintains that the plan of salvation has been the same from the very beginning and that Christ was the propitiation for sins under the old covenant, an allusion to Hebrews 9:15. Hodge writes: 'Men were saved then as now by faith in Christ; that this mode of salvation was revealed to Abraham and understood by him, and taught by Moses and the prophets.'[11] The solution to the apparent contradiction between the two principles is to recognize that the Mosaic covenant had a number of different purposes and therefore has to be viewed from various perspectives.

Hodge offers three points. First, he argues: 'The law of Moses was, in the first place, a re-enactment of the covenant of works.' He explains that a covenant is simply a promise suspended upon a condition, and in this case the covenant of works is the promise of eternal life upon the condition of perfect obedience. To support

---

10. Charles Hodge, *1 & 2 Corinthians* (1857, 59; Edinburgh: Banner of Truth, 1994), 432-33.

11. Hodge, *1 & 2 Corinthians*, 433.

this contention, Hodge appeals to Luke 10:26-28 and Christ's use of Leviticus 18:5 and concludes: 'This is the covenant of works.' Hodge argues that there is an immutable principle that in the absence of sin there is no condemnation, but where sin is present the consequence is condemnation. He maintains: 'Viewed under this aspect it is the ministration of condemnation and death.'[12] Hodge echoes Paul's characterization of the Mosaic covenant as a 'ministry of death' and Ezekiel's identification of God's laws as 'not good' (Ezek. 20:25).

Second, Hodge carefully situates the Mosaic economy within God's covenantal dealings, not merely with individuals, but with the nation of Israel as a whole: 'The Mosaic economy was also a national covenant; that is, it presented national promises on the condition of national obedience. Under this aspect also it was purely legal.'[13] One need only look at Israel's exile to confirm this point. Like Adam cast from God's presence in the garden, Israel was hurled into exile away from God's dwelling place. What Hodge describes as a 'national covenant' is older nomenclature by which we would now describe the typological relationship between Israel and Christ.[14] That is, Israel, as a nation, typifies the person and work of Christ. In this case, their corporate failure to remain in the land serves as a typological antithetical parallelism to Christ's successful probation and attainment of eternal life on behalf of the elect.

Third, the Princetonian does not ignore the fact that the Mosaic covenant also reveals the gospel: 'As the gospel contains a renewed revelation of the law, so the law of Moses contained a revelation of the gospel.'[15] Within the Mosaic economy we find instructions for the priesthood, sacrifices, and the like, which

---

12. Hodge, 1 & 2 Corinthians, 433-34; for similar comments on 2 Corinthians 3:9 see John Owen, Exposition of Hebrews, vol. 6 (1854-55; Edinburgh: Banner of Truth, 2010), 85-86.

13. Hodge, 1 & 2 Corinthians, 434.

14. Hodge likely gleans the idea of a national covenant from Herman Witsius. Cf. Herman Witsius, Economy of the Covenants Between God and Man, 2 vols. (rep.; Escondido, CA: Den Dulk Foundation, 1991), IV.iv.47-57.

15. Hodge, 1 & 2 Corinthians, 434.

Hodge explains are shadows and types of Christ. Hodge then offers a summary explanation of how these three different aspects relate one to another:

> When therefore the apostle spoke of the old covenant under its legal aspect, and especially when speaking to those who rejected the gospel and clung to the law of Moses as law, then he says, it kills, or is the ministration of condemnation. But when viewing it, and especially when speaking of those who viewed it as setting forth the great doctrine of redemption through the blood of Christ, he represented it as teaching his own doctrine. The law, in every form, moral or Mosaic, natural or revealed, kills.[16]

Like his Reformed predecessors, and echoing principles set forth in the Westminster Confession, Hodge links the moral law to the various epochs of pre-redemptive and redemptive history and accounts for how it functions, not abstractly, but redemptive-historically, or covenantally.

Theological Implications

There are four important issues that arise from the foregoing exploration of the relationship between the Adamic and Mosaic covenants. First, when we read the Scriptures and contemplate the role of the law, the three uses of the law as they function in the new covenant apply primarily to believers but do not provide an exhaustive hermeneutical account of how the law functions in every administration of the covenant of grace. The covenant of works reappears to highlight the need for the fulfillment of the broken covenant of works. The covenant reappears to remind Israel that the curse of the broken covenant still requires a remedy. The remedy for the broken covenant of works is the work of Christ. Christ's passive obedience addresses the covenant's transgression, but His active obedience addresses the fulfillment of the covenant of works.

In this respect, the Westminster Confession explains that, far from being abrogated, the covenant of works is still binding upon sinners: 'The moral law doth forever bind all, as well as justified persons as others, to the obedience thereof' (XIX.v). The moral

---

16. Hodge, *1 & 2 Corinthians*, 434.

law, which was covenantally administered to Adam as the covenant of works (XIX.i), is still binding and still holds out the possibility of eternal life for anyone who fulfills it. Note the language in Westminster Confession XIX.vi, which confirms this point: 'Although true believers be not under the law, as a covenant of works, to be thereby justified, or condemned ...' In other words, if a person is outside of Christ and still in Adam, he is still under the law as a covenant of works. John Owen (1616-1683) points out that one of the chief reasons the Mosaic covenant revived the covenant of works was to remind the people of its sanction and keep the people under its bondage.[17] The reappearance of the covenant of works at Sinai, consequently, presents sinners, not merely with the bare law, but with their federal failure in Adam's broken covenant of works, one that is replayed on the grand stage of redemptive history in Israel's failed probation in the land. With remarkable parallels between Adam's and Israel's respective exiles, it seems like readers would naturally be drawn to see some sort of repetition of Adam's state in the garden in Israel's tenure in the land.

The second implication is that the reappearance of the covenant of works highlights sinful man's inability to merit eternal life through his obedience; not only did God's son, Adam, fail but so did God's other son, Israel. Geerhardus Vos (1862-1949) explains the connections between the reappearance of the covenant of works at Sinai specifically as it connects to Christ's active obedience:

> Everyone will have to agree that for Adam, perfect keeping of the law for a fixed period of time was the means to acquire eternal beatitude that cannot be lost. When the covenant of works was broken, God could have rescinded this promise. He was no longer bound to honor it. Nevertheless, He allowed the promise and the condition to stand and repeatedly be published anew, especially by the proclamation of the Sinaitic law (Lev. 18:5, 'The one who does them will live by them'; cf. Rom. 10:5, 'For Moses describes the righteousness that is by the law,' etc.; Gal. 3:12). Fulfillment of this condition from man's side was no longer conceivable; thus the repetition must have had a different significance. This significance can only be that after the

---

17. John Owen, *An Exposition Upon Psalm CXXX*, in *The Works of John Owen, D. D.*, vol. 14 (London: Richard Baynes, 1826), 183.

fall God gave His covenant of grace, in which the same demand and promise are fulfilled in the Meditator.[18]

In other words, the covenant of works requires someone to fulfill it in order to lay hold of the promised reward of eschatological life. Adam and Israel were God's faithless sons but Jesus is God's faithful Son, the one in whom the Father is well pleased (Matt. 3:17; Mark 1:17; Luke 3:22). Christ actively fulfilled the law – He completed the covenant of works.

On the heels of the Father's declaration of approbation, the Spirit led Jesus into the wilderness for forty days, evocative of Israel's forty-year Spirit-led wanderings, but with one massive difference – where Israel was disobedient Jesus was obedient.[19] Christ fulfilled the broken covenant of works both by paying the penalty for its violation (passive obedience) and by His positive fulfillment of the law (active obedience). Notably, Paul states that Christ was born 'under the law, to redeem those who were under the law' (Gal. 4:4-5). In context, Paul's reference is to the Mosaic covenant (Gal. 3:12-25; 4:21-28), but did Christ only come to redeem Israelites? Did He also not come to redeem Gentiles? Gentiles were not under the Mosaic covenant but they were under the covenant of works. Israel's reception of the Mosaic covenant with the publication of the moral law was a reappearance of the universally binding covenant of works along with the gospel. That the covenant of works reappears at Sinai therefore shows that Christ redeems both Israel, which is a microcosm of humanity at large, and Gentiles. Jesus came to deliver both Jews and Gentiles out from under the law in both of its covenantal administrations.

The third issue is, What is the best way to explain the relationship between the Adamic and Mosaic covenants? To say that the covenant of works reappears at Sinai only speaks to the large-scale issue. Part I illustrated the many different ways

---

18. Geerhardus Vos, *Reformed Dogmatics*, 5 vols., trans. and ed. Richard B. Gaffin Jr. (Bellingham, WA: Lexham Press, 2012-15), III:132.

19. See, e.g., Craig L. Blomberg, 'Matthew,' in *Commentary on the New Testament Use of the Old Testament*, ed. G. K. Beale and D. A. Carson (Grand Rapids: Baker, 2007), 14-18; Brandon D. Crowe, *The Last Adam: A Theology of the Obedient Life of Jesus in the Gospels* (Grand Rapids: Baker Academic, 2017), 1-82.

that theologians have explained the connection, and individually evaluating these views lies beyond the scope of this chapter. Nevertheless, there are several key principles that should always remain carefully guarded: (a) any position that maintains that fallen sinners can somehow merit eternal life should be rejected; (b) any view that diminishes or attenuates the role of the moral law as binding upon all people throughout pre-redemptive and redemptive history should be rejected; and (c) any view that argues that God changes the way that He deals with sinners in the different covenantal administrations should be rejected (i.e., salvation is always by grace alone through faith alone in Christ alone). Given these principles, how should one account for the relationship between the Adamic and Mosaic covenants?

The apostle Paul provides a way forward in Colossians 2:17. In reference to the Mosaic laws regulating food and drink, festivals, and the Sabbath, Paul says, 'These are a shadow of the things to come, but the substance belongs to Christ.' The distinction between the shadow (σκιὰ) and substance (σῶμα) finds parallels in the Hellenistic literature of Plato (ca. 428–ca. 348 B.C.) and Philo (20 B.C.–ca. A.D. 50). In his allegory of the cave Plato contrasts shadows (*skia*) with images (*eikon*) or form; Paul's use of *soma* ('substance') is a similar idea. Likewise, Philo spoke of the letter of the Old Testament as the shadow and his own allegorical interpretations as the substance, or what really and truly exists. These sets of terms were used to contrast between appearance and reality.[20] The shadow-substance relationship is how the Westminster divines explain the differences between the covenant of grace under the time of the Law (Old Testament) versus the Gospel (New Testament):

> Under the law, it was administered by promises, prophecies, sacrifices, circumcision, the paschal lamb, and other types and ordinances delivered to the people of the Jews, all foresignifying Christ to come …. Under the gospel, when Christ, the substance, was exhibited, the ordinances in which this covenant is dispensed are the preaching of the Word, and the administration of the sacraments (VII.v-vi).

---

20. Douglas J. Moo, *The Letters to the Colossians and to Philemon*, PNTC (Grand Rapids: Eerdmans, 2008), 222.

The divines cite Colossians 2:17 to support the idea that Christ's advent renders the Mosaic covenant obsolete, and thus it vanishes away (Heb. 8:13).[21] In other words, at its core the Mosaic covenant is the covenant of grace but its externals are accidental and thus expire.

The substance-accidents distinction lies behind explanations like those of Heinrich Bullinger (1504-1575) and Calvin when they clarify the relationship between the testaments. Recall Bullinger's explanation: 'In the very substance [substantia], truly, thou canst find no diversity: the difference which is betwixt them doth consist in the manner of administration [modo administrandi], in a few accidents [accidentibus], and certain circumstances [circunstantiis].'[22] Likewise, Calvin writes: 'The covenant [foedus] made with all the fathers is so far from differing from ours in reality and substance [substantia et re], that it is altogether one and the same: still the administration [administratio] differs.'[23] By the late seventeenth century theologians employed the same substance-accidents distinction but factored the covenant of works as a refinement of earlier Reformation-era formulations. Thus, Francis Turretin (1623-1687) writes that God administered the covenant of grace at Sinai 'under a rigid legal economy' (rigida oeconomia legali). There was a twofold relation (schesis), legal and evangelical, 'through which by a new promulgation of the law and of the covenant of works [nova Legis et foederis oeprum promulgatione], with an intolerable yoke of ceremonies, he wished to set forth what men owed and what was to be expected by them on account of duty unperformed.'[24]

---

21. The divines cite both Colossians 2:17 and Hebrews 8, 9, and 10 (The Humble Advice of the Assembly of Divines, Now By Authority of Parliament Sitting at Westminster, Concerning a Confession of Faith [London: Company of Stationers, 1647].

22. Bullinger, Decades, III.viii (vol. II, p. 293); idem, Sermonum Decades Quinque de Potssimis Christianae Religionis Captibus, in Tres Tomos (Zurich: Christoph Froschoverus, 1557), 148.

23. John Calvin, Institutes of the Christian Religion, trans. Henry Beveridge (Grand Rapids: Eerdmans, 1957), II.x.2; idem, Institutio Religionis Christianae (Geneva: Robert Stephanus, 1559). Cf. Andrew A. Woolsey, Unity and Continuity in Covenantal Thought: A Study in the Reformed Tradition to the Westminster Assembly (Grand Rapids: Reformation Heritage Books, 2012), 253-343, esp. 253-76.

24. Francis Turretin, Institutes of Elenctic Theology, trans. George Musgrave Giger, ed. James T. Dennison, Jr. (Phillipsburg, NJ: P & R, 1992-97), XII.vii.31; idem, Institutio Theologiae Elencticae, 3 vols. (Edinburgh: John D. Lowe, 1847).

In the early twentieth century, Vos expressed this same principle in terms echoing Bullinger, Calvin, and Turretin when he writes: 'The old dispensation of the covenant of grace bore a legal character for Israel as a nation and, therefore, in its external form once more kept the covenant of works in view, although the core of what God established with Israel was of course the continuation of the Abrahamic revelation of the covenant of grace.'[25] Vos speaks of the external form versus the core of the Mosaic covenant, which echoes the earlier substance-accidents distinction. The substance-accidents distinction is a useful way to explain how the covenant of works reappears with the Mosaic covenant; the distinction allows one to factor the presence of both the covenants of works and grace. And with the Westminster Confession, one may also acknowledge that the accidental presence of the covenant of works serves the purpose, among others, of foresignifying Christ to come – the last Adam who would fulfill the abandoned work of the first Adam.

As Part I demonstrated, there are other legitimate ways to express the relationship between the Adamic and Mosaic covenants. Westminster divines Samuel Bolton (1606-1654) and Jeremiah Burroughs (1599-1646) argue that the Mosaic covenant is distinct and subservient to the covenant of grace. Their view recognizes that God substantively deals with Israel on the basis of the covenant of grace but that the Mosaic covenant is accidental.[26] True, they deny that the Mosaic covenant is part of the covenant of grace, but such a point seems semantic rather than material. Herman Witsius (1636-1708) makes similar claims when he calls the Mosaic economy a 'covenant of sincere piety,' which is neither of the covenants of works or grace.[27] But he also argues that the Mosaic covenant was national and corporate and not merely for individual rank-and-file Israelites.[28]

---

25. Vos, *Reformed Dogmatics*, II:36.

26. Samuel Bolton, *The True Bounds of Christian Freedome* (London: P. S., 1656), 130-31; Jeremiah Burroughs, *Gospel Conversation* (London: Peter Cole: 1653), 47.

27. Witsius, *Economy of the Covenants*, IV.iv.54.

28. Witsius, *Economy of the Covenants*, IV.iv.54.

Another Westminster divine, Anthony Burgess (1600-1663), took a different approach when he looked at the Mosaic covenant from two different perspectives: either broadly or narrowly. Broadly considered, the Mosaic covenant is part of the covenant of grace; narrowly considered, it is the covenant of works.[29] Thomas Boston (1676-1732) uses the language of subservience like Burroughs and Bolton but in a different manner because he maintains that the Mosaic covenant is part of the covenant of grace. But he nevertheless claims that the covenant of works was added to the Mosaic covenant.[30] Similarly, John Colquhoun (1748-1827) argues that the covenant of works was *displayed* at Sinai, which preserves the integrity of the covenant of grace. He then goes on to list seven reasons why the Israelites received the covenant of grace and seven reasons why the covenant of works was also displayed.[31] Robert Shaw (1795-1863) claims the law was published as *a* covenant of works, not *the* covenant of works.[32] Along these lines James Buchanan (1791-1857) stipulates that the covenant with Israel is a *national* covenant of works, not *the* covenant of works, which is similar to Hodge's view.[33]

Whether they employ substance-accidents, subservience, broad versus narrow, display, *a* versus *the* covenant of works, or a national covenant of works, all of the aforementioned theologians strive to maintain the purity of the covenant of grace in God's dealings with Israel. In all of these formulations God's underlying mechanism for saving Israelite sinners is the covenant of grace and the Adamic and Mosaic covenants evaporate under the bright light of the saving

---

29. Anthony Burgess, *Vindiciae Legis: or, A Vindication of the Morall Law and the Covenants* (London: Thomas Underhill, 1647), lect. XXIV (p. 233).

30. Thomas Boston, *The Marrow of Modern Divinity in Two Parts by Edward Fisher with Notes by Mr. Thomas Boston*, 8th ed. (Falkirk: Patrick Mair, 1789), 74.

31. John Colquhoun, *A Treatise on the Law and the Gospel* (New York: Wiley & Long, 1835), 53, 55-62, 64-69.

32. Robert Shaw *An Exposition of the Confession of Faith of the Westminster Assembly of Divines*, 8th ed. (Glasgow: Blackie and Son, 1857), 195.

33. James Buchanan, *The Doctrine of Justification: An Outline of Its History in the Church and of Its Exposition from Scripture* (1867; Edinburgh: Banner of Truth, 1991), 38-39; Hodge, *1 & 2 Corinthians*, 434.

work of Christ, the last Adam, who fulfills both. All of these views have their merits and are compatible, but tracing Paul's shadow-substance language from Colossians best explains the relationship, in my judgment, between the Adamic and Mosaic covenants.

Fourth, questions arise regarding the apparent contradiction between the *ordo* and *historia salutis*. That is, how can a regenerate Israelite interact with the Mosaic covenant that also carries the covenant of works along with it? How can a regenerate Israelite seemingly exist under two covenantal economies? Recall that the Westminster Confession (XIX.vi) explains that true believers are not under the law as a covenant to be either justified or condemned but rather as a rule of life that informs them of the will of God, their duty, and directs and binds them to live accordingly. Thus, truly believing Israelites were only under the economy of the covenant of grace. Recall, the covenant of works reappears but is not re-administered. At this point, however, the Confession chiefly addresses questions related to the *ordo salutis*. It does not address issues related to the *historia salutis*. Moses and Daniel, for example, were both united to Christ and therefore engaged the Mosaic covenant as a rule of life vis-à-vis the *ordo salutis*. Like Abraham, both Moses and Daniel were justified by faith alone in Christ alone; they were participants in the covenant of grace. The reappearance of the covenant of works with the Mosaic covenant, however, reminded them of their failure in Adam and their own inabilities to fulfill the requirements of the law; both of these truths consequently pointed and drove them to Christ, the last Adam, as the one who would remedy these problems. But, if Moses and Daniel were saved and united to Christ, why then did they both suffer the curses of the Mosaic covenant?

Why did God prevent Moses from entering the promised land? God told Moses: 'Because you broke faith with me in the midst of the people of Israel at the waters of Meribah-kadesh, in the wilderness of Zin, and because you did not treat me as holy in the midst of the people of Israel. For you shall see the land before you, but you shall not go there, into the land that I am giving to the people of Israel' (Deut. 32:51-52). The promised land was a type of heaven (Heb. 11:9-10). Why was Moses precluded from the promised land if he was washed, justified, sanctified, and united to Christ (1 Cor. 6:11)? Similarly, Daniel was a righteous man (Ezek. 14:14), and yet he was carted off to Babylon to live in exile from the presence of God despite his union with Christ. Moses and Daniel suffered the curses of the covenant because they participated in the Mosaic covenant, which was a unique event in redemptive history. The Mosaic economy was God's covenant solely with His people Israel, which among other soteriological purposes, was also supposed to foresignify Christ to come, to borrow the language from the Westminster Confession (VII.v). Or in the formulation of Hodge, Buchanan, and Shaw, the Mosaic covenant was a national covenant of works. Hence, Daniel was individually saved and justified but he was connected to the nation and thus prayed: 'All Israel has transgressed your law and turned aside, refusing to obey your voice. And the curse and oath that are written in the Law of Moses the servant of God have been poured out upon us, because we have sinned against him' (Dan. 9:11). Like Adam, God expelled Israel from His presence and Daniel along with the rest of Israel suffered this curse of the covenant.

The fact that redeemed Israelites could suffer the curse of the covenant is evidence that warrants Turretin's characterization of the Mosaic covenant as a 'a rigid legal economy.' Even though it was part of the covenant of grace, there was nevertheless a new accidental promulgation of the law and of the covenant of works.[34] In this sense both Moses and Daniel served as types of the Messiah as they bore the curses of the covenant despite their justified state. As such, they foreshadowed that the last Adam would not merely bear the curses in a typological sense but really and truly. As Paul writes, 'Christ redeemed us from the curse of the law by becoming a curse for us' (Gal. 3:13). Unlike Old Testament believers who could suffer the curses of the covenant, New Testament believers are no longer subject to covenant curses. Those who are truly united to Christ are no longer liable to curse. If they sin, they might fall under God's fatherly displeasure and discipline, but not His curse (Heb. 12:7; WCF XI.v). The Mosaic covenant along with the

---

34. Turretin, *Institutes*, XII.vii.31.

reappearance of the covenant of works has become obsolete in the wake of the advent of Christ. Christ as the true Israel has fulfilled the national covenant of works.[35] He has fulfilled the intolerable yoke of ceremonies of the rigid legal economy.

Conclusion

This chapter's thesis is that the covenant of works reappears in the Mosaic covenant in order to demonstrate humanity's inability to merit eternal life, to remind Israelite sinners that they stand under the condemnation of the broken covenant of works, and to foreshadow the active obedience of Christ. The following points support this thesis:

1. As Part I demonstrates, the historical evidence is abundantly clear that Reformed theologians have wrestled with the presence of legal elements within the Mosaic covenant, which led many to posit that the Mosaic covenant repeats the covenant of works in some sense.

2. The Reformed appeal to Leviticus 18:5 as a proof text for the covenant of works is one of the simplest sources to explain why Reformed theologians appeal to legislation of the Mosaic covenant to argue for the covenant made with Adam. They were using intra-canonical exegesis to understand both the Adamic and Mosaic covenants.

3. The earliest Jewish interpreters of Scripture observed the parallels between Eden // Promised Land and Adam // Israel. This led them to suggest that Israel recapitulated Adam's probation in the garden. These conclusions are warranted, at a minimum, by the parallels between Adam, Israel, and Christ that Scripture itself identifies. To deny the reappearance of the covenant of works at Sinai in any sense runs against the grain of the clear statements of Scripture and drives an unnecessary wedge between Adam, Israel, and Christ.

4. A number of biblical texts support the idea that the covenant of works reappears at Sinai. Leviticus 18:5 is one of the more prominent as it reappears in later portions of Scripture: Ezekiel 20,

---

35. Gladd, *Adam and Israel*, 83.

Nehemiah 9:29, Romans 10:5, Galatians 3:12, and Luke 10:25-28. Other relevant texts include Romans 5:12-14, Galatians 4:24-25, and 2 Corinthians 3.[36]

5. There are numerous ways by which Reformed theologians have explained the relationship between the Adamic and Mosaic covenants. The best explanation, however, traces Paul's shadow-substance language from Colossians 2:17 and recognizes that the Mosaic covenant is part of the covenant of grace – this is its substance. The reappearance or display of the covenant of works is accidental.

The covenant of works is a vital doctrine, but we must not believe that once Adam fell it was no longer relevant or present in redemptive history. Until the last Adam came to fulfill the covenant of works, it has always loomed large over redemptive history. Blessedly, because of Christ, we no longer engage the moral law as a covenant but rather only as a rule. Christ has delivered sinners, Jew and Gentile alike, from the Adamic and Mosaic covenants, and thus we are free from its curses. While we may indeed return to the dust because of Adam's transgression of the covenant of works, we are nevertheless heaven-bound dust because Christ has redeemed us from the curses of the Adamic (Gentiles) and Mosaic (Jews) covenants through His life, death, and resurrection.

---

36. For other arguments, see Bryan D. Estelle, J. V. Fesko, and David VanDrunen, eds., *The Law is Not of Faith: Essays on Works and Grace in the Mosaic Covenant* (Phillipsburg: P & R, 2009).

~: III.3 :~

Justification and the Covenant of Works

Introduction

Early modern non-conformist pastor Thomas Brooks (1608-1680) once wrote: 'The first covenant is called a covenant of works, because this covenant required working on our part as the condition of it, for justification and happiness, "The man that doth these things shall live."'[1] Brooks explicitly mentions one of the chief elements of the covenant of works, namely, the doctrine of justification. At first glance such a doctrine may seem out of place given how prominently justification features in God's post-fall dealings with sinners. In specific theological terms, the doctrine is a key benefit of the covenant of grace and our union with Christ. As true as this observation is, what the historic Reformed tradition has rightly understood is that the doctrine of justification has roots in God's initial covenantal dealings with Adam. This chapter explores the bond between justification and the covenant of works in order to take the Reformed tradition's insight and amplify its implications. Rather than innovating or resorting to novelty, shining a light on forgotten and dormant aspects of the historic Reformed covenant of

---

1. Thomas Brooks, *Paradise Opened*, in *The Complete Works of Thomas Brooks*, vol. 5 (Edinburgh: James Nichol, 1867), 296.

works can be a fruitful endeavor and lead to refined understandings of other related doctrines. In particular, this chapter defends the thesis that the covenant of works carries with it the doctrines of justification and eschatology. The doctrine of justification does not have its foundation in the covenant of grace and eschatology does not enter redemptive history in the days immediately preceding Christ's return.

Justification is a judicial and forensic declaration that reveals whether a person does or does not conform to the moral standard of God's law. Justification does not merely deal with redeemed sinners but also has relevance to Adam and even Christ, the last Adam. Would Adam fulfill God's command to be fruitful, multiply, fill the earth, and subdue it, all the while refraining from eating from the tree of knowledge? Would God therefore justify Adam and declare him righteous regarding His commands? And would this declaration consummate the age and usher in the eschaton? Adam, of course, forsook this path and so God sent another Adam to take up the discarded work. God justified this Son and He initiated the new heavens and earth through His ministry. The two Adams and their respective covenants serve as the proper context for rightly understanding the doctrine of justification and its correlation to eschatology. In short, the covenant of works, justification, and eschatology walk hand-in-hand.

In order to demonstrate these links, the chapter begins with a brief sampling of a number of early modern and contemporary views regarding the covenant of works and justification. The chapter then analyzes the claims to demonstrate their exegetical and theological soundness. With the relationship established between justification and the covenant of works, the chapter explores three noteworthy consequences: (1) eschatology precedes soteriology, (2) how justification is not a mixture of faith and obedience, and (3) that sanctification precedes justification in the covenant of works, whereas in the covenant of grace justification precedes sanctification in the order of salvation. The chapter concludes with summary observations about the interconnections between justification, eschatology, and the covenant of works.

Various Formulations

Among recent expositors of the doctrine of justification some have linked it to the Adamic context. John Murray (1898-1975), for example, rightly contends that one of Adam's goals in the initial creation context was to seek justification through his obedience.[2] But given Murray's rejection of the covenant of works, he naturally does not link Adam's justification to the doctrine of the covenant. Others have explicitly trussed covenant and justification in the creation context. Numerous early modern Reformed theologians make the connection explicit. Westminster divine Samuel Rutherford (1600-1661) argued that God promised Adam eternal life, something that he could have achieved through his obedience. Rutherford explains: 'Our first *Adams* Element is Justification by works, in which we love to live and die.'[3] Fellow divine Thomas Goodwin (1600-1680) makes the connection between justification and the covenant of works unambiguous, though he argues for a slightly different conclusion. Goodwin embraced the Cameronian view that Adam's reward was temporal, extended life in the garden, and not eternal life. Nevertheless, he states: 'That the covenant of works, the justification of Adam by that covenant, and the reward of his obedience, were all natural.'[4] The difference between justification under the covenants of works and grace lies in their material causes, nature versus grace. In his analysis of Romans 4:4, Goodwin argues that Paul highlights the different bases of justification. Under the covenant of works justification is κατὰ ὀφείλημα ('according to debt'), whereas under the covenant of grace it is κατὰ χάριν ('according to grace'). Lest there be misunderstanding, Goodwin stipulates that Adam's reward is a *debitum naturale*, that is, owed

---

2. John Murray, 'The Adamic Administration,' in *The Collected Writings of John Murray*, vol. 2, *Systematic Theology* (Edinburgh: Banner of Truth, 1991), 47.

3. Samuel Rutherford, *The Covenant of Life Opened* (Edinburgh: Robert Broun, 1654), I.vii (p. 46).

4. Thomas Goodwin, *Of the Creatures, and the Condition of Their State of Creation*, in *The Works of Thomas Goodwin*, 10 vols. (Eureka, CA: Tanski Publications, 1996), VII:48. For a similar view by James Ussher, see Harrison Perkins, *Catholicity and the Covenant of Works: James Ussher and the Reformed Tradition* (Oxford: Oxford University Press, 2020), 73-80, 225-43.

to him by virtue of the covenantal condescension, not 'a debt of retribution in a mercenary way.'[5] Similar connections between the covenant of works and justification appear in other early modern documents such as the Formula Consensus Helvetica (1675).[6] Geerhardus Vos (1862-1949) has also explicitly connected justification to the covenant of works when he writes: 'If Adam had remained unfallen and kept the probation command, then God would have justified him – that is, God would have taken into account Adam's holy and steadfast condition and would have had a state of immutable righteousness follow.'[7]

In recent years some have assembled a number of the pieces of the puzzle but do not complete it. Brian Vickers, for example, offers one of the few biblical-theological treatments of the doctrine of justification. He rightly begins with creation and argues that God and Adam were in covenant.[8] He also properly notes that the covenant of works introduced eschatology on to the stage of pre-redemptive history because God wove the goal of Adam's covenantal labors into the very fabric of creation: 'Before the fall of Adam and the subsequent unfolding of redemption, there was an end for which God created the world.' The tree of life was the symbol of the creation's goal.[9] Vickers correctly argues that eternal life would be the fruit of Adam's successful probationary obedience.[10] Vickers therefore presents all of the right elements: covenant, justification, and eschatology. But he does not take these individual pearls and place them on a single strand so they can create a beautiful doctrinal necklace. Instead, he quickly proceeds to the work of

---

5. Goodwin, *Of the Creatures*, VII:49.

6. Martin Klauber, 'The Helvetic Formula Consensus (1675): An Introduction and Translation,' *TrinJ* 11NS (1990): 103-23, esp. art. XXIII.

7. Geerhardus Vos, *Reformed Dogmatics*, 5 vols., ed. Richard B. Gaffin Jr. (Bellingham, WA: Lexham Press, 2012-17), IV:138.

8. Brian Vickers, *Justification by Grace Through Faith: Finding Freedom from Legalism, Lawlessness, Pride, and Despair*. Explorations in Biblical Theology (Phillipsburg, NJ: P & R, 2013), 13-23.

9. Vickers, *Justification by Grace*, 13.

10. Vickers, *Justification by Grace*, 19.

the last Adam without thoroughly fleshing-out the connections between covenant, justification, and eschatology.

The aforementioned views all originate from within the Reformed church, but others outside this community of faith have made similar arguments. Mary Sylvia C. Nwachukwu, a Roman Catholic, draws similar connections in her *Creation-Covenant Scheme and Justification by Faith*.[11] Nwachukwu's overall case is slightly different than the previously surveyed views. She argues that Paul's doctrine of justification has a creation background that focuses upon both the initial creation (Gen. 1–11) and the broader covenantal structure of the Old Testament, especially Israel's failure to meet her covenantal obligations.[12] On the whole, she believes that creation theology lies behind Paul's doctrine of justification.[13] She spirals in on the creation context by first noting that Paul does not locate his doctrine in Hellenistic or Jewish backgrounds, but in the Old Testament, evident from Paul's statements in Romans 1:1-2 and 3:21, by which he invokes the authorities of the law and the prophets.[14] She closes in on Paul's foundation when she notes that Genesis 2:4–11:9 identifies man as the source of evil that disrupted the creation's original goodness and subjected it to God's curse.[15] Paul's arguments in Romans 9–11 ultimately highlight that God rescues elect sinners by means of the God-human relationship He has established in creation.[16] In this vein Nwachukwu appeals to God's cosmic covenant with the creation in Genesis 9:8-17, which provides the framework for His interaction with a post-flood world. The covenant offers a structure for understanding the entire primeval history (Gen. 1–11).[17] More specifically, Nwachukwu

---

11. Mary Sylvia C. Nwachukwu, *Creation-Covenant Scheme and Justification by Faith: A Canonical Study of the God-Human Drama in the Pentateuch and the Letter to the Romans* (Rome: Editrice Pontificia Università Gregoriana, 2002).

12. Nwachukwu, *Creation-Covenant Scheme and Justification*, 7.

13. Nwachukwu, *Creation-Covenant Scheme and Justification*, 13.

14. Nwachukwu, *Creation-Covenant Scheme and Justification*, 27.

15. Nwachukwu, *Creation-Covenant Scheme and Justification*, 33.

16. Nwachukwu, *Creation-Covenant Scheme and Justification*, 37.

17. Nwachukwu, *Creation-Covenant Scheme and Justification*, 106.

contends that God's covenant with Abraham receives its foundation from this creation-covenant scheme where the themes of blessing, judgment, promise, and covenant all coalesce. This context provides Paul with the fundamental building blocks of his doctrine of justification.[18]

Analysis

The above-surveyed views rightly contend that the doctrine of justification has its roots in creation, though Nwachukwu argues for a wider understanding of covenant since she locates the origins of covenant in Genesis 9 rather than Genesis 1–2. Nevertheless, her overall observations are correct even if inexact for several reasons. First, Paul reaches back to Abraham to expound his doctrine of justification, which is undoubtedly early in the Genesis narrative. The Abrahamic narrative, however, has more than historical connections to the creation. As others have noted, God's covenant with Abraham quietly whispers that this covenant addresses Adam's failure in the covenant of works. Adam and Eve's covenantal labor was the divine command to be fruitful, multiply, fill all the earth, and subdue it, which means that the covenant of works has a global scope. Adam and Eve were supposed to fill the earth with divine image bearers as they extended the garden order throughout the creation.[19] When Abraham appears on the scene, the narrative quietly insists that he inherits the role of Adam and Eve.[20] But rather than the command to be fruitful, God promises Abraham, 'I will make you fruitful' (Gen. 17:6; cf. Gen. 28:3; 48:4). And like the original command to fill the world, God would bless 'all the nations of the earth' through Abraham (Gen. 22:18; cf. Matt. 28:18-20). The Abrahamic covenant has Adamic roots, but the difference between the two covenants lies in the differentiation between the covenants of works and grace. In the former, God commands Adam to be fruitful whereas in

18. Nwachukwu, *Creation-Covenant Scheme and Justification*, 117.

19. G. K. Beale, *The Temple and the Church's Mission: A Biblical Theology of the Dwelling Place of God* (Downers Grove, IL: IVP Academic, 2004), 81-87.

20. N. T. Wright, *The New Testament and the People of God* (Philadelphia: Fortress Press, 1992), 263.

the latter God promises Abraham He will make him fruitful. This disparity exhibits the difference between law versus gospel. If God justified Adam by his obedience (law), then He would justify Abraham by faith in Christ (gospel).

Second, Paul locates the foundation for the doctrine of justification in the work of Christ, but Jesus does not appear *de novo* on the stage of redemptive history but comes as the last *Adam* (1 Cor. 15:45). Adam was a type of the one to come (Rom. 5:14). Adam was a living typological antithetical parallelism; that is, his disobedience as our federal covenant head stands in antithesis to Jesus' obedience as the federal covenant representative of those who are in Him. This is Paul's chief point in Romans 5, 'For as by the one man's disobedience the many were constituted as sinners, so by the one man's obedience the many will be constituted as righteous' (v. 19, trans. mine). Where Adam failed Christ succeeded, but Jesus does not introduce a new work with His ministry. As Herman Bavinck (1854-1921) notes, redemption does not introduce eschatology into the creation. According to Bavinck, grace

> does not grant anything beyond what Adam, if he had remained standing, would have acquired in the way of obedience. The covenant of grace differs from the covenant of works in the road, not in its final destination. The same benefits are promised in the covenant of works and freely given in the covenant of grace. Grace restores nature and raises it to its highest fulfillment, but it does not add a new, heterogeneous component to it.[21]

In other words, God does not re-write Adam's covenantal vocation to fill the earth and subdue it but instead sends one who will faithfully fulfill it.[22] Eternal life is the goal and there are only two paths to it: through obedience to the Adamic covenant of works or through faith in the work of the last Adam and the covenant of grace.

---

21. Herman Bavinck, *Reformed Dogmatics*, 4 vols., ed. John Bolt, trans. John Vriend, 4 vols. (Grand Rapids, MI: Baker Academic, 2004-07), II:577.

22. N. T. Wright, *The Resurrection of the Son of God* (Minneapolis, MN: Fortress Press, 2003), 334, 336.

Theological Implications

There are three key implications for recognizing the connections between the covenant of works, eschatology, and justification: (1) eschatology precedes soteriology, (2) justification is not a mixture of faith and works, and (3) sanctification precedes justification in the pre-fall state, whereas it follows justification in the post-fall state.

Eschatology Precedes Soteriology

The above-surveyed theologians are correct to align creation, covenant, and eschatology. The Genesis 1:28 command is one of the two legal pillars of the covenant of works; the other is, of course, the prohibition of eating from the tree of knowledge (Gen. 2:16-17). God interweaves creation, covenant, and eschatology.[23] This means that the early modern Reformed tradition fundamentally understood that the covenant of works was pregnant with the eschaton. In a more succinct formulation, Vos has noted that the Sabbatical principle was the embodiment of the covenant of works.[24] Adam would have halted his labors and enjoyed an anticipatory taste of the coming eternal Sabbath rest of God that awaited him at the conclusion of his work. Vos elsewhere writes: 'In so far as the covenant of works posited for mankind an absolute goal and unchangeable future, the eschatological may be even said to have preceded the soteric religion.'[25] Eschatology is therefore older than soteriology; there was no need for salvation prior to the entrance of sin into the world. Consequently, eschatology is not an exponent of soteriology and thus something that enters theology at the end, a locus that only deals with the last days immediately preceding the second advent of Christ and consummation of the age. Instead, eschatology is the exponent of protology, or creation; or more specifically, eschatology is the intended goal of the covenant of works. Adam was supposed to secure eschatological life by means

---

23. Brian G. Mattson, *Restored to Our Destiny: Eschatology and the Image of God in Herman Bavinck's Reformed Dogmatics* (Leiden: Brill, 2012), 240.

24. Geerhardus Vos, *Biblical Theology* (1948; Edinburgh: Banner of Truth, 1996), 140.

25. Geerhardus Vos, *The Pauline Eschatology* (1930; Phillipsburg, NJ: P & R, 1994), 325 n. 1.

of his obedience to the covenantal commands. Upon his successful covenantal probation, God would have justified him – declared him righteous. His justification would have ushered in the eschaton, the new heavens and earth. As important as connecting the doctrine of justification to the Abrahamic narrative is, one must push past this layer of the covenant of grace and look to the covenant of works.

In God's plan, justification and eschatology are therefore inseparably joined together at the hip and not even the fall can rend them asunder. The eschatological verdict that should have fallen upon Adam comes instead upon Christ, the last Adam. Paul spells this out in his précis of Christ's work: 'Great indeed, we confess, is the mystery of godliness: He was manifested in the flesh, justified by the Spirit, seen by angels, proclaimed among the nations, believed on in the world, taken up in glory' (1 Tim. 3:16, trans. mine).[26] God passed the verdict of the final judgment over His Son, which means that He inaugurated the new heavens and earth through His obedience and fulfillment of the requirements of the covenant of works. Correlatively, anyone united to Christ by grace alone through faith alone also has right to this eschatological verdict in the present, in the midst of the present evil age (Gal. 1:4). Justified sinners enter into the eternal Sabbath rest that Adam only knew by way of shadow rather than reality.

Justification is Either by Works or Faith
This leads to a second implication, namely, given the protological roots of justification, it cannot rest on a mixture of faith and works. One of the most common errors regarding justification is to argue that God justifies sinners on the basis of faith and works. This was the error of the Judaizers, who tried to augment faith in Christ with circumcision. The same fault hobbles Roman Catholic views, which construe justification as a combination of grace and works, the culmination of a life-long process. Sinners receive their initial justification through baptism but only secure their final justification by faith working through love. As the Council of Trent summarizes

---

26. Vos, *Pauline Eschatology*, 151; G. K. Beale, *A New Testament Biblical Theology: The Unfolding of the Old Testament in the New* (Grand Rapids, MI: Baker Academic, 2011), 492-93.

this, believers 'through the observance of the commandments of God and of the Church, faith co-operating with good works, increase in that righteousness which they have received through the grace of Christ, and are still further justified.'[27] Yet, in the pre-fall state the covenant of works does not admit a mixture of faith and works. Stated in blunt terms, *believing* does not fill the earth and subdue it; only *doing* accomplishes this work. God does not justify the last Adam by His faith and works but only according to His works: 'By the one man's obedience the many will be constituted righteous' (Rom. 5:19b, trans. mine).

Christ fulfills the abandoned covenant of works through His obedience, not through His faith. This is why there are only two mutually exclusive paths to justification: either through obedience to the covenant of works or faith in the works of the last Adam. To argue that justification rests in an amalgamation of faith in Christ and the believer's good works fails to recognize the protological origins of justification. Mixing faith and works in justification is an effort to turn back the redemptive-historical clock, wipe the slate clean, and return redeemed sinners to the garden for a mulligan on Adam's failed covenantal labors. Rather, the last Adam secures an immutable, indefectible, and irresistible eschatological state for those in union with Him. As Bavinck notes, Jesus

> came not only to bear our punishment for us but also to obtain for us the righteousness and life that Adam had to secure by his obedience. He delivered us from guilt and punishment and placed us at the end of the road that Adam had to walk, not at the beginning. He gives us much more than we lost in Adam, not only the forgiveness of sins and release from punishment but also and immediately—in faith—the not-being-able to sin and not-being-able to die.[28]

We do not return to the proton to relive the covenantal probation but instead rest in the last Adam's completed work and thus step into the eschaton.

---

27. 'Canons and Decrees of the Council of Trent,' Fifth Session, § 2, in Philip Schaff, *Creeds of Christendom*, 3 vols. (1931; Grand Rapids: Baker Books, 1990), II:99.

28. Bavinck, *Reformed Dogmatics*, III:394-95.

There are two likely objections against the claim that eschatological life required obedience, or works: Did not Adam's state require faith and thus in some sense his successful covenantal probation would have consisted in a combination of faith and works? Correlatively, does not the New Testament speak of the faith of Christ, and thus in some sense was not Christ's work a mixture of faith and works? The first question regarding Adam's faith employs an equivocal use of the term *faith*. In the covenant of grace, for example, Reformed theologians have defined saving faith as 'accepting, receiving, and resting upon Christ alone for justification, sanctification, and eternal life, by virtue of the covenant of grace' (WCF XIV.ii). Faith is resting and trusting in the work of another, namely, Jesus. As Vos notes, 'For Adam, there was no thought of saving faith as the elect sinner learns to exercise it.'[29] The apostle Paul, for example, highlights this point in Romans 4 by using the words *faith* (πίστις) or *believe* (πιστεύω) sixteen times in twenty-five verses (Rom. 4:3, 5, 9, 11, 12, 13, 14, 16, 18, 19, 20, 22, 24). Stunning in this respect is Romans 4:5, 'And to the one who does not work but believes in him who justifies the ungodly, his faith is counted as righteousness.' God did not tell Adam to rest in the work of another – to exercise his faith and trust someone else to accomplish the work on his behalf. As noted in Part I, when Reformed theologians have spoken of Adam's faith, they carefully distinguish between the function of faith under the covenants of works versus grace. Theologians speak of legal versus evangelical faith. Legal faith is interchangeable with justification through obedience to the law whereas evangelical faith seeks justification through the gospel.[30] Legal faith (*fides legalis*) simply believes the promises of the law, namely, the one who does them will live in them.[31] These distinctions parallel Paul's own vocabulary when he contrasts the law of works versus the law of faith (Rom. 3:27).[32]

---

29. Vos, *Reformed Dogmatics*, IV:201.

30. Antonius Walaeus, *Loci Communes S. Theologiae Autor D. Antonio Walaeo* (Leiden: Adrian Whyngarden, 1647), 416.

31. Johannes Cocceius, *Summa Theologiae Ex Scripturis Repetita* (Geneva: Samuel Chouët, 1665), VIII.xxii.46 (p. 278).

32. Charles Hodge, *A Commentary on the Epistle to the Romans* (Philadelphia, PA: Henry Perkins, 1836), 82; Douglas J. Moo, *The Letter to the Romans*, 2nd ed. (Grand Rapids, MI: Eerdmans, 2018), 269-70.

Second, the idea of Christ's faith treads upon the hotly contested question of the meaning of *pistis Christou*, which can be translated as faith *in* Christ or the faith *of* Christ depending on whether one interprets the lexeme as an objective or subjective genitive (see, e.g., Rom. 3:22, 26; Phil. 3:9; Gal. 2:16, 20; 3:22; James 2:1). There is a growing body of literature on this subject that far exceeds the scope of this modest section. Nevertheless, there are good reasons to dismiss the subjective genitive translation of *pistis Christou* ('faith of Christ'). Moisés Silva provides five key reasons for opting for the objective genitive: (1) the Eastern Greek-speaking church fathers opted for the objective genitive; (2) human faith is a significant theme in the New Testament; (3) Paul regularly uses the term *pistis* vis-à-vis the Christian's faith but the other occurrences as they might relate to Christ are ambiguous at best; (4) Galatians 2–3 consistently uses the verb πιστεύω to refer to the Christian's faith, not Christ's; and (5) there is no reason to suggest that highlighting faith in Christ somehow negates salvation apart from works. The whole point of justification *sola fide* is for people to abandon their own works and rest in the works of Christ.[33] While we may speak of Christ's faith as a general trust in His heavenly Father, we must note that like Adam's faith in the promises of the law, Christ believed His Father's Word that the one who does the law will live in it (Lev. 18:5).[34] Christ was not looking to another to fulfill the law on His behalf. But even then, while Christ had faith in His Father, the New Testament is silent regarding this matter. It never once speaks of or explains it; this stands in stark contrast to the copious statements and explanations of the faith of believers.[35]

---

33. Moisés Silva, 'Faith Versus Works of Law in Galatians,' in *Justification and Variegated Nomism*, vol. 2, *The Paradoxes of Paul*, ed. D. A. Carson, Peter T. O'Brien, and Mark A. Seifrid (Grand Rapids, MI: Baker Academic, 2004), 217-48, esp. 228-34.

34. Cf. Michael Allen, *Justification and the Gospel: Understanding the Contexts and Controversies* (Grand Rapids, MI: Baker Academic, 2013), 101-26; idem, *The Christ's Faith: A Dogmatic Account* (London: T & T Clark, 2009); Robert Letham, *The Work of Christ* (Downers Grove, IL: IVP Academic, 1993), 117-18.

35. For those in favor of the subjective genitive, see Richard B. Hays, *The Faith of Jesus Christ: The Narrative Substructure of Galatians 3:1–4:11*, 2nd ed. (Grand Rapids, MI: Eerdmans, 2002); also N. T. Wright, 'The Letter to the

Along similar lines as the *pistis Christou* argument, Norman Shepherd (b. 1933) has maintained that Christ's faith was integral to His work as mediator. Concerning the fulfillment of the covenant promise to Abraham, Shepherd writes that, 'All of this is made possible through the covenantal righteousness of Jesus Christ. His was a living, active, and obedient faith that took him all the way to the cross. This faith was credited to him as righteousness.'[36] While this statement is laced with biblical language and for that reason seems to ring true, Shepherd erroneously applies it to Christ. Nowhere does the New Testament state that Christ's faith was credited to Him as righteousness. When Paul puts forth an example of faith, he appeals to Abraham, not Christ (Rom. 4:3). Instead, the New Testament is replete with references to Christ obeying the will of His Father, not His faith (Matt 3:15; 5:18-19; John 4:34; 6:38-40; 17:3-6; Rom. 5:12-21; Gal 4:4-5). That Christ saves His people by His works or obedience, is why Paul places faith and works in stark antithesis (Rom. 2:13; Gal 3:10; cf. Deut. 6:24; 27.26). Again, while Christ undoubtedly has faith, His is of a different order than saving faith. As Bavinck notes:

> Naturally faith for Christ was not, as it is for us, trust in the grace and mercy of God, for this feature is something faith only obtained as a result of the state of sin in which we find ourselves. By nature faith for Adam and Christ was nothing other than the act of clinging to the word and promises of God, a holding on to the Invisible One. And that is what Jesus did as well (Matt. 27:46; Heb. 2:17-18; 3:2).[37]

Galatians: Exegesis and Theology,' in *Between the Two Horizons*, ed. Joel B. Green and Max Turner (Grand Rapids, MI: Eerdmans, 2002), 218); and Douglas Harinck, *Paul Among the Post-Liberals* (Grand Rapids, MI: Brazos, 2003), 26-30, 40-45. Note the pro and con collection of essays presented in Michael F. Bird and Preston M. Sprinkle, *The Faith of Jesus Christ: The Pistis Christou Debate* (Grand Rapids, MI: Baker Academic, 2010). For the objective genitive case, see James D. G. Dunn, 'Once more, Pistis Christou,' in *Pauline Theology*, vol. 4, ed. D. M. Hay and E. E. Johnson (Atlanta, GA: Scholars Press, 1997), 61-81; J. V. Fesko, *Justification: Understanding the Classic Reformed Doctrine* (Phillipsburg, NJ: P & R, 2008), 157-60.

36. Norman Shepherd, *Call of Grace: How the Covenant Illuminates Salvation and Evangelism* (Phillipsburg, NJ: P & R, 2002), 19.

37. Bavinck, *Reformed Dogmatics*, III:312.

Vos similarly states: 'Of the specific form that faith, as saving faith, takes within the sinner, nothing can be seen in the sinless Christ.'[38] Justification in the covenant of works is therefore by obedience and in the covenant of grace it is *sola fide*.

The Ordo Salutis and the Covenant of Works

The third issue relates to the order of salvation. The *ordo salutis* is a common staple in historic Reformed theology despite recent criticisms against it.[39] A common *ordo salutis* entails the following: election, effectual calling, faith, justification, adoption, sanctification, perseverance, and glorification.[40] One should note, however, that the *ordo* is a concomitant of the covenant of grace; that is, the *ordo* is part of soteriology and thus not part of the covenant of works. This does not mean that there are no connections between the *ordo salutis* and the covenant of works. If the arguments presented above concerning the eschatological nature of the covenant of works and justification are true, then one must factor eschatology and the *ordo*. Eschatology does not enter the *ordo* with glorification, as some have erroneously alleged regarding the traditional Reformed view.[41] Rather, the whole *ordo* is a concomitant of the eschatological advent of the last Adam, the completion of His work, and the last days' outpouring of the Spirit. Moreover, in the covenant of grace the fact that Christ has completed the abandoned work of the covenant of works means that, as noted above, Jesus places redeemed sinners in a higher state than Adam. Adam was in a protological state whereas believers irreversibly step into the eschaton by faith and through union with Christ. Jesus 'does not bring us back to the point on the road where Adam stood

---

38. Vos, *Reformed Dogmatics*, III:60.

39. For an examination of the claims of critics, the historic Reformed understanding, and an exegetical defense, see J. V. Fesko, 'Romans 8:29-30 and the Question of the *Ordo Salutis*,' *JRT* 8 (2014): 35-60.

40. E.g., Louis Berkhof, *Systematic Theology: New Combined Edition* (1932, 1938; Grand Rapids, MI: Eerdmans, 1996), 415-20; John Murray, *Redemption Accomplished and Applied* (Grand Rapids, MI: Eerdmans, 1955), 81-90

41. Richard B. Gaffin Jr., *Resurrection and Redemption: A Study in Paul's Soteriology* (Phillipsburg, NJ: P & R, 1987), 137-38; see also David B. Garner, *Sons in the Son: The Riches and Reach of Adoption in Christ* (Phillipsburg, NJ: P & R, 2016), 219-53, 287-314.

but has covered the whole journey for us to the very end.[42] Because of the indefectible nature of justification, Reformed theologians have therefore typically placed justification prior to sanctification in the *ordo salutis*.[43] Bavinck explains, 'Logically justification comes first in this connection (Rom. 8:30; 1 Cor. 1:30), for it is an evangelical kind of justification, an acquittal on the basis of the righteousness of God granted in faith and not on the basis of the works of the law.'[44]

The priority of justification to sanctification appears on the grand stage of redemptive history in the shift from the Sabbath to the Lord's Day, or the last day of the week to the first. Recall, the pre-fall Sabbath embodies the covenant of works – it was a token of the eternal rest that awaited Adam upon the completion of his labors. Thus, first work, then rest. Once Christ completed His work and

---

42. Bavinck, *Reformed Dogmatics*, III:577.

43. See Fesko, 'Romans 8:29-30,' 41-50.

44. Bavinck, *Reformed Dogmatics*, IV:249. For other theologians who prioritize justification to sanctification see, e.g., Perkins, *Catholicity and the Covenant of Works*, 242-48; Heinrich Bullinger, *The Decades of Henry Bullinger*, 2 vols. (1849-52; Grand Rapids: Reformation Heritage Books, 2004), III.ix (vol. II, pp. 326, 330); John Calvin, *Institutes of the Christian Religion*, trans. Henry Beveridge (Grand Rapids, MI: Eerdmans, 1957), III.xi.1; Peter Martyr Vermigli, *Predestination and Justification*, The Peter Martyr Library, vol. 8, trans. and ed. by Frank A. James III (Kirksville: Thomas Jefferson University Press, 2003), 92, 144, 151; Girolamo Zanchi, *De religione Christiana Fides – Confession of Christian Religion*, 2 vols., ed. Luca Baschera and Christian Moser (Leiden: Brill, 2007), XIX.iii (vol. I, pp. 338-39); William Perkins, *A Commentary on Galatians*, ed. Gerald T. Sheppard (1617; New York: Pilgrim Press, 1989), 128-29; John Owen, *The Doctrine of Justification* in, *The Works of John Owen*, ed. William Goold, 24 vols. (Edinburgh and London: Johnstone and Hunter, 1850-53); V:133; Francis Turretin, *Institutes of Elenctic Theology*, ed. James T. Dennison Jr., trans. George Musgrave Giger (Phillipsburg, NJ: P & R, 1992-97), XVI.ii.4; Herman Witsius, *Conciliatory, or Irenical Animadversions on the Controversies agitated in Britain, under the Unhappy Names of Antinomians and Neonomians*, trans. Thomas Bell (Glasgow: W. Lang, 1807), VI.v, xi, xvi (pp. 70, 168, 171-72); Wilhelmus à Brakel, *The Christian's Reasonable Service*, 4 vols, trans. Bartel Elshout (Morgan, PA: Soli Deo Gloria, 1992), II:405-06, 612, 615; John Brown of Haddington, *Questions and Answers on the Shorter Catechism* (1846; Grand Rapids, MI: Reformation Heritage Books, 2006), 166. For further exegetical and theological argumentation, see J. V. Fesko, 'The Priority of Justification to Sanctification,' in *Being Saved: Explorations in Human Salvation*, ed. Marc Cortez, Joshua R. Farris, S. Mark Hamilton (London: SCM Press, 2018), 185-200.

fulfilled the fractured covenant of works by paying the penalty for its transgression and completing its obligations, there was a seismic shift in redemptive history where the people of God now rest on the first day of the week.[45] God initiated the protological creation on the first day of the week; Christ's resurrection as the last Adam constitutes the cornerstone of the eschatological creation, and like the proton, Jesus launches the new heavens and earth on the first day of the week rather than the last. Therefore, in the wake of Christ's completed work the people of God first rest and then work. We first rest as a token and reminder that the last Adam has been justified and secured right and title to eternal life for His people. As Paul writes: 'Therefore, as one trespass led to condemnation for all men, so one act of righteousness leads to justification that results in life for all men' (Rom. 5:18, trans. mine). Succinctly stated, 'justification brings life in its train.'[46] Given this state of affairs, in the covenant of grace justification precedes sanctification because salvation rests entirely in the finished work of Christ and not in the believer's sanctification. This is not to say that sanctification is superfluous. On the contrary, there is an unbreakable bond between justification and sanctification. Instead, to say that justification precedes sanctification is to recognize the fact that believers are sanctified because they are justified; they are not, however, justified because they are sanctified.[47] As Vos has argued, 'The rule is firm that there cannot be genuine Christian sanctification that does not grow on the root of justification.'[48] Or, in scriptural terms, God justifies the *ungodly* (Rom. 4:5) and salvation is 'not a result of works' (Eph. 2:9).[49]

---

45. J. V. Fesko, *Last Things First: Unlocking Genesis 1–3 with the Christ of Eschatology* (Fearn: Mentor, 2007), 183-204.

46. Bavinck, *Reformed Dogmatics*, IV:249.

47. Vos, *Reformed Dogmatics*, IV:6-7.

48. Vos, *Reformed Dogmatics*, IV:68.

49. Calvin, *Institutes*, III.xiii.2, 5; idem, *Galatians, Ephesians, Philippians, & Colossians*, CNTC (Grand Rapids: Eerdmans, 1996), comm. Eph. 2:8-10 (pp. 144-45); Lancelot Ridley, *A Commentary in Englyshe upon Sayncte paules Epystle to the Ephesyans for the Instruccyon of Them That Be Unlearned in Tonges* (London: Robert Redeman, 1540), comm. Eph. 2:8-10 (no pagination in this edition); Vermigli,

In the pre-fall state, however, justification functions differently given the absence of sin and Adam's uprightness by virtue of bearing the unblemished image of God. Strictly speaking, Adam's sanctification is different than the sanctification of the *ordo salutis*. The Westminster Shorter Catechism, for example, defines sanctification as 'the work of God's free grace, whereby we are renewed in the whole man after the image of God, and are enabled more and more to die unto sin, and live unto righteousness' (q. 35). The soteriological doctrine of sanctification presupposes fallen human beings and thus does not apply to the pre-fall state. That being said, because Adam was created in God's image, he possessed both holiness and righteousness. There are a number of exegetical considerations in this respect. When God created Adam, He pronounced him very good (Gen. 1:31). Proverbs uses a synonymous parallelism to show that to be good is also to be righteous: 'So you will walk in the way of the good and keep to the paths of the righteous' (Prov. 2:20). The apostle Paul uses these adjectives to describe the law of God but also coordinates them with holiness: 'The law is holy, and the commandment is holy and righteous and good' (Rom. 7:12). Given that God created Adam upright (Eccles. 7:29), he was therefore righteous and holy, or sanctified. Especially significant in this regard is that Adam was a type of the one who was to come (Rom. 5:14), which means he anticipates Jesus, 'the holy and righteous one' (Acts 3:14).[50] In fact, when Paul speaks of the renewal of God's image by the work of Christ, he tells the Ephesians they have 'put off the old man,' that is, their existence in Adam, and have put on the new man, 'created after the likeness of God in true righteousness and holiness' (Eph. 4:22-24; cf. Luke 1:75).[51] Christ restores what was lost in Adam's fall, but of course, He redeems to a superior, eschatological, not protological, state. The Westminster Shorter

---

Predestination and Justification, 109; S. M. Baugh, *Ephesians*, Evangelical Exegetical Commentary (Bellingham, WA: Lexham Press, 2016), 158-65.

50. Brandon Crowe, *The Last Adam: A Theology of the Obedient Life of Jesus in the Gospels* (Grand Rapids, MI: Baker Academic, 2017), 114-15.

51. Baugh, Ephesians, 368-73.

Catechism succinctly presents Adam's original state as being created after God's 'own image, in knowledge, righteousness and holiness, with dominion over the creatures' (q. 10).[52]

This means that prior to the fall, Adam's sanctification preceded his justification. As Bavinck explains: 'The first person, therefore, was created after God's image in righteousness and holiness and needed neither justification nor sanctification, though he had to be obedient to the law to be justified by works of the law and to receive eternal life (legal justification).'[53] Or, in the words of Brooks: 'Adam was invested and endowed with righteousness and holiness in his first glorious estate; with righteousness, that he might carry it fairly, justly, evenly, and righteously towards man; and with holiness, that he might carry it wisely, lovingly, reverentially, and holily towards God, and that he might take up in God as his chiefest good, as in his great all.'[54] In the pre-fall state, therefore, Adam's sanctification was supposed to fuel his justification. Or, alternatively stated, Adam's obedience was the path to his justification and eschatological life.

Recognizing how justification and sanctification relate in the pre- and post-fall contexts is vital to preserving the integrity of both. A failure to understand that a pre-fall sanctification preceded Adam's justification undermines the fact that in the covenant of works Adam 'had freedom, and power to will and do that which was good and well pleasing to God' (WCF IX.ii). God created Adam with the ability and capacity to fulfill the covenant of works and he tragically squandered his blessed state and opportunity – he wasted his sanctified existence. Conversely, the failure to recognize that in the post-fall context justification precedes sanctification destabilizes the eschatological character of justification and the solely sufficient work of Christ as the last Adam as its foundation. To say that in the post-fall context sanctification precedes justification returns redeemed sinners to the covenant of works and Adam's

---

52. A. A. Hodge, *A Commentary on the Confession of Faith* (Philadelphia, PA: Presbyterian Board of Publication, 1901), 124.

53. Bavinck, *Reformed Dogmatics*, IV:249.

54. Brooks, *Paradise Opened*, 297.

probation. In redemptive historical terms, such an error tries to do the impossible by rewinding the clock to the time before Christ had completed the work of redemption—to cease to rest on the first day of the week and instead worship on the Sabbath, the last day of the week—as if the work was not done. Vos summarizes these points in the following manner:

> Adam, as he was in the covenant of works, was perfectly holy; in all his characteristics and inclinations there was perfect devotion to God. Still, on the basis of this perfect holiness, righteousness had first to be acquired by Adam; his condition expressing itself in works would be indicative of his state, of his righteousness. In the covenant of grace, this is reversed. Here, by faith, the sinner is first transferred into the state of righteousness, so that he is much further than Adam before the fall; inasmuch as Adam's state was not secure, the sinner's is. And now, following on this righteousness, the state of holiness appears, produced through the work of sanctification.[55]

Rather than beginning the week in the knowledge that the work has been completed by the last Adam, we foolishly try to return to the Sabbath and are told that the work must still be completed.

Conclusion

Eschatology is not something that enters the stage of redemptive history in the days immediately preceding the return of Christ. Rather, in pre-redemptive history the covenant of works was laden with the promise of eschatological life and awaited Adam's successful probation, his justification. Adam's fall did not abrogate God's promise to grant confirmed eternal life to the one who would faithfully fulfill the covenant of works. Rather, God sent a faithful Son of Man, one like Adam, who would complete the abandoned covenantal task. Our redemption is all by God's grace in Christ, the last Adam, but He accomplished this salvation entirely by His works. Christ fulfilled the covenant of works so that we take a step into the new heavens and earth the moment we believe. We receive a foretaste of that eternal eschatological rest each and every

---

55. Vos, *Reformed Dogmatics*, IV:193.

Lord's Day as we celebrate the completed work of Christ—we first rest—and enter the remainder of the week in the knowledge and hope that the work has been done. We can only begin to enter this eternal rest solely by the completed work of Christ—His obedience alone—not our own. To try to mix our good works with Christ's as the means by which we enter God's eternal rest is an alchemy doomed to failure.

~: III.4 :~

Grace and Merit in the Covenant of Works

Introduction

'*G*od is love' and 'God so loved the world' are statements that hide in plain sight in the pages of holy writ (1 John 4:16; John 3:16). Theologians regularly and rightly invoke these truths in their explanations of God's response to the fall and human sin. Who cannot but revel in the fact that 'God shows his love for us in that while we were still sinners, Christ died for us,' and that 'God's love has been poured into our hearts through the Holy Spirit who has been given to us' (Rom. 5:8, 5). Reformed theologians have readily acknowledged God's love in redemption as well as in His covenantal relationship with Adam, despite inaccurate criticisms to the contrary. Westminster divine William Strong (d. 1654), for example, stretches a canopy of love across the landscape of pre- and post-fall creation when he writes: 'To give our first Parents a being, and so glorious a Covenant, and all the Creatures for their use, to have dominion over them all, was great love from God; but here is a higher act of love, to give sinners a Son: *so God loved the world, that he did not spare his only begotten Son.*'[1] Wilhelmus

---

1. William Strong, *A Discourse of the Two Covenants: Wherein the Nature, Differences, and Effects of the Covenant of Works and of Grace Are Distinctly, Rationally, Spiritually and Practically Discussed* (London: Francis Tyton, 1678), 32.

à Brakel (1635-1711) characterizes the commands Adam received as 'the law of love,' and Johannes Heidegger (1633-1698) argued that Adam was supposed to love God with his whole heart, soul, and strength.[2] In the contemporary period, Geerhardus Vos (1862-1949) likewise comments: 'In establishing the covenant of works the motivation was God's love and benevolence toward unfallen man.'[3] A rushing stream of love flows out of the covenant of works and provides an important source for watering our understanding of God's pre-fall dealings with Adam.

But in spite of the regular appeal to God's love and benevolence in the covenant of works, theologians have historically also appealed to God's grace as a requirement for pre-fall anthropology. God either had to give Adam a gift of grace so that he would desire the beatific vision, or receive Adam's obedience in grace because it was meager and insufficient in comparison with the extravagant reward of eternal life. As common as such explanations are, this chapter defends the thesis that God's love and benevolence are the preferred categories to understand how a human being could secure eternal life through his finite obedience. As common as it is for Reformed theologians to invoke God's grace to describe the covenant of works, in the post-Barthian world where Christology devours everything, there is little, if any place, for the very good creation that God has made. In the rush to summon grace, God's love and benevolence receive less attention. Moreover, at a minimum, one can say that God gave Adam His grace, but he must quickly stipulate that it is different from the grace that we receive in Christ. Even though he received God's grace, Adam nevertheless fell – this grace was resistible and ineffectual. Rather than grace, a better way forward is to say that God poured out unmerited love by giving Adam the gifts of creation, existence, the divine image, and the covenant of works, the arena in which Adam was supposed to love God and his fellow human beings. But rather than love Him, Adam spurned God's gifts and

---

2. Wilhelmus à Brakel, *The Christian's Reasonable Service*, 4 vols., trans. Bartel Elshout (Morgan, PA: Soli Deo Gloria, 1992), I:359; Johannes Heidegger, *Medulla Theologiae Christianae* (Zurich: David Gessner, 1697), IX.vii (pp. 70-71).

3. Geerhardus Vos, *Reformed Dogmatics*, 5 vols., ed. Richard B. Gaffin Jr. (Bellingham, WA: Lexham Press, 2014-17), II:93.

idolatrously loved himself. In a stunning response, even though God had every right to condemn His covenant servant, He responded with grace – His demerited favor. In other words, in spite of Adam's demerit, his sin, God gave him a deeper manifestation of His love – His grace and mercy.

To defend the thesis that divine love and benevolence present a better way to account for God's pre-fall relationship to Adam, the chapter begins with a brief overview and critique of past appeals to grace. In lieu of grace, this first section factors the goodness of pre-fall human nature and creation as divine gift as key pillars for an optimal formulation of the covenant of works. Second, the chapter delves into the related question of whether Adam could merit eternal life. As common as it is for theologians to appeal to merit, the category is hobbled by complex arguments of condign and congruent merit, questions of proportionality of work to reward, and whether anyone can truly merit anything from God. Instead of merit, a better route lies immediately at hand in the covenant of works. Rather than begin from below and try to explain how a finite creature can merit an infinite reward, covenant reorients the discussion by locating Adam's ability to secure eternal life in the liberality of God's promise. We can set aside questions of grace and Adam's (in)abilities as a finite creature and instead affirm that God voluntarily condescended to Adam in the covenant of works. Adam's obedience, therefore, is not primary; rather, God's promise is. The third and final section addresses potential objections, such as why employing the *donum superadditum* ('super added gift') and grace are less than ideal options, and why the rise of Karl Barth's (1886-1968) theology necessitates a greater degree of precision in formulating the pre-fall covenant. The chapter concludes with summary observations.

Grace

Historical Overview and Analysis

In the history of doctrine many theologians have appealed to the concept of grace to account for pre-fall anthropology. As documented in Part I, various theologians have proposed several different grace-based explanations. The dominant paradigm for nearly one thousand years was the Augustinian-Thomist nature-grace construct. Thomas Aquinas (1225-1274) argued that human reason was subject to God because of a supernatural endowment of grace.[4] Aquinas based this idea partially upon the views of Augustine (354-430), who maintained that when Adam and Eve sinned, they lost their gift of divine grace.[5] Apart from grace, Adam only had the power and desire for a natural end (e.g., extended life in the garden) but grace elevated both nature and desire to make them fit for a supernatural end (eternal life and the beatific vision).[6] The following summary from Part I reminds us of the different options:

1. Carry over an Augustinian-Thomist nature-grace construct (John Calvin, Peter Martyr Vermigli, the Gallican and Belgic confessions).

2. Reject the nature-grace construct and argue that righteousness was completely natural to Adam given his status as a creature made in God's image (Luther).

3. Employ the doctrine of the covenant, maintain the opposition between grace and works in the pre-fall context, but nevertheless contend that Adam was unable to merit truly anything before God, which is similar to the doctrine of congruent merit (Robert Rollock), though all of the elements of *ex pacto* merit are present as with later Reformed theologians (Turretin, Witsius, Pictet, Van Til, Braun, and à Brakel).

4. Employ the doctrine of the covenant to explain Adam's pre-fall estate but still retain the Augustinian-Thomist nature-grace construct either in terms of natural and supernatural gifts (Johannes Wollebius, Jacob Arminius, Francis Junius, Anthony Burgess, and John Ball) or the divine elevation of the efficacy of Adam's obedience (Samuel Rutherford).

---

4. Thomas Aquinas, *Summa Theologica* (rep.; Allen, TX: Christian Classics, 1948), Ia q. 95 art. 1.

5. Augustine, *City of God*, XIII.13, in NPNF[1], II:251.

6. Thomas Aquinas, *Truth*, 3 vols. (1952; Eugene, OR: Wipf & Stock, 2008), q. 18 art. 2.

5. Explain Adam's ability to merit in terms of divinely given grace, but distinguish between pre- and post-fall grace. The former is imperfect and lacks the grace of perseverance, while the latter is perfect and contains said grace (John Owen).

Based on his own exploration of Reformed views, Richard Muller has concluded: 'Virtually all of the Reformed theologians of the era recognized, albeit in varying degrees, that there could be no relationship between God and the finite, mutable creature apart from grace. This was also the burden of the medieval doctrine of the *donum superadditum*, particularly in its full Augustinian form, a doctrine most probably at the root of the idea of the covenant of works.'[7] Hence, while invoking pre-fall grace has respectable pedigree and even confessional precedent, the covenant of works contributed to introducing a viable and arguably preferable alternative.

As documented in Part I, when some Reformed theologians explained the doctrine of the covenant of works, they did not resort to pre-fall grace but instead to divine promise. Theologians avoided categories of grace to explain how Adam's finite obedience could merit the infinite reward of eternal life. Instead, Adam's ability to merit eternal life was *ex pacto*, that is, there was no inherent worth in Adam's act of obedience but rather his capability to attain eternal life was by virtue of God's covenant promise (so Witsius, Pictet, Van Til, Braun, and à Brakel).[8] There are several important exegetical and theological reasons why *ex*

---

7. Richard A. Muller, *After Calvin: Studies in the Development of a Theological Tradition* (Oxford: Oxford University Press, 2003), 183. See similar comments in Ernest F. Kevan, *The Grace of Law: A Study in Puritan Theology* (Ligonier, PA: Soli Deo Gloria, 1993), 112.

8. Note, that appealing to *ex pacto* obedience ('through or on the basis of the covenant') arguably has its roots in the Scotist and nominalist view of the efficacy of the sacraments. And though Reformed theologians who employ this concept would deny it, some propose that it has close similarities to the concept of congruent merit (Richard A. Muller, *Dictionary of Latin and Greek Theological Terms: Drawn Principally From Protestant Scholastic Theology*, 2nd ed. [1985; Grand Rapids: Baker Academic, 2017], s. v. *ex pacto* [p. 114]. See also Richard Cross, 'John Duns Scotus,' in *Christian Theologies of the Sacraments: A Comparative Introduction*, ed. Justin S. Holcomb [New York: New York University Press, 2017], 100-18).

pacto obedience has greater explanatory power in contrast to the common Augustinian-Thomist pre-fall nature-grace construct. This section explores these issues under the following four considerations to demonstrate covenant as the preferable category in lieu of appealing to pre-fall grace: (1) Pre-fall human nature in church history; (2) the goodness of pre-fall human nature; (3) creation as gift; and (4) covenant and love.

Pre-Fall Human Nature in Church History

The first consideration involves understanding Adam's pre-fall human nature. A tried-and-true staple of Catholic and Reformed soteriology is that grace perfects nature.[9] Applying the nature-grace construct, however, to the pre-fall state is an arguably problematic proposition.[10] As common as it is among Catholic and Reformed theologians to posit the necessity of pre-fall grace, it suggests that there is some sort of defect inherent in unfallen human beings. Early modern Roman Catholic theologian Robert Bellarmine (1542-1621), for example, contends that God created Adam from flesh and spirit, and thus had elements in common with animals and angels. Flesh and spirit

---

9. Aquinas, *Summa Theologica*, Ia q. 1 art. 8 ad. 2; Francis Junius, *A Treatise on True Theology*, trans. David C. Noe (Grand Rapids: Reformation Heritage Books, 2014), thesis 36 (pp. 90, 218); idem, *The Mosaic Polity*, trans. Todd M. Rester, ed. Andrew M. McGinnis (Grand Rapids: CLP Academic, 2015), 68, 92; Herman Witsius, *Economy of the Covenants Between God and Man*, 2 vols. (rep.; Escondido, CA: Den Dulk Foundation, 1991), III.xii.26, IV.xii.55-58; Francis Turretin, *Institutes of Elenctic Theology*, 3 vols., trans. George Musgrave Giger, ed. James T. Dennison Jr. (Phillipsburg, NJ: P & R, 1992-97), I.ix.15, xiii.3; XIX.xxvii.8; David Sytsma, "'As a Dwarfe Set Upon a Gyants Shoulders,' John Weems (ca. 1579-1636) on the Place of Philosophy and Scholasticism in Reformed Theology,' in *Die Philosophie der Reformierten*, Melanchthon-Schriften der Stadt Bretten, eds. Günter Frank and Herman Selderhuis (Stuttgart: Frommann-Holzboog, 2012), 299-321, esp. 309 n. 49; Herman Bavinck, *Reformed Dogmatics*, trans. John Vriend, ed. John Bolt, 4 vols. (Grand Rapids: Baker Academic, 2003-08), I:322, III:226, 577; David VanDrunen, *Divine Covenants and Moral Order: A Biblical Theology of Natural Law* (Grand Rapids: Eerdmans, 2014), 26-38. Protestants have criticized Thomas on nature and grace because they have often misunderstood his view. For a corrective, see Arvin Vos, *Aquinas, Calvin, and Contemporary Protestant Thought: A Critique of Protestant Views on the Thought of Thomas Aquinas* (Washington D. C: University of America Press, 1985), 123-60.

10. Turretin, *Institutes*, V.xi.4; Herman Bavinck, 'Calvin and Common Grace,' *PTR* 7/3 (1909): 437-65, esp. 440-45.

were contradictory propensities; thus, God remedied the imbalance by a gift of grace.[11] Whether one posits that Adam required God's infused grace to elevate nature to make him desire a supernatural end, or that God evaluated Adam's obedience on the basis of grace rather than justice, Adam's person and work are in some sense inherently deficient in the pre-fall state. Aquinas, for example, makes his case based upon two biblical texts and an Aristotelian presupposition of proportionality. Aquinas appeals to 1 Corinthians 2:9, 'What no eye has seen, nor ear heard, nor the heart of man imagined, what God has prepared for those who love him.' He claims that eternal life and the desire for the beatific vision exceed the heart and imagination of human beings. In order for human beings to desire the beatific vision, God must provide a supernatural gift, which He calls grace.[12] Aquinas makes similar claims regarding 2 Corinthians 5:5, 'He who has prepared us for this very thing is God, who has given us the Spirit as a guarantee.' Our desire to preserve our earthly tabernacle (our physical bodies) is a natural desire; the only way to seek something above nature is if God provides His superadded grace.[13]

Inherent in Aquinas' exegesis is the presupposition of Aristotelian proportionality, to which he adds the distinction of passive and obediential potency. That is, a work must be proportionate to its reward. Thus, a passive potency can only be realized through its own active power. Apart from divine grace human beings can only attain a natural end, as this lies within their passive potency. But obediential potency, on the other hand, means that humans can achieve eternal life if aided by divine grace. In other words, a stone only has a passive potency to lie still or fall if dropped from a height, but it has an obediential potency of becoming a human being if God so wills it.[14] While later Reformed theologians do not

---

11. Robert Bellarmine, *De Gratia Primi Hominis*, I.v, in *De Controversiis Christianae Fidei*, vol. 4 (Naples: Joseph Giuliano, 1585), 24; see also Turretin, *Institutes*, V.xi.5.

12. Aquinas, *Summa Theologica*, IaIIae q. 114 art. 2.

13. Thomas Aquinas, *Commentary on the Letters of Saint Paul to the Corinthians* (Lander, WY: Aquinas Institute for the Study of Sacred Doctrine, 2012), comm. 2 Cor. 5:5, chp. 5, lect. II (§ 160).

14. Lawrence Feingold, *The Natural Desire to See God According to St. Thomas and His Interpreters* (Ave Maria, FL: Sapientia Press, 2004), 107.

necessarily argue the need for pre-fall grace in this precise Thomist fashion, they virtually assume these categories as unquestioned facts. But this Thomistic exegesis and philosophical assumption generates several questions. Has Aquinas correctly exegeted the apostle Paul's statements? And must one assume an Aristotelian concept of proportionality in the relationship between a work and reward?

On the one hand, given the fact of the fall, in the big picture what Aquinas says about nature and grace is true. Human beings have no natural desire in a sin-fallen state for the beatific vision and eternal life – far from it. Paul states this truth succinctly: 'No one seeks God' (Rom. 3:11b). Thus, Thomas rightly appeals to 1 Corinthians 2:9, namely, that no one has 'imagined what God has prepared for those who love him,' if he refers to fallen human beings. The same may be said of 2 Corinthians 5:5, in that Paul's context is soteriological, not protological, as Paul states: 'For while we are still in this tent, we groan, being burdened – not that we would be unclothed, but that we would be further clothed, so that what is mortal may be swallowed up by life' (2 Cor. 5:4). Adam was not mortal until he ate the fruit of the tree of knowledge. Aquinas' error lies in the way that he appeals to passages that deal specifically with soteriology, or a post-fall human condition that is in need of redemption, where grace must perfect (or redeem) nature.

A second fault in Aquinas' argument is his uncritical appeal to Aristotle's principle of proportionality between work and reward. Aquinas' assumption may be correct, but there are normal instances when there is a disproportionality between work and reward. When a waiter, for example, serves a wealthy person she might receive a larger gratuity in comparison with serving a person of lesser means. The same labor receives a different reward based upon the relative financial status of the person served. There is significant disproportionality between work and reward when one compares the labors of a brain surgeon to a professional baseball player. A brain surgeon performs work that pays quite handsomely, but one can argue that his reward is proportionate to the nature of his work. Brain surgeons operate on brains! The baseball player, on the other hand, receives significant compensation for hitting a small ball with a wooden stick, which can be quite entertaining and fun to watch, but pales in comparison to the brain surgeon's labor. Nevertheless, people commonly accept the baseball player's compensation because such is the nature of professional sports. So, if one can uncritically appeal to Aristotle's concept of proportionality apart from exegetical argumentation, then why not instead import a concept of legitimate disproportionality to explain the relationship between Adam's finite work and his infinite reward? Such a question should not rely upon an uncritical use of any principle but rather should ideally rest on exegesis. To what texts, therefore, might one draw to explain the nature of Adam's pre-fall anthropology and the relationship between his work and reward?

Anthropology, Gift, and Love

The various texts to which we must look fall under three rubrics: (1) the goodness of Adam's pre-fall nature, (2) creation as gift, and (3) covenant and love.

The Goodness of Pre-fall Human Nature

The first pillar of rightly formulating pre-fall anthropology is recognizing the inherent goodness of the creation and especially the goodness of human beings in their natural state. When God created human beings, He issued a forensic verdict over them when He said they were 'very good' (Gen. 1:31). God created Adam and Eve upright and holy; to be declared *good* is another way of saying that the first human beings were righteous (Prov. 2:20; Eccles. 7:29; Rom. 7:12; Acts 3:14; Eph. 4:22-24). Significant in this respect is that Jesus asked one of His interlocutors why he called Him good, 'No one is good except God alone' (Luke 18:19). In a post-fall world this statement is undoubtedly true and for this reason the apostle Paul echoes Christ's teaching, 'None is righteous, no, not one … no one does good, not even one' (Rom. 3:10, 12c). But in the pre-fall context, God Himself says that Adam is good, even 'very good.' At this point, some might object by stipulating that Adam is good not simply because of his unfallen state but also because of the *donum superadditum* (Aquinas), or natural and supernatural gifts (Calvin), or the pre-fall grace of God (Rutherford).

Relevant at this point are Paul's statements in 1 Corinthians 15:44-46, 'It is sown a natural body; it is raised a spiritual body. If there is a natural body, there is also a spiritual body. Thus it is written, "The first man Adam became a living being"; the last Adam became a life-giving Spirit. But it is not the spiritual that is first but the natural, and then the spiritual.' Paul provides a redemptive historical overview of the work of the two Adams and characterizes them as the difference between the *natural* (ψυχικόν) and the *spiritual* (πνευματικόν). While Paul sets his exposition of the resurrection within the context of soteriology, he addresses the nature of the eschaton. But recall that eschatology is not the exponent of soteriology but chiefly, first and foremost, of protology. In other words, when Paul contrasts the natural and spiritual the transition is primarily from the protological to the eschatological. In the post-fall world, the protological must account for soteriology given the entrance of sin into the world. If we correlate Adam's goodness (righteousness and holiness) with the fact that he was in a natural state, then this means that Adam by nature had both the desire and capacity for the beatific vision. Another way of stating this truth is that by virtue of Adam's status as a divine image bearer, he had both the capacity and desire for eternal life. When Adam and Eve sinned, they hid themselves from the face of God: 'And they heard the sound of the LORD God walking in the garden in the Spirit of the day, and the man and his wife hid themselves from the face [מִפְּנֵי] of the LORD God among the trees of the garden' (Gen. 3:8, trans. mine). God's presence and beholding His face, the beatific vision, was not out of place in the garden; Adam and Eve's sin was the intruder.

When God created Adam and Eve in His image, God gave them dominion over the fish of the sea, the birds of the air, and the creatures of the land (Gen. 1:26). As noted in earlier chapters, the dominion mandate defines the nature of God's image. Just as God was sovereign over the cosmos, so now humans as image bearers were God's viceregents over the creation: 'You have given him dominion over the works of your hands; you have put all things under his feet' (Ps. 8:6). I have argued in previous chapters that one may distinguish between the material and formal causes of the covenant of works, but we should not separate them. Those who press the question of whether Adam was created *in* or *for* covenant posit a false dichotomy; Adam's status as an image bearer is just as necessary as the commands of the covenant of works. Nevertheless, for the sake of argument we can isolate the formal cause of the covenant of works to demonstrate what Adam would have known by virtue of his creation. In other words, what did Adam know by means of general versus special revelation?[15] God specially revealed the dominion mandate and the prohibition not to eat from the tree of knowledge to Adam and Eve through His verbal commands, which would have given them explicit knowledge of the eschatological goal of their labors. But what apart from this special revelation would they have known by means of general revelation?

Adam and Eve would have known three chief things. First, they would have known the natural law of God inscribed upon their hearts (Rom. 2:15). Second, they would have known of God's existence and of His attributes. As the apostle Paul explains, even fallen human beings know of God's 'invisible attributes, namely, his eternal power and divine nature' (Rom. 1:20). This means that Adam would have naturally known of God's eternality, and as an image-bearer, he would therefore presumably have a natural desire for the beatific vision. As Vos notes: 'Man is said to have been made in the image of God, and obviously the underlying idea is that in his very constitution he is adapted and designed for communion with God.'[16] Gregory of Nyssa (335-394) reflects on what Adam would have known through the creation when he writes that God prepared a 'royal lodging for the future king' because 'all kinds of wealth had been stored in this palace,' namely, the creation. The 'bosom of the earth' was a 'royal treasure-house,' and God 'thus manifests man in the world, to be the beholder of some of the wonders therein, and the lord of others; that by his enjoyment he

15. Geerhardus Vos, *Biblical Theology* (1948; Edinburgh: Banner of Truth, 1975), 20, 22.

16. Geerhardus Vos, 'The Scriptural Doctrine of the Love of God,' *PRR* 13/49 (1902): 1-37, esp. 6.

might have knowledge of the Giver, and by the beauty and majesty of the things he saw might trace out that power of the Maker which is beyond speech and language.'[17] Third, Adam and Eve would have naturally known of their relationship to God as His offspring. Once again, this is knowledge that even fallen human beings know. In his address to the philosophers at Mars Hill Paul quoted pagan poets: '"In him we live and move and have our being"; as even some of your own poets have said, "for we are indeed his offspring"' (Acts 17:28). These different exegetical considerations lead to the conclusion that Adam did not require the grace of God in the pre-fall state. Rather, as the Westminster Confession states, God created Adam and Eve 'having the law of God written in their hearts, and the power to fulfill it' (IV.ii). But the question of whether Adam required God's grace in the pre-fall context does not rest upon anthropology alone. There are two other important factors, namely, creation and covenant.

Creation as Gift

A second key pillar is the doctrine of creation *ex nihilo*. The doctrine of creation addresses how the triune God formed the heavens and the earth and exercises His lordship over all. But it also testifies that God gave the creation to Adam and Eve as a multifaceted gift. The Scriptures teach creation *ex nihilo*, which is a doctrinal sentry against pantheism. If the creation was in any way merely an extension of God, then it would be a necessary part of God and thus not truly a free gift to humanity. In fact, apart from creation *ex nihilo*, human beings would in some sense be divine because they would be a necessary extension of God's being. As St. Augustine (354-430) observes, 'In the beginning, that is from yourself, in your wisdom which is begotten of your substance, you made something and made it out of nothing. For you made heaven and earth not out of your own self, or it would be equal to your only-begotten Son and therefore to yourself.'[18] But the fact that the triune God created out of nothing means that the creation's

---

17. Gregory of Nyssa, *On the Making of Man*, II.i, in NPNF[2], V:390.

18. Augustine, *Confessions*, trans. Henry Chadwick (Oxford: Oxford University Press, 1991), XII.vii (p. 249).

reception by humanity is the blessing of an unmerited gift. Before the world's creation, donation, and reception, there was nothing.[19] After the creation, God gave everything in the world for human beings for the completion of their covenantal work.[20] The creation itself expresses the disproportion of the creator versus the creature; or to borrow the terms of the Westminster Confession of Faith (1647), the creation is another 'voluntary condescension' of the creator to human beings (VII.i).[21] Or in the words of the apostle Paul, 'The God who made the world and everything in it, being Lord of heaven and earth, does not live in temples made by man, nor is he served by human hands, as though he needed anything, since he himself gives to all mankind life and breath and everything' (Acts 17:24-25). God needs nothing from human beings but yet gives to them the creation as a gift.

The creation is a reflection of who God is, though some theologians have spoken far more bluntly. John Calvin (1509-1564), for example, writes that the creation manifests God's 'perfections in the whole structure of the universe' and that the cosmos daily places God in our view so that 'we cannot open our eyes without being compelled to behold him.'[22] Every time people look at the world they behold the theater of God's glory. But Calvin goes even further when he writes, 'I admit, indeed, that the expression, "Nature is God [*Naturam esse Deum*]," may be piously used, if dictated by a pious mind; but as it is inaccurate and harsh, (Nature being more properly the order which has been established by God,) in matters which are so very important, and in regard to which special reverence is due, it does harm to confound the Deity with the inferior operations of his hands.'[23] Calvin was willing to say that nature is God, so long as it was 'piously used,' that is, so long

---

19. Kenneth L. Schmitz, *The Gift: Creation*, The Aquinas Lecture, 1982 (Milwaukee, WI: Marquette University Press, 2011), 33.

20. Similarly, Schmitz, *The Gift*, 34.

21. Similarly, Schmitz, *The Gift*, 65, 74.

22. John Calvin, *Institutes of the Christian Religion*, trans. Henry Beveridge (Grand Rapids: Eerdmans, 1957), I.v.1.

23. Calvin, Institutes, I.v.5; idem, Institutio Christiane Religionis (Geneva: Robert Stephanus, 1559). Similarly, Schmitz, *The Gift*, 59.

as one did not skid into pantheism. But the point stands, that there is a sense in which the creation itself is a self-giving of God unto humanity.

The self-giving of God through the creation is evident in several passages. Think, for example, about Christ's teaching regarding loving one's enemies. Christians are supposed to love and pray for their enemies so that they emulate their heavenly Father. How does God love His enemies? 'For he makes his sun rise on the evil and on the good, and sends rain on the just and on the unjust' (Matt. 5:45b). In other words, the natural actions of the creation, sunlight and rain, are manifestations of God's love to both believer and unbeliever alike.[24] This means that when God told Adam and Eve, 'You may surely eat of every tree of the garden' (Gen. 2:16), that He gave them gifts of His love. The creation is a synthesis of power and love, the power of creating out of nothing and lovingly giving this gift to Adam and Eve.[25] While Calvin could say that 'nature is God' to express the close relation between God and the creation, a sounder route lies in acknowledging its sacramental character. God made the cosmos, placed Adam and Eve in the garden, and then gave them the world to provide for their every need. The world was a divine gift that did not exist for its own sake but in order to be transformed, to become life, and thus to be given back to God as humanity's gift to God.[26] To acknowledge the sacramental character of the creation recognizes that the creation is not itself God but points beyond to Him, but it also highlights the creation as a gift and demonstration of God's love.[27] In the words of Dumitru Staniloae (1903-1993), 'As gift of God to us, the world becomes the meeting place and bridge of our meeting with God. The world itself is not for us the source of growth in respect of eternal being, yet

---

24. Vos, 'Doctrine of the Love of God,' 22.

25. Schmitz, *The Gift*, 92.

26. Alexander Schmemann, 'The World as Sacrament,' in *Church, World, Mission: Reflections on Orthodoxy in the West* (Crestwood, NY: St. Vladimir's Seminary Press, 1979), 217-27, esp. 223.

27. Schmemann, 'The World as Sacrament,' 227.

its being grants us a love which guarantees us eternal love and mediates the communication of that love.'[28]

Once again, the doctrine of creation *ex nihilo* underscores the undeserved nature of God's love, His voluntary condescension to humans. As Aquinas observes: 'The fact of saying that God made all things by his Word excludes the error of those who say that God produced things by necessity. When we say that in him there is a procession of love, we show that God produced creatures not because he needed them, nor because of any other extrinsic reason, but on account of the love of his own goodness.' That God, for example, created light and then declared that it was good was proof, according to Aquinas, of the divine love.[29] God bathed Adam and Eve in love by giving them the gift of His creation, a sacramental reflection of His very being, and in a sense, a giving of Himself to them. Such a self-giving finds its formal meeting place in the covenant that God made with Adam.

Covenant and Love

The third pillar of rightly understanding pre-fall anthropology and the relationship between Adam's work and reward is factoring the covenant between God and Adam. Within the modern period critics of the covenant of works have decried the early modern doctrine for supposedly confusing the categories of contract and covenant, the former being legal and the latter promissory. Part I explored these claims and demonstrated that they were unsound because of a failure to read carefully primary source texts and importing a modern notion of contract into early modern texts. Part II also surveyed a number of biblical texts to show how necessary it is to read the creation account within the broader context of the Pentateuch, especially against the backdrop of Deuteronomy, Israel's covenantal charter. Within the context of Deuteronomy, the themes of covenant, law, and love coalesce. These subjects converge both in Deuteronomy as well as in Genesis 1–2. Recognizing the connection between covenant and love is vital to Adam's pre-fall anthropology and the nature of his work.

---

28. Dumitru Staniloae, 'The World as Gift and Sacrament of God's Love,' *Sorbonost* 9 (1969): 662-73, esp. 666.

29. Aquinas, *Summa Theologica*, Ia q. 32 art. 1.

Deuteronomy contains Israel's covenantal commission: 'Hear, O Israel: The LORD our God, the Lord is one. You shall love the LORD your God with all your heart and with all your soul and with all your might. And these words that I command you today shall be on your heart' (Deut. 6:4-6). It may strike modern readers as odd that God would command His people to love Him, but the cognitive dissonance has to do with contemporary misunderstandings of the nature of love and an unfamiliarity with the biblical concept. In the contemporary period notions of love have been predominated by an incomplete and feminized perspective by connecting love with emotion and feeling rather than with concrete action.[30] To be sure, there are affective aspects of love, but its primary characteristic is action, not feeling. William Moran compares the covenant of Deuteronomy against the background of Ancient Near Eastern literature and comes to the following observation:

> Love in Deuteronomy is a love that can be commanded. It is also a love intimately related to fear and reverence. Above all, it is a love which must be expressed in loyalty, in service, and in unqualified obedience to the demands of the Law. For to love God is, in answer to a unique claim (6:4), to be loyal to him (11:1, 22; 30:20), to walk in his ways (10:12; 11:22; 19:9; 30:16), to keep his commandments (10:12; 11:1, 22; 19:9), to do them (11:22; 19:9), to heed them or his voice (11:13; 30:16), to serve him (10:12; 11:1, 13). It is in brief, a love defined by and pledged in the covenant – a covenantal love.[31]

This description of Israel's obligation to love God characterizes all of God's covenants with His people, whether with Adam in the garden, Israel at Sinai or in the promised land, or with His people in the new covenant. Christ, for example, cites the *Shema* when asked what the greatest commandment is (Matt. 22:37-38). Jesus, moreover, quite succinctly states: 'If you love me, you will keep my commandments' (John 14:15). Thus, the covenantal love of God means following His commandments and walking in His

---

30. Francesca M. Cancian, 'The Feminization of Love,' *Signs* 11/4 (1976): 692-709.

31. William L. Moran, 'The Ancient Near Eastern Background of the Love of God in Deuteronomy,' *CBQ* 25/1 (1963): 77-87, esp. 78.

ways.[32] Covenantal obedience becomes acts of personal fidelity, faithfulness to the personal God and not just the right things to do.[33] As noted in earlier chapters, Adam's chief failure was one of love. He idolatrously loved himself more than his covenant Lord. Coordinating covenant, law, and love sets important contextual parameters for understanding Adam's pre-fall anthropology and the relationship between his work and reward.

In terms of Adam's pre-fall anthropology, the covenant is the space in which God pours out His love upon His servant but it is also the same stage on which Adam was supposed to return God's love. God manifests His love to Adam both by giving him the gift of creation and by entering into a covenant with him, a covenant in which Adam is clearly the inferior party. God first loved Adam so that Adam could then love God by obeying His commands.[34] In this vein medieval rabbi Rashi (1040-1105) explains the nature of service to God that is relevant to the Adamic context: 'You should not say, "I will carry out the commandments of my Creator so that He will supply me with all my needs," but, instead, serve out of love.'[35] The last Adam takes up the failed work of the first, and His own obedience to the Father helps us to understand what Adam's obedience was supposed to be: 'As the Father has loved me, so have I loved you. Abide in my love. If you keep my commandments, you will abide in my love, just as I have kept my Father's commandments and abide in his love' (John 15:9-10). The covenant of works, therefore, was God's call to Adam to love Him. Adam's reward of eternal life was never a cold *quid pro quo* but rather it was supposed to be God the Father's gift to Adam, His son (Luke 3:38). Jon Levenson's comments about covenantal punishment and reward apply both to Israel and to Adam when he writes: 'The selfless disregard of reward brings the greatest reward. There is room for reward and punishment within a structure of

---

32. Jon D. Levenson, *The Love of God: Divine Gift, Human Gratitude, and Mutual Faithfulness in Judaism* (Princeton, NJ: Princeton University Press, 2016), 13.

33. Levenson, *The Love of God*, 14.

34. Similarly, Levenson, *The Love of God*, 61.

35. As cited in Levenson, *The Love of God*, 67; see also Vos, 'Doctrine of the Love of God,' 7.

covenantal love, but there is no room for genuine covenantal love premised on reward and punishment alone.'[36] Covenant and love set the context for obedience and reward.

Love and covenant also address matters related to Adam's desires. One of the chief places that speaks of love and desire is the Song of Songs. To appeal to the Song of Songs may seem odd but there are intra-canonical connections between Genesis 1–3 and the Song that provide an inter-textual explanation of Adam's relationship to God in the pre-fall context. Establishing the Genesis-Song of Songs connection requires a few brief exegetical observations.[37] First, Song of Songs has a preponderance of garden imagery, which echoes the garden of Eden (Song 4:12, 15, 16; 5:1; 6:2; 8:13).[38] Second, God's presence dictates that the garden is the first earthly temple.[39] The garden, of course, was filled with every kind of tree that was 'pleasant to the sight and good for food' (Gen. 2:9, 15), a visual theme repeated in the subsequent Solomonic temple (1 Kings 6:18; 7:18-19), and one that appears in the Song of Songs (1:17; 2:16; 3:9-10; 4:3). Third, the over-arching narrative of the Song is that the relationship between husband and wife gives concrete expression to the marital bond between God and His people, whether with Adam and Eve in the garden of Eden, Israel in the land of promise (e.g. Hosea), or Christ and His bride, the church.[40] As the apostle Paul comments regarding the marriage between Adam and Eve (Gen. 2:7), 'This mystery is profound, and I am saying that it refers to Christ and the church'

---

36. Levenson, *The Love of God*, 68.

37. For what follows, see Ellen Davis, 'Reading the Song Iconographically,' in *Scrolls of Love: Ruth and Song of Songs*, ed. Peter S. Hawkins and Lesleigh Cushing Stahlberg (New York: Fordham University Press, 2006), 172-84.

38. Iain Duguid, *The Song of Songs*, TOTC (Downers Grove, IL: IVP Academic, 2015), 40, 118.

39. See G. K. Beale, *The Temple and the Church's Mission: A Biblical Theology of the Dwelling Place of God* (Downers Grove, IL: InterVarsity Press, 2004); J. V. Fesko, *Last Things First: Unlocking Genesis with the Christ of Eschatology* (Fearn: Mentor, 2007), 57-76; L. Michael Morales, *Cult and Cosmos: Tilting Toward a Temple-Centered Theology* (Leuven: Peeters, 2014).

40. Similarly, Levenson, *The Love of God*, 133, 134; see also Duguid, *Song of Songs*, 41, 80.

(Eph. 5:32). Fourth, the Song portrays an idealized marriage, that which existed between Adam and Eve in the initial creation, and that which should ultimately exist between God and His people.

Given the connections between Genesis 1–3 and the Song, there are two exegetical factors that inform the nature of Adam's relationship to God. The Song does not speak in terms of obedience and disobedience but in terms of intimacy and its potential loss. Adam and Eve lost the intimacy they had with God prior to their fall into sin. Their sin disrupted the harmony that existed between them and God, as bride and husband, the concord that Adam and Eve had with one another, and the peace that existed between them and the creation. In the wake of the fall, God cast Adam and Eve into exile given their breach of the covenant. There was discord between Adam and Eve; Adam tried to blame Eve for his sin (Gen. 3:12). And sin brought disharmony between humans and the creation (Gen. 3:16). The Song, therefore, provides a retrospective echo of Eden that prospectively projects into the future and anticipates a restored connection between God and His people through Christ. This redemption restores the ruptured relationships between God and man, husband and wife, and humanity and creation.

But a second exegetical factor is the Song's description of the desire that exists between the husband and her bride. We read in Songs 7:10, 'I am my beloved's, and his desire is for me.' The term *desire* (תשוקה) is a deliberate echo of Eve's cursed desire for Adam, 'Your desire shall be contrary to your husband' (Gen. 3:16). The Song inverts and restores the desire between husband and wife to its proper pre-fall state.[41] Adam's desire should have been for his bride within the covenant of works – his love for God should have become manifest in his love for his wife. Related to this theme of desire is the woman's repeated phrase in the Song, *whom my soul loves*. This phrase first appears in chapter 1: 'Tell me, you whom my soul loves, where you pasture your flock' (v. 7)? It then materializes four more times in rapid succession in chapter 3:

> On my bed by night I sought him whom my soul loves; I sought him, but found him not. I will rise now and go about the city, in

---

41. Duguid, *Song of Songs*, 147.

the streets and in the squares; I will seek him whom my soul loves. I sought him, but found him not. The watchmen found me as they went about in the city. 'Have you seen him whom my soul loves?' Scarcely had I passed them when I found him whom my soul loves. I held him, and would not let him go until I had brought him into my mother's house, and into the chamber of her who conceived me (vv. 1-4).

The bride's search for her husband by describing him to the watchmen as 'him whom my soul loves' hardly meets the criteria for a missing person's report. This phrase, however, echoes the description of one person: 'You shall love the Lord your God with all your heart and *with all your soul* and with all your might' (Deut. 6:5, emphasis). The Song echoes the first and greatest commandment in its idealized presentation of the marriage relationship between God and His people, a love and desire that was supposed to mark Adam and Eve's love for God. This means that Adam's desire for God and the beatific vision was a natural correlate given his status as an image-bearer and covenant servant. Moreover, as the representative of the bride of God, Adam was supposed to adorn himself with obedience, 'as a bride adorns herself with her jewels' (Isa. 61:10; cf. Ezek. 16:11-13; 1 Pet. 3:3-5).[42]

Summary

Claiming that God gave Adam grace in the pre-fall context may be one way to account for the creator-creature relationship, but a preferable way takes the Adamic anthropology and contextualizes it within the matrix of covenant, law, and love. Reading the Adamic covenant within the framework of Deuteronomy and the close associations between love and obedience illuminates the importance of love for understanding the nature of Adam's work and reward. Within this covenantal context God voluntarily condescends to Adam and showers him with gifts in the creation, a sacramental manifestation of His love. God gave of Himself in love to Adam and looked for Adam to return this love to Him. As Vos notes: 'What God desires of His people is that they shall answer to the love which

---

42. Similarly, Levenson, *Love of God*, 138-39.

He bears them with a like affection.[43] In loving and obeying his covenant Lord, Adam would have received the reward of eternal life. Adam did not require God's grace to accomplish this obedience, as he was unfallen and very good. As Martin Luther (1483-1546) rightly observes: 'Righteousness was not a gift which came from without, separate from man's nature, but that it was truly part of his nature, so that it was Adam's nature to love God, to believe God, to know God, etc. These things were just as natural for Adam as it is natural for the eyes to receive light.'[44] The Song of Songs casts light upon Genesis 1–3 and reveals that it was natural for Adam to desire and love God. Factoring God's love and benevolence for Adam sets the stage for a better understanding regarding how Adam could secure eternal life through his obedience.

Merit

The concept of merit is complicated and fraught with many twists and turns. Roman Catholics have historically employed the distinction between *condign* and *congruent* merit. In the simplest of terms, condign merit is when a person actually secures a reward because he has earned it outright. Conversely, congruent merit is when God grades a person's work on a curve; he has not actually earned the reward in a strict sense, but God nevertheless rewards the effort as if he did.[45] Only Christ merits salvation condignly whereas God rewards believers congruently. Historically, Reformed theologians have rejected this distinction. The Westminster Confession, for example, states:

> We cannot by our best works merit pardon of sin, or eternal life at the hand of God, by reason of the great disproportion that is between them and the glory to come; and the infinite distance that is between us and God, whom, by them, we can neither profit, nor satisfy for the debt of our former sins, but when we have done all we can, we have done but our duty, and are unprofitable servants:

---

43. Vos, 'Doctrine of the Love of God,' 16.

44. Martin Luther, *Lectures on Genesis*, comm. Gen. 3:7, in LW 1:165.

45. See Muller, *Dictionary*, s. v. *meritum de condigno, meritum de congruo* (pp. 217-18); also Aquinas, *Summa Theologica*, IaIIae qq. 111, 114.

and because, as they are good, they proceed from his Spirit; and as they are wrought by us, they are defiled, and mixed with so much weakness and imperfection, that they cannot endure the severity of God's judgment (XVI.v; cf. WLC q. 193).

In their sin-fallen state believers cannot merit pardon, whether condignly or congruently. Why? Because of several factors: (1) the great distance between God and the creature; (2) at best we are unprofitable servants; (3) good works ultimately proceed from the Spirit; and (4) our good works are mixed with sin.

In more technical terms, Westminster divine Obadiah Sedgwick (1600-1658) explains the nature of merit before God and that it must be an:

1. *Opus indebitum*: the work must be more than what is required.

2. *Opus perfectum*: it must be a perfect work.

3. *Opus infinitum*: a work of infinite value and worth.

Given these three requirements, the only person that can merit anything is Jesus.[46] Reformed theologians generally follow this pattern and regularly invoke *merit* to characterize the work of Christ. The Belgic Confession (1561) states that believers by true faith embrace Jesus 'with all his merits' (XXII) and that they do not claim anything for themselves or their merits (XXIII). Likewise, 'we do good works, but not for merit – for what would we merit?' And the only place to rest is on the 'merit of the suffering and death of our Savior' (XXIV). Similar statements appear in the Canons of Dort (1618-19).[47] Reformed theologians such as William Perkins (1558-1602) argue that merit is any work that secures God's favor and everlasting life and that merit is absolutely necessary to secure salvation, but that Christ is the only root and fountain of all merit.[48] Other Reformed theologians such as Zacharias Ursinus

---

46. Obadiah Sedgwick, *The Bowels of Tender Mercy Sealed in the Everlasting Covenant* (London: Edward Mottershed, 1661), II.v.1 (p. 460).

47. See Canons of Dort, II, rej. of errors, 1, 3, 4; V.8.

48. William Perkins, *A Reformed Catholike* (London: John Legat, 1598), 102-03.

(1534-1583) make similar claims.[49] There is a sense in which the Reformed agree with Roman Catholics, in that they acknowledge the possibility of condign merit but that only Christ can offer it; but they reject the category of congruent merit. While these discussions about merit pertain to the post-fall context, Reformed theologians often carry them into the covenant of works. Adam could not merit eternal life because of the distance between God and the creature and thus Reformed theologians speak of the necessity of God's grace as Part I has documented.[50]

A shift occurred, however, once discussions about the pre-fall context began to factor the doctrine of the covenant. As noted in Part I, the Westminster Confession's language of voluntary condescension harmonizes with the claim that Adam required God's grace but it does not necessitate it. Instead, it also accommodates the idea that Adam's obedience and reward were *ex pacto*. That is, one need not enter the labyrinth of whether God had to elevate Adam's nature, obedience, or explain complex notions of what constitutes merit. The doctrine of the covenant can cut the Gordian knot by factoring three key elements set within the context of God's love and the gift of creation. First, God freely gives the creation and covenant; He creates *ex nihilo*, which stresses the creator-creature distinction and the inequality of the covenanting parties. Adam is not God's equal. Second, God sets the terms of the covenant. This is not a question of condign or congruent merit. That is, has Adam offered a work that is not required, perfect, and infinite, to borrow Sedgwick's description? To say that a work must be infinite

---

49. Zacharias Ursinus, *The Commentary of Dr. Zacharias Ursinus on the Heidelberg Catechism*, trans. G. W. Williard (rep.; Phillipsburg, NJ: P & R, n.d.), 485-88.

50. Part I's survey ended with early modern views, but the trend persists among modern Reformed theologians. See, e.g., Robert L. Dabney, *Syllabus and Notes of the Course of Systematic and Polemic Theology*, 3rd ed. (Asbury Park, NJ: Presbyterian Publishing Company, 1885), 302; Anthony Hoekema, *Created in God's Image* (Grand Rapids: Eerdmans, 1986), 119; John Murray, 'Adamic Administration,' in *Collected Writings of John Murray*, vol. 2 (Edinburgh: Banner of Truth, 1977), 49, 56; Michael D. Williams, *Far as the Curse is Found: The Covenant Story of Redemption* (Phillipsburg, NJ: P & R, 2005), 72-74. Cf. Charles Hodge, *Systematic Theology*, 3 vols. (rep.; Grand Rapids: Eerdmans, 1993), II:364-65.

and therefore proportionate to the infinite reward fails to account for the free nature of the covenant. God has set the terms and has stipulated that He will reward a finite work of obedience with an infinite reward. This is not a question of a finite creature somehow indebting an infinite creator. Rather, God has benevolently lavished love upon Adam and thus his reward ultimately rests in the cradle of the liberality of God's promise, not in the worthiness of Adam's obedience. Third, rather than speak of pre-fall infused habits, super added gifts, or the necessity of God's grace, a preferable route is to recover a trinitarian understanding of the covenant of works. This third and final point invites further exposition.

If love characterizes the covenant of works as I have argued above, then this naturally summons the person and work of the Holy Spirit as a vital participant. The apostle John clearly and succinctly states, 'God is love' (1 John 4:8), so recognizing that the triune God is love is supremely biblical. At the same time, theologians have historically argued that the Holy Spirit is the bond of love among the Trinity.[51] The Father predestines the elect in love (Eph. 1:4-5); He sent His Son in love (John 3:16; Rom. 5:8). And Christ's outpouring of the Spirit at Pentecost was equally an outpouring of love: 'God's love has been poured into our hearts through the Holy Spirit who has been given to us' (Rom. 5:5; cf. Titus 3:5-6; Acts 2:17). It stands to reason, then, that within the pre-temporal covenant of redemption, the Father's oath to give His Son the Spirit to carry out His mission as covenant surety was a promise to anoint Him with love.[52] The Father poured out the Spirit and anointed Him in love that Christ might render His obedience in love, and this loving obedience gave the Son the right to unleash the outpouring

---

51. Augustine, *On the Trinity*, VI.v, in NPNF[1] III:100; Aquinas, *Summa Theologica*, Ia q. 37 art. 2. See also, Coffey, 'Holy Spirit as the Mutual,' 193-229; Dimitru Staniloae, *Theology and the Church* (Crestwood: St. Vladimir's Seminary Press, 1980), 96; Boris Bobrinskoy, 'The Filioque Yesterday and Today,' in *Spirit of God, Spirit of Christ: Ecumenical Reflections on the Filioque Controversy*, ed., Lukas Vischer (London: SPCK, 1981), 142-43.

52. For a detailed explanation of the covenant of redemption and the Spirit's role, see J. V. Fesko, *The Trinity and the Covenant of Redemption* (Fearn: Mentor, 2016), 143-94, 319-26.

of the Spirit, another manifestation of trinitarian love. The Father promised to anoint His Son with the Spirit in order to equip Him for His mission, that He might have the requisite gifts to carry out His role as Messiah and covenant surety.[53] We can also say that the Spirit's willingness to be the one to anoint the Son was also the Spirit's expression of love for the Son.

The complex of biblical passages that speak to the Messiah's anointing with the Holy Spirit are naturally relevant. The Father would anoint the Son with a Spirit of wisdom, understanding, counsel, might, knowledge, and especially the 'fear of the LORD' (Isa. 11:2).[54] The fear of the Lord is the beginning of wisdom and knowledge (Ps. 111:10; Prov. 1:7; 9:10), a fountain of life (Prov. 14:26-27), and the motivating factor behind obedience, *hesed*, or covenant love and faithfulness (Prov. 16:6; Exod. 20:20), the reward for which is 'riches and honor and life' (Prov. 22:4; cf. 19:23; 3:16; 15:33; 18:12; 1 Kings 3:12-14).[55] Noteworthy is the fact that the Spirit-anointed Servant would possess the fear of Yahweh. Isaiah invokes the tetragrammaton, the covenant name of God, which has connections to God's law (Exod. 3:14).[56] The Servant's anointing with the Spirit means that He would, with all certainty, yield His life in loving obedience to the will of His heavenly Father. The anointing of the Spirit burst onto the scene of redemptive history when the Father poured out the Spirit upon His Son at His baptism at the Jordan. In the wake of the rending of the heavens, Christ read Isaiah: 'The Spirit of the Lord GOD is upon me, because the LORD has anointed me to bring good news to the poor' (Isa. 61:1; Luke 4:18-21).[57] That Christ

---

53. For the Spirit's participation in Christ's mission, see John Owen, *Pneumatologia: A Discourse Concerning the Holy Spirit*, in *The Works of John Owen*, 16 vols. (1850-53; Edinburgh: Banner of Truth, 1994), III:162-83.

54. J. Alec Motyer, *The Prophecy of Isaiah: An Introduction and Commentary* (Downers Grove: InterVarsity, 1993), 122.

55. Bruce K. Waltke, *The Book of Proverbs*, 2 vols., NICOT (Grand Rapids: Eerdmans, 2005), I:202-03; cf. Edward J. Young, *The Book of Isaiah*, 3 vols., NICOT (Grand Rapids: Eerdmans, 1965), I:383.

56. Tremper Longman, *Proverbs*, BCOTWS (Grand Rapids: Baker, 2006), 101.

57. David W. Pao, *Acts and the Isaianic New Exodus* (Grand Rapids: Baker, 2000), 70-84.

read this passage and claimed to fulfill it meant He was conscious of His messianic character, mission, and pneumatic anointing.[58]

Historically, the Reformed tradition has acknowledged the Spirit's role in the work of Christ evident in this summary statement from the Westminster Confession:

> The Lord Jesus, in his human nature thus united to the divine, was sanctified, and anointed with the Holy Spirit, above measure, having in him all the treasures of wisdom and knowledge; in whom it pleased the Father that all fullness should dwell; to the end that, being holy, harmless, undefiled, and full of grace and truth, he might be thoroughly furnished to execute the office of a mediator, and surety (WCF VIII.iii).

In short, the last Adam carried out His ministry and work in the power of the Spirit.[59] The Spirit-Son connection illuminates the nature of Adam's state in the garden because of several factors. First, the covenant of works is the mirror image of the *pactum salutis*, as it is a typological portrait of the Son's threefold office (prophet, priest, and king) and work as surety in the covenant of grace. The covenant of redemption and its fulfillment in the covenant of grace bookend the covenant of works:

Covenant of Redemption	Covenant of Works	Covenant of Grace
God promises to anoint the Son with the Spirit to equip Him with the requisite gifts to carry out His mission (e.g., Isa. 42:1; 61:1-3).	Adam is a type of the one who is to come (Rom. 5:14).	The Father anoints the Son with the Spirit at His baptism (Matt. 3:16-17; Luke 4:16-21).

On either side we find the promise to anoint the Son with the Spirit to carry out His mission and the Father's anointing of the Son. Second, recall Paul's designation of Adam as a type of the

---

58. Geerhardus Vos, *The Self-Disclosure of Jesus: The Modern Debate about the Messianic Consciousness* (Phillipsburg: P & R, 1953), 114.

59. See Bavinck, *Reformed Dogmatics*, III:290-95; Vos, *Reformed Dogmatics*, III:56-60. Note, Vos speaks of 'habitual graces or gifts.' The latter term *gifts* is preferable given what I have argued in this chapter.

one to come (Rom. 5:14). The connections between the persons and works of Adam and Christ find their verbal linkage in the fact that Paul calls Jesus the *last Adam* (1 Cor. 15:45). Third, God does not re-write Adam's vocation but rather sends Jesus, the faithful last Adam, to fulfill his abandoned work.

Given the Adam-Christ connections and the Spirit's role in Christ's ministry, it seems that the better way to account for the relationship between Adam's obedience and reward is factoring the Holy Spirit's role in the covenant of works. Rather than appealing to the *donum superadditum* or grace, we should instead coordinate covenant and Spirit. That is, God promised to reward Adam's obedience by virtue of the covenant. But we must first account for Adam's reception of the Spirit, particularly as it relates to the image of God. The triune God executed the work of creation; the Father sent the Son and Spirit to carry out this work (John 1:1-4; Col. 1:15-17). The opening words of Genesis attest to the work of the Spirit: 'The earth was without form and void, and darkness was over the face of the deep. And the Spirit of God was hovering over the face of the waters' (Gen. 1:2). Latter portions of the Old Testament echo the tandem work of the Son and Spirit: 'By the word of the LORD the heavens were made, and by the Spirit of his mouth all their host' (Ps. 33:6, trans. mine). God's Word and breath, His *nephesh* or *pneumati* (LXX), 'Spirit' created the heavens and earth.[60] Similarly Job attests to the Spirit's role: 'By his Spirit [ברוחו] the heavens were made fair' (Job 26:13, trans. mine). Elihu echoes the creation of Adam when he professes: 'The Spirit of God has made me, and the breath of the Almighty gives me life' (Job 33:4). Likewise, the Psalmist attests to the cosmic work of the Spirit: 'When you send forth your Spirit, they are created, and you renew the face of the ground' (Ps. 104:30). Regarding the magnitude of the creation, Isaiah proclaims: 'Who has measured the Spirit of the LORD, or what man shows him his counsel?' (Isa. 40:13). This canonical witness testifies to the fact that the Spirit played a significant role in the creation, and thus His role must be factored in the covenant of works.[61]

---

60. Abraham Kuyper, *The Work of the Holy Spirit*, trans. Henri De Vries (New York: Funk & Wagnalls, 1900), 24.

61. Kuyper, *Holy Spirit*, 27.

To this end, the Genesis account reveals the specific connection to Adam in his creation. Just as Elihu recognized that the Spirit made him, and the breath of the Almighty gave him life, we see the first instance of the Spirit giving Adam life when God formed him from the dust of the earth: 'Then the LORD God formed the man of dust from the ground and breathed into his nostrils the breath of life, and the man became a living creature' (Gen. 2:7). The synonymous parallelism in Job 33:4 and similar statements in Psalm 33:6 confirm that God breathed the Spirit into Adam, which resulted in the gift of life. Echoing Genesis 2:7 and Job 33:4, Jesus performed a living parable when He breathed upon His disciples: 'Peace be with you. As the Father has sent me, even so I am sending you. And when he had said this, breathed on them and said to them, "Receive the Holy Spirit"' (John 20:21-22).[62] God was creating the new heavens and earth through the Spirit and the last Adam, but this creative activity has its precedence in the Son's and Spirit's first work of creation both in the cosmos at large and in the microcosmic creation of Adam.[63]

The Spirit participated in giving to Adam the image of God, as the Genesis narrative explains: 'Then God said, "Let us make man in our image, after our likeness"' (Gen. 1:26). The 'us' of this statement is not a plural of majesty, or God speaking to His heavenly court, even though, of course, the angels attend the triune God in the celestial court, but rather this is intra-trinitarian dialogue.[64] The triune God created and impressed His image and likeness into the first man, which means by his immediate creation Adam received the divine image, a likeness that was natural, intact, whole, holy, righteous, and desirous of eternal communion with the source of his image, the triune God. While the triune God created Adam, the inbreathing of life was especially the work of the Spirit.[65] In

---

62. Kuyper, *Holy Spirit*, 29, 34.

63. Contra Calvin, who argues that God merely animated Adam with His breath; Calvin knowingly disagreed with the 'ancients,' or church fathers on this point (John Calvin, *Genesis* [rep.; Grand Rapids: Baker Book House, 1993], comm. Gen. 2:7).

64. See the Excursus on Genesis 1:26 at the end of this chapter.

65. Kuyper, *Holy Spirit*, 35-36.

this matter, Clement of Alexandria (150-215) makes an important observation when he writes: 'The love-charm is within the human being – that which indeed is called a breath of God.'[66] God gave Adam His very own Spirit, which forms a tangible communion between Adam and his maker. The protological indwelling of the Spirit attracted Adam to God and gave him the desire for the *visio Dei*, or the beatific vision. As Presbyterian theologian and New Testament scholar, George Smeaton (1814-1889), observes: 'Adam had the Spirit in the state of integrity, not only for himself, but for his seed; and he walked after the Spirit as long as he stood in his integrity.'[67] The Spirit's protological indwelling was also the most intimate of bonds between Adam and the triune God. Factoring Adam's communion with the Spirit is essential for rightly assessing the efficacy of Adam's obedience. Adam was the subject of divine complacency in his sinless nature and a temple of the Holy Spirit. Again, Smeaton rightly avers: 'The deep ground-thought presupposed by Christianity is, that Adam had the divine image and life from the Spirit of Life. It follows, accordingly, that the elements were already deposited in him by which he was in a position to reach the full perfection of his being, as he was.'[68]

Adam's responsibility was to love God in the power of the Spirit. John Owen (1616-1683) maintains:

> Adam may be said to have had the Spirit of God in his innocency. He had him in these peculiar effects of his power and goodness; and he had him according to the tenor of that covenant whereby it was possible that he should utterly lose him, as accordingly it came to pass. He had him not by especial inhabitation, for the whole world was then the temple of God. In the covenant of grace, founded in the person and on the mediation of Christ, it is otherwise.[69]

---

66. Clement of Alexandria, *Pedagougus*, I.iii, in ANF, II:211; see also Nonna Verna Harrison, 'The Human Person as Image and Likeness of God,' in *The Cambridge Companion to Orthodox Christian Theology*, ed. Mary B. Cunningham and Elizabeth Theokritoff (Cambridge: Cambridge University Press, 2008), 79.

67. George Smeaton, *The Doctrine of the Holy Spirit* (Edinburgh: T & T Clark, 1882), 11.

68. Smeaton, *Holy Spirit*, 12.

69. Owen, *Pneumatologia*, in *Works*, III:102-03.

Owen's statement requires some nuance, as the entire world was not the temple of God. Rather, the garden was the temple and Adam was supposed to expand the garden-temple order throughout the entire world.[70] This garden-expansion work lies at the heart of the covenant of works: be fruitful, fill all the earth, and subdue it (Gen. 1:28). But Owen makes an insightful point when he distinguishes between Adam's protological possession of the Spirit and our eschatological reception of the Spirit in the covenant of grace. He does not use the specific terminology, but he differentiates between protology and eschatology. The first Adam had a protological dispensation of the Spirit whereas the last Adam bestows the gift of the eschatological Spirit. Stated in simpler terms, Christ places believers on a higher plane than Adam; He does not return us to the garden but places us in the new creation (2 Cor. 5:17; Gal. 6:15).

Owen's congregational colleague, Thomas Goodwin (1600-1680), makes similar insights regarding the Spirit's role in the covenant of works:

> Adam had the Spirit as well as we, and the Holy Ghost was at the making of him, and wrote the image of God upon his heart; for where holiness was, we may be sure the Spirit was too. The Holy Ghost was at that consultation—'Let us make man'—and one of the *us* spoken unto. Yea, and that Spirit that 'moved upon the waters,' who also is sent forth to 'renew the face of the earth' (Ps. 104), the same Spirit was in Adam's heart to assist his graces, and cause them to flow and bring forth, and to move him to live according to those principles of life given him.[71]

Like Owen, Goodwin coordinates creation and the image of God as constituent elements of the covenant of works but links them to the work of the Spirit. He also rightly distinguishes between the protological and eschatological states.

Lest one confound the covenants of works and grace, he stipulates that Adam had the Spirit by condition whereas we receive Him by irrevocable promise:

---

70. Beale, *Temple and the Church's Mission*, 81-122.

71. Thomas Goodwin, *The Work of the Holy Ghost in Our Salvation*, in *The Works of Thomas Goodwin* (1861-66; Eureka, CA: Tanski Publications, 1996), VI:54.

Hence Adam retained the Spirit according to the tenor of the covenants (which is but that equal law of creation between God and the creature), whereby he held a continuance of the privileges given him at the creation, even as he did life in God's sight, upon works of obedience: 'Do this and live.' And as by one act of disobedience he forfeited life ('Cursed is he that continueth not in all things'), and so in like manner the Spirit was forfeited by him upon the same terms. Even as in a man that comes from Adam, one mortal stab causeth the soul to depart, so here, one act of sinning cause the soul to depart; for the bond of the union ceased .... The gift of the Spirit, to a truly converted soul, is an absolute gift, and not upon conditions on our parts, but to work and maintain in us what God requires of us. The gift of the Spirit is not founded upon qualifications in us, to continue so long as we preserve grace in our souls, and do not sin it away.[72]

Goodwin's explanation is beneficial because he incorporates the work of the Spirit in the covenant of works and preserves the parallels between Adam and the last Adam; he also notes the differences concerning the protological and eschatological states. More will be said about this below, but correlating the Spirit's work in the covenants of works and grace is the difference between God's unmerited love and benevolence in an unfallen world and His demerited grace and mercy in response to sin.

Summary

Theologians have appealed to super added gifts, grace, and condign and congruent merit, to account for the disparity between creator and creature, how a creature can attain an infinite reward through finite obedience. Appealing to grace in the pre-fall context is understandable but it seems that the better approach is to acknowledge the goodness of Adam's creation and that it was perfectly natural for him to love and desire God because he was made in His image. God benevolently showered him with His abundant love, evident in the world created *ex nihilo* and His covenantal bond, a realm where God revealed His own *hesed* through the Holy Spirit, their bond of union and communion. God would extravagantly reward Adam's labors because

---

72. Goodwin, *The Work of the Holy Ghost*, VI:55.

He loved him, and the extravagance of this reward was due to God's promise and magnanimity, not the intrinsic value of Adam's obedience. Smeaton's assessment of Adam's status as an imager-bearer is salient: 'The representations of man from a Biblical point of view are to the effect that he had, from the first, realized and formed within him the divine idea to such an extent that he needed nothing more than the required probation in order to his being confirmed, and then exalted to an immensely higher degree, according to the promised reward.'[73] In spite of all of this, Adam loved himself more than his faithful covenant Lord and plunged the world into darkness. Blessedly, his apostasy was not the last word as God promised that one like the Son of Man, a son of Adam, would faithfully fulfill his failed work – the last Adam would love His Father more than Himself.

Potential Objections

Some might object to sidestepping the concept of grace to explain pre-fall anthropology and the nature of the Creator-creature relationship. Given the appeal to the concept among both Roman Catholic and Reformed theologians, why remove the idea? There are two chief reasons for drawing on divine love and gift rather than grace in the pre-fall context.

First, as noted above, to appeal to the *donum superadditum* to overcome the supposed imbalance between flesh and spirit implies that there is a defect in humanity's initial creation, which fails to recognize the significance of the unfallen image of God. Reformed theologians therefore rightly reject the *donum superadditum* but still nonetheless appeal to grace to explain the creator-creature divide. Most simply invoke the concept and rarely explain what they mean by it. John Owen, however, is an exception to this general rule. Owen argued that Adam's obedience had to be undergirded by grace given its disproportion to the reward.[74] But Owen also acknowledged that the two covenants contained different degrees of

---

73. Smeaton, *Holy Spirit*, 14.

74. John Owen, *An Exposition of the Epistle to the Hebrews*, vol. 6, in *The Works of John Owen*, vol. 22, ed. William H. Goold (1855; Edinburgh: Banner of Truth, 2010), 69.

grace. The covenant of grace is 'ordered in all things,' which means that it contains everything necessary to ensure the salvation of the elect. By contrast, 'The first covenant with Adam was ordered in grace, but not in all grace; it was ordered in righteousness, holiness, and innocency, but not ordered in the grace of perseverance: and failing in that grace, the whole covenant failed.'[75] One can re-state Owen's point by saying that the grace of the covenant of works is resistible and ineffectual, as Adam disobeyed and fell; conversely, the grace of the covenant of grace is irresistible and effectual because the elect receive the gift of perseverance. Moreover, the grace of the covenant of works comes apart from the mediator, whereas the grace of the covenant of grace comes through Christ. The grace of the covenant of works, then, is quite different than the grace of the covenant of grace. At a minimum, if one invokes pre-fall grace, he should explain all of these qualifications so the differences between the two types of grace are clear. But why appeal to such a highly qualified concept of grace when invoking God's love and benevolence is the shorter, simpler, and straighter path?

Second, in the wake of the theology of Barth greater clarity regarding pre-fall grace is necessary because of the radically Christocentric nature of his claims. Barth rejected the covenant of works because it supposedly corrupted the story of redemption with anthropocentrism. In reference to the covenant of works, Barth writes:

> This is that biblical exegesis had been invaded by a mode of thought in which this history, however extraordinary the course it took, could only unfold itself and therefore only begin as the history of man and his works, man who is good by nature and who is therefore in covenant with God – a God who pledged to him by virtue of his goodness. To this mode of thinking it became more and more foreign to think of the history as conversely the history of God and His works, the God who originally turns to man in grace, and therefore as from the very first the history of the covenant of grace.[76]

---

75. Owen, 'Everlasting Covenant,' IX:419.

76. Karl Barth, *Church Dogmatics*, 14 vols., eds. G. W. Bromiley and T. F. Torrance (Edinburgh: T & T Clark, 1936-68), IV/1:62.

Barth believed that the covenant of works turned the church's gaze away from the Father's grace in Christ and instead erroneously focused it on humanity. Barth therefore swept away the covenant of works and everything associated with it such as natural law – there is no law inherent in humans or written in the cosmos.[77] In his assessment, natural law like the covenant of works destroyed the grace of God.[78]

In Barth's mind, the only manner by which God deals with humans is through the covenant of grace, or exclusively through Christ. God makes this one covenant with Adam even in his pre-fall state, the patriarchs, Abraham, and the people of Israel.[79] Although, one should note that Barth all but denied the historicity of Adam:

> Adam has no existence on the plane of history and of psychological analysis. He exists as the first Adam, as the type of the second Adam who is to come, as the shadow cast by His light. He exists as the 'Moment' which forms the background from which Christ advances to victory, the scene where the world and mankind are transformed from fall to righteousness, from death to life, and from old to new. Adam has no separate, positive existence. He does not revolve round his own pole; he is not a second factor. He exists only when he is dissolved, and he is affirmed only when in Christ he is brought to naught.[80]

Barth believed that Genesis 1–11 was *saga*, which means that it is not history.[81] For Barth, creation was simply the external aspect of the covenant of grace, by which he ultimately reduced Adam to non-being.[82] Adam is only a literary, a-historical precursor to Christ and a mythic type of humanity.[83] In short, Barth's Christology

---

77. Barth, *Church Dogmatics*, IV/1:140.

78. Barth, *Church Dogmatics*, IV/1:58.

79. Barth, *Church Dogmatics*, III/1:267.

80. Karl Barth, *The Epistle to the Romans*, 6th ed., trans. Edwyn C. Hoskyns (1933; Oxford: Oxford University Press, 1968), 171.

81. Barth, *Church Dogmatics*, III/1:81.

82. Barth, *Church Dogmatics*, III/1:42-228.

83. Barth, *Church Dogmatics*, III/1:81, 92, 252-53; idem, *Christ and Adam: Man and Humanity in Romans 5*, trans. T. A. Smail (1956; Eugene, OR: Wipf & Stock,

swallows creation, Adam, and the covenant of works and the only thing left is God's grace in Christ.[84]

From one vantage point, Barth's christocentrism sounds devout and resonates in the minds of redeemed sinners who only know of a saving relationship with the triune God solely through the grace of Christ. But upon closer examination there are defects in Barth's construction. Barth famously rejected natural law, natural theology, and the covenant of works because it supposedly was anthropocentric; he wanted to ensure that all of God's dealings with humans were through Christ and the one covenant of grace. But does such a move arise from the exegesis of the Scriptures or the imposition of philosophical principles of Idealism upon the sacred text? Barth's commitment to German Idealism emerges in his description of how a theological system must begin with a fundamental principle: 'If this view is really to be the basis for the development of this type of system, it must first be expounded definitively in the form of a concretely formulated first principle or a whole series of such first principles, and then the development of the system will consist in the analysis of these *a priori* principles.'[85] For Barth, the fundamental *a priori*, the principle from which he deduced his entire system of theology was Christ: 'Therefore dogmatics must actually be Christology and only Christology.'[86] For Barth, an expansive Christology was undeniably the center of dogmatic theology.[87] This means that all theology is Christology and humans, fallen or not, can only know of grace in Christ. At

---

2004), 17, 23, 34-35, 46; cf. Carl Trueman, 'Original Sin and Modern Theology,' in *Adam, the Fall, and Original Sin: Theological, Biblical, and Scientific Perspectives*, ed. Hans Madueme and Michael Reeves (Grand Rapids: Baker Academic, 2014), 167-86, esp. 176-79.

84. Concerning humanity's initial pre-fallen condition: 'Salvation is the perfect being which is not proper to created being as such but is still future. Created being as such needs salvation, but does not have it' (Barth, *Church Dogmatics*, IV/1:8; cf. Barth, *Church Dogmatics*, III/2:146-47). My thanks to Harrison Perkins for alerting me to these passages.

85. Barth, *Church Dogmatics*, I/2:861.

86. Barth, *Church Dogmatics*, I/2:872.

87. Barth, *Church Dogmatics*, I/2:872.

least two problems arise with Barth's christocentrism: (a) grace presupposes nature, and (b) Christology presupposes anthropology.

'Grace presupposes nature' is a dictum that goes back at least to Aquinas, but in what might be a surprise to some it is also a common principle in Reformed theology. Aquinas writes: 'Faith presupposes natural knowledge as grace presupposes nature.'[88] Francis Turretin (1623-1687) makes this same point: 'The special knowledge of true Faith (by which believers please God and have access to him, of which Paul speaks) does not exclude but supposes the general knowledge from nature.'[89] Others such as Abraham Kuyper (1837-1920) have made the same observation:

> It is, therefore, of the greatest importance, to see clearly, that *special* theology may not be considered a moment without *natural* theology, and that on the other hand natural theology of itself is unable to supply *any* pure knowledge of God. That special revelation (*revelatio specialis*) is not conceivable without the hypothesis of natural theology, is simply because *grace* never creates one single new reality.[90]

Herman Bavinck (1854-1921) makes the same point when he writes:

> Natural morality is the presupposition of faith. The world is the field in which the seed of the Word, prepared by the Holy Spirit, is sown, germinates, and bears fruit (Matt. 13:38). Regeneration presupposes natural birth, re-creation presupposes creation, and Scripture presupposes nature. The world, the earth, is the foundation of the church; without the one the other would be impossible, just as revealed theology (*theologia revelata*) is impossible without natural theology (*theologia naturalis*).[91]

Turretin, Kuyper, and Bavinck have not fallen prey to the infection of Aristotelian synthesis thinking as Barth or Cornelius Van Til

---

88. Aquinas, *Summa Theologica*, Ia q. 2 art. 2 ad. 1; see also Rudi te Velde, *Aquinas on God: The 'Divine Science' of the Summa Theologiae* (Aldershot: Ashgate Publishing, 2006), 150-60.

89. Turretin, *Institutes*, I.iii.10.

90. Abraham Kuyper, *Principles of Sacred Theology*, trans. J. Hendrik de Vries (Grand Rapids: Eerdmans, 1963), 373.

91. Herman Bavinck, *Reformed Ethics*, vol. 1, ed. John Bolt (Grand Rapids: Baker Academic, 2019), 234. See also Richard A. Muller, 'Kuyper and Bavinck on Natural Theology,' *TBR* 10 (2019): 5-35, esp. 12, 32.

(1895-1987) have erroneously alleged. That is, trying to combine pagan and Christian thought, which produces a supposed nature-grace dualism. In Barth's mind, the covenant of works introduced the so-called nature-grace dualism.[92] Rather, Turretin, Kuyper, and Bavinck maintain a vital catholic and Reformed idea of the necessity of creation: 'In the beginning, God created the heavens and earth' (Gen. 1:1).

Multiple Reformed confessions have echoed this truth, such as the Gallican Confession (1559), 'God reveals himself to men; firstly, in his works, in their creation' (II), the Belgic Confession (1561), 'We know God by two means: First, by the creation ... since the universe is before our eyes like a beautiful book' (II), or even the opening words of the Westminster Confession (1646), 'Although the light of nature ...' (I.i). Creation is not merely the external basis of the covenant of grace but instead the manifestation of His love to humans, those who bear His image. The creation is an expression of God's goodness. God spoke to Adam through creation—to see the unseen and invisible God through the visible—a message that called out to Adam and continues to call out to his fallen children.[93] God spoke to Job out of the whirlwind to explain that the creation is abundant and mysterious, and humanity is only one part of it – not its equal, let alone its overlord.[94] Adam was not creation's master but a custodian of God's gift. If Adam had contemplated his proper place and role within the creation, he would have seen himself as a tiny part of the massive cosmos and rejoiced in the abundant outpouring of divine love and especially reveled in the gift of the Spirit.[95]

---

92. Barth, *Church Dogmatics*, IV/1:55-66; idem, 'No!' in *Natural Theology: Comprising 'Nature and Grace'* (1946; Eugene, OR: Wipf & Stock, 2002), 100-01, 103; Cornelius Van Til, *Common Grace and the Gospel* (Phillipsburg, NJ: P & R, 1972), 2, 34, 93-94; idem, *Herman Dooyeweerd and Reformed Apologetics*, 3 parts (Philadelphia, PA: Westminster Theological Seminary, 1972), III:17.

93. Richard Giannone, 'Introduction,' in *Flannery O'Connor: Spiritual Writings*, ed. Robert Ellsberg (Mary Knoll, NY: Orbis Books, 2003), 35.

94. Wendell Berry, 'The Body and the Earth,' in *The Art of the Commonplace: The Agrarian Essays of Wendell Berry*, ed. Norman Wirzba (Berkeley, CA: Counterpoint, 2002), 93-134, esp. 94.

95. See similar comments in Berry, 'The Body and the Earth,' 95.

Augustine insightfully explains the nature of the gift of the Spirit when he writes:

> Love, then, which is from God and is God, is properly the Holy Spirit, through whom the charity of God is poured forth in our hearts, through which the whole Trinity dwells in us. For this reason the Holy Spirit, since He is God, is also most rightly called the Gift of God. What else is to be understood by the Gift in the strict sense except charity which leads to God, and without which any other gift, no matter which, does not lead to God?[96]

Augustine's comments address the post-fall work of the Spirit and thus our reception of Him is an outpouring of charity, or grace, but in the pre-fall context the Spirit would be a gift of love. Nevertheless, instead of resting in the power of the Spirit to love God, he wanted to be a god himself; he believed that equality with God was a thing to be grasped (Phil. 2:6). Such is the nature of the Psalmist's words of praise: 'When I look at your heavens, the work of your fingers, the moon and the stars, which you have set in place, what is man that you are mindful of him, and the son of man that you care for him?' (Ps. 8:3-4). In the simplest of terms, there is no redemption without creation, there is no grace apart from nature. This applies both to our knowledge of God (general and special revelation) as well as to our redemption, especially as it pertains to Christology.

Christology presupposes anthropology. This is the assumption embedded in the Psalmist's reflections upon Adam's creation: 'You have given him dominion over the works of your hands; you have put all things under his feet' (Ps. 8:6). The Psalmist's words are not merely a wistful look back upon the creation, let alone a reflection upon an ahistorical saga – a gaze into the mythic mist as Barth contends. Rather, the Psalmist goes back to the future, as Adam's creation points forward to Christ's finished work: 'For as in Adam all die, so also in Christ shall all be made alive. But each in his own order: Christ the firstfruits, then at his coming those who belong to Christ. Then comes the end, when he delivers the kingdom to God the Father after destroying every rule and every authority and power.

---

96. Augustine, *The Trinity*, The Fathers of the Church, trans. Stephen McKenna (Washington D. C: The Catholic University of America Press, 1963), XV.xviii (32).

For he must reign until he has put all his enemies under his feet' (1 Cor. 15:22-25, emphasis). The apostle Paul looks back to Adam through the lens of Psalm 8 and recognizes that the work of the last Adam presupposes the work of the first. The engine behind Barth's theology is the notion of Christ as the sole elected and rejected person. Christ's election undergirds the notion that all theology is Christology, but in his effort to guard the doctrine of Christ he undermines it.

Beginning with Christology leaves no room for creation, for Adam, which strikes at the heart of the man in the God-*man*. How can you have a last *Adam* if you have no Adam to begin with? By eliminating the natural order, Adam, the covenant of works, natural law, and natural theology, Barth collapses history into eternity and veers into the arms of Eutyches (ca. 375-454) and monophysitism. Barth does not provide 'the resources we need if we are to say that Jesus of Nazareth's complex, contingent, particular, creaturely humanity, which is utterly and entirely not-God, is nevertheless united with God so as to become God's humanity.'[97] In Barth's formulation we lose Nicaea's (325) claims that Christ 'was made human' and Chalcedon's (451) affirmation that Christ was 'truly man.' George Hunsinger argues that Barth maintains a Chalcedonian christology, but the reason he has been accused of compromising this creedal line is 'rooted mainly in a failure to appreciate that he employs a dialectical strategy of juxtaposition.'[98] But Barth's use of dialectical juxtaposition (trying to combine the contradictory in the effort to underscore mystery) invites scorn. As G. K. Chesterton (1874-1936) once remarked: 'The honest man is he who is always trying to utter the unutterable, to describe the indescribable; but the quack lives not by plunging into mystery, but by refusing to come out of it.'[99]

---

97. Mike Higton, *Christ, Providence and History: Hans W. Frei's Public Theology* (London: T & T Clark, 2004), 60, also 5-6, 39-64, esp. 54-59.

98. George Hunsinger, 'Karl Barth's Christology: Its basic Chalcedonian Character,' in *The Cambridge Companion to Karl Barth*, ed. John Webster (Cambridge: Cambridge University Press, 2000), 132.

99. G. K. Chesterton, 'The Mystagogue,' in *In Defense of Sanity: The Best Essays of G. K. Chesterton*, ed. Dale Ahlquist, et al. (San Francisco, CA: Ignatius Press, 2011), 65-68, esp. 66.

In his haste to rest in the hope of the Christ of heaven, Barth has devalued the Christ of earth.[100]

In the post-Barthian theological landscape, does speaking of grace in the pre-fall context shed greater light or ambiguity? To say that Barth merely spoke of grace the way the Reformed tradition has done is to compare apples to oranges. The early modern Reformed tradition is saying something quite different than Barth. As noted above, when Owen invokes grace, he clarifies that it is a different degree and kind of grace than that received through Christ. Moreover, in a dramatically different manner, early modern theologians would neither think to deny Adam's historicity, nor allow Christology to swallow the rest of theology. The early modern Reformed appeal to grace is thus objectively superior to Barth's understanding because it suffers from none of his faults. But even so, the rise of erroneous teaching always requires greater precision in doctrine. In this case, in the post-Barthian world, rather than speaking of grace, the better option lies in speaking of divine love, benevolence, and gift. In this sense, we can speak of God showering Adam with unmerited favor by creating the world *ex nihilo*, giving the creation to him as a gift, creating Adam and Eve in His image, and entering into a covenant with them that had a remarkable reward of eternal life. But on the heels of the fall, God mercifully poured out His grace upon Adam and Eve, His demerited favor that granted to them the blessing of eternal life in spite of their demerit (sin) by the work of the last Adam, Jesus Christ.

Conclusion

While speaking of pre-fall grace may be one way to account for Adam's relationship to God, reserving grace for Christ and the post-fall world best preserves the differences between the proton and the eschaton. In his natural state, Adam was holy, righteous, in communion with the triune God through the Spirit, bore the divine image, and therefore naturally loved God and desired the beatific vision. Had Adam obeyed, God would have rewarded him with

---

100. Similarly Fritz Oehlschlaeger, *The Achievement of Wendell Berry: The Hard History of Love* (Lexington, KY: The University Press of Kentucky, 2011), 196.

the gift of eternal life and the eschatological dispensation of the Spirit. Sadly, we all know the rest of the story. Adam's fall, however, exposes one of the greatest mysteries in all of theology: How does a perfectly righteous and holy image-bearer with a natural desire to love God and for the beatific vision turn away from his covenant Lord? The question poses an enigma for the ages. À Brakel has offered sage advice. Rather than trying to navigate the labyrinth of why Adam fell and made us all subject to sin, 'Let us be more concerned how we may be delivered from sin rather than how we became involved in it.'[101] 'Therefore,' writes à Brakel, 'one must make Christ in the covenant of grace the foundation for all rest and comfort and seek holiness from Him as a principal element of salvation.'[102]

---

101. À Brakel, *The Christian's Reasonable Service*, I:374.

102. À Brakel, *The Christian's Reasonable Service*, I:380.

~: III.4a :~

Excursus on Genesis 1:26

Introduction

*I*nterpreters have presented different explanations for the seemingly peculiar grammar of Genesis 1:26, 'Then God said [singular], "Let us make [plural] man in our image, after our likeness".' What explains the shift between the singular and the plural? Some have dismissed this as a reference to the Trinity and instead argue that it represents God as a monarch and the 'use of "we" in God's speaking is that it is the royal "we." God the king creates us in his image so that we can rule in his stead.'[1] But as other commentators have noted, the royal 'we' rarely, if at all, occurs in the Old Testament.[2] In fact, Hermann Günkel (1862-1932) noted that the plural of majesty was first introduced by the Persians, long after the composition of Genesis (see Ezra 4:18; 1 Macc. 10:19).[3] In the history of interpretation, therefore, the two most viable views are that Genesis 1:26 reveals God speaking with His heavenly court of angels or that this verse refers to the

---

1. Catherine Clark Kroeger and Mary J. Evans, eds., *The IVP Women's Bible Commentary*, ed. (Downers Grove, IL: InterVarsity Press, 2002), 4; C. F. Keil and Franz Delitzsch, *Commentary on the Old Testament*, 10 vols. (1866-91; Peabody, MA: Hendrickson, 1996), I:39.

2. Eugene J. Pentiuc, *Jesus the Messiah in the Hebrew Bible* (Mahwah, NJ: Paulist Press, 2006), 6.

3. Hermann Günkel, *Genesis*, trans. Mark Biddle (Macon, GA: Mercer University Press, 1997), 112.

Trinity.[4] That is, Genesis 1:26 is an intra-trinitarian deliberation over the creation of humans. This excursus defends the thesis that Genesis 1:26 refers to intra-trinitarian dialogue, specifically the Father addressing the Son. The excursus defends this thesis in the following manner: (1) a brief overview of the two views with their respective adherents and explanations; (2) exegetical rationale for the superiority of the trinitarian interpretation; and (3) the theological significance of Genesis 1:26.

Kline on Genesis 1:26

Meredith Kline (1922-2007) argues that the 'let us' and 'our image' of Genesis 1:26 refers to God addressing His angelic council. He believes this is an exegetically sound answer because whenever the first-person plural fiat appears in Scripture, it is within the context of the heavenly council.[5] So, for example, 'Then the LORD God said, "Behold, the man has become like one of us knowing good and evil"' (Gen. 3:22). In Kline's view, God addressed the cherubim mentioned in Genesis 3:24.[6] Likewise, when God determined to judge a city such as Babel or Sodom, plural and singular forms of speech appear: 'Let us go down' (Gen. 11:7). When God spoke, 'I will go down,' the following verse indicates that 'men turned from there and went toward Sodom' (Gen. 18:21-22). When Isaiah encountered the enthroned Lord flanked by the seraphim, God asked: 'Whom shall I send, and who will go for us?' (Isa. 6:8). Though the seraphim are distinct from the divine council, they nevertheless belong to the heavenly court as evident from its appearance in Revelation 4. Kline, therefore, believes that Genesis 1:26 is God's speech to His divine council, although he does recognize that the Trinity appears in Genesis 1:2 with mention of the Spirit hovering over the waters of creation.

According to Kline, those who want to connect the Trinity with Genesis 1:26 have missed the council idiom in the Bible, which was

---

4. For a brief survey of other views, see Bruce K. Waltke, *An Old Testament Theology: An Exegetical, Canonical, and Thematic Approach* (Grand Rapids: Zondervan, 2007), 212-13.

5. Meredith G. Kline, 'Creation in the Image of the Glory-Spirit,' *WTJ* 39 (1976-77): 250-72, esp. 259.

6. Kline, 'Creation in the Image,' 259-60.

common to Canaanite texts of the Mosaic age.[7] Kline admits the Son's participation in the creation (Heb. 1:3) as well as the image-bearing-son connections (Gen. 5:1-3); Scripture reveals that the eternal Son was the archetypal referent for the sonship aspect of God's image in humanity.[8] So, Kline sees the Trinity in Genesis 1, and the triune God makes humans in His image. But based on God's speech to the heavenly council, the angels also share in the divine image. The fact that angels share in the divine image is evident from other council contexts, which designate angels as 'sons of God' (Job 1:6, 2:1; 38:7; Pss. 29:1; 89:6).[9] Further confirmation of this claim appears in the Psalmist's reflections on Genesis 1:26 when he compares humans to angels: 'You have made him a little lower than the heavenly beings and crowned him with glory and honor' (Ps. 8:5). Kline explains: 'That man in his likeness to God is like members of the divine council suggests that to bear the image of God is to participate in the judicial function of the divine Glory.'[10]

Other advocates of a view similar to Kline include Richard Middleton, David VanDrunen, Bruce Waltke, Gordon Wenham, Randall Garr, Gerhard von Rad, Hermann Günkel, and among Jewish commentators Nahum Sarna, Umberto Cassuto, and ancient Rabbinic interpreters.[11] For example, *Midrash Rabbah* states: 'Rabbi Hanina said, "When God set out to create the first human being,

---

7. Kline, 'Creation in the Image,' 260.

8. Kline, 'Creation in the Image,' 253, 260-61.

9. Kline, 'Creation in the Image,' 264.

10. Kline, 'Creation in the Image,' 265.

11. J. Richard Middleton, *The Liberating Image: the Imago Dei in Genesis 1* (Grand Rapids: Brazos Press, 2005), 55-60; David VanDrunen, *Divine Covenants and Moral Order* (Grand Rapids: Eerdmans, 2014), 538-42; Bruce Waltke, *An Old Testament Theology: An Exegetical, Canonical, and Thematic Approach* (Grand Rapids: Zondervan, 2011), 127; idem, *Genesis: A Commentary* (Grand Rapids: Zondervan, 2016), 64-65; Gordon J. Wenham, *Genesis 1-15*, Word Biblical Commentary (Waco, TX: Word Books, 1987), 28; W. Randall Garr, *In His Own Image and Likeness: Humanity, Divinity, and Monotheism* (Leiden: Brill, 2003), 51-92; Gerhard von Rad, *Genesis*, OTL (Philadelphia, PA: Westminster, 1972), 58; Günkel, *Genesis*, 112; Nahum Sarna, *Genesis*, JPSTC (Philadelphia, PA: Jewish Publication Society, 1989), 12; similarly Umberto Cassuto, *Genesis*, Part One, *Adam to Noah*, trans. Israel Abrahams (Jerusalem: Magness Press, 1998), 55.

he consulted with the ministering angels. He said to them, "Let us make man."'[12] Likewise Philo of Alexandria (b. 25 B.C.) writes: 'For it seemed to be unfitting to God, the ruler of all, that the road to wickedness within the reasonable soul should be of his making, and therefore he delegated the forming of this part to his inferiors.'[13] In other words, the participation of the angels in the creation of humanity accounts for their sins, not God's creative act.[14]

The Trinity

Historically, the most common interpretation of Genesis 1:26 is to understand the 'let us' and the 'our image' as a reference to the Trinity – the divine intra-trinitarian council. This view has been held by numerous church fathers, theologians of the Middle Ages, Protestant Reformers, and post-Reformation theologians including: Augustine (354-430), Cyril of Alexandria (378-444), Fulgentius of Ruspe (460-533), Peter Lombard (1096-1160), Thomas Aquinas (1225-1274), Johannes Brenz (1499-1570), Wolfgang Musculus (1497-1563), John Calvin (1509-1564), Andrew Willet (1562-1621), John Downame (1571-1652), John Davenant (1572-1641), James Ussher (1581-1656), Edward Leigh (1602-1671), Thomas Goodwin (1600-1680), Thomas Watson (ca. 1620-1686), John Edwards (1637-1716), George Smeaton (1814-1889), and Anthony Hoekema (1913-1988), to name some.[15] A variant of this is that some argue

---

12. *Midrash Rabbah*, 8:3-4, as cited in Pentiuc, *Jesus the Messiah*, 7.

13. Philo, *On the Confusion of Tongues*, in *Philo*, LCL, vol, 4, trans. F. H. Colson and G. H. Whitaker (Cambridge, MA: Harvard University Press, 1985), 179 (p. 109).

14. Pentiuc, *Jesus the Messiah*, 7.

15. Augustine, *The Trinity*, The Fathers of the Church, trans. Stephen McKenna (Washington D. C: The Catholic University of America Press, 1988), Vii.iv.12 (p. 204); Cyril of Alexandria, *Against Julian*, I.xxix, in *Cyril of Alexandria*, ed. Norman Russell (New York: Routledge, 2000), 196; Fulgentius of Ruspe, in *Genesis 1-11*, ACCS, ed. Andre Louth (Downers Grove, IL: InterVarsity Press, 2001), 31; Peter Lombard, *The Sentences*, vol. 1, trans. Giulio Silano (Toronto: PIMS, 2007), 14-15; Thomas Aquinas, *Summa Theologica* (rep.; Allen, TX: Christian Classics, 1948), IIa-IIae q. 2 art. 8 ad 3; Johannes Brenz, *Commentary on Genesis*, 1:26-27, in *Genesis 1-11*, ed. John L. Thompson, RCS (Downers Grove, IL: InterVarsity Press, 2012), 41; Wolfgang Musculus, *Commentary on Genesis*, 1:26-27, in *Genesis 1–11*, ed. Thompson, 42; John Calvin, *Genesis*, CTS (rep.; Grand Rapids: Baker Books,

that the dialogue is specifically between the Father and Son: so Ambrose (ca. 340-397), Hilary of Poitiers (ca. 310-367), Prudentius (348-413); Marius Victorinus (290-364), Clement of Alexandria (150-215), John Chrysostom (349-407), and Ephrem the Syrian (306-373).[16] Advocates of this view contend that the Son is the image of God and thus the Father and Son deliberate and determine to make human beings after the image of the Son. The Son is the eternal uncreated image of God, whereas humans are the finite, temporal, created image. In contrast to Kline's argument, who largely appeals to Old Testament texts to confirm his interpretation, advocates of a trinitarian reference appeal to New Testament texts to understand Genesis 1:26. Ephrem the Syrian, for example, asks the question, 'To whom was God speaking,' when He said, 'Let us make man in our image'? Ephrem appeals to John and Paul: 'For by him all things were created, in heaven and on earth' (Col. 1:16) and 'All things were made through him, and without him was not anything made that was made' (John 1:3).[17] Pre-modern commentators were aware

---

1991), comm. Gen. 1:26 (pp. 92-93); Andrew Willet, *A Sixfold Commentary Upon Genesis* (London: John Norton, 1605), 20; John Downame, *The Summe of Sacred Divinity* (London: William Barret, 1620), 29; *An Exposition of the Epistle of St. Paul to the Colossians* (London: Hamilton, Adams, and Co., 1627), 209; James Ussher, *A Body of Divinity* (London: Jonathan Robinson, 1645), 77; Edward Leigh, *A Treatise of Divinity Consisting of Three Books* (London: William Lee, 1646), 116; Thomas Goodwin, *A Discourse of Election* (London: Thomas Goodwin Jr., 1683), 127; Thomas Watson, *A Body of Practical Divinity* (London: Thomas Parkhurst, 1692), 66; John Edwards, *Theologia Reformata: Or, The Body and Substance of the Christian Religion* (London: John Lawrence, et al., 1713), 293; George Smeaton, *The Doctrine of the Holy Spirit* (Edinburgh: T & T Clark, 1882), 11; Anthony A. Hoekema, *Created in God's Image* (Grand Rapids: Eerdmans, 1986), 12.

16. Ambrose, *Exposition of the Christian Faith*, I.vii.53, I.xvii.111, NPNF², X:209, 219; Hilary of Poitiers, *On the Trinity*, V.vii-viii, NPNF², IX:87-88; Prudentius, *Poems*, in *Genesis 1-11*, ed. Louth, 29; *Against Arius*, IA.20, in *Genesis 1-11*, ed. Louth, 29; Clement of Alexandria, *Exhortation to the Greeks*, 10, in *Genesis 1-11*, ed. Louth, 29; John of Chrysostom, *Homilies on Genesis 1-17*, Fathers of the Church, trans. Robert C. Hill (Washington, D. C: The Catholic University of America Press, 1999), Homily XIV.xvi (p. 189); Ephrem the Syrian, *Commentary on Genesis*, in *St. Ephrem The Syrian: Selected Prose Works*, trans. Edward G. Mathews Jr. and Joseph P. Amar, ed. Kathleen McVey (Washington, D.C: The Catholic University of America Press, 1994), 93-94.

17. Ephrem the Syrian, *Commentary on Genesis*, 93-94.

of the 'council idiom' but believed there was a better explanation of this exegetical phenomenon. Augustine, for example, thought that only humans bear the image of God but in settings of judgment God did address His angels.[18]

Exegetical Rationale for a Trinitarian Interpretation

Given these two options, which is the preferable interpretation? Does Genesis 1:26 reveal that God consults with His heavenly court or is this a reference to the Trinity? While the heavenly court interpretation has its merits, a trinitarian reading is the superior choice for several reasons: (1) it pays closer attention to the immediate context of Genesis 1:26; (2) rests on the whole canon of Scripture rather than only the Old Testament; and (3), employs a biblically-sourced hermeneutic rather than one more indebted to historical-critical presuppositions. First, elements within Genesis 1:26 point away from understanding this as God speaking to His heavenly court. On the one hand, no one should doubt the presence of the heavenly court; Scripture attests to its existence: 'Around the throne were twenty-four thrones, and seated on the thrones were twenty-four elders, clothed in white garments, with golden crowns on their heads' (Rev. 4:4). Nevertheless, Kline states: 'In the creative fiat addressed to the heavenly council, "Let us make man in our image", angels are identified as sharing in the image-likeness to God.' He also appeals to passages where the Old Testament refers to angels as 'sons of God' to support his interpretation (Job 1:6; 2:1; 38:7; Pss. 29:1; 89:6). The idea here is that sons are image bearers (Gen. 5:3).[19] Some proponents of Kline's view demur from his claim that angels also share in the divine image.[20] It seems, therefore, that Kline's view entails that the angels were in some sense co-creators of humans because humans and angels share the divine image. Yet, Kline does not deal with the fact that when God says, 'Let us make man in our image' (Gen. 1:26), that He personally

---

18. Augustine, *City of God*, trans. Marcus Dods (New York: Random House, 1993), XVI.vi.

19. Kline, 'Creation in the Image,' 265.

20. So VanDrunen, *Divine Covenants*, 541.

carries it out: 'So God created [ויברא] man in his own image, in the image of God he created [ברא] him; male and female he created [ברא] them' (Gen. 1:27). Genesis 1:27 has a threefold repetition of the verb *bara*, 'to create.' Notable is that this verb only has God as its subject throughout the Old Testament (Gen. 1:1; 1:21, 27; 2:3; 2:4; 5:1; 6:7; 34:10; Num. 16:30; 4:32; Isa. 4:5; 40:26, 28; 41:20; 42:5; 43:1; 43:7; 43:15; 45:7; 45:8; 45:12, 18; 48:7; 54:16; 57:19; 65:17-18; Jer. 31:22; Ezek. 21:30; 28:13, 15; Amos 4:13; Mal. 2:10; Pss. 51:10; 89:12, 47; 102:18; 104:30; 148:5; cf. Eccles. 12:1). The Old Testament never connects this verb with angels. Genesis 1:27 uses the threefold repetition to highlight the fact that humans bear the image of God alone, and that no other creature participated in this act. If God is therefore the sole actor, then how does this inform the statement, 'Let us make man in *our* image, after *our* likeness' (Gen. 1:26, emphasis)? The divine court is likely present during this act but God acts alone and does not consult His heavenly retinue.

Second, the trinitarian interpretation rests upon the whole canon of Scripture. In his interpretation of Genesis 1:26, Kline largely only appeals to the Old Testament. Within the larger scope of his essay, he refers to a number of New Testament passages as he rightly locates the Trinity in the opening pages of the Bible. Kline explains, for example, that the Son participates in the creation according to Hebrews 1:2-3, John 1:3, and Colossians 1:16ff.[21] He also looks to other New Testament passages such as John 17:5 and Hebrews 2:6ff to explain the Son's close association with the Spirit's work in creation and new creation.[22] And he rightly connects Christ's parabolic breathing on His disciples as an allusion to Adam's reception of the Spirit (John 20:22; Gen. 2:7).[23] So Kline offers a trinitarian exegesis of the opening chapters of Genesis *except* for when he explains Genesis 1:26. Rather than speaking to the Son and Spirit, God 'was addressing himself to the angelic council of elders, taking them into his deliberative council.'[24] At this point Kline only interprets Genesis 1:26 by other

---

21. Kline, 'Creation in the Image,' 253.
22. Kline, 'Creation in the Image,' 254.
23. Kline, 'Creation in the Image,' 259.
24. Kline, 'Creation in the Image,' 259.

Old Testament texts (Gen. 3:22, 24; 11:7; 18:2, 21; 19:1 Isa. 6:8).[25] To be clear, Kline believes that the Trinity is involved in the creation of humans, as the Son and the Spirit constitute the archetypal image, and thus humans reflect the image of God. But Kline nevertheless avers:

> The use of the idiom of the divine council in the Genesis 1:26 fiat thus alerts us to the involvement of the Glory-Spirit in this episode. Those who have sought to explain the plural as a reflection of the trinitarian nature of God and in particular as an allusion to the Spirit of Genesis 1:2, though missing the proper explanation found in the council idiom, have been correct in finding the antecedent of the Genesis 1:26 usage in the Spirit of Genesis 1:2. The Glory theophany, in which God was present as Logos-Wisdom [Son] and Spirit-Power [Spirit], stood as archetype at the creation of man as God's image.[26]

In other words, the Trinity appears in Genesis 1–2 but not specifically in Genesis 1:26. According to Kline, advocates of intra-trinitarian deliberation miss the council form of address and thus misunderstand this one verse. Yet, one should ask why the other cited New Testament texts weigh less than the Old Testament texts to which Kline appeals?

Stated in other terms, should not later New Testament Scripture that more clearly reveals the events of Genesis 1–2 take precedent over the less clear statements? While the other Old Testament passages likely invoke the 'council idiom' as Kline suggests, none of them appear in context with Genesis 1:27, 'So God created man in his own image, in the image of God he created him; male and female he created them.' In this immediate context Genesis makes statements followed straightaway by subsequent interpretive declarations. Such is the nature of the dominion mandate: 'Then God said, "Let us make man in our image, after our likeness. And let them have dominion over the fish of the sea and over the birds of the heavens and over the livestock and over all the earth and over every creeping thing that creeps on the earth' (Gen.1:26). The second sentence of the verse explains the first; having dominion over

---

25. Kline, 'Creation in the Image,' 259-60.

26. Kline, 'Creation in the Image,' 260.

the earth defines the nature of image-bearing. Likewise, Genesis 1:27 explains the plurals of Genesis 1:26, 'Let *us* make man in *our* image, and after *our* likeness' (emphasis). On this connection, St. Augustine reasons that God may have uttered the 'Let us make' to the angels 'had He not added "in our image."' He adds: 'We cannot believe that man was made in the image of angels, or that the image of God is the same as that of angels, it is proper to refer this expression to the plurality of the Trinity.'[27] Kline stands beside a stream of crystal-clear water from which he can quench his exegetical thirst but instead wanders off into the biblical forest to find other puddles of water. But the greatest weakness in Kline's argument is that the rest of Scripture, especially the New Testament, does not confirm his interpretation.

Nowhere in the New Testament do we find God consulting with the heavenly court regarding the creation of humans. Instead, the New Testament places special emphasis upon the Son. Echoing Genesis 1:1, John writes: 'In the beginning was the Word, and the Word was with God, and the Word was God. He was in the beginning with God. All things were made through him, and without him was not any thing made that was made' (John 1:1-3).[28] When Paul specifically invokes the concept of the divine image, he does not refer to the heavenly court but to the Son and His role in creation: 'He is the image of the invisible God, the firstborn of all creation. For by him all things were created, in heaven and on earth, visible and invisible, whether thrones or dominions or rulers or authorities – all things were created through him and for him' (Col. 1:15-16). In Colossians 1:15-16 Paul specifically alludes to Genesis 1:27.[29] More specifically, the apostle Paul draws attention to the triune God and not the heavenly council when he writes: 'Do not lie to one another, seeing that you have put off the old man with its practices and have put on the new man, which is being renewed in the knowledge after the image of its creator [κατ᾽εἰκόνα τοῦ

---

27. Augustine, *City of God*, XVI.vi.

28. G. K. Beale and D. A. Carson, eds., *Commentary on the New Testament Use of the Old Testament* (Grand Rapids: Baker Academic, 2007), 421.

29. Beale and Carson, *Commentary*, 851-53.

κτίσαντος αὐτόν]' (Col. 3:9-10, emphasis, trans. mine). Paul's Greek invokes the Septuagint of Genesis 1:26-27b, 'Then God said, "Let us make man in our image"... in the image of God he created him; male and female he created him [κατ᾽ εἰκόνα θεοῦ ἐποίησεν αὐτόν, ἄρσεν καὶ θῆλυ ἐποίησεν αὐτούς]' (emphasis). The bolded Greek text highlights the parallels between the two statements.[30] Once again, Paul does not appeal to the heavenly council but specifically to the Son when he invokes Genesis 1:26-27. Paul makes similar arguments in Ephesians 4:22-24 when he tells his recipients, 'Put off your old man, which belongs to your former manner of life and is corrupt through deceitful desires and to be renewed in the spirit of your minds, and to put on the new man, created after the likeness of God in true righteousness and holiness' (trans. mine). Likewise, the Son, image, and creation all converge in Hebrews 1:2-3 when the author says that God has spoken to us by His Son, by 'whom he appointed the heir of all things, through whom also he created the world. He is the radiance of the glory of God and the exact imprint of his nature, and he upholds the universe by the word of his power' (Heb. 1:2-3).

Third, the trinitarian interpretation employs a biblically-sourced hermeneutic. At this point, the views of Kline are not in view as he readily acknowledges the Trinity's presence in Genesis 1–2. But there are other Evangelical interpreters who dismiss the Trinity either because it supposedly puts doctrine before exegesis or because the tenets of scientific and grammatico-historical exegesis forbid appeal to the Trinity.[31] Among higher-critical commentators the so-called J(ahwehist) and E(lohist) sources would have never dreamed or imagined of the doctrine of the Trinity. Such assumptions have contributed to the vanishing of the trinitarian understanding of Genesis 1:26 in the present day. Yet, these objections fail because they do not employ a biblically-sourced mode of interpretation but arguably rely on unbiblical methods. How so? When one interprets

---

30. G. K. Beale, *A New Testament Biblical Theology: The Unfolding of the Old Testament in the New* (Grand Rapids: Baker Academic, 2011), 450; Beale and Carson, *Commentary*, 865-66.

31. So, e.g., Waltke, *Old Testament Theology*, 86-87.

the Bible, he must do so in accord with its own principles. In this case, to argue that we cannot appeal to the doctrine of the Trinity in Genesis fails to account for the divine authorship of the Scriptures. Yes, there are human authors but the ultimate author is the triune God. Interpretation should not be limited by what the human author may or may not have understood, as Scripture itself acknowledges that the biblical authors sometimes wrote more than they knew: 'Concerning this salvation, the prophets who prophesied about the grace that was to be yours searched and inquired carefully, inquiring what person or time the Spirit of Christ in them was indicating when he predicted the sufferings of Christ and the subsequent glories' (1 Pet. 1:10-11).[32] This does not mean readers should ignore the original historical context, but rather they must factor both the human and divine authorship of Scripture. The triune God speaks throughout all of Scripture, not just the New Testament. Any interpretation of Scripture, whether Old or New Testament, must account for the double agency of scriptural revelation.[33]

This means that a person's doctrine of God forms his principles of interpretation: 'That shape is determined by the nature of the God who speaks to us through Christ and covenant, the nature of Holy Scripture, and the nature of Christian renewal in the church.'[34] In other words, everyone brings theological presuppositions to interpret the Bible, so it is not a question of setting aside all presuppositions but rather bringing the correct ones to the table. To say that the Genesis 1–3 narratives are part of an evolutionary development of Israel's religion from polytheism to monotheism as the use of different terms for God supposedly suggests (*Elohim*, 'gods' vs. *Yahweh*), reads the canon of Scripture in a manner contrary to its own self-interpretation. Paul, for example, does not read the Old Testament in this manner. Thus, the only proper method of interpreting the Bible is to recognize that the triune

---

32. Craig A. Carter, *Interpreting Scripture with the Great Tradition: Recovering the Genius of Premodern Exegesis* (Grand Rapids: Baker Academic, 2018), 44, 57-58, 168, 170.

33. Scott R. Swain, *Trinity, Revelation, and Reading: A Theological Introduction to the Bible and its Interpretation* (London: T & T Clark, 2011), 36-39.

34. Swain, *Trinity, Revelation, and Reading*, 119.

God speaks therein and does so through the various covenants that He makes with His people.[35] Philo's heavenly court interpretation, for example, naturally follows his own Neo-Platonic doctrine of God where God must employ intermediaries to create, and thus Philo can lay the blame for the fall at the feet of God's angelic contractors.[36] Philo's Neo-Platonic doctrine of God unsurprisingly produces a Neo-Platonic interpretation of Genesis 1:26.

The same pattern unfolds with the interpretation of higher critics who reject numerous tenets of orthodox theology; higher critical interpreters simply do not believe the biblical text. This stands in marked contrast to pre-critical readings of Scripture.[37] As Craig Carter has recently argued, higher critics bring neo-pagan metaphysical assumptions of the Enlightenment to biblical interpretation rather than seeking to read the Old Testament the way the New Testament authors do. Carter draws attention to the fact that 'Great Tradition' (pre-critical interpreters) read the Bible in a similar fashion as the New Testament authors; they read the whole canon within the framework of the ecumenical creeds.[38] Thus, the Eastern and Western patristics, theologians of the Middle Ages, the Reformers, and like-minded post-Reformation theologians see no problem with Genesis 1:26 referring to the Trinity. This third point regarding reading the Bible in a manner consistent with the Bible's own self-interpretation raises an important question. Namely, to what extent have higher critical presuppositions driven Evangelical interpreters away from a trinitarian reading of Genesis 1:26? I offer no answers but merely pose the question given the fact that the trinitarian explanation of Genesis 1:26 has become unpopular even among conservative Christian commentators despite its dominance among pre-critical interpreters.

---

35. Swain, *Trinity, Revelation, and Reading*, 7.

36. Roberto Radice, 'Philo's Theology and Theory of Creation,' in *The Cambridge Companion to Philo*, ed. (Cambridge: Cambridge University Press, 2010), 124-45.

37. David C. Steinmetz, 'The Superiority of Pre-Critical Exegesis,' *Theology Today* 37 (1980): 27-38.

38. Carter, *Great Tradition*, 14. For a history of the interpretation of Genesis 1:26-27, see Claus Westermann, *Genesis 1–11* (Minneapolis, MN: Fortress Press, 1994), 147-72.

Theological Significance of Genesis 1:26 for the Covenant of Works

In Kline's interpretation, Genesis 1:26 does not refer to an intra-trinitarian deliberation but to the triune God conferring with His heavenly court. If Kline admits the Trinity in Genesis 1–2, of what significance is his omission of the triune God from Genesis 1:26? Is this not a minor and insignificant point? As seemingly small as the difference is, Kline's exegesis sidelines an important element within the creation narrative that reveals an on-going covenantal dialogue throughout the biblical canon. Within Kline's interpretation, God's speech to His heavenly court is a theological cul-de-sac. The importance and rationale of this speech ends in the early pages of the Pentateuch, as he never explains how this bears upon later New Testament revelation. Others, such as VanDrunen, argue that God's exhortation to His heavenly council shows that angels participate in the divine-judicial work, and thus humans have this divine and angelic characteristic. Unlike Kline, VanDrunen suggests that angels do not possess the divine image, but humans nevertheless resemble them in some respects: 'For my lord the king is like the angel of God to discern good and evil' (2 Sam. 14:17).[39] But even then, the appeal to angels seems superfluous. Why is the New Testament silent about this supposedly important angelic quality that humans possess? A trinitarian interpretation, however, presents a narrative that unfolds and endures throughout the various biblical covenants from the proton to the eschaton.

Among early modern Reformed theologians, Genesis 1:26 is a commonly cited text in support of the covenant of redemption.[40] In other words, Genesis 1:26 is a part of the revealed intra-trinitarian dialogue among Father, Son, and Holy Spirit to plan and execute the redemption of the elect. Jesus told His disciples, 'My Father

---

39. VanDrunen, *Divine Covenants*, 541.

40. John Owen, 'Exercitation XXVII: The Original of the Priesthood of Christ in the Counsel of God,' in *The Works of John Owen*, vol. 19, ed. William H. Goold (1862; Edinburgh: Banner of Truth, 1991), 43; John Gill, *Body of Divinity*, II.vi (p. 211); Thomas Goodwin, *Three Several Ages of Christians in Faith and Obedience*, in *The Works of Thomas Goodwin*, vol. 7 (1861-66; Eureka, CA: Tanski Publications, 1996), VI (p. 540); Jonathan Edwards, 'Covenant of Redemption,' 442.

covenanted to me a kingdom' (Luke 22:29b, trans. mine), which means that before the foundations of the world, the Father told the Son, 'You are a priest forever after the order of Melchizedek' (Ps. 110:4; Heb. 7:21).[41] Because the Son was willing to go and redeem His bride, to lay down His life for her, the Father said: 'Out of the anguish of his soul he shall see and be satisfied; by his knowledge shall the righteous one, my servant, make many to be accounted righteous, and he shall bear their iniquities. Therefore I will divide him a portion with the many, and he shall divide the spoil with the strong, because he poured out his soul to death and was numbered with the transgressors' (Isa. 53:11-12). When Christ was born and began His ministry, He told His Father: 'I delight to do your will, O my God; your law is within my heart' (Ps. 40:8; Heb. 10:7-10).[42] The Father was delighted with His Son's love and obedience and thus thundered out of the heavens: 'This is my beloved Son, with whom I am well pleased' (Matt. 3:17), words that undoubtedly encouraged Jesus.

In the midst of His ministry Jesus told His disciples: 'For the works that the Father has given me to accomplish, the very works that I am doing, bear witness about me that the Father has sent me' (John 5:36). And near the end of His ministry Jesus prayed to His Father: 'I glorified you on earth, having accomplished the work that you gave me to do' (John 17:4). Even then, Christ still had the cross before Him, a path that He enquired if it was avoidable: 'My Father, if it be possible, let this cup pass from me; nevertheless, not as I will, but as you will' (Matt. 26:39). Christ's obedience led Him to the cross where He uttered His last words to His Father: 'My God, my God, why have you forsaken me?' (Matt. 27:46; Ps. 22:1). But even in His suffering, He never forsook His path of obedience unto His very last words to His Father: 'Father, in your hands I commit my spirit!' (Luke 23:46). Even though the Father and the creation were silent while Christ was in the tomb, God spoke volumes when He raised Jesus from the dead, by which Jesus 'was declared to be the Son of God in power according to the

---

41. Beale and Carson, *Commentary*, 967-68.

42. Beale and Carson, *Commentary*, 977-78

Spirit of holiness' (Rom. 1:4). The resurrection was the Father's way of saying to the Son: 'You are my Son; today I have begotten you' (Ps. 2:7; Acts 13:32-33).[43] When Christ ascended, His Father told Him: 'Sit at my right hand, until I make your enemies your footstool' (Ps. 110:1; Acts 2:35). In fact, these words were never uttered to any of the angels but only to the Son (Heb. 1:13).

Within the canon, the Bible reveals an ongoing dialogue between Father and Son that stretches from before the foundations of the world to the consummation until 'all things are subjected to him, then the Son Himself will also be subjected to him who put all things in subjection under him, that God may be all in all' (1 Cor. 15:28). This on-going discourse between Father and Son is the proper context for Genesis 1:26. Indeed, one can borrow words from Hebrews 1:13 and combine them with Genesis 1:26: 'To which of the angels has he ever said,' 'Let us make man in our image, after our likeness'? Interpreters who argue that Genesis 1:26 is intra-trinitarian dialogue are correct, but those who maintain that this verse is specifically the Father's words to the Son hit the target dead center. Genesis 1:26 finds a New Testament counterpart in Romans 5:14, when Paul states that Adam 'was a type of the one who was to come.' That is, in the covenant of redemption the triune God determined to create and redeem a people, and this plan became manifest in the covenant of works, when the Father told the Son, 'Let us make man in our image, after our likeness,' so that Adam would foreshadow the last Adam. When Adam and Eve fell, God made the covenant of grace with them and carried out the rest of the plan of redemption, which has culminated in the incarnation, life, death, and resurrection of the Son as the 'exact imprint' of the Father (Heb. 1:3), the 'image of the invisible God' (Col. 1:15).

Conclusion

Interpretations of Genesis 1:26 that rest solely on the supposed grammatico-historical interpretation or higher critical assumptions about the biblical text should be set aside because they do not read

---

43. Beale and Carson, *Commentary*, 584-85.

the Bible in a manner consistent with its own self-interpretation. Higher critics bring neo-pagan theological assumptions to the biblical text that drive them away from a right understanding. On the other hand, conservatives such as Kline, have proposed the heavenly court interpretation based largely on an Old Testament intra-textual reading that has some warrant and may be true. But a broader canonical reading of Genesis 1:26 presents a thicker reading of the text, exegesis that pays closer attention to the immediate context and the New Testament's subsequent reading. Rather than God's communication to His heavenly court, Genesis 1:26 is part of the on-going intra-trinitarian conversation between Father, Son, and Spirit that begins in the covenant of redemption, is manifest in the covenant of works, and is consummated in the covenant of grace. 'Let us make man in our image, after our likeness' takes us through the fall and bearing 'the image of the man of dust' but ultimately and blessedly leads us to receiving 'the image of the man of heaven' (1 Cor. 15:49).

Conclusion

FAR from being a foreign intrusion on the texts of Scripture, the covenant of works is a doctrine that rests upon a broad canonical footing. The term *covenant of works* obviously does not appear in the biblical text, but is instead a theological rubric that explains numerous passages. Part I explored key issues in the doctrine's history such as terminology, the history of the exegesis of Leviticus 18:5, the nature of Adam's faith, covenant versus contract, the question of grace in the pre-fall context, and the relationship between the Adamic and Mosaic covenants. These chapters revealed that the common objections to the covenant of works fall short because of a superficial reading of primary-source texts. Modern interpreters such as Barth, Murray, Torrance, and McGowan misunderstood the early modern term *contract* and did not read its nuanced use in its historical-theological context. In short, contracts were also promises, but in the wake of the Enlightenment philosophers stripped contracts of their promissory character. Moreover, for as much as critics chide the Reformed tradition for supposedly building the doctrine from Hosea 6:7 alone, Part I's overview revealed that advocates engaged many passages of Scripture to support the covenant of works. Rather than isolating Genesis 1–3 from the rest of Scripture, advocates of the covenant of works read the opening pages of the Bible within the context of the canon.

Part II examined eight strategic texts to demonstrate that the covenant of works is a biblical doctrine: Romans 2:14-15, Genesis 2:16-17, Leviticus 18:5, Isaiah 24:5, Hosea 6:7, Galatians 4:24,

Romans 5:12-21, and Romans 7:1-6. John Murray is correct to say that the term *covenant* does not appear in Genesis 1–3, but other parts of Scripture certainly attest to its presence. Hosea 6:7 tells us, 'Like Adam they [Israel] transgressed the covenant,' and Isaiah states: 'The earth lies defiled under its inhabitants; for they have ... broken the everlasting covenant' (24:5). And Paul distinguishes between sin (ἁμαρτία) in general and Adam's covenantal transgression (παράβασις) (Rom. 5:14). Other passages of Scripture such as Leviticus 18:5 and its intra-canonical interpretation reveal that eternal life is the reward for perfect obedience to the law, an interpretation confirmed by Christ Himself: 'You have answered correctly; do this, and you will live' (Luke 10:28). The obedience-eternal life connection is an idea that Paul echoes in his own letters: 'The law is not of faith, rather "The one who does them shall live by them"' (Gal. 3:12). Read against the backdrop of the Pentateuch when God commanded Adam and Eve to take dominion over the earth and not to eat from the tree of knowledge, these imperatives were not naked commands. Rather, they were dressed in the robes of covenant, as with all of God's administration of His law.

Part III established that covenant and law do not exclude love, but are the very cradle in which love is supposed to lie. At the heart of covenant is God's love for His creation. Creation *ex nihilo*, giving human beings the image of God, and dwelling in communion with them through the presence of the Spirit revealed that love permeated God's covenant with Adam. God showered Adam and Eve with love and they were supposed to return that love to Him. Instead, Adam and Eve forsook the love of the triune God and plunged the world into sin by seeking to grasp equality with Him (Phil. 2:6). In the words of Abraham Kuyper, 'Adam's sin consisted in this, that he banished all of the love of God from his heart. Now it is impossible to be neutral or indifferent toward God. When Adam ceased to love God, he began *to hate* Him. And it is this hatred of God which now lies at the bottom of the heart of every child of Adam.'[1] God imputed Adam's covenantal transgression to

---

1. Abraham Kuyper, *The Work of the Holy Spirit*, trans. Henri De Vries (New York: Funk & Wagnalls, 1900), 344.

all of his offspring but He did not leave his fallen children without hope. Adam was a type of the one who was to come (Rom. 5:14). Adam accounts for the *man* of the God-*man*, the seed of the woman, the seed of Abraham, Isaac, and Jacob, and the seed of David. Jesus, the last Adam, entered the world to take up Adam's vocation and faithfully carry it out. In contrast to Adam and Israel, God's faithless sons, the last Adam told His disciples: 'I do as the Father has commanded me, so that the world may know that I love the Father' (John 14:31). The last Adam was obedient unto death, even death on the cross (Phil. 2:8). The covenant of works, therefore, is the framework for rightly comprehending Christ's obedience as the last *Adam*. Only when we understand Adam's work can we appreciate Christ's work.

Having an accurate assessment of salvation rests in knowing the difference between law and gospel, the covenants of works and grace. Only when we comprehend the covenant of works will we fully appreciate the words of Paul: 'The first man was from the earth, a man of dust; the second man is from heaven. As was the man of dust, so also are those who are of the dust, and as is the man of heaven, so also are those who are of heaven. Just as we have borne the image of the man of dust, we shall also bear the image of the man of heaven' (1 Cor. 15:47-49). Only when we factor Adam and the covenant of works, can we appreciate Jesus as the faithful last Adam, ruling over the creation the way that the first Adam should have.[2] The creation amounts to the great unfinished portrait of old Adam.[3] As the Psalmist looks back upon this painting and asks, 'What is man that you are mindful of him, and the son of man that you care for him?' he ultimately looks to Jesus, the Son of Man, to complete Adam's covenant (Ps. 8:4). As the prophet Daniel received a vision of Psalm 8, he also saw God completing this Adamic portrait through Christ: 'I saw in the night visions, and behold, with the clouds of heaven there came one like a son

---

2. G. K. Beale, *A New Testament Biblical Theology: The Unfolding of the Old Testament in the New* (Grand Rapids: Baker Academic, 2011), 782.

3. Marilynne Robinson, *The Givenness of Things: Essays* (New York: Farrar, Straus and Giroux, 2015), 256.

of man,' one like Adam, 'and to him was given dominion and glory and a kingdom, that all peoples, nations, and languages should serve him; his dominion is an everlasting dominion, which shall not pass away, and his kingdom one that shall not be destroyed' (Dan. 7:13-14).

The Bible opens with the creation and Adam's covenant and concludes with a new creation and the covenant of the last Adam. We come full circle but to a higher state. In the words of the poet John Donne (1572-1631):

> We think that Paradise and Calvarie
> Christs Crosse, and Adams tree, stood in one place;
> Looke Lord, and find both *Adams* met in me;
> As the first *Adams* sweat surrounds my face,
> May the last *Adams* blood my soule embrace.[4]

The Bible concludes with the book of Revelation, the only other place in Scripture that speaks of the tree of life, the original sacrament of the covenant of works. What Adam and Eve lost in the covenant of works, Jesus restores to the fallen children of Adam that are in union with Him: 'Blessed are those who wash their robes, so that they may have the right to the tree of life and that they may enter the city by the gates' (Rev. 22:14).

But the last Adam does not merely wipe the slate of sin clean and return us to Adam's probation. On the contrary, as English poet John Milton (1608-1674) once wrote:

> I who e're while the happy Garden sung,
> By one mans disobedience lost, now sing
> Recover'd Paradise to all mankind,
> By one mans firm obedience fully tri'd
> Through all temptation, and the Tempter foil'd
> In all his wiles, defeated and repuls't,
> And *Eden* rais'd in the wast Wilderness.[5]

---

4. John Donne, *The Complete Poems of John Donne*, vol. 2 (London: Robson and Sons, 1873), 340.

5. John Milton, *Paradise Regained*, I.1-7, in *The Major Works including Paradise Lost*, ed. Stephen Orgel and Jonathan Goldberg (Oxford: Oxford University Press, 2008), 619.

In other words, Jesus the last Adam loved the Father and obeyed where Adam failed and thus gave eternal life to His bride, the church. In technical terms, Jesus offers His passive obedience to address Adam's violation of the covenant and His active obedience to fulfill the covenant's original eschatological goal. Christ does not merely restore us to Adam's place but He irreversibly positions believers in the new heavens and earth. This is why J. Gresham Machen (1881-1937) sent the short but powerful telegram from his deathbed to his colleague John Murray (1898-1975): 'I'm so thankful for the active obedience of Christ; no hope without it.'[6] If Christ merely places us back in the garden, we are doomed to failure like Adam before us. If Adam in a perfect world, free from sin, failed, what chances do his fallen children have?

One of the fundamental elements of the covenant of works that has been lost in the present day is the principle that eschatology precedes soteriology. This is an insight that rests in early modern expositions of the covenant of works but has largely been lost. This is why the church must recover the covenant of works. While many in the Reformed church embrace and teach the doctrine, it is often a thin account. The covenant of works is merely the occasion of the fall, disobedience, and the reason for Christ's incarnation. As true as these things are, early modern discussions also stress that the covenant of works is about love, promise, and Adam's justification. Recovering these truths can provide needed insights in the present. In the words of J. R. R. Tolkien (1892-1973), 'Some things that should not have been forgotten were lost.'[7]

In their efforts to protect Christ and the gospel from a supposed encroaching Pelagianism, critics of the doctrine unwittingly weakened the connections between Adam and Christ, the covenants of works and grace, and the relationship between law and gospel. Instead, the covenant of works is of the greatest importance. We

---

6. J. Gresham Machen, *God Transcendent*, ed. Ned B. Stonehouse (Edinburgh: Banner of Truth, 1998), 14.

7. *The Lord of the Rings: The Fellowship of the Ring*, New Line Productions Inc., WingNut Films, Directed by Peter Jackson, Screen Play by Fran Walsh. 2001, based on the novel, J. R. R. Tolkien, *The Fellowship of the Ring*, 2nd ed. (Boston: Houghton Mifflin Company, 1965).

come full circle and close with the comments of Wilhelmus à Brakel (1635-1711) that opened this book: 'For whoever errs here or denies the existence of the covenant of works will not understand the covenant of grace, and will readily err concerning the mediatorship of the Lord Jesus. Such a person will readily deny that Christ by his active obedience has merited a right to eternal life for the elect.'

❧BIBLIOGRAPHY☙

À Brakel, Wilhelmus. *The Christian's Reasonable Service*, 4 vols., trans. Bartel Elshout. (Morgan, PA: Soli Deo Gloria, 1992).

A Solemn League and Covenant, for Reformation, and Defence of Religion (London: Edward Husbands, 1643).

Allen, R. Michael. *The Christ's Faith: A Dogmatic Account* (London: T & T Clark, 2009).

_____. *Justification and the Gospel: Understanding the Contexts and Controversies* (Grand Rapids: Baker Academic, 2013).

Ames, William. *The Marrow of Sacred Divinity* (London: Henry Oberton, 1642).

_____. *The Marrow of Theology*, trans. John Dykstra Eusden (Grand Rapids: Baker, 1968).

Andersen, Francis I. and David Noel Freedman. *Hosea*, AB, vol. 24 (New York: Doubleday, 1980).

Annesley, Samuel. *The Morning Exercises at Cripplegate*, vol. 6 (1675; London: Thomas Tegg, 1844).

Annotations Upon All the Books of the Old and New Testaments (London: Evan Tyler, 1657).

Aquinas, Thomas. *Commentary on the Letters of St. Paul to the Corinthians*, trans. F. R. Larcher (Lander, WY: Aquinas Institute for the Study of Sacred Doctrine, 2012).

_____. *Commentary on the Letters of St. Paul to Galatians and Ephesians*, Latin / English Edition of the Works of St. Thomas Aquinas, trans. F. R. Larcher (Lander, WY: The Aquinas Institute for the Study of Sacred Doctrine, 2012).

_____. *Commentary on the Letters of St. Paul to the Philippians, Colossians, Thessalonians, Timothy, Titus, and Philemon*, Latin / English

Edition of the Works of St. Thomas Aquinas, trans. F. R. Larcher (Lander, WY: The Aquinas Institute for the Study of Sacred Doctrine, 2012).

_____. *Commentary on the Letters of St. Paul to the Romans*, Latin / English Edition of the Works of St. Thomas Aquinas, trans. F. R. Larcher (Lander, WY: The Aquinas Institute for the Study of Sacred Doctrine, 2012).

_____. *Summa Contra Gentiles*, 5 vols. (1956; Notre Dame: University of Notre Dame Press, 1975).

_____. *Summa Theologica* (Allen, TX: Classic Reprints, 1948).

_____. *Truth*, 3 vols. (1952; Eugene, OR: Wipf & Stock, 2008).

Arminius, Jacob. *Opera Theologica* (Leiden: Godefridus Basson, 1629).

_____. *The Works of James Arminius*, 3 vols. (1875; Grand Rapids: Baker, 1996).

Augustine. *Augustine on Romans: Propositions from the Epistle to the Romans Unfinished Commentary on the Epistle to the Romans*, trans. Paul Frederiksen Landes (Chico, CA: Scholars Press, 1982).

_____. *City of God*, trans. Marcus Dods (New York: Random House, 1993).

_____. *Confessions*, trans. Owen Chadwick (Oxford: Oxford University Press, 1991).

_____. *The Trinity*, The Fathers of the Church, trans. Stephen McKenna (Washington D. C: The Catholic University of America Press, 1988).

Auld, Graeme. 'Imago Dei in Genesis: Speaking in the Image of God,' *ExpT* 116 (2005): 259-62.

Baius, Michael. *Prima Hominis Justitia*, in *Michaelis Baii Opera* (Colon: Baltharsar Egmont, 1696).

Ball, John. *A Treatise of the Covenant of Grace* (London: G. Miller, 1645).

Ballor, Jordan J. *Covenant, Causality, and Law: A Study in the Theology of Wolfgang Musculus* (Göttingen: Vandenhoeck & Ruprecht, 2012).

Barcellos, Richard C. *The Covenant of Works: Its Confessional and Scriptural Basis* (Palmdale, CA: Reformed Baptist Academic Press, 2016).

_____. *Getting the Garden Right: Adam's Work and God's Rest in Light of Christ* (Cape Coral, FL: Founders Press, 2017).

Barnes, Albert. *Notes, Explanatory and Practical, On the Epistle of Romans* (New York: Leavitt, Lord, and Co., 1834).

Barr, James. 'Reflections on the Covenant with Noah,' in *Covenant as Context: Essays in Honour of E. W. Nicholson*, ed. A. D. H. Mayes and R. B. Salters (Oxford: Oxford University Press, 2003), 11-22.

Barrett, C. K. *Acts*, vol. 1, ICC (Edinburgh: T & T Clark, 1998).

_____. *The Epistle to the Romans*, 2nd ed., BNTC (Peabody, MA: Hendrickson, 1991).

_____. *The Second Epistle to the Corinthians*, BNTC (1973; Peabody: Hendrickson, 1997).

Barrett, Matthew. *Canon, Covenant and Christology: Rethinking Jesus and the Scriptures of Israel* (Downers Grove, IL: IVP Academic, 2020).

Barth, Karl. *Church Dogmatics*, 14 vols., ed. G. W. Bromiley and T. F. Torrance (Edinburgh: T & T Clark, 1936-68).

Bastingius, Jeremias. *An Exposition Upon the Catechisme of the Lowe Countryes* (Cambridge: John Legat, 1589).

Baugh, S. M. *Ephesians*, Evangelical Exegetical Commentary (Bellingham, WA: Lexham Press, 2016).

Baur, Michael. 'Law and Natural Law,' in *The Oxford Handbook of Aquinas*, eds. Brian Davies and Eleonore Stump (Oxford: Oxford University Press, 2012), 238-54.

Bavinck, Herman. 'Calvin and Common Grace,' *PTR* 7/3 (1909): 437-65.

_____. *Reformed Dogmatics*, 4 vols., trans. John Vriend, ed. John Bolt (Grand Rapids: Baker Academic, 2003-08).

_____. *Reformed Ethics*, vol. 1, ed. John Bolt (Grand Rapids: Baker Academic, 2019).

Baxter, Richard. *Aphorismes of Justification, With their Explication annexed. Wherein also is opened the nature of the Covenants, Satisfaction, Rightousnesse, Faith, Works, &tc* (London: Francis Tyton, 1649).

_____. *Christian Directory* (1846; Morgan, PA: Soli Deo Gloria, 1996).

Beach, J. Mark. *Christ and the Covenant: Francis Turretin's Federal Theology as a Defense of the Doctrine of Grace* (Göttingen: Vandenhoeck & Ruprecht, 2007).

Beale, G. K. *A New Testament Biblical Theology: The Unfolding of the Old Testament in the New* (Grand Rapids, MI: Baker Academic, 2011).

_____. 'The Descent of the Eschatological Temple in the Form of the Spirit at Pentecost: Part I,' *TynB* 56/1 (2005): 73-102.

_____. 'The Descent of the Eschatological Temple in the Form of the Spirit at Pentecost: Part II,' *TynB* 56/2 (2005): 63-90.

_____. *The Temple and the Church's Mission: A Biblical Theology of the Dwelling Place of God* (Downers Grove: IVP Academic, 2004).

_____. 'The Use of Hosea 11:1 in Matthew 2:15: One More Time,' *JETS* 55/4 (2012): 697-715.

Beale, G. K. and D. A. Carson, eds. *New Testament Commentary on the Use of the Old Testament* (Grand Rapids: Baker, 2007).

Beardslee, John W., ed. *Reformed Dogmatics*, trans. John W. Beardslee (Oxford: Oxford University Press, 1965).

Beeke, Joel and Mark Jones. *A Puritan Theology: Doctrine for Life* (Grand Rapids: Reformation Heritage Books, 2012).

Belcher Jr., Richard P. *The Fulfillment of the Promises of God: An Explanation of Covenant Theology* (Fearn: Mentor, 2020).

Bell, Thomas. *A View of the Covenants of Works and Grace* (Glasgow: Edward Khull & Co., 1814).

Bellarmine, Robert. *De Controversiis Christianae Fidei*, vol. 3 (Lyon: Johannes Pillehotte, 1610).

_____. *De Controversiis Christianiae Fidei*, vol. 4 (Naples: Joseph Giuliano, 1585).

Belleville, Linda. '"Under law": Structural Analysis and the Pauline Concept of Law in Galatians 3:21-4:11,' *JSNT* 16 (1986): 53-78.

Berkhof, Louis. *Systematic Theology: New Combined Edition* (1932, 1938; Grand Rapids: Eerdmans, 1996).

Berry, Wendell. *The Art of the Commonplace: The Agrarian Essays of Wendell Berry*, ed. Norman Wirzba (Berkely, CA: Counterpoint, 2002).

Betz, Hans Dieter. *Galatians: A Commentary on Paul's Letter to the Churches in Galatia* (Philadelphia: Fortress, 1979).

Beza, Theodore. *Iesu Christi D. N. Novum Testamentum* (Geneva: Jacob Stadot, 1616).

Bierma, Lyle D., ed. *An Introduction to the Heidelberg Catechism: Sources, History and Theology* (Grand Rapids: Baker, 2005).

Bird, Michael, and Preston M. Sprinkle. *The Faith of Jesus Christ: The Pistis Christou Debate* (Grand Rapids, MI: Baker Academic, 2010.

Blake, Thomas. *Vindiciae Foederis; or, A Treatise of the Covenant of God Entered with Man-Kinde*, 2nd ed. (London: Abel Roper, 1658).

Blenkinsopp, Joseph. *Isaiah 1–39*, AB (New York: Doubleday, 2000).

_____. 'P and J in Genesis 1:1–11:26: An Alternative Hypothesis,' in *Fortunate Are the Eyes that See*, ed. Astrid B. Beck, et al. (Grand Rapids: Eerdmans, 1995), 1-15.

Block, Daniel. *The Book of Ezekiel Chapters 1–24*, NICOT (Grand Rapids: 1997).

Bobrinskly, Boris. 'The Filioque Yesterday and Today,' in *Spirit of God, Spirit of Christ: Ecumenical Reflections on the Filioque Controversy*, ed. Lukas Vischer (London: SPCK, 1981), 133-48.

Bock, Darrell L. *Luke*, 2 vols., BECNT (Grand Rapids: Baker, 1996).

Bolton, Samuel. *The True Bounds of Christian Freedome: Whereunto is annexed a discourse of the learned John Camerons, touching the three-fold covenant of God with man, faithfully translated* (London: P. S., 1656).

_____. *The True Bounds of Christian Freedom* (Edinburgh: Banner of Truth, 2001).

Boston, Thomas. *A View of the Covenant of Works from the Sacred Records*, 2nd ed. (Edinburgh: John Gray, 1775).

_____. *The Marrow of Modern Divinity in Two Parts by Edward Fisher with Notes by Mr. Thomas Boston*, 8th ed. (Falkirk: Patrick Mair, 1789).

Bovell, Carlos. 'Genesis 3:21: The History of Israel in a Nutshell,' *ExpT* 115 (2004): 361-66.

Braun, Johannes. *Doctrina Foederum sive Systema Theologiae* (Amsterdam: Abraham van Somer, 1691).

Breckinridge, Robert J. *The Knowledge of God Objectively Considered Being the First Part of Theology Considered as a Science of Positive Truth, Both Inductive and Deductive* (New York: Robert Carter & Brothers, 1885).

Briggs, Charles Augustus. *A Critical and Exegetical Commentary on the Book of Psalms*, ICC, 2 vols. (Edinburgh: T & T Clark, 1976).

Brooks, Thomas. *Paradise Opened*, in *The Complete Works of Thomas Brooks*, vol. 5 (Edinburgh: James Nichol, 1867).

Brown, Michael. *Christ and the Condition: The Covenant Theology of Samuel Petto (1624-1711)* (Grand Rapids: Reformation Heritage Books, 2012).

Brown, Michael and Zach Keele. *Sacred Bond: Covenant Theology Explored*, 2nd ed. (Grand Rapids: Reformed Fellowship, 2019).

Brown, William P. *The Ethos of the Cosmos: The Genesis of Moral Imagination in the Bible* (Grand Rapids: Eerdmans, 1999).

Brown of Haddington, John. *A Compendious View of Natural and Revealed Religion in Seven Books* (Glasgow: John Bryce, 1782).

———. *Questions and Answers on the Shorter Catechism* (1846; Grand Rapids, MI: Reformation Heritage Books, 2006).

Bruce, F. F. *The Epistle to the Galatians: A Commentary on the Greek Text* (Grand Rapids: Eerdmans, 1982).

Brueggemann, Walter. *Isaiah 1–39* (Louisville, KY: Westminster John Knox Press, 1998).

———. *Tradition for Crisis: A Study in Hosea* (Richmond, VA: John Knox Press, 1968).

Brunner, Emil. *The Christian Doctrine of Creation*, trans. Olive Wyon (London: Westminster Press, 1952).

Brunner, Emil and Karl Barth. *Natural Theology: Comprising 'Nature and Grace' by Professor Dr Emil Brunner and the reply 'No!' by Dr Karl Barth* (rep.; Eugene, OR: Wipf & Stock, 2002).

Bucanus, Guillaume. *Institutiones Theologicae* (Geneva: Jacob Stoer, 1625).

Buchanan, James. *The Doctrine of Justification: An Outline of Its History in the Church and of its Exposition from Scripture* (1867; Edinburgh: Banner of Truth, 1991).

Bullinger, Heinrich. *The Decades of Henry Bullinger*, 2 vols., trans. Thomas Harding (1849-52; Grand Rapids: Reformation Heritage Books, 2004).

———. *Sermonum Decades Quinque de Potssimis Christianae Religionis Captibus, in Tres Tomos* (Zurich: Christoph Froschoverus, 1557).

Bultmann, Rudolph. *Kerygma and Myth*, ed. Hans Werner Bartsch (New York: Harper & Row, 1961).

Burgess, Anthony. *Vindicae Legis: or, A Vindication of the Morall Law and the Covenants* (London: Thomas Underhill, 1647).

Burroughs, Jeremiah. *An Exposition of the Prophecy of Hosea*, ed. Thomas Hall, Edward Reynolds, and James Sherman (1643, 1843; Beaver Falls, PA: Soli Deo Gloria, n.d).

———. *Gospel Conversation* (London: Peter Cole: 1653).

Buxtorf Sr., Johannes. *Lexicon Hebraicum et Chaldaicum* (Basil: Johannes Konig, 1663).

Byfield, Nicholas. *The Pattern of Wholesome Words* (London: Samuel Mun, 1618).

Calamy, Edmund. *Two Solemn Covenants* (London: Thomas Banks, 1645).

Calvin, John. *Antidote to the Council of Trent*, in *Tracts*, vol. 3, trans. Henry Beveridge (Edinburgh: Calvin Translation Society, 1851).

_____. *The Book of Psalms*, vol. 2, CTS (rep.; Grand Rapids: Baker, 1981).

_____. *Commentaires sur le Prophete Isaïe* (Genève: Adam Rivery & Jean Rivery, 1552).

_____. *Commentarii in Epistolam Pauli ad Galatas* (Geneva: Jean Girard, 1548).

_____. *Commentarii Ioannis Calvini in Quinque Libros Mosis. Genesis Seorsum: Reliqui Quatvor in Formam Harmonias Digesti* (Geneva: Gaspar de Hus, 1573).

_____. *Commentariorum in Isaiam Prophetam, 1–39*, in *Joannis Calvini Opera Quae Supersunt Omnia*, vol. 42, ed. Edouard Cunitz, et al. (Braunschweig: C. A. Schwetschke, 1863).

_____. *Commentary on Genesis*, CTS (rep.; Grand Rapids: Baker, 1993).

_____. *Commentary on Hosea*, CTS (rep.; Grand Rapids: Baker, 1993).

_____. *Commentary on the Book of the Prophet Isaiah*, vol. 1, CTS (rep.; Grand Rapids: Baker, 1993).

_____. *Commentary on the Last Four Books of Moses Arranged in the Form of a Harmony*, trans. Charles William Bingham, CTS, vol. 3 (rep.; Grand Rapids: Baker, 1993).

_____. *Commentaries on the Prophet Ezekiel*, 2 vols., CTS (rep.; Grand Rapids: Baker, 1993).

_____. *Galatians, Ephesians, Philippians, & Colossians*, CNTC, eds. David W. Torrance and T. F. Torrance (1960; Grand Rapids: Eerdmans, 1996).

_____. *A Harmony of the Gospels: Matthew, Mark and Luke*, and James and Jude, eds. CNTC, vol. 2, David W. Torrance and T. F. Torrance (1960; Grand Rapids: Eerdmans, 1996).

_____. *Institutes of the Christian Religion*, 2 vols., trans. Henry Beveridge (Edinburgh: Calvin Translation Society, 1845).

_____. *Institutio Christianae Religionis* (Geneva: Robert Stephanus, 1559).

_____. *John 1-10*, CNTC (1960; Grand Rapids: Eerdmans, 1996).

_____. *Romans and Thessalonians*, CNTC, eds. David W. Torrance and T. F. Torrance (1960; Grand Rapids: Eerdmans, 1996).

_____. *The Second Epistle of Paul the Apostle to the Corinthians and the Epistles of Timothy, Titus and Philemon*, CNTC, eds. David Torrance and T. F. Torrance (1960; Grand Rapids: Eerdmans, 1996).

_____. *Sermons de M. Jean Calvin sure le V. livre de Moyse nommé Deuteronome* (Geneva: 1567).

_____. *Sermons on Deuteronomy*, trans. Arthur Golding (London: Henry Middleton, 1583).

_____. *Sermons on Galatians*, trans. Arthur Golding (1574; Audubon, NJ: Old Paths Publications, 1995).

Cameron, John. *Ioh. Cameronis S. Theologiae in Academia Salmuriensi Nuper Professoris, Praelectionum Tomus Tertius et Ultimus* (Saumur: Cl. Giorarg & Dan. Lerpiner, 1628).

Campbell, Douglas A. *The Deliverance of God: An Apocalyptic Rereading of Justification in Paul* (Grand Rapids: Eerdmans, 2009).

Cancian, Francesca. 'The Feminization of Love,' *Signs* 11/4 (1976): 692-709.

Carson, D. A. 'Adam in the Epistles of Paul,' in *In the Beginning*, ed. Nigel M. de Cameron (Glasgow: Biblical Creation Society, 1980), 28-44.

_____. *Matthew: Chapters 13–28*, EBC (Grand Rapids: Zondervan, 1995).

Carter, Craig A. *Interpreting Scripture with the Great Tradition: Recovering the Genius of Premodern Exegesis* (Grand Rapids: Baker Academic, 2018).

Cartwright, Thomas. *Cartwrightiana*, ed. Albert Peel and Leland H. Carlson (London: George Allen and Unwin Ltd., 1951).

Caryl, Joseph. *The Nature, Solemnity, Grounds, Property, and Benefits of a Sacred Covenant* (London: John Rothwell, 1643).

Cassuto, Umberto. *A Commentary on the Book of Genesis: Part One* (Jerusalem: Magnes Press, 1998).

Charlesworth, James H., ed. *The Old Testament Pseudepigrapha*, 2 vols. (New York: Doubleday, 1983).

Chesterton, G. K. *In Defense of Sanity: The Best Essays of G. K. Chesterton*, ed. Dal Ahlquist, et al. (San Francisco, CA: Ignatius Press, 2011).

Chisholm, Robert B. 'The "Everlasting Covenant" and the "City of Chaos": Intentional Ambiguity and Irony in Isaiah 24,' *CTR* 6/2 (1993): 237-53.

Chrysostom, John of. *Homilies on Genesis 1–17*, Fathers of the Church, trans. Robert C. Hill (Washington, D. C: The Catholic University of America Press, 1999).

Cicero. *On the Republic, On the Laws*, LCL, vol. 16, trans. C. W. Keyes (Cambridge: Harvard University Press, 1943).

Clines, D. J. A. *Job 21–37*, WBC, vol. 18a (Nashville, TN: Thomas Nelson, 2006).

_____. 'The Tree of Knowledge and the Law of Yahweh,' *VT* 24 (1974): 8-14.

Cocceius, Johannes. *The Doctrine of the Covenant and Testament of God*, trans. Casey Carmichael (Grand Rapids: Reformation Heritage Books, 2016).

_____. *Lexicon et Commentarius Sermonis Hebraici et Chaldaici* (Frankfurt: Balthasar Christophor Wust, 1689).

_____. *Summa Theologiae Ex Scripturis Repetita* (Geneva: Samuel Chouët, 1665).

Collins, C. John. 'Echoes of Aristotle in Romans 2:14-15: Or, Maybe Abimelech Was Not So Bad After All,' *JMM* 13/1 (2010): 123-73.

Colquhoun, John. *A Treatise on the Covenant of Works* (Edinburgh: Thomsons Brothers, 1821).

_____. *A Treatise on the Law and the Gospel* (New York: Wiley & Long, 1835).

Cooke, G. A. *The Book of Ezekiel*, ICC (1936; Edinburgh: T & T Clark, 1970).

Cranfield, C. E. B. *Romans*, ICC, 2 vols. (Edinburgh: T & T Clark, 2001).

Crisp, Oliver. *Revisioning Christology: Theology in the Reformed Tradition* (Aldershot: Ashgate, 2011).

Crisp, Tobias. *Christ alone Exalted: Being the Compleat Works of Tobias Crisp, D. D. Containing XLII Sermons*, 2 vols. (London: William Marshall, 1690).

Cross, Richard. 'John Duns Scotus,' in *Christian Theologies of the Sacraments: A Comparative Introduction*, ed. Justin S. Holcomb (New York: New York University Press, 2017), 100-18.

Crowe, Brandon D. *The Last Adam: A Theology of the Obedient Life of Jesus in the Gospels* (Grand Rapids: Baker Academic, 2017).

Cunningham, William. *Historical Theology: A Review of the Principal Doctrinal Discussions in the Christian Church Since the Apostolic Age*, vol. 2, 3rd (Edinburgh: T & T Clark, 1870).

Cyril of Alexandria. *Commentary on the Twelve Prophets*, vol. 1, trans. Robert C. Hill, The Fathers of the Church (Washington, D. C: Catholic University of America Press, 2007).

_____. *Cyril of Alexandria*, ed. Norman Russell (New York: Routledge, 2000).

Dahl, Nils Alstrup. *Studies in Paul: Theology for the Early Christian Mission* (1977; Eugene, OR: Wipf & Stock, 2002).

Dahood, Mitchell. *Psalms II: 51–100*, AB (New York: Doubleday, 1968).

Daneau, Lambert. *A Fruitfull Commentarie on the Twelve Small Prophets* (Cambridge: University of Cambridge, 1594).

Das, A. Andrew. *Galatians* (St. Louis: Concordia, 2014).

_____. *Paul, the Law, and the Covenant* (Grand Rapids: Baker, 2000).

Davenant, John. *An Exposition of the Epistle of St. Paul to the Colossians*, trans. Josiah Allport (London: Hamilton, Adams, and Co., 1831).

Davidson, Richard M. *Typology in Scripture: A Study of Hermeneutical τύπος Structures* (Berrien Springs, MI: Andrews University Press, 1981).

Davies, W. D. and D. C. Allison. *Matthew*, ICC, 3 vols. (London: T & T Clark, 2006).

Davis, Ellen F. 'Reading the Song Iconographically,' in *Scrolls of Love: Ruth and Song of Songs*, ed. Peter S. Hawkins and Lesleigh Cushing Stahlberg (New York: Fordham University Press, 2006), 172-84.

_____. *Swallowing the Scroll: Textuality and the Dynamics of Discourse in Ezekiel's Prophecy* (Sheffield: Sheffield Academic Press, 1989).

De Boer, Martinus C. 'The Meaning of the Phrase *ta stoicheia tou cosmou* in Galatians,' *NTS* 53 (2007): 204-24

De Greef, Wulfurt. *The Writings of John Calvin, Expanded Edition: An Introductory Guide*, trans. Lyle D. Bierma (Louisville: Westminster John Knox, 2008).

De la Faye, Antoine. *In D. Pauli Apostoli Epistolam ad Romanos Commentarius* (Geneva: Peter and Jacob Chouet, 1608).

De Lubac, Henri. *The Mystery of the Supernatural* (1967; New York: Herder & Herder, 1998).

De Witte, Petrus. *Catechizing Upon the Heidelberge Catechisem, of the Reformed Christian Religion* (Amsterdame: Gillis Joosten Saeghman, 1664).

Dempster, Stephen G. *Dominion and Dynasty: A Theology of the Hebrew Bible* (Downers Grove, IL: InterVarsity Press, 2003).

Denlinger, Aaron C. 'Robert Rollock's Catechism on God's Covenants,' *MAJT* 20 (2009): 105-29.

_____. *Omnes in Adam Ex Pacto Dei: Ambrogio Catarino's Doctrine of Covenantal Solidarity and Its Influence on Post-Reformation Reformed Theologians* (Göttingen: Vandenhoeck & Ruprecht, 2010).

Denzinger, Heinrich, ed. *Compendium of Creeds, Definitions, and Declarations on Matters of Faith and Morals*, 43rd ed. (San Francisco: Ignatius Press, 2012).

DeRoche, Michael. 'The Reversal of Creation in Hosea,' *VT* 31/4 (1981): 400-09.

Dickson, David. *An Exposition of All St. Pauls Epistles with an Explanation of Those Other Epistles of the Apostles, St. James, Peter, John & Jude* (London: Francs Eglesfield, 1659).

_____. *Truths Victory Over Error* (Edinburgh: John Reid, 1684).

Diodati, Giovanni. *Pious and Learned Annotations Upon the Holy Bible* (London: Nicolas Fussell, 1651).

Domning, Daryl P. and Monika K. Hellwig. *Original Selfishness: Original Sin and Evil in the Light of Evolution* (Aldershot: Ashgate, 2006).

Donne, John. *The Complete Poems of John Donne*, vol. 2 (London: Robson and Sons, 1873).

_____. *Donne: Poems and Prose* (New York: Alfred A. Knopf, 1995).

Donnelly, John Patrick. *Calvinism and Scholasticism in Vermigli's Doctrine of Man and Grace* (Leiden: Brill, 1976).

Douglas, Mary. *Purity and Danger: An Analysis of the Concepts of Pollution and Taboo* (London: Routledge & Kegan Paul, 1966).

Downame, John. *The Christian Warfare Against the Devill World and Flesh Wherein is Described Their Nature, the Maner of their Fight and Meanes to Obtaine Victory* (London: William Stansby, 1634).

_____. *Lectures Upon the Foure First Chapters of the Prophecie of Hosea* (London: William Welby, 1608).

_____. [see also Finch, Henry] *The Summe of Sacred Divinitie* (London: William Stansby, 1625?).

_____. *A Treatise of Justification* (London: Nicolas Bourne, 1633).

Duby, Steven J. 'Working with the Grain of Nature: Epistemic Under-pinnings for Christian Witness in the Theology of Herman Bavinck,' *TBR* 3 (2012): 60-84.

Duguid, Iain. *The Song of Songs*, TOTC (Downers Grove, IL: IVP Academic, 2015).

Dumbrell, William J. *Covenant and Creation: A Theology of the Old Testament Covenants* (1984; Carlisle: Paternoster Press, 2000).

Duncan, James. *A Treatise on the Covenant of Works, Man's Fall and his Recovery through Jesus Christ* (Pittsburgh, PA: S. Engles & Co., 1813).

Dunn, James D. G. *The Epistle to the Galatians*, BNTC (Peabody, MA: Hendrickson, 1993).

____. 'Once more, Pistis Christou,' in *Pauline Theology*, vol. 4, ed. D. M. Hay and E. E. Johnson (Atlanta, GA: Scholars Press, 1997), 61-81.

____. James D. G. Dunn, *Romans 1–8*, WBC, vol. 38a (Dallas, TX: Word Books, 1988).

____. *The Theology of Paul the Apostle* (Grand Rapids: Eerdmans, 1998).

Dunson, Ben C. *Individual and Community in Paul's Letter to the Romans* (Tübingen: Mohr Siebeck, 2012).

Eagleton, John. *Thoughts on the Covenant of Works: An Epistolary Address to Junior Ministers of the Gospel of All Denominations* (Edinburgh: R. Baynes, 1829).

Edwards, Jonathan. *History of the Work of Redemption* (Edinburgh and Boston: Draper & Folsom, 1782).

Eichrodt, Walther. *Ezekiel* (Philadelphia: Westminster, 1965-66).

Ellingworth, Paul. *The Epistle to the Hebrews*, NIGTC (Grand Rapids: Eerdmans, 1993).

Ellis, Brannon. 'The Eternal Decree in the Incarnate Son: Robert Rollock on the Relationship Between Christ and Election,' in *Reformed Orthodoxy in Scotland: Essays on Scottish Theology 1550-1700*, ed. Aaron C. Denlinger (London: Bloomsbury T & T Clark, 2014), 45-65.

Ellis, E. Earle. *The Gospel of Luke*, NCBC (1966; Grand Rapids: Eerdmans, 1996).

Engberg-Pedersen, Troels. *Paul and the Stoics* (Louisville, KY: Westminster John Knox Press, 2000).

Enns, Peter. *The Evolution of Adam: What the Bible Does and Doesn't Say About Human Origins* (Grand Rapids: Brazos, 2012).

Ephrem (the Syrian). *St. Ephrem The Syrian: Selected Prose Works*, trans. Edward G. Mathews Jr. and Joseph P. Amar, ed. Kathleen McVey (Washington, D.C: The Catholic University of America Press, 1994).

Erskine, John. *Theological Dissertations* (London: Edward and Charles Dilly, 1765).

Estelle, Bryan D., J. V. Fesko, and David VanDrunen, eds. *The Law is Not of Faith: Essays on Works and Grace in the Mosaic Covenant* (Phillipsburg, NJ: P & R, 2009).

Feingold, Lawrence. *The Natural Desire to See God According to St. Thomas Aquinas and His Interpreters* (Ave Maria, FL: Sapientia Press, 2010).

Ferry, Brent C. 'Works in the Mosaic Covenant: A Reformed Taxonomy' (ThM Thesis: Westminster Theological Seminary, 2009).

Fesko, J. V. *The Covenant of Redemption: Origins, Development, and Reception* (Göttingen: Vandenhoeck & Ruprecht, 2015).

_____. *The Covenant of Works: Origins, Development, and Reception* (Oxford: Oxford University Press, 2020).

_____. *Death in Adam, Life in Christ: The Doctrine of Imputation* (Fearn: Mentor, 2016).

_____. 'Do This and Live: The Reformation of Biblical Exegesis,' *HapTR* 6 (2017): 9-28.

_____. *Justification: Understanding the Classic Reformed Doctrine* (Phillipsburg, NJ: P & R, 2008).

_____. *Last Things First: Unlocking Genesis 1–3 with the Christ of Eschatology* (Fearn: Mentor, 2007).

_____. 'The Priority of Justification to Sanctification,' in *Being Saved: Explorations in Human Salvation*, ed. Marc Cortez, Joshua R. Farris, S. Mark Hamilton (London: SCM Press, 2018), 185-200.

_____. *Reforming Apologetics: Retrieving the Classic Reformed Approach to Defending the Faith* (Grand Rapids: Baker Academic, 2019).

_____. 'The Republication of the Covenant of Works,' *CP* 8 (2012): 197-212.

_____. 'Romans 8:29-30 and the Question of the *Ordo Salutis*,' *JRT* 8 (2014): 35-60.

_____. *The Theology of the Westminster Standards: Historical Context and Theological Insights* (Wheaton, IL: Crossway, 2014).

_____. *The Trinity and the Covenant of Redemption* (Fearn: Mentor, 2016).

[Finch, Henry; see also Downame, John]. *The Summe of Sacred Divinitie* (London: William Stansby, 1625?).

Fisher, Edward. *The Marrow of Modern Divinity* (London: G. Calvert, 1645).

Fitzmyer, Joseph. *The Gospel According to Luke (X-XXIV)*, AB (New York: Doubleday, 1985).

_____. *Romans*, AB (New York: Doubleday, 1992).

Fretheim, Terence E. *The Pentateuch* (Nashville, TN: Abingdon, 1996).

Furnish, Victor P. *II Corinthians*, AB (New York: Doubleday, 1984).

Gaberel, J. P. *Histoire de L'Eglise de Geneve*, 3 vols. (Geneva: Joël Cherbuliez, 1858-62).

Gaffin Jr., Richard B. *Resurrection and Redemption: A Study in Paul's Soteriology* (Phillipsburg, NJ: P & R, 1987).

Gale, Theophilus. *The True Idea of Jansenisem, Both Historick and Dogmatick* (London: E. Calvert, 1669).

Garner, David B. *Sons in the Son: The Riches and Reach of Adoption in Christ* (Phillipsburg, NJ: P & R, 2016).

Garrett, Duane. *Hosea, Joel*, NAC, vol. 19a (Nashville, TN: Broadman and Holman, 1997).

Gathercole, Simon. 'A Law Unto Themselves: The Gentiles in Romans 2.14-15 Revisited,' *JSNT* 85 (2002): 27-49.

_____. 'Torah, Life, and Salvation: Leviticus 18:5 in Early Judaism and the New Testament,' in *From Prophecy to Testament: The Function of the Old Testament in the New*, ed. C. A. Evans (Peabody, MA: Hendrickson, 2004), 126-45.

Gemser, B. 'The Importance of the Motive Clause in Old Testament Law,' *VT Supplement* 1 (1953): 50-66.

Genesis Rabbah: The Judaic Commentary to the Book of Genesis, trans. Jacob Neusner, 3 vols. (Atlanta: Scholars Press, 1985).

Gesenius, Wilhelm. *Commentar über den Jesaia* (Leipzig: Freidrich Christian Willhelm Vogel, 1821).

Gib, Adam. *Kaina Ka Palaia. Sacred Contemplations* (Edinburgh: Neill and Company, 1788).

Gillespie, Patrick. *The Ark of the Covenant Opened* (London: Tho. Parkhurst, 1677).

_____. *Ark of the Testament Opened, or The Secret of the Lords Covenant Unsealed in a Treatise of the Covenant of Grace* (London: R. C., 1681).

Gladd, Benjamin L. *From Adam and Israel to the Church: A Biblical Theology of the People of God* (Downers Grove, IL: InterVarsity Press, 2019).

Gomarus, Franciscus. *Opera Theologica Omnia* (Amsterdam: Joannis Janssonius, 1664).

Goodwin, Thomas. *The Works of Thomas Goodwin*. 12 vols. (1861-66; Eureka, CA: Tanski Publications, 1996).

Goppelt, Leonhard. *Typos: The Typological Interpretation of the Old Testament in the New* (Grand Rapids: Eerdmans, 1982).

Gordley, James. *The Philosophical Origins of Modern Contract Doctrine* (Oxford: Oxford University Press, 1991).

Gordon, T. David. *Promise, Law, Faith: Covenant-Historical Reasoning in Galatians* (Peabody, MA: Hendrickson, 2019).

Gouge, William. *A Learned and Very Useful Commentary on the Whole Epistle to the Hebrewes* (London: T. W. and S. G. for Joshua Kirton, 1655).

Grabill, Stephen. *Rediscovering the Natural Law in Reformed Theological Ethics* (Grand Rapids: Eerdmans, 2006).

Greenberg, Moshe. *Ezekiel 1-20*, AB (New York: Doubleday, 1983).

_____. 'Some Postulates of Biblical Criminal Law,' in *A Song of Power and the Power of Songs: Essays on the Book of Deuteronomy*, ed. Duane L. Christensen (Winona Lake: Eisenbrauns, 1993), 283-300.

Grotius, Hugo. *On the Law of War and Peace*, ed. Stephen C. Neff (Cambridge: Cambridge University Press, 2012).

Gunkel, Herman. *Genesis* (Macon, GA: Mercer University Press, 1997).

Haak, Theodore, ed. *The Dutch Annotations Upon the Whole Bible* (London: Henry Hills, 1657).

Hagner, Donald A. *Matthew 14–28*, WBC, vol. 33b (Dallas, TX: Word Books, 1995).

Hahn, Scott W. *Romans*, CCSS (Grand Rapids: Baker, 2017).

Haldane, Robert. *Romans* (1874; Edinburgh: Banner of Truth, 1996).

Hall, Joseph. *The Works of Joseph Hall B. of Norwich* (London: M. Flesher, 1647).

Harinck, Douglas. *Paul Among the Post-Liberals* (Grand Rapids, MI: Brazos, 2003).

Harris, Murray J. *The Second Epistle to the Corinthians*, NIGTC (Grand Rapids: Eerdmans, 2005).

Hartley, John E. *Leviticus*, WBC (Dallas: Word, 1992).

Hays, Richard B. *The Faith of Jesus Christ: The Narrative Substructure of Galatians 3:1–4:11*, 2nd ed. (Grand Rapids, MI: Eerdmans, 2002).

Heidegger, Johannes. *Corpus Theologiae Christianiae*, 2 vols. (Zurich: Heideggerian Office, 1732).

_____. *Medullae Theologiae Christianiae* (Zurich: David Gessner, 1697).

Henry, Matthew. *A Commentary on the Whole Bible: Romans to Revelation* (London: The Religious Tract Society, 1835).

Herzer, Mark A. 'Adam's Reward: heaven or Earth?' in *Drawn into Controversie: Reformed Theological Diversity and Debates within Seventeenth-Century British Puritanism*, eds. Michael A. G. Haykin and Mark Jones (Göttingen: Vandenhoeck & Ruprecht, 2011), 162-82.

Higton, Mike. *Christ, Providence and History: Hans W. Frei's Public Theology* (London: T & T Clark, 2004).

Hilderbrand, Hans J., ed. *The Oxford Encyclopedia of the Reformation*. 4 vols. (Oxford: Oxford University Press, 1996).

Hobbes, Thomas. *Leviathan*, ed. Richard Tuck (Cambridge: Cambridge University Press, 1996).

Hodge, A. A. *A Commentary on the Confession of Faith* (Philadelphia, PA: Presbyterian Board of Publication, 1901).

_____. *Outlines of Theology* (1860; Edinburgh: Banner of Truth, 1991).

Hodge, Charles. *1 & 2 Corinthians* (1857-59; Edinburgh: Banner of Truth, 1994).

_____. *Romans* (1835; Edinburgh: Banner of Truth, 1989).

_____. *Systematic Theology*, 3 vols. (New York: Scribner, Armstrong, and Co., 1876).

Hoekema, Anthony A. *Created in God's Image* (Grand Rapids: Eerdmans, 1986).

Hoeksema, Herman. *Reformed Dogmatics* (1966; Grand Rapids: Reformed Free Publishing Association, 1985).

Hogg, James. *A Letter to a Gentleman Detecting the Errors Vented at this Time* (Edinburgh: William Brown and William Dicky, 1716).

Holmes Jr., Oliver Wendall. *The Common Law* (London: Macmillan & Co., 1882).

Hubbard, David Allan. *Hosea: An Introduction and Commentary*, Tyndale Old Testament Commentary (Downers Grove: InterVarsity Press, 1989).

Hugenburger, Gordon. *Marriage as a Covenant: Biblical Law and Ethics as Developed from Malachi* (Grand Rapids: Baker, 1998).

Hume, David. *Political Essays*, ed. Knud Kaakonssen (Cambridge: Cambridge University Press, 1994).

———. *A Treatise of Human Nature* (1888; Mineola, NY: Dover Publications, 2003).

Hunnius, Aegedius. *Calvinus Iudaizans* (Wittenberg: Welacus, 1593).

———. *Judaizing Calvin*, trans. Paul A. Rydecki (Bynum, TX: Repristination Press, 2012).

Hunsinger, George. 'Karl Barth's Christology: Its basic Chalcedonian Character,' in *The Cambridge Companion to Karl Barth*, ed. John Webster (Cambridge: Cambridge University Press, 2000), 127-42.

Ibbetson, David. 'Sixteenth Century Contract Law: *Slade's Case* in Context,' *Oxford JLS* 4/3 (1984): 295-317.

Ibn Ezra, *The Commentary of Ibn Ezra on Isaiah*, vol .1, ed. M. Friedländer (London: Society of Hebrew Literature, 1873).

Janzen, Cornelius. *Cornelii Iansenii Episcopi Iprensis Augustinus*, vol. 2 (Louvain: Jacob Zeger, 1640).

Jewett, Robert. *Romans* (Minneapolis: Fortress, 2007).

Johnson, Dan. *From Chaos to Restoration: An Integrative Reading of Isaiah 24-27*, JSOT Sup 61 (Sheffield: Journal for the Study of the Old Testament, 1988).

Johnson Jr., S. Lewis. 'Romans 5:12—An Exercise in Exegesis and Theology,' in *New Dimensions in New Testament Study*, eds. Richard N. Longenecker and Merrill C. Tenney (Grand Rapids: Zondervan, 1974), 298-316.

Jones, Mark. 'The "Old" Covenant,' in *Drawn into Controversie: Reformed Theological Diversity and Debates Within Seventeenth-Century British Puritanism*, eds. Michael A. G. Haykin and Mark Jones (Göttingen: Vandenhoeck & Ruprecht, 2011), 183-203.

Junius, Francis. *The Mosaic Polity*, trans. Todd M. Rester, ed. Andrew M. McGinnis (Grand Rapids: CLP Academic, 2015).

———. *A Treatise on True Theology*, trans. David Noe (Grand Rapids: Reformation Heritage Books, 2014).

Kahn, Victoria. *Wayward Contracts: The Crisis of Political Obligation in England, 1640-1674* (Princeton: Princeton University Press, 2004).

Käsemann, Ernst. *Commentary on Romans* (Grand Rapids: Eerdmans, 1980).

Kearney, Peter J. 'Creation and Liturgy: The P Redaction of Ex 25-40,' *ZAW* 89 (1977): 375-87.

Keil, C. F. and Franz Delitzsch. *Commentary on the Old Testament*, 10 vols. (1866-91; Peabody, MA: Hendrickson, 1996).

Kelly, John. *The Divine Covenants: Their Nature and Design; or, The Covenants Considered as Successive Stages in the Development of the Divine Purposes of Mercy* (London: Jackson, Walford, & Hodder, 1851).

Kevan, Ernest F. *The Grace of Law: A Study in Puritan Theology* (Ligonier, PA: Soli Deo Gloria, 1993).

Kidner, Derek. *Love to the Loveless: The Message of Hosea* (Downers Grove: InterVarsity Press, 1981).

_____. *Psalms 73-150*, TOTC (Downers Grove: InterVarsity Press, 1973).

Kitz, Anne Marie. *Cursed Are You! The Phenomenology of Cursing in Cuneiform and Hebrew Texts* (Winona Lake: Eisenbrauns, 2014).

Klauber, Martin. 'The Helvetic Formula Consensus (1675): An Introduction and Translation,' *TrinJ* 11NS (1990): 103-23.

Kline, Meredith G. 'Creation in the Image of the Glory-Spirit,' *WTJ* 39 (1976-77): 250-72.

_____. *Essential Writings of Meredith G. Kline*, ed. Jonathan G. Kline (Peabody, MA: Hendrickson, 2017).

_____. *Genesis: A New Commentary*, ed. Jonathan G. Kline (Peabody, MA: Hendrickson, 2016).

_____. *Images of the Spirit* (1980; Eugene, OR: Wipf & Stock, 1999).

_____. *Kingdom Prologue: Genesis Foundations for a Covenantal Worldview* (Overland Park, KS: Two Age Press, 2000).

_____. *Treaty of the Great King: The Covenant Structure of Deuteronomy* (Grand Rapids: Eerdmans, 1963).

Knight III, George W. *The Pastoral Epistles*, NIGTC (Grand Rapids: Eerdmans, 1992).

Kolb, Robert. 'Luther's Hermeneutics of Distinctions: Law and Gospel, Two Kinds of Righteousness, Two Realms, Freedom and Bondage,' in *The Oxford Handbook of Martin Luther's Theology*, ed. Robert Kolb, Irene Dingel, and L'Ubomír Batka (Oxford: Oxford University Press, 2014), 168-86.

Kraus, Hans-Joachim. *Psalms 60–150* (Minneapolis: Fortress, 1993).

Kroeger, Catherine Clark and Mary J. Evans, eds. *The IVP Women's Bible Commentary*, ed. (Downers Grove, IL: InterVarsity Press, 2002).

Kuyper, Abraham. 'The Natural Knowledge of God,' *TBR* 6 (2015): 73-112.

_____. *Principles of Sacred Theology*, trans. J. Henrick de Vries (Grand Rapids: Eerdmans, 1963).

_____. *The Work of the Holy Spirit*, trans. Henri De Vries (New York: Funk & Wagnalls, 1900).

Landy, Francis. *Hosea* (Sheffield: Sheffield Academic Press, 1995).

Lane, William. *Hebrews*, vols. 47a-b, WBC (Dallas, TX: Word, 1991).

Lañyez, Diego. *Jacob Lainez Disputationes Tridentiae*, vol. 2, ed. Harmannus Grisar. (Regensberg: Felicianaia Rauch, 1886).

Lapide, Cornelius à. R. P. *Cornelii A Lapide e Societate Jesu, Sacrae Scripturae Olim Lovanni, Postea Romae Professoris, Commentaria in Duodecim Prophetas Minores* (ex Typographia Balleoniana, 1761).

Lawne, William. *An Abridgment of the Institution of Christian Religion Written by M. John Calvin* (Edinburgh: Thomas Vaultrollier, 1585).

Lee, Brian J. *Johannes Cocceius and the Exegetical Roots of Federal Theology: Reformation Developments in the Interpretation of Hebrews 7–10* (Göttingen: Vandenhoeck & Ruprecht, 2009).

Leigh, Edward. *A Treatise of the Divine Promises. In Five Books* (London: George Millar, 1633).

Letham, Robert. *The Work of Christ* (Downers Grove, IL: IVP Academic, 1993).

Levenson, Jon D. *The Love of God: Divine Gift, Human Gratitude, and Mutual Faithfulness in Judaism* (Princeton, NJ: Princeton University Press, 2016).

Levering, Matthew. *Biblical Natural Law: A Theocentric and Teleological Approach* (Oxford: Oxford University Press, 2012).

Levering, Matthew and Michael Dauphinais, eds. *Reading Romans with St. Thomas Aquinas.* (Washington D. C: The Catholic University of America Press, 2012).

Levine, Baruch A. *Leviticus*, JPSTC (Philadelphia: Jewish Publication Society, 1989).

Leydekker, Melchior. *Melchioris Leydeckeri de Historia Jansenismi* (Utrecht: Francis Halmam, 1695).

_____. *Synopsis Theologiae Christianae, Libris VII* (Utrecht: Rudolph à Zyll, 1689).

Lillback, Peter. *The Binding of God: Calvin's Role in the Development of Covenant Theology* (Grand Rapids: Baker, 2001).

Lim, Won Taek. 'The Covenant Theology of Francis Roberts' (PhD Diss., Calvin Theological Seminary, 2000).

Little, Joyce A. 'Paul's Use of Analogy: A Structural Analysis of Romans 7:1-6,' *CBQ* 46 (1984): 82-90.

Lohfink, Norbert. *The Christian Meaning of the Old Testament* (Milwaukee: Bruce Publishing Co., 1968).

Long, Stephen. *Natura Pura: On the Recovery of Nature in the Doctrine of Grace* (New York: Fordham University Press, 2010).

Longenecker, Richard. *The Epistle to the Romans*, NIGTC (Grand Rapids: Eerdmans, 2016).

_____. *Galatians*, WBC (Dallas: Word, 1990).

Longman III, Tremper. *The Book of Ecclesiastes*, NICOT (Grand Rapids: Eerdmans, 1998).

_____. *Job*, Baker Commentary on the Old Testament Wisdom and Psalms (Brand Rapids: Baker Academic, 2012).

Louth, Andrew, ed. *Genesis 1–11*, ACCS (Downers Grove, IL: InterVarsity Press, 2001).

Love, John. *The Covenant of Works: Its Nature and End. A Discourse* (Aberdeen: G. & R. King, 1848).

Lusk, William. *Discourses on the Covenant of Works, the Fall of Man, and Original Sin* (Troy, NY: N. Tuttle, 1832).

Luther, Martin. *D. Martin Luthers Werke*, vol. 42 (Weimar: Herman Böhlaus, 1911).

_____. *Disputation on Justification*, in LW, vol. 34, ed. Lewis Spitz (Philadelphia: Muhlenberg Press, 1960).

_____. *Lectures on Genesis: Chapters 1–5*, in LW, vol. 1, ed. Jaroslav Pelikan (St. Louis: Concordia Publishing House, 1958).

_____. *Lectures on Genesis 12–20*, LW, vol. 3 (St. Louis, MO: Concordia, 1961).

_____. *Lectures on the Minor Prophets*, Luther's Works, vol. 18, ed. Hilton C. Oswald (St. Louis, MO: Concordia, 1975).

Luzaraga, J. *Las Tradiciones de La Nube en la Biblia y en el Judaismo Primitivo* (Rome: Biblical Institute Press, 1973).

Maccovius, Johannes. *Distinctiones et Regulae Theologicae ac Philosophicae* (Oxford: Robert Blagravius, 1656).

_____. *Scholastic Discourse: Johannes Maccovius (1588-1644) on Theological and Philosophical Distinctions and Rules*, eds. Willem van Asselt, et al. (Apeldoorn: Instituut voor Reformatienderzoek, 2009).

Machen, J. Gresham. *God Transcendent*, ed. Ned B. Stonehouse (Edinburgh: Banner of Truth, 1998).

Macintosh, A. A. *Hosea: A Critical and Exegetical Commentary* (Edinburgh: T & T Clark, 1997).

Marshall, I. Howard. *The Gospel of Luke*, NIGTC (Grand Rapids: Eerdmans, 1978).

____. *The Pastoral Epistles*, ICC (Edinburgh: T & T Clark, 1999).

Martens, J. W. 'Romans 2.14-16: A Stoic Reading,' *NTS* 40 (1994): 55-67.

Martyn, Louis. *Galatians*, AB (New York: Doubleday, 1997).

Mason, Steven D. 'Another Flood? Genesis 9 and Isaiah's Broken Eternal Covenant,' *JSOT* 33/2 (2007): 177-98.

____. *'Eternal Covenant' in the Pentateuch: The Contours of an Elusive Phrase* (New York: T & T Clark, 2008).

Mastricht, Peterus Van. *Theoretica-Practica Theologia*, 9th ed., vol. 1 (Utrecht: W. van der Water, et al., 1724).

Mattson, Brian G. *Restored to Our Destiny: Eschatology and the Image of God in Herman Bavinck's Reformed Dogmatics* (Leiden: Brill, 2012).

May, Larry. 'Hobbes,' in *Ethics in History of Western Philosophy*, ed. Robert J. Cavalier, James Gouinlock, and James P. Sterba (New York: St. Martin's Press, 1989), 125-54.

Mays, James Luther. *Hosea: A Commentary* (Philadelphia: The Westminster Press, 1969).

McConville, J. G. *Deuteronomy*, AOTC (Downers Grove: IVP, 2002).

McGowan, A. T. B. *Adam, Christ and Covenant: Exploring Headship Theology* (London: Apollos, 2016).

McGrath, Alister. *Iustitia Dei: The Christian Doctrine of Justification*, 3rd ed. (Cambridge: Cambridge University Press, 2005).

McGraw, Ryan M. *A Heavenly Directory: Trinitarian Piety, Public Worship and a Reassessment of John Owen's Theology* (Göttingen: Vandenhoeck & Ruprecht, 2014).

Melanchthon, Philip. *Commentary on Romans* (St. Louis, MO: Concordia Publishing House, 1992).

Mettinger, Trygve N. D. *The Eden Narrative: A Literary and Religio-Historical Study of Genesis 2–3* (Winona Lake: Eisenbrauns, 2007).

Middleton, J. Richard. *The Liberating Image: The Imago Dei in Genesis 1* (Grand Rapids: Brazos, 2005).

461

Midrash Rabbah, Numbers, vol. 1 (London: The Soncino Press, 1983).

Milgrom, Jacob. *Leviticus,* AB, 3 vols. (New Haven: Yale University Press, 1991-2000).

Millbank, John. *The Suspended Middle: Henri de Lubac and the Renewed Split in Modern Catholic Theology,* 2nd ed. (Grand Rapids: Eerdmans, 2005).

Milton, John. *The Major Works including Paradise Lost,* ed. Stephen Orgel and Jonathan Goldberg (Oxford: Oxford University Press, 2008).

Moberly, R. W. L. 'Did the Serpent Get it Right?' *JTS* 39/1 (1988): 1-27.

Moo, Douglas J. *The Epistle to the Romans,* NICNT (Grand Rapids: Eerdmans, 1996).

———. *Galatians,* BECNT (Grand Rapids: Baker, 2013).

———. *The Letters to the Colossians and to Philemon,* PNTC (Grand Rapids: Eerdmans, 2008).

———. *The Letter of James,* PNTC (Grand Rapids: Eerdmans, 2000).

Morales, L. Michael. *Cult and Cosmos: Tilting Toward a Temple-Centered Theology* (Leuven: Peeters, 2014).

———. *The Tabernacle Pre-Figured: Cosmic Mountain Ideology in Genesis and Exodus* (Leuven: Peeters, 2012).

Moreland, J. P., et al., eds. *Theistic Evolution: A Scientific, Philosophical, and Theological Critique* (Wheaton, IL: Crossway, 2017).

Motyer, J. Alec. *The Prophecy of Isaiah: An Introduction and Commentary* (Downers Grove: InterVarsity Press, 1993).

Muller, Richard A. *After Calvin: Studies in the Development of a Theological Tradition* (Oxford: Oxford University Press, 2003).

———. *Calvin and the Reformed Tradition: On the Work of Christ and the Order of Salvation* (Grand Rapids: Baker Academic, 2012).

———. 'Demoting Calvin: The Issue of Calvin and the Reformed Tradition,' in *John Calvin, Myth and Reality: Images and Impact of Geneva's Reformer,* ed. Amy Nelson Burnett (Eugene, OR: Cascade, 2011), 3-17.

———. *Dictionary of Latin and Greek Theological Terms: Drawn Principally from Protestant Scholastic Theology,* 2nd ed. (1985; Grand Rapids: Baker Academic, 2017).

———. 'Divine Covenants, Absolute and Conditional: John Cameron and the Early Orthodox Development of Reformed Covenant Theology,' *MAJT* 17 (2006): 11-56.

———. 'Kuyper and Bavinck on Natural Theology,' *TBR* 10 (2019): 5-35.

_____. *Post-Reformation Reformed Dogmatics*. 4 vols. (Grand Rapids, Baker, 2003).

_____. 'Review of David Weir, *Origins of the Federal Theology,*' *TJR* 72/4 (1992): 597-98.

Muller, Richard A. and Rowland S. Ward. *Scripture and Worship: Biblical Interpretation and the Directory for Worship* (Phillipsburg, NJ: P & R, 2007).

Murray, John. *Collected Writings*, 4 vols. (Edinburgh: Banner of Truth, 1977).

_____. *The Covenant of Grace* (London: Tyndale Press, 1954).

_____. *The Epistle to the Romans*, New International Commentary on the New Testament, vol. 2 (Grand Rapids: Eerdmans, 1965).

_____. *Redemption Accomplished and Applied* (Grand Rapids, MI: Eerdmans, 1955).

Musculus, Wolfgang. *Common Places of Christian Religion* (London: 1563).

_____. *In Esaiam Prophetam Commentarii* (Basil: ex Officina Heruagianus, 1557).

Neusner, Jacob. *The Halakha: Historical and Religious Perspectives* (Leiden: Brill, 2002).

Niehaus, Jeffrey J. 'An Argument against Theologically Constructed Covenants,' *JETS* 50/2 (2007): 259-73.

Nietzsche, Friedrich. *Human, All Too Human: A Book for Free Spirits* (Cambridge: Cambridge University Press, 1996).

Nihan, Christophe. *From Priestly Torah to Pentateuch: A Study in the Composition of the Book of Leviticus* (Tübingen: Mohr Siebeck, 2007).

Novak, David. *Natural Law in Judaism* (Cambridge: Cambridge University Press, 1998).

Nowell, Alexander. *A Catechism Written in Latin by Alexander Nowell, Dean of St. Paul's*, trans. Thomas Norton (1570; Cambridge: Cambridge University Press, 1853).

Nwachukwu, Sylvia C. *Creation-Covenant Scheme and Justification by Faith: A Canonical Study of the God-Human Drama in the Pentateuch and the Letter to the Romans* (Rome: Editrice Pontifica Università Gregoriana, 2002).

Nygren, Anders. *Commentary on Romans* (Philadelphia: Muhlenberg Press, 1944).

O'Brien, Peter T. *Colossians, Philemon*, WBC, vol. 44 (Waco, TX: Word Books, 1982).

O'Connor, Flannery. *Flannery O'Connor: Spiritual Writings*, ed. Robert Ellsbert (Mary Knoll, NY: Orbis Books, 2003).

Oehlschlaeger, Frtiz. *The Achievement of Wendell Berry: The Hard History of Love* (Lexington, KY: The University Press of Kentucky, 2011).

Oeming, Manfred. 'To Be Adam or Not to Be Adam: The Hidden Fundamental Anthropological Discourse Revealed in an Intertextual Reading of *adam* in Job and Genesis,' in *Reading Job Intertextually*, ed. Katharine Dell and Will Kynes (New York: Bloomsbury, 2013), 19-29.

Oepke, Albrecht. Καθίστημι, in *Theological Dictionary of the New Testament*, vol. 3, ed. Gerhard Kittel (Grand Rapids: Eerdmans, 1965), 445.

Origen, *Commentary on the Epistle to the Romans: Books 6–10*, trans. Thomas P. Scheck (Washington, D. C.; The Catholic University of America Press, 2002).

Oswalt, John N. *The Book of Isaiah: Chapters 1–39*, NICOT (Grand Rapids: Eerdmans, 1986).

Owen, John. *The Works of John Owen*, 23 vols. ed. William H. Goold (1850-53; Edinburgh: Banner of Truth, 1998).

Pak, Sujin. *Judaizing Calvin: Sixteenth-Century Debates over the Messianic Psalms* (Oxford: Oxford University Press, 2009).

Pareus, David. *Davids Parei in Divinam ad Romanos S. Pauli Apostoli Epistolam Commentarius* (Geneva: Paulus Marcellus, 1617).

Parker, Heather. '"At their perfect age": Elite Child Betrothal and Parental Control, 1430-1560,' in *Children and Youth in Premodern Scotland*, eds. Janay Nugent and Elizabeth Ewan (Woodbridge, Suffolk, UK: The Boydell Press, 2015), 173-86.

Pedersen, J. *Israel, Its Life and Culture*, vol. 1/1-2 (Oxford: Oxford University Press, 1926).

Pederson, Randall J. *Unity in Diversity: English Puritans and the English Reformation, 1603-1689* (Leiden: Brill, 2014).

Pelagius. *Pelagius's Commentary on St. Paul's Epistle to the Romans* (Oxford: Clarendon, 1998).

Pelikan, Jaroslav and Valerie Hotchkiss, eds. *Creeds and Confessions of Faith in the Christian Tradition*, 3 vols. (New Haven, CT: Yale University Press, 2003).

Pentiuc, Eugene. *Jesus the Messiah in the Hebrew Bible* (Mahwah, NJ: Paulist Press, 2006).

Pererius, Benedict. *Secundus Tomus Disputationum in Sacram Scripturam Continens Centum Octoginta Octo Disputationes Super Eipstola Beati Pauli ad Romanos* (Ingolstadt: Adam Sartorius, 1603).

Perkins, Harrison. *Catholicity and the Covenant of Works: James Ussher and the Reformed Tradition* (Oxford: Oxford University Press, 2020).

_____. 'Meritum ex pacto in the Reformed Tradition: Covenantal Merit in Theological Polemics,' *MAJT* 31 (2020): forthcoming.

_____. 'Reconsidering the Development of the Covenant of Works: A Study in Doctrinal Trajectory,' *CTJ* 53/2 (2018): 289-317.

Perkins, William. *Armilla Aurea, id est, Theologiae Descriptio Mirandam Seriem Causarum et Salutis et Damnationis Iuxta Verbum Des Proponens* (Cambridge: John Legatt, 1591).

_____. *A Commentarie or Exposition, Upon the Five First Chapters of the Epistle to the Galatians* (Cambridge: John Legat, 1604).

_____. *A Golden Chaine, or The Description of Theologie, Containing the Order of the Causes of Salvation and Damnation, According to Gods Woord* (London: Edward Alde, 1595).

_____. *A Reformed Catholike* (Cambridge: John Legat, 1598).

Philo. *Philo*, LCL, vol. 1, trans. F .H. Colson and G. H. Whitaker (1929; Cambridge: Harvard University Press, 1991).

_____. *Philo*, LCL, vol. 9, trans. F. H. Colson (1941; Cambridge: Harvard University Press, 1985).

Pictet, Benedict. *Christian Theology* (London: R. B. Seeley and W. Burnside, 1834).

_____. *Theologia Christiana* (London: R. Baynes, 1820).

Placaeus, Josua. *De Imputatione Primi Peccatis Adami Josue Placaei in Academia Salmuriensi S. s. Theologiae Professoris Disputatio* (Saumur: Ioannem Lesnerium, 1661).

Plummer, Alfred. *The Gospel According to S. Luke*, ICC (1901; Edinburgh: T & T Clark, 1977).

Polanus, Amandus. *Partitiones Theologicae* (Geneva: Peter Albertus, 1623).

Polaski, Donald C. 'Reflections on a Mosaic Covenant: The Eternal Covenant (Isaiah 24:5) and Intertextuality,' *JSOT* 77 (1998): 55-73.

Pollock, Darren M. *Polemical Hermeneutics: Andrew Willet's 1611 Hexapla on Romans* (Göttingen: Vandenhoeck & Ruprecht, 2017).

Pope, James. *The Substance of Christian Religion, Soundly Set Forth in Two Bookes* (London: John Oxbridge, 1595).

_____. *Syntagma Theologicae Christianae* (Hanau: Johannes Aubrius, 1615).

_____. *The unveiling of Antichrist. Or, Antichrist stript naked out of all his Scripture-attyre, by Which He Hath Deceived the Christian World* (London: Henry Overton, 1646).

Postell, Seth D. *Adam as Israel: Genesis 1–3 as the Introduction to the Torah and Tanakh* (Cambridge: James Clarke and Co., 2012).

Preston, John. *The New Covenant or the Saints Portion* (London: Nicolas Bourne, 1639).

Radice, Roberto. 'Philo's Theology and Theory of Creation,' in *The Cambridge Companion to Philo*, ed. (Cambridge: Cambridge University Press, 2010), 124-45.

Rashi, *Leviticus*, The Pentateuch and Rashi's Commentary, trans. Abraham ben Isaiah and Benjamin Sharfman (Brooklyn: S. S. & R. Publishing, 1949).

Rehnman, Sebastian. 'Is the Narrative of Redemptive History Trichotomous or Dichotomous?' *NAK* 80/3 (2000): 296-308.

Reicke, Bo. 'The Law and This World According to Paul,' *Journal of Biblical Literature* 70/4 (1951): 259-76.

Rendtorff, Rolf. *The Covenant Formula: An Exegetical and Theological Investigation* (Edinburgh: T & T Clark, 1998).

Ridderbos, Herman N. *The Epistles of Paul to the Churches of Galatia*, NICNT (Grand Rapids: Eerdmans, 1953).

Ridley, Lancelot. *A Commentary in Englyshe upon Sayncte paules Epystle to the Ephesyans for the Instruccyon of Them That Be Unlearned in Tonges* (London: Robert Redeman, 1540).

Riissen, Leonard. *Summa Theologiae Didactico-Elencticae* (Berne: Daniel Tschiffel, 1703).

Roberts, Francis. *Mysterium et Medulla Bibliorum. The Mysterie and Marrow of the Bible* (London: George Calvert, 1657).

Robinson, Marilynne. *The Givenness of Things: Essays* (New York: Farrar, Straus and Giroux, 2015).

Rollock, Robert. *Analysis Dialectica ... in Pauli Apostolis Epistolam ad Romanos* (Edinburgh: Robert Waldegrave, 1594).

_____. *Analysis Logica in Epistolam Pauli ad Galatas* (London: Felix Kyngston, 1602).

_____. *Quaestiones et Responsiones Aliquote de Foedere Dei* (Edinburgh: Henry Charter, 1596).

_____. *Select Works of Robert Rollock*, 2 vols., ed. William M. Gunn (1844-49; Grand Rapids: Reformation Heritage Books, 2008).

_____. *Some Questions and Answers about God's Covenant and the Sacrament That is a Seal of God's Covenant*, trans. and ed. Aaron Clay Denlinger (Eugene, OR: Pickwick Publications, 2016).

Runge, Steven E. *Discourse Grammar of the Greek New Testament: A Practical Introduction for Teaching and Exegesis* (Peabody, MA: Hendrickson, 2010).

Russell, David. *A Familiar Survey of the Old and New Covenants* (Edinburgh: Waugh and Innes, 1824).

Rutherford, Samuel. *The Covenant of Life Opened: or, A Treatise of the Covenant of Grace* (Edinburgh: Robert Broun, 1655).

Sailhammer, John H. *The Pentateuch as Narrative* (Grand Rapids: Zondervan, 1995).

Sarna, Nahum. *Genesis*, Jewish Publication Society Torah Commentary (Philadelphia: Jewish Publication Society, 1989).

Sarpi, Paolo. *Historia del Concilio Tridentino* (London: Giovani Billio, 1619).

_____. *The Historie of the Councel of Trent*, trans. Nathanael Brent (London: Robert Barker and John Bill, 1620).

Schaff, Philip, ed. *Creeds of Christendom*, 3 vols., 6ᵗʰ ed. (1931; Grand Rapids: Baker, 1990).

Scharpius, Johannes. *Cursus Theologicus in Quo Controversiae Omnes de Fidei Dogmatibus* (Geneva: Francis Nicolaus, 1622).

Schmemann, Alexander. 'The World as Sacrament,' in *Church, World, Mission: Reflections on Orthodoxy in the West* (Crestwood, NY: St. Vladimir's Seminary Press, 1979), 217-27.

Schmitz, Kenneth L. *The Gift: Creation*, The Aquinas Lecture, 1982 (Milwaukee, WI: Marquette University Press, 2011).

Schreiner, Susan. *Are You Alone Wise? The Search for Certainty in the Early Modern Era* (Oxford: Oxford University Press, 2010).

Schreiner, Thomas R. *Galatians*, ZECNT (Grand Rapids: Zondervan, 2010).

_____. *Romans*, BECNT (Grand Rapids: Baker, 1998).

Schweizer, Eduard. 'Slaves of the Elements and Worshipers of Angels: Gal 4:3, 9 and Col 2:8, 18, 20,' in *JBL* 107/3 (1988): 455-68.

Sedgwick, Obadiah. *The Bowels of Tender Mercy Sealed in the Everlasting Covenant*. London: Adoniram Byfield, 1661.

Seitz, Christopher R. *Isaiah 1–39* (Louisville, KY: John Knox Press, 1993).

Selden, John. *John Selden and His Table Talk*, ed. Robert Waters (New York: Eaton & Mains, 1899).

Shaw, Robert. *An Exposition of the Confession of Faith of the Westminster Assembly of Divines*, 8th ed. (Glasgow: Blackie and Son, 1857).

Shedd, W. G. T. *Discourses and Essays* (Andover: W. F. Draper, 1856).

_____. *Dogmatic Theology*, 3 vols. (1888; Grand Rapids: Zondervan, 1969).

Shepherd, Norman. *Call of Grace: How the Covenant Illuminates Salvation and Evangelism* (Phillipsburg, NJ: P & R, 2002).

Silva, Moisés. 'Faith versus Works of the Law in Galatia,' in *Justification and Variegated Nomism*, vol. 2, ed. D. A. Carson, et al. (Grand Rapids: Baker, 2004), 217-48.

_____. *Interpreting Galatians: Explorations in Exegetical Method*, 2nd ed. (Grand Rapids: Baker, 2001).

Simpson, A. W. B. *A History of the Common Law of Contract: The Rise of the Action of Assumpsit* (Oxford: Clarendon Press, 1987).

Skinner, Quentin. 'Meaning and Understanding in the History of Ideas,' *History and Theory* 8/1 (1969): 3-53.

Smeaton, George. *The Doctrine of the Holy Spirit* (Edinburgh: T & T Clark, 1882).

Smith, Henry Boynton. *System of Christian Theology*, 2nd ed. (New York: A. C. Armstrong & Son, 1884).

Snaith, John G. *Ecclesiasticus: or The Wisdom of Jesus Son of Sirach* (Cambridge: Cambridge University Press, 1974).

Son, Sang-Won (Aaron). *Corporate Elements in Pauline Anthropology: A Study of Selected Terms, Idioms, and Concepts in the Light of Paul's Usage and Background* (Rome: Pontifico Instituto Biblico, 2001).

Sprinkle, Preston M. *Law and Life: The Interpretation of Leviticus 18:5 in Early Judaism and in Paul*, WUNT (Tübingen: Mohr Siebeck, 2008).

St. Germain, Christopher. *The Doctor and the Student*, ed. William Muchall (Cincinnati: Robert Clarke and Co., 1886).

Staniloae, Dumitru. 'The World as Gift and Sacrament of God's Love,' *Sorbonost* 9 (1969): 662-73.

Steinmetz, David. *Calvin in Context*, 2nd ed. (Oxford: Oxford University Press, 2010).

_____. 'The Superiority of Pre-Critical Exegesis,' *Theology Today* 37 (1980): 27-38.

Steymans, Hans Ulrich. 'The Blessings in Genesis 49 and Deuteronomy 33: Awareness of Intertextuality,' in *South African Perspectives on the Pentateuch Between Synchrony and Diachrony*, ed. Jurie le Roux and Eckart Otto (London: T & T Clark, 2007), 71-89.

Stordalen, T. *Echoes of Eden: Genesis 2–3 and Symbolism of the Eden Garden in Biblical Hebrew Literature* (Leuven: Peeters, 2000).

Streett, Daniel R. 'As It Was in the Days of Noah: The Prophets' Typological Interpretation of Noah's Flood,' *CTR* 5 (2007): 42-46.

Strong, William. *A Discourse of the Two Covenants: Wherein the Nature, Differences, and Effects of the Covenant of Works and of Grace Are Distinctly, Rationally, Spiritually and practically Discussed* (London: Francis Tyton, 1678).

Stuart, Douglas. *Hosea-Jonah*, WBC, vol. 31 (Waco, TX: Word Books, 1987).

Swain, Scott R. *Trinity, Revelation, and Reading: A Theological Introduction to the Bible and Its Interpretation* (London: T & T Clark, 2011).

Sytsma, David. '"As a Dwarfe Set Upon a Gyants Shoulders," John Weems (ca. 1579-1636) on the Place of Philosophy and Scholasticism in Reformed Theology,' in *Die Philosophie der Reformierten*, Melanchthon-Schriften der Stadt Bretten, eds. Günter Frank and Herman Selderhuis (Stuttgart: Frommann-Holzboog, 2012), 299-321.

Tate, Marvin E. *Psalms 51–100*, WBC, vol. 20 (Dallas, TX: Word, 1990).

Telfer, Charles. *Wrestling with Isaiah: The Exegetical Methodology of Campegius Vitringa (1659-1722)* (Göttingen: Vandenhoeck & Ruprecht, 2016).

The Bible and Holy Scriptures Conteyned in the Olde and Newe Testament (Geneva: Rouland Hall, 1560).

The Confession of Faith and Catechisms of The Orthodox Presbyterian Church (Willow Grove, PA: The Committee on Christian Education of the Orthodox Presbyterian Church, 2005).

The Humble Advice of the Assembly of Divines, Now by Authority of Parliament Sitting at Westminster, Concerning a Confession of Faith (London: Company of Stationers, 1647).

The Humble Advice of the Assembly of Divines, Now by Authority of Parliament Sitting at Westminster, Concerning a Larger Catechisme (London: A. M. 1648).

The Humble Advice of the Assembly of Divines, Now by Authority of Parliament Sitting at Westminster, Concerning a Shorter Catechisme (London: J. F. 1648).

Thompson, J. A. *Deuteronomy*, TOTC (Downers Grove: IVP, 1974).

Thompson, John. L. *Genesis 1–11*, RCS (Downers Grove, IL: InterVarsity Press, 2012).

Thornwell, James H. *Collected Writings*, vol. 1, ed. John B. Adger (Richmond: Presbyterian Committee of Publication, 1871).

Thrall, Margaret E. *The Second Epistle to the Corinthians*, vol. 1, ICC (Edinburgh: T & T Clark, 1994).

Thronveit, Mark A. *Ezra-Nehemiah* (Louisville, KY: John Knox Press, 1992).

Tigay, Jeffrey H. *Deuteronomy*, JPSTC (Philadelphia: JPS, 2003).

Tolkien, J. R. R. *The Fellowship of the Ring*, 2nd ed. (Boston: Houghton Mifflin Company, 1965).

Torrance, James B. 'The Concept of Federal Theology – Was Calvin a Federal Theologian?' in *Calvinus Sacrae Scripturae Professor: Calvin as Confessor of Holy Scripture*, ed. Wilhelm H. Neusner (Grand Rapids, MI: Eerdmans, 1994), 15-40.

_____. 'Covenant or Contract? A Study of the Theological Background of Worship in Seventeenth-Century Scotland,' *Scottish Journal of Theology*, 23 (1970): 51-76.

Trelcatius, Lucas. *A Briefe Institution of the Common Places of Sacred Divinitie* (London: Francis Burton, 1610).

Trueman, Carl. 'Original Sin and Modern Theology,' in *Adam, the Fall, and Original Sin: Theological, Biblical, and Scientific Perspectives*, ed. Hans Madueme and Michael Reeves (Grand Rapids: Baker Academic, 2014), 167-86.

Turner, Kenneth J. *The Death of Death in the Death of Israel: Deuteronomy's Theology of Exile* (Eugene: Wipf & Stock, 2010).

Turretin, Francis. *Institutes of Elenctic Theology*, 3 vols., trans. George Musgrave Giger, ed. James T. Dennison Jr. (Phillipsburg, NJ: P & R, 1992-97).

_____. *Institutio Theologicae Elencticae*. Edinburgh: Robert Carter, 1847.

Ursinus, Zacharias. *The Commentary of Dr. Zacharias Ursinus on the Heidelberg Catechism* (1852; Phillipsburg: P & R, n. d.).

———. *Der Heidelberger Katechismus und Vier Verwandte Katechismen* (Leipzig: Georg Böhme, 1907).

———. *The Summe of Christian Religion*, trans. D. Henrie Parry (Oxford: 1601).

Ussher, James. *A Body of Divinitie, or The Summe and Substance of Christian Religion* (London: Tho. Downs and Geo. Badger, 1645).

Van Asselt, Willem. *The Federal Theology of Johannes Cocceius (1603-69)* (Leiden: Brill, 2001).

Van Mastricht, Petrus. *Theoretica-Practica Theologia*, 9th ed., vol. 1 (Utrecht: W. van der Water, et al., 1724).

Van Steters, John. *Prologue to History: The Yahwehist as Historian in Genesis* (Louisville: Westminster John Knox, 1992).

Van Til, Cornelius. *Common Grace and the Gospel* (Phillipsburg, NJ: P & R, 1972).

———. *Herman Dooyeweerd and Reformed Apologetics*, 3 parts (Philadelphia, PA: Westminster Theological Seminary, 1972).

Van Til, Salomon. *Theologiae Revelatae Compendium*, in *Theologiae Utrisque Compendium* (Leiden: Jordan Luchtmans, 1704).

Van Vliet, Jan. *The Rise of Reformed System: The Intellectual Heritage of William Ames* (Milton Keynes: Paternoster, 2013).

VanDrunen, David. *A Biblical Case for Natural Law* (Grand Rapids: Acton Institute, 2006).

———. *Divine Covenants and Moral Order: A Biblical Theology of Natural Law* (Grand Rapids: Eerdmans, 2014).

———. *Natural Law and the Two Kingdoms: A Study in the Development of Reformed Social Thought* (Grand Rapids: Eerdmans, 2009).

VanDrunen, David and Manfred Svensson, eds. *Aquinas Among the Protestants* (Oxford: Wiley Blackwell, 2018).

Vanhoozer, Kevin. *First Theology: God, Scripture, and Hermeneutics* (Downers Grove: InterVarsity Press, 2002).

Velde, Rudi te. *Aquinas on God: The 'Divine Science' of the Summa Theologiae* (Aldershot: Ashgate Publishing, 2006).

Venema, Cornelis. *Accepted and Renewed in Christ: The Twofold Grace of God and the Interpretation of Calvin's Theology* (Gottingen: Vandenhoeck & Ruprecht, 2007).

_____. 'The Mosaic Covenant: A "Republication" of the Covenant of Works?' *MAJT* 21 (2010): 35-101.

Venema, Herman. *Dissertationum Sacrarum, Libri Tres* (Leiden: Samuel and Johannes Luchtmans, 1771).

Vermigli, Peter Martyr. *Commentary on Aristotle's Nicomachean Ethics* (Kirksville, MO: Truman State University Press, 2006).

_____. *The Common Places of the Most Famous and Renowned Divine Doctor Peter Martyr*, trans. Anthonie Marten (London: 1583).

_____. *In Epistolam S. Paul Apostoli ad Rom. D. Petir Martyris Vermiliji*, 3rd ed. (Basil: Peter Pernius, 1568).

_____. *Loci Communes D. Petri Martyris Vermilii* (London: Thomas Vautroller, 1583).

_____. *Most Learned Commentaries of D. Peter Martir Vermilius ... Upon the Epistle of S. Paul to the Romanes* (London: John Daye, 1558).

_____. *Predestination and Justification*, The Peter Martyr Library, vol. 8, ed. Frank A. James III (Kirksville, MO: Sixteenth Century Essays and Studies, 2003).

Vickers, Brian. *Jesus' Blood and Righteousness: Paul's Theology of Imputation* (Wheaton: Crossway, 2006).

_____. *Justification by Grace through Faith: Finding Freedom from Legalism, Lawlessness, Pride, and Despair* (Phillipsburg, NJ; P & R, 2013).

Virel, Matthieu. *La Religion Chrestienne* (Geneva: Eustace Vignon, 1586).

Vitringa, Campegius. *Commentarius in Librum Jesiae*, vol. 2 (Leeuwarden: Franciscus Halma, 1720).

Von Rad, Gerhard. *Genesis*, rev. ed. (Philadelphia: The Westminster Press, 1961).

Vos, Arvin. *Aquinas, Calvin, and Contemporary Protestant Thought: A Critique of Protestant Views on the Thought of Thomas Aquinas* (Washington D. C: University of America Press, 1985).

Vos, Geerhardus. *The Pauline Eschatology* (1930; Phillipsburg, NJ: P & R, 1994).

_____. *Redemptive History and Biblical Interpretation: The Shorter Writings of Geerhardus Vos*, ed. Richard B. Gaffin, Jr. (Phillipsburg, NJ: P & R, 1980).

_____. *Reformed Dogmatics*, 5 vols., ed. Richard B. Gaffin, Jr., et al. (Bellingham, WA: Lexham Press, 2012-14).

_____. *The Self-Disclosure of Jesus: The Modern Debate about the Messianic Consciousness* (Phillipsburg, NJ: P & R, 1953).

____. 'The Scriptural Doctrine of the Love of God,' *PRR* 13/49 (1902): 1-37.

____. 'Some Doctrinal Features of the Early Prophecies of Isaiah,' *PRR* 8 (1897): 444-63.

Wagner, J. Ross. *Heralds of the Good News: Isaiah and Paul in Concert in the Letter to the Romans* (Leiden: Brill, 2003).

Walaeus, Antonius. *Loci Communes S. Theologiae Autore D. Antonio Walaeo* (Leiden: Adrian Whyngarden, 1647).

Walker, George. *The Manifold Wisedome of God: In the Divers Dispensation of Grace by Jesus Christ.* London: John Bartlet, 1640.

____. *Socinianisme in the Fundamentall Point of Justification Discovered and Confuted* (London: John Bartlet, 1641).

Waltke, Bruce K. *Genesis: A Commentary* (Grand Rapids: Zondervan, 2001).

____. *An Old Testament Theology: An Exegetical, Canonical, and Thematic Approach* (Grand Rapids: Zondervan, 2007).

Warburton, William. *The Divine Legation of Moses Demonstrated in Nine Books*, 10th ed., 3 vols. (London: A. Millar and J. and R. Tonson, 1765).

Ward, Rowland S. *God and Adam: Reformed Theology and the Creation Covenant*, 2nd ed. (2003; Lansvale, Australia: Tulip Publishing, 2019).

Warfield, B. B. 'Hosea VI.7: Adam or Man?' in *The Selected Shorter Writings*, 2 vols., ed. John E. Meeter (rep.; Phillipsburg, NJ: P & R, 2001), I:116-29.

____. 'The Idea of Systematic Theology,' in *Studies in Theology* (Oxford: Oxford University Press, 1932), 49-87.

Waters, Guy P., Nicholas Reid, and John R. Muether, eds. *Covenant Theology: Biblical, Theological, and Historical Perspectives* (Wheaton, IL: Crossway, 2020).

Watson, Thomas. *A Body of Practical Divinity* (London: Thomas Parkhurst, 1692).

Watts, John D. *Isaiah 1–33*, WBC, vol. 24 (Nashville, TN: Thomas Nelson, 1985).

Watts, Isaac. *Faith and Practice Represented in Fifty-Four Sermons on the Principle Heads of the Christian Religion*, vol. 1 (London: John Oswald, 1739).

Wawrykow, Joseph P. *God's Grace and Human Action: 'Merit' in the Theology of Thomas Aquinas* (Notre Dame: University of Notre Dame Press, 1995).

Webster, John. *The Culture of Theology*, ed Ivor J. Davidson and Alden C. McCray (Grand Rapids: Baker Academic, 2019).

Weinfeld, Moshe. Weinfeld, Moshe. *Deuteronomy 1–11*, AB (New York: Doubleday, 1991).

_____. 'Sabbath, Temple and Enthronement of the Lord,' in *Mélanges Bibliques et Orientaux en l'honneur de M. Henri Cazelles*, ed. A. Caquot and M. Delcor (Neukirchen-Vluyn: Neukirchener Verlag, 1981), 501-12.

Weir, David. *Origins of Federal Theology in Sixteenth-Century Reformation Thought* (Oxford: Oxford University Press, 1990).

Weiser, Arthur. *The Psalms: A Commentary* (Philadelphia: The Westminster Press, 1998).

Wenham, Gordon J. *Genesis*, WBC, 2 vols. (Dallas, TX: Word Books, 1994).

_____. 'Sanctuary Symbolism in the Garden of Eden Story,' in *I Studied Inscriptions from Before the Flood: Ancient Near Eastern, Literary and Linguistic Approaches to Genesis 1–11*, eds. Richard S. Hess and David Toshio Tsumura (Winona Lake, IN: Eisenbrauns, 1994), 399-404.

Westerholm, Stephen. *Israel's Law and the Church's Faith: Paul and His Recent Interpreters* (Grand Rapids: Eerdmans, 1988).

Westermann, Claus. *Genesis 1–11*, trans. John J. Scullion, S. J. (Minneapolis: Fortress, 1994).

Whitaker, William. *Tractatus de Peccato Originali* (London: Johannes Legat, 1600).

Willet, Andrew. *Hexapla: That Is, A Six-fold Commentarie upon the most Divine Epistle of the Holy Apostle S. Paul to the Romanes* (London: Leonard Greene, 1620).

Williams, Michael. 'Adam and Merit,' *Presbyterion* 35/2 (2009): 87-94.

Wilson, David. *Palæmon's Creeds Reviewed and Examined*, 2 vols. (London: George Keith, 1762).

Wilson, Thomas. *A Christian Dictionarie* (London: W. Iaggard, 1612).

Witherington III, Ben. *Grace in Galatia: A Commentary on Paul's Letter to the Galatians* (Grand Rapids: Eerdmans, 1998).

Witsius, Herman. *Conciliatory, or Irenical Animadversions on the Controversies agitated in Britain, under the Unhappy Names of Antinomians and Neonomians*, trans. Thomas Bell (Glasgow: W. Lang, 1807).

_____. *De Oeconomia Foederum Dei Cum Hominibus*, 2nd ed. (Leeuwarden: J. Hagenaar, 1685).

_____. *Economy of the Covenants Between God and Man*, 2 vols., trans. William Crookshank (1822; Escondido, CA: Den Dulk Foundation, 1992).

Wolf, Hans Walter. *Hosea* (Minneapolis: Fortress, 1974).

Wollebius, Johannes. *Compendium Theologiae Christianae* (Basil: Joh. Jacob Genathus, 1633).

Woolsey, Andrew A. *Unity and Continuity in Covenantal Thought: A Study in the Reformed Tradition to the Westminster Assembly* (Grand Rapids: Reformation Heritage Publishing, 2012).

Wright, N. T. *The Day the Revolution Began: Reconsidering the Meaning of Jesus's Crucifixion* (San Francisco, CA: Harper One, 2016).

_____. 'The Law in Romans 2,' in *Paul and the Mosaic Law*, ed. James D. G. Dunn (Grand Rapids: Eerdmans, 1996), 131-50.

_____. 'The Letter to the Galatians: Exegesis and Theology,' in *Between the Two Horizons*, ed. Joel B. Green and Max Turner (Grand Rapids, MI: Eerdmans, 2002), 205-36.

_____. *The New Testament and the People of God* (Philadelphia: Fortress Press, 1992).

_____. *Paul and the Faithfulness of God*. 2 vols. (Minneapolis, MN: Fortress Press, 2013).

_____. *The Resurrection of the Son of God* (Minneapolis, MN: Fortress Press, 2003).

_____. *Romans*, NIB, vol. 10 (Nashville, TN: Abingdon, 2002).

_____. *What St. Paul Really Said: Was Paul of Tarsus the Real Founder of Christianity?* (Grand Rapids: Eerdmans, 1997).

Wuellner, Bernard. *Dictionary of Scholastic Philosophy* (Fitzwilliam, NH: Loreto Publications, 2012).

Xenophon. *Xenophon: Memorabilia and Economics*, trans. E. C. Marchant, LCL (1923; Cambridge: Harvard University Press, 1959).

Young, E. J. *The Book of Isaiah*, 3 vols. (Grand Rapids: Eerdmans, 1969).

_____. 'Confession and Covenant,' in *Scripture and Confession: A Book About Confessions Old and New*, ed. John H. Skilton (Phillipsburg, NJ: P & R, 1973), 31-66.

Zanchi, Girolamo. *De religione Christiana Fides – Confession of Christian Religion*, 2 vols., ed. Luca Baschera and Christian Moser (Leiden: Brill, 2007).

❖ SUBJECT INDEX ❖

Page numbers with the suffix 'n'
(e.g. 85n) indicate information
in the footnotes. Cov. stands for
covenant. All other abbreviations
are from pages viii-x.

A

À Brakel, Wilhelmus .... xxvi, 60, 102,
103-4, 245-6, 329,
378, 417, 440
Abimelech 172, 173, 234
Abraham
and Abimelech 172, 234
justification of 18, 178-9, 276,
353, 362-3, 365, 369
Abrahamic covenant
cov. of grace ... 145, 228, 268, 275-6,
279, 344, 351, 353, 362-3
cov. terminology 62
exegesis Isa. 24:5 .... 222-3, 228
Mosaic cov. 156, 267-70, 275,
279, 344, 351
Sarah 228, 267-8, 275, 344
accidentals
see substance-accidents
active obedience, of
Christ 346-8, 355, 439-40
active potency 89-90, 383
Adam
faith of 49-54, 367-8
historicity of 293, 296, 410, 416

revelation to 44-7, 51-2, 116,
283, 387
and the Spirit 44, 45, 47, 114,
386, 413-14, 416-17, 425
telos 47, 49, 122-3, 299,
359-60, 387
term used for
'man' 241-2, 245, 247, 251-3
see also Adam's obedience; beatific
vision; imputation; last Adam;
pre-fall anthropology; tree of
the knowledge of good and evil
Adam-Israel parallels
doctrine 321-2, 331-2,
340-2, 345, 347
exegesis 191-7, 235, 241-2,
253-8, 261, 277, 284-5, 300
Adam (place) 240, 251, 258-9
Adamic Administration 1, 162, 201
Adamic covenant
death 18, 29-30, 35, 174-5,
188-91, 194-5, 218, 230-1, 235-7
exegesis 217-19, 230-7, 240-8
terminology 1-12, 318
see also condescension; dominion
mandate; Mosaic covenant link
to Adamic covenant; tree of life;
tree of the knowledge of good
and evil
Adam's obedience
cov. of works 6, 12, 58, 318

and faith................................ 49, 51-2
love for God...........................329-30
ordo salutis.....................................374
pre-fall grace.................. 92-7, 378-9,
383, 408
Trinity and
Spirit............. 399-400, 403, 405
allegory 16, 19, 266-7, 304, 349, 410
Ambrogio Catharinus...................... 242
Ames, William............................. 59, 72
Anderson, Francis 251
angelic council .. 419, 420-2, 424-7, 431
Annotations of Dort................. 74-5, 223
antecedent conditions, definition.65-6
Aquinas, Thomas 15-19, 26-7, 34-5,
47, 70, 79-86, 89-90, 95, 96,
290, 380, 383-4, 385, 391, 412
Aristotle.................. 70, 82-4, 87, 168-9,
384-5, 412
Arminius, Jacob 93-4, 105
Augustine of Hippo ..... xxix, 28, 29, 66,
80, 83, 85, 86-7, 167, 191, 292,
294, 304, 380, 388, 414, 424, 427
Augustinian-Thomism
see nature-grace dualism
Augustinus (Jansen) 101

B
Baius, Michael 100
Ball, John 36-7, 59, 96-7, 105, 133
Barth, Karl .... xviii-xx, xxii, 161,
409-13, 414-16, 435
Bavinck, Herman .... xxxiii, 319, 325,
363, 366, 369, 371, 374, 412-13
beatific vision
doctrinal history..............79-82, 84,
85, 95-6
doctrine.......378, 380, 383-4, 386-7,
396, 405, 416-17
Belgic Confession (1561) 88-9, 104,
323, 398, 413
Bell, Thomas.................... 151, 263, 264
Bellarmine, Robert............31, 127, 382
berith .... xix, 63, 64, 73, 74
Berkhof, Louis.......................... 162, 247
Beza, Theodore...........................88, 304

bilateral covenants.............57, 60, 235n
Blake, Thomas................. 134, 156, 158
Blenkinsopp.................................... 235n
Bolton, Samuel.......... 38-9, 127-8, 130,
131, 132, 156, 351
Boston, Thomas 144-5, 154, 156,
246, 253, 254, 352
Brakel, Wilhelmus à........ xxvi, 60, 102,
103-4, 245-6, 329,
378, 417, 440
Braun, Johannes 103
Bres, Guy de..................................... 88
Brooks, Thomas 357, 374
Bruce, F. F. 266-7
Buchanan, James 150-2, 156, 352
Bulkeley, Peter..........................133, 156
Bullinger, Heinrich... 109-10, 156, 350
Burges, Cornelius...............................70
Burgess, Anthony...........94-5, 105, 107,
128-30, 132, 139, 156, 352
Burroughs, Jeremiah 128-9, 130-1,
156, 252-3, 351, 352
Buxtorf, Johannes, Sr. 63
Byfield, Nicholas............................. 120

C
Cain.. 234
Calamy, Edmund 36, 128-30,
132, 134, 156
Calvin, John .... xx, 14, 19-27, 33, 38,
39, 52, 58, 61, 77, 84-7, 88,
90, 91, 104, 110-13, 115,
117, 122, 123, 156, 165,
170-1, 220, 223-5, 226, 242,
276-7, 294, 303, 330, 342,
350, 385, 389-90
Cameron, John....... 5, 36, 44, 47-9, 108,
122-3, 130, 133, 140,
145, 156, 158
Campbell, Douglas .... xx-xxi
Carter, Craig................................... 430
Cartwright, Thomas...................3-4, 11
Caryl, Joseph.....................................70
Cavendish, Margaret 69
Chalcedon, Council of (451)...........415
Chesteron, G. K. 415

Christ Jesus
    cov. of grace 118, 148, 177,
            264, 309, 310, 348, 370,
            402, 405, 417, 433-4
    death of 74, 232-3, 292, 303,
            306-9, 356, 370-1,
            398, 432, 433, 437
    faith of...................................368-70
    foreshadowed by priests/
        ceremonies 111, 112, 136-7,
            153, 250, 277, 345-6, 432
    grace 21, 135, 148, 152, 274
    imputation of His
        righteousness......................8, 282,
            291-2, 295-300
    mediator .. 86, 118, 123, 136-7, 440
    merit.......................................398-9
    obedience of 306, 313, 346-8,
            355, 366-7, 376, 439-40
    teaching on eternal life:
        Luke 10:25-28......... 35, 153, 180,
            208-9, 211, 214,
            229, 328, 336, 436
    teaching on eternal life:
        Matt. 19:16...... 15-17, 19, 23, 28,
            30, 33, 35, 39, 209
    type/antitype with
        Israel 321-2, 342, 345, 348
    union with 167, 177, 301, 303,
            307-8, 310, 336, 353-4, 365
    see also last Adam; Trinity
Christology ....xxxii, 299, 378,
            409-12, 414-16
Chrysostom, John 28, 29, 31,
            304, 423
Church Dogmatics (Barth) .... xix, 161,
            409-11, 413
Cicero.. 168
circumcision............. 146, 229, 265, 275,
            334, 365
City of God (Augustine)....................427
Clement of Alexandria............405, 423
Cocceius, Johannes 53, 63, 102,
            244, 301-2
Colquhoun, John.................. 145-9, 156,
            246, 352

common law............................... 71, 219
concomitant conditions,
    definition 65-6
condescension
    doctrinal history......... 7, 64-5, 73-4,
            98, 105-6
    doctrine...............325, 337, 360, 379,
            389, 391, 396
condign merit.............. 79, 97, 102, 103,
            379, 397-9
congruent merit............. 79, 92, 97, 103,
            379, 380, 397-9
conscience.........162, 163, 167, 171, 173,
            177, 181, 219, 310, 323
contract, use of term...... 1, 55-60, 62-3,
            66-72, 75, 224, 435
cosmic mediation 85n, 86, 91
Council of Trent..................242, 365-6
covenant, use of term......7, 9-10, 55-66,
            69-70, 72-5, 183-4, 197, 312
covenant name of
    God...........................190, 320-1, 401
covenant of faith................8-9, 53, 65-6
covenant of grace (foedus gratiae)
    Abrahamic cov............145, 228, 268,
            275-6, 279, 344,
            351, 353, 362-3
    Christ 118, 148, 177, 264,
            309, 310, 348, 370, 402,
            405, 417, 433-4
    cov. of redemption 58, 400, 402,
            431, 433, 434
    faith 41, 43-53, 65, 367
    justification.....................358-9, 364,
            367, 370, 372
    Lev. 18:5.....200, 201, 203, 214, 342
    one and only cov............. 58, 61, 344,
            409-11
    ordo salutis..........367, 370, 372, 375
    Sarah 112, 117, 264, 266-7,
            275-6, 278, 279, 344
    terminology................. 2-11, 55, 118
    trans-testamental cov.........111, 115,
            124, 141, 276
    unconditional...........................73-4
    WCF........52, 127-38, 336, 349, 367

see also Mosaic covenant as covenant of grace; new covenant
covenant of life.................. 1, 6-7, 12, 95, 201, 322, 329
Covenant of Life Opened (Rutherford) 95-6, 133, 359
covenant of nature (*foedus naturae*) 5-6, 8-10, 11, 34, 46, 47-9, 128
see also natural covenant (*foedus naturale*)
covenant of redemption............. 58, 400, 402, 431, 433, 434
covenant of works
   summary............. 318, 337-8, 437-40
   telos 6-7, 11, 12, 43, 49, 99, 186, 208, 335, 359-60, 363, 364, 387, 439
   terminology.................... 1-2, 4, 5-12, 115-18, 121-2, 318
   see also Adamic covenant; Mosaic covenant; Mosaic covenant link to Adamic covenant; rule of life
creation *ex nihilo*................ xxvi, 388-91, 399, 416, 436
creation law 271, 272-3
Crisp, Tobias............... 136-9, 156, 158
Cum Occasione (papal bull)............. 100
Curtis, Byron 255-6, 258-9
Cyril of Alexandria............. 241-2, 422

D

Daneau, Lambert..............................243
Daniel 353-4, 437-8
Davenant, John..........................32, 422
David, covenant with Jonathan.......................xxvi, 57, 60-1
Davidic covenant............. 187, 226, 228, 237, 334
De Status Purae Naturae (Jansen) .. 100
death
   of Christ............74, 232-3, 292, 303, 306-9, 356, 370-1, 398, 432, 433, 437
   end of contract/cov................ 62, 74, 304-5, 311-12

exile as..........194-5, 331-2, 334, 345
   of Jacob and Moses...................... 196
'ministry of death' 147, 152-3, 215, 308, 343, 345
penalty of Adamic cov. 18, 29-30, 35, 174-5, 188-91, 194-5, 218, 230-1, 235-7
penalty of Mosaic cov. 6, 15, 117, 121, 125, 147, 152-3, 194-5, 215, 279, 308, 343, 345
debts.........10, 65, 67, 102, 359-60, 400
Decades (Bullinger) 109-10
Decalogue
   doctrinal history........ 114-17, 125-7, 134-5, 144-6, 149
   exegesis......... 176, 179-80, 188, 190, 194, 198, 202, 283-4, 332
diatheke 57-8, 60, 64, 73
Dickson, David......................35, 58, 72
Diodati, Giovanni..........................33-4
divine image
   see image of God
dominion mandate
   Adam 186, 189-90, 283, 300, 322-4, 328-30
   for all humanity......296, 318, 326-7
   image of God.......... 186, 322-4, 326, 328, 386-7, 426
Domning, Daryl.............................. 293
Donne, John.................................... 438
donum superadditum.......... 46, 325, 379, 381, 385, 403, 408
Downame, John....... 49, 72, 126-7, 422
Durham, James..................................58

E

Eagleton, John 61, 246-7, 260
Eden
   see Garden of Eden
English Civil War 71
Ephrem the Syrian...........................423
eschaton (new creation)
   eschatology precedes soteriology ....xxxii, 358, 364-5, 386, 439

Mosaic cov. 264, 271-2, 274
relationship to protological
    state...... 264, 274-5, 311-12, 366,
        370, 372, 373, 375, 386, 406-7
eternal life
Christ's teaching:
    Luke 10:25-28 .... 35, 153, 180,
        208-9, 211, 214, 229,
            328, 336, 436
Christ's teaching:
    Matt 19:16.............15-17, 19, 23,
        28, 30, 33, 35, 39, 209
faith 43-4, 47, 50
Lev. 18:5.................... 15-17, 19, 21-3,
    25, 28-30, 32-5, 39, 41, 180,
    204, 208-9, 211-12, 214-16,
    229, 328, 336, 342, 436
merit and grace 78, 81, 91,
    92, 99-100, 104-5,
        363, 367, 381, 386
Mosaic cov. 112, 119-22,
    141-3, 149, 157
see also tree of life
evangelical covenant (foedus
    evangelicum) 5, 8-9, 11, 33,
        111-12, 115, 119,
        122-3, 124, 276-7
evangelical faith................ 49, 51-4, 367
evangelical obedience 36-8, 41, 200
Eve 45, 188, 194, 292, 322, 330, 395
Ex Omnibus Afflictionibus
    (papal bull) 100
exile
    Adam.............................334, 337, 395
    Adam foreshadows Israel 191-6,
        235, 261, 321-2,
        331-2, 345, 347
    Cain 234
    Daniel... 354
    Israel................................... 206, 249

F
faith
    Adam's faith................. 49-54, 367-8
    Christ's faith...........................368-70
    covenant of faith 8-9, 53, 65-6

doctrine.............. 318, 328, 344, 353,
    363, 365-70, 412
Lev. 18:5....................17-18, 20-8, 31,
    34-5, 38, 209-15
Mosaic cov. 110, 127, 144
natural/supernatural 44-9, 51-2
Romans............................ 178-9, 312
fides legalis (legal faith) 49-54, 367
Finch, Henry 6, 11, 68-9
first and second covenants 2-3
Fisher, Edward.......... 62, 108, 113, 125,
    126, 144, 156, 301, 309
foedus evangelicum
    see evangelical covenant (foedus
        evangelicum)
foedus gratiae
    see covenant of grace (foedus
        gratiae)
foedus legale
    see legal covenant (foedus legale)
foedus naturae
    see covenant of nature (foedus
        naturae)
foedus naturale
    see natural covenant (foedus
        naturale)
foedus operum ...6, 10-11, 115-19, 121-2
Formula Consensus
    Helvetica (1675) 140, 158, 360
Freedman, David Noel.....................251

G
Gallican Confession (1559) 88, 104,
    105, 413
garden of Eden
    first temple/communion
        with God.............. xxvi, 331, 333
    parallels with promised land 185,
        192, 196, 202, 218, 235,
        240-1, 321, 331-3, 340-1,
            347, 355
    parallels with Song of
        Songs 394-5
    see also tree of life; tree of the
        knowledge of good and evil
Genesis Rabbah.................. 191-2, 240-1

Gentiles
    definition 164-6
    Galatians 272-4
    Isaiah 203, 219-21, 227, 237
    Rom. 2:14-15 .... 115, 126, 162-7,
                 168n, 170-3, 180, 219,
                 233, 273-4, 323
    Rom. 7:1-6 .... 303, 310-11, 312-13
Gesenius, Wilhelm 219, 234
Golden Chaine (Perkins)............. 116-17
Gomarus, Franciscus...................4-5, 32
Gomer.......................................249, 305
Goodwin, Thomas 5, 36, 43, 44-9,
         52, 156, 359, 406-7, 422
gospel and law distinction
    see law and gospel distinction
gospel faith 49, 51-4, 367
Gouge, William...............................74
government covenant/contract ...68-70
grace 378-88, 408-9, 416
    see also covenant of grace (*foedus*
         gratiae); Mosaic covenant as
         covenant of grace; nature-grace
         dualism
Gregory of Nyssa 387
Grotius, Hugo 68
Günkel, Hermann 419, 421

H
Hagar 112, 117, 263-4, 266-8,
         275, 276, 278-9, 344
Heidegger, Johannes...............6, 11, 12,
         139-40, 156,
         158, 244, 378
Hellwig, Monica 293
historia salutis............................ 291, 353
Hobbes, Thomas............................ 70-1
Hodge, Charles 152-3, 156, 295,
         302, 312, 343-6, 354
Holmes, Oliver Wendell...................68
Holy Spirit
    see Spirit
Hosea 248-9, 256, 258, 261, 305
human beings
    see image of God; pre-fall
         anthropology

Hume, David 71
Hunsinger, George 415

I
Ibn Ezra, Abraham
    ben Meir 219, 234
Idealism .... xxii, 161, 162, 411
image of God
    all humanity 45, 171-2
    angels............. 419, 420-2, 424-7, 431
    and cov. 116, 185-6, 322-30,
         386-7, 407-8
    nature-grace dualism 86, 88,
         93, 97, 99, 104
    ordo salutis................................373-4
    Trinity/Son/
         Spirit........404, 406, 416-17, 421,
         423-4, 425-8, 433, 436
    WCF...................................... 35, 99
imputation
    Adam's guilt.... 118, 175, 232-3, 235,
         242, 283, 318, 326-7
    of Adam's guilt and Christ's
         righteousness.....................8, 282,
         291-2, 295-300
Innocent X, Pope 100
Institutes of the Christian Religion
    (Calvin) 86, 87, 109, 110, 277
Irish Articles (1615) 185, 324
Isaac 228, 266, 267, 275, 437
Ishmael 266, 275
Israel
    exegesis Hosea 6:7 .... 241-2, 245,
         249-50, 252-8, 261
    exegesis Isa. 24:5 ....219-20, 223,
         224-5, 230, 235, 237
    exegesis Lev. 18:5........... 200, 202-8,
         212, 215-16
    exegesis Rom. 5:12-21... 284-5, 300
    exegesis Rom. 7:1-6 ....305, 310-11
    type/antitype with Christ...... 321-2,
         342, 345, 348
    see also Adam-Israel parallels;
         Mosaic covenant

J
Jacob........................ 187, 196, 310, 437

Jansen, Cornelius 100-1
Jerome of Stridonium 241, 243, 248
Jerusalem 112, 142, 266-8, 275
Jesus Christ
   see Christ Jesus
Jews, definition 164-6
Johnson, Thomas C. 233
Jonathan, covenant with
   David .... xxvi, 57, 60-1
Judaizers 201, 265, 269, 272, 274,
                           275-6, 279, 365
Junius, Francis 4-5, 93-4, 105
justification
   doctrinal history 18, 19, 21-8, 35,
            37, 46, 49-53, 65-6, 127, 141
   doctrine 328, 343, 353, 357-75
   exegesis Gal. 4:24 ...... 266, 270, 276
   exegesis Lev. 18:5 ....209, 213
   exegesis Rom. 2:14-15 .... 166, 177,
                                       178-9
   exegesis Rom. 5:12-21 298,
                              299, 300
   exegesis Rom. 7:1-6 302-3,
                              306-7, 311-12
   relationship to
      sanctification 26-7, 306, 358,
                              364, 370-5

K
Kahn, Victoria.....................................69
Käsemann, Ernst 168n
Kidner, Derek................................. 254
Kline, Meredith 229, 230, 231-2,
                           233, 237, 420-1,
                           424-7, 431, 434
Kuyper, Abraham 412-13, 435

L
La Faye, Antoine de 30
Landy, Francis 255
Lañyez, Diego................................. 2-3
Lapide, Cornelius à 241
last Adam
   doctrine...........321-2, 336, 342, 358,
                     363, 365-6, 403, 415-
                     16, 433, 437-40
   exegesis. 192, 292, 294-300, 311-12

law
   Aquinas 15-19, 26-7, 290
   Calvin............................ 20-7, 111-12
   defined using Lev. 18:5 .... 15, 17-42,
                              113, 178, 201-16
   and love 329-30
   vs. promise........38, 40, 268-70, 278
   reveals sin 111-12, 121, 148-9,
                     157, 166, 177, 279, 308
   terminology...............................285-91
   see also common law; contract,
      use of term; covenant, use
      of term; creation law; legal
      covenant (foedus legale);
      marriage covenant/contract;
      moral law; natural law;
      statute, use of term
law and gospel distinction
   doctrine............................... 437, 439
   Mosaic cov. 119-22, 124, 127,
                     140, 146, 152-3
   Reformation.........3-4, 6, 22-3, 26-7,
                     28, 29, 31, 32, 277-9
   post-Reformation 39-40
law of nature
   see natural law
legal covenant (foedus legale)......5, 8-10,
                     26, 33, 111-12, 117-19,
                     122, 276-9, 345-6, 350
legal faith (fides legalis) 49-54, 367
legal obedience 37, 200
legalism.........................xx, 41-2, 59, 201
Leigh, Edward 5, 108, 124, 156, 422
Levenson, Jon...............................393-4
Leviathan (Hobbes)........................ 70-1
Lex Rex (Rutherford) 59
Lord's Day 371, 375-6
love
   God's love for humanity 377-9,
                     388-91, 399, 413, 416
   and obedience 329-30, 392-6
Luther, Martin 3, 89-90, 104,
                     105, 243, 397

M
Maccovius, Johannes 33
Machen, J. Gresham 439

marriage covenant/contract
doctrinal history..... 57, 62, 63, 68-9
doctrine............................394-6, 439
exegesis.................... 172-3, 288, 301,
304-6, 308, 312-13
Marrow of Modern Divinity, The
(Fisher/Boston) 62, 108, 113,
125-6, 144-5, 154, 301, 352
McGowan, Andrew.... xxi-xxii, 61, 435
mediate imputation 295
Melanchthon, Philip 3, 304
merit
condign/congruent...........79, 92, 97,
103, 379, 380, 397-9
ex pacto 92, 102-3, 104,
106, 380-2, 399
pre-fall Adam and
grace........ xxii-xxiii, 65, 78, 80-1,
92, 96-9, 105
Trinity and pre-fall
Adam 397-408
objections to Trinitarian
approach............................408-16
meritum ex pacto 92, 102-3, 104,
106, 380-2, 399
Midrash Rabbah 421-2
Milton, John...................................... 438
'ministry of death' 147, 152-3, 215,
308, 343, 345
Moo, Douglas.................................. 285
moral law
doctrinal history..............114, 125-7,
134-9, 149, 155, 157
doctrine................323-4, 346-7, 356
exegesis............. 163, 174-80, 309-11
Moran, William 392
Mosaic covenant
and Abrahamic cov. 156, 267-70,
275, 279, 344, 351
and death 6, 15, 117, 121, 125,
147, 152-3, 194-5, 215,
279, 308, 343, 345
exegesis......................223-6, 249-50,
286-8, 303-7
law reveals sin ... 111-12, 121, 148-9,
157, 166, 177, 279, 308

priests/ceremonies foreshadow
Christ 111, 112, 136-7, 153,
250, 277, 345-6, 432
third cov. (*tertium quid*) ... 39, 122-3,
128-33, 143, 145, 156, 158
see also Decalogue; national
covenant
Mosaic covenant as covenant of grace
doctrinal history......... 122-4, 132-9,
140-7, 149, 152, 156, 158
doctrine..................... 340, 342, 344,
350-4, 356
exegesis........................ 176, 180, 214,
268, 276-7, 308-9
Mosaic covenant link to
Adamic covenant
doctrinal history......107-10, 113-15,
119-21, 123, 127-31,
144, 154-6
doctrine....... 320-1, 323, 334-5, 339,
341-2, 346-9, 353
exegesis Gal. 4:24 ....264, 270-9
exegesis Gen. 2:16-17.......... 189-98
exegesis Hosea 6:7......................257
exegesis Isa. 24:5 ....220-2, 225,
227, 229-30, 237
exegesis Lev. 18:5.................. 214-15
exegesis Rom. 2:14-15.............174-6,
179-81
exegesis Rom. 5:12-21....... 290, 300
exegesis Rom. 7:1-6 310-13
Moses.............16, 20-1, 24, 28, 31, 111,
118, 196, 272, 353-4
Motyer, Alec 225-6, 237
Muller, Richard.......................... 60, 381
Murray, John.....xix-xx, 1, 41-2, 61, 162,
168n, 183-4, 200-3, 205,
247, 252, 359, 435, 439
Musculus,
Wolfgang...... 91, 113-15, 223, 422

N

national covenant..... 142-4, 145-6, 149,
150, 153, 154, 156,
345, 352, 354-5
natural covenant (*foedus
naturale*) 3, 4-5, 11

see also covenant of nature (*foedus naturae*)

natural faith 44-6, 48-9, 51-2

natural gifts 47, 80, 86-9, 93-4, 97, 104-5, 385

natural law
  doctrinal history............35, 70-1, 91, 113-14, 115, 125-6, 134
  doctrine................323-4, 328-9, 387, 410, 411, 415
  exegesis Isa. 24:5 ....219, 222, 223, 233-5
  exegesis Rom. 2:14-15........ 161, 163, 167-76, 179-81
  exegesis Rom. 7:1-6............303, 305, 310-11

natural potency 83, 85, 87

natural revelation....................161, 186, 328-9, 412

nature-grace dualism
  Aquinas 78, 79-86, 89-90, 95, 96, 383-4, 385, 412
  Reformation............................84-91
  Early Orthodoxy 91-4
  High and Late Orthodoxy... 94-101
  overlap of alternative approaches...........................104-5

Neusner, Jacob....................................341

new covenant
  doctrinal history................124, 129, 137-8, 156
  doctrine...................334, 343-4, 346
  exegesis Gal. 4:24......... 267, 269-70, 275
  exegesis Isa. 24:5 ... 226, 228, 236-7
  exegesis Rom. 5:12-21....... 286, 298
  exegesis Rom. 7:1-6 .... 306, 308

new creation
  see eschaton (new creation)

New Testament
  see trans-testamental covenant

Nicaea, Council of (325) 415

Nicomachean Ethics (Aristotle) 87, 169

Noahic covenant 220, 221-2, 226, 228, 230-1, 232, 235-7, 255

nomos-governed states 282, 283, 284-5

Novak, David.................................... 234

Nowell, Alexander............................243

Nwachukwu, Mary Sylvia C........ 361-2

O

obedience
  of Christ......... 306, 313, 346-8, 355, 366-7, 376, 439-40
  legal/evangelical 36-8, 41, 200
  and love 392-6
  see also Adam's obedience

obediential potency ...82-4, 85, 87, 383

Old Testament
  see trans-testamental covenant

On the Law of War and Peace (Grotius) 68

ontology.................. 78-9, 84, 91, 93, 96, 98, 102, 105, 106, 293

ordo salutis 291, 353, 370-5

Origen of Alexandria 29, 304

Owen, John 98, 105, 156, 347, 405-6, 408-9, 416

P

passive obedience, of Christ 346, 348, 439

passive potency...........82-4, 89-90, 383

Paul
  and cov. terminology................ 5, 10
  Aquinas 15, 17-19, 26, 81
  Calvin..............20-3, 25, 26, 33, 112, 165, 170-1
  further Reformed introduction to 27-8, 29, 31-2, 37, 41-2, 53, 113, 115, 147-8, 150, 152

Pelagianism................................ xix, 439

Pelagius.................................... 167, 293

Pererius, Benedict...............................30

Perkins, William.........92, 108, 115-20, 121-2, 156, 398

Petto, Samuel 156

Philo of Alexandria.................169, 349, 422, 430

Pictet, Benedict 102-3, 104

pistis Christou 368
Pius V, Pope 100
Placaeus, Josua 295
Plato 349
Polanus, Amandus 108, 120-2, 156
political covenant/contract 68-70
Pope, James 128-9, 156
pre-fall anthropology
   in church history 382-5
   God's love for humanity 377-9,
        388-91, 399, 413, 416
   imitative link to Adam 293-4
   see also merit; nature-grace dualism
pre-fall covenant
   see Adamic covenant
Preston, John 59, 62
priests
   Adamic cov. 194
   Mosaic cov. 111, 112, 136-7, 153,
        250, 277, 345-6, 432
Prima Hominis Justitia (Baius) 100
promised land
   Moses precluded from 353-4
   parallels with Eden 185, 192,
        196, 202, 218, 235,
        240-1, 321, 331-3,
        340-1, 347, 355
   return from exile 206
   Song of Songs 394
proportionality 79, 82, 84, 95,
        102-3, 105, 379, 383-5, 400
protology
   indwelling of the Spirit 405-6
   Mosaic cov./law 264, 270, 271-2,
        274-5
   roots of justification 358, 360,
        365-6
   and soteriology 370, 386

Q

quadriga 16-17, 18-20, 26-7, 31, 41

R

Rashi, Rabbi 393
regeneration 45, 66, 86, 92,
        310, 353

revelation
   to Abraham 344
   to Adam ...44-7, 51-2, 116, 283, 387
   at Sinai 133, 134-5, 149, 153,
        156, 272, 345
   see also natural revelation; special
      revelation; supernatural
      revelation
Ridderbos, Herman 210n
Roberts, Francis 37, 53, 64-6
Rollock, Robert 6, 12, 91, 104,
        105, 119
Roman Catholicism
   Adamic cov. Hosea 6:7 241-2,
        248, 260
   Adam's pre-fall state 46-7,
        100-1, 105
   condign/congruent
      merit 79, 92, 97, 103,
        379, 380, 397-9
   justification 23, 24, 65-6,
        127, 365-6
rule of life
   doctrinal history 139, 146,
        148-9, 154
   doctrine 353, 356
   exegesis 176-7, 265, 278, 309-10
Rutherford, Samuel 43, 50, 59, 95-6,
        105, 133-4, 156, 359, 385

S

Sabbath
   doctrine 318-19, 320, 334, 335,
        349, 364-5, 371, 375
   exegesis 186, 229, 309
salvation
   doctrinal history 59, 65-6, 86,
        110-11, 146, 150
   doctrinal history Lev. 18:5 .... 21, 24,
        25, 27, 39
   doctrine 291, 344, 353, 367,
        370-5, 437
   exegesis Gal. 4:24 .... 264-5, 268,
        274, 276, 278
   exegesis Lev. 18:5 211-12,
        214, 215-16

exegesis Rom. 2:14-15........ 164, 167, 178-9
exegesis Rom. 5:12-21................ 292
exegesis Rom. 7:1-6 312
see also soteriology
sanctification, relationship to
justification 26-7, 306, 358, 364, 370-5
Sarah
and Abimelech 172, 173
Abrahamic cov.................228, 267-8, 275, 344
cov. of grace 112, 117, 264, 266-7, 275-6, 278, 279, 344
Scharpius, Johannes 124, 156
second covenant
see first and second covenants
Sedgwick, Obadiah 6, 12, 156, 158, 398
Selden, John 69
sexual immorality 172, 203, 204
shadow-substance
relationship 349, 353, 356
Shaw, Robert 149, 156, 352
Shepherd, Norman.......................... 369
signs of covenants........59, 85, 188, 190, 320, 334-5
Silva, Moisés 368
Simpson, Sydrach 128-9, 156
sin
angels... 422
imitation of Adam...................293-5
revealed by law.............. 111-12, 121, 148-9, 157, 166, 177, 279, 308
terminology 233, 285-91, 436
see also imputation
Skinner, Quentin 56
Smeaton, George.............405, 408, 422
Smith, Henry Boynton 295
Solemn League and
Covenant (1638) 70
soteriology
preceded by eschatology.......... xxxii, 358, 364-5, 386, 439
and protology.... 370, 373, 384, 386
special revelation 219, 226, 233-4, 283-4, 326, 387, 412, 414

Spirit
Adam 44, 45, 47, 114, 386, 413-14, 416-17, 425
Christ 348, 365, 370
cov. of works 332-5
new cov............ 275, 306-7, 312, 343
Trinity 400-7, 425-6
spiritual covenant (spirituale
foedus) 33, 111-12, 277
St. Germain, Christopher 67
Staniloae, Dumitru 390
statute, use of term 222, 229-30
Strong, William.............. 301, 309, 377
substance-accidents 109-12, 124, 135-6, 137, 141, 156, 277, 350-1
Sum of Saving Knowledge, The
(Dickson and Durham) 58
Summa Contra Gentiles
(Aquinas) 82, 89-90
suntheke 57, 60, 73
supernatural covenant...................... 4-5
supernatural faith 44-9, 51-2
supernatural gifts............ 44, 47, 80, 81, 86-9, 93-4, 97, 104-5, 383, 385
supernatural grace 47, 48, 80-1, 84, 104
supernatural revelation 47, 161, 172, 174, 176, 179-81, 186-7, 328
Syntagma Theologiae (Polanus)........121

T
telos
Adam 47, 49, 122-3, 299, 359-60, 387
covenant of works............6-7, 11, 12, 43, 49, 99, 186, 208, 335, 359-60, 363, 364, 387, 439
temporal blessings
and eternal life 142, 143, 204
extended life 43, 44, 122-3, 359
Lev. 18:5......................15, 17-18, 25, 28-9, 32, 36, 39, 212
testament, use of term 64, 73-5
third covenant (tertium
quid).....................39, 122-3, 128-33, 143, 145, 156, 158
Tolkien, J. R. R. 439

Torrance, James B. ....xx-xxi, 55-62, 69, 75, 435

trans-testamental covenant 111, 115, 124, 141, 276

transgression, use of term.........285-91

tree of life 84-5, 87, 90, 116, 190, 327, 329, 335, 360, 438

tree of the knowledge of good and evil

  Adam's eschatological goal.........387

  and Adam's image-bearer role 322, 326-30

  Adam's mortality 174-5, 384

  evidence of Adamic cov. 113-14, 116, 183, 187-8, 190, 198, 300, 312, 318, 320-1, 326-30, 334-5

  parallels with Mosaic cov./ Decalogue 198, 283, 284, 321, 341

Trelcatius, Lucas 33

Tremellius, Immanuel..................... 252

Trinity.................. 322, 337, 388, 400-7, 411, 414, 419-33

Turretin, Francis 7-9, 11, 34-5, 101-2, 104, 139-41, 156, 158, 184, 244, 277-8, 295, 350, 354, 412-13

U

unilateral covenants...........57-8, 60, 68

Ursinus, Zacharias 3, 59, 92, 125

Ussher, James................. 11, 33, 50, 181, 185, 324, 422

V

Van Til, Salomon 102, 103, 104, 412

VanDrunen, David 221-2, 228, 229, 236, 237, 421, 431

Vatable, François 252

Vermigli, Peter Martyr 14, 27-8, 87-8, 104, 108, 114-15

Vickers, Brian 360

Vindiciae Legis (Burgess) 94-5, 107, 132, 139, 352

Viret, Pierre 88

Vitringa, Campegius.................219, 234

Vos, Geerhardus.......180, 231, 247, 317, 318-19, 326, 347, 351, 360, 364, 370, 372, 375, 378, 387, 396-7

W

Waleaus, Antonius..............................53

Walker, George....................4, 6, 11, 12, 132-3, 156

Warfield, Benjamin B. 247, 317

Webster, John .... xiii, xiv

Wellhausen, Julius 251

Westminster Confession of Faith

  Adam pre-fall 98-100, 105-6, 323-8, 374, 388, 413

  condescension 7, 73-4, 98, 105-6, 325, 389

  cov. of grace 52, 136, 336, 367

  cov. of works 2, 7, 13, 240, 243-4, 260, 318, 320, 351, 354

  imputation...............295, 318, 326-7

  merit...............................397-8

  moral law 114, 126-7, 134-5, 137, 139, 155, 174-80, 309-10, 323-4, 346-7

  Mosaic cov. 114, 126-7, 134-6, 139, 146, 148-9, 154, 346-7, 354

  Trinity 402

Westminster divines...............7, 124-39, 176-7, 223, 349-50

Westminster Larger Catechism 1, 6-7, 244, 323, 329

Westminster Shorter Catechism........1, 6-7, 134-5, 179, 244, 318, 322, 372-3

Whitaker, William 243

Willet, Andrew........ 14, 29-32, 73, 422

Williams, Michael................... xxii-xxiii

Wilson, David.........................xvii-xviii

Wilson, Thomas 63

Witsius, Herman 9-11, 34, 59, 60, 102, 104, 141-3, 156, 244, 329, 351

Witte, Petrus de 32

Wollebius, Johannes 32, 93, 105

works

  see covenant of works

Wright, N. T. ....xxiii-xxiv

Y

Young, E. J....................................218-20

Z

Zwingli, Ulrich 109

❧ SCRIPTURE INDEX ☙

OLD TESTAMENT

Genesis
1 255
1-2 .... xxiii, xxxii, 362,
    391, 426, 428, 431
1-3 .... 183-5, 189-95,
    197, 284, 320-1, 327,
    331, 394, 397, 429
1-11 ....195, 361, 410
1-26 433
1:1 ....413, 425, 427
1:1-2:4 195
1:2 .... 332, 333, 403,
    420, 426
1:3 311
1:3-4 186
1:3-6 326
1:18 326
1:21 425
1:26 .... 35, 244, 260,
    386, 404, 419-34
1:26-27 .... 125, 174,
    175, 428
1:26-28 326
1:27 425-7
1:28 ....174, 184-5, 186,
    189, 190, 194, 196,
    214, 256, 283, 284,
296, 300, 312, 318, 320,
    322, 326, 364, 406
1:30 256
1:31 ..292, 312, 373, 385
2:1-4 186
2:3 318

2:3-4 425
2:4 ....189, 320
2:4-11:9 361
2:7 .... 232, 322, 333,
    394, 404, 425
2:8 394
2:8-15 340
2:9 ....87, 320, 321
2:15 .... 194, 225, 394
2:16 ....37, 189, 190, 390
2:16-17 .... 174, 183-98,
    214, 231, 244, 272,
    283, 284, 300, 312,
    318, 321, 322, 326,
    327, 364
2:17 ....35, 121, 125,
    174, 175, 244, 260,
    303, 320, 330, 341
2:18-19 186
2:22-23 322
3:6 ....188, 194,
    255, 292, 334
3:7 331
3:7-8 253
3:8 .... 193, 341, 386
3:11 243
3:12 395
3:14-19 .... 193, 194
3:15 ....162, 340
3:16 395
3:17 ....218, 231
3:17-18 225
3:18 256
3:19 331
3:21 193

3:22 .... 162, 420, 426
3:22-24 194
3:23-24 196
3:24 ....420, 426
5:1 425
5:1-3 421
5:3 424
5:5 330
6:4 229
6:5 195-6
6:5-8 226
6:7 425
6:9 172
6:18 .... 75, 183, 261
7:11 236
7:16 236
8:2 ....221, 236
8:7 221
8:11 221
8:21 ....196, 236
8:21-22 221
8:22 222
9 362
9:6 35
9:8-17 361
9:9-11 220
9:10 255
9:13-16 ....188, 320
9:16 ....226, 228,
    236, 334
11:7 ....420, 426
12:3 189
15 .... xxxii, 267
15:6 178
15:9-10 64

15:14......................144
15:17..........................64
15:18......................288
17:1 .... 144, 172
17:2 226
17:4 63
17:6 362
17:7 .... 62, 144, 228
17:7-8......................255
17:9 223
17:9-14...............188, 320
17:11-12...................334
17:13 .... 63, 223,
                              228, 229
17:14 223
17:19 228
18:2............................426
18:5............................194
18:21..........................426
18:21-22 420
19:1............................426
20:6-7........................172
20:9............................172
20:11 172
22:17.........................255
22:18.........................362
26:5..........222, 226, 229
27:29.........................189
28:3............................362
34:10..........................425
47:22.........................230
47:26.........................230
47:29-30 196
48:4............................362
49 196
49:30..........................196
50 196

Exodus
3:14............................401
3:14ff................ 189, 320
4:22........................... 340
6:4............................. 288
13:21.......................... 333
19:5......................63, 121
19:6............................224
19:21..........................254
20......................144, 323
20:1-17 ....190, 194,
                   200, 283, 284
20:5............................188
20:7.................188, 189

20:11 188
20:12-16.................. 209
20:13 188
20:13-15...................320
20:17..........................194
20:18-21 193
20:19-23:22 284
20:20..........................401
20:26..........................193
21:12-17 283
24 ....64, 223
24:7-8........................223
24:8............................334
25-34 193
29:45..........................224
31:12..........................320
31:13................ 188, 335
31:14 189
31:16..........................229
31:16-17 334
32:8........................... 288
33:28..........................254
34:27 117

Leviticus
11-15.........................193
11:8............................194
16:21-22 296
18:2.......................... 202
18:5 .... xxx, 13-42,
      53, 96, 113, 120, 127,
      147, 154, 155, 158,
      162, 165, 175, 178,
      180, 199-216, 229,
      265, 269, 276, 279,
      328, 336, 342, 344,
      345, 347, 355, 368,
                     435, 436
18:5 (LXX) 208
18:6-23 203
18:24-28................... 202
18:26..........................203
18:29.......................... 204
19:18........208, 209, 330
19:23.......................... 341
20:9............................. 15
24:8..................226, 229
24:16..........................189
25:3............................259
26:12 .... 224, 341
26:16..........................225
26:25-45 226

26:40....................... 288
26:42 288

Numbers
3:7-8..........................194
4:23-24......................194
4:26............................194
4:32............................425
5:1-4 332
5:12 288
5:19-20...................... 288
5:20............................305
5:29 288
5:29 (LXX) 305
9:15-16 333
11:25..........................333
12:1-15.......................332
14:41 288
15:28..........................136
16:30..........................425
22:18.......................... 288
24:5-9 340
24:9............................189
24:13 288
27:14.......................... 288
30:8-9........................226
35:55..........................218

Deuteronomy
1:43 288
4:1 165
4:3............................332
4:20-31......................249
4:25-28......................332
5 323
5:2 121
5:6-21 200
5:21............................194
6:4.....................328, 396
6:4-6................. 329, 392
6:5...................xxvii, 208
6:24 369
6:24ff........................205
6:25 213
7:12-13 341
8:19............................341
9:12 288
9:15 (LXX) 64
9:16 288
10:4.................. 135, 179
10:12..........................392
11:1............................392

11:13.........................392
11:16.......................... 288
11:22.........................392
11:26-28...................226
11:26-29...................189
13:2-6.......................332
13:7-11.....................332
13:13-16..................332
14:8...........................194
17:2-7.......................332
17:20....................... 288
19:9...........................392
19:21.........................332
20:12-14...................214
21:19.........................218
24:1-4.......................305
27:1-28:68................ 321
27:26........... 34, 38, 120,
141, 144, 147,
184, 278, 369
28-34............... 185, 191,
195, 261
28:1-6.......................250
28:1-68................... 206
28:14....................... 288
28:15....... 225, 272, 332
28:15-35...................250
28:15-68...................194
28:15ff......................226
28:20........................332
28:58-68..................332
29-34............... 195, 197
29:12.........................189
29:21................263, 304
29:24........................332
30:6.......... 134, 193, 322
30:12.......................31-2
30:15.................. 25, 30
30:15-19...................205
30:16.........................392
30:19..........23, 189, 327
30:20............. 331, 392
31:1...........................250
31:14........................196
31:16........................196
31:20........196, 226, 288
31:21........................196
31:27-29 196
31:51-52 353
32:1-43.....193, 322, 331
32:8..........................245
32:49 196

33 196
33:2 (LXX) 270
34 196
34:1-5 196

Joshua
3:16........................... 251
7 296
7:11..........288, 289, 290
7:15...................288, 289
8:25..........................254
11:15....................... 288
23:16........288, 289, 290
24:22 143

Judges
2:1............................229
8:10..........................254
12:6..........................254
20:44 254
20:46 254

1 Samuel
4:10..........................254
12:21....................... 288
14:24........................190
15:24....................... 288
18:3.....................xxvi, 61
20:8 61
23:18......................... 61
31:8..........................254

2 Samuel
1:19..........................254
1:25..........................254
1:27..........................254
3:38..........................254
7:14ff........................187
7:16..........................334
11:7 254
13:13-14 338
14:17 431
21:9..........................254
23:1..........................259
23:5..................226, 228
24 296

1 Kings
3:12-14 401
6:18..........................394
7:18-19 394

8:21...........................121
8:31..........................190
22:20 254

2 Kings
7:3-8 332
18:12........288, 289, 290
23:3........................... 143

1 Chronicles
1:1 245
16:17 228
21 296

2 Chronicles
6:22 190
15:12........................ 143

Ezra
4:18..........................419

Nehemiah
9:5-37 207
9:6-30...................... 206
9:19-20......................333
9:29..............206-8, 216,
342, 356
9:38............................ 63
10:29........................ 143

Job
1:1 172
1:6 .... 421, 424
1:8 172
2:1 .... 421, 424
2:3 172
14:15-17 288
25:4........................... 36
26:13 403
28:18 .... 244, 260
28:28 .... 125, 175
31:1 75
31:33............... 162, 245,
246, 252, 253
33:4.......... 333, 403, 404
34:11........................164
34:14-15 334
34:19........................103
38:7................. 421, 424

Psalms
2:7 433
3:6 404

8 .... 312, 415
8:3-4 414
8:4 437
8:5 421
8:6 .... 386, 414
19:7-8 188
22:1 432
23:6 331
25:10 63
25:14 63
27:4 331
29:1 .... 421, 424
33:6 403
40:6-8 xxvii
40:8 432
51:10 425
62:12 164
68:17 270
78:10 304
81:7 VUL 254
82:1 254
82:7 .... 246, 254
89:6 .... 421, 424
89:12 425
89:47 425
101:3 288
101:6 288
102:18 425
104:30 .... 403, 425
105:10 ....226, 228
106:3 37
106:38 218
110:1 433
110:4 432
111:5 229
111:9 229
111:10 401
112:1 37
119:1-2 37
119:6 143
119:89 223
119:119 288
143:2 .... 166, 265
147:18-19 187
147:19-20 310
148:5 425
148:5-6 187

Proverbs
1:7 401
2:20 .... 373, 385
3:16 401

5:5 332
5:20-23 332
6:24 305
6:29 305
7:21-27 332
9:10 401
14:26-27 401
15:33 401
16:6 401
18:12 401
19:23 401
22:4 401
26:17 339

Ecclesiastes
7:29 ....35, 125, 175,
244, 260, 328,
373, 385
7:30 .... 80, 88
12:1 425
12:14 164

Song of Songs
1:7 395
1:17 394
2:9-10 394
2:12 259
2:16 394
3:1-4 395-6
4:3 394
4:12 394
4:15-16 394
5:1 394
6:2 394
7:10 395
8:13 394

Isaiah
1:12-17 250
1:19 18
4:5 425
6:8 ....420, 426
11:2 401
13-23 .... 221, 227,
234-5, 237
14:12 254
19:8-9 334
23:17 227
24-27 .... 222, 227,
230-1, 232
24:1-3 230
24:1-4 227

24:1-6 237
24:4 .... 231, 233
24:5 ......xxx, 217-37, 288,
289, 290, 304, 436
24:5-6 .... 218, 235-6
24:5-6a 233
24:6 .... 221, 225,
231, 235
24:13-16 226
24:17 221
24:18 236
24:20 233
25:6-8 230
25:8 ....231, 232, 237
26:16-19 231
26:20 .... 221, 236
27:8-9 232
40:13 403
40:26 425
40:28 425
41:20 425
42:1 402
42:5 425
43:1 425
43:7 425
43:15 425
45:7-8 425
45:12 425
45:18 425
48:7 425
53:11-12 .... 296, 432
53:11b 298
54:5 305
54:16 425
55:3 ....226, 228
57:19 425
61:1 401
61:1-3 402
61:8 228
61:10 ....296, 396
62:5 305
63:11-14 333
65:17-18 425
66:24 288

Jeremiah
3:1 305
3:9 218
5:28 288
11:2 223
11:4 223
17:10 164

20:4 255
31:20 235
31:22 425
31:31 .... 137, 267, 306
31:31-33 .... 117, 118, 304
31:31-34 298
31:33 171
31:35-36 222
32:40 .... 63, 228
33:20-21 222
33:25-26 187
34:18-20 64
50:5 228

Ezekiel
14:14 354
16:11-13 396
16:59 .... 288, 289, 290
16:60 228
17:15-16 .... 288, 289
17:18 .... 288, 289, 290
18:9 205
18:17 205
18:19 205
18:21 205
20 .... 24-5, 28, 40,
        41, 216, 342, 355
20:1-26 204-6
20:11 .... 25, 35, 52,
        120, 127, 162,
        184, 214
20:12 335
20:13 .... 15, 35, 162, 214
20:20 .... 162, 335
20:21 214
20:23-26 215
20:25 .... 30, 206, 345
21:30 425
28:13 425
28:15 425
33:15 205
36-37 214
36:37 333
37 331
37:26 228
44:7 .... 288, 290

Daniel
7 296
7:13 312
7:13-14 438
9 203

9:5 288
9:11 .... 226, 354

Hosea
1:2 258
1:2-3:5 249
1:4-5 258
1:6-8 258
1:9-10 255
2:18 .... 255, 256
2:20 MT 255
2:21 256
2:23 255
2:25 MT 255
3:1-5 305
4-14 249
4:3 256
6:1-3 249
6:4 250
6:4-11:11 249
6:6 .... 250, 255, 261
6:7 .... xxiv, xxix, xxx,
        13, 162, 191-2, 235,
        239-61, 288, 289, 290,
        299, 300, 344, 436
6:9 251
8:1 .... 288, 289
9:6 256
10:8 256
11:1 .... 340, 342
11:12-12:14 249
12:2 164

Amos
3:3 65
4:13 425
5:21-24 250

Micah
6:6-8 250

Habakkuk
2:4 .... 18, 21-2, 210,
        211-12, 214, 265,
        276, 279

Haggai
2:4-5 333

Zechariah
3:1-5 296

5:3 226

Malachi
2:10 425
2:14 .... 63, 288, 305
7:21 36

**DEUTERO-
CANONICAL
BOOKS**

1 Maccabees
10:19 419

4 Maccabees
12:13 270

2 Baruch
54:19 293

Sirach
11-12 191
14:17 191
16:26-28 273
17:1 191

NEW TESTAMENT

Matthew
2:15 342
3:15 369
3:16-17 402
3:17 .... 348, 432
5:17 .... 215, 311
5:18 223
5:18-19 .... 329, 369
5:45b 390
7:12 120
9:13 250
12:7 250
15:2-3 287
18:15 295
18:17-19 144
19:10-15 209
19:16 .... 15-16, 28, 30
19:16-17 .... 17, 23, 34,
        39, 41, 209
19:16-19 120
19:17 .... 32, 35, 127, 184
19:17-19 147
19:18-19 209

19:26......................210
22:37-38..................392
22:37-40..................179
25:1-13 306
25:46 209
26:28 ....298, 334
26:39 432
26:64 312
27:46 .... 369, 432
28:18-20.......... 334, 362

Mark
1:17 348
10:17-22.................. 209
14:24................298, 334
14:62......................312

Luke
1:75 373
3:22........................ 348
3:38................340, 393
4:16-21 402
4:18-21 401
10:25.............. 211, 214
10:25-28..................144,
208-10, 216,
328, 336,
342, 356
10:26-28..................153,
180, 345
10:27....................... 208
10:28......... 35, 162, 208,
211, 229, 436
10:29....................... 209
17:10 ....92, 96, 99,
102, 103
17:26-37 236
18:18-23 209
18:19.......................385
19:16-17 165
22:20 ....298, 306, 334
22:29 288
22:29b......................432
22:69 312
23:46 432

John
1:1-2......................427
1:1-3 85
1:1-4.......................403
1:3 425
1:13 423

1:17 ....20-1, 148,
270, 290
3:16..........127, 377, 400
3:28-29..................... 306
4:34.........................369
5:14 295
5:24.........................432
6:38-40 369
10:34.......................254
14:15 392
14:18 xxvii
14:31 437
15:9-10 .... xxvii, 393
17:3-6 369
17:4 432
17:5 425
20:21-22.................. 404
20:22 425

Acts
1:25.........................287
2:3-4........................333
2:17 400
2:35.........................433
3:14 .... 373, 385
6:7..............................49
7:8 229
7:53 270
13:32-33 433
13:38.......................127
16:31 127
17:24-25 389
17:26.......................324
17:28....................... 388
21:24.......................271

Romans
1-2 310
1:1-2 361
1:3-4 312
1:4 433
1:16-17...................164
1:17 ....18, 21
1:18-32 ..... 164, 167, 176
1:19-21 273
1:20.........................387
1:32 ....167-8, 273
2:2...........................164
2:3 37
2:5...........................164
2:6-11 164
2:7 37

2:12.................. 166, 173,
274, 310
2:13.............23, 141, 166,
213, 278, 369
2:14...........................233
2:14-15 ....35, 45, 113,
115, 125, 126, 134,
161-81, 219, 244,
260, 273, 274, 323
2:15...........................387
2:16 174
2:23.................. 257, 286
2:27..........................152
3:1-20......................167
3:3...............................49
3:10.........................385
3:11b........................384
3:12 361
3:12c........................385
3:19 165
3:19-20 121
3:20..........127, 167, 300
3:20-21 35
3:21-5:11 299
3:21-22 ....27, 50
3:22 368
3:23 36
3:26 368
3:27 .... 10, 53, 127,
178, 367
3:27-28 300
3:28............35, 127, 178
3:29.........................36
4:1-8.........................276
4:2 ....18, 27
4:2-3 178
4:3 .... 367, 369
4:4 .... 102, 359
4:4-5.........................318
4:5 .... 367, 372
4:9...........................367
4:11-14......................367
4:15 .... 257, 286, 299
4:16..........................367
4:18-20 367
4:22..........................367
4:24..........................367
5:1-11.......................292
5:4...........................377
5:5 400
5:8...................... 377, 400
5:12............36, 125, 174,

175, 233, 244,
260, 292, 294
5:12-13 ... 35
5:12-14 ...283, 290,
307, 356
5:12-21 ... xxxi, 162,
232, 233, 237,
256, 281-300,
307, 322, 369
5:13-14 ... 284
5:13-14a ...285, 290
5:14 ... xxvii, 192, 235,
252, 257, 272, 294,
297, 321, 342, 344,
363, 373, 402, 403,
433, 436, 437
5:15 ...294
5:16 ...294, 298
5:17 ...37, 294
5:18 ...294, 372
5:19 ...125, 174, 175,
243, 257, 294, 295,
298, 307, 363, 366
5:19-20 ...243, 244, 260
5:20-21 ...212, 308
5:20a ...287
6:2-3 ...307
6:4-6 ... 308
6:6-7 ...303
6:7 ... 306
6:8 ... 308
6:9 ...305
6:11 ... 308
6:14 ... 274-5, 302,
306, 307
6:14b ...309
6:20-23 ... 304
6:23 ... 35
7:1 ... 303, 310
7:1-6 ...xxxi, 301-13
7:2-3 ... 304
7:4 ... 306
7:4-6 ... 62, 301
7:5-6 ...307
7:6 ... 152, 167
7:7-11 ... 121
7:10 ... 34, 162, 306, 328
7:12 ...206, 269, 373, 385
8:2 ...178
8:2-3 ... 35
8:3 ... 39
8:4 ... 167

8:8 ...102
8:10 ...328
8:22-23 ... 231
8:30 ... 371
9-11 ... 232, 361
9:4 ... 63, 298
9:26-27 ...232
9:30-31 ... 212, 214
10 ... 32, 213
10:1 ...212
10:3 ...212
10:3-4 ... 27
10:4 ... 212, 269, 309
10:5 ...13, 14, 15, 18,
23, 24, 27, 29, 34, 35,
37, 117, 119, 120, 125,
127, 134, 147, 152,
154, 162, 165, 174,
175, 179, 180, 212-14,
216, 229, 243-4, 260,
264, 268, 328, 336,
342, 344, 347, 356
10:5-6 ... 25, 38
10:6-10 ... 213-14
11:27 ...298
11:35 ...92
12:6 ...49
13:8 ...269, 278
13:8-10 ... 167
13:10 ...269, 278
13:10b ...330

1 Corinthians
1:30 ...371
2:9 ... 81, 82, 84, 383
3:16 ...333
6:11 ...354
6:19 ...333
11:25 ...298, 306
15:20-28 ...312
15:21-22 ... 244
15:22 ...37, 322
15:22-25 ...415
15:28 ...433
15:34 ...295
15:42-49 ...312
15:42-58 ...237
15:44-46 ...386
15:45 ... 299, 322, 363,
403, 434
15:45-49 ...232
15:45-56 ... 5

15:45ff ...44
15:47 ... 37
15:47-49 ...437
15:54 ...232
15:56 ...313

2 Corinthians
2:9 ...384
3 ... 343, 344, 356
3:1-11 ...342-6
3:3 ...118
3:6 ...19, 152, 158,
267, 298, 306
3:7 ...215
3:7-18 ... 308
3:14 ...267, 298, 343
3:18 ... 47
5:4 ...292, 384
5:5 ...81, 82, 84,
383, 384
5:7 ... 47
5:17 ... 406
11:3 ...292

Galatians
1:4 ... 307, 365
2-3 ... 368
2:6-7 ... 103
2:16 ... 35, 265, 368
2:20 ... 368
3-4 ...269
3:2 ...49
3:3 ...152
3:5 ... 167
3:10 ... 38, 120, 125,
141, 144, 147, 152,
154, 175, 244, 260,
264, 278, 369
3:10-11 ...216, 268
3:10-12 ... 21, 23, 210-12,
269, 342, 344
3:10-13 ... 35
3:10-14 ... 165, 276
3:11 ... 167
3:11-12 ... 17-18, 26,
33, 328
3:12 ...13, 17, 24, 35,
37, 125, 127, 144,
148, 152, 166, 175,
178, 184, 214, 229,
243, 244, 260, 336,
347, 356, 436

3:12-25 348
3:13 .... 52, 162, 354
3:15-18 267
3:15-29 268
3:17 .... 147, 298
3:17-18 144
3:18 270
3:19 .... 257, 266,
286, 287
3:19-20 270
3:19-26 269
3:22 ....121, 368
3:23 49
3:24 .... 140, 149,
270, 277
3:29 266
4:1ff 313
4:3 .... 270, 274,
309, 344
4:4 .... 215, 229, 311
4:4-5 ....348, 369
4:4b-5 274
4:8-9 273
4:9 ....270, 344
4:21-23 266
4:21-27 304
4:21-28 348
4:21a 274
4:24 .... xxx, 112, 117,
118, 144, 147,
148, 155, 158,
263-79, 298
4:24-25 ....344, 356
4:24b-26 267
4:26-29 266
5:3 329
5:6 22
5:14 ....269, 330
5:18 167
5:23 121
5:25b 271
6:15 406
6:16 271

Ephesians
1:4-5 400
2:1-3 331
2:3 296
2:9 372
2:12 ....166, 298
2:22 333
4:11 xiv

4:22-23 428
4:22-24 373
4:24 35
4:24-25 45
5:23-33 306
5:32 395
22:24 385

Philippians
2:6 .... 414, 436
2:8 437
3:9 27
3:12 292

Colossians
1:15 433
1:15-16 427
1:15-17 403
1:16 423
1:16ff 425
2:8 271
2:11-12 334
2:11-14 308
2:17 ....309, 349-50,
356
2:21-22 272
3:9-10 .... 35, 428

1 Timothy
2:13 322
2:13-14 292
2:14 .... 257, 287
3:16 365
3:16-17 312

Titus
3:5-6 400
3:11 295

Philemon
3:9 35

Hebrews
1:2-3 ....425, 428
1:3 .... 421, 433
1:13 433
2:2 ....257, 270, 286
2:6ff 425
2:13 286
2:17-18 369
3:2 369
4:3 .... 141, 278

4:9 .... 141, 278
6:4-5 47
7:21 432
8:6 .... 118, 137
8:8 306
8:9 121
8:13 ....306, 350
9:10 15
9:12 118
9:15 ....257, 286-7, 298,
306, 344
9:16-17 74
9:17 73
10:1 .... 140, 277,
309
10:5-7 xxvii
10:7-10 432
10:28 15
10:38 18
11 50
11:1 47
11:9-10 353
12:7 354
12:24 306

James
1:25 ....36, 37
2:1 368
2:8 278
2:10 ....120, 329
2:21 18

1 Peter
1:10-11 429
3:3-5 396

2 Peter
3:1-7 236
3:10 271
3:16 339

1 John
4:8 400
4:16 377

Revelation
4:4 424
19:7 306
22:14 .... 36, 438

Also available by J.V. Fesko...

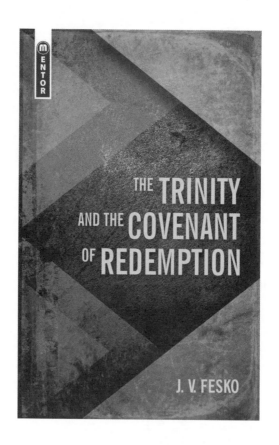

ISBN 978-1-7819-1765-7

The Trinity and the Covenant of Redemption

J. V. Fesko

When Christians reflect on the gospel, their attention is rightly drawn to the cross and empty tomb. But is this it? Or is there much more to the story? In a ground–breaking work, J. V. Fesko reminds us that the great news of this gospel message is rooted in eternity, whereby a covenant was made between the persons of the Trinity in order to redeem sinners like you and me. J. V. Fesko, in the first of a three part series on covenant theology featuring Redemption, Grace and Works, aims to retrieve and recover classic Reformed covenant theology for the church.

... by engaging in Scripture exegesis, historical reflection, and interaction with modern trends in theology, Fesko admirably puts the covenant of redemption back in its rightful place in Reformed theology.

Ryan M. McGraw
Morton H. Smith Professor of Systematic Theology,
Greenville Presbyterian Theological Seminary, Greenville,
South Carolina

Some books today exegete the shining truths of the Holy Scriptures, others mine the treasures of Reformed orthodoxy, and yet others interact with influential theologians of the modern era. This book is one of the few that does all three, and does them well.

Joel R. Beeke
President, Puritan Reformed Theological Seminary, Grand
Rapids, Michigan

Christian Focus Publications

Our mission statement —

STAYING FAITHFUL

In dependence upon God we seek to impact the world through literature faithful to His infallible Word, the Bible. Our aim is to ensure that the Lord Jesus Christ is presented as the only hope to obtain forgiveness of sin, live a useful life and look forward to heaven with Him.

Our books are published in four imprints:

CHRISTIAN
FOCUS

Popular works including biographies, commentaries, basic doctrine and Christian living.

CHRISTIAN
HERITAGE

Books representing some of the best material from the rich heritage of the church.

MENTOR

Books written at a level suitable for Bible College and seminary students, pastors, and other serious readers. The imprint includes commentaries, doctrinal studies, examination of current issues and church history.

CF4•K

Children's books for quality Bible teaching and for all age groups: Sunday school curriculum, puzzle and activity books; personal and family devotional titles, biographies and inspirational stories — because you are never too young to know Jesus!

Christian Focus Publications Ltd,
Geanies House, Fearn, Ross-shire,
IV20 1TW, Scotland, United Kingdom.
www.christianfocus.com
blog.christianfocus.com